FUNDAMENTALS OF
RADIATION ONCOLOGY

FUNDAMENTALS OF RADIATION ONCOLOGY

PHYSICAL, BIOLOGICAL, AND CLINICAL ASPECTS

THIRD EDITION

HASAN MURSHED, M.D., M.S

Medical Director
Hope Regional Cancer Center
Panama City, Florida, United States

ELSEVIER

ACADEMIC PRESS
An imprint of Elsevier

Library of Congress Cataloging-in-Publication Data
A catalog record for this book is available from the Library of Congress

British Library Cataloguing-in-Publication Data
A catalogue record for this book is available from the British Library

ISBN: 978-0-12-814128-1

For information on all Academic Press Publications visit our website at
https://www.elsevier.com/books-and-journals

Working together
to grow libraries in
developing countries

www.elsevier.com • www.bookaid.org

Publisher: Stacy Masucci
Acquisition Editor: Rafael E. Teixeira
Editorial Project Manager: Tracy I. Tufaga
Production Project Manager: Poulouse Joseph
Designer: Mark Rogers

Typeset by TNQ Technologies

Dedication

This book is dedicated to my children Ishraq and Ishmam.

Their faces remind me every day that "may I always act so as to preserve the finest traditions of my calling and may I long experience the joy of healing those who seek my help."*

—*Hippocratic Oath, Modern version, Louis Lasagna, MD, 1964

Contents

PART I

BASIC SCIENCE OF RADIATION ONCOLOGY

3. Radiation Biology   57

JIMMY CAUDELL, RICHARD C. MILLER AND BARRY ROSENSTEIN

4. Molecular Cancer Biology   89

JIMMY CAUDELL, RICHARD C. MILLER AND BARRY ROSENSTEIN

PART II

TECHNIQUES AND MODALITIES OF RADIATION ONCOLOGY

PART III

CLINICAL RADIATION ONCOLOGY

PART IV

PALLIATIVE CARE AND RADIATION TREATMENT TOXICITY

Foreword—
James A. Bonner

Once again, Dr. Murshed has done an excellent job of producing an information-packed textbook that can be used in the day-to-day practice of radiation oncology. This new issue of *Fundamentals of Radiation Oncology* is an important compilation of the new and established literature that affects routine and complex decision-making in our clinics. Since the last edition of *Clinical Fundamentals for Radiation Oncologists*, there have been many new advances in radiation oncology. These advances have occurred in almost every disease site. This wealth of new information is difficult to summarize in a concise manner, but Dr. Murshed and all the contributors have artfully accomplished this goal. This edition is filled with crucial information for the busy practitioner.

Since the publication of the last edition, there have been breakthroughs in stereotactic radiosurgery, proton therapy, and immunotherapy to name just a few innovative areas. This textbook provides detailed information regarding new applications of radiotherapy, while still maintaining a strong backbone of basic principles of radiation oncology, radiobiology, and physics. The textbook creatively organizes and summarizes the major clinical trials, frequently using helpful tables, in each disease site.

It is also important to note that Dr. Murshed has substantially increased the number of contributing authors for this edition of the text. This edition includes contributions from 48 experts in the field. These experts have been able to encapsulate the major advances in a manner that highlights the most significant issues that frequently arise on a daily basis. This is the beauty of this textbook. It is also noteworthy that the contributors represent programs from all over the world and these authors provide a comprehensive perspective to radiation oncology care.

Therefore, Dr. Murshed has done a very thorough job of presenting the basic and detailed issues that are associated with all oncologic disease sites. He has made this information relevant for the daily practice of radiation oncology. Dr. Murshed has always had a strong interest in the educational aspects of our field. This fact was obvious during his residency at The University of Alabama at Birmingham. He has continued this interest over the past 20 years, and this updated version of *Fundamentals of Radiation Oncology* is a great testament to his commitment to our field. I believe that all radiation oncologists will find this textbook a "must have" in their armamentarium.

James A. Bonner, M.D.
Merle M. Salter Professor and Chairman
Department of Radiation Oncology
University of Alabama at Birmingham
Birmingham, Alabama, United States
June, 2018

Foreword—
Thomas A. Buchholz

I would like to personally acknowledge and thank Dr. Hasan Murshed for providing our community with an outstanding Third Edition of the *Fundamentals of Radiation Oncology*. This comprehensive textbook includes 26 chapters authored by a variety of thought-leaders. It is unique in including chapter authors from around the world in addition to notable authorities in the United States.

The field of radiation oncology is rapidly changing, and this new edition provides a single source that captures the many conditions seen by radiation oncologists. In addition, it provides much of the foundational science behind the field of radiation oncology. Selected chapters are also dedicated to the importance of technique, including describing the role of newer proton techniques and the important evolving role of stereotactic treatments for intracranial and extracranial disease. Finally, exciting new materials are provided regarding the interactions of radiation oncology and immunotherapy, an area that is likely to significantly increase in importance over the next decade.

One hallmark that has impressed me about this textbook is its comprehensive content and ease of use. The structure and design allow for this book to use for an immediate reference or to address an immediate clinical question. However, it also serves as an outstanding comprehensive study guide for the field of radiation oncology.

I am sure that many will share my very high opinion of this impressive work. More importantly, I am sure that this textbook will help bring forward the many clinical and technical advances in radiation oncology to centers around the world, and in doing so, help raise the standard of care. On behalf of the radiation oncology community and the patients who benefit from their excellent care, I say thank you to Dr. Murshed and the nearly 50 contributing authors.

Thomas Buchholz, M.D.
Professor Emeritus
University of Texas, MD Anderson Cancer Center
Medical Director
Scripps MD Anderson Cancer Center
La Jolla, California, United States
June, 2018

Preface

Cancer management, specifically Radiation Oncology, has undergone ground breaking changes over the past several years. The AJCC 8th staging system has been implemented, and new tools for cancer diagnosis, and novel radiation modalities and techniques are now available. Most importantly, new studies and their associated data have led to rapid changes in recommendations for cancer treatment, requiring this third edition of *Fundamentals of Radiation Oncology*.

This new edition continues to provide current, concise, and a readily available source of clinical information for busy practicing radiation oncologists. The book consists of 26 chapters, divided into four parts.

Part I describes the basic science of radiation oncology, with discussions of radiation physics, radiation protection, and radiation biology, as well as molecular biology.

Part II describes techniques and modalities of radiation oncology including brachytherapy, intensity-modulated radiation therapy (IMRT), stereotactic radiotherapy (SRS), stereotactic body radiation therapy (SBRT), and proton therapy. Significant recent advances made in the areas of immunotherapy and combined modality therapy; as such, these chapters have also been added to this new edition.

Part III describes the clinical science of radiation oncology including risk factors, symptoms/signs, and investigations needed for the cancer diagnosis and up-to-date treatment recommendations in accordance with the new AJCC staging system. In addition, radiation treatment techniques, with an emphasis on IMRT, have been expanded to all the chapters. Also included in this version of the book is a chapter on benign diseases. Updated annotated bibliographies of latest landmark studies providing evidence-based rationale for the recommended treatments are presented at the end of each chapter.

Part IV describes palliative radiation treatments to improve the quality of life for cancer patients and the management of side effects from radiation treatment.

This updated edition was made possible through an international collaboration of contributing authors from Australia, Canada, India, Turkey, United Kingdom, and United States. I am immensely indebted to all of the contributing authors; without their assistance, this book would not be. I am especially grateful to Ugur Selek, M.D., who contributed several chapters to this edition. I am also thankful for his continuing friendship over the past 16 years.

In addition, I sincerely thank all of the excellent reviewers of this book for their thoughtful input in updating the clinical chapters. Finally, I wish to thank Tracy Tufaga, Rafael Teixeira and Poulouse Joseph at Elsevier for their commitment to excellence and expert editorial contribution to this book.

May this updated edition provide you, the reader, the best knowledge, excellent skills, and the compassion to *"cure sometimes, treat often, comfort always."**

Hasan Murshed, M.D.
June 2018

---

*Hippocrates Asclepiades (460 BC–370 BC).

Contributors

Kamran Ahmad M.D. Assistant Member, Radiation Oncology, Moffitt Cancer Center, Tampa, FL, USA

Hilary P. Bagshaw M.D. Assistant Professor, Radiation Oncology, Stanford University, Stanford, CA, USA

Andrew Bang M.D. Clinical Fellow, Radiation Oncology, University of Toronto, Princess Margaret Cancer Centre, Toronto, ON, Canada

Astrid Billfalk-Kelly M.D. Clinical Fellow, Radiation Oncology, University of Toronto, Princess Margaret Cancer Centre, Toronto, ON, Canada

Drexell Boggs M.D. Assistant Professor, Radiation Oncology, University of Alabama, Birmingham, AL, USA

Yasemin Bolukbasi M.D. Associate Professor, Radiation Oncology, Koc University, Istanbul, Turkey

Ivan Brezovich Ph.D. Professor, Radiation Oncology, University of Alabama, Birmingham, AL, USA

Mark K. Buyyounouski M.D., M.S. Professor, Radiation Oncology, Stanford University, Stanford, CA, USA

Allan Caggiano M.S. Chief Medical Physicist, Sr. Patricia Lynch Regional Cancer Center, Teaneck, NJ, USA

Jimmy Caudell M.D., Ph.D. Adjunct Assistant Professor, Radiation Oncology, University of Alabama, Birmingham, AL, USA

Nulifer Kilic Durankus M.D. Consultant, Radiation Oncology, Koc University, Istanbul, Turkey

Timothy W. Dziuk M.D. Consultant, Radiation Oncology, Texas Oncology, San Antonio, TX, USA

Molly Gabel M.D. Adjunct Associate Professor, Radiation Oncology, SMG MD Anderson Cancer Center, Berkeley Heights, NJ, USA

Saumil Gandhi M.D., Ph.D. Assistant Professor, Radiation Oncology, University of Texas, MD Anderson Cancer Center, Houston, TX, USA

Kent Gifford Ph.D. Assistant Professor, Radiation Physics, University of Texas, MD Anderson Cancer Center, Houston, TX, USA

Jayant Sastri Goda M.D. Professor, Radiation Oncology, Tata Memorial Centre, Mumbai, India

Melis Gultekin M.D. Associate Professor, Radiation Oncology, Hacettepe University, Ankara, Turkey

Dorothy Guzral MBChB, Ph.D. Consultant, Clinical Oncology, Imperial College Healthcare NHS Trust, London, UK

Jerry Jaboin M.D., Ph.D. Associate Professor, Radiation Medicine, Oregon Health and Science University, Portland, OR, USA

Rojymon Jacob M.D. Associate Professor, Radiation Oncology, University of Alabama, Birmingham, AL, USA

Rakesh Jalali M.D. Medical Director, Radiation Oncology, Apollo Proton Cancer Center, Chennai, India

Jonathan Leeman M.D. Clinical Instructor, Radiation Oncology, Brigham and Women's Hospital/Dana Farber Cancer Institute, Boston, MA, USA

John Leung M.B.B.S. Associate Professor, Radiation Oncology, University of Adelaide, Adelaide, Australia

Richard Miller M.D. Associate Professor, Radiation and Cellular Oncology, the University of Chicago, Chicago, IL, USA

Blair Murphy M.D. Resident, Radiation Medicine, Oregon Health and Science University, Portland, OR, USA

Robert Oldham M.D. Clinical Professor, University of Missouri, Columbus, MO, USA

Berrin Pehlivan M.D. Associate Professor, Radiation Oncology, Istanbul Kemerburgaz University, Istanbul, Turkey

Andrew Pippas M.D. Consultant, Medical Oncology, John B Thomas Cancer Center, Columbus, GA, USA

Richard Popple Ph.D. Professor, Radiation Oncology, University of Alabama, Birmingham, AL, USA

Nicolas D. Prionas M.D., PhD. Resident, Radiation Oncology, Stanford University, Stanford, CA, USA

David Reisman M.D., Ph.D. Consultant, Hematology Oncology, Baptist Medical Group, Pensacola, FL, USA

Barry Rosenstein Ph.D. Professor, Radiation Oncology, Icahn School of Medicine at Mount Sinai, New York, NY, USA

Naomi Schechter M.D. Associate Professor, Radiation Oncology, Keck Medical Center of USC, Los Angeles, CA, USA

Timothy Schultheiss Ph.D. Professor, Radiation Physics, City of Hope Medical Center, Duarte, CA, USA

Ugur Selek M.D. Professor, Radiation Oncology, Koc University, Istanbul, Turkey

Duygu Sezen M.D. Consultant, Radiation Oncology, Koc University, Istanbul, Turkey

David Smith Ph.D. Research Professor, Radiation Physics, City of Hope Medical Center, Duarte, CA, USA

Shen Sui Ph.D. Professor, Radiation Oncology, University of Alabama, Birmingham, AL, USA

Kim Sunjune M.D., Ph.D. Assistant Member, Radiation Oncology, Moffitt Cancer Center, Tampa, FL, USA

Neil Taunk M.D., M.S. Assistant Professor, Radiation Oncology, University of Pennsylvania, Philadelphia, PA, USA

Erkan Topkan M.D. Professor, Radiation Oncology, Baskent University, Adana, Turkey

Jefferson Trupp M.D. Consultant, Radiation Oncology, Hope Regional Cancer Center, Panama City, FL, USA

Derek Tsang M.D. Assistant Professor, Radiation Oncology, University of Toronto, Princess Margaret Cancer Centre, Toronto, ON, Canada

Matthew Williams MBChB, Ph.D. Consultant, Clinical Oncology, Imperial College Healthcare NHS Trust, London, UK

Jack Yang Ph.D. Director, Medical Physics, Monmouth Med Ctr/RWJBarnabas Health, Long Branch, NJ, USA

Guler Yavas M.D. Associate Professor, Radiation Oncology, Selcuk University, Konya, Turkey

Gozde Yazici M.D. Associate Professor, Radiation Oncology, Hacettepe University, Ankara, Turkey

Berna Akkus Yildirim M.D. Consultant, Radiation Oncology, Baskent University, Adana, Turkey

Reviewers

Aziz Ahmad M.D.   General Surgeon, Lynn Haven Surgical Center, Lynn Haven, FL, USA

Penny Anderson M.D.   Professor, Radiation Oncology, Fox Chase Cancer Center, Philadelphia, PA, USA

Michael Asare-Sawiri B.S.   Medical Dosimetrist, Hope Regional Cancer Center, Lynn Haven, FL, USA

Kin-Sing Au M.D.   Consultant, Radiation Oncology, Island Cancer Centre, Guam, USA

Jerry Barker, Jr. M.D.   Radiation Oncologist, Texas Oncology, Fort Worth, TX USA

James Beggs M.D.   Otolaryngologist, Gulf Coast Facial Plastics and ENT Center, Panama City, FL, USA

Donald Buchsbaum Ph.D.   Professor, Radiation Oncology, University of Alabama, Birmingham, AL, USA

Hans Caspary M.D.   Otolaryngologist, Head & Neck Associates, Panama City, FL, USA

Jason Cundiff M.D.   General Surgeon, Bay Medical Sacred Heart, Panama City, FL, USA

Daniel Daube M.D.   Otolaryngologist, Gulf Coast Facial Plastics and ENT Center, Panama City, FL, USA

Cyril DeSilva M.D.   Neurosurgeon, Bay Medical Center, Panama City, FL, USA

Gregory England M.D.   Cardiothoracic Surgeon, Coastal Cardiovascular Surgeons, Panama City, FL, USA

Robert Finlaw M.D.   Gastroenterologist, Digestives Diseases Center, Panama City, FL, USA

Brian Gibson M.D.   Otolaryngologist, Gulf Coast Facial Plastics and ENT Center, Panama City, FL, USA

Moses Hayes M.D.   Medical Oncologist, Sacred Heart Medical Oncology Group, San Destin, FL, USA

Heather Headstrom M.D.   Neurosurgeon, Panama City Neurosurgery, Panama City, FL, USA

Bret Johnson M.D.   Dermatologist, Dermatology Associates, Panama City, FL, USA

N. Alex Jones M.D.   General Surgeon, Emeralds Bay Surgical Associates, Panama City, FL, USA

Mariusz Kiln M.D.   Gastroenterologist, Emerald Coast Gastroenterology, Panama City, FL, USA

Charles Kovaleski M.D.   Dermatologist, Dermatology Associates, Panama City, Florida, USA

Glen MacAlpin M.D.   General Surgeon, Sacred Heart Medical Group, Port St Joe, FL, USA

Lawrence Margolis M.D.   Professor Emeritus, Radiation Oncology, University of San Francisco, San Francisco, California, USA

William Mckenzie M.D.   Pulmonologist, Lung and the Sleep Center, Panama City, FL, USA

Pierre Mechali M.D.   Consultant, Hope Urology Center, Panama City, FL, USA

Angel Nunez M.D.   Pulmonologist, Panama City Pulmonary, Panama City, FL, USA

Christopher Nutting M.D., Ph.D.   Professor, Radiation Oncology, Royal Marsden Hospital NHS Foundation, London, UK

Marwan Obid M.D.   Pulmonologist, Obid Allergy and Respiratory Center, Panama City, FL, USA

Jesus Ramirez M.D.   Pulmonologist, Bay Clinic and Sleep Disorder lab, Panama City, FL, USA

Shilpa Reddy M.D.   Gastroenterologist, Digestive Diseases Center, Panama City, FL, USA

George Reiss M.D.   General Surgeon, Surgical Associates-NW Florida, Panama City, FL USA

Albibi Riyad M.D.   Gastroenterologist, Digestive Diseases Center, Panama City, FL, USA

Sharon Spencer M.D.   Professor, Radiation Oncology, University of Alabama, Birmingham, AL, USA

Quang Tran M.D.   Otolaryngologist, Head & Neck Associates, Panama City, FL, USA

Maciej Tumial M.D.   Gastroenterologist, Panama City Gastroenterology, Panama City, FL, USA

Richard Wilson M.D.   General Surgeon, Surgical Associates-NW Florida, Panama City, FL USA

Larry Wong D.O.   General Surgeon, Bay Medical Sacred Heart, Panama City, FL, USA

Kristina Woodhouse M.D.   Assistant Professor, Radiation Oncology, University of Texas, MD Anderson Cancer Center, Houston, TX, USA

Ibrahim Yazji M.D.   Cardiothoracic surgeon, Coastal Cardiovascular Surgeons, Panama City. FL, USA

PART I

BASIC SCIENCE OF RADIATION ONCOLOGY

1

Radiation Physics, Dosimetry, and Treatment Planning

Wilhelm Roentgen discovered X-rays in 1895 while experimenting with a gas-filled cathode tube; Henri Becquerel discovered radioactivity in 1896 while experimenting with uranium salts. Soon after these discoveries, radiation was used to treat cancer and other diseases. To effectively use radiation, it is important to understand its basic properties, which are addressed in this chapter.

FUNDAMENTAL PHYSICAL QUANTITIES

Mass, energy, charge, and force all have key roles in radiation physics.

Mass

Mass is the amount of matter within any physical object. Mass is measured as weight and the standard international (SI) unit of mass is the kilogram (kg), represented by a lump of platinum–iridium alloy kept in Paris, France. In the much smaller realm of atomic physics, weights are expressed as atomic mass units (amu or u). An amu is equivalent to 1/12th the mass of one atom of carbon (C^{12} isotope).

Einstein's theory of relativity ($E = mc^2$) suggests that mass (m) can be converted into energy (E), as a function of the speed of light squared (c^2). One amu of mass is converted into 931 MeV of energy. The mass of a moving object, its "relativistic mass," is larger than its mass at rest because the kinetic energy associated with its motion adds to the resting mass.

Energy

Energy is the ability of a system to perform work. There are two types of energy—potential energy and kinetic energy. One electron volt (eV) is the energy acquired by an electron when it moves across a potential of 1 V. One million electron volts are designated by MeV.

Fundamentals of Radiation Oncology
https://doi.org/10.1016/B978-0-12-814128-1.00001-5

Charge

Electric charge is the property of matter that causes it to experience a force in the presence of an electromagnetic field. Charges are positive or negative with an electron being the smallest unit of negative charge (-1) and the proton being the smallest unit of positive charge ($+1$). The SI unit of charge is the Coulomb (6.25×10^{18} elementary charges).

Force

A force is an interaction that can change the direction or velocity of an object. Coulomb force (electromagnetic force) is the force between two charged bodies. Protons and electrons are held together by the Coulomb force. Gravitational force is the attraction between two masses. It is a very weak force unless the masses are very large, like the earth or the sun. Strong force holds particles together in the atomic nucleus (protons, neutrons, and quarks), is the strongest known fundamental physical force, but only acts over atomic distances. Weak force is the force that is responsible for particle decay processes (beta decay) and is approximately one-millionth of the strong force.

ATOMIC STRUCTURE

The atom consists of three fundamental particles: protons, neutrons, and electrons. The particles are bound together by the abovementioned four fundamental forces.

Atomic Models

In the Rutherford model of the atom, protons and neutrons reside in the center (nucleus), whereas electrons revolve around the nucleus in circular orbits. The Bohr model of the atom introduced four refinements to the Rutherford model.

1. Electrons can only occupy certain discrete orbits while revolving around the nucleus.
2. When electrons are in stationary orbits, they do not emit radiation as predicted by classical physics.
3. Each stationary orbit has a discrete energy associated with it.
4. Radiation is only emitted whenever an electron moves from a higher orbit to a lower orbit, and radiation is absorbed whenever an electron moves from a lower orbit to a higher orbit.

Electron Binding Energy

Because negative electrons are bound to the positive nucleus by the Coulomb force, it requires a certain amount of energy to remove an electron from the atom. This energy is called "ionization energy."

Atomic Shell Filling Rules

Electron shells are labeled from the nucleus outward either by the letters K, L, M, N... or by the numbers 1, 2, 3, 4... (principal quantum numbers, n). The maximum number of electrons allowed in a given atomic shell is given by:

Maximum number of electrons in a given shell $= 2n^2$ where n is the principal quantum number.

Characteristic Radiation

When an electron acquires enough energy from an incident photon to leave an inner orbit of the atom, a vacancy is created in that shell, which is immediately filled by an outer shell electron, emitting the excess energy as a photon. This photon is a "characteristic X-ray."

Auger Electrons

The characteristic X-ray can leave the atom or it can displace an outer shell electron. The displaced electron is called as "Auger electron," and its kinetic energy is equal to the energy of the characteristic X-ray that displaced it minus the energy required to remove the electron from its shell.

Nuclear Binding Energy

The particles contained in the nucleus are bound together by the strong and the weak nuclear forces discussed above. The mass of a nuclide is always less than the mass of the constituent components. This deficiency of mass is called the mass defect. The energy required to separate the nucleus into its constituent particles is called the nuclear binding energy. It can be computed using Einstein's equation.

NUCLEAR STRUCTURE

Atoms are identified by their atomic symbols $^A_Z X$, where X is the atomic symbol, A is the mass number (number of protons plus neutrons), and Z is the atomic number (number of protons). The number of neutrons (N) in an atom can be determined by the equation $N = A - Z$.

Special types of nuclei are defined as follows:

- **Isotopes:** Isotopes are atoms that have the same number of protons (Z), but a different number of neutrons (A − Z). Examples of two isotopes are $^{12}_5 C$ and $^{14}_6 C$.
- **Isobars:** Isobars are atoms with nuclei that have the same number of total particles (A), but a different number of protons (Z) and neutrons (A − Z). Example of isobars are $^{40}_{19} K$ and $^{40}_{20} Ca$.
- **Isotones:** Isotones are nuclides that have the same number of neutrons (A − Z) and a different number of protons (Z). Examples of isotones are $^{14}_6 C$ and $^{15}_7 N$.
- **Isomers:** Isomers are atoms with nuclei that have the same number of total particles (A) and the same number of protons (Z), but different levels of energy in the nucleus. Examples of isomers are $^{99}_{43} Tc$ and $^{99m}_{43} Tc$.

RADIOACTIVE DECAY

Radioactivity is the process by which an unstable nucleus is transformed by giving off the excess energy and forming a new stable element. The transformation may involve the emission of electromagnetic radiation or emission of particles, involving mechanisms such as beta decay, alpha decay, or isomeric transitions. Examining the ratio of neutrons to protons in all stable nuclei, the following conclusions can be made (see Fig. 1.1):

If Z is less than or equal to 20, the ratio of neutrons to protons is 1.

If Z is greater than 20, the ratio becomes greater than 1 and increases with Z.

As more protons are added to the nucleus, the effects of the Coulomb force begin to overwhelm the strong nuclear forces, which can make an atom unstable. This unstable nucleus will tend to lose energy by different decay mechanisms, described in the next section, to reach a more stable state.

MODES OF RADIOACTIVE DECAY

Alpha Decay

Radionuclides that have a Z greater than 82 are decayed most frequently by the emission of a helium nucleus, or alpha particle (α). The alpha particle is identical to the nucleus of a helium atom, ^4_2He.

Beta Decay

By this process, a radioactive nucleus emits either an electron or a positron. There are two types of beta decay: β^- (beta minus or negatron emission) and β^+ (beta plus or positron emission).

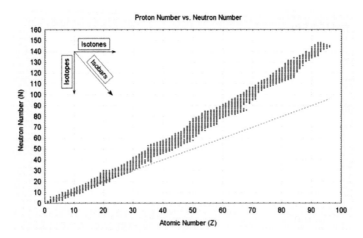

FIGURE 1.1   Neutron versus proton in stable nucleus.

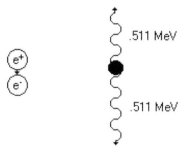

FIGURE 1.2 The conversion of mass into energy; the annihilation radiation is traveling in the opposite direction.

- Negatron emission: If a radionuclide has a high number of neutrons (high n/p ratio), it tends to reduce the n/p ratio by converting a neutron into a proton, negatron, and antineutrino.
- Positron emission: If a radionuclide has a deficit of neutrons (low n/p ratio), it tends to increase the n/p ratio, either by converting a proton into a neutron and a positron (positron emission) or by capturing an orbital electron (electron capture). In positron emission, a proton is converted into a neutron, positron, and a neutrino. The creation of a positron requires 1.02 MeV of energy to be available from the nuclear decay. The positron is an unstable antiparticle of the electron, possessing the same mass but opposite charge. Once the traveling positron has slowed down enough, the positron and another electron will annihilate each other, and their rest masses are converted into energy (1.02 MeV). This energy appears as two 0.511 MeV annihilation photons traveling in opposite directions (see Fig. 1.2).

Electron capture: This process competes with positron emission. An orbital electron is captured by the nucleus, which then rearranges its structure and transforms a proton into a neutron in order to reach electronic stability. Because an orbital electron has been removed from its orbital, an electron from a higher orbital fills this void and characteristic X-rays and/or Auger electrons are emitted from the atom as a result.

Gamma Emission

In gamma emission, the nucleus releases the excess energy by emission of one or more gamma rays. Gamma emission occurs with alpha or beta decay. Gamma emission is isomeric as there is no change in atomic mass or number.

Isomeric Transitions

The most stable arrangement of the nucleus in an atom is called its ground state. In some nuclear decays, the daughter nucleus stays in a more excited state (metastable state) for some period of time. The only difference between the metastable state and the final ground state is a difference in energy; hence the two states are called isomers and the transition from the metastable state to the ground state is called an isomeric transition. There are two competing methods by which a nucleus can lose excess energy during an isomeric transition: gamma emission and internal conversion.

Internal Conversion

The gamma ray displaces an electron from its orbital by transferring all of its energy to the electron (the gamma ray ceases to exist). The displaced electron is called an "internal conversion electron." Characteristic X-rays follow as the shell from which the electron was displaced is filled by electrons from outer shells.

Mathematics of Radioactive Decay

The mathematics of radioactive decay depends on the observation that in a large collection of N radioactive atoms, the number of decays ΔN that occur in a time interval Δt is found to be proportional to Δt and to the total number N of radioactive nuclei. The proportionality constant λ is called the decay (or disintegration) constant and gives the rate at which a radionuclide is disintegrating per unit time. The units of the decay constant are s^{-1} (or disintegrations per second).

If we solve the difference equation:

$$\Delta N = -\lambda N \Delta t$$

After making this difference equation into a differential equation and solving, the final result is an equation that allows us to calculate the number of radioactive atoms N(t) at any time t:

$$N(t) = N_0 e^{-\lambda t},$$

where N(t) is the number of atoms remaining at time t, N_0 is the number atoms at time $t = 0$, e is the mathematical constant 2.718, λ is the decay constant, and t is the elapsed time (see Fig. 1.3.)

The decay constant gives the rate at which a radionuclide is disintegrating per unit time. The units are s^{-1} (or disintegrations per second).

Activity

Activity is the rate of decay of a radioactive material at any given point in time. The activity (A) is related to the number of disintegrations by:

$$A(t) = -\lambda N(t)$$

The equation for N(t) can be rewritten in terms of activity A(t):

$$A(t) = A_0 e^{-\lambda t}$$

where A(t) is the activity remaining at time t, A_0 is the activity at time $t = 0$, e is the mathematical constant 2.718, λ is the disintegration constant, and t is the elapsed time.

The original unit of activity was the curie (Ci). The curie is defined as the number of disintegrations given of by 1 g of radium (^{226}Ra) and is equal to 3.7×10^{10} disintegrations per second (dps). The newer SI unit of activity is the becquerel (Bq), defined by:

$$1 \, \text{Bq} = 1 \, \text{dps}$$

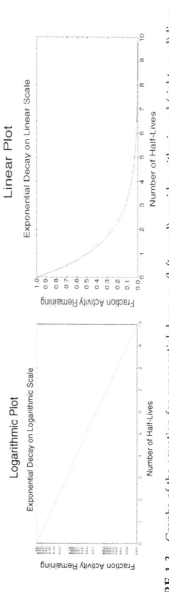

FIGURE 1.3 Graphs of the equation for exponential decay on (left panel) semi logarithmic and (right panel) linear scale.

The relationship between the curie and the becquerel is then given by:

$$1\,\text{Ci} = 3.7 \times 10^{10}\,\text{Bq}$$

Half-life: The half-life, $t_{1/2}$, of a radionuclide is the time it takes for one-half of the atoms in a given sample to decay. It is denoted by $t_{1/2}$ and can be calculated from the disintegration constant by:

$$t_{1/2} = \frac{0.693}{\lambda}$$

Mean life: The mean (average) life is the average amount of time a nucleus lives before it decays. It is given by:

$$t_{\text{avg}} = 1.44 t_{1/2}$$

Equilibrium

In radioactive decay, a "parent" radionuclide decays gives rise to a "daughter" radionuclide. If the half-life of the daughter species is considerably shorter than that of the parent, then the activity of the daughter increases from zero until it reaches the activity of the parent. Decay then continues with the activity of the parent. This is called **secular equilibrium** and is attained after about five half-lives of the daughter species. An example of secular equilibrium is the decay of ^{226}Ra as shown below (Fig. 1.4):

$$^{226}\text{Ra}(t_{1/2} = 1620\ \text{y}) \rightarrow\ ^{222}\text{Rn}(t_{1/2} = 4.8\ \text{d}).$$

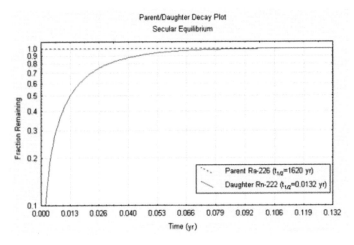

FIGURE 1.4 A secular equilibrium plot showing the activity of the parent and daughter for different times t.

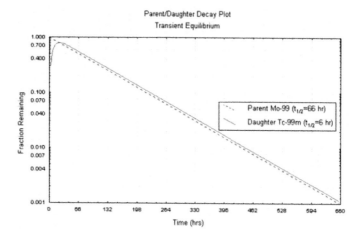

FIGURE 1.5 A transient equilibrium plot showing the activity of the parent and daughter for different times t.

If the half-life of the daughter is slightly shorter than that of the parent, then **transient equilibrium** is reached after some time whereby the activity of the daughter builds till equals that of the parent and then slightly exceeds the activity of the parent. Subsequently, the activity of the daughter follows the activity of the parent but remains slightly higher. An example of transient equilibrium is given by the decay of ^{99}Mo to ^{99m}Tc as shown below (Fig. 1.5):

$$^{99}Mo(t_{1/2} = 66\ h) \rightarrow {}^{99m}Tc(t^{1/2} = 6\ h).$$

ELECTROMAGNETIC RADIATION AND PROPERTIES OF INTERACTION

X-ray and gamma radiation are a part of a larger set of photon radiation called the electromagnetic spectrum. Fig. 1.6 shows the types of radiation in the spectrum.

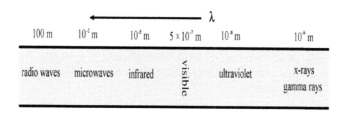

FIGURE 1.6 The electromagnetic spectrum. *Reprinted from McDermott PN, Orton CG. The physics & technology of radiation therapy. Madison, WI: Medical Physics Publishing; 2010, Fig. 2.13, p. 2–18, © 2010, with permission from the author.*

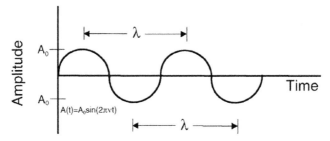

FIGURE 1.7 Illustration of an electromagnetic wave showing the wavelength and frequency.

All photons have two fundamental parameters (Fig. 1.7):

Wavelength (λ): The wavelength of a photon is the distance from one point on the photon wave to the next identical point on the wave.

Frequency (ν): The frequency of a photon is the number of times the wave oscillates per second.

Photons are known to travel at a constant velocity in space equal to the speed of light (c), which is 3×10^8 meters per second (m/s) in a vacuum.

The relationship between the frequency ν of a photon and its wavelength λ is given by:

$$\nu = \frac{c}{\lambda}$$

where ν is the frequency of the photon, λ is the wavelength of the photon, and c is the speed of light.

Photons are known to have zero mass and zero charge but do have energy given by:

$$E = h\nu$$

where ν is the frequency of the photon (in units of s^{-1} or Hz [hertz]), and h is the physical constant called Planck's constant (6.62×10^{-34} J-s).

The energy of a photon can be rewritten in terms of wavelength by:

$$E = \frac{hc}{\lambda}$$

Photon Interaction Process, Kerma, Absorbed Dose

As photons travel through material, they can displace atomic orbital electrons along their paths. These freed electrons (primary electrons) are responsible for most of the energy deposition that occurs in therapeutic photon beams. Photon interactions with matter are a two-step process:

1. Energy transfer and kerma
   An incident photon interacts with an orbital electron in the atom of the material through photon interaction mechanism such as photoelectric, Compton, or pair production (described later). During these interactions, photons transfer some or all of their energy to an atomic orbital electron. This orbital electron can gain enough kinetic energy to leave the atomic orbital and become a primary electron.

This process of energy transfer (uncharged photons to charged electrons) is called kerma (**k**inetic **e**nergy **r**eleased in **ma**tter). The SI unit for kerma is joules per kilogram (J/kg) or gray (Gy).

2. Energy absorption and absorbed dose

Primary electrons released during the energy transfer process interact with other orbital electrons, thereby ionizing and exciting atoms along their irregular tracks. Also, primary electrons displace other electrons as they travel through matter, called "delta rays." Energy deposited per unit mass of matter is called "absorbed dose."

The old unit of absorbed dose is the rad (radiation absorbed dose). The rad has been replaced in the SI system with the gray (Gy). They are related as follows:

$$100 \text{ rad} = 1 \text{ J/kg} = 1 \text{ Gy}.$$

Because the gray is large compared to the rad, the centiGray (cGy) is often used:

$$1 \text{ rad} = 1 \text{ cGy}.$$

Modes of Photon Interaction

Mechanisms of interaction for photons are described below. These interactions transfer energy from photons to the irradiated material, where it is ultimately dissipated as heat.

Coherent scattering is dominant interaction in the low-energy region (<50 keV) and in high Z materials. Photons interact with electrons of an atom causing them to oscillate. This oscillation energy is reradiated by another photon of the same energy as the incident photon, but at a different angle. No net energy is transferred.

Photoelectric absorption occurs when an incident photon is totally absorbed by an electron, typically one from an inner shell. It has dominant interaction in the 10−26 KeV. If the energy of the photon exceeds the binding energy of the electron, the electron is ejected from the atom as a "photo electron," which has energy equal to the incident photon minus the binding energy. The probability for photoelectric absorption increases rapidly with the atomic number of the atom where the interaction occurs. This is the main interaction responsible for diagnostic imaging (Fig. 1.8A).

Compton scattering occurs when only part of the incident photons are transferred to the electron, which is emitted at an angle φ relative to the incoming photon. It has dominant interaction in the 26 KeV−24 MeV. The remaining energy accompanies the photon that is scattered at an angle θ. The electron's kinetic energy equals the energy of the incident photon minus the energy of the scattered photon minus the binding energy of the electron. Compton scattering is the dominant interaction at therapeutic photon energies (Fig. 1.8B).

Pair production occurs when incident photons interact with the nuclear field and is completely absorbed. It has dominant interaction above 10 MeV. Part of its energy is converted into matter by creating an electron−positron pair. The remaining energy is kinetic energy associated with the electron and the positron. The positron is antimatter and as it slows down while traveling in matter, it combines with an electron forming two photons known as "annihilation photons," each having energy of 0.51 MeV. Because the resting energy of an electron and a positron is 0.51 MeV each, pair production cannot occur unless the incident photon has at least 1.02 MeV energy (Fig. 1.8C).

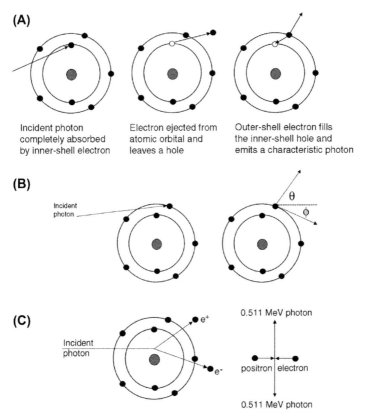

FIGURE 1.8 (A) Photon interaction of photoelectric absorption. (B) Photon interaction of Compton scattering. (C) Photon interaction of pair production.

Photodisintegration occurs when high-energy photons are absorbed by the nucleus. It has interaction above 8–16 MeV. The energy can be used to eject a neutron, a proton, or an alpha particle or to break the nucleus into several components.

Mathematics of Photon Attenuation

The mathematics of attenuation of radiation is identical to the decay of radioactive nuclides. The process of photon attenuation is a random event that must be treated statistically and depends on the assumption that as N photons pass through a material of thickness x, a given fraction μ will be removed from the photon beam per unit path length.

Stated in mathematical terms:

$$\frac{\Delta N}{\Delta x} = -\mu N$$

where μ is a constant and is called the linear attenuation constant.

The linear attenuation constant μ gives the rate at which photons are removed from a material per unit thickness. The units are cm^{-1}.

If we integrate this differential equation, we arrive at a formula that can be used to calculate the number of photons that will remain after a photon beam has passed through a thickness x of material, given by:

$$N(x) = N_0 e^{-\mu x}$$

where $N(x)$ is the number of photons remaining after passing through a material of thickness x, N_0 is the number photons with no material in the beam (x = 0 cm), e is the mathematical constant 2.718, and μ is the linear attenuation coefficient for the photon beam energy and material irradiated.

This algebraic equation states that if we know μ, N_0, and x, we can solve for $N(x)$. This type of attenuation is known as *exponential attenuation.* It is known that the amount of attenuation for the same thickness x of material is different for different density materials; it follows that μ depends on the density p of the material. If we divide μ by p, we obtain the mass attenuation coefficient (μ/p). The **mass attenuation coefficient** has units of cm^2/g and is independent of density.

PARTICULATE RADIATION PROPERTIES AND INTERACTIONS

Particulate radiation consists of particles that possess resting mass. Its interaction with matter is different from the interaction of photons with matter. Particulate radiation has mass but may or may not possess electric charge. Interactions of electrons, neutrons, and heavy particles are described below.

Interactions of Electrons

Because of their charge, electrons displace other electrons from their orbits and thereby cause ionization as they travel through matter. Because electrons are relatively light, their original paths are substantially altered ("scattered"), as they interact with other electrons. Because of their strong scattering, the Bragg peak, which is associated with heavier particles, is not observed with electrons. Occasionally an electron transfers enough energy to another electron that the new electron can cause ionization on its own. The new electron is called a "delta ray." Free electrons can interact with atomic electron or with nuclei as below:

- Interactions with atomic electrons: Free electrons interact with other atomic electrons predominantly by inelastic collisions, causing excitation and ionization of the atom along their tracks. Excitation is the promotion of an orbital electron to a higher energy level in the atom, without the ejection of the orbital electron. On the other hand, if the incident electron had enough energy to eject the orbital electron, then the interaction is called an ionization (see Fig. 1.9).

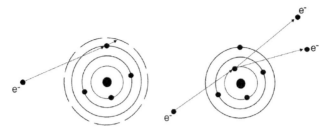

FIGURE 1.9 Excitation and ionization of an atom.

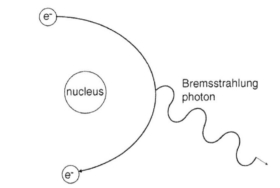

FIGURE 1.10 Creation of bremsstrahlung radiation.

- Interactions with nuclei (bremsstrahlung): Electrons with kinetic energy will interact with atomic nuclei, mostly by inelastic collisions. As the electron is bent from its original path by the Coulomb force of the atomic nucleus, it decelerates and loses energy in the form of a photon. This photon is called a bremsstrahlung photon (see Fig. 1.10).

Interactions of Neutrons

Because neutrons have no charge, they cannot cause ionization directly. Their main interaction of interest in radiation therapy is their collision with protons that lead to further ionization. Furthermore, neutron interactions typically produce a wide range of subatomic particles, recoil nuclei, and photons. These particles deposit energy in very different ways, producing differing biological effects. Slow (thermal) neutrons have energy around 0.025 eV and fast neutrons have much higher energy of KeV and MeV.

Interactions of Heavy Charged Particles

Heavy charged particles generally include any charged particles with resting masses greater than that of electrons. These include protons, heavy ions, and pions. Heavy charged particles do not change direction appreciably while traveling through matter.

Heavy charged particles with large amounts of kinetic energy generally interact with matter by undergoing inelastic collisions with atomic electrons. In this process, they give up a portion of their energy with each interaction, finally giving up a large portion of energy at the end of their range, causing the Bragg peak.

THE PHYSICS OF DOSIMETRY

The radiation dose prescribed by a radiation oncologist for a patient must be quantified by a dosimetrist or medical physicist to determine monitor unit (MU) settings. It is important to understand the basic parameters used for dosimetry calculations and treatment planning. A brief review of the major concepts in dose calculation leading to MU settings follows.

Inverse Square Law

The inverse square law can be derived by considering a point source that is emitting radiation equally in all directions; two spheres are centered on this source with radii r_1 and r_2 ($r_2 > r_1$). The intensity I of the photons emitted from the source is defined as the number N of photons going through a spherical surface per unit area A per unit time of the sphere:

The inverse square law: r1 is the distance from the point source to a sphere of area A_1, and r_2 is the distance from the point source to a sphere of A_2. It is assumed that no photons are lost due to absorption as they travel away from the source, so: $N_1 = N_2$. Noting that the area of a sphere is $A = \pi r^2$; solving these equations yields:

$$\frac{I_2}{I_1} = \left(\frac{r_1}{r_2}\right)^2,$$

As can be seen from equation, the ratio of intensities of a photon beam is inversely proportional to the square of the ratio of the distances from the source. This decrease in the number of photons at a function of increasing distance is known as the inverse square law.

Backscatter Factor

Consider the following two experimental arrangements. In Fig. 1.11, situation (A) illustrates an exposure calibration of a photon beam in air. Situation (B) illustrates the irradiation conditions of the phantom. The reading on the electrometer in (B) is increased considerably compared with (A). This increase in dose, caused by radiation that was scattered back toward the probe from the phantom/patient, is called backscattered radiation. The factor used to correct this effect is called the backscatter factor (BSF). The BSF is defined as:

$$BSF = \frac{\text{Exposure at phantom surface}}{\text{Exposure at same point with no phantom present}}$$

The BSF increases as the energy approaches a maximum value in the orthovoltage range and then decreases. It also increases as the field size increases; however, it is independent of SSD (source-to-surface distance).

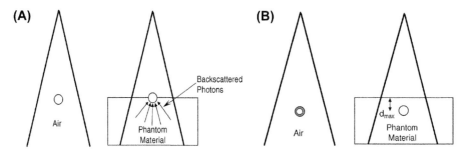

FIGURE 1.11   The left panel shows backscatter factor measurement: (A) dose measurement in air; (B) dose measurement in phantom surface at the same point. The right panel shows peak scatter measurement. The buildup cap placed around the chamber in air measurement is to give dose in free space.

Peak Scatter Factor

The BSF only applies to low-energy photon radiation. With the use of megavoltage radiation, a buildup effect occurred that shifts the depth maximum dose, d_{max}, from the surface to a new depth. A quantity similar to the BSF was defined and called the peak scatter factor (PSF) (Fig. 1.11):

$$PSF = \frac{\text{Dose at depth } d_{max} \text{ in phantom}}{\text{Dose in free space at same point}}$$

where d_{max} is the maximum dose and dose in free space is the dose to an ionization chamber with a small amount of buildup material wrapped around it to provide electronic equilibrium.

Depth of Maximum Dose (d_{max})

The radiation dose deposited within the first few millimeters of the patient's skin is highly variable because of the lack of electronic equilibrium, which is a function of the PSF. The first few millimeters are also known as the buildup region. d_{max} is the depth in tissue where the electronic equilibrium occurs for a radiation beam. This depth, d_{max}, is a function of energy (Table 1.1). As nominal energy increases, d_{max} also increases.

Percentage Depth Dose

One of the most used quantities in dosimetry is the dose at any depth along the central axis of the radiation beam or percentage depth dose (PDD) (Figs. 1.12 and 1.13) [3,4]. The PDD is defined by:

$$PDD = \frac{\text{Dose at depth } d \text{ along central axis}}{\text{Dose at depth of maximum dose along central axis}}$$

TABLE 1.1 Depth of d_{max} Variation With Nominal Beam Energy ($10 \times 10 \text{ cm}^2$)

Energy	Nominal d_{max} (cm)
Co-60	0.5
4 MV	1.0
6 MV	1.5
10 MV	2.5
15 MV	3.0
20 MV	3.5
25 MV	4.0
34 MV	5.0

Data from Jani SK. Handbook of dosimetry data for radiotherapy. Boca Raton, FL: CRC Press; 1993. p. 63, Table 1.I1.

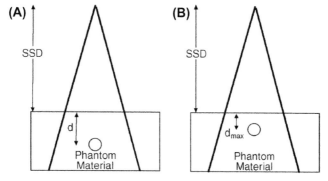

FIGURE 1.12 Percentage depth dose measurement: (A) dose measured at depth of central axis; (B) dose measured at d_{max} along central axis. *SSD*, source-to-surface distance.

The PDD is a function of beam energy, depth of measurement, beam field size, and the SSD.

The PDD depends on the following parameters:

Energy: As beam energy increases, the PDD (for a fixed depth) also increases. This results from the greater penetrating power of the photon beam.

Depth: As depth of the measurement increases, PDD decreases (with the exception of the buildup region). This is due to exponential attenuation of the photon beam as it passes through the patient.

Field size: As field size increases, PDD increases. This result from increased scatter because of the larger collimator and patient area irradiated.

SSD: As SSD increases, PDD increases due to the definition of the PDD and the inverse square law.

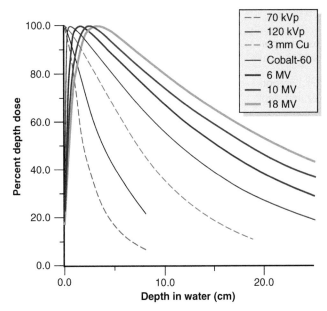

FIGURE 1.13 Central axis depth dose distribution for different-quality photon beams. Field size, 10 × 10 cm; source-to-surface distance (SSD) = 100 cm for all beams except for 3.0 mm Cu half-value layer (HVL), SSD = 50 cm. *(Reproduced from Fig. 6.36 from Clinical Radiation Oncology by Gunderson and Tepper, fourth edition, 2016, Elsevier).*

Tissue—Air Ratio

The PDD was used as the primary dosimetric variable when treatment techniques were predominantly SSD.

When newer machines became available, which rotated around an isocenter, it became possible to treat patients using isocentric techniques. In an isocentric technique, the distance from the source to the center of the target volume is held constant, whereas the distance from the source to the surface of the patient changes for each beam orientation. A new quantity was then defined to address isocentric treatment calculations, called the tissue—air ratio, or TAR. The TAR is defined as:

$$TAR = \frac{\text{Dose at depth d in phantom}}{\text{Dose in free space at the same point.}}$$

Note that the TAR varies like the PDD with respect to the beam energy,

depth and field size. It is independent of SSD.

Scatter—Air Ratio

TAR can be divided in to a two-component model. In this model, the absorbed dose to any point in the patient is the sum of two components:

$$\text{Total dose} = \text{primary dose} + \text{scatter dose.}$$

- Primary dose component: It consists of all photons that come from the head of the machine that contributes dose to the point of interest.
- Scatter dose component: It consists of all photons that are scattered from the machine and the patient that deliver dose to the point of interest.

The scatter component can be found by subtracting the zero- area TAR from all other TARs at that depth (a field that contains only scatter), given by:

$$SAR = TAR - TAR_0.$$

This quantity is called the scatter-air ratio (SAR) and is utilized in the calculation of dose in irregular fields.

Tissue–Phantom Ratio, Tissue–Maximum Ratio

Tissue–phantom ratio (TPR) is a new dosimetric quantity introduced for high-energy photon beams, because TAR is difficult to measure above 3 MeV. TPR is defined as:

$$TPR = \frac{\text{Dose at a depth d in phantom}}{\text{Dose at a specified reference depth in phantom,}}$$

where the specified reference depth is 5, 7, or 10 cm.

If the specified reference depth of the above TPR definition is redefined to be at the d_{max}, then we have a special case of a TPR called the tissue–maximum ratio (TMR). TMR is nearly independent of SSD and is the most often used dosimetric quantity (Fig. 1.14):

$$TMR = \frac{\text{Dose at a depth d in phantom}}{\text{Dose at a depth of maximum dose in phantom}}$$

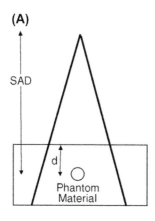
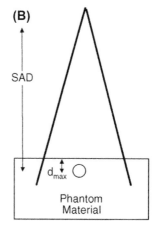

FIGURE 1.14 Tissue–maximum ratio (TMR) measurement: (A) dose measured at depth d in phantom; (B) dose measured at d_{max} in phantom.

LINAC CALIBRATION

The calibration procedure for a linear particle accelerator (linac) is to deliver an output of 1 cGy/MU (centiGray per monitor unit) for the reference field size, reference depth, and reference distance from the source (Fig. 1.15). This calibration is done as per the AAPM TG 51 protocol [5]. Typically the reference field size is 10 cm × 10 cm and the reference depth is 10 cm for photons and varies with electron energy. The reference distance is SSD + ref depth or Source Axis Distance (SAD). This is called factor CAL (calibrated output).

Types of Calibration

The two ways to perform treatment unit calibration are as follows (Fig. 1.15):

Output calibration (SSD): The calibration point is located at some reference depth in phantom.

Output calibration (SAD): The calibration point is located at a reference depth in the phantom at the isocenter.

Field Size Correction Factors

Because it is not practical to calibrate every possible field size, a table of field size correction (FSC) factors is used. These FSC factors allow us to get from the calibrated output to the output for the field size of interest. Notice that there is no mention of depth at this point.

The FSC factor, also known as the relative dose factor or output factor, is defined as:

$$\text{FSC} = \frac{\text{Dose for field size r at calibration depth}}{\text{Dose at calibration field size at calibration depth}}$$

Collimator Scatter Factor and Phantom Scatter Factor

Sometimes the FSC factor is broken into two smaller components:

1. Collimator scatter factor S_c

The radiation dose originating only from scatter of the collimator and head of the machine is defined as:

$$S_c = \frac{\text{Dose in Air for Field size r}}{\text{Dose in Air for Reference Field size}}$$

The open field size is used for calculating S_c in treatment time calculations, even if field blocking is present.

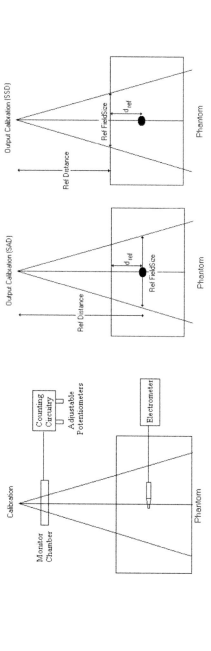

FIGURE 1.15 Right panel showing a typical calibration setup; the left panel showing the difference between the SAD and SSD calibration setup. *SSD*, source-to-source distance.

2. Phantom scatter factor S_p

The radiation dose originating only from scatter from the patient is defined as:

$$S_p = \frac{\text{Dose in Phantom Only for Field size r}}{\text{Dose in Phantom Only for Reference Field size}}$$

When blocking is in the field, the blocked field size is used for S_p in time calculations.

3. Collimator–phantom scatter factor $S_{c,p}$:

Because the phantom dose cannot be measured, we define the collimator–phantom scatter factor as scattered radiation originating from the collimator, head, and/or patient:

$$S_{c,p} = \frac{\text{Dose in Phantom for Field size r}}{\text{Dose in Phantom for Reference Field size}}$$

This factor (equivalent to the original FSC factor) is given by:

$$S_{c,p} = S_c S_p$$

Therefore,

$$S_p = \frac{S_{c,p}}{S_c}$$

Note that $S_{c,p}$ is equivalent to our FSC factor.

Beam Modifier Factors

Next, the effect of any beam modifiers (Lucite trays and wedges) must also be taken into account because these devices cause a decrease in the output of the machine.

To compensate for beam attenuation, tray factors (TF) and wedge factors (WF) are used.

They are defined as:

$$TF = \frac{\text{Dose with tray in field}}{\text{Dose without tray in field}}$$

$$WF = \frac{\text{Dose with wedge in field}}{\text{Dose without wedge in field}}$$

These factors relate the calibrated output (10 × 10) to the output with the tray and/or wedge in the field.

Patient Attenuation Factors

Another factor in the dose rate is the patient attenuation factor (PAF). These factors account for the attenuation caused by the patient when they are in the useful beam. These factors can be the PDD, TAR, TPR, or TMR.

The choice of the PAF for use in a treatment time calculation is dependent on which treatment technique is used (SSD or SAD).

The proper choices are:

1. SSD → PDD
2. SAD → TAR, TMR, TPR

If blocking is present in the field, then the blocked field size is used to calculate the PAF in a time calculation.

Calculation of Monitor Units and Treatment Time

The monitor unit is given by:

$$MU\ (Time) = \frac{\text{Dose prescribed at the prescription point}}{\text{Dose rate of the unit at the prescription point}}$$

where:

Dose rate of the unit at the prescription point $= (CAL)\ (S_c)\ (S_p)\ (WF)\ (TF)\ (PAF)$
or,

$$MU\ (Time) = \frac{\text{Dose prescribed at the prescription point}/(IDL)}{(CAL)(ISF)(Sc)(Sp)(WF)(TF)(PAF)}$$

So for photon treatments, the equation is given by:

$$MU\ (Time) = \frac{(TD/\%IDL)}{(CAL)(ISF)(S_c)(S_p)(WF)(TF)(PAF)}$$

While for electron treatments, it is given by:

$$MU\ (Time) = \frac{(TD/\%IDL)}{(CAL)(ISF)(RCF)(CF)}$$

Electron Beam Dosimetry

Electrons behave differently from X-rays. Because of their unique interaction with matter, they demonstrate a rapid dose fall-off, a finite range, and X-ray contamination. Unlike high-energy X-rays, electrons have less skin sparing and a high surface dose. As such, in addition to the depth of maximum dose denoted as R100, electron beams are described by other unique parameters such as R90, Rp, and X-ray component as seen in Fig. 1.16 and Table 1.2.

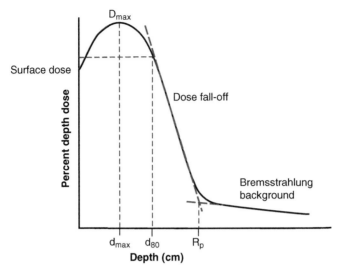

FIGURE 1.16 Electron depth dose curve showing the definition of R90, R50, and Rp. *PDD*, percentage depth dose. *Reprinted from Figure 6-40 from Clinical Radiation Oncology by Gunderson and Tepper, 4th edition, 2016, Elsevier.*

TABLE 1.2   Electron Beam Dose of Maximum Depth, R90, and Rp Varies With Beam Energy

Electron Beam Central Axis Depth Dose Data, SSD = 100 cm			
Nominal energy (MeV)	R100 (dmax) (cm)	R90 (cm)	Rp (cm)
6	1.3	1.7	2.88
9	1.8	2.6	4.32
12	2.3	3.5	5.85
15	2.5	4.4	7.26
18	2.5	5.2	9.25

Data from Jani SK. Handbook of dosimetry data for radiotherapy. Boca Raton, FL: CRC Press; 1993. p. 76, Table 2.A1.

- **R90** is the depth of 90% dose level and is the recommended therapeutic range of the electron beam depth dose.
- **Rp** is the practical range of the electron beam, or the maximum distance it can penetrate. This is the depth where the fall-off tangent of the electron beam depth dose curve intersects with the bremsstrahlung component line.

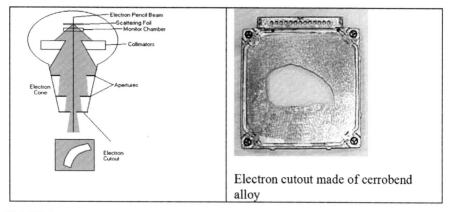

Electron cutout made of cerrobend alloy

FIGURE 1.17 Left panel showing a schematic diagram of the electron cone setup and the right panel showing an electron cutout.

- Because of the interaction of the electron beam with the accelerator head components, bremsstrahlung X-rays are produced. This is known as bremsstrahlung contamination of the electron beam and produces a tail in the electron beam depth dose. The bremsstrahlung component of the electron beam is calculated by extrapolating the bremsstrahlung tail to the Rp.

Because electrons are easily scattered in air, close collimation near the patient's surface is necessary to accurately define the radiation field (Fig. 1.17). An electron cone is inserted in the linear accelerator close to the patient's skin (either 95 or 100 cm). This cone will define the field size at the patient.

Note that if further custom collimation is necessary, one can fabricate an electron cutout to be placed at the end of the cone or tertiary collimation at the patient's surface may be used in the form of lead sheet. Note that this blocking affects the electron beam output and the beam PDD. Electron custom block output is routinely measured before clinical use.

Electron beams are clinically useful to treat superficial tumors, such as skin cancers, chest wall tumors, and tumor beds. With proper attention to the choice of electron beam energy and beam modifiers such as cutout and skin bolus, electron beams are very effective in treating superficial targets.

THE PHYSICS OF RADIATION TREATMENT PLANNING AND DELIVERY

Radiation treatments can be performed in two different ways:

1. External beam radiation therapy: radiation is given from a linear accelerator.
2. Brachytherapy (internal radiation): radiation is given by implanting a radioactive source into the patient.

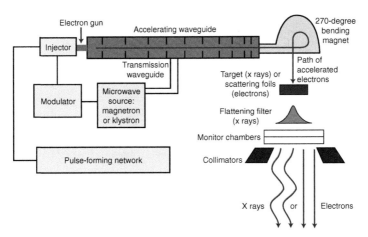

FIGURE 1.18   Schematic diagram of a linear accelerator. *Reprinted from Figure 6-5 from Clinical Radiation Oncology by Gunderson and Tepper, fourth edition, 2016, Elsevier.*

External Beam Radiation

Modern external beam radiation therapy is performed via a linear accelerator (Fig. 1.18), which accelerates electrons to very high energies. The electrons strike a tungsten target to produce bremsstrahlung X-rays, which are then used to treat patients. Alternatively, high-energy electrons can also be used for the patient's treatment. Better skin sparing and better penetration of the tissue make a linear accelerator an optimum tool for radiation treatments.

- Modern linear accelerators can produce low- and high-energy photons (6 and 18 MV photons, respectively) and electrons ranging from 4 to 20 MeV.
- In addition, modern linear accelerators are equipped with dual asymmetrical jaws, a multileaf collimator (M LC), and electronic portal imaging devices (EPIDs). The dual asymmetric jaws are used to generate dynamic wedges with nominal wedge angles (10–60 degrees) and can therefore be used for treatment planning and treatments as opposed to fixed physical wedges.
- The standard M LC consists of individual collimator leaves of 0.5–1 cm at the isocenter, which are individually controlled by a computer. Although initially designed to replace Cerrobend blocks, the M LC is now used to modulate the beam intensity to perform intensity-modulated radiation therapy (IMRT).
- The record and verify (R&V) system controls the various patient treatment parameters to be used. This type of system allows the linac parameters to be set and verified before the patient is treated, thereby avoiding errors such as incorrect gantry, collimator, couch, field size, dose per fraction, total dose, and treatment accessories.
- In addition, EPIDs are now in routine clinical use along with new imaging technologies. Not only automating the portal imaging to verify patient positioning, EPIDs are also essential to perform image-guided radiation therapy (IGRT) for more accurate delivery of the radiation.

Internal Radiation

Internal radiation is also called brachytherapy. Radioactive sources, such as 125I seeds, 137Cs capsules, or 192Ir ribbons, are placed inside the patient in the treatment areas. These radioactive sources deliver high-dose radiation to the tumor with a rapid dose fall-off, sparing the surrounding normal critical structures from the high dose of radiation. Brachytherapy can be interstitial or intracavitary and can be temporary or permanent.

RADIATION TREATMENT PLANNING

After a patient is counseled and a decision has been made for external beam radiation treatment, a planning process is set into motion. For a conformal radiation therapy (CRT) technique, the patient is CT simulated, which involves the following process:

- The patient is set in the treatment position that is dictated by the treating physician. This may include specific positioning of the patient such as supine or prone position of the head, arms, and legs. A treatment aid such as a breast board or belly board may be required, depending on the site of the treatment. To reproduce the treatment setup, the patient be in a comfortable position.
- Immobilization of the patient: Immobilization devices ensure setup reproducibility on a daily basis. These devices include thermoplastic face masks for brain, head, and neck patients, wing boards for lung patients, and body molds for breast and prostate patients. Immobilization devices are custom-made, thus offering reproducibility and rigidity.
- CT scanning: The superior and inferior limits of the CT scan are noted by the treating physician, and orally or intravenously administered contrast may be used for greater precision of tumor localization. All surgical scars are usually marked by radiopaque wires for identification on CT images. Depending on the no-shift or shift methods, reference marks may be placed on the patient before CT scans.
- Transfer of the CT dataset to the treatment planning station: Once the CT scan is complete, its dataset is transferred to the planning station, where the data are prepared by the dosimetrist for a virtual simulation. This involves the orientation of the patient/treatment coordinate system without the presence of the patient. The three-dimensional dataset (3D CT) enables the radiation oncologist to make treatment planning decisions that he/she would have been unable to make during conventional simulation. In addition, secondary imaging datasets such as diagnostic CT, magnetic resonance imaging (MRI), or positron emission tomography (PET) can be registered and fused with the primary CT dataset for greater localization of the target volume.

At this point, the CT simulation process is concluded and the planning process begins, involving the following steps:

- Contouring structures: Once the dataset is prepared by the dosimetrist at the planning station, the treating physician contours the critical structure and target volumes. Presently, physicians are using the International Commission on

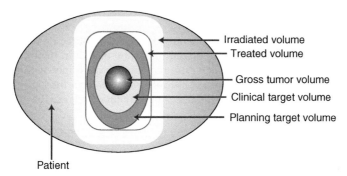

FIGURE 1.19 Different target volumes as defined by the International Commission on Radiation Units and Measurements. *CTV*, clinical target volume; *GTV*, gross tumor volume; *ITV*, internal target volume; *PTV*, planning target volume. *Reprinted from Figure 6-46 from Clinical Radiation Oncology by Gunderson and Tepper, 4th edition, 2016, Elsevier.*

Radiation Units and Measurements (ICRU), reports 50 and 62 [7,8] definitions for different target volumes (Fig. 1.19). Briefly, gross tumor volume is the gross disease seen clinically or in imaging studies, clinical target volume (CTV) is the clinically suspected extension of the tumor beyond the gross disease, internal target volume is CTV, which provides a margin to account for the internal movement of the CTV, whereas planning target volume (PTV) is the margin needed to compensate for any setup error for the patient. In addition to target volumes, critical structures, organ at risk (OAR) volume has also been defined by the ICRU. Once the critical structures are outlined by the radiation oncologist, a margin is added to the OAR for the uncertainty of the setup error for the patient. This is called the planning organ at risk volume (PRV).

- Beam placement and design of the treatment fields: Once all of the critical structures and target volumes have been contoured, the dosimetrist initiates the radiation beam placement as per the physician's instruction. Standard setup treatments such as the four-field box pelvis require only four beams coming from AP/PA and RT/LT lateral beams, whereas other treatments such as the nine-field IMRT may require more complex beam arrangements. Modern treatment planning systems use M LCs and dynamic wedges for normal tissue blocking rather than Cerrobend blocks and physical wedges used previously. Depending on the target volumes and prescription, appropriate treatment fields are then designed by the dosimetrist. These fields should be verified by the physician before initiation of the dose calculation.
- Dose calculation and isodose generation: The next step in radiation treatment planning is the generation of the 3-D dose distribution for the patient. Sophisticated computer software is used to derive an optimized treatment plan for each patient. In general, isodose distribution in all three axes and a dose—volume histogram (DVH) are generated for the physician to review, evaluate, and approve the plan.

- Treatment plan verification and quality assurance (QA): The final step treatment planning is to verify the plan that has been designed for an individual patient. For a simple setup, this may involve taking only setup verification films before initiating the radiation treatment to verify the bony landmarks. For more complex IMRT plans, detailed measurements of the fluence map are needed.

  Once the planning is complete and approved by the radiation oncologist, the necessary QA is then performed by the medical physicist. The treatment planning information is then transferred to the R&V system for delivery of the radiation therapy by the linear accelerator.

EXTERNAL BEAM RADIATION THERAPY

Radiation treatment planning has matured considerably over the past 20 years. Powerful computer hardware, coupled with sophisticated software, now enables radiation treatment planning to provide state-of-the-art image processing, precise target localization, and innovative 3-D dose computation. Commercially available radiation dose calculation algorithms now range from pencil beam algorithms to the most precise Monte Carlo algorithm. The following sections describe radiation treatment modalities.

3-D Conformal Radiation Therapy

Three-dimensional conformal treatment employs 3-D patient anatomy data to generate 3-D dose distribution to conform the target volume being treated. Computer-generated reconstruction of the ICRU-defined target volumes and surrounding OARs are derived directly from CT/MRI data.

- The dosimetrist/radiation oncologist team uses a beam's-eye view (relationship of target and normal tissue as seen by the radiation beam) to arrange radiation fields in preparation for noncoplanar/coplanar radiation therapy to treat the tumor. Three-dimensional CRT (3-D CRT) is a forward planning technique.
- This is a manual trial-and-error iterative process performed by the dosimetrist, who continuously evaluates treatment plans by altering beam parameters (beam directions, weights, modifiers, etc.) until a satisfactory plan is achieved. 3-D CRT dose calculations are more accurate because the dose computation algorithm uses 3-D datasets from the CT scan, thus providing comprehensive patient anatomy. Three-dimensional dose corrections are also performed, which take into account tissue heterogeneities.

  To perform a 3-D CRT plan evaluation, isodose distribution in three-dimensional planes is most useful as it aids the radiation oncologist in determining the spatial relationship between the radiation dose, the target, and the OARs. However, because the biologic effect of the radiation is also a function of the volume of the organ irradiated, a DVH becomes a critical tool for treatment plan evaluation. It is the cumulative DVH, which plots the target's volume and critical structures as a function of dose, which is most useful to the radiation oncologist. An optimized treatment plan should include >95% of the PTV within the 100% of the prescribed isodose line, while maintaining all of the critical structural constraints set forth by the physician.

Intensity-Modulated Radiation Therapy

IMRT is a newer technology in radiation oncology that delivers highly conformal radiation to the tumor while improving normal tissue sparing. It combines two advanced concepts to deliver 3-D conformal radiation.

1. Inverse treatment planning utilizes techniques such as simulated annealing or gradient optimization. Most inverse optimization problems in radiation therapy are simple and straightforward and can be solved using a gradient optimization technique, which is much faster and is used by many treatment planning systems.
2. Computer-controlled intensity modulation of the radiation beam: In IMRT, radiation is broken into many "beamlets"; the intensity of which can be adjusted individually and is achieved by the treatment planning program.
   - All target volumes and OARs are outlined, five to nine equally spaced coplanar beams are placed around the patient and a low photon beam energy of 6 MV is usually selected energy. The large number of beam orientations may nullify any requirement for beam angle optimization for the IMRT planning.
   - The radiation oncologist then mathematically quantifies the desired dose distribution within the patient by defining some objective functions such as assigning minimum and maximum doses acceptable for treating the targets and minimum and maximum limiting doses for the OARs. For example, a prescription plan for prostate cancer IMRT treatment might be prostate PTV dose 180 cGy/fx to 7920 cGy, the rectal constraint V70 < 25% and V40 < 35%, and bladder constraint V75 < 25%. This type of plan optimization is known as dose—volume—based optimization for IMRT.
   - The plan evaluation is accomplished by reviewing isodose distribution in axial, coronal, and sagittal planes and by reviewing the cumulative DVH. However, very careful attention must be given to IMRT plan evaluation, as unexpected high doses can be deposited in unintended locations within the patient. An optimized treatment plan should include at least 95% of the PTV within the 100% of the prescribed isodose line, while maintaining all the critical structural constraints established by the physician. The minimum and the maximum dose constraints for the PTV should be within 5% of the prescribed dose. This helps achieve a more homogeneous dose distribution within the target volume.
   - After the IMRT plan is approved by the radiation oncologist, the nonuniform beam fluence map is then converted into the M LC sequence for the accelerator. The beams are delivered by computer-controlled opening and closing of the M LC leaves.
   - There are two primary types of IMRT delivery systems: (1) static multileaf collimation (sM LC), commonly known as the step-and-shoot technique and (2) dynamic multileaf collimation (dM LC), commonly known as the sliding window technique. In the sM LC technique, although the gantry is in one angle, the nonuniform fluence is delivered by using a sequence of fixed, multiple (20—100), small subfields. The radiation stops while the M LC pattern changes from one subfield to the next at each gantry angle. In the dM LC technique, the M LC leaves are continuously moving while the radiation beam is on. It is the slow and fast variable speeds of the M LC leaves that cause the high and low intensity of the nonuniform fluence of the beam during the treatment.

The potential advantages of IMRT are the creation of multiple targets and multiple critical avoidance structures using new accelerated fractionation schemes, such as simultaneous integrated boost treatments. IMRT is the most important advance in radiotherapy since the invention of the linear accelerator.

Volumetric Modulated Arc Therapy

Volumetric modulated arc therapy (VMAT) is a new and advanced form of IMRT. This technique delivers continuous radiation while rotating the gantry around the patient as opposed to fixed beam IMRT. During treatment machine rotation, three parameters are varied: the speed of rotation around the patient, the dimension of the beam shaping aperture MLC to fit the size and shape of the tumor/target, and the rate at which the radiation dose is delivered to the patient. VMAT is much faster than fixed beam IMRT owing to its continuous delivery of radiation during the arcs. By shortening the treatment time, the effect of patient breathing and patient involuntary movements during treatment are minimized, thus improving tumor targeting accuracy.

Image-Guided Radiation Therapy

Setup errors and organ motion contribute significant uncertainties during radiation therapy delivery. To overcome this problem, modern linear accelerators are equipped with portal vision and/or an on-board imager. This allows the radiation oncologist to move from 2-D setup verification portal films to 3-D volumetric soft tissue target imaging for treatment verification.

- During the treatment planning process, the dosimetrist generates a digitally reconstructed radiograph (DRR) based on the CT simulated images.
- During treatments, either MV or kV diagnostic quality images are taken immediately before the treatments. These images are taken with EPID and are registered with the DRRs. They allow the patient to reproduce the setup on a daily basis.
- To visualize soft tissue tumors, patients undergo cone beam CT (CBCT) immediately before treatment. CBCT is created with a gantry-mounted kV imager and EPID. The CBCT images are then registered with CT simulation images, and the patient must reproduce the setup on a daily basis.

The use of IMRT coupled with IGRT allows for smaller PTV margins, thereby enabling the radiation oncologist to deliver a higher radiation dose to the tumor, which improves sparing of normal critical structures safely.

BRACHYTHERAPY

In modern radiation oncology, a large number of patients are treated with brachytherapy. Radioactive sources that are implanted into the tumor give conformal and very high radiation doses to the tumor and a low dose to the surrounding tissues. This is a consequence of the inverse square law and the attenuation of radiation by the tissue. As the distance from the radioactive source increases, rapid dose decay in the surrounding normal tissue is observed. Brachytherapy can utilize an interstitial, intracavitary, or other techniques.

Interstitial Brachytherapy

In this technique, the radioactive sources are implanted directly into the tumorous tissue. They can be in the form of seeds, needles, or ribbons and can be removed from the tissue after a specific dose. In the case of temporary implants, these radioactive sources are removed from the tissue after a specific dose has been given. Alternatively, the sources can remain in the implanted tissue as a permanent implant.

- One of the most common uses of an interstitial implant is that of treating prostate cancer. Prostate cancer implants can be temporary or permanent. The permanent implant is most commonly performed with either 125I or 103Pd radioactive seeds. Table 1.3 lists their dosimetric characteristics.
- Data in Table 1.3 clearly demonstrate that radioactive sources used for permanent implants have short half-lives and low radiation energies because the majority of the radiation dose is given over a short period of time to a limited volume of tissue.
- On the other hand, radioactive sources used for temporary implants have longer half-lives and higher radiation energies. For temporary prostate cancer implants, the radioactive isotope 192Ir is commonly used. It has an HVL of 3 cm of lead, average energy of 380 keV, and a half-life of 73.2 days with a dose rate constant of 4.55 cGy/mCi h.

HDR units are now commercially available, showing the progress made since the early days of brachytherapy (Paterson–Parker or Manchester system tables that were developed for dosimetric treatments in the early days of brachytherapy planning).

TABLE 1.3   Dosimetric Characteristics for 125I and 103Pd

	^{125}I	^{103}Pd
HVL tissue	2 cm (0.025 mm lead)	1.6 cm (0.008 mm lead)
Average energy	28 keV	21 keV
Half-life	59.4 d	16.97 d
Dose rate constant	1.16 cGy/mCi h[1]	0.95 cGy/mCi h
Dose rate	7 cGy/h	21 cGy/h
Primary dose	145 Gy	115 Gy
mCi	0.31–0.37 mCi/seed	1.4 mCi/seed
Boost dose	108 Gy	90 Gy
mCi	0.25–0.31 mCi/seed	1 mCi/seed

Intracavitary Brachytherapy

With this technique, hollow stainless steel applicators hold the radioactive sources in the desired configuration for the brachytherapy treatments. This technique is most commonly used for cervical and uterine cancer treatments.

- Fletcher–Suit applicators (the most commonly used) have a tandem that is inserted into the uterine canal and colpostats that are inserted into the vaginal fornices, which are then secured with a locking mechanism. Once the applicators are stabilized with packing and verified with X-ray images, they are loaded with radioactive sources.
- Intracavitary low dose rate (LDR) brachytherapy is commonly performed with 137Cs radioactive sources. 137Cs has an HVL of 6 mm of lead, average energy of 662 keV, and a half-life of 30 years. Its dose rate constant is 3.09 cGy/mC h.
- A high activity 10 Ci source of 192Ir with a dose rate of about 100 cGy/min, known as high dose rate (HDR), is now available for temporary implants used for prostate and other cancers. HDR implantation is often done using a remote after-loading technique, which permits the brachytherapy treatment time to be short (e.g., minutes). This minimizes radiation exposure of personnel and, with the aid of sophisticated treatment planning software to manipulate the source dwell times, adds the necessary flexibility to customize the brachytherapy treatments.

OTHER RADIATION THERAPY MODALITIES

Modern radiation oncology employs many other radiation therapy techniques for patient treatments including the following:

- **Stereotactic radiosurgery (SRS)** is a technique that allows the radiation oncologist to focus beams of radiation precisely to treat tumors in a single-fraction treatment. Radiosurgery can be performed using X-rays from linear accelerators or gamma rays from ^{60}Co radioactive sources from a Gamma Knife unit. SRS is primarily used for brain tumors and metastatic brain lesions. Similar to SRS, stereotactic body radiotherapy uses a very small field over three to five fractions and has recently been used to treat lesions of the spinal cord, liver, adrenal gland, lung, and pancreas.
- **Particle radiation therapy** using proton and neutron beams is now used to treat certain tumors that are very difficult to cure with photon radiation therapy alone. Proton beams deposit most of the radiation dose at a certain depth within the body (Bragg peak), which then more effectively spares the underlying normal tissue. Neutron beams typically have a greater relative biological effectiveness on the tumor than a similar dose of photon radiation therapy.
- A **nonsealed radionuclide** such as 153Sm is administered intravenously to treat widespread painful bony metastatic lesions. 153Sm beta particles have a maximum range of 3 mm in soft tissue, 1.7 mm in bone, an average energy of 0.23 MeV, and a half-life of 1.9 days. On the other hand, radioimmunotherapy is a form of infusible treatment available for lymphoma cancer patients. Radioimmunotherapy uses cell-specific monoclonal antibodies, which are radiolabeled with 111In, 90Y, or 131I. These antibodies then bind to specific cancer cells (CD20 positive) and deliver radiation directly to the cancer cell.

A newer generation of external beam radiation therapy techniques has recently become available. These techniques include Halcyon and the CyberKnife.

Halcyon uses a cone beam intensity-modulated beam delivered from a rotating linear accelerator mounted on a ring gantry. The patient is inside the ring gantry while the radiation beam is on. This system combines a low energy (6 MV) accelerator with MV CBCT and kV CBCT scanning modes for imaging. For MV CBCT, the accelerator utilizes a LDR mode of the 6 MV beam, and the frames captured via the EPID are reconstructed into a volumetric image. For kV CBCT, a large 43 cm × 43 cm imaging kV panel that was custom-designed for the Halcyon kV application is paired with a kV X-ray tube typically used in the diagnostic imaging applications. The images are reviewed in real time to make patient positional adjustment by moving the treatment table automatically in order to put the patient exactly where he/she needs to be, the same way every day within millimeter accuracy. For beam shaping, a dual-layer MLC was developed for the Halcyon system in order to eliminate the need for backup jaws and leaf carriages while reducing leakage radiation and increasing patient clearance. The Halcyon is a newest approach to deliver image-guided—intensity-modulated radiation therapy.

The CyberKnife uses a noninvasive image—guided localization system and robotic delivery of SRS to treat patients. The robotic arm of the CyberKnife gives this technique unprecedented access to tumor sites with an ease that is very difficult to achieve with conventional radiation therapy techniques. Currently, this system is being tested to treat prostate cancer patients with four to five fractions of treatments in hypofractionated fashion, similar to the HDR brachytherapy treatments for prostate cancer.

In the future, these exciting newer generation radiation therapies will allow us to treat cancer patients with higher radiation doses, thus increasing the likelihood of cure, while minimizing side effects from the radiation treatments.

References

Ref 1. *McDermott PN, Orton CG. The physics & technology of radiation therapy. Madison, WI: Medical Physics Publishing; 2010.*

Ref 2. *Jani SK. Handbook of dosimetry data for radiotherapy. Boca Raton, FL: CRC Press; 1993.*

Ref 3. *Khan F. The physics of radiation therapy. 3rd ed. Philadelphia: Lippincott Williams & Wilkins; 2003.*

Ref 4. *Sterling TD, Perry H. Derivation of mathematical expres- sion for the percent depth dose surface of cobalt 60 beams and visu- alization of multiple field dose distribution. Br J Radiol 1964;37:544.*

Ref 5. *Almond PR, Biggs PJ, Coursey BM, Hanson WF, Huq MS, Nath R, Rogers DWO. AAPM's TG-51 protocol for clinical reference dosimetry of high-energy photon and electron beams. Med Phys 1999;26:1847—70.*

Ref 6. *Gunderson L, Tepper J. Clinical radiation oncology. 1st ed. , London: Churchill Livingstone; 2000.*

Ref 7. *International Commission on Radiation Units and Measurements (ICRU) Report 50. Prescription, recording and reporting photon beam therapy. Bethesda, MD: ICRU; 1993.*

Ref 8. *International Commission on Radiation Units and Measurements (ICRU) Report 62. Prescription, recording and reporting photon beam therapy (supplement to ICRU report 50). Bethesda, MD: ICRU; 1999.*

Ref 9. *Levitt SH, Purdy JA, Perez CA, Vijayakumar S. Technical basis of radiation therapy: practical clinical applications. 4th revised edition. New York: Springer; 2006.*

2

Radiation Protection and Safety

Radiation has been safely used for cancer treatments for more than a century. The potential hazards of ionizing radiation were realized early on, leading to precautions that limit the exposure of workers and the public to radiation. It is important that radiation oncologists have an understanding of the principles of radiation safety, especially regarding the safe handling of X-rays and radioactive materials as they apply to the practice of radiation oncology.

MEASUREMENT OF RADIATION QUANTITIES

Radiation safety standards are necessary to define radiation protection quantities and are discussed in detail by several publications of National Council on Radiation Protection and Measurements (NCRP) and International Commission on Radiological Protection (ICRP) [1–4]. A brief description of commonly used radiation protection terms follows.

Radiation Exposure

Radiation exposure is the absolute value of the total charge of one sign produced in a small mass of air, when all electrons liberated by photons in air are completely stopped in air, divided by the mass of air:

$$X = dQ/dm.$$

The original unit of exposure is roentgen (R). The unit of exposure in the International System of Units (SI) is the coulomb per kilogram (C/kg). They are related as follows.

$$1\,R = 2.58 \times 10^{-4} C/kg.$$

Fundamentals of Radiation Oncology
https://doi.org/10.1016/B978-0-12-814128-1.00002-7

Absorbed Dose

Absorbed dose is the mean energy imparted by ionizing radiation to a mass, dm:

$$D = dEaverage/dm.$$

The original unit of absorbed dose is the rad, which is an acronym for radiation absorbed dose. The unit of absorbed dose in the SI system is the gray (Gy) and its relation to the rad is

$$1 \, Gy = 100 \, rad.$$

Effective Dose Equivalent

The biological effect of radiation exposures from different types of radiation (photons, neutrons, protons, as well as other particles) can be different because of the distinct ways in which different radiation interacts with matter and the manner in which energy is deposited in the matter.

- This difference in biological effects is taken into account by a quantity called the effective dose equivalent. The effective dose equivalent to a tissue T that is irradiated by different types of radiation R is defined as

$$H_T = \sum(W_R D_{T,R}),$$

where H_T is the effective dose equivalent, W_R is a weighting factor of radiation R, and $D_{T,R}$ is the absorbed dose received by tissue T from radiation R.
- Note that quality factors were defined in ICRP Report 27 [3] and NCRP Report 91 [1], but they were replaced by radiation weighting factors, W_R, in NCRP Report 116 [2] as shown in Table 2.1. The product of Q and N is called the radiation weighting factor, W_R.

Effective Dose

In addition to the biological differences in radiation exposure, one must also consider how different types of tissues/organs respond to radiation.

- To account for these differences in tissue/organ sensitivity, the NCRP and ICRP have adopted the concept of the effective dose [2,3].
- Each organ is given a weighting factor (W_T) based on radiation-induced cancer incidence data collected from atomic bomb survivors or occupational exposures such as radium dial painters and underground miners. The effective dose is defined as

$$E = \sum(W_T H_T),$$

where E is the effective dose, W_T is a weighting factor of tissue T, and H_T is the mean dose equivalent received by tissue T.

TABLE 2.1   Radiation Quality Factors and Radiation Weighting Factors

Radiation	Q NCRP 91	W$_R$ NCRP 116
X-rays, gamma rays, electrons	1	1
Thermal neutrons	5	—
Neutrons other than thermal	20	—
Neutrons other than thermal <10 keV	—	5
Neutrons 10 to 100 keV	—	10
Neutrons > 100 to 2 MeV	—	20
Protons > 2 MeV	—	2–5
Alphas, fission fragments, heavy nuclei	20	20

Data from National Council on Radiation Protection and Measurements (NCRP) Report No. 116. Limitation of Exposure to Ionizing Radiation. Bethesda, MD: NCRP; 1993. p. 7, NCRP Report No. 116. Table 1.1.

RADIATION PROTECTION PRINCIPLES

The goal of radiation protection is to prevent the nonstochastic (deterministic) effects, such as erythema and radiation sickness, and to limit the stochastic effects, such as cancer and genetic defects. External radiation exposure to humans can be minimized by the following three factors:

- **Time:** Minimizing time of radiation exposure reduces the total dose.
- **Distance:** Maximizing the distance from the radiation source reduces the total dose.
- **Shielding:** Maximizing the thickness of any shielding barriers between the radiation source and the point of exposure reduces the total dose.

These principles are used in radiation oncology practice on a daily basis to reduce occupational exposure, medical exposure, and exposure to the general public. For example, an interstitial or intracavitary brachytherapy procedure can be performed by using an afterloading technique, which is accomplished much faster than a preloading/manual loading technique, thereby minimizing the time of exposure to personnel. High dose rate (HDR) brachytherapy is performed remotely, thus maximizing the distance from the radioactive source to personnel and minimizing the time proximal to the source. The linear accelerators are housed in heavily shielded vaults having up to 6–10 feet of concrete in the primary shielding. This reduces the occupational exposure to the radiation therapist and to the general public.

ORGANIZATIONS

Radiation protection standards are set by two governing radiation protection bodies: the ICRP and the NCRP, which are nongovernmental organizations in the United States. The protection standards set by these two organizations are adopted into US law by the following federal agencies:

- **Nuclear Regulatory Commission (NRC):** The NRC oversees the licensing of all nuclear reactor—produced materials known as by-product materials. In 2007, the NRC began regulating all discrete sources of naturally occurring radioactive materials and accelerator-produced radioactive materials. Most states have entered into agreements with the NRC to enforce their regulations. They are called Agreement States.
- **Individual State Agencies:** State agencies oversee the licensing of individuals and institutions that handle electronic X-ray generators, such as diagnostic X-ray units and linear accelerators.
- **Department of Transportation:** The Department of Transportation (DOT) oversees the transportation of radioactive materials.
- **Food and Drug Administration:** The Food and Drug Administration (FDA) oversees the pharmaceutical aspects of radioactive material as well as patient safety of linacs and X-ray machines.

REGULATIONS

The NRC and individual states are responsible for regulating radioactive materials.

- **NRC's regulations:** In 2002, the NRC adopted a new set of regulations for the medical use of radioactive by-product materials [5]. They are based on a risk-based approach involving procedures that the NRC deems to be high risk in nature, such as
  1. gamma stereotactic radiosurgery and
  2. teletherapy units and
  3. HDR remote afterloading.
- **Dose limits to the public:** The total effective dose equivalent to the public cannot exceed 1 mSv/individual per year [2]. However, visitors to hospitalized radiation treatment patients are allowed to receive single dose greater than 1 mSv if the dose received by the visitor does not exceed 5 mSv and the Radiation Safety Officer (RSO) has predetermined appropriateness for the visit. In that case, approval can be given based on the time limitation if the visitor remains seated or standing at a distance designated as safe.
- **Medical event definitions** [6]: A medical event is any event, except for patient intervention, in which the administration of a by-product material or radiation from a by-product material occurs in an amount that exceeds specific criteria set by the Code of Federal Regulations 10 CFR 35.2 misadministration sections (1) through (6).

  Some of these criteria include radiopharmaceuticals differing from the total dose delivered more than 20%, a gamma stereotactic radiosurgery doses delivered differing from the prescribed dose by more than 10%, a teletherapy total dose delivered differing from the prescribed dose by more than 20%, a brachytherapy total dose delivered differing from the prescribed dose by more than 20%, the administration of a dose to the wrong individual, wrong site, wrong pharmaceutical or radioisotope, or the wrong route of administration.

- **Medical event reporting requirements:** If a medical event occurs, the following tasks must be completed:
  - The NRC Operations Center (in an Agreement State the pertinent State Agency) must be notified by telephone no later than the next calendar day after discovery of the medical event.
  - A written report must be submitted to the appropriate NRC Regional Office (in an Agreement State the pertinent State Agency) within 15 days after discovery of the medical event.
  - The treating physician must notify the referring physician and also notify the individual who is the subject of the medical event no later than 24 h after its discovery.
- **Administrative requirements:** The management of the institution must appoint a RSO, who is responsible for implementing the radiation protection program. Institutions that use two or more types of by-product material must establish a Radiation Safety Committee to oversee all uses of by-product material permitted by the license. The licensee must have a written quality management program. The licensee must retain all records for a period of 3 years.
  - The institution must use a written directive for any therapeutic dose of radiation from by-product material. The written directive must contain the patient's name and the following minimum information, shown in Table 2.2.
- **Technical requirements**:
  - Full calibration of the gamma stereotactic unit, the teletherapy unit and the HDR unit must be performed before the first medical use if a spot check measurement differs by more than 5% after replacement of sources, after any repair and annually.
  - Spot check calibration for the gamma stereotactic unit, the teletherapy unit, and the HDR unit must be performed daily before clinical use, monthly, and after source changes.
  - The institution must possess radiation-detecting instruments. Instruments must be calibrated after any repair and annually.
  - The institution must perform semiannual physical inventory and leak testing of all brachytherapy sources. If a source shows activity greater than 185 Becquerel (Bq) (0.005 μCi), then the source is deemed leaking and must not be used for patient treatment.
  - After a permanent brachytherapy implant, the institution must survey and account for sources that have not been implanted. After a temporary brachytherapy implant, the institution must survey the patient to make sure that all sources have been removed.
  - The institution must provide initial and annual radiation safety training to all personnel caring for brachytherapy patients. The training must include size and appearance of the sources, and the operating procedure for the HDR unit. It must also include safe handling and shielding instructions, patient and

TABLE 2.2   Written Directives Requiring Treatment-Specific Information

Type of Therapy	Required Information
Unsealed by-product material other than sodium iodide 131I	Radioactive drug Dosage Route of administration
Gamma stereotactic	Total dose Target coordinate settings for each distinct treatment site
Teletherapy	Total dose Dose per fraction, number of fractions, treatment site
High dose rate remote Afterloading	Radionuclide Treatment site, dose per fraction, number of fractions, total dose
Brachytherapy (before implant)	Radionuclide treatment site Total dose
Brachytherapy (after implant)	Radionuclide treatment site Total dose Number of sources Total source strength

visitor control, notification of the RSO if the patient has a medical emergency or expires, and emergency procedure drill for the operator, medical physicist, and the authorized user.
- The institution must not release a patient with a permanent brachytherapy implant until the measured dose from the patient at 1 m is less than 5 mrem/h. Patients with a temporary brachytherapy implant must not be released until all sources have been removed from the patient. All patients must be surveyed before their release from the institution.

OCCUPATIONAL AND GENERAL PUBLIC DOSE LIMITS

The NCRP Report 116 [2] recommendations of exposure limits are based on the following criteria:

- At low radiation levels the nonstochastic effects are essentially avoided.
- The predicted risk for stochastic effects should not be greater than the average risk of accidental death among workers in "safe" industries. This accidental death rate in safe industries is given in the 1991 data published by the National Safety Council as 0.90 "f 10^{-4} deaths per year [7].
- The ALARA (As Low As Reasonably Achievable) principle should be followed. This principle states that radiation risks should be kept as low as reasonably

achievable, taking into account the current state of technology and economics of improvement in relation to public health safety.
- The effective dose equivalent limits shown in Table 2.3 are based on NCRP Report 116 [2]. They do not include exposures received from medical procedures or natural background.
- The cumulative dose equivalent of an exposed person over his lifetime is limited by the individual radiation worker's lifetime effective dose, not to exceed his or her age in years times 10 mSv (Table 2.3):

$$H_{cum} = 10 \text{ mSv} \times \text{Age(years)}.$$

TABLE 2.3   Annual Effective Dose Equivalent Limits

Type	Dose Equivalent (mSv)
OCCUPATIONAL EXPOSURES	
Radiation workers	50
Lens of eye	150
Skin, hands, feet	500
PUBLIC EXPOSURES	
General public—Infrequent	5
General public—Continuous or frequent	1
Lens of eye	15
Skin, hands, feet	50
Unrestricted Area	0.02 mSv/h
CHILD (<18 Y)/EDUCATIONAL EXPOSURES	
Child(<18 y)/students	1
Lens of eye	15
Skin, hands, feet	50
EMBRYO/FETUS EXPOSURES	
Embryo/fetus	5
Embryo/fetus (after declared pregnancy)	0.5 monthly

Data from National Council on Radiation Protection and Measurements (NCRP) Report No. 116. Limitation of Exposure to Ionizing Radiation. Bethesda, MD: NCRP; 1993. p. 56, Table 19.1.

ALARA AND RADIATION-INDUCED BIOLOGICAL EFFECTS

The interaction of radiation with living matter releases energy within the matter and causes damage to the tissues. These can be broadly characterized as nonstochastic (deterministic) and stochastic effects [8]. As noted previously, the goal of the radiation protection program is to prevent the nonstochastic effects and to limit the stochastic effects.

- **Nonstochastic effects** are characterized by the following:
  1. Severity of the effect varies with the dose.
  2. Threshold dose after which the effect is observed.
  3. Clear, causal relationship between dose and effect is observed.
  4. Examples include skin erythema and radiation sickness.
- **Stochastic effects** are characterized by the following:
  1. The severity of the effect does not vary with the dose.
  2. The probability of the effect varies with the dose.
  3. A linear function is assumed with no threshold.
  4. These effects occur among unexposed and exposed individuals.
  5. Examples include cancer and genetic effects from radiation.

The stochastic effects relevant to radiation protection are primarily radiation-induced carcinogenesis, teratogenesis, and mutagenesis. As a stochastic effect has no threshold, it is important to maintain exposures ALARA. This ALARA principle can be applied on a daily basis to any radiation oncology practice, including constructing properly designed radiation facilities, performing area surveys, and monitoring personnel doses. A brief description of these is given below.

RADIATION TREATMENT ROOM DESIGN

Modern high-energy linear accelerators (linacs) are housed in heavily shielded vaults with up to 6–10 feet of concrete because occupational exposure from the accelerator to the radiation therapist and general public is not to exceed the maximum permissible dose (MPD) as noted in Table 2.3. The guidelines for designing treatment room shielding are detailed in NCRP Reports 49, 51, and 116 [2,9,10]. However, a brief description of the basic factors for such shielding and other technical requirements to design a treatment room is as follows.

Given the above, the design of a megavoltage unit treatment room should include the following considerations [11,12] (Fig. 2.1):

- **Primary radiation shielding**: The primary radiation shielding is the barrier that is sufficient to attenuate the primary radiation to the required limit. Primary radiation is the radiation that exits through the collimation system of the linear accelerator and is used to treat patients. Generally, primary shielding is the thickest because of the high energy of the primary beam.
- **Secondary radiation shielding**: The secondary radiation shielding is the barrier that is sufficient to attenuate secondary radiation to the required limit. Secondary

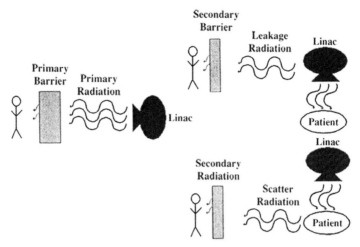

FIGURE 2.1   Primary and secondary barriers protecting persons from primary, leakage, and scatter radiation.

radiation consists of any leakage and scatter radiation. Leakage radiation is any radiation that escapes from the treatment machine that is not part of the primary beam. It has equivalent energy to that of primary radiation. Scatter radiation, on the other hand, is the radiation that is scattered from the machine and from the patient in all directions and is lower in energy than primary and leakage radiation.

- **Neutron shielding for high-energy photon and electron beams**: When a photon beam is produced with an energy exceeding 10 MV, the beam will become contaminated with neutrons that are produced as a result of the photodisintegration process that occurs in the target and collimators. At 15 MV, neutrons become an important issue for shielding calculations.

The following factors must be taken into account when performing primary and secondary shielding calculations:

- **Workload (W)**: The workload gives the amount of beam-on time and is usually given in terms of gray (Gy) at 1 m from the source. This is calculated by multiplying the amount of radiation dose given to a patient by the total number of patients treated per week. A typical value for W in a department is 500 to 1000 Gy/week at a distance of 1 m from the source, depending on the number of patients treated at the facility.
- **Use factor (U)**: The use factor gives the fraction of the operating time during which radiation is striking a particular barrier. When treating a patient, the radiation beam is delivered from many different angles by pointing the beam to the walls, floor, and ceiling. Recommended values for the use factor are given in Table 2.4. Note that, because of the multidirectional nature of leakage and scatter radiation, the use factor for the leakage and scatter radiation is always 1.

TABLE 2.4 Typical Use Factors for Primary Barrier

Barrier	Use Factor (U)
Floor	1
Walls	1/4
Ceiling	1/4–1/2

Data from National Council on Radiation Protection and Measurements (NCRP) Report No. 49. Structural shielding design and evaluation for medical use of x-rays and gamma rays of energies up to 10 MV. Bethesda, MD: NCRP; 1976. p. 64, Table 3.

- **Occupancy factor (T):** The occupancy factor gives the fraction of the operating time during which the area adjacent the treatment room is occupied by an individual. Depending on what is on the other side of the treatment room wall, such as offices, nurse stations, rest rooms, or parking lots, the typical values for the occupancy factor recommended is given in Table 2.5.
- **Distance (d):** This is the distance in meters from the isocenter of the radiation source to the area to be protected. The inverse square law applies to both primary and scatter radiation. The greater the distance from the source of the radiation, the smaller the dose received by the adjacent area on the other side of the treatment wall, thus requiring less shielding.
- **Dose equivalent limit (P):** The dose equivalent limits for the uncontrolled and the controlled areas around a treatment room are 0.1 mSv/week (0.01 rad/week) and 1.0 mSv/week (0.1 rad/week), respectively.

TABLE 2.5 Occupancy Factors for Shielding Design

Type of Occupancy	Occupancy Factor (T)
Full (office, nurse station, laboratories, etc.)	1
Partial (hallway, unoccupied parking lot, etc.)	1/4
Occasional (toilets, patient waiting room, stairways, outside pedestrian area, etc.)	1/8–1/16

Data from National Council on Radiation Protection and Measurements (NCRP) Report No. 49. Structural shielding design and evaluation for medical use of x-rays and gamma rays of energies up to 10 MV. Bethesda, MD: NCRP; 1976. p. 65, Table 4.

Considering all of the above, the barrier transmissions for the primary and the secondary barriers are given by the following formulas:

- **Primary radiation barrier:** The primary barrier transmission B is given by

$$B = \frac{Pd^2}{WUT}$$

where P is the maximum permissible dose for the area adjacent to the barrier; W is the workload of the unit; U is the use factor for the barrier; T is the occupancy factor for the area adjacent to the barrier, and d is the distance from the isocenter to the barrier.
- **Leakage radiation barrier:** The leakage barrier transmission BL is given by

$$B_L = \frac{Pd^2}{0.001\ WT}$$

where P is the maximum permissible dose for the area adjacent to the barrier and d is the distance from isocenter to the barrier. Leakage radiation cannot exceed 0.1% (0.001) of the primary beam. The use factor for leakage radiation is always 1 because leakage radiation is always present in the room when the unit is operational. Leakage radiation is assumed to be at the same energy as the primary beam.
- **Scatter radiation barrier:** The scatter barrier transmission BS is given by

$$B_s = \left(\frac{P}{\alpha WT}\right)\left(\frac{400}{F}\right)\ d_1^2 d_2^2,$$

where α is the fractional scatter at 1 m from the point of scatter; F is the area of the beam; d_1 is the distance from the source to the point of scatter; d_2 is the distance from the point of scatter to the area of interest; P is the maximum permissible dose for the area adjacent to the barrier; W is the workload of the unit; and T is the occupancy factor for the area adjacent to the barrier. Note that the use factor U for a scatter barrier is always 1 because scattered radiation is always present in the room when the unit is operational. Values of α are given in Table 2.6.
- Once the transmission factors B, B_L, and B_S are calculated, the barrier thickness can easily be determined from the broad beam attenuation curves for the given beam energies from NCRP 51 [10]. The thicknesses of the shielding barriers are given by NCRP 51 as a function of beam energies and the transmission factors.
- **Neutron radiation barrier:** Neutrons become shielding problems at energies of greater than 15 MV because of increased photodisintegration in interactions. Concrete has high hydrogen content, making it a very effective barrier for neutron shielding.

  Borated polyethylene also has high hydrogen content and is another effective material to slow down fast neutrons. It should be noted that if a slow neutron is absorbed by a nucleus, a photon may be ejected from the excited nucleus as it returns to its ground state. This ejected photon is called a capture gamma and is important for door construction. When dealing with the neutron shielding needed for the door construction, the order in which materials are put into the door is

TABLE 2.6 Ratio of Scattered to Incident Exposure α

Scattering Angle from Central Ray (degrees)	6 MV
30	0.007
45	0.002
60	0.001
90	0.001

Data from ref National Council on Radiation Protection and Measurements (NCRP) Report No. 49. Structural shielding design and evaluation for medical use of x-rays and gamma rays of energies up to 10 MV. Bethesda, MD: NCRP; 1976. p. 59, Table B-2.

very important. A lead sheet is usually added to the door to shield scattered X-rays. The borated polyethylene should always precede the lead so as to shield these capture gammas produced in the borated polyethylene.

It should also be noted that IMRT (Intensity Modulated Radiation Treatment) treatments increase the amount of monitor units (MU) needed to deliver the same dose of radiation to a patient when compared with conformal therapy. This increase in MU has an impact on the leakage barrier and causes an increase in the thickness of the leakage barrier. This lack of efficiency can be taken into account by the IMRT ratio, which can vary between 5 and 10 MU/cGy. To take into account how IMRT treatments modify the leakage barrier, we calculate the IMRT factor, given by

IMRT Factor $= [(\% \text{ of IMRT used at facility})(\text{IMRT Ratio}) + (1 - \text{IMRT Ratio})]/100.$

IMRT factors can range from 1.5 (dual energy with 50% treatments under 10 MV) to 5 (all IMRT facility). This IMRT factor is then multiplied into the leakage calculated through the leakage formula, and the thickness of the leakage barrier is increased accordingly.

In addition to appropriate shielding for the treatment room, a variety of other safety measures are taken to provide protection to the treating radiation therapist and the public:

(1) radiation warning signs to indicate radiation areas, (2) warning lights to indicate when the radiation beam is on, (3) door interlocks to turn the treatment machine off if the treatment room door is open during the treatment, (4) constant visual and audio contact with the patient in the treatment room during treatment via a closed circuit camera and speaker, (5) multiple emergency shut-off buttons located at several locations within and outside the treatment room. State regulations usually govern these safety measures, and these requirements vary from state to state.

SIGNAGE AND LABELING REQUIREMENTS

The areas surrounding a treatment room are of two types [11,12]:

- **Uncontrolled area:** The exposure of persons in an uncontrolled area is not under the supervision of the RSO. The dose equivalent limit for an uncontrolled area is 0.02 mSv/week.
- **Controlled area:** The exposure of persons in a controlled area is under the supervision of the RSO. The dose equivalent limit for a controlled area is 0.1 mSv/week. Persons in a controlled area are required to be badged.
- **Signage for radiation areas:** Any area where radiation is being emitted, such as radiation treatment rooms, must have a sign indicating the amount of radiation present within the area. The signage for these radiation areas is usually designated as shown in Table 2.7 and Fig. 2.2.
- **Signage for radioactive material area:** Any area that would contain radioactive sources, such as a hot lab, must have sign stating that radioactive materials are present, as shown in Fig. 2.3.
- **Shipping labeling for radioactive sources:** The DOT sets the requirements for labeling of radioactive material shipments. Labeling for shipping of radioactive materials is determined by the transport index (TI). The TI is the dose rate at 1 m from package surface, as shown in Table 2.8 and Fig. 2.4. After receiving a radioactive source, performing a wipe test is necessary.

TABLE 2.7   Dose Rate Limits for Different Radiation Signs[a]

Type or Area	Dose Rate Limits
Controlled	0.02 mSv/h
Radiation area	0.05 mSv/h
High radiation area	1 mSv/h
Very high radiation area	5 Gy/h

[a]*For high doses and high dose rates, it is appropriate to use units of absorbed dose instead of dose equivalent. Data from Federal Register, Code of Federal Regulations. Part 20 (CFR 10.1003); 1996.*

FIGURE 2.2   Radiation signs for the controlled area and radiation areas: Symbols are printed in magenta over a yellow background. *Reproduced from Code of Federal Regulations. Part 20, 10 CFR 20.1901–20.1904); 1996.*

FIGURE 2.3   Symbols are printed in purple, magenta, or black over a yellow background.

TABLE 2.8   Dose Rate Levels for Radiation Packages

Type of Package	Dose Rate at 1 M
White	Background
Yellow II	0–1 mR/h
Yellow III	1–10 mR/h

FIGURE 2.4   Symbols showing shipping labels for radioactive materials. *From Code of Federal Regulations, 49 CFR 172.436–172.440, 1989.*

EQUIPMENT AND AREA MONITORING

The basic measurement device for detecting radiation is a gas-filled detector (Fig. 2.5A and B).

- **Ionization chamber** ("cutie-pie"): Ionization chambers are used for measurements of radiation in low-level areas. They have large volumes for good sensitivity. These meters are excellent choices for quantitative measurements of radiation, such as routine area surveys and surveys of patients (Fig. 2.5A).

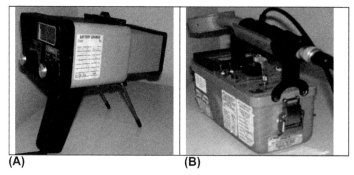

FIGURE 2.5 (A and B) "Cutie-pie" type ionization chamber, Keithley model 36100 and Geiger–Mueller (GM) counter with pancake GM detector, Ludlum [14]C.

- **GM counters:** GM counters are much more sensitive than ionization chamber survey meters. GM counters are the preferred choice for qualitative measurements of radiation protection, such as locating lost sources, finding holes in shielding, and contamination surveys, but are not a good choice for quantitative measurements of radiation because of their large energy dependence and long dead times (Fig. 2.5B).
- **Neutron detectors:** Neutron detectors are similar to GM counters; however, the tubes are filled with boron trifluoride (BF_3) gas. Neutrons cannot directly ionize a gas, so neutron detection takes place by converting neutrons into alpha particles, which can then directly ionize the gas in proportion to the neutron dose received by the neutron detector.

PERSONNEL MONITORING

Personnel monitoring must be used in controlled areas for occupationally exposed individuals. NCRP Report No. 33 [13] recommends using personnel monitoring for individuals who may receive a dose exceeding 25% of the MPD. The NRC requires that personnel monitoring be used for individuals who may receive a dose exceeding 10% of the MPD.

Types of personal dosimeters may be

- **Thermoluminescent dosimeter (TLD) badge:** TLDs are used for body and ring badges. Irradiated TLDs trap electrons, which when heated emit visible light. The amount of visible light is proportional to the radiation received by the TLD (Fig. 2.6A).
- **Film badge:** Films are common dosimeters for body badges. The optical density of the irradiated film is related to the radiation received by the film and is a measure of the radiation dose received by the person wearing the film badge.
- Note that TLDs and film badges may contain two separate pieces of TLD or films. One set may have a filter over it to give an indication of the penetrating ability of the radiation that passed through.

(A)

(B)

FIGURE 2.6   Different types of radiation dosimeters: (A) TLD body and ring badges and (B) an electronic dosimeter.

- **Electronic dosimeter:** More recently, electronic dosimeters are gaining popularity because they can quantitatively measure radiation exposure on a real-time basis and produce a readout immediately, as opposed to the TLD or film dosimeters (Fig. 2.6B).

The goal of any radiation safety program is to maintain a safe environment for patients, workers, and the public. A radiation safety program should always strive for ALARA. Every reasonable step must be taken to maintain radiation exposures as far as possible below the maximal permissible dose limits for individuals in a radiation oncology department.

References

Ref 1. *National Council on Radiation Protection and Measurements (NCRP). Report No. 91. Recommendations on the limits for exposure to ionizing radiation. Bethesda, MD: NCRP; 1987.*

Ref 2. *National Council on Radiation Protection and Measurements (NCRP). Report No. 116. Limitation of exposure to ionizing radiation. Bethesda, MD: NCRP; 1993.*

Ref 3. *International Commission on Radiological Protection (ICRP). Publication 27. Problems involved in developing an index of harm. Oxford, UK: Pergamon Press; 1977.*

Ref 4. *International Commission on Radiation Units, Measurements (ICRU). Report 33. Quantities and units. Washington, DC. 1980.*

Ref 5. *Code of Federal Regulations. Part 35—Medical Use of Byproduct Material. Federal Register 67, no. 79 (Wednesday, April 24, 2002).*

Ref 6. *Title 10, Part 35.2 Code of federal regulations. Washington, DC: U.S. Government Printing Office; 1993. p. 551—4.*

Ref 7. *National Safety Council (NSC). Accident facts. Chicago, IL. 1991 Edition 1991.*

Ref 8. *National Council on Radiation Protection and Measurements (NCRP). Report No. 115. Risk estimates for radiation protection. Bethesda, MD: NCRP; 1993.*

Ref 9. *National Council on Radiation Protection and Measurements (NCRP). Report No. 49. Structural shielding design and evaluation for medical use of x-rays and gamma rays of energies up to 10 MV. Bethesda, MD: NCRP; 1976.*

Ref 10. *National Council on Radiation Protection and Measurements (NCRP). Report No. 51. Radiation protection design guidelines for 0.1—100 MeV particle accelerator facilities. Washington, DC: NCRP; 1977.*

Ref 11. *Cember H. Introduction to health physics. 2nd ed. New York: Pergamon Press; 1984.*

Ref 12. *Khan FM. The physics of radiation therapy. 2nd ed. Baltimore, MD: Williams & Wilkins; 1994.*

Ref 13. *National Council on Radiation Protection and Measurements (NCRP). Report No. 33. Medical X-ray and gamma-ray protection for energies up to 10 MeV — Equipment design and use. Washington, DC: NCRP; 1968.*

Radiation Biology

The response of cells, tissues, organs, and whole organisms to ionizing radiation is a complex phenomenon. The different responses due to interactions of radiation with the biologic tissues can include DNA and chromosome lesions, cell killing, cell cycle disruption, systemic radiation damage, early and late normal tissue effects, effects on embryos, and genetic and somatic effects. Optimization of radiation therapy requires the radiation oncologist to understand the basic principles and parameters of radiation biology and its application in clinical radiation oncology.

RADIOBIOLOGICAL QUANTITIES

Directly and Indirectly Ionizing Radiation

- Directly ionizing radiations (e.g., electrons, protons, nuclear fragments) have charge and, when interacting with the cell, can cause ionization directly, thereby altering the chemical properties of molecules in the cell, resulting in biological effects.
- Indirectly ionizing radiations (e.g., X-rays, neutrons) have no charge and therefore must collide with an atom's orbiting electrons or nucleus to transfer energy [1,2]. This collision results in ejection of charged particles, which then in turn produces direct ionizations.

Deposition of Ionizations Along Tracks

When an ionizing particle passes through absorbing matter, energy is not deposited uniformly along its path but in small packages as either spurs or blobs.

- Spurs (4 nm, three ion pairs) are associated with low—linear energy transfer (LET) radiation.

    95% of X- and gamma-ray deposition of energy appears as spurs. Each ion pair involves ~ 33.7 eV of energy.

- Blobs (7 nm, 12 ion pairs) are associated with high-LET radiation and are more likely produced with neutrons and alpha particles.

Fundamentals of Radiation Oncology
https://doi.org/10.1016/B978-0-12-814128-1.00003-9

Direct and Indirect Effects of Radiation

- Direct effects occur when atoms of the critical target, such as DNA, are directly ionized by radiation, causing damage. About one-third of all biological damage results from direct action with low-LET photons but increases to nearly 100% with high-LET radiations.
- Indirect effects occur when a nontarget material, typically H_2O, is ionized (ejection of an electron) by radiation and free radicals are produced that damage a critical target, such as DNA. Hydroxyl free radicals (OH·) have a half-life of 10^{-9} s and a diffusion distance of about 1 nanometer (nm). About two-thirds of all biological damage results from indirect action with low-LET photons but decreases to nearly zero with high-LET radiations.

Linear Energy Transfer

- LET describes the rate at which the energy is transferred per unit length of track (keV/μm).
- X-rays and gamma rays are low-LET radiation as compared with alpha particles, which are high-LET radiations (Table 3.1).
- As particle energy increases, LET decreases.
- As particle charge and atomic number increases, LET increases.
- As LET increases, relative biological effectiveness (RBE) increases and maximizes around 100 KeV/μm, and then RBE decreases with LET.
- On the other hand, oxygen enhancement ratio (OER) decreases with higher LET and is 1 at 100 KeV/μm.

Relative Biological Effectiveness

With the advent of linear and particle accelerators, higher-energy X-rays, protons, and carbon ions have become available for clinical use. Comparisons of the biologic effects of these newer forms of radiation with the older low-energy superficial X-rays led to the concept of relative biologic effectiveness [2,4].

- RBE measures the same biological effect of a test radiation efficiency in relation to the standard radiation of 250 kVp X-rays:

$$RBE = \frac{\text{Dose of 250 KVp X} - \text{rays to produce a biological effect}}{\text{Dose of a test radiation to produce the same biological effect}}$$

As noted above, maximum RBE is seen at an LET of ∼100 keV/μm. At LET values >200 kev/μm, the ionization densities within the cells are more than needed for optimum cell kill; as such RBE decreases for very high-LET radiations. Table 3.2 shows that RBE is a function of several parameters such as dose, number of fractions, dose rate, and LET.

TABLE 3.1 Approximate LETs and RBEs of Several Types of Radiation

Radiation Type	LET (keV/μm)	RBE
Linac X-rays (6–15 MeV)	0.3	~0.8
Beta particle (1 MeV)	0.3	0.9
Cobalt-60 γ-rays	0.2	0.8–0.9
250 kVp X-rays (standard)	2	1.0
150 MeV protons (therapy energies)	0.5	~1.1
Neutrons	0.5–100	1–2
Alpha particles	50–200	5–10
Carbon ions (in spread out Bragg peak)	40–90	2–5

LET, linear energy transfer; RBE, relative biological effectiveness.
Modified from Coia LR, Moylan DE. Introduction to clinical radiation oncology. 3rd ed. Madison, WI: Medical Physics Publishing; 1996.p. 24, Table 2.1, © *1996 with permission.*

TABLE 3.2 Relationship of RBE as a Function of Changing Radiation Parameters

	RBE
↑ Dose	↓
↑ Number of fractions	↑
↓ Dose rate	↑
↑ LET	↑

Therapeutic Ratio

The goal of radiation therapy is to achieve sufficient damage to the tumor to either cause it to regress or at least cease growth while minimizing toxicity to normal tissue. Therapeutic ratio (TR) is a function of the probability of tumor control and the probability of normal tissue complication (Fig. 3.1) [3]. One way of quantifying the TR is as below:

$$TR = TCP \times (1 - NTCP)$$

As treatment dose increases, tumor control probability (TCP) improves, but the normal tissue complication probability (NTCP) also increases. The TR is often defined as the ratio of TCP and NTCP at a specified dose level, although it may also be

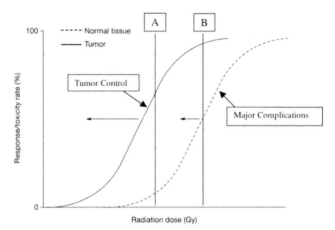

FIGURE 3.1 Therapeutic ratio. Sigmoid curves of tumor control and complications. Line A shows dose for tumor control with minimum toxicity; line B shows dose for maximum tumor control with significant complications. *Modified from Seiwert TY, Salama JK, Vokes EE. The concurrent paradigm—general principles. Nat Clin Pract Oncol 2007;4:86—100 , © 2007 with permission from Wolters Kluwer Health and Coia LR, Moylan DE. Introduction to clinical radiation oncology. 3rd ed. Madison, WI: Medical Physics Publishing; 1996. p. 46, Fig. 2.4, © 1998, with permission.*

calculated as the ratio of doses at a specified level of response. The further the NTCP curve lies in a higher dose range compared with the TCP response, the greater the TR and therefore the less likely that effective radiotherapy will result in normal tissue toxicity.

The probability of normal tissue complication is dependent on the volume of tissue irradiated and radiation sensitivity ("steepness") of normal tissue cells. A number of models have been proposed to predict and evaluate normal tissue complications:

- One of the popular models has been the Lyman model, which assumes uniform dose across the volume of interest in the treatment field.
- Another model in radiation therapy practice is the dose—volume histogram (DVH). This summarizes information on nonuniform dose distributions in an organ. With the DVH, the assumption is that limiting the volume of critical structures irradiated to specific doses will protect against complications. Use of this concept assumes that the location of the radiation dose within an organ is unimportant, as the spatial distribution of voxels within the organ is lost in the DVH.

The goal of modeling NTCP is to distribute an unavoidable dose to critical normal tissues optimally; that is, maximize the dose to the target region and quantify differences on the basis of models of dose—volume distributions and dose—response relationships. However, it is important to consider that there may be heterogeneity in the radiosensitivity across different portions of a particular organ.

RADIATION EFFECTS ON CHROMOSOMES

DNA is the critical target for radiation-induced damages, leading to cell killing [1,2,6]. A variety of DNA lesions can be induced by radiation as follows:

- Single-strand break (SSB): This involves the breaking of one sugar/phosphate backbone of the DNA molecule. For every 1 gray (Gy) of radiation, 1000 SSBs are created, but these alterations are repaired, without long-term cellular damage.
- Double-strand break (DSB): This involves breaking of both backbones of the DNA molecule. This is likely to occur when each strand break is less than three nucleotides apart. For every 1 Gy of radiation, 40 DSBs are created. Some of these alterations are not repaired or misrepaired, leading to biological effects including cell death and mutations.
- Locally multiply damaged sites: The area in which a DSB is induced is usually accompanied by a number of base damages and SSBs.

Chromosome-Type Aberrations

Chromosome-type aberrations occur when cells are irradiated in G1 phase before DNA duplication in S phase. Breaks occurring in a single strand of DNA will be replicated in S phase and seen later when cells are in M phase. Typical aberrations of special interest include the following:

- Translocations: Generally nonlethal and stable and therefore can be detected many years following irradiation. These types of chromosomal aberrations are associated with some cancers.
- Dicentric chromosomes: Lethal, asymmetrical aberration; scoring of these aberrations after as little as 0.25 Gy can be used as a biological dosimeter.
- Ring chromosomes: Lethal.
- Deletions: May or may not be lethal, depending on content deleted.

Chromatid-Type Aberrations

Chromatid-type aberrations occur when cells are irradiated after S phase has been completed when DNA material has already been replicated. Radiation may damage one but not both associated chromatids. The aberrations that may be observed in M phase are as follows:

- Anaphase bridges: Lethal.
- Deletions: May or may not be lethal depending on the DNA content lost.

Telomeres and Telomerase

Telomeres are repeat nucleotide sequences (TTAGGG) and protein on the ends of chromosomes that prevent degradation and end–end ligation. They act as natural caps and prevent chromosomes from fusing together. Telomere length is progressively reduced with each cell division until the cell becomes senescent.

- Hayflick phenomenon—normal human cells divide only 50–60 times before undergoing growth arrest; likely the result of telomere shortening.
- Telomerase is a ribonucleoprotein enzyme that adds repeat sequences to the 3' end of DNA. Telomerase is active in germ cells, stem cells, and immortal (cancer) cells.
- Joining between short telomeres and DNA breaks may contribute to chromosomal instability during tumorigenesis by formation of nonreciprocal translocations and other rearrangements.

Repair of Radiation Damage

Following DNA breaks, repair mechanisms are initiated, as described below [7–9]:

- Base excision repair (BER) may lead to increased mutation but not usually changes in cell sensitivity. BER acts to repair SSBs and base damages (Fig. 3.2).
- Nucleotide excision repair (NER) is efficient repair of pyrimidine dimers induced by ultraviolet radiation and bulky chemical damages. Mutated NER genes do not result in hypersensitivity to ionizing radiation but increase sensitivity to ultraviolet radiation and certain anticancer chemical (e.g., alkylating agents that induce bulky adducts), leading to known disorders resulting from NER gene mutations including xeroderma pigmentosum and Cockayne syndrome (Fig. 3.3).
- Mismatch repair (MMR) genes remove base—base and small insertion—deletion mismatches after DNA replication. MMR can result in genomic instability and lead to colon and endometrial cancers, for example (Fig. 3.4).

Because DSBs are the critical lesion leading to biological effects in cells exposed to ionizing radiation, their repair is critical. Four major pathways are involved in the repair of DSBs as follows:

- Homologous recombinational repair (HRR) occurs in mid- to late S phase and G2 cells (following DNA replication when sister chromatids are present). Co-located undamaged DNA strands are used to assist with repair of the damaged strand, thus resulting in generally error-free repair. HRR is less frequent than nonhomologous end joining (NHEJ). The basic steps involved first entail DNA end resection at the site of the DSB to generate single-stranded DNA overhangs. A recombinational event then takes place, which is mediated by creation of a nucleoprotein filament that catalyzes homology search, strand pairing, and strand exchange with the unbroken homologous chromosome. DNA synthesis then takes place with the donor sequence serving as a template, and finally, resolvases complete the process by resolving the Holliday junctions and the DNA sequence around the DSB is restored.
- Classical nonhomologous end joining (C-NHEJ) is a pre—S phase event. In this process, a series of enzymes first brings the broken DNA ends together, following which there may be removal of a small number of nucleotides through pairing of short homologous stretches of DNA. The broken ends are then ligated to form an intact DNA double strand.

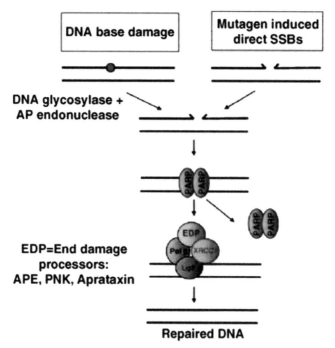

Repaired DNA

FIGURE 3.2 Diagram showing base excision repair (BER) mechanism. Damaged base processing is initiated by a specific DNA glycosylase, which removes the damaged base creating an abasic site (AP site). AP endonuclease (APE) then cleaves the phosphodiester bond 5′ to the AP site. Both AP endonuclease induced and direct strand break are recognized by PARP-1 dimer. PARP-1 then dissociates from DNA, the release of which exposes SSB to the end damage processors (EDPs), DNA polymerase β (Pol β), and XRCC1−DNA ligase IIIα, which perform the remainder of the repair. After "cleaning" of the SSB ends (if required), Pol β then adds one nucleotide to the 3′ end and DNA ligase completes the repair by sealing DNA ends. *Reprinted from Sharma RA, Dianov GL. Targeting base excision repair to improve cancer therapies. Mol Aspects Med 2007;28(3−4):345−74,* © *2007 with permission from Elsevier.*

Single-strand annealing (SSA) is typically initiated when DSBs occur at genomic loci where extensive homology exists between sequences at either side of the DSB and mediates the rejoining of the two ends. SSA is a mutagenic process that often results in large deletions of up to several hundred base pairs as well as translocations. Similar to HRR, SSA is initiated by DNA end resection, but unlike HRR the overhangs do not initiate repair synthesis. Instead, the two homologous DNA stretches are annealed while the generated tails are removed and the resulting nicks ligated.

Alternative end joining (alt-EJ) involves DNA resection that reveals microhomologies that facilitate the alignment of DNA ends for ligation. Because alt-EJ requires pairing of only small homologous DNA sequences, either small deletions and/or insertions can result depending on how the repair is orchestrated.

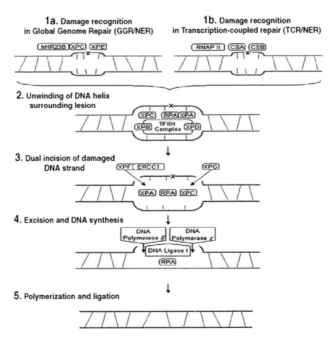

FIGURE 3.3　Diagram showing NER mechanism. Note that the initial step, DNA damage recognition, differs within the global genome repair (GGR/NER) and transcription-coupled repair (TCR/NER). The remaining steps are identical. *Reprinted from Saldivar JS, Wu X, Follen M, Gershenson D. Nucleotide excision repair pathway review I: Implications in ovarian cancer and platinum sensitivity." Gynecol Oncol 107(1 Suppl 1):S56–71, © 2007 with permission from Elsevier.*

Various types of mammalian cell DNA repair processes and diseases associated with their deficiency are described in Table 3.3.

CELL SURVIVAL CURVES

Target Theory

As radiation dose increases, the probability of cell inactivation also increases. Poisson statistics can be used to predict the probability of cell inactivation resulting from a certain number of "lethal events" per cell. For example, if an average of one lethal event per cell is produced by a particular dose of radiation, approximately 37% of the cells will have zero lethal events and survive. Cell survival data plotted on a semilogarithmic scale reveal there is an initial linear portion, followed by a curved section, which then resumes linearity at higher doses (Fig. 3.5). Although several survival curve models are described, such as single hit—single target model and single-hit—multitarget

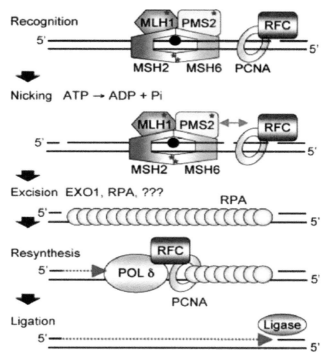

FIGURE 3.4 Diagram showing MMR. Recognition of a mismatch by MutSα (MSH2−MSH6) or MutSβ (MSH2−MSH3, not shown), and MutLα (MLH1−PMS2) results in the formation of a ternary complex. PCNA may play an important role in the recruitment of MMR proteins to the vicinity of the replication fork. Nicking by the endonuclease function of PMS2 may establish strand discrimination targeting repair to the newly synthesized strand. MMR is bidirectional and can be 5′-directed as well. Excision by EXO1 leads to the formation of a replication protein A (RPA)-coated single-strand gap. Resynthesis by replicative polymerase (polδ) and ligase restore the integrity of the duplex. *Reprinted from Hsieh P, Yamane K. DNA mismatch repair: molecular mechanism, cancer, and ageing. Mech Ageing Dev 2008;129(7−8):391−407, © 2008 with permission from Elsevier.*

model, the most widely used liner quadratic model fits the survival data dose–response curves best and is discussed below:

The Linear-Quadratic (L-Q) Model

The most widely used in radiobiology is the linear-quadratic model. It is based on early work with radiation-induced chromosomal aberrations data that introduced the concept of the dual-radiation action (two components to cell killing with one proportional to the dose and the other proportional to the square of the dose).

- The L-Q formula describes the shape of cell survival curves where SF is the surviving fraction, N is the number of cells remaining following exposure to dose D, N0 is the number of cells at $D = 0$ Gy, and e is the mathematical constant 2.718, while α and β are parameters of radiosensitivity:

$$SF = N/N0 = e^{-(\alpha D + \beta D2)}$$

TABLE 3.3 Selected Human Diseases With Defective DNA Repair Capacities

Disorder	Gene Mutated	DNA Repair Pathway	Cancer Risk
AUTOSOMAL RECESSIVE DISORDERS			
Ataxia telangiectasia	ATM	Double-strand break signaling	+
Seckel syndrome	ATR	UV and replication damage signaling	?
AT-like disorder	MRE11	Double-strand break repair	−
Nijmegen breakage syndrome	NBS1	Double-strand break repair	+
Bloom syndrome	BLM	Regulation of recombination	+
Werner syndrome	WRN	Maintenance of genome stability	+
Rothmund−Thomson syndrome	RECQL4	Double-strand break repair	+
Fanconi anemia and interstrand cross-link repair	FANCA −N	Homologous recombination	+
Xeroderma pigmentosa (NER)	XPA−G	Nucleotide excision repair	+
XPF-ERCC1 progeroid syndrome	XPF	NER	?
Xeroderma pigmentosum variant	XPV	Translesion synthesis	+
Cockayne syndrome	CSA, CSB	Transcription coupled (TC)-NER	−
Trichothiodystrophy	XPD, XPB, TTDA, TTDN1	TC-NER	−
Lig4 syndrome	LIG4	V(D)J recombination and NHEJ	+
Radiation-sensitive SCID artemis	XLF, LIG4	V(D)J recombination and NHEJ	+/?
Spinocerebellar ataxia with neuropathy	TDP1	Single-strand break repair	−
Ataxia with oculomotor apraxia	APTX	Single-strand break repair	−
Lynch syndrome, MSH2, MSH6	MLH1,	Mismatch repair	+

TABLE 3.3 Selected Human Diseases With Defective DNA Repair Capacities—cont'd

Disorder	Gene Mutated	DNA Repair Pathway	Cancer Risk
Hereditary breast cancer-2	BRCA1,	Homologous recombination repair	+
Li-Fraumeni syndrome	TP53	DNA-damage signaling	+

Reproduced from Ouyang KJ, Woo LL, Ellis NA. Homologous recombina- tion and maintenance of genome integrity: cancer and aging through the prism of human RecQ helicases." Mech Ageing Dev 2008 129(7–8):425–40, © 2008 with permission from Elsevier.

- The dual action of radiation model promulgated by Rossi and Kellerer hypothesized that the αD component of cell killing results from single track of radiation each producing two chromosomal breaks that may misrepair to form a lethal chromosomal aberration. In contrast, the βD^2 component represents the portion of cell killing due to the production of two chromosomal breaks resulting from two separate tracks of radiation. Thus, delivery of radiation over a series of small fractions or low-dose rates does not affect the αD component of cell killing but results in a diminished βD^2 component because repair of the initial chromosomal break could be accomplished before the occurrence of the second chromosomal break.
- The dose at which the contribution to killing from the αD component (nonrepairable damage) is equal to that of the βD^2 component (repairable damage) represents the α/β ratio (Fig. 3.6). The α/β ratio indicates the ability of the cell to repair radiation-induced damage and therefore the impact of fractionation or irradiation at a low dose rate. Typically, tissues that respond to radiation quickly, acute responses, are characterized by a high α/β ratio and therefore show only modest sparing with fractionation. In contrast, tissues that respond more slowly, late responses, (typically more than 3 months following the completion of a clinical radiotherapy treatment) are characterized by a low α/β ratio and therefore show substantial sparing with fractionation (Table 3.4).

The Four "R's" of Radiobiology

The impact of multiple fractionated radiation therapy is generally superior to single fractionated radiation therapy, which can be explained largely by the Four "R's" of radiobiology.

Repair: Fractionation permits repair sublethal and potential lethal damage and is advantageous when the α/β ratio is large for the tumor and small for the tissues/ organs in the radiation field that results in the critical complications resulting from radiotherapy.

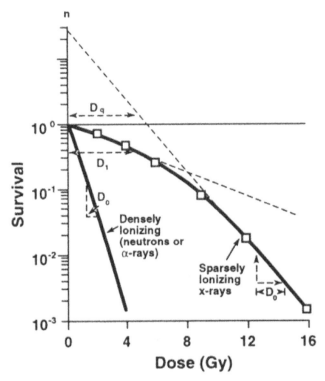

FIGURE 3.5 For high-LET radiations, the dose–response curve is a straight line on an exponential scale. In contrast, for low-LET radiations, the dose–response curve has an initial slope followed by a portion in which the slope is changing with dose and finally resulting in a terminal linear portion at high doses. The Do ($-1/D37$) is an indicator of the inherent radiosensitivity of the biologic specimen. n and Dq indicate the extent of the initial slope of the survival curve, which predicts sparing of cells from low-dose rate radiation. *Reproduced from Coia LR, Moylan DE. Introduction to clinical radiation oncology. 3rd ed. Madison, WI: Medical Physics Publishing; 1996. p. 33, Fig. 2.1A, © 1996 with permission.*

Reoxygenation: Fractionation is advantageous particularly when tumors possess significant volumes of hypoxic tissue, thus providing the opportunity for reoxygenation.

Reassortment: Fractionation is advantageous because it permits tumor cells in resistant portions of the cell cycle that survive an initial dose of radiation to move into a more sensitive phase of the cell cycle when subsequent doses of radiation are delivered.

Repopulation: Fractionation may not be advantageous if it extends the length of a protocol allowing tumors to repopulate during the course of radiotherapy.

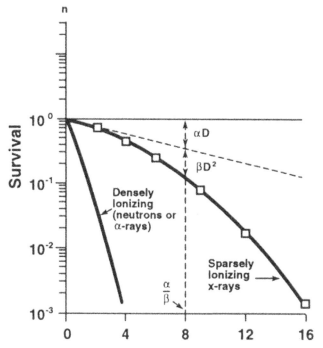

FIGURE 3.6 This diagram shows L-Q model cell survival curve with an α/β ratio of 8 Gy. At the dose of 8 Gy, the portion of cell killing due to the linear component of irreparable lesions is equal to the portion of cell killing due to quadratic component from the accumulation of sublethal lesions. *Reproduced from ref Coia LR, Moylan DE. Introduction to clinical radiation oncology. 3rd ed. Madison, WI: Medical Physics Publishing; 1996. p. 33, Fig. 2.1B, © 1996 with permission.*

TABLE 3.4 Typical α/β Ratios for Early and Late Reacting Tissues

Early Reacting Tissues	α/β Values (Gy)
Skin (epidermis), jejunum, colon, testis	6–13
Average value	10
Late Reacting Tissues	
spinal cord, kidney, lung, bladder	1–7
Average value	3–4

Data modified from Hall EJ, Giaccia AJ. Radiobiology for the radiologist. 8th ed. 2019, Table 23.1, p. 422, Wolters Kluwer, 2019.

FRACTIONATION PROTOCOLS USED IN CLINICAL RADIOTHERAPY

Standard treatment: Use of fraction sizes of 1.8–2.0 Gy that are typically delivered once a day, 5 days/week over a 4–6 week period.

- **Concomitant boost**: Two fractions per day, one fraction to the larger RT field and a second fraction to the boost field.
- **Simultaneous integrated boost**: One fraction per day, a lower dose to the larger RT field and higher dose to the boost field.

Hyperfractionation: The number of fractions is increased, the time is kept the same, the dose per fraction is less than 1.8 Gy. Typically two fractions per day are delivered. The rationale is either to increase the dose a modest amount to spare late responding tissues or increase the dose by a large amount in order to increase the probability of tumor cure.

Hypofractionation: The dose per fraction is higher than 2.2 Gy with a reduced total number of fractions. The rationale is to more effectively treat tumors with a low α/β ratio compared with the normal tissue. An additional rationale for use of hypofraction in clinical scenarios when the α/β for the tumor and normal tissue in the radiation field may be similar is to both improve patient convenience and lower the cost of therapy through use of a smaller number of treatments.

Accelerated fractionation: Shorter overall treatment time, dose per fraction of 1.8 to 2 Gy (but may be lower), more than 10 Gy per week delivered. The rationale is to overcome accelerated tumor repopulation.

Stereotactic radiation: Radiation therapy using relatively large fraction sizes using stereotactic localization technique. Stereotactic radiosurgery (given in 1 fx); stereotactic body radiotherapy (SBRT) also referred to as stereotactic ablative radiotherapy (SABR) (given in 3–5 fxs); fractionated stereotactic radiation therapy (given in more than 5 fxs).

- One of the main applications of the L-Q model is the calculation of tolerance doses of different fractionation regimens (given in the same overall time), where the total dose of a regimen and the corresponding α/β ratio are known. This is based on the principle that treatment regimens that are isoeffective have the same biologically effective (equivalent) dose (BED). Typically, for tumors and early-reacting tissues, an α/β value of 10 Gy is used for BED calculations, whereas for late-reacting tissue, an α/β value of 3 Gy is typically assumed. This relationship is shown in the following equation:

$$BED = nd[1 + (d/\alpha/\beta)]$$

where n is the number of fractions and d is the dose/fraction.
- To calculate the new total dose D2 for a new protocol with a specified dose per fraction of d2 to be isoeffective with a previous protocol with a dose per fraction of d1 and total dose D1, the following equation can be used based on the BED formula:

$$D2 = D1 \, (d1 + \alpha/\beta)/(d2 + \alpha/\beta)$$

It should be noted that for protocols in which the total radiotherapy dose is delivered over substantially different time periods, it may be necessary to also take into account cellular proliferation correction in the calculation of the BED by adding a proliferation term. Also for hyperfractionation regimens when repair may be incomplete between the fractions, an incomplete repair factor such as Thames H-factor is included for the BED calculation.

In addition, it should be noted that the LQ model may not be accurate for the very large fraction sizes used for SRS and SBRT. For SRS/SBRT, other mechanisms such as direct cell death due to damage of the critical target, such as DNA; vascular damage causing endothelial cell death; and vascular dysfunction leading to indirect cell death may be mechanisms for cell killing and cell survival.

DOSE RATE EFFECT AND REPAIR OF DAMAGE

Cell survival curves illustrate the repair process within the cell after irradiation. There are two types of "operationally defined" cell repair processes: sublethal damage (SLD) repair and potentially lethal damage (PLD) repair.

Sublethal Damage

SLD is characterized by split-dose irradiation experiments [11], in which surviving cells are exposed to a second irradiation after time has elapsed between fractions. It demonstrates reconstruction of the shoulder region so that a higher total dose is required to achieve the same biological effect as a single-dose regimen. The increase in survival is likely due to SLD repair. Repair is rapid and is largely complete in about 2–6 h depending on the tissue irradiated.

The overall response to a split-dose regimen is a combination of three factors: repair, redistribution, and repopulation, as described below.

Repair (primarily late S phase cells) is rapid and is 90% complete in about 2 h. There is good correlation between the size of the shoulder of a survival curve and the magnitude of repair of SLD. In terms of the α/β ratio, broad shoulders have small ratios and good repair of SLD.

Redistribution or reassortment involves the movement of cells in an irradiated tissue, typically from a radioresistant phase of the cell cycle to a more sensitive phase of the cell cycle. Hence, this process is typically thought to be advantageous in terms of tumor treatment since cancer cells are generally cycling and therefore will be in a more sensitive phase of the cell cycle when the next fraction of radiation is delivered. In contrast, cells comprising late responding tissues are not usually actively cycling and therefore will not be in a more sensitive phase of the cell cycle when a subsequent radiation dose is delivered.

Repopulation can occur when cells eventually progress through the mitotic block and go through mitosis and divide.

SLD and its repair are important for sparing normal tissue from radiation treatment complications.

Potentially Lethal Damage

PLD is the damage that has the potential to become lethal if the post-irradiation conditions are suitable, such as with complete nutrition and at optimal temperature. This is because the optimal environment allows the cells to divide and thus have inadequate time to repair DNA damage that occurred due to the irradiation. However in suboptimal ambience, such as depleted nutrition or in room temperature, cell survival increases as cell entry into mitosis is delayed, which then allows time to repair radiation-induced DNA damage.

There is very little PLD repair after exposure to high-LET radiations.

THE OXYGEN EFFECT AND REOXYGENATION

Oxygen enhances the response of cells to radiation, making it a radiosensitizer. Free radicals are produced as radiation ionizes H_2O. Free radicals then react with the organic molecule DNA to produce R'. The reactive (broken DNA) molecule can repair itself in time unless O_2 reacts with the damaged DNA.

- The OER is:

$$OER = \frac{\text{Dose of radiation under hypoxic conditions to produce a particular biological effect}}{\text{Dose of radiation in the presence of oxygen to produce the same level of effect}}$$

- Oxygen enhances low- but not high-LET radiation effects, because extensive damage by high-LET radiation does not require O_2 fixation of damage to attain maximum effect. The OER is about 2.5 for low-dose fractions in treatment, especially with hyperfractionation compared with irradiations compared with a somewhat greater value for OER following irradiation with a larger dose.

  The oxygen enhancement of cells to radiation mainly occurs between oxygen tension of 0 and 20 mm of mercury (mmHg). Beyond 40 mmHg, no further increase in radiation sensitivity is noted. During or within 5 msec of radiation exposure, an O_2 concentration of 0.5% (3−4 mmHg) will shift the survival curve to half way toward the fully aerated condition, but at least 2% (15 mmHg) O_2 is required to see the full oxygen effect as seen in Fig. 3.7.

- Once a nest of cancer cells expands to about 1−2 mm in diameter, it must develop a blood supply in order to continue to grow. Diffusion is no longer adequate to supply cells with oxygen and nutrients and waste removal. The diffusion distance for oxygen is ~70 μm from blood vessels, resulting in hypoxic zones within the tumor.

  Hypoxic tumor cells are radioresistant, and reoxygenation between the treatment fractions makes them radiosensitive. Hypoxia can be chronic or intermittent.

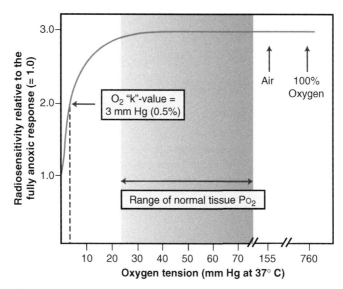

FIGURE 3.7 This diagram shows that the cell radiosensitivity increases as a function of the oxygen concentration. The oxygen concentration of 3 mmHg or of 0.5% results in radiosensitivity of halfway between anoxia and full oxygenation, and at full oxygenation of 30 mmHg, the cells reach the maximum radiosensitivity. *Modified from ref Gunderson LL, Tepper JE. The biologic basis of radiation oncology: clinical radiation oncology. 4th ed. Philadelphia: Elsevier; 2016. pp. 2–40, Fig. 1.23, p. 22.*

RADIOSENSITIZERS AND RADIOPROTECTORS

Radiosensitizers are agents that increase the effects of radiation. Effectiveness is measured in terms of the enhancement ratio (ER).

$$ER = \frac{\text{Radiation dose for a given biological effect in the absence of the sensitizer}}{\text{Radiation dose to achieve the same effect in the presence of the sensitizer}}$$

To be useful clinically, a radiosensitizer must show a therapeutic gain for tumors versus normal tissues. Gain could result from selective uptake, differential absorption rate, or biological half life. They must be effective at systemically nontoxic dosages (minimal side effects). Examples of radiosensitizers currently in use are cisplatin and gemcitabine, although many molecularly targeted agents are currently under investigation as potential radiosensitizers.

Radioprotectors are agents that protect cells (organs, organisms) from the damaging effects of ionizing radiation. These agents reduce the effective dose of the radiation, measured in terms of the dose reduction factor (DRF).

$$DRF = \frac{\text{Radiation dose in the presence of drug to produce a given biological effect}}{\text{Dose in absence of drug to obtain the same biological effect}}$$

Sulfhydryl compounds (e.g., amifostine) are radioprotectors that contain free SH groups, which interrupt the chain of events that utilizes free radicals to indirectly damage target molecules (i.e., free radical scavengers).

CELL AND TUMOR CELL KINETICS

Molecular and Biology Techniques

Cell growth characteristics
- Cell survival curves: As described in Chapter 2.
- Cell adhesive matrix assay: Tissue culture plate is coated with fibronectin and fibrinopeptides. Cells are grown for 2 weeks and stained with crystal violet to image cell growth.
- Courtenay—Mills assay: Growth of cells in soft agar.

Cell metabolism
- MTT assay: Only living cells reduce a tetrazolium compound (MTT). Measured spectrophotometrically.

Cytogenetic analysis
- Fluorescent in situ hybridization: Used to detect and localize the presence or absence of specific DNA sequences on chromosomes. Uses fluorescently labeled cDNA probe that will bind to the gene of interest on the chromosome. Often used to identify her2/neu amplification in breast cancer.
- Micronucleus assay: Micronuclei are acentric chromosomal fragments that are correlated with DNA damage. These are visible at mitosis and are seen as nuclear material in the cytoplasm and stain similarly to the nucleus. The micronuclear material may be, for example, the remnants of dicentric chromosomal aberrations.
- Single cell electrophoresis/comet assay: Fluorescent microscopic method to examine DNA damage and repair of a single cell. Specimen is loaded on an electrophoretic gel; DNA migration is directly proportional to the amount of DSBs. By altering the pH, DSB (neutral) and SSBs (alkaline) can be examined. Can also be used to test for oxidative DNA damage or DNA cross-links.

Hypoxia
- Sensitizer adducts: Nitroimidazoles are bioreduced in hypoxic areas while they are cleared from aerobic tissues. These radio- or immunolabeled nitroimidazoles can then be imaged.

Gel electrophoresis: A process by which agarose or polyacrylamide is used to separate DNA cut by nucleases or proteins [1,2]. It consists of a series of pores for the DNA, RNA, or protein to migrate through when an electric current is applied. Once the DNA, RNA, or proteins are separated by size, they are assayed by labeled probes or antibodies. The following procedures may be performed to transfer material to nitrocellulose paper for ease of use in assaying the probes.
- Southern blot: Transfer of DNA from a gel onto nitrocellulose paper where it can be detected by hybridization with a labeled cDNA probe.
- Northern blot: Transfer of RNA from a gel onto nitrocellulose paper with subsequent detection by hybridization with a labeled cDNA probe.
- Western blot: Transfer of protein from a gel onto nitrocellulose paper for easy detection with radioactive or immunologically labeled antibodies.

Other techniques

- Polymerase chain reaction: Used to amplify a DNA sequence. The process denatures DNA, nucleotide primers are then hybridized, and then a heat stabile DNA polymerase (Taq) copies the desired DNA. Successive rounds of heating and cooling amplify the gene of interest.
- Restriction fragment length polymorphism: DNA is cut with an endonuclease (an enzyme that cuts DNA at a specific sequence, generating DNA fragments). The DNA is then run on a gel, and the patterns are compared. It is used to identify deletions, insertions, and tandem repeats.
- Single-stranded conformation polymorphism: This is useful for detecting single base-pair changes.
- Chloramphenicol acetyl transferase (CAT) assay: Used to study promoters. The promoter is ligated to the bacterial CAT gene and introduced into cells. Mutations are made to determine the essential segments of the promoter for its activity.
- Gel shift assay: A short radioactive oligonucleotide probe identical to a portion of the promoter is added to a cell extract containing DNA-binding proteins and then run on a polyacrylamide gel. Retardation of the probe indicates binding with the DNA segment.
- Microarrays: Used to study gene expression patterns in mass numbers to correlate gene relationships; they may be of value in predicting patient response to therapies.

Immunofluorescence of phosphorylated γH2AX at the gamma position is used to visualize foci of DNA double-strand breaks and repair-related proteins. It is seen early in the damage/repair process and declines in magnitude shortly after the initial damage.

MicroRNAs

Mature microRNAs (miRNAs) are naturally occurring, 22-nucleotide, noncoding RNAs that mediate posttranscriptional gene regulation. miRNAs play an important role in many biological processes, including differentiation and development, cell signaling, and response to infection. Overwhelming evidence indicates that dysregulation of miRNA expression is a cause or indicator of several disease processes, including many cancers. The discovery that circulating miRNAs are detectable in serum and plasma, and that their expression varies as a result of disease, presents great potential for circulating miRNA expression signatures to be used as biomarkers in disease diagnosis and prevention.

Cell Cycle Kinetics

Several kinetic parameters are used to describe the response of a tumor to radiation treatment [1]:

- Mitotic index (MI): Proportion of cells undergoing mitosis to the total number of cell.

$$MI = \lambda Tm/Tc$$

where λ is the correction factor for the nonlinear distribution of cells through the cell cycle (typical value is 0.693), Tm is the length of mitosis and Tc is the length of the cell cycle.
- Labeling index (LI): Proportion of cells in the S phase of the growth cycle.

$$LI = \lambda Ts/Tc$$

where Ts is the length of the S phase and Tc is the length of the cell cycle.
- Growth fraction (GF): Proportion of viable cells in active cell division. GF is calculated by the following formula:

$$GF = \text{proliferating cell}/\text{proliferating cell} + \text{quiescent cells}$$

- Cell loss factor (CLF): Rate of cell loss from a tumor. CLF is estimated by comparing the rate of production of new cells with the observed growth of the tumor.

$$CLF = 1 - Tpot/Tvol$$

where Tpot is the potential doubling time and Tvol is the volume doubling time. If CLF = 1, then there is no tumor growth.
- Potential volume doubling time (Tpot): The volume doubling time that would be measured in the absence of cell loss.

$$Tpot = \lambda Ts/LI$$

where Ts is the duration of S phase, LI is the labeling index, and λ is the age distribution correction factor (varies from 0.7 to 1).
- Tumor doubling time (Tvol): Tvol is much larger than Tpot because tumor GF < 100% and because of continuous CLF. In small tumors where all cells may be dividing and differentiating at a constant rate, there is good correlation between Tvol and Tpot. In large tumors, Tvol is much larger than Tpot because the CLF increases.

By using flow cytometry (labeling of S phase cells with BrdUrd, and staining total DNA with propidium iodide to quantity the relative content of DNA), both TS and LI can be determined from a single sample.

Effects on Tumor Cells

Tumor growth: Tumors are cell renewal systems in which cell production exceeds loss. Stem cells capable of self-renewal that may be responsible for tumor regrowth after treatment represent less than 1% of the population (growth fractions range from 20% to 60% in the majority of tumors with an average of 30%). Although human tumors are monoclonal, heterogeneity exists due to:
- differentiation
- microenvironmental factors
- generation of new sublines due to continuous mutations

Tumor regression:

- Rapid regression: Tumors with a high proliferation index (large growth fraction and small Tpot) typically regress rapidly during and after irradiation, regardless of whether the tumor was fast (low cell loss) or slow (high cell loss) growing before irradiation. Patients with tumors that regress rapidly may have good prognosis (low clonogenic numbers, high cell loss), or poor prognosis (early cell loss but rapid regrowth), or neither since the combination of growth fraction, cell loss, Tpot, and repopulation determine the ultimate outcome.
- Slow regression: Slow regression may result from low proliferation, low cell loss, residual stroma, or treatment failure. Examples are prostate cancer, some nodular sclerosing Hodgkin disease, teratocarcinomas of the testis, and soft-tissue sarcomas.

Tumor repopulation: Repopulation occurs when the rate of cell loss decreases after irradiation treatment begins. Proliferation may now exceed cell loss, and tumors with high proliferation and high cell loss may regrow early and rapidly. Small tumors grow more rapidly than large tumors (Gompertzian growth is characterized by a sigmodal shape when tumor diameter is compared with time post-irradiation). Tumor cell repopulation begins early after the start of treatment but is masked by the regression of the tumor bulk (result of high cell loss).

NORMAL TISSUE KINETICS AND PROLIFERATION STATUS

Response of tissues and organs to radiation is determined to some degree by their state of developmental differentiation and functional role. Aside from cells such as lymphocytes that are susceptible to undergoing apoptotic death, less differentiated cells are generally more sensitive to radiation (as mitotic activity increases, sensitivity also increases). The time interval between irradiation of early-reacting tissues and its expression as tissue damage depends on the life span of the mature functional cells rather than the dose. The time interval between irradiation and expression of damage in late-reacting tissues depends on the life span of the mature functional cells and total dose (the greater the dose, the shorter the expression time).

Effects on Normal Tissues

The etiology of normal tissue injury from radiation treatment is complex. It includes the concept of functional subunits (FSUs) and numerous radiation-induced cellular signaling cascades releasing cytokines, as described below.

Functional Subunits

- FSUs are self-contained units that comprise an organ, which may or may not be structurally distinct. Examples of distinct FSUs are kidney nephrons, whereas non-structurally distinct FSUs are present in the skin. Thus, migration of surviving cells from outside the irradiated field can assist with recovery.

  Radiation sensitivity depends on intrinsic cellular radiosensitivity and the number of target cells in a subunit. If an FSU has a small number of cells, low doses of radiation can destroy sufficient numbers of cells to compromise the unit.

Variation in total numbers of cells in each subunit appears to correlate with tolerance doses of some organs. For example, hair depigmentation occurs at a lower dose than skin depigmentation because hair follicles have fewer melanocytes.

- Organs with FSUs arranged in series (e.g., spinal cord) display complications following a large dose to a small volume. Once the threshold volume has been exceeded, further increases in the treated volume have little effect.
- Organs with FSUs arranged in parallel (e.g., lung, liver, kidney) are resistant to the development of complications when a small volume is irradiated, even with a large dose of radiation. However, with increasing volume exposed, the probability for the development of toxicity increases following irradiation with a particular dose.

Michalowski's H Type and F Type Classification

The following classification systems have been used to correlate sensitivity and proliferative ability [2]:

Hierarchal-type tissues (H-type): Rapid division to replenish cells with a short mature life. Cell types include epithelial lining of the GI tract, bone marrow stem cells, skin, and mucosa. Loss of tissue function results from the inability of damaged stem cells to replace depleted functional cells. Increased severity of damage may be caused by increased dose, which results in increased numbers of damaged stem cells and hence longer regeneration times.

Flexible-type tissues (F-type): Cell types include liver, kidney, lung, and spinal cord. Most cells in these tissues are not in the cell cycle because their life span is long and they are performing a specific function. Because these cells have a long life span and are not programmed for proliferation, response is delayed (late reacting tissue). As dose increases, the time interval between irradiation and complications decreases.

Radiation and Cytokines

Radiation can induce cytokines and growth factors, which can act as radioprotectors or proinflammatory.

- Interleukin-1 (IL-1) and IL-6 are inflammatory cytokines. Radiation treatment induces IL-1 and IL-6 in macrophages. They are radioprotectors of hematopoietic cells.
- Basic fibroblast growth factor (bFGF) acts in angiogenesis by inducing endothelial cell growth, thereby limiting microvascular damage. It is a radioprotector of endothelial cells, which reduces the likelihood of apoptosis (reduces late effects). bFGF responds to stress (heat, shock, hypoxia, chemicals, and radiation). In slowly proliferating normal tissues, damage to vessels is responsible for radiation-induced late effects.
- Platelet derived growth factor-beta (PDGF-β) increases damage to vascular tissue. Transforming growth factor-beta (TGF-β) is a fibrotic cytokine. It is produced by inflammatory cells and induces a strong inflammatory response (e.g., pneumonitis) while also stimulating growth of connective tissue and inhibiting epithelial cell growth. Fibrosis and vascular changes are associated with late radiation effects due to this factor.

- Tumor necrosis factor (TNF-α) is produced by monocytes and tumor cells. It is a radioprotector of hematopoietic cells while sensitizing tumor cells to radiation. It binds to cell surface receptors and induces proliferation of fibroblasts, inflammatory cells, and endothelial cells and so is associated with complications such as microvascular obliteration. In clinical trials, administration of TNF causes fatigue, anorexia, weight loss, and transient leukopenia. Increased serum TNF concentrations are associated with severe interstitial pneumonitis, hepatic dysfunction, renal insufficiency, and demyelination. TNF may also contribute to the pathophysiology of radiation CNS symptoms.

EARLY AND LATE REACTING TISSUES: SPECIFIC ORGANS

Early Reacting Tissues

Skin: Manifestations of normal tissue damage can be complex. In skin, acute erythema can occur within 2 days after 2−6 Gy; erythema and epilation can occur within 3 weeks after 5−10 Gy; desquamation can occur within 3 weeks after 15−20 Gy; and reepithelialization takes place after 6−8 weeks. Late effects include atrophy, fibrosis, necrosis, and telangiectasia.

Hematopoietic tissue: A localized dose of 10 Gy has only a transient effect on stromal function. But after 20 or more Gy, aplasia with severe sinusoidal damage occurs (dilated sinuses with hemorrhage). Total body irradiation (TBI) for autologous or allogeneic transplantation involves 5−16 Gy. TBI is given as a single dose or in fractions of 1.2−4 Gy per fraction.

Lymphoid tissue and the immune system: Lymphocytes are susceptible to apoptotic death (apoptosis) and therefore strongly influence the radiation response for much of the immune system. A total body dose of 3.5−4.5 Gy inhibits the immune response.

Digestive tract:

- In oral cavity irradiation, doses of 50−60 Gy cause acute radiation mucositis.
- Esophagus irradiation doses of 20−25 Gy cause symptoms of substernal burning and painful swallowing. Late effects on the muscle layer include necrosis and inflammatory cells and a thickening of the epithelium.
- Stomach irradiation can cause nausea and often vomiting and happen immediately after treatment. Delayed gastric emptying and epithelial denudement are the two main early radiation effects. Peptic ulceration is seen in patients receiving more than 40 Gy to the upper abdomen. Dyspepsia occurs within 6 months to 4 years. Gastritis occurs in 1−12 months.
- In the small intestine, atrophy of the villi occurs 2−4 days postirradiation. Epithelial denudation is responsible for the acute gut reactions. Late bowel reactions involve all tissue layers and are caused by atrophy of the mucosa because of vascular injury with subsequent breakdown resulting from mechanical irritation and bacterial infection, and hence an acute inflammatory response.

Testes: Temporary sterility with acute exposures is seen after about 0.15 Gy but may not be manifested for 1−2 months following irradiation. Permanent sterility is produced by doses between 3.5 and 6 Gy.

Female reproductive system:
- Vulvar skin tolerance dose is 50–70 Gy.
- Vaginal acute effects include erythema, moist desquamation, and confluent mucositis, leading to loss of vaginal epithelium that persists up to 6 months. Gross abnormalities in the vagina include pale color with a thin atrophic mucosa, inflammation, and tissue necrosis with ulceration that can progress to fistula. There is a tolerance dose of 90 Gy before ulceration and more than 100 Gy for fistula.
- Cervical/uterine dose may reach 200 Gy before effects are seen as atrophy of endometrial glands and stroma and ulceration.
- Ovary/reproduction/endocrine: An acute dose of 2.5–12 Gy induces sterility, depending on age with the closer the woman to menopause, the lower the dose to produce sterility.

Late Reacting Tissues

Lung: The threshold for pneumonitis is about 20–25 Gy and it appears in 1–3 months. Symptoms include shortness of breath, dry cough, and low-grade fever. When radiation and chemotherapy are concurrent, pneumonitis develops earlier and is usually more severe. Time course of pathology:
- Acute phase: Lasts 1–2 months post-RT. Vascular congestion, edema, inflammatory response, and vacuolization of the endothelium. This exudative phase is clinically silent.
- Intermediate phase: From 2 to 9 months post-RT. Hyaline membrane forms and damages endothelial cells. Type II cells proliferate and cell death induces an immune response.
- Reparative phase: From 6 to 9 months post-RT. Congestion and vessel occlusions with capillary regeneration. Mononuclear cell infiltration and laying down of connective tissue continue.
- Late/chronic phase: Greater than 9 months post-RT. May occur with acute pneumonitis. Damaged type I pneumocytes are replaced with scar tissue.

Urinary tract:
- Symptoms of radiation nephropathy are hypertension and anemia.
- Ureteral stricture and secondary hydronephrosis are late radiation-induced effects. The risk tends to increase with the length of the ureter irradiated. Although early bladder reactions may occur, it is the late effects that are of greater concern. These include epithelial denudation, ulceration, hemorrhage, contraction, telangiectasis, and fistula formation.

Liver: Radiation-induced liver damage reduces the liver's capacity to metabolize certain chemotherapeutic agents, leading to longer half-lives and heightened toxicity. Veno-occlusive disease is characteristic of radiation-induced damage to the liver.

Thyroid: Hypothyroidism can result from radiation treatment to the head and neck area.

Central nervous system:
- Four types of damage are seen in the spinal cord:
  - Transient demyelination mediated by damage of the oligodendrocytes

- White matter necrosis with a latency of <30 weeks and requiring doses >20 Gy
- Vascular damage with a latency of >30 weeks and requiring <20 Gy
- Nerve root necrosis caused by damaged Schwann cells
- Brain damage
  - White matter necrosis: Presumably secondary to damage of glial cell precursors
  - Vascular damage: Leads to ischemic necrosis

Heart: Coronary artery disease appears to be the most common effect resulting from exposure of the heart to moderate doses of radiation <10 Gy.

Bone: Humeral and femoral heads develop necrosis and femoral neck fracture. Mandible and temporomandibular joint develop osteoradionecrosis.

Blood vessels (late effects): Endothelial cells of the vessels are moderately radiosensitive and irradiation causes permeability, occlusions of small vessels, detachment of the endothelial cells from the basement membrane, cell pyknosis, thrombosis, and rupture of the capillary wall.

Cataracts:

- The radiation threshold dose to induce a cataract was originally estimated to be 2 Gy for a single exposure but is now considered to be < 0.5 Gy. Higher doses are tolerated when delivered in a series of small doses.
- The severity and latency of cataract formation is dose-dependent. Large RBE values are seen for neutrons at low dose (RBE approaches 50 at very low dose).
- Radiation-induced cataracts follow a specific course of progression (posterior subcapsular region). Most other nonradiation cataracts progress differently, so at early stages of development, radiation-induced cataracts are distinctive.

ACUTE EFFECTS OF WHOLE-BODY IRRADIATION

Prodromal Syndrome

The threshold for early symptoms is about 1 Gy. As radiation dose increases, the severity of symptoms increases and the onset time decreases from a few hours to a few minutes. Symptoms include gastrointestinal (anorexia, nausea, vomiting, diarrhea, cramps, salivation, fluid loss) and neuromuscular (fatigue, apathy, sweating, fever, headache). The whole-body dose that would result in the death of 50% of a population of irradiated humans in 60 days (LD50/60) is 3–4 Gy. With less than 2 Gy, no treatment is required; with doses between 2 and 4 Gy, survival is good with appropriate treatment. For doses between 4 and 10 Gy, survival is possible with intervention, whereas survival is not possible following acute doses above 10 Gy.

Hematopoietic Syndrome

The dose range for symptoms is about ∼3–8 Gy. Symptoms may include depression of blood components, chills, fatigue, petechial hemorrhages in the skin, ulceration of the mouth, and epilation. The latency period depends on life span of the mature functional cells. Depression of blood components can be measured in a few days. Patient symptoms appear in 14—21 days with most deaths occurring between 30 and 60 days. As the dose increases, mean survival time decreases.

Treatment: With less than 2 Gy exposure, watch carefully but only treat in response to specific symptoms (antibiotics for infection, fresh platelets for local hemorrhage, etc.). Following an exposure to 2—8 Gy, careful nursing, antibiotics, and platelets are appropriate. Bone marrow transplants may be useful if a good match is found; otherwise, it may do more harm than good. Transplants are likely useful only in a narrow range of dose exposure of 8—10 Gy.

Gastrointestinal Syndrome

The threshold for symptoms is about 5 Gy. Symptoms may include nausea, vomiting, diarrhea, loss of appetite, fatigue, and dehydration. The latency period depends on the transit time of mature cells migrating up intestinal villi. By day 2, electrolytes and fluids exit, while bacteria and other microbes enter and the patient presents with symptoms. Death follows in about 3—10 days.

Central Nervous Syndrome/Cerebrovascular Syndrome

The threshold for symptoms is >20 Gy. Symptoms include severe nausea and vomiting in minutes, then disorientation, loss of muscle control, respiratory distress, diarrhea, convulsive seizures, coma, and death. Latency period is from a few hours (near threshold dose) to minutes (higher doses). As dose increases, mean survival time decreases. The mechanism of action may be disruption of nerve impulses and/or leakage of vessels causing an increase in fluid content of the brain.

DETERMINISTIC AND STOCHASTIC EFFECTS OF RADIATION

Deterministic Effects

- There is a minimum or threshold dose below which, for all practical purposes, the induction of the effect cannot be detected.
- The severity of the effect is dose-dependent.
- Examples: Organ and tissue damage and fetal effects.

Stochastic Effects

- Any dose, however small, may cause the effect; however, the probability for the induction of the effect is dose-dependent. Hence, a threshold does not exist for induction of the effect.
- The severity of the effect is not related to dose.
- Examples: Carcinogenesis and genetic effects, although a no-threshold model for radiation carcinogenesis is not universally accepted.

TABLE 3.5   Cancers Documented in Humans due to Radiation Exposure

Cancer Type	Human Data
Skin	X-ray workers
Lung	Pitchblende miners (radon daughters)
Bone	Radium dial painters
Liver	Thorotrast exposure
Thyroid	Japanese survivors, Marshall Islanders, children receiving radiotherapy for enlarged thymus and tinea capitis, Chernobyl
Breast	Japanese A-bomb survivors, TB sanitariums due to fluoroscopic exam
Bone marrow	Japanese survivors, Chernobyl, ankylosing spondylitis (British study of leukemia), radiologists (pre-1922)

Data compiled from Hall EJ, Giaccia AJ. Radiobiology for the radiologist, 6th ed., 2006, Hall EJ, Radiobiology for the Radiologist, fifth edition, Lippincott Williams & Wilkins, pp. 144–163, 2000; Travis, EL. Primer of medical radiobiology, 2nd ed. Chicago: Year Book Medical Publishers; 1989. pp. 163–82.

Carcinogenesis

Radiation is a cancer-inducing agent. This has been documented in humans after occupational exposure, atomic bomb survivors, medical exposure, and from fallout testing grounds, is presented in Table 3.5.

- Latency: Leukemia has the shortest latency period (peaks ~7–12 years) and solid tumors in ~10–50 years.
- The younger the person, the more susceptible to radiation-induced malignancies; this is particularly pronounced for females and breast cancer susceptibility.
- Chronic lymphatic leukemia is not induced by radiation, as opposed to acute lymphatic or myelogenous leukemia or chronic myelogenous leukemia. Solid tumors appear approximately four to six times more frequently than leukemia.
- Radiation risk varies with cancer site, age at exposure, and gender.

EFFECTS OF RADIATION ON THE EMBRYO AND FETUS

Radiation causes damage to the embryo and fetuses depending on the total dose, dose rate, mode of delivery, and gestation stage of the embryo/fetus [12,13].
Gestation is divided into preimplantation, organogenesis, and fetal periods.

- Irradiation doses as low as 5–15 cGy in mice during the preimplantation phase cause embryonic death.
- Irradiation during organogenesis (2–6 weeks in humans) causes temporary growth retardation and congenital abnormalities.

- Irradiation during the fetal period causes permanent growth retardation.
- Irradiation before 8 weeks can cause microcephaly (0.1–0.2 Gy).
- Irradiation during 8–15 weeks of gestation causes cognitive disability. During this gestational age, the risk of severe cognitive disability is a linear function of radiation dose with a risk coefficient of 0.4 per 1 Gy [14,15].
- The decrease in IQ is estimated to be at a rate of 30 points per Gy.
- Cancer induction (leukemia): The results of the Oxford survey [16] are consistent with an association between leukemia and in utero exposure to diagnostic X-rays. Doll and Wakeford suggest that even low-dose radiation, particularly in the third trimester, increases the risk of childhood cancer. An X-ray exam increases cancer risk by 40%, and the absolute excess risk is ~6% per Gy.
- Occupational exposure of women: The maximum permissible dose to the fetus during the entire gestation is 5 mSv with monthly exposures not to exceed 0.5 mSv as recommended by the NCRP Report 116 [17]. Female radiation workers should be counseled by their radiation safety officer but cannot be compelled to stop working in their current position.
- Pregnant patient: 0.1 Gy during the sensitive period of 10 days to 26 weeks is suggested as the cutoff point before therapeutic abortion should be considered.

RADIATION-INDUCED HERITABLE CHANGES

Radiation damage to DNA can cause gene mutation or chromosomal aberration in germ cells of the gonads. This can be inherited causing mutations in future generations. However, radiation-induced mutations are no different from spontaneous mutations, such as polydactyly, color blindness, and Down syndrome. Doubling dose is the dose necessary to double the spontaneous mutation frequency. The Committee on Biological Effects of Ionizing Radiation (BEIR V) [19] estimates the doubling dose to be 1 Sv (1 Gy).

To study the genetic effects from radiation, the Megamouse project [20,21] was performed that used several million irradiated mice with easily identifiable mutations such as change of coat color. This study revealed the following:
- Large variation in results, so averages were used and uncertainty at low doses.
- Dose-dependent effect with mutations increases linearly with dose.
- Dose rate dependent with fewer mutations as the rate at which the dose was delivered decreased.
- No threshold dose in that every dose, however small, appeared to be mutagenic.
- Male mice appear to be more sensitive than females. At low-dose rates, it is difficult to see mutations with exposure of females, even after several Gy. Therefore, at low-dose rates, almost all genetic burden is due to male exposure.
- Lengthening the interval between irradiation and conception reduces mutation risk. This forms the basis for the recommendation that in humans, 6 months should be allowed to elapse between significant gonadal radiation exposure and a planned conception.

- The human data that drive risk assessment and radiation protection from the Japan experience did not reveal any significant increase in genetic effects of children born to atomic bomb–exposed Japanese. The studies included untoward pregnancies, death rate in live-born children through age 17 years, sex chromosome abnormalities, and frequency of mutations examined by 2D electrophoretic protein patterns. Therefore, BEIR V and the United Nations Scientific Committee on the Effects of Atomic Radiation (UNSCEAR) [22] used the Megamouse data to estimate human genetic risk.

The genetically significant dose (GSD) is the dose equivalent to the gonads weighted for age and sex of exposed individuals expected to have offspring.

SOURCES OF RADIATION EXPOSURE

All US individuals are exposed to a variety of sources of radiation. Table 3.6 lists these and provides the average effective dose for each source received by people living in the U.S. on an annual basis.

As seen in Table 3.6, the annual effective dose from the background radiation for US population is 3.11 mSv/person-year. The annual effective dose from the man made radiation for the exposed person is about 3.13 mSv/personyear.

So the total annual effective dose from the background radiation combining with the man-made radiation is now 6.24 mSv/year (624 mrem/year) [13]. This increase in

TABLE 3.6   Sources and Annual Effective Dose Values for the US Population

Sources	Dose (mSv)	Percent (%)
Radon and Thoran	2.28	37
CT	1.47	24
Nuclear medicine	0.77	12
Interventional fluoroscopy	0.43	7
Space	0.33	5
Conventional radiography	0.33	5
Internal	0.29	5
Terrestrial	0.21	3
Consumer	0.13	2
Occupational	0.005	<0.1
Industrial	0.003	<0.1
Total	6.24	100

NCRP Report 160, Ionizing Radiation Exposure of the Population of the United States 2009, with permission from National Council on Radiation Protection and Measurements.

annual effective dose to US population since the publication of NCRP Report 93 is mainly attributed to man-made radiation increase.

Although the annual effective dose to US population increased over the last three decades, it is expected not to increase significant genetic risk to off springs, as human gene pool may be able to take in higher radiation damage.

References

Ref 1. Gunderson LL, Tepper JE. *The biologic basis of radiation oncology: clinical radiation oncology. 4th ed. Philadelphia: Elsevier; 2016. p. 2—40. 2016.*

Ref 2. Hall EJ, Giaccia AJ. *Radiobiology for the radiologist. 6th ed. 2006.*

Ref 3. Coia LR, Moylan DE. *Introduction to clinical radiation oncology. 3rd ed. Madison, WI: Medical Physics Publishing; 1996.*

Ref 4. Johns HE, Cunningham JR. *The physics of radiology. 4th ed. Springfield, IL: Charles C Thomas; 1983.*

Ref 5. Seiwert TY, Salama JK, Vokes EE. *The concurrent paradigm—general principles. Nat Clin Pract Oncol 2007;4:86—100.*

Ref 6. Perez CA, Brady LW. *Biologic basis of radiation theraoy: principles and practice of radiation oncology. 6th ed. Baltimore, MD: Lippincott Williams & Wilkins; 2013. p. 61—88. 2013.*

Ref 7. Sharma RA, Dianov GL. *Targeting base excision repair to improve cancer therapies. Mol Aspects Med 2007;28(3—4):345—74.*

Ref 8. Saldivar JS, Wu X, Follen M, Gershenson D. *Nucleotide excision repair pathway review I: implications in ovarian cancer and platinum sensitivity. Gynecol Oncol 2007; 107(1 Suppl. 1):S56—71.*

Ref 9. Hsieh P, Yamane K. *DNA mismatch repair: molecular mech- anism, cancer, and ageing. Mech Ageing Dev 2008;129(7—8):391—407.*

Ref 10. Ouyang KJ, Woo LL, Ellis NA. *Homologous recombina- tion and maintenance of genome integrity: cancer and aging through the prism of human RecQ helicases. Mech Ageing Dev 2008;129(7—8):425—40.*

Ref 11. Elkind MM, Sutton-Gilbert H, Moses WB, Alescia T, Swain RW. *Radiation response of mammalian cells in culture. V. tem- perature dependence of the repair of x-ray damage in surviving cells (aerobic and hypoxic). Radiat Res 1965;25:359—76.*

Ref 12. Russell LB, Russell WL. *An analysis of the changing radi ation response of the developing mouse embryo. J Cell Physiol 1954;43(suppl. 1):103—49.*

Ref 13. National Council on Radiation Protection and Measurements (NCRP) Report 160. *Ionizing Radiation Exposure of the Population of the United States. Bethesda, MD: National Council on Radiation Protection and Measurements; 2009.*

Ref 14. Otake M, Schull WJ. *In utero exposure to A-bomb radiation and mental retardation; a reassessment. Br J Radiol 1984;57:409—14.*

Ref 15. *Stewart A, Kneale GW. Radiation dose effects in relation to obstetric x rays and childhood cancers. Lancet 1970;1:1185—8.*

Ref 16. *Doll R, Wakeford R. Risk of childhood cancer from fetal irradiation. Br J Radiol 1997;70(830):130—9.*

Ref 17. *National council on radiation protection and measurements NCRP Report 116. Limitation of exposure to ionizing radiation. Bethesda, MD: NCRP; 1993.*

Ref 18. *Travis EL. Primer of medical radiobiology. 2nd ed. Chicago: Year Book Medical Publishers; 1989. p. 163—82.*

Ref 19. *BEIR V. Committee on the biological effects of ionizing radiation: Health effects of exposure of low level of ionizing radiations. Washington, DC: National Academies of Science/National Research Council; 1990.*

Ref 20. *Russell WL. Genetic hazards of radiation. Proc Am Phil Soc 1963;107:11—7.*

Ref 21. *Russell WL. Studies in mammalian radiation genetics. Nucleonics 1965;23:53—6.*

Ref 22. *United Nations Scientific Committee on the Effects of Atomic Radiation UNSCEAR. Ionizing radiation sources and biological effects. New York: United Nations; 1988.*

Molecular Cancer Biology

Cancer is abnormal and uncontrolled growth of cells and tissues. It is caused by a series of genetic changes involving cell division, genetic instability, apoptosis, local and distant invasion, and evasion of body's immune system, leading to fundamental changes of normal properties of cells and tissues. Optimization of radiation therapy requires that the radiation oncologist have a basic understanding of the principles and parameters of molecular cancer biology and its application in clinical radiation oncology. A brief discussion of the molecular and cellular biology of carcinogenesis and its implication in cancer treatment follows.

CELL CYCLE CONTROL

The cell cycle is an orderly process regulated by protein kinases and cyclins. Once cells pass the G1 point, they enter S phase, then move through the G2 phase, and eventually exit the M phase (Fig. 4.1).

G1 → S

- Cyclin D combines with CDK4/6 to move cells through the G1 restriction point. This complex is inhibited by p16, p21, and p27. Cyclin E combines with CDK2 in late G1 to assist with movement to the S phase.
- Cyclin/CDK4/6 complex phosphorylate the RB protein (RB1D) that causes its decoupling from E2F, which is a transcription factor that activates many genes essential during S phase.
- DNA damage can activate p53, which in turn can activate p21 (waf1/cip1), causing cell cycle arrest.
- CDC25A phosphatase is also capable of removing inhibitory phosphorylation residues on CDK2 in the later G1 phase, resulting in additional phosphorylation of RB1 and release of E2F, thereby promoting G1/S transition.

G2 → M

- Cyclin A/CDK2 facilitates progression through S phase into G2.
- The cyclin B/CDK1 complex causes breakdown of the nuclear envelope and initiation of mitosis. CDK1 is also known as cdc2.

Fundamentals of Radiation Oncology
https://doi.org/10.1016/B978-0-12-814128-1.00004-0

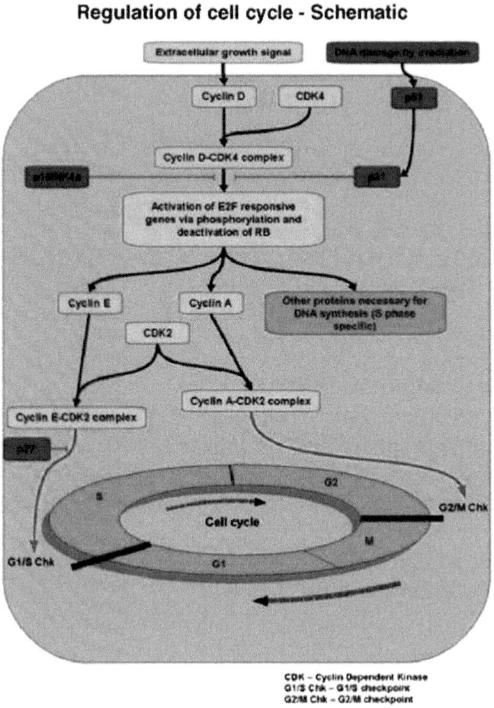

Regulation of cell cycle - Schematic

FIGURE 4.1   Protein kinases activated by cyclins that regulate cell cycle progression. *Reproduced from, Wikipedia, the Free Encyclopedia. Regulation of Cell Cycle. Wikimedia Foundation, Inc.; 2009. http://en. wikipedia.org/wiki/Cell cycle. Source: National Center for Biotechnology Information (NCBI) document "Science Primer."*

- Separation of chromosomes at anaphase requires the anaphase-promoting complex (APC), which consists of E3 ubiquitin ligase causing the degradation of cyclin B to allow exit from M phase.

CARCINOGENESIS AND METASTASIS

Carcinogenesis is a multistage process involving cancer initiation, progression, and metastasis (Fig. 4.2) [2,3]. Following is the mechanism that describes the development of the tumor metastasis when malignant cells travel from the primary tumor to a different organ and create additional tumors.

Matrix Metalloproteinases

- Matrix metalloproteinases (MMPs) and tissue inhibitors of metalloproteinases (TIMPS) degrade the extracellular connective tissue aiding development of tumor metastasis. In particular, gelatinase a (MMP-2) and gelatinase b (MMP-9) degrade type IV collagen (basement membrane) and is associated with metastases.

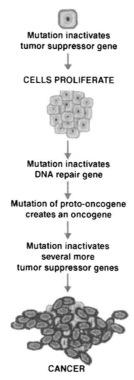

FIGURE 4.2 Depiction of the multiple mutations required by cancer. *Reproduced from, Wikipedia, the Free Encyclopedia. Carcinogenesis. Wikimedia Foundation, Inc.; 2009. p. 1. http://en.wikipedia.org/wiki/Carcinogenesis.*

- In addition to MMPs, the plasminogen activator degrades type I collagen (interstitial material) and is associated with tumor cell migration through tissue barriers. Metastatic cells use urokinase plasminogen activator (uPA) through a cascade (including plasmin) of events, eventually converting procollagenase IV to its active form.
- Tissue inhibitors of metalloproteinase (TIMP-2) inactivate collagenase IV.
- Loss of the epithelium-specific cell-to-cell adhesion molecule E-cadherin (antimetastatic protein) is a key step in the development of metastases.

Integrins

- Integrin receptors bind directly to extracellular matrices and are altered in response to environmental signals. Cell cycle regulation is broadly controlled by three things: mitogens, contact with other cells, and adherence to a substratum. Because cell cycle progression is contact inhibited and adherence dependent (cell-to-cell contact via cadherins and bound to a substratum by integrins), integrins play an important role in carcinogenesis.

- For cells to migrate, adhesion receptors such as integrins bind to extracellular molecules and cytoskeleton. Cells that express the vitronectin receptor become invasive. Specific integrins associated with increased metastases differ according to the origin of the tumor cells and may influence to which organs the cell can spread.

The mechanism with which a tumor cell travels to a distant organ and survives in a foreign microenvironment is extremely complex. It is anticipated that an elucidation of this process at the molecular level will eventually lead to development of antimetastatic cancer treatments.

TUMOR SUPPRESSOR GENES

Cancer-inducing mutations appear to behave in a recessive fashion by inactivating tumor suppressor genes [2,5,6]. Both copies of the gene must be lost or inactivated for expression of the malignant phenotype; therefore they are "loss-of-function" mutations.

- Tumor suppressor gatekeepers: These genes control cell division and cell death and directly regulate growth of tumors by inhibiting cell division or promoting cell death (rate limiting for tumor growth).
- Tumor suppressor caretakers: These genes oversee the integrity of the genome. Therefore, they control the mutation rate of cells.

The following is an incomplete list of tumor suppressor genes.

- *APC* (adenomatous polyposis of the colon): Involved in multiple cellular processes including cell division, cell–cell attachment, and mitosis. Involved in the WNT signaling pathway through beta-catenin. Mutations seen in familial adenomatous polyposis of the colon. Located on chromosome 5q21-q22.
- *BRCA1*: Involved in DNA damage repair, ubiquitination, transcriptional regulation, and other various functions. Mutations associated with familial breast and ovarian cancer gene located on chromosome 17q21.
- *BRCA2*: Involved in the repair of chromosomal damage. Mutation observed in familial breast and ovarian cancer gene. Located on chromosome 13q12.3.
- *MLH1* and *MSH2*: Involved in mismatch repair and genomic stability. Mutations associated with HNPCC (hereditary nonpolyposis colorectal cancer). Patients with these syndromes develop colorectal, ovarian, and endometrial cancers. Located on chromosomes 3p21.3 and 2p22-p2.
- *NF1*: Encodes neurofibromin 1, a GTPase-activating enzyme that is a negative regulator of the RAS signal transduction pathway. Mutations result in neurofibromatosis type 1 (von Recklinghausen disease), involved in neurofibromas, gliomas, pheochromocytomas of the nervous system and myeloid leukemia. Located on chromosome 17q11.2.
- *NF2*: Encodes neurofibromin 2, a membrane/cytoskeleton scaffolding protein. Mutations are seen in neurofibromatosis type 2, which may result in bilateral acoustic neuromas, meningiomas, schwannomas, and ependymomas of the nervous system. Located on chromosome 22q12.2.

- *TP53*: Protein has multiple functions including activation of DNA repair, G1/S cell cycle checkpoint, and apoptosis induction following DNA damage. Germline mutations cause Li−Fraumeni syndrome, and somatic mutations are seen in a wide variety of tumors. Located on chromosome 17p13.1.
- *PTEN*: A phosphatase which negatively regulates the AKT signal transduction pathway. Important in apoptosis and blocking cell division. Mutations result in Cowden's syndrome, certain hamartomas, gliomas, and prostate and endometrial cancers. Located on chromosome 10q23.3.
- *RB1*: A cell cycle checkpoint gene. Binds to and inhibits E2F, which is necessary for entry into the S phase. Mutations occur in familial retinoblastoma. Also a target of many viral oncoproteins. Located on chromosome 13q14.1-q14.2.
- VHL (von Hipple−Lindau): An E3 ubiquitin ligase that marks proteins for degradation. Mutations associated with renal cell carcinomas, hemangiomas, and pheochromocytomas. Located on chromosome 3p26-p25.
- *WT1*: A transcription factor important in the development of the urogenital system. Mutations seen in Wilms tumor. Located on chromosome 11p13.

DNA REPAIR GENES

DNA damage can be created by natural sources, such as reactive oxygen/nitrogen species, or environmental causes, such as radiation or toxic chemicals. However, multiple DNA repair mechanisms function, including NER, BER, MMR, DSBR. DNA repair pathways ensure that genetic information is accurately copied during cell division. However, mutations in DNA repair genes may cause an accumulation of mutations in genes associated with carcinogenesis, such as proto-oncogenes. Genes such as *BRCA1*, *BRCA2*, *MSH2*, *MLH1*, *XP*, and *BLM* encode proteins that have DNA repair functions. Mutations in these genes can lead to tumor formation.

PROTO-ONCOGENES AND ONCOGENES

More than 150 genes, generally referred to as proto-oncogenes, perform fundamental roles in the regulation of cell growth or differentiation. Mutations can convert proto-oncogenes into active oncogenes [2,5,6] and range from subtle changes (e.g., single-nucleotide substitutions) to gross rearrangements (insertions, deletions, gene amplifications, and/or chromosomal translocations). They could be induced by a variety of physical, chemical, or viral agents and may affect the level of gene expression, the nature of the gene product, or both. Activated oncogenes have been identified in >30% of human cancers.

Oncogenes are "gain of function" mutations; that is, alteration of only one copy is required to cause activation and therefore function in a dominant fashion. The following is an incomplete list of oncogenes. As shown in Fig. 4.3, genes found in similar signal transduction pathways acting in a similar fashion could also be construed as oncogenes (e.g., *PDGF*, *EGF*, *CDK2*, *MDM*).

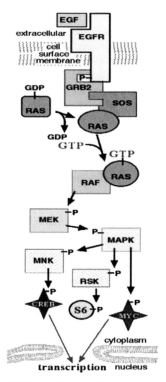

FIGURE 4.3   Example of EGF signal transduction cascade, with many of the above proteins capable of becoming oncogenes. *Reproduced from, Wikipedia, the Free Encyclopedia. MAP/ERK Signal Transduction Pathway. Wikimedia Foundation, Inc.; 2008. p. 1. http://en.wikipedia.org/wiki/MAPK/ERK_pathway a. Source: Drawn by John W. Schmidt.*

Growth Factors

- Vascular endothelial growth factor (VEGF): Binds VEGFR and promotes growth and endothelial cell proliferation. Implicated in breast cancer, colon cancer, and angiosarcoma.

Receptor Tyrosine Kinases

- Epidermal growth factor receptor (*EGFR*): Encodes the protein that binds growth factor ligands (e.g., EGF) and transmits signal intracellularly via autophosphorylation. Overexpression or mutations are associated with a variety of cancers including head and neck, glioblastoma, lung, and colon cancers.
- *Her2/neu*: Member of the *EGFR* family. Amplification can be detected in 15%–20% of breast cancers.
- *VEGFR*: Encodes a receptor that binds VEGF ligands.
- *RET*: Encodes receptor for the glial cell line–derived neurotrophic factor. Mutations are seen in medullary thyroid carcinoma.

- *KIT*: Encodes receptor for cytokine stem cell factor. Overexpression and mutations are identified in seminomas, GIST, and leukemia.

Regulatory GTPases

- *RAS*: Encodes a family of intracellular proteins that are part of signal transduction cascades, often transmitting signals from receptor tyrosine kinases to cytoplasmic kinases. May be overexpressed or mutated such that the active form (RAS-GTP) is constitutively present. The *RAS* oncogene is found altered in a variety of cancers, including pancreas, colon, and lung.

Other Kinases

- *SRC*: Encodes a tyrosine kinase involved in a signal transduction pathway between receptor tyrosine kinases and other downstream effectors. Mutations associated with colon cancer.
- *RAF*: Encodes a serine/threonine kinase; member of the mitogen-activated protein kinase (MAPK) family. Downstream effector of RAS. Alterations identified in multiple human cancers.
- *ABL*: Encodes a cytoplasmic tyrosine kinase involved in cell differentiation, division, and adhesion. In chronic myelogenous leukemia (CML), a translocation (Philadelphia chromosome) causes the BCR-ABL fusion protein, which is constitutively active.
- *CDK4*: Encodes a serine/threonine kinase which controls cell cycle progress. Activation seen in lung and pancreatic cancers. Other cyclin-dependent kinases as well as their cyclin regulatory subunits have been implicated in a number of cancers.

Transcription Factors

- *MYC*: Upon activation, MYC dimerizes with MAX to regulate transcription by binding to DNA at sequence-specific sites. Deregulation may occur via translocation, amplification, overexpression, or abnormal signaling. Activations are seen in bladder, breast, neuroblastoma, and ovarian cancers.
- *FOS*: Encodes a transcription factor activated by the MAP/ERK signal transduction pathway. Combines with JUN to form the AP-1 transcription factor.

APOPTOSIS

Apoptosis, a form of programmed cell death, can occur following radiation and differs from cell necrosis [2,8]. During cell necrosis, there is a flow of ions into the cell, resulting in swelling due to loss of osmotic pump function, followed by organelle swelling and chromatin breakdown. This is followed by cell and nuclear membrane breakdown resulting in an inflammatory response. In contrast, apoptosis is characterized by (Fig. 4.4) [1] organized compaction and segregation into delineated masses [2], followed by condensation of the cytoplasm and convolution of the nuclear and cellular membrane [3], resulting in the creation of apoptotic bodies that are phagocytosed and digested by the adjacent cells and wandering macrophages.

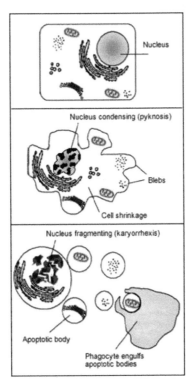

FIGURE 4.4 The characteristic morphological changes of apoptosis and the organized degradation of cellular organelles into apoptotic bodies, which are eventually
phagocytosed. *Reproduced from, Wikipedia, the Free Encyclopedia. Apoptosis. Wikimedia Foundation, Inc.; 2008. p.
3. http://en.wikipedia.org/wiki/Apoptosis.*

Apoptosis can occur in 4—6 h (secondary apoptosis is seen in cells undergoing reproductive death in 24—96 h).

The morphological and biochemical hallmarks of apoptosis generally result from
activation of proenzyme proteases called caspases. Caspases can be divided into two
broad groups:

- "Initiator" caspases are activated by death signals to cleave and activate
- "Effector" or "executioner" caspases that act on multiple substrates

There are two discrete pathways by which caspases are activated—distinguished by
use of different initiator caspases:

- Intrinsic pathway from the mitochondria—activates caspase 9
- Extrinsic pathway from the microenvironment acting through TNFR family
  members—activates caspase 8

Intrinsic Apoptotic Pathway

Radiation triggers the intrinsic pathway by causing either

- activation of p53 by radiation or
- generation of the lipid ceramide—although cell type dependent, radiation affects plasma membranes and activates sphingomyelinase, which increases levels of ceramide by hydrolysis of sphingomyelin or
- direct action of radiation on mitochondria

These actions result in release of cytochrome c from the mitochondria, which binds to apaf-1 (apoptosis protease activation factor 1) and procaspase 9 to form the apoptosome, resulting in activated caspase 9.

Regulation of the mitochondrial events occurs through members of the BCL-2 family of proteins. The BCL-2 proteins regulate mitochondrial membrane permeability and can be either proapoptotic or antiapoptotic.

- Proapoptotic gene products:
  - BAX, BAK, BIK, BIM, BLK, BAD, Bcl-xs, BID, HRK, MTD/BOK
  - p53 (a transcription factor) induces BAX, PUMA, NOXA, and PERP
  - BID and BAX make mitochondrial membranes more permeable to cytochrome c
- Antiapoptotic gene products:
  - BCL-2, BCL-xl, MCL-1, BCL-w, BAG-1, BFL-1, BRAG-1, BCL2A1

The above proteins determine if the cell commits to apoptosis or aborts apoptosis, such as BCL-2 blocks the release of cytochrome c from mitochondria and therefore aborts apoptosis in this pathway.

Extrinsic Apoptotic Pathway

The extrinsic pathway [8,10] encompasses transmembrane receptor—mediated interactions involving death receptors such as engagement of FAS by its ligand FASL. This leads to recruitment of the adaptor protein FADD to the cytoplasmic tail of FAS. The FAS—FADD interaction is mediated by their respective death domains. This interaction allows recruitment of procaspase 8 and formation of the death-inducing signaling complex. This results in the formation of active caspase 8 with subsequent processing of downstream effector caspases (CASP3, CASP6, and CASP7) that can then cleave various cellular proteins leading to apoptotic cell death.

- The effector caspases activate cytoplasmic endonucleases, which degrade chromosomal DNA, and proteases that degrade the nuclear and cytoskeletal proteins. These lead to cytomorphological changes, such as chromatin and cytoplasmic condensation (pyknosis), nuclear fragmentation (karyorrhexis), ultimately forming the apoptotic bodies.
- Phagocytic uptake of apoptotic cells is the final component of apoptosis. This process does not involve release of cellular materials and therefore does not cause an inflammatory response.

- NFκB (a mediator of immune and inflammatory responses) may play a role in regulating apoptosis. It is usually localized in the cytoplasm and remains transcriptionally inactive until stimulated by inflammatory cytokines or peptide growth factors. NFκB translocates into the nucleus and regulates the expression of target genes with key roles in the regulation of apoptosis, tumor growth, and activation of inflammatory responses.

Understanding the apoptotic process is important because cells that readily undergo apoptotic death are generally radiosensitive. Thus, if apoptosis can be upregulated in cancer cells, it may render a tumor more susceptible to control by radiation.

Necroptosis

Necroptosis represents a programmed form of necrosis. In necroptosis, the TNFR-associated death protein TRADD signals to RIPK1, which recruits RIPK3 forming the necrosome. This drives oligomerization of MLKL resulting in permeabilization of the plasma membranes and a necrotic form of cell death.

ANGIOGENESIS

Angiogenesis is the formation and differentiation of blood vessels. Oxygen can diffuse from a blood vessel approximately 70 μm. Without blood supply tumors can only grow to a few millimeters in size. Tumors often upregulate genes involved in angiogenesis to provide their own blood supply.

The process of angiogenesis occurs as an orderly series of events [8]:
- Growing tumors or injured tissues produce and release angiogenic growth factors (VEGF, TGFβ) into nearby tissues.
- These growth factors bind to specific receptors on the endothelial cells of nearby blood vessels.
- Binding to the receptors activates the endothelial cells. Signals are then sent from the cell's surface to the nucleus.
- Enzymes create openings in the sheathlike covering (basement membrane) surrounding all existing blood vessels (hyperpermeability).
- The endothelial cells then proliferate and migrate through the holes of the existing vessel toward the diseased tissue or tumor.
- Integrins, which are specialized adhesion molecules, serve as grappling hooks to help pull the sprouting new blood vessel toward the tumor or injured site.
- Additional enzymes including MMPs are produced to degrade the tissue in front of the developing vessel tip to accommodate its growth.
- Developing endothelial cells roll up to form a blood vessel tube. Individual blood vessel tubes connect to form blood vessel loops that can circulate blood.
- Finally, newly formed blood vessel tubes are stabilized by specialized cells (smooth muscle cells, pericytes) that provide structural support. Blood flow then begins.

THERAPEUTICS

Chemotherapeutics

In cancer treatment, chemotherapy plays a very significant role. Often chemotherapy is given sequentially before or after radiation therapy or concurrently with radiation therapy. Following is a list of the cytotoxic agents that have been in clinical use for a long period of time:

- Bleomycin: Binds DNA, generating free radicals and promoting scission reactions between base pairs. Dose limiting toxicity is lung fibrosis.
- Carboplatin: Binds to DNA causing intra-/interstrand cross-linking. Side effects include nephrotoxicity, ototoxicity, nausea and vomiting, and neurotoxicity.
- Carmustine (BCNU): Alkylates and cross-links DNA and carbamoylates proteins. Not cell cycle dependent. Crosses the blood−brain barrier. Other agents of this class include CCNU. Toxicity includes myelosuppression.
- Cisplatin: Binds to DNA causing intra-/interstrand cross-links. Side effects include nephrotoxicity (ATN), ototoxicity, nausea, vomiting, and neurotoxicity (neuropathy).
- Cyclophosphamide: Nitrogen mustard alkylating agents which can cause DNA cross-linking. Ifosfamide is another agent in this class. Toxicities include hemorrhagic cystitis, myelosuppression, nausea, and vomiting.
- Dacarbazine (DTIC): DNA synthesis inhibition by its action as a purine analogue and interaction with SH (sulfhydryl) groups. Common side effects include loss of appetite, vomiting, low white blood cell count, and low platelets.
- Docetaxel: Inhibits microtubule disassembly causing G2/M arrest. Other members of the taxane class include paclitaxel, navelobine, and eribulin. Toxicities include myelosuppression.
- Doxorubicin (Adriamycin): DNA intercalator; interacts with topoisomerase II, blocking DNA replication/repair and RNA and protein synthesis. Also produces free radicals. Side effects include cardiotoxicity (which has memory lasting years such that it can synergize with radiation given years after chemotherapy).
- Etoposide (VP-16): Inhibits topoisomerase II, causing accumulation of single- and double-strand DNA breaks. Acts primarily at S/G2. Can cause myelosuppression.
- Fluorouracil: Pyrimidine analogue that is metabolized to F-UMP. F-UMP is incorporated into RNA and DNA, inhibiting RNA processing (faulty protein production) and DNA replication, blocking cell growth. Also blocks thymidylate synthetase, reducing the availability of TTP (thymidine triphosphate) necessary for DNA synthesis. Toxicities include myelosuppression, GI side effects, mucositis, oral ulcers, and diarrhea.
- Gemcitabine: Competes for incorporation into DNA, thus blocking DNA one nucleotide past the drug. Also inhibits ribonucleotide reductase. Kills at S phase, blocks at G1/S. Side effects include anemia, thrombocytopenia, and nausea/vomiting.
- Irinotecan (CPT-11): Interacts with topoisomerase I, preventing the relegation of SSB (single-strand break), thus increasing the incidence of DSB (double-strand break). Can cause diarrhea and immunosuppression. Class includes topotecan.

- Methotrexate: Inhibitor of DHFR gene, which results in inhibition of purine and thymidylate synthetase inhibition of DNA and RNA synthesis. Can cause stomatitis, leucopenia, and nausea.
- Mitomycin C: Binds to DNA, leading to cross-linking and inhibition of DNA synthesis and function. Mitomycin is cell cycle phase–nonspecific. Side effects include bone marrow damage, lung fibrosis, and renal damage.
- Oxaliplatin: Binds to DNA, causing intra-/interstrand cross-links. Side effects include nephrotoxicity, ototoxicity, nausea/vomiting, and neurotoxicity.
- Temozolamide: An oral alkylating agent used in gliomas. Its efficacy is related to the methylation state of MGMT gene (if methylated, temozolamide is more effective). Side effects include neutropenia, anemia, thrombocytopenia, and constipation.
- Vinblastine: Binds tubulin, preventing microtubule formation. Results in M phase arrest. Side effects include peripheral neuropathy and bone marrow suppression.
- Vincristine: Binds to the microtubular proteins of the mitotic spindle, leading to crystallization of microtubules and mitotic arrest or cell death. Side effects include hair loss, constipation, difficulty walking, headaches, neuropathic pain, lung damage, and low white cell count.

Targeted Therapies

In contrast to chemotherapy, targeted therapy targets specific aspects (overexpressed proteins) of cancer cells that differ from normal cells to tailor individualized cancer treatment. Following are recent targeted therapy agents listed in alphabetical order used for cancer treatments:

- Afatinib: EGFR and HER2 inhibitor approved for treatment of non–small cell lung cancer (NSCLC) whose tumors have EGFR exon 19 deletions or exon 21 (L858R) substitution mutations.
- Alemtuzumab: Monoclonal antibody targeting CD-52. Used in chronic lymphocytic leukemia (CLL) and T-cell lymphoma.
- Axitinib: VEGF-R inhibitor used for treatment of renal cell carcinoma.
- Bevacizumab: Monoclonal antibody against VEGF, which inhibits its binding to VEGF-R, thus suppressing vascular growth. Indicated for colon cancer, lung cancer, and glioblastoma multiforme (GBM). Can cause infusion reactions, nausea, and rash.
- Blinatumomab: Bispecific CD19–directed CD3 T-cell engager that binds to CD19 expressed on the surface of cells of B-lineage origin and CD3 expressed on the surface of T cells. Activates endogenous T cells by connecting CD3 in the T-cell receptor complex with CD19 on benign and malignant B cells. Mediates formation of a synapse between the T cell and the tumor cell, upregulation of cell adhesion molecules, production of cytolytic proteins, release of inflammatory cytokines, and proliferation of T cells, which result in redirected lysis of CD19 + cells. Used for treatment of acute lymphoblastic leukemia.
- Bortezomib, carfilzomib, and ixazomib: Proteasome inhibitors approved for treatment of multiple myeloma.

- Brentuximab vedotin: Antibody—drug conjugate comprised of an anti-CD30 antibody joined by an enzyme cleavable linker to a monomethyl auristatin E (MMAE). It releases the toxic MMAE upon internalization into CD30-expressing tumor cells. Approved for treatment of Hodgkin and anaplastic large cell lymphoma.
- Cabozantinib: Multiple tyrosine kinase inhibitor approved for treatment of renal and medullary thyroid cancer.
- Ceritinib and alectinib: Selective inhibitors of anaplastic lymphoma kinase (ALK). Approved for treatment of ALK positive NSCLC.
- Cetuximab and necitumumab: Monoclonal antibodies targeting EGF-R, used for treatment of solid tumors.
- Cobimetinib: Mitogen-activated protein kinase/extracellular signal—regulated kinase (MEK) inhibitor used in combination with a BRAF inhibitor for treatment of melanoma.
- Crizotinib and brigatinib: In approximately 5% of patients with NSCLCs, typically younger individuals who never smoked. The tumor possesses an interstitial deletion and inversion within chromosome 2p that results in fusion of the N-terminal portion of the protein encoded by the echinoderm microtubule-associated protein-like 4 (EML4) gene with the intracellular signaling portion of the anaplastic lymphoma kinase (ALK) gene. EML4-ALK undergoes constitutive dimerization through interaction between the coiled-coil domain within the EML4 region of each monomer, thereby activating ALK and generating oncogenic activity. Tumor cells expressing EML4-ALK are "addicted" to its continued function. These drugs are inhibitors of the receptor tyrosine kinase activity of ALK and EGFR (brigatinib) and are used for treatment of NSCLCs characterized by an EML4-ALK translocation.
- Daratumumab: Human monoclonal antibody (IgG1κ) that binds to CD38, which is a transmembrane glycoprotein expressed on the surface of hematopoietic cells, including multiple myeloma. Inhibits the growth of CD38-expressing tumor cells by inducing apoptosis directly through Fc-mediated cross-linking and immune-mediated tumor cell lysis.
- Denosumab: Binds to and inhibits RANK ligand. Denosumab increases osteoclast activity, is stimulated by RANKL, and is a mediator of bone pathology in solid tumors with osseous metastases.
- Dinutuximab: Binds to the glycolipid GD2, which is expressed on neuroblastoma cells and induces cell lysis.
- Elotuzumab: Humanized IgG1 monoclonal antibody that specifically targets the SLAMF7 protein, which is expressed on multiple myeloma cells and facilitates the interaction with NK cells to mediate the killing of myeloma cells through antibody-dependent cellular cytotoxicity.
- Gefitinib and erlotinib: Small molecule inhibitors of EGF-R tyrosine kinase signaling.
- Gemtuzumab: Binds to the CD33 antigen, which is expressed on the surface of leukemic blasts in more than 80% of patients with AML. Causes internalization of calicheamicin inside the lysosomes, which then causes DNA double-strand breaks and cell death.

- Ibrutinib and acalabrutinib: Selective inhibitors of Bruton's tyrosine kinase (Btk). Forms a covalent bond with a cysteine residue in the BTK active site, leading to inhibition of BTK enzymatic activity. Used for treatment of mantle cell lymphoma and CLL.
- Idelalisib and copanlisib: Small molecule inhibitors of phosphoinositide-3 kinase (PI3K) delta approved for treatment of relapsed CLL, follicular B-cell NHL, small lymphocytic lymphoma (idelalisib), and PI3K-alpha and PI3K-delta approved for treatment of follicular lymphoma (copanlisib).
- Imatinib, dasatinib, nilotinib, ponatinib, and bosutinib: Multityrosine kinase inhibitors used for treatment of CML possessing a translocation (Philadelphia chromosome) causes the bcr-abl fusion protein.
- Lapatinib and neratinib: Small molecule inhibitors of EGFR and HER2 used for treatment of HER2-positive breast cancer.
- Lenvatinib: Multiple tyrosine kinase inhibitor used for treatment of renal cell and thyroid cancer.
- Midostaurin: Semisynthetic derivative of staurosporine, an alkaloid derived from the bacterium *Streptomyces staurosporeus* that inhibits FLT3 activity. Approved for treatment of FLT3 mutation−positive acute myeloid leukemia.
- Ofatumumab: Anti-CD20 monoclonal antibody that targets CD20 on B cells. Used for treatment of CLL.
- Obinutuzumab: Monoclonal antibody that targets the CD20 antigen expressed on the surface of B-lymphocytes and mediates B-cell lysis. Used for lymphoma treatment.
- Olaparib, rucaparib, and niraparib: Poly (ADP-ribose) polymerase (PARP) inhibitor. Selectively binds to and inhibits PARP, which enhances the cytotoxicity of DNA-damaging agents, particularly in cells with mutant BRCA, resulting in synthetic lethality. Approved for treatment of either BRCA-mutated ovarian cancer (olaparib and rucaparib) or ovarian, fallopian tube, or primary peritoneal cancers (niraparib).
- Olaratumab: PDGF-R blocking antibody used for treatment of soft tissue sarcoma.
- Osimertinib: EGFR inhibitor used for treatment of NSCLC possessing a T790M mutation.
- Palbociclib, abemaciclib, and ribociclib: CDK4/6 inhibitor approved for treatment of HER2-negative and hormone receptor−positive breast cancer.
- Pazopanib: VEGFR tyrosine kinase inhibitor approved for treatment of renal cell carcinoma and soft tissue sarcoma.
- Ramucirumab: Recombinant human IgG1 monoclonal antibody that specifically binds to VEGF receptor 2. Used for treatment of solid tumors.
- Regorafenib: Multikinase inhibitor including VEGFR2 and TIE2 that is used for treatment of gastrointestinal, stromal, liver and colorectal tumors.
- Rituximab: Anti-CD20 antibody. CD20 is a protein found on the surface of B cells at certain stages in their life cycle. CD20 initiates B-cell lysis and is indicated for lymphoma.
- Romidepsin, belinostat, and panobinostat: Histone deacetylase inhibitors that result in histone hyperacetylation, thereby affecting gene expression. Romidepsin and belinostat were approved for treatment of T-cell lymphoma and panobinostat for multiple myeloma.

- Sunitinib and sorafinib: Small molecule multiple tyrosine kinase inhibitors. Indicated for renal cell and several other cancers.
- Temsirolimus and everolimus: Bind to the intracellular protein, FKBP-12, resulting in an inhibitory complex formation and inhibition of mTOR kinase activity. Used for treatment of renal cell carcinoma.
- Tositumomab and ibritumomab tiuxetan: Anti-CD20 antibody conjugated to ^{131}I and ^{90}Y, respectively. Used to treat non-Hodgkin's lymphoma.
- Trastuzumab and pertuzumab: Monoclonal antibodies that bind to the HER2 receptor and prevent growth factors from stimulating a growth signal. Ado-trastuzumab emtansine is an HER2-targeted antibody—drug conjugate composed of the humanized anti-HER2 IgG1, trastuzumab, and the small molecule cytotoxin, DM1, which is a microtubule inhibitor. Upon binding to the HER2 receptor, the drug undergoes receptor-mediated internalization and subsequent lysosomal degradation, resulting in intracellular release of DM1-containing cytotoxic catabolites. Binding of DM1 to tubulin disrupts microtubule networks in the cell. These drugs are used for treatment of HER2-positive breast cancer.
- Vandetanib: VEGF-R, EGF-R, and RET-inhibitor used for treatment of medullary thyroid cancer.
- Vemurafenib, dabrafenib, and trametinib: Used to treat melanomas with a mutation that results in the substitution of glutamic acid for valine at codon 600 (BRAF V600E).
- Venetoclax: Selective small-molecule inhibitor of BCL-2, an antiapoptotic protein approved for treatment of CLL with a 17p chromosomal deletion.
- Vismodegib and sonidegib: Binds to and inhibits smoothened, a transmembrane protein involved in Hedgehog signal transduction used for treatment of basal cell carcinoma.
- Ziv-aflibercept: Recombinant fusion protein consisting of VEGF-binding portions from the extracellular domains of human VEGF receptors 1 and 2 fused to the Fc portion of the human IgG1. By binding to these endogenous ligands, it inhibits the binding and activation of their cognate receptors. This inhibition can result in decreased neovascularization and vascular permeability. Approved for treatment of colorectal cancer.

References

Ref 1. *Wikipedia, the Free Encyclopedia. Regulation of cell cycle. Wikimedia Foundation, Inc.; 2009. http://en.wikipedia.org/wiki/Cell cycle.*

Ref 2. *Michael B, et al. Molecular cancer and radiation biology. In: Perez CA, Brady LW, editors. Principles and practice of radiation oncology. 6th ed. Baltomore (MD): Lippincott Williams & Wilkins; 2013. p. 89—101.*

Ref 3. *Keleg S, Büchler P, Ludwig R, Büchler MW, Friess H. Invasion and metastasis in pancreatic cancer. Mol Cancer 2003;2:14.*

Ref 4. *Wikipedia, the Free Encyclopedia. Carcinogenesis. Wikimedia Foundation, Inc.; 2009. http://en.wikipedia.org/wiki/Carcinogenesis.*

Ref 5. *Hall EJ. In: Baltimore MD, editor. Radiobiology for the radiologist. 5th ed. Lippincott Williams & Wilkins; 2000. See also Hall EJ, Giaccia AJ. Radiobiology for the Radiologist, 6th edition, 2006.*

Ref 6. *Kufe DW, editor. Cancer medicine 7 (Holland-Frei). Philadelphia: BC Decker Inc./ American Association for Cancer Research (AACR); 2006.*

Ref 7. *Wikipedia, the Free Encyclopedia. MAP/ERK signal transduction Pathway. Wikimedia Foundation, Inc.; 2008. http://en.wikipedia.org/wiki/MAPK/ERK_pathway a.*

Ref 8. *Stevenson MA, et al. Molecular and cellular biology. In: Gunderson LL, Tepper JE, editors. Clinical radiation oncology. 4th ed. Philadelphia, (PA): Elsevier; 2016. p. 41–50.*

Ref 9. *Wikipedia, the Free Encyclopedia. Apoptosis. Wiki media Foundation, Inc.; 2008. http://en.wikipedia.org/wiki/Apoptosis.*

Ref 10. *Elmore S. Apoptosis: a review of programmed cell death. Toxicol Pathol 2007;35(4):495–516.*

TECHNIQUES AND MODALITIES OF RADIATION ONCOLOGY

5

Brachytherapy

Brachytherapy is a short-distance method of treating malignant disease using localized irradiation from small sealed (encapsulated) radioactive sources. Brachytherapy provides a highly conformal and very intense, localized radiation dose to the tumor while having rapid dose falloff in the surrounding normal tissue. This rapid dose falloff with distance spares the surrounding normal tissues from high doses of radiation, improving the therapeutic ratio. A large number of patients are treated with brachytherapy in modern radiation oncology. This chapter covers the basic principles of brachytherapy physics [1] and its application in radiation oncology.

TECHNIQUES OF BRACHYTHERAPY

Brachytherapy can be performed utilizing the following techniques:

Interstitial: In this technique the radioactive sources are implanted directly into the cancerous tissue. Radioactive sources can be in the form of seeds, needles, or ribbons. In a temporary implant, these radioactive sources can be removed from the tissue after a specific dose has been given. Alternatively, the sources can be left in the implanted tissue as a permanent implant. One of the common uses of an interstitial implant is prostate cancer treatment. Prostate cancer implants can be permanent or temporary. The permanent implant is most commonly performed with either ^{125}I or ^{103}Pd radioactive seeds and temporary implants utilize ^{192}Ir sources.

Intracavitary and intraluminal: With the intracavitary technique, hollow stainless steel applicators hold the radioactive sources in the desired configuration for brachytherapy treatments. This technique is most commonly used to treat cervical and uterine cancers. Fletcher-Suit applicators (most common) have a tandem that is inserted into the uterine canal and colpostats that are inserted into the vaginal fornices, which are then secured with a locking mechanism. Once the applicators are stabilized with packing and verified with X-ray images, the applicators are then loaded with radioactive sources either with low dose rate (LDR) ^{137}Cs or with high dose rate (HDR) ^{192}Ir sources for treatments.

Surface mold: In this technique an applicator holding radioactive sources in geometric arrangements is placed on the skin or mucosal surface. The radioactive sources give uniform distributions of radiation dose to a specified depth to a skin or mucosal surface cancer. This technique is mostly used for skin cancer and oral cavity cancers.

Fundamentals of Radiation Oncology
https://doi.org/10.1016/B978-0-12-814128-1.00005-2

PHYSICS AND BIOLOGY OF BRACHYTHERAPY SOURCES

Radioactive Sources

Radium-226: Since early 1900, ^{226}Ra was the only radionuclide source extensively used for brachytherapy for cancers. Due to the decay of ^{226}Ra, gaseous products are generated. Gaseous products cause excess pressure in sealed ^{226}Ra sources, causing leakage of radioactive radon gaseous ^{222}Ra.

Cesium-137: To avoid the disadvantage of high photon energy and radon leakage, cesium-137 source was developed to replace ^{226}Ra sources. ^{137}Cs is a by-product of nuclear fission and is generated in nuclear reactors. ^{137}Cs sources are encapsulated stainless steel tubes with a half-life of 30 years and a physical length of 2 cm for intracavitary brachytherapy. In clinical application, the activity of the ^{137}Cs sources must be adjusted for the decay of ^{137}Cs over time (date of calibration when purchased to the date of treatment).

Iridium-192: It is produced when stable ^{191}Ir (37% abundance) absorbs a neutron [2]. It has a range of photon energies averaged at ~ 380 keV compared with 662 keV, emitted from ^{137}Cs. ^{192}Ir requires less shielding for radiation workers' protection and public safety. ^{192}Ir sources can be made with very high concentrations of ^{192}Ir, which is desirable for the HDR remote afterloader unit (~ 10 Ci) because it can be fabricated into a very small volume source, ^{191}Ir has been clinically used for intravascular brachytherapy.

Iodine-125: Has a half-life of 59.6 days and emits gamma rays of 35.5 keV and characteristic X-rays in the range of 27–32 keV. Because of the lower energy photon emissions, the radiation exposure around the patient to workers and the public can be easily managed, compared with other radionuclide sources. The half value layer thickness for the photons emitted by encapsulated ^{125}I sources is about 0.025 mm of lead. ^{125}I seeds are widely used in interstitial brachytherapy, on an outpatient basis.

Palladium-103: It has a similar clinical application as that for ^{125}I seeds, with similar physical size and encapsulation as that of ^{125}I seeds [2]. Average photon energy is about 21 keV. ^{103}Pd has a shorter half-life of 17 days, compared with 60 days of ^{125}I. Because of its relative shorter half-life, ^{103}Pd may have a biological advantage for delivering HDR to the implanted target volume, compared with that of ^{125}I. Characteristics of some of the radionuclides widely used in brachytherapy, historically or currently, are summarized in Table 5.1.

In principle, radioactive sources used for permanent implants are desirable to have low photon energies for the safety of radiation workers and public safety. Shorter half-lives are desired to achieve adequate dose rates for tumor control. By contrast, longer half-life radionuclides are desired for temporary implants, as they reduce the frequency of source exchange. The emission energy level for radioactive sources is tolerated by use of radiation barriers or shielding during placing temporary implants.

Source Strength Specifications

To properly define the characteristics of brachytherapy sources, there are several terminologies as the followings [4].

- Exposure rate (dX/dt) at a specified distance. The quantity of exposure, usually symbolized by X, and commonly expressed in units of roentgens (R) or

TABLE 5.1 Characteristics of Some Radionuclide Sources Used in Brachytherapy

	$T_{1/2}$	Half Value Layer Lead [3]	Γ (R cm^2/mCi h)	E (keV)	Decay	Typical Source Design
^{226}Ra	1622 y	12	8.25	830	To ^{222}Rn with $t_{1/2}$ and final ^{206}Pb. By α, β emission	Ra-sulfate or RaCl, 1 cm long, 0.5 mm Pt filter
^{137}Cs	30 y	6	3.26	662	To ^{137}Ba, by β, γ emission	Ceramic microsphere labeled, in stainless steel capsule
^{192}Ir	74 d	3	4.69	380	To ^{192}Pt and ^{192}Os, by beta emission and electron capture	Alloy, 30% Ir and 70% Pt, wire or seed in 3 mm long 0.5 mm diameter
^{125}I	60 d	0.025	1.45	27–35	To ^{125}Te, γ, electron capture, internal conversion, leading char X-ray	Model 6711 seed, active silver rod AgI, visible in radiograph. Titanium capsule filter electron and X-ray <5 keV
^{103}Pd	17 d	0.008	0.65	21	^{103}Rh, electron capture, and char X-ray	Titanium tube with ^{103}Pd graphite cylinders and a lead rod X-ray marker

milliroentgens (mR), is a quantity that reflects the extent of ionization events taking place when air is irradiated by ionizing photons (gamma radiation and/or X-rays). Exposure rate constant (Γ) is defined by the International Commission on Radiation Units and Measurements (ICRU) as exposure rate (R/h) at 1 cm from a point source of 1 mCi and has the unit R cm^2/mCi hr.

- Radioactivity. The source strength is specified in terms of the number of radioactive disintegrations per second, such as, millicuries (mCi) or megabecquerel (MBq).
- Apparent activity. Specified in terms of exposure rate at 1 m for radioactivity of a bare source. It is determined by the ratio of exposure rate at 1 m to the exposure rate constant of the unfiltered source at 1 m.
- Equivalent mass of radium. Specified in terms of effective equivalent mass of ^{226}Ra, with equivalent exposure as ^{226}Ra. The conversion is simply by comparing exposure rate constant for one radioactive source to that of ^{226}Ra.
- Air kerma strength. Reference to help avoid errors due to uncertainty in the relationship between the source activity and the radiation emitted. Reference air kerma rate (RAKR), defined by ICRU 38, as "the kerma rate to air, in air, at a reference distance of 1 m, corrected for air attenuation and scattering" [3]. The total reference air kerma is the sum of the products of the reference air kerma rate and the duration of the application for each source. American Association of Physicists in Medicine (AAPM) recommends using air kerma strength for the source strength specification. Air kerma strength is specified in terms of air kerma rate at the point along the transverse axis of the source in free space.

$$S_K = K(d)d^2$$

where S_K is the air kerma strength, measured in U, d is the distance from the source, and K(d) is the kerma in air. The 1 U = 1 unit of air kerma strength = 1 cGy cm^2/h.

Source Strength Calibration

Traceability to national standards: The National Institute of Standards and Technology (NIST) calibrates a "primary" standard of each type (^{137}Cs, ^{60}Co-60, ^{125}I, ^{192}Ir) using open-air geometry and a series of spherical graphite cavity chambers. In North America, clinical calibration of radioactive sources is traceable to national standards through a chain connecting clinics to an Accredited Dosimetry Calibration Laboratory (ADCL). ADCL provides secondary standard calibrations to clinical users for instruments and radioactive sources for brachytherapy dosimetry [5]. Clinical calibration (assay) uses a "reentrant"-type ion chamber. The walls of the chamber surround the source, approximating 4π measurement geometry. This well-type ionization chamber should bear a calibration factor determined by an ADCL using a secondary source of the same type, shape, and geometry. The chamber-specific source holder and electronic meter are calibrated together by an ADCL every 2 years.

Brachytherapy Dose Calculation: Calculation of Dose Using TG-43 Formalism

Classical dose calculations based on point sources or Sievert integrals for line sources are not adequate because they ignore scatters, anisotropic and radiation shielding from encapsulation. AAPM TG-43 proposed that effects of several physical factors on dose rate distribution are considered separately and are divided into several modules [2,6].

$$\dot{D}(r, \theta) \; = \; \Lambda S_k \frac{G(r, \theta)}{G(1, \pi/2)} F(r, \theta) g(r)$$

- Dose rate constant, Λ. Includes effects of encapsulation and self-filtration within the source, scattering in water surrounding it. Λ is defined as dose rate per unit air kerma strength (U) at 1 cm along the transverse axis in water.
- Geometry factor, $G(r, \theta)$ (cm^{-2}). Accounts for variation of relative dose due to the only spatial distribution of activity within the source. When the distribution of radioactivity can be approximated by a point source, then $G(r, \theta)$ reduces to

$$G(r, \theta) \; = \; 1/r^2$$

When the distribution of radioactivity can be approximated by a line source of length L, then $G(r, \theta)$ is reduced to

$$G(r, \theta) \; = \; \frac{\beta}{L \, r \, \sin\theta}$$

where L is the active length of the source and β is the angle subtended by the active source with respect to the calculation point (r, θ) [2].
- Anisotropic factor, $F(r, \theta)$. Two-dimensional function gives the angular variation of dose rate due to primary photons' self-filtration, oblique filtration through the encapsulating material, and scattering of photons in the medium. $F(r, \theta)$ is normalized at $\theta = \pi/2$ (transverse axis), that is, $F(r, \pi/2) = 1$.
- Radial dose function, $g(r)$. Accounts for the effects of absorption and scatters in the medium along the transverse axis of the source. The radial dose function applies only to transverse axis of the source, at $\theta = \pi/2$.

The TG-43 dosimetry system is currently used in many of the treatment planning systems in clinics [6–8]. TG-43 is a water-based dosimetry system, considering everything outside the brachytherapy sources as water. Because of this, MRI images of the patient can be directly used for brachytherapy dose computation, without concerning for electron density information as that in external beam dose calculation. This water-based simplification works well for many clinical cases, especially for intracavitary GYN brachytherapy, where bones or the air-to-tissue interface is outside the treatment volume or far away from the brachytherapy sources. The TG-43 formalism remains the standard of practice for dose optimization.

However, recent advances in dose calculation (detailed in AAPM TG-186) have facilitated the improvement of dose calculation algorithms. There are certain clinical deficiencies in the implementation of TG-43. One of the challenges is the medium inhomogeneity. Tissue, bone, and air cavity interfaces often diminish the dose distribution just as shown in the external beam treatment planning systems. Oncentra Brachy® is close to clinical reality with the addition of its new advanced collapsed cone engine (ACE). This dose calculation algorithm for brachytherapy is based on the TG-186 recommendations published by the AAPM workgroup in 2012. ACE has been fully integrated into Oncentra Brachy®, focused on areas between tissue, air, and bone, and accounts for tissue heterogeneities, lack of backscatter from locations where there is no tissue appearing as well following applicator attenuation and shielding. The accuracy is similar to Monte Carlo (MC) process, but the calculation time is less when compared with the full blown MC calculations, which require different orders of computing power. ACE can provide better insight into the actual dose distribution, compared with TG-43, thereby enabling the brachytherapy HDR planning to make informed and accurate treatment decisions.

General rules of ACE are determined as a sum from several components:

$$D = D_{prim} + D_{1sc} + D_{msc}$$

in which D_{prim} is the dose from the primary photons, D_{1sc} is the dose from first-order scattered photons, and D_{msc} is the dose from summation of all higher-order scattered photons.

The calculations are performed sequentially, in which dose from lower scatter order photons are used to represent the fluence for higher order dose calculations. The algorithm naturally yields $D_{m,m}$, which is the dose to the local medium of the radiation transported through the medium. While the primary dose calculations are performed by a ray tracing algorithm, the scatter dose is calculated using the collapsed cone superposition convolution method. There are possible benefits of implementing TG-186 for the current practice; however, due to the difficulty in acquiring MC data and the hardware upgrade with lengthy calculation time, the full implementation of TG-186 is yet to be completed [9,10].

Brachytherapy Dose Rate

- LDR brachytherapy includes dose rates between 0.4 and 2 Gy/h. However, in routine clinical practice, LDR brachytherapy is usually delivered at dose rates between 0.3 and 1 Gy/h.
- Medium dose rate (MDR) brachytherapy is performed using dose rates of 2–12 Gy/h.
- HDR brachytherapy utilizes dose rates ≥12 Gy/h. Only automatic afterloading can be used for clinical HDR because the source activity is very high. For gynecological implants using conventional prescription, the dose rate to the prescription "point A" is higher than 12 Gy/h, because the distances from point A to all dwell positions are >2 cm. On the other hand when interstitial needles or catheters are used to deliver the dose rate to a prescription point (0.5 cm from a needle or a catheter) can also be higher for the same HDR source.

Radiobiology of High Dose Rate and Low Dose Rate

Biologically, HDR is defined in terms of duration of exposure. Treatment duration is short compared with the half-time of sublethal radiation damage repair. Typical half-time for normal tissue to be repaired is ~1.5 h and a time interval of 6 h is generally considered to be adequate for repair. In principle, LDR brachytherapy uses dose rates low enough for normal tissues to be repaired during the treatment. In contrast, HDR brachytherapy uses fewer dose fractionations, separating each fractionation by time intervals long enough to allow normal tissue repair. As expected, biological effective dose (BED) calculations suggest that HDR for cervical cancer using practical fraction numbers, such as n = 3−5, has an inferior BED therapeutic ratio (tumor-to-normal tissue) compared with that of LDR, which delivers 60 Gy in 72 h [11]. Additional geometric sparing factors are needed to compensate for the inferior radiobiological effectiveness. This geometric sparing factor may be introduced using packing material to spare organs at risk during HDR.

$$f_{gs} = \frac{\text{Geometric Spared OAR Dose}}{\text{Tumor Dose}}$$

For HDR to be radiobiologically equivalent to LDR, the required numerical value for f_{gs} can be calculated using BED based on the linear quadratic model [12,13] as follows.

BED for HDR is defined as

$$BED_{HDR} = n\,d\left(1 + \frac{d}{\alpha/\beta}\right)$$

where, d is dose per fraction in Gy for HDR, n is the number of fractions, and α/β is the characteristic ratio for the tissue considered. Typically, $\alpha/\beta = 3$ Gy for late responding tissue and 10 Gy for responding tissue.

During continuous irradiation at an LDR, the BED_{LDR} is

$$BED_{LDR} = D\left(1 + \frac{gD}{\alpha/\beta}\right)$$

$$g = \frac{2}{\mu T}\left[1 - \frac{1}{\mu T}(1 - e^{-\mu T})\right]$$

where, D is LDR dose in Gy, T is the duration of LDR in hours, μ equals $0.693/T_{repair}$. Typically, T_{repair} equals 1.5 h for late responding tissue and 0.5 h for early responding tissue.

High-Dose-Rate Remote Afterloader

HDR remote afterloader automatically administers ^{192}Ir source directly into the treatment volume or near the treatment volume, eliminating the radiation exposure to hospital staff. The HDR remote afterloader uses a stepping (traveling) source dosimetry system to deliver the radiation dose at various positions inside applicators/catheters

TABLE 5.2   Key Features of Some High-Dose-Rate Remote Afterloaders

	GammaMed 12i	VariSource	microSelectron (Flexitron)
Number of channels	24	20	18
Adjustable height	Yes		Yes
Step width	1–10 mm	Variable	2.5, 5 mm
Source diameter	0.9 mm	0.6 mm	1.1 mm

inside or around target volume. The HDR unit provides the freedom to manipulate both dwell position and dwell time so that the reference isodose surface can cover the target volume. Typical step size for the source is 5 mm in clinical planning and treatment, with a minimum dwell time of 0.1 s (Table 5.2).

The advantages of HDR include the following:

- Treatment as an outpatient
- Elimination of exposure to personnel
- More stable applicator position relative to target during treatment
- Possibility of holding normal tissue away from the applicators
- Tailor dose distribution to the target volume by adjusting dwell time and position
- Smaller source leads smaller applicators and leads more comfortable for patient during treatment

The disadvantages of HDR include the following:

- More labor intensive (requires large staff during the procedure)
- Radiobiologically inferior therapeutic ratio compared with LDR
- Increased probability of errors with more complicated procedure
- Requires substantial initial capital investment [14].

Computerized Treatment Planning Process

1. Source position localization: In brachytherapy, the sources are placed directly into the treatment volume or near the treatment volume. There is a rapid dose falloff with distance from the sources due to the inverse square law. Because of the short distances from the sources and the inverse square law, the accuracy for localizing the source position plays an important role in brachytherapy dosimetry and treatment planning.
2. Radiographic image planning: Traditionally, radiographic simulator using a pair of X-ray films can be used to localize the position of applicators, seeds, or other radiopaque landmarks within the patient. More recently, films have been replaced by a pair of X-ray images acquired with conventional simulator equipped with

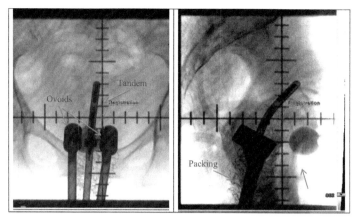

FIGURE 5.1   A pair of low-dose-rate Fletcher applicator in a patient acquired by a conventional simulator. The left panel shows an anterior—posterior view and the right panel shows a right-lateral view of the implant.

onboard imager (OBI). In Fig. 5.1, a pair of orthogonal images, in anterior—posterior (AP) and right-lateral (RLT) direction, were acquired by a conventional simulator. Dummy ^{137}Cs sources can be visualized and digitized to reconstruct three-dimensional (3D) images of these sources inside applicators. Reference "point A" can be digitized as a point 2 cm lateral to the tandem applicator inside the uterus and 2 cm up from the mucous membrane of the lateral fornix or the surface of ovoid applicators [15]. Anatomical landmarks, such as the "bladder reference point," defined by the location of the Foley catheter balloon [15], were also clearly visualized and digitized. The 3D position of the "bladder reference point" can be reconstructed from its projection in AP and RLT images.

3. Ultrasound images planning: Ultrasound imaging systems provide a relatively low-cost modality to visualize the soft organ structure relative to the position of seeds. Ultrasound imaging systems have been widely used in prostate cancer volume assessment, treatment planning, and real-time monitored seed implants. Using ultrasound imaging systems, prostate gland, adjacent normal structures, the urethra, rectum, and bladder can be identified by an experienced user. Recently, ultrasound based, real-time intraoperative treatment planning for HDR prostate brachytherapy has become more attractive due to much improved delivery efficiency to complete the whole procedure.

4. CT images planning: Nowadays, localization of source position and treatment planning are mainly based on CT images. Reconstructed CT images in three fundamental views (axial, sagittal and coronal) greatly help identification/digitization of the seed, catheter, and applicator. CT provides 3D volume information, and brachytherapy dose distributions are truly calculated in 3D treatment volume. Normal tissues and target volumes (if visible) can be readily contoured and dose volume histogram can be calculated. In general, thin slice thickness (1 mm) and higher X-ray energy (140 keV) are recommended for brachytherapy planning using CT images. Fig. 5.2 shows CT-based brachytherapy planning for a cervical cancer patient.

(A)   **(B)**   **(C)**

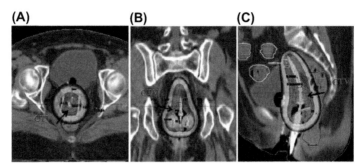

FIGURE 5.2   Dose distribution of CT-based brachytherapy application in (A) axial, (B) coronal, and (C) sagittal images. The dose is prescribed to target volume (CTV) (*arrow*). The prescribed dose was demonstrated in red area. *From Onal and Oymak (2011). "CT-Guided Brachytherapy Planning," Chapter 6, Computed tomography - special applications: InTech; Chapters published November 21, 2011 under CC BY 3.0 license. p. 113.*

One important limitation of CT planning is that certain types of tumor volumes cannot be clearly visualized in CT. For example, the target volume for GYN cervical cancer cannot be identified from CT images. Magnetic resonance imaging (MRI) provides better soft tissue contrast to identify target volumes. It is advised to have an MRI with the compatible applicators in place. Accurate target definition is important to define the margin of primary tumor and/or residual disease. For this purpose Gynecological GEC-ESTRO Working Group published their recommendations for image-guided brachytherapy (MRI-based) [16].

- GTV: Macroscopic tumor at brachytherapy, high signal intensity mass(es) (FSE, T2) in cervix/corpus, parametria, vagina, bladder, and rectum.
- High-risk Clinical Target Volume (CTV): Includes GTV, whole cervix, and presumed extracervical tumor extension and gray zones in parametria, uterine corpus, vagina, rectum, and bladder.
- Intermediate-risk CTV: Encompasses HRCTV with margins added according to tumor size and regression. Minimum margins of 5–15 mm for extensive disease with good remission HRCTV and initial tumor extension.

As MRI imaging becomes more available to the brachytherapy community, more clinics will use MRI for image-guided brachytherapy planning and treatment for cervical and other types of cancers.

CLINICAL INDICATION OF BRACHYTHERAPY

Breast Cancer

Breast conserving management is now the standard of care for early-stage breast cancer patients. This involves lumpectomy followed by post-op radiation treatment (RT). Recently, HDR brachytherapy as post-op RT has become popular. HDR brachytherapy can be used to boost the dose after completion of whole breast RT. In selected cases,

HDR brachytherapy can be used as accelerated partial breast irradiation to deliver RT to the lumpectomy bed. Most common techniques of breast brachytherapy are as follows:

- Interstitial breast brachytherapy: Involves temporary placement of catheters into the breast across the tumor bed for placement of radioactive sources. The CTV is lumpectomy bed +2 cm margin (PTV = CTV). Usually ^{192}Ir source, either LDR or HDR, is used.
   Dose
   LDR iridium-192
   Primary treatment 50 cGy/h to 45–50 Gy
   Boost treatment 50 cGy/h to 15–20 Gy
   HDR iridium-192
   Primary treatment 3.4 Gy/fx to 34 Gy in 10 fractions over 5 treatment days
   Boost treatment 5 Gy/fx to 10 Gy in two fractions over 1–2 treatment days
- Intracavitary breast brachytherapy: A balloon is placed into the lumpectomy bed after the procedure. The CTV is defined at 1 cm from expanded balloon surface. The balloon is then connected to an HDR ^{192}Ir afterloader for radiation delivery. The balloon consists of either single channel or multichannel geometry.
   Dose
   HDR iridium-192
   Primary treatment 3.4 Gy/fx to 34 Gy in 10 fractions over 5 treatment days (BID)
   Boost treatment 5 Gy/fx to 10 Gy in two fractions over 1–2 treatment days

Prostate Cancer

Low-risk prostate cancer patients are good candidates for brachytherapy alone. However, low- and intermediate-risk prostate cancer patients are candidates for boost brachytherapy as well. It is recommended that patients with prostate gland volumes of 60 cc or more receive cytoreductive hormonal treatment to optimize the brachytherapy. Prostate brachytherapy can be permanent LDR brachytherapy with ^{125}I or ^{103}Pd. Temporary HDR brachytherapy uses ^{192}Ir.
   Dose
   Low Dose Rate
   ^{125}I monotherapy 145 Gy minimum peripheral dose (mPD)
   Boost 108–110 Gy mPD (with 41.4–50.4 Gy EBRT)
   ^{103}Pd monotherapy 125 Gy mPD
   Boost 90–100 Gy mPD (with 41.4–50.4 Gy EBRT)
   High Dose Rate
   Monotherapy
   8.5–9.5 Gy/fx × 4 or 6.0–7.5 Gy/fx × 6
   Boost
   9.5–10.5 Gy/fx × 2 (with 40–50 Gy EBRT)
   4.0–6.0 Gy/fx × 4 (with 36–50 Gy EBRT)

Endometrial Cancer

The primary treatment for early-stage endometrial cancer is surgery. However, patients with high risk factors (grade 3 tumor and >50% myometrial invasion) benefit from post-op RT by reducing the risk of vaginal cuff recurrences. Vaginal cuff brachytherapy is an excellent alternative to EBRT, as it provides local control without causing EBRT side effects. Most commonly, the treatment is delivered with a single-channel vaginal cylinder. HDR ^{192}Ir is commonly used for treatment.

Dose

Monotherapy 7 Gy/fx to 21 Gy to 0.5 cm depth

Boost 6 Gy/fx to 12−18 Gy Gy to vaginal surface (EBRT dose 45 Gy)

Cervical Cancer

Concurrent chemoRT is now standard of care for locally advanced cervical cancer patients and patients with stage IB2-IVA. Radiation treatment involves EBRT to 45−50.4 Gy to the pelvis followed by brachytherapy to the cervical cancer. Brachytherapy can be LDR manually loaded or remote afterloader using ^{137}Cs or ^{192}Ir or HDR remote afterloader using ^{192}Ir. Recently, CT- and/or MRI-based treatment planning is recommended for cervical cancer brachytherapy.

Dose (Pelvic EBRT to 45−50 Gy)

Low dose rate

40−60 cGy/h to a cumulative dose of 40−45 Gy, Goal TD should be >85 Gy

High dose rate

5.5−6 Gy/fx x 5 to 27.5−30 Gy or 7 Gy/fx x 4 to 28 Gy

Vaginal cancer

Treatment for vaginal cancer involves surgical resection followed by post-op RT as indicated. For organ preserving radiation treatment involves EBRT and intracavitary and/or interstitial brachytherapy. Tumor thickness <0.5 cm use intracavitary brachytherapy; tumor >0.5 cm treat whole pelvis RT followed by intracavitary or interstitial brachytherapy boost.

Intracavitary technique uses acrylic dome cylinder for the treatment. The cylinder can be loaded with 137Cs sources in configuration of 20-10-20 mgs or similar distribution with HDR 192Ir source.

For Interstitial technique a Syed/Neblett template is most commonly used, although variety of templates are available. The template has a central opening for a vaginal obturator and an opening for a tandem through the obturator. Multiple openings for plastic, steel, or titanium needles in a circumferential pattern around the central opening are also present. In addition, needles can also be loaded on vaginal obturator.

Dose

Low dose rate

Intracavitary: prescribed to 0.5 cm depth if >0.5 cm residual thickness, 60 Gy to the entire vaginal mucosa with additional boost doses of 10−15 Gy to the gross disease site.

Interstitial: low dose 192Ir sources for a dose rate of 30–55 Gy/h, making sure that the periphery of the entire tumor volume is enclosed within the prescription isodose line. If treated after EBRT, then the implant boost dose is 30–35 Gy (with 45-50 Gy EBRT).

High dose rate
HDR boost dose is 4.5-5.5 Gy x5 fractions to 22.5-27.5 Gy (with 45-50 Gy EBRT)

Soft Tissue Sarcoma

High-grade soft tissue sarcoma (STS) has high risk local failure. As such, post-op RT is indicated for extremity or trunk STS patients. Brachytherapy can be used as either monotherapy postoperatively or in combination with EBRT. However, for post-op positive margins, a combination of brachytherapy and EBRT is recommended. Both LDR and HDR brachytherapies are used for post-op sarcoma treatments. During surgery, catheters are placed at the tumor bed to cover CTV + 1–2 cm margin. Single-plane or multiplane implants may be indicated. LDR ^{192}Ir ribbons or HDR ^{192}Ir are used for treatments.

Dose

Low dose rate
50 cGy/h to 45–50 Gy for monotherapy, 15-25 Gy for boost (with 45-50 Gy EBRT)
High dose rate
2–4 Gy/fx to 30–54 Gy for monotherapy, 12-20 Gy for boost (with 45-50 Gy EBRT)

Palliative Brachytherapy

The highly conformal and very intense, localized radiation dose from brachytherapy to the tumor, while having rapid dose fall-off in the surrounding normal tissue is ideal for palliative treatment for cancers. As such locally recurrent symptomatic cancers from head and neck, trachea, bronchus, esophagus, and cervix can all be treated with minimal side effects, and in short treatment time.

Endobronchial brachytherapy: Cough, dyspnea, airway obstruction and hemoptysis can be palliated with brachytherapy. Usually a 6 French after loading catheter is used for the brachytherapy treatment. Depending on the location of the cancer, multiple catheters may need to be used. The RT dose is prescribed 1 cm from the center of the source to 2 cm proximal and distal margins. Treatments are given in 1 weekly intervals.

Dose

Monotherapy: HDR 6 Gy/fx to 24 Gy in 4 fractions or 7.5 Gy to 22.5 Gy in 3 fractions or 10 Gy/fx to 20 Gy in 2 fractions
Boost: 4 Gy/fx to 16 in 4 fractions or 5 Gy/fx to 15 Gy in 3 fractions or 7.5 Gy/fx to 15 Gy in 2 fractions (with 30 Gy EBRT)

Esophageal brachytherapy: Dysphagia, odynophagia, and chest pain can be treated effectively with brachytherapy. The applicator can be a nasogastric tube or a special esophageal brachytherapy applicator with an external diameter of 6-10 mm. The RT dose is prescribed 1 cm from center of the source to 2 cm proximal and distal margins.

Dose

Monotherapy: LDR 0.4-1 Gy/hr to 25-40 Gy or HDR 5-7.5 Gy to 15-20 Gy in 2-4 fractions

Boost: LDR 0.4-1 Gy/hr to 20-25 Gy or HDR 5-7 Gy/fx to 10-14 Gy x1-2 fractions (with 30 Gy EBRT)

Cervical brachytherapy: A ring applicator can be used to treat acute severe vaginal bleeding in cervical cancer patients.

Dose

HDR 5 Gy/fx to 10 Gy x2 fractions at 1 week interval to the surface of the cervix

In summary, because brachytherapy sources are placed directly into or near the treatment volume, they deliver the most conformal radiation therapy to the target. There is also rapid dose falloff with distance from the source, minimizing radiation dose to the surrounding normal tissues and hence improving the therapeutic ratio. In addition to LDR brachytherapy, the HDR brachytherapy is now making outpatient treatment practical. Advanced imaging with CT or MRI is now used routinely for brachytherapy as well. Most importantly, positive clinical outcomes with brachytherapy treatments make this modality of radiation treatment very useful for many cancer treatments.

References

Ref 1. Burmeister J, et al. The American Society for radiation Oncology's 2015 Core physics Curriculum for radiation oncology Residents. Int J Radiat Oncol Biol Phys 2016;95(4):1298–303.

Ref 2. Nath R, et al. Dosimetry of interstitial brachytherapy sources: recommendations of the AAPM radiation therapy Committee Task Group No. 43. American Association of Physicists in Medicine. Med Phys 1995;22(2):209–34.

Ref 3. International Commission on Radiation Units & Measurements. Dose and volume specification for reporting intracavitary therapy in gynecology. In: International Commission on Radiation Units & Measurements, editor. International Commission on Radiation Units and Measurements: Bethesda, Md., U.S.A; 1985.

Ref 4. Nath RAL, Jones D, Ling C, Loevinger R, Hanson W. Specification of Brachytherapy Source Strength Report of AAPM Task Group No. 32. New York: American Association of Physicists in Medicine; 1987.

Ref 5. Lanzl LH. World radiation therapy dosimetry network. Int J Radiat Oncol Biol Phys 1982;8(9):1607–15.

Ref 6. Rivard MJ, et al. Update of AAPM Task Group No. 43 Report: a revised AAPM protocol for brachytherapy dose calculations. Med Phys 2004;31(3):633–74.

Ref 7. *Rivard MJ, et al. Supplement to the 2004 update of the AAPM Task Group No. 43 report. Med Phys 2007;34(6):2187—205.*

Ref 8. *Rivard MJ, et al. Supplement 2 for the 2004 update of the AAPM Task Group No. 43 report: Joint recommendations by the AAPM and GEC-ESTRO. Med Phys 2017;44(9):e297—338.*

Ref 9. *Zourari K, Major T, Herein A, et al. A retrospective dosimetric comparison of TG-43 and a commercially available MBDCA for an APBI brachytherapy patient cohort. Phys Med 2015;31:669—76.*

Ref 10. *Ahnesjo A, van Veelen B, Tedgren A, et al. Collapsed cone dose calculations for heterogeneous tissues in brachytherapy using primary and scatter separation source data. Comput Meth Progr Biomed 2017;139:17—29.*

Ref 11. *Liversage WE. A general formula for equating protracted and acute regimes of radiation. Br J Radiol 1969;42(498):432—40.*

Ref 12. *Dale RG. The application of the linear-quadratic dose-effect equation to fractionated and protracted radiotherapy. Br J Radiol 1985;58(690):515—28.*

Ref 13. *Stitt JA, et al. High dose rate intracavitary brachytherapy for carcinoma of the cervix: the Madison system: I. Clinical and radiobiological considerations. Int J Radiat Oncol Biol Phys 1992;24(2):335—48.*

Ref 14. *Kubo HD, et al. High dose-rate brachytherapy treatment delivery: report of the AAPM radiation therapy Committee Task Group No. 59. Med Phys 1998;25(4):375—403.*

Ref 15. *Nag S, et al. The American Brachytherapy Society recommendations for low-dose-rate brachytherapy for carcinoma of the cervix. Int J Radiat Oncol Biol Phys 2002;52(1):33—48.*

Ref 16. *Haie-Meder C, et al. Recommendations from Gynaecological (GYN) GEC-ESTRO Working Group (I): concepts and terms in 3D image based 3D treatment planning in cervix cancer brachytherapy with emphasis on MRI assessment of GTV and CTV. Radiother Oncol 2005;74(3):235—45.*

Intensity-Modulated and Image-Guided Radiation Therapy

Intensity-modulated radiation therapy (IMRT) is an advanced form of conformal therapy that delivers high doses of radiation to target volumes while minimizing exposure of normal tissues. The term conformal refers to multiple shaped beams having direction and intensity chosen to conform a therapeutic radiation dose to a three-dimensional (3D) target volume constructed using 3D imaging modalities [1,2]. IMRT uses clinical objectives, such as the dose prescribed to the tumor and dose–volume constraints of normal tissues. It is modeled using a mathematical objective and computer optimization to determine the beam shapes and intensities resulting in the desired conformal dose distribution.

TARGET VOLUMES, MARGINS AND DOSE–VOLUMES FOR INTENSITY-MODULATED RADIATION THERAPY

Target volumes: Currently, physicians use the International Commission on Radiation Units and Measurements (ICRU) reports 50, 62, 83 [3–5] definitions for different target volumes (Fig. 6.1).

Gross target volume (GTV) is the gross disease seen clinically or in imaging studies and includes primary gross tumors (GTV-T), nodal gross tumors (GTV-N), and metastatic gross tumors (GTV-M).

Clinical target volume (CTV) is the clinically suspected extension of the tumor beyond the gross disease.

Internal target volume (ITV) is the CTV and a margin to account for internal movement of the CTV.

Planning target volume (PTV) is the margin needed for the uncertainty of the setup error for the patient.

Organs at risk (OAR) volume has also been defined by the ICRU as the margin added to the OAR for the uncertainty of setup error for the patient to create a planning organ at risk volume (PRV).

Tissues not defined as CTV or OARs are considered remaining volume at risk (RVR).

Fundamentals of Radiation Oncology
https://doi.org/10.1016/B978-0-12-814128-1.00006-4

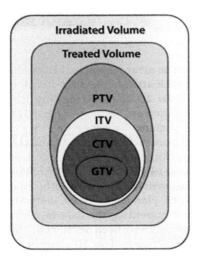

FIGURE 6.1   Different target volumes as defined by the International Commission on Radiation Units and Measurements (ICRU). *Reprinted from Shepard DM, Cao D, Afghan MK, et al. An arc-sequencing algorithm for intensity modulated arc therapy. Med Phys 2007;34:464–470; Levitt SH, Purdy JA, Perez CA, Vijayakumar S. Technical basis of radiation therapy: practical clinical applications. 4th ed. Fig. 9.13, p. 188, © 2006 with permission of Springer Science and Business Media.*

Treated volume is the area enclosed by an isodose line specified by the physician/planner, and irradiated volume is the volume enclosed by the 50% isodose line.

Margin: A margin around the GTV, CTV, and ITV volumes is necessary to account for setup uncertainty. The PTV margin is determined from systemic and random errors around the target. van Herk et al. calculated the PTV margin using 2.5S + 0.7s, where S and s are the systematic and random errors, respectively [6,7]. Margins can be reduced by proper patient immobilization techniques, and daily image guidance.

Dose-Volume specification: ICRU 83 recommends dose-volume specification when reporting target dose coverage for an IMRT treatment plan, rather than a simple point dose. ICRU 83 defines Dv as the absorbed dose encompassing a specified volume v of a structure and recommends the following [5,8]:

Dv—the absorbed dose encompassing a specified volume v of the target

Dmedian—the median dose, D50%, this represents absorbed dose to the PTV

Dnear-min—D98%, the near-minimum absorbed dose to the PTV

Dnear-max—D2%, the near-maximum absorbed dose to the PTV

For normal tissue structures, ICRU 83 recommends reporting the following:

D2%—for serial structure OARs, such as spinal cord

Dmean—for parallel structure OARs, such as parotid gland

Dmean, D2%, Vd—for OARs that combine serial and parallel structure OARs, such as lungs

TCP, NTCP, EUD—not recommended for routine use

HI, CI—not recommended for routine use

INVERSE PLANNING INTENSITY-MODULATED RADIATION THERAPY

In IMRT, an inverse problem-solving technique is used to work backward from a dose prescription goal and the normal tissue constraints to a treatment plan [9,10]. Modern software are available to calculate the beam intensities and the leaf sequences necessary to achieve the desired dose distribution. Mathematical objective and cost functions defining the desired dosimetric and clinical outcomes are solved by working backward to calculate the beam intensities. The objective function translates the dose-volume goals and constraints into a numerical value that is minimized when all of the goals and constraints are met. An inverse planning process involves the following steps:

- **Imaging**: A 3D image of the patient via a CT simulation is necessary for the IMRT treatment planning process. Additional imaging modalities such as magnetic resonance imaging (MRI) and positron emission tomography; scans may be needed for fusing the tumor volume with the CT-simulated data set for accurate localization of the tumor volume.
- **Contouring**: All target volumes (GTV, CTV, and PTVs) and normal critical structures that are needed for the optimization process must be defined by the radiation oncologist/planner. In inverse planning, radiation to defined normal structures is avoided to prevent any possible normal structure exposure.
- **Dose prescription**: The planner assigns the beam energies, number of beams, and beam directions. In general, 5—9 noncoplanar fixed beams or multiple 2—5 arcs are a sufficient number for IMRT. Opposing beams are typically avoided because they do not improve the plan quality significantly compared with an unopposed beam. Furthermore, high-energy (>10 MV) beams are not necessary for IMRT since neutron dose negates a small or negligible dosimetric advantage. Cost functions and dose constraints are defined by the physician/planner. A typical prescription plan example would be (7920 cGy) for prostate cancer. IMRT treatment might be the following: prostate PTV D95% $\geq$ 7920 cGy, D2% $<$ 8500 cGy, rectum V70 $<$ 25% and V40 $<$ 35%, and bladder V75 $<$ 25%.
- **Dose calculation and plan optimization**: Once the cost functions are defined by the planner, the radiation dose is calculated. Radiation beams are divided into small segments of beamlets. Small multileaf collimators (MLCs) move across the beams' pathway to block the radiation beam for a part of the treatment time, creating radiation intensity across the target volume (s). The beam intensity or fluence per beamlet is modulated by varying the speed and pattern of the MLCs, meeting the cost functions and the dose constraints of the specific treatment prescription. Modern computer software use model-based dose calculation algorithms to provide dose calculation. Generally, the dose calculation algorithm used during optimization uses an iterative process designed for rapid calculation, which sacrifices accuracy for speed iterations are performed until the beamlet intensities produce an acceptable conformal dose distribution. Once the optimal beam intensities and dose distribution are achieved, the MLC leaf sequence that will generate the optimized beamlet intensities is calculated. The final dose calculation is performed with a more accurate algorithm, such as convolution superposition or Monte Carlo simulation to produce the final dosimetry accuracy.

- **IMRT QA and delivery**: Patient-specific QA is part of the IMRT plans. This involves measurement of plan-generated absorbed dose in a phantom and comparing it with the computer-generated plan and an independent absorbed dose calculation. Typically, measurements must be within 95% tolerance with a gamma index of 3% or 3 mm to be acceptable for patient treatment. Additional evaluation and tolerance criteria may be set by the medical physics team, following the RTOG or other IMRT QA guidelines.

Volumetric-Modulated Arc Treatment

Volumetric-modulated arc treatment (VMAT) is an advanced form of IMRT. Radiation treatment is delivered while the gantry is rotating around the patient. Three parameters are modulated simultaneously while the beam is on:

- Gantry rotation speed
- MLC aperture shape
- Dose rate

VMAT uses the same inverse planning process and intensity modulation as IMRT [11–13], except that a different optimization strategy is needed for the VMAT planning. This is because the simultaneous MLC motion during the arc rotation poses additional machine constraints, such as the maximum leaf and the maximum gantry speed, for the optimizer. To ensure that the machine constraints are reliable, a direct aperture optimization (DAO) algorithm is used to optimize the leaf positions and the aperture intensities. DAO does not require a leaf-sequencing step after optimization and results in fewer monitor units (MUs) (less modulation) and less treatment time. However, DAO is more computationally intensive than beamlet intensity modulation and thus requires more time for planning because the machine characteristics and limitations could affect the planning outcomes dramatically.

VMAT plans have comparable quality to fixed-gantry IMRT. The benefits of VMAT are shorter treatment time and fewer MUs. The reduction in MUs results in less out-of-field dose, and for high-energy beams, fewer neutrons if higher energies (>10 MV) are used.

IMAGE-GUIDED RADIOTHERAPY

Image-guided radiotherapy (IGRT) involves patient imaging before and during radiation treatments to guide radiation to the targets accurately. Over the years, radiation treatment now has advanced from 3DCRT to IMRT, stereotactic radiosurgery, stereotactic body radiation therapy, and brachytherapy with high conformity of dose to the target volumes requiring accurate patient positioning. Setup error is the displacement of the target position relative to its position during the initial CT simulation. Setup error has two components—systematic and random. Systematic errors are the same for every treatment, such as offsets in the setup marks. Random errors are variation of the target position around a mean value. Examples of random errors include day-to-day variation of the bladder and rectum fullness and day-to-day variation of the positional changes in the breast.

IGRT helps to reduce both systematic and random errors [14—16]. The IGRT process involves CT simulation of the patient, and after treatment planning the treatment position is verified using IGRT, correction of treatment position as needed, reverification the treatment position using IGRT, and finally, delivering treatment to the target.

IGRT techniques can be based on ionizing radiation and/or nonionizing techniques.

Radiation-based methods include the following:

- Electronic portal imaging device (EPID): An amorphous-silicon (A-Si) flat panel imager used to image either MV radiation produced by the treatment head or kV radiation generated by gantry or room-mounted X-ray sources. MV images are low-contrast, whereas kV images have diagnostic quality.
- Cone beam CT (CBCT): Volumetric CT images of the patient produced by a gantry-mounted KV X-ray tube and an EPID A-Si flat panel imager. In some commercial systems, MV volumetric CBCT images are also available for IGRT.
- CT on rail: Movable CT scanner that slides on rails in the treatment room.
- Tomotherapy: An integration of a low-energy (6 MV) accelerator with an MV CT scanner into a ring gantry structure. The accelerator produces a low-energy MV beam, and the CT detector then reconstructs the volumetric images. IGRT is performed before the radiation delivery, with the same mechanical and radiation isocenter.
- Fiducial markers: Inert fiducial markers can be implanted within the tumor, which can be used to enhance tumor targeting using radiation-based methods. Surgical clips and stents can also be used.

Non—radiation-based methods:

- US: Ultrasound transducers are used to transmit and receive sound waves to detect tissue interfaces. This is used for prostate patient IGRT.
- Camera: Video cameras are used to reconstruct surface images of the patient for both initial setup and monitoring position during radiation treatment.
- RF beacons: Small radiofrequency transponders are implanted within or near the tumor. An antenna positioned in proximity to the patient is used to monitor the transponder position during both initial setup and radiation treatment.
- MRI: MRI units are installed in the treatment vault, either separately or integrated with the accelerator and used to scan a patient in the treatment position who is treated immediately. MRI/linear accelerator units can be used to visualize tumor motion in real time during the treatment.

Other:

- 4D tracking/respiratory gating: An external device is used during the CT simulation to track respiratory motion, permitting reconstruction of a 4D-CT data set for planning. During treatment, the respiratory motion can be used to start and stop the radiation beam (gating) depending on the respiratory phase, which is assumed to correlate with position of the target. Monitoring devices also include camera-based monitoring of the chest position and spirometry.

IGRT images acquired before the treatment delivery can be processed either online or offline. Systematic error is reduced by offline reviewing of IGRT images after multiple treatments, analyzing trends of the error, and taking corrective action to avoid possible target offset. Proper QA of IGRT is required to minimize systamatic error introduced by the IGRT system. Random errors are reduced by daily imaging and online correction coupled with proper immobilization.

The planned radiation dose calculated on the CT simulation data set may not match the actual dose delivered during the radiation therapy course because of setup and internal positioning uncertainties. As such, PTV margins must be sufficient to account for these errors. IGRT can minimize the setup uncertainty thereby minimizing the margin needed for the PTV. Margin reduction reduces the volume of normal tissue irradiated, either reducing side effects or allowing higher doses to the target volume, which may improve control of the disease [17–20]. In other words, IGRT may improve the therapeutic ratio for cancer treatments. This is one of the most significant benefits of IGRT. As such, IGRT can benefit patients treated with 3DCRT, IMRT, and SBRT, for which critical structures are of concern. The future of IGRT may be evolving into adaptive radiation therapy. Serial daily imaging confirms change of a target volume and or patient anatomy requiring replanning of the treatment plan. This adaptation of the treatment according to the decrease or increase in the tumor volume or change in the adjacent normal tissue due to weight loss may correct variation of the planned dose to the target accordingly. IGRT can thus help in the delivery of a modified and updated treatment plan throughout the entire radiation treatment course.

CLINICAL EXPERIENCE OF INTENSITY-MODULATED RADIATION THERAPY AND VOLUMETRIC-MODULATED ARC TREATMENT

Brain Cancer

IMRT has demonstrated superior target dose conformality and homogeneity compared with the 3D conformal technique for intracranial tumors. IMRT also reduced normal tissue doses to critical structures such as the optic nerves, optic chiasm, and brainstem [21–24]. A study comparing VMAT with coplanar fixed-field IMRT showed that VMAT resulted in equal or significantly better target coverage, with improved sparing of normal OAR [25]. However, noncoplanar IMRT and VMAT techniques provided better sparing of the contralateral optic structures than coplanar IMRT and VMAT techniques [26].

Fig. 6.2A and B shows 2-arc VMAT planning for multiple brain metastases lesions.

Head and Neck Cancer

In PARSPORT trial by using IMRT decreased xerostomia was achieved by sparing of parotid glands by using IMRT [27]. However, fixed-beam IMRT requires complex treatment planning and longer treatment time. Longer treatment times result in less accuracy of the treatment because of intrafractional patient motion on the treatment table. In addition, more MUs are needed for IMRT when compared with 3D conformal treatment, which may increase the risk of secondary malignancies [28]. On the other hand, VMAT techniques require less treatment time and fewer MUs. The plan quality is comparable with IMRT technique [29,30]. Several studies by Scorsetti et al. [31] showed that clinical outcome with VMAT treatment for head and neck (H&N) cancer

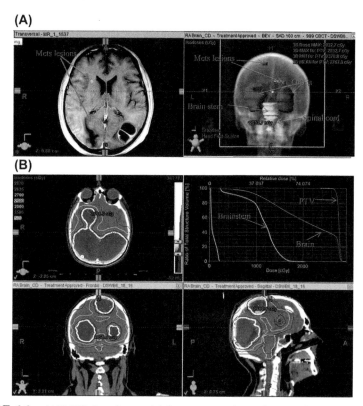

FIGURE 6.2   (A) MRI showing multiple metastatic brain lesions, fused with planning CT scan to delineate target volumes and critical normal structures. (B) A 47-year-old man with history of SCCa of head and neck (H&N), status post chemoRT to 7000 cGy. An MRI brain scan shows multiple metastatic lesions. Previous H&N RT field overlaps the WB field. As such, a volumetric-modulated arc treatment (VMAT) technique used to treat the brain lesions with a dose of 3000 cGy followed by a boost dose of 2000 cGy is given to targets. The VMAT plan achieved prescription dose and all normal structure constraints.

was encouraging. Smet et al. [32] noted survival data favoring VMAT compared with IMRT, and by Guo et al. [33] reported that 36-month locoregional relapse-free survival of 94% and a 36-month OS of 97%. Preliminary results in locally advanced H&N cancer treated with VMAT demonstrated a favorable toxicity profile, even while using concomitant chemotherapy [33].

Fig. 6.3A and B shows a 2-arc VMAT planning for a locally advanced right tonsil H&N cancer patient.

Breast Cancer

In dosimetric studies, VMAT plans demonstrated reduction in the mean dose to the heart, ipsilateral lung, and contralateral breast compared with IMRT [34,35]. Scorsetti

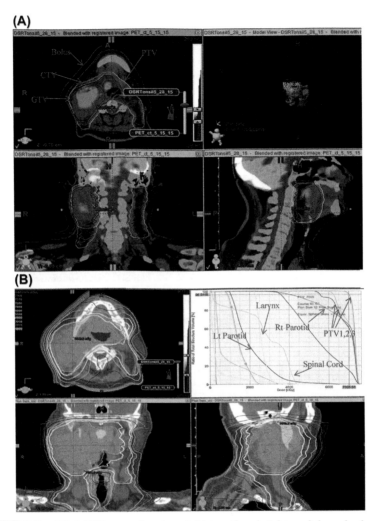

FIGURE 6.3   (A) A PET scan showing right tonsil and right neck lymphadenopathy is fused with the planning CT scan to distinguish target volumes and normal structures. (B) A 65-year-old man with T2N3M0, IVB right tonsil cancer. He is prescribed Chemo/RT to a total final dose of 7000 cGy. A volumetric-modulated arc treatment (VMAT) plan that met treatment and constraints was designed for the patient. Left parotid gland V26 = 25%, spinal cord = 43 Gy, larynx = 35 Gy. (a) PET scan fusion with planning CT scan for target volume delineation. (b) VMAT plan isodose lines and dose volume histogram (DVHs) for the critical structures. The right parotid gland did not meet the constraint.

et al. [35] reported a phase II trial using a 3-week VMAT—SIB course after breast-conserving surgery showed that the technique is well tolerated with optimal local control [36]. In a study by De Rose et al. [36] VMAT—SIB (40.5 Gy on the whole breast, 48 Gy on surgical bed) showed a very favorable acute and late toxicity profile and optimal 2-year local control. A study by Kim et al. [37], which delivered up to 50 Gy to the whole breast and up to 60—70 Gy on tumor sites, noted late grade ≥2 toxicity of 3.2%.

Fig. 6.4 shows a hybrid IMRT plan for a left breast cancer patient.

Lung Cancer

Grills et al. reported a dosimetric benefit of increasing higher RT dose while meeting the OAR constraints by using IMRT versus 3DCRT in node-positive non—small cell lung cancer (NSCLC) patients [38]. Chapet et al. reported heart sparing with IMRT technique for lung cancer patients [39]. Murshed et al. also showed that IMRT decreased the total lung V10 and V20, which corresponded to a reduction of >2 Gy in the mean total lung dose and a 10% decrease in the risk of radiation pneumonitis [40]. Yom et al. [41] compared 3DCRT with the IMRT technique for NSCLC and noted reduction in v20 from 38% to 35% and reduction in > grade 3 treatment-related pneumonitis from 32% to 8% ($P < .001$) at 12 months with the use of IMRT. Liao et al. [42] noted significant reduction in ≥ grade 3 treatment-related pneumonitis by IMRT (approximate numbers derived from figures, ∼25% at 12 months in 3DCRT vs. ∼10% at 12 months in IMRT, $P = .017$). Liao et al. also noted median survival of 10.2 months in 3DCRT versus 16.8 months in IMRT ($P = .039$), which may not be directly related to IMRT.

Fig. 6.5 shows a hybrid VMAT plan involving AP/PA and two arcs for a lung cancer patient.

Prostate Cancer

The use of IMRT allowed dose escalation in prostate cancer to improve outcomes and reducing treatment-related toxicities [43—45]. VMAT planning studies done by Palma et al. [46,47] showed that both IMRT and VMAT plans improved OAR sparing compared with 3DCRT. VMAT treatment also reduced MUs by 42% and lowered doses to the OARs compared with the fixed-field IMRT plans. The reduction of treatment time with VMAT [48—50], minimizes the intrafraction motion of the prostate mostly by applying a single-arc VMAT treatment delivered in 1—1.5 min compared with 5—10 min with a 5- or 7-field fixed-beam IMRT treatment. Spratt et al. [51] reported long-term data of high-dose IMRT (86.4 Gy) for patients with localized prostate cancer at 7 years. Early grade 2 or higher late gastrointestinal and genitourinary toxicities were 4.4% and 21.1%, respectively, and late grade 3 gastrointestinal and genitourinary toxicity was 0.7% and 2.2%, respectively. Of the 427 men reporting as fully potent at baseline, 74% of them preserved their sexual function at time of last follow-up.

Fig. 6.6 showing a two-arc VMAT planning for a prostate cancer patient.

The use of IMRT coupled with IGRT now allows for tighter PTV margins, ideally enabling the radiation oncologist to deliver a higher radiation dose to the tumor and improve sparing of normal critical structures safely. IMRT is the most important advance in radiotherapy since the invention of the linear accelerator for radiation treatments.

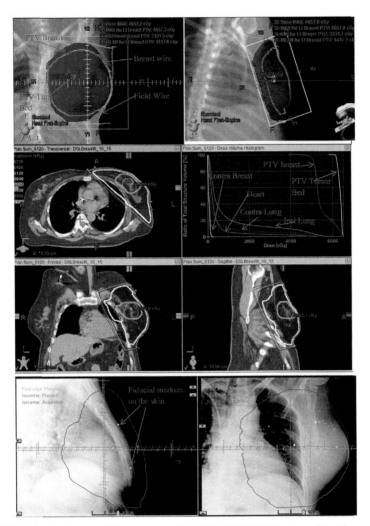

FIGURE 6.4   A 49-year-old woman with IDC pT1cN0M0, stage IA. She is ER/PR positive, and HER2-positive. She received Taxol, carboplatin, and Herceptin. She presented for post-op RT and was planned with a hybrid IMRT inverse planning to a total final dose of 6120 cGy. Hybrid IMRT plan met prescription dose and constraints. Hot spot = 5%, total lung v20 < 6%, and heart V30 < 3%. The **upper panel** shows the planning target volume (PTV) in pink within the green border wires on the skin in AP and left medial view of two open and two IMRT tangent fields; the **middle panel** shows isodose lines and DVHs; and the **lower panel** shows daily X-ray IGRT matching the fiducial markers on the breast from the CTsim, with the fiducial markers during the daily treatments.

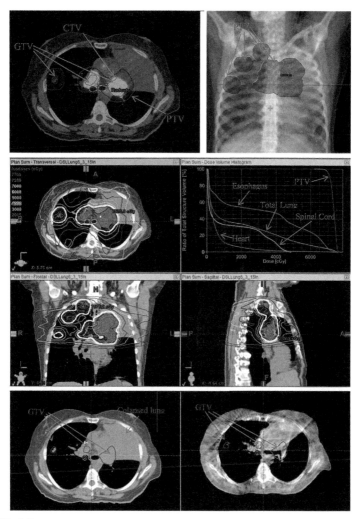

FIGURE 6.5   A 61-year-old woman with a history of left breast invasive ductal cancer, status post lumpectomy and radiation therapy diagnosed with right lung non−small cell lung cancer, T2aN3M1a, stage IV. The patient was planned ChemoRT to 7000 cGy concurrently with chemotherapy CarboTaxol every week ×7 cycles. A hybrid treatment plan of AP/PA and VMAT met treatment prescription and normal structure constraints. Total lung v20 = 33%, V10 = 39%, heart v30 = 3%, and spinal cord = 46 Gy. The **upper panel** shows PET scan fused with planning CT scan for planning target volume (PTV) delineation (pink color), the **middle panel** shows isodose lines conforming PTV and DVH, and the **lower panel** shows daily cone beam CT with tumor response to treatment.

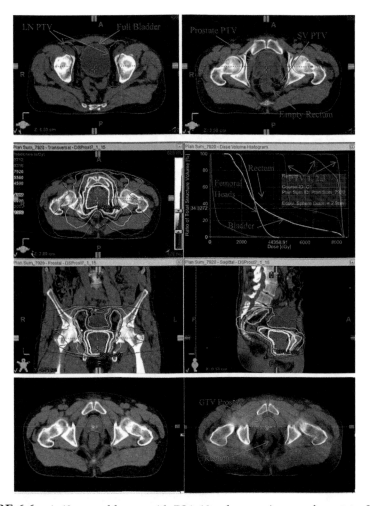

FIGURE 6.6   A 68-year-old man with PSA 19, adenocarcinoma of prostate, 2 out of 12 scores positive with gleason score of $4 + 5 = 9$. A volumetric-modulated arc treatment (VMAT) plan was designed to a total final dose of 7920 cGy. The VMAT plan met prescription and normal structure constraints. Rectum v75 = 8%, v70 = 13%, v50 = 29%, bladder v75 = 8%, v70 = 9%, v65 = 12%, femoral heads = 4000 cGy, v45 < 0%, and penial bulb mean dose = 19 Gy. The **upper panel** shows full bladder, empty rectum, and target PTV; the **middle panel** shows isodose lines and DVH; the **lower left panel** is CTSim scan and **lower right panel** shows daily CBCT with empty rectum and GTV prostate.

References

Ref 1. *Frass BA, Eisbruch A. Mfang: intensity modulated and image guided radiation therapy. In: Gunderson LL, editor. Clinical radiation oncology. New York: J E Tepper Elsevier Publishing; 2016.*

Ref 2. *Levitt SH, Purdy JA, Perez CA, Vijayakumar S. Technical basis of radiation therapy: practical clinical applications, 4th revised edition. New York: Springer; 2006.*

Ref 3. *International commission on radiation units and measurements (ICRU) report 50. Prescription, recording and reporting photon beam therapy. Bethesda, MD: ICRU; 1993.*

Ref 4. *International commission on radiation units and measurements (ICRU) report 62. Prescription, recording and reporting photon beam therapy (supplement t o ICRU report 50). Bethesda, MD: ICRU; 1999.*

Ref 5. *International commission on radiation units and measurements (ICRU) report 83 prescribing, recording, and reporting photon-beam intensity-modulated radiation therapy (IMRT). Bethesda, MD: ICRU; 2010.*

Ref 6. *van Herk M, Remeijer P, Rasch C, et al. The probability of correct target dosage: dose-population histograms for deriving treatment margins in radiotherapy. Int J Radiat Oncol Biol Phys 2000;47:1121—35.*

Ref 7. *Siebers JV, Keall PJ, Wu QW, et al. Effect of patient setup errors on simultaneously integrated boost head and neck IMRT treatment plans. Int J Radiat Oncol Biol Phys 2005;63:422—33.*

Ref 8. *Holmes T, Das R, Low D, et al. American Society of Radiation Oncology recommendations for documenting intensity-modulated radiation therapy treatments. Int J Radiat Oncol Biol Phys 2009;74:1311—8.*

Ref 9. *Bortfeld T, Burkelbach J, Boesecke R, et al. Methods of image reconstruction from projection applied to conformation radiotherapy. Phys Med Biol 1990;35:1423—34.*

Ref 10. *Fraass BA, Steers JM, Matuszak MM, et al. Inverse-optimized 3-D conformal planning: minimizing complexity while achieving equivalence with beamlet IMRT in multiple sites. Med Phys 2012;39:3361—74.*

Ref 11. *Shepard DM, Cao D, Afghan MK, et al. An arc-sequencing algorithm for intensity modulated arc therapy. Med Phys 2007;34:464—70.*

Ref 12. *Otto K. Volumetric modulated arc therapy. IMRT in a single gantry arc. Med Phys 2008;35:310—7.*

Ref 13. *Crijns W, Budiharto T, Defraene G, Verstraete J, Depuydt T, Haustermans K, et al. IMRT-based optimization approaches for volumetric modulated single arc radiotherapy planning. Radiother Oncol 2010;95:149—52.*

Ref 14. *Dawson LA, Sharpe MB. Image-guided radiotherapy: rationale, benefits, and limitations. Lancet Oncol 2006;7(10):848—58.*

Ref 15. *Michalski J, et al. Radiation therapy oncology group. Research plan 2002-2006. Image-guided radiation therapy committee. Int J Radiat Oncol Biol Phys 2001;51(3 Suppl. 2):60—5.*

Ref 16. *Gupta M, et al. Effect of imaging frequency on PTV margins and geographical miss during image guided radiation therapy for prostate cancer. Pract Radiat Oncol 2017.*

Ref 17. *Wortel RC, et al. Acute toxicity after image-guided intensity modulated radiation therapy compared to 3D conformal radiation therapy in prostate cancer patients. Int J Radiat Oncol Biol Phys 2015;91(4):737—44.*

Ref 18. *Wortel RC, et al. Late side effects after image guided intensity modulated radiation therapy compared to 3D-conformal radiation therapy for prostate cancer: results from 2 prospective cohorts. Int J Radiat Oncol Biol Phys 2016;95(2):680—9.*

Ref 19. *Huang CM, et al. A retrospective comparison of outcome and toxicity of preoperative image-guided intensity-modulated radiotherapy versus conventional pelvic radiotherapy for locally advanced rectal carcinoma. J Radiat Res 2017;58(2):247—59.*

Ref 20. *Raziee H, et al. Improved outcomes with dose escalation in localized prostate cancer treated with precision image-guided radiotherapy. Radiother Oncol 2017;123(3):459—65.*

Ref 21. *MacDonald SM, Ahmad S, Kachris S, et al. Intensity modulated radiation therapy versus three-dimensional conformal radiation therapy for the treatment of high grade glioma: a dosimetric comparison. J Appl Clin Med Phys 2007;8(2):47—60.*

Ref 22. *Narayana A, Yamada J, Berry S, et al. Intensity-modulated radiotherapy in high-grade gliomas: clinical and dosimetric results. Int J Radiat Oncol Biol Phys 2006;64(3):892—7.*

Ref 23. *Wagner D, Christiansen H, Wolff H, Vorwerk H. Radiotherapy of malignant gliomas: comparison of volumetric single arc technique (RapidArc), dynamic intensity-modulated technique and 3D conformal technique. Radiother Oncol 2009;93(3):593—6.*

Ref 24. *Amelio D, Lorentini S, Schwarz M, Amichetti M. Intensity-modulated radiation therapy in newly diagnosed glioblastoma: a systematic review on clinical and technical issues. Radiother Oncol 2010;97(3):361—9.*

Ref 25. *Shaffer R, Nichol AM, Vollans E, et al. A comparison of volumetric modulated arc therapy and conventional intensity-modulated radiotherapy for frontal and temporal high-grade gliomas. Int J Radiat Oncol Biol Phys 2010;76(4):1177—84.*

Ref 26. *Panet-Raymond V, Ansbacher W, Zavgorodni S, Bendorffe B, Nichol A, Truong PT, Beckham W, Vlachaki M. Coplanar versus noncoplanar intensity-modulated radiation therapy (IMRT) and volumetric-modulated arc therapy (VMAT) treatment planning for fronto-temporal high-grade glioma. J Appl Clin Med Phys July 5, 2012;13(4):3826.*

Ref 27. *Nutting CM, Morden JP, Harrington KJ, et al. PARSPORT trial management group. Parotid-sparing intensity modulated versus conventional radiotherapy in head and neck cancer (PARSPORT): a phase 3 multicentre randomised controlled trial. Lancet Oncol 2011;12:127—36.*

Ref 28. *Hall EJ. Intensity-modulated radiation therapy, protons, and the risk of second cancers. Int J Radiat Oncol Biol Phys 2006;65:1—7.*

Ref 29. *Verbakel WF, Cuijpers JP, Hoffmans D, Bieker M, Slotman BJ, Senan S. Volumetric intensity-modulated arc therapy vs. conventional IMRT in head-and-neck cancer: a comparative planning and dosimetric study. Int J Radiat Oncol Biol Phys 2009;74:252—9.*

Ref 30. *Vanetti E, Clivio A, Nicolini G, et al. Volumetric modulated arc radiotherapy for carcinomas of the oro-pharynx, hypo-pharynx and larynx: a treatment planning comparison with fixed field IMRT. Radiother Oncol 2009;92:111−7.*

Ref 31. *Scorsetti M, Fogliata A, Castiglioni S, et al. Early clinical experience with volumetric modulated arc therapy in head and neck cancer patients. Radiat Oncol 2010;5:93.*

Ref 32. *Smet S, Lambrecht M, Vanstraelen B, Nuyts S. Clinical and dosimetric evaluation of RapidArc versus standard sliding window IMRT in the treatment of head and neck cancer. Strahlenther Onkol 2015;191:43−50.*

Ref 33. *Guo R, Tang LL, Mao YP, et al. Clinical outcomes of volume-modulated arc therapy in 205 patients with nasopharyngeal carcinoma: an analysis of survival and treatment toxicities. PLoS One 2015;10:e0129679.*

Ref 34. *Popescu CC, Olivotto IA, Beckham WA, et al. Volumetric modulated arc therapy improves dosimetry and reduces treatment time compared to conventional intensity-modulated radiotherapy for locoregional radiotherapy of left-sided breast cancer and internal mammary nodes. Int J Radiat Oncol Biol Phys 2010;76:287−95.*

Ref 35. *Scorsetti M, Alongi F, Fogliata A, et al. Phase I−II study of hypofractionated simultaneous integrated boost using volumetric modulated arc therapy for adjuvant radiation therapy in breast cancer patients: a report of feasibility and early toxicity results in the first 50 treatments. Radiat Oncol 2012;7:145.*

Ref 36. *De Rose F, Fogliata A, Franceschini D, et al. Phase II trial of hypofractionated VMAT-based treatment for early stage breast cancer: 2-year toxicity and clinical results. Radiat Oncol 2016;11:120.*

Ref 37. *Kim YJ, Kim K, Lee R, et al. Two-year follow-up of volumetric-modulated arc therapy for treating internal mammary nodes in locally advanced breast cancer. Anticancer Res 2016;36:4847−51.*

Ref 38. *Grills IS, Yan D, Martinez AA, Vicini FA, Wong JW, Kestin LL. Potential for reduced toxicity and dose escalation in the treatment of inoperable non-small-cell lung cancer: a comparison of intensity-modulated radiation therapy (IMRT), 3D conformal radiation, and elective nodal irradiation. Int J Radiat Oncol Biol Phys 2003;57:875−90.*

Ref 39. *Chapet O, Khodri M, Jalade P, N'Guyen D, Flandin I, D'Hombres A, et al. Potential benefits of using non coplanar field and intensity modulated radiation therapy to preserve the heart in irradiation of lung tumors in the middle and lower lobes. Radiother Oncol 2006;80:333−40.*

Ref 40. *Murshed H, Liu HH, Liao Z, Barker JL, Wang X, Tucker SL, et al. Dose and volume reduction for normal lung using intensity-modulated radiotherapy for advanced-stage non-small-cell lung cancer. Int J Radiat Oncol Biol Phys 2004;58:1258−67.*

Ref 41. *Yom SS, Liao Z, Liu HH, Tucker SL, Hu CS, Wei X, et al. Initial evaluation of treatment-related pneumonitis in advanced-stage non-small-cell lung cancer patients treated with concurrent chemotherapy and intensitymodulated radiotherapy. Int J Radiat Oncol Biol Phys 2007;68:94−102.*

Ref 42. *Liao ZX, Komaki RR, Thames Jr HD, Liu HH, Tucker SL, Mohan R, et al. Influence of technologic advances on outcomes in patients with unresectable, locally advanced non-small-cell lung cancer receiving concomitant chemoradiotherapy. Int J Radiat Oncol Biol Phys 2010;76:775−81.*

Ref 43. *Dearnaley DP, Sydes MR, Graham JD, Aird EG, Bottomley D, Cowan RA, et al. RT01 collaborators. Escalated-dose versus standard-dose conformal radiotherapy in prostate cancer: first results from the MRC RT01 randomised controlled trial. Lancet Oncol 2007;8:475−87. 45.*

Ref 44. *Zelefsky MJ, Fuks Z, Hunt M, Yamada Y, Marion C, Ling CC, et al. High-dose intensity modulated radiation therapy for prostate cancer: early toxicity and biochemical outcome in 772 patients. Int J Radiat Oncol Biol Phys 2002;53:1111−6.*

Ref 45. *Zelefsky MJ, Levin EJ, Hunt M, Yamada Y, Shippy AM, Jackson A, et al. Incidence of late rectal and urinary toxicities after three-dimensional conformal radiotherapy and intensity-modulated radiotherapy for localized prostate cancer. Int J Radiat Oncol Biol Phys 2008;70:1124−9.*

Ref 46. *De Meerleer GO, Vakaet LA, De Gersem WR, De Wagter C, De Naeyer B, De Neve W. Radiotherapy of prostate cancer with or without intensity modulated beams: a planning comparison. Int J Radiat Oncol Biol Phys 2000;47:639−48.*

Ref 47. *Palma D, Vollans E, James K, Nakano S, Moiseenko V, Shaffer R, et al. Volumetric modulated arc therapy for delivery of prostate radiotherapy: comparison with intensity-modulated radiotherapy and three-dimensional conformal radiotherapy. Int J Radiat Oncol Biol Phys 2008;72:996−1001.*

Ref 48. *Yoo S, Wu QJ, Lee WR, Yin FF. Radiotherapy treatment plans with RapidArc for prostate cancer involving seminal vesicles and lymph nodes. Int J Radiat Oncol Biol Phys 2010;76:935−42.*

Ref 49. *Rao M, Yang W, Chen F, Sheng K, Ye J, Mehta V, et al. Comparison of Elekta VMAT with helical tomotherapy and fixed field IMRT: plan quality, delivery efficiency and accuracy. Med Phys 2010;37:1350−9.*

Ref 50. *Wolff D, Stieler F, Welzel G, Lorenz F, Abo-Madyan Y, Mai S, et al. Volumetric modulated arc therapy (VMAT) vs. serial tomotherapy, step-and-shoot IMRT and 3Dconformal RT for treatment of prostate cancer. Radiother Oncol 2009;93:226−33.*

Ref 51. *Spratt DE, Pei X, Yamada J, Kollmeier MA, Cox B, Zelefsky MJ. Long-term survival and toxicity in patients treated with high-dose intensity modulated radiation therapy for localized prostate cancer. Int J Radiat Oncol Biol Phys March 1, 2013;85(3):686−92.*

Stereotactic Radiation: Cranial Lesions

Stereotactic radiation is a technique of delivering high doses of radiation in one to five fractions to a defined small target with the goal of killing cancer cells and eradicating the tumor. The technique integrates stereotactic localization of the target to guide high doses of radiation with little or no extra margin to exclude the surrounding normal structures from radiation. This chapter reviews the radiobiology, techniques, and clinical applications of stereotactic radiation for brain tumors.

RADIOBIOLOGY OF STEREOTACTIC RADIATION

The cell death mechanism of stereotactic radiation is different from that of conventional fractionated radiation therapy. The linear quadratic model using repair, repopulation, reoxygenation, and redistribution may not apply to stereotactic high-dose radiation [1,2]. The current data show the following as the mechanisms of action for stereotactic radiation:

1. Direct cell death due to damage of the critical target, such as DNAs that are directly ionized by radiation, causing damage.
2. Vascular damage causing endothelial cell death and vascular dysfunction leading to indirect cell death.
3. Immunocytokine activation due to antigen release from death of tumor cells causing indirect cell death of the nonirradiated tumors.

In addition, because of very high dose of conformity and very steep dose gradient at the target margins, the conventional therapeutic ratio may not apply to the stereotactic radiation treatments as with a conventional fractionation scheme.

STEREOTACTIC RADIOSURGERY TECHNIQUE

Stereotactic radiosurgery (SRS) is a single fraction of high-dose radiation to treat intracranial tumors. Various SRS machines and techniques are available as described below [3]:

- Gamma Knife: It uses ionizing radiation from ^{60}Co sources. The Gamma Knife machine typically uses 201 total sources, each with 30 Ci and a total activity of

Fundamentals of Radiation Oncology
https://doi.org/10.1016/B978-0-12-814128-1.00007-6

6000 Ci. The ^{60}Co sources are arranged in an annular fashion with the source beams converging on a single point (isocenter) at the center of the annulus, 40 cm from the sources.
- Stereotactic linear accelerator: It uses cones or multileaf collimators (MLCs) to shape the radiation beams to conform to the target volume. Typically, 5–11 isocentric fixed beams or arcs are used for planning and treatments.
- CyberKnife: Recently, a robot-controlled CyberKnife is a variant of the 6-MV linear accelerator, which is mounted on a robotic arm with nonisocentric radiation beams using the principles of linear accelerators for the SRS.
- Stereotactic tomotherapy: The helical tomotherapy technique uses a narrow intensity-modulated beam delivered from a rotating linear accelerator mounted on a ring gantry. The patient moves through the ring gantry while the radiation beam is on, producing a helical form of radiation therapy, thereby eliminating multiple fields and field junctions.
- Stereotactic proton therapy: Protons from particle accelerators, such as cyclotrons and synchrotrons are used for SRS. In this technique, the Bragg peak from one proton beam is used repeatedly to treat the target.

PATIENT IMMOBILIZATION AND SETUP

Patient immobilization is of critical importance in minimizing the intra- and interfraction patient movements. This is accomplished by using fixed type invasive frames or noninvasive masks (Fig. 7.1). The SRS setup is based on the Cartesian 3D coordinate system, which transfers x, y, and z setup coordination from the rigidly attached invasive frame to the head of the patient to the isocenter within the target volume. For mask-based immobilization, the image guidance is used to minimize the intra- and interfraction movements. Ultimately, 1-mm setup accuracy is achievable for SRS and submillimeter accuracy for the invasive methodology.

IMAGING

CT and MRI are performed with the positional frame attached to the patient. Images with slice thickness of <2 mm are recommended for SRS planning. Fusion of MRI

 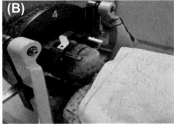

FIGURE 7.1 Patient immobilization and positioning during treatment of patients with (A) linac-based modality and use of face mask and (B) Gamma Knife SRS with the use of an invasive frame.

with CT is recommended for target delineation. Images are fused by using fiducial markers on CT and MRI, or by image registration algorithms such as mutual information.

TARGET VOLUME DELINEATION

T1- and T2-weighted MRI and FLAIR sequences are fused with the CT images (Fig. 7.2). GTV includes only the contrast-enhanced tumor volume on MRI. No surrounding edema is included in the GTV. For the fixed frame-based SRS technique, CTV and PTV are the same as GTV without any additional margin. For the frameless SRS technique, CTV is the same as GTV and a 1–2 mm margin is added to the CTV to delineate PTV [4].

Delineation of OAR Volumes

For a typical intracranial SRS, the brain, brainstem, optic chiasm, optic nerves, and cochlea are delineated as OARs (Fig. 7.2):

- **Brain:** Brain represents the entire structure within the bony skull from the vertex to the lower border of foramen magnum or alternatively the upper border of the first cervical vertebrae.
- **Brainstem:** The brainstem is comprised of the midbrain, pons, and medulla oblongata. The brainstem starts from the level of the superior border of the posterior clinoid inferiorly to the border of the foramen magnum, which is at the level of the superior border of the first cervical vertebrae.
- **Optic chiasm:** Located in the forebrain, the optic chiasm is an X-shaped structure directly in front of the hypothalamus. The optic chiasm is in direct contact with

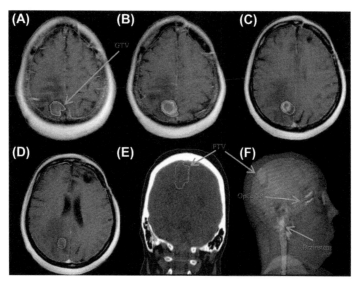

FIGURE 7.2 Target volume and organs at risk contouring: GTV: gross tumor volume; PTV: planning target volume; optic nerves and brainstem.

cerebrospinal fluid anteriorly within the subarachnoid space and posteriorly within the third ventricle. Inferiorly, the optic chiasm lies over the body of the sphenoid bone, typically above the diaphragma sellae and rarely within the sulcus chiasmatis.

- **Optic nerves:** The optic nerves are comprised of four segments: (1) The intraocular segment within the posterior retina emerging through the scleral opening (lamina cribrosa), (2) the intraorbital segment passes posteriorly and centrally within the orbit, (3) intracanalicular segment constitutes the portion where the optic nerves exit through the tendinous ring and optic canal (optic foramen) inferior to the ophthalmic artery, and (4) intracranial or cisternal segment enters the middle cranial fossa and passes within the suprasellar cistern with the anterior cerebral artery at its superolateral aspect to join the contralateral optic nerve at the optic chiasm.
- **Cochlea:** The cochlea is a shell-shaped spiral that turns between two-and-a-half and two-and-three-quarters times around the modiolus (a central column of bone). The cochlea resides in a bony cavity in the petrous portion of the temporal bone. Its base lies against the lateral end of the internal acoustic meatus, its basal coil forms the promontory of the middle ear, and its apex is directed anterolaterally. A bony core, the modiolus, transmits the cochlear nerve and contains the spiral ganglion, the sensory ganglion for this nerve.

TREATMENT PLAN

The recommended target volume size limitation for SRS is < 3–4 cm. SRS is not recommended for tumors near cranial nerves or within deep gray matter of the brainstem. The planner determines the following:

- Isocenter position for Gamma Knife SRS (GK-SRS). Larger or irregular targets typically require multiple isocenters.
- Number of fields or arcs of 9–11 beams for linac SRS, steep dose gradient is achieved by circular stereotactic collimators or micro MLCs. When using circular collimators to treat large or irregular targets, multiple isocenters are commonly used.
- Gantry and table positions for linac SRS.
- Treatment dose within the target volume—D0 is surface isodose completely encompassing PTV, Dmin, and Dmax to PTV.
- RT dose is 6–25 Gy per fraction in one to five fractions.

GK-SRS and linac-based SRS plans can be monoisocentric or have multiple isocenters, creating multiple spherical isodose distributions (Fig. 7.3). This result in hot spots and a nonuniform dose distribution within the target volumes. For GK-SRS, the radiation dose prescribed is to 50%–80% isodose lines because dose falloff outside the prescription isodose lines is the characteristic of GK-SRS. For linac-based SRS, the dose usually prescribed is to 70%–80% isodose line encompassing the target volume, which describes the percentage of the maximum dose that encircles the borders of the target (Fig. 7.4) [5]. Because the target volume has no OAR, hot spots of 20%–100% within the target do not cause any normal tissue complications.

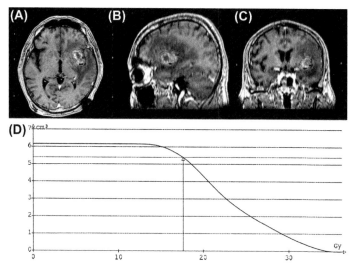

FIGURE 7.3   Gamma Knife SRS plan: (A) Axial; (B) Sagittal; (C) Coronal view; and (D) Related dose–volume histogram showing high dose inhomogeneity within the tumor by the DVH tail.

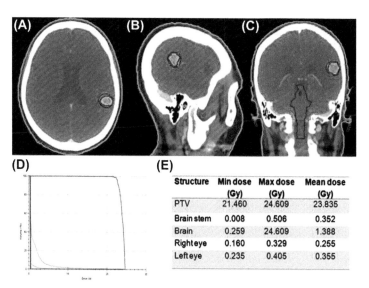

FIGURE 7.4   Linac-based SRS plan: (A) Axial; (B) Sagittal; (C) Coronal view; (D) Dose–volume histogram; and (E) Evaluation metrics.

TREATMENT PLAN ASSESSMENT

The SRS treatment plan is evaluated by three-dimensional isodose distribution, DVHs, conformity index (CI), homogeneity index (HI), tumor control probability, and normal tissue control probability. The RTOG guidelines for SRS treatment plan evaluation are presented below (Tables 7.1 and 7.2) [6−8]:

1. Conformity index (CI): the volume of prescription isodose line divided by the target volume. The ideal CI value is 1, meaning that the prescription isodose line matches perfectly the target volume without doses beyond the PTV.
2. Homogeneity index (HI): the ratio of the maximum point dose in the target volume to the prescription isodose line. Desired HI is 2 or less.
3. Coverage quality (Q): the ratio of minimum dose in the target volume to the prescription isodose. Desired coverage is 90% of the isodose line covering the PTV.

TABLE 7.1   Commonly Used Indices in Evaluation of Stereotactic Radiosurgery Planning Results

Dose Plan Indices	Formula	Acceptable Value
Conformity index (CI)	PIV/TV	1−2 (0.9−3.5)
Paddick conformity index ($CI_{Paddick}$)	$TV_{PTV}^2 / TV \times PTV$	1
CI_{Lomax}	TV_{PIV}/TV	0−1
Homogeneity index (HI)	D_{max}/PD	1(1.1−2.5)
Coverage (Q)	D_{min}/PD	0.9−1
Selectivity index (SI)	TV_{PIV}/PIV	1
Gradient index (GI)	$PIV_{X\%}/PIV_{(X/2)\%}$	<3

D_{max}, maximum dose point in the treatment volume; D_{min}, minimum dose point in the treatment volume; PD, prescription dose; PIV, volume of prescription isodose; TV, target volume; TV_{PIV}, volume of prescription isodose in the target; X/2, isodose which carries half of the prescription isodose; X, isodose which carries the prescription isodose.
Modified from Shaw LS, et al. Radiosurgery for the treatment of previously irradiated recurrent primary brain tumors and brain metastases: initial report of radiation therapy oncology protocol (90-05). Int J Radiat Oncol Biol Phys 1996;34(3): 647−54; Souhami WS, et al. Randomized comparison of stereotactic radiosurgery followed by conventional radiotherapy with carmustine to conventional radiotherapy with carmustine for patients with glioblastoma multiforme: report of Radiation Therapy Oncology Group 93-05 protocol. Int. J. Rad. Oncol. Biol. Phys 2004;60(3):853−60; Andrews CS, et al. Whole brain radiation therapy with or without stereotactic radiosurgery boost for patients with one to three brain metastases: phase III results of the RTOG 9508 randomized trial. Lancet 2004;363:1665.

TABLE 7.2   Typical Stereotactic Radiosurgery Plan Assessment Specifications

Parameter	No Variation	Minor Variation (Acceptable)	Major Variation (Unacceptable)
Dose QA (lesion size, PD)	2.0 cm: 20 Gy	–	–
	2.1–3.0 cm: 18 Gy	–	–
	3.1–4.0 cm: 15 Gy	–	–
Dose conformity CI (PIV/TV)	1.0–2.0	0.9–1.0 or 2.0–3.5	<0.9 or >3.5
Dose homogeneity HI (MD/PD)	≤2	2–2.5	>2.5
Target coverage Q	The 90% isodose line (90% of the PD, not TD) completely encompassed target	80% isodose line covers the target	80% isodose line does not cover the target

MD, maximum dose; PD, prescription dose; PIV, volume of prescription isodose line; QA, quality assurance; TD, total dose; TV, target volume.
Modified from Shaw LS, et al. Radiosurgery for the treatment of previously irradiated recurrent primary brain tumors and brain metastases: initial report of radiation therapy oncology protocol (90-05). Int J Radiat Oncol Biol Phys 1996;34(3): 647–54; Souhami WS, et al. Randomized comparison of stereotactic radiosurgery followed by conventional radiotherapy with carmustine to conventional radiotherapy with carmustine for patients with glioblastoma multiforme: report of Radiation Therapy Oncology Group 93-05 protocol. Int. J. Rad. Oncol. Biol. Phys 2004;60(3):853–60; Andrews CS, et al. Whole brain radiation therapy with or without stereotactic radiosurgery boost for patients with one to three brain metastases: phase III results of the RTOG 9508 randomized trial. Lancet 2004;363:1665.

CLINICAL INDICATION OF CRANIAL STEREOTACTIC RADIATION

Stereotactic Radiosurgery for Single Brain Metastases

For metastatic brain tumors, whole brain radiation is the most common treatment. However, for one to three brain lesions, WBRT may be overtreatment and cause neurocognitive side effects. Therefore, SRS may be indicated as primary or boost treatments for these patients and salvage treatments after WBRT.

Dose: tumor size <2 cm is 24 Gy, <2–3 cm is 18 Gy, >3–4 cm is 15 Gy.

Acoustic Neuroma

Acoustic neuroma is a benign intracranial growth that develops from the Schwann cells of the eighth cranial nerve. It arises from the vestibular portion of the vestibulocochlear nerve. The patients may present with headaches, vertigo/tinnitus and unilateral hearing loss. Treatment options are microsurgery or SRS.

Dose: 12–13 Gy.

Pituitary Adenoma

These are benign tumors of the pituitary gland. Tumors smaller than 10 mm are microadenoma, and tumor more than 10 mm are macroadenoma. Tumors that actively overproduce prolactin, growth hormone, or cortisol are called functioning adenoma, whereas tumors without hypersecretory symptoms of acromegaly or Cushing syndromes are called nonfunctioning adenoma.

Dose: for nonfunctioning adenoma 12–20 Gy, for functioning adenoma, 15–30 Gy.

Skull-Based Meningioma

Meningioma is an extra axial tumor that originates from the meninges. Most meningiomas are benign (WHO grade I), atypical (WHO grade II), or malignant (WHO grade III). Malignant meningiomas are identified by pathologic evaluation (brain invasion, anaplasia, mitosis). These tumors are clinically more aggressive (rapid growth, frequent recurrences, invasiveness). Maximal safe resection is recommended treatment. However, for skull-based meningioma SRS is an excellent treatment option.

Dose: 12–14 Gy.

Arteriovenous Malformation and Cavernous Hemangioma

Arteriovenous malformation (AVM) is a congenital disorder of the vascular system in which abnormally thin-walled blood vessels form between arteries and veins in the brain. As such the AVM nidus may pose intracranial bleeding leading to fatality. On the other hand, the Cavernous Hemangioma is a vascular malformation where dilated thin walled blood vessels form benign tumors. Surgery is the treatment of choice; however if the locations of the lesions within the brain is high risk for surgery, then SRS is an option of treatment.

Dose: tumor size <4 cm is 20–25 Gy.

Trigeminal Neuralgia

Trigeminal neuralgia is a chronic pain syndrome of the trigeminal nerve (fifth cranial), possibly due to loss of the myelin sheath of the trigeminal nerve. Patient may present with pain episodes due to touch or exposure to cold temperature. Treatment options are medical management with carbamazepine, balloon compression, microvascular decompression, and SRS. The SRS target is the trigeminal nerve anterior to the pons.

Dose: 70–90 Gy.

Parkinson's Disease

Parkinson's disease is a chronic degenerative disorder of the central nervous system. The motor symptoms of Parkinson's disease are due to the lack of dopamine due to cell death from the midbrain area of substantia nigra. Treatment options are medical managements with levodopa, MAO-B inhibitors, thalamotomy/pallidotomy, and SRS. The SRS target is globus pallidus interna and ventralis intermedius nucleus.

Dose: 120—140 Gy.

STEREOTACTIC RADIOSURGERY TOXICITY

Acute complications occur within the first 90 days of SRS. They include headache, nausea, vomiting, seizures, transient neurologic deterioration, vertigo, regional alopecia, and fatigue. Most SRS side effects are temporary and self-limiting. SRS-induced nausea and vomiting are rare and treated by antiemetic. Seizures may occur in 2%—6% patients and for cortical lesions may need anticonvulsant treatment. Peritumoral edema is related with larger lesions or higher doses outside the target volume and is managed with steroids.

Chronic complications occur months or years after SRS. Radiation necrosis is a chronic toxicity and is of high risk due to prior RT history, higher radiation doses, and large tumor or multiple tumor volumes. Radiation necrosis incidence peaks between 12 and 15 months from SRS. It is difficult to differentiate between necrosis and tumor recurrence. Necrosis may require surgical interventions. The dose tolerance limits for normal structures are given in Table 7.3.

CLINICAL TRIALS OF STEREOTACTIC RADIOSURGERY FOR METASTATIC BRAIN CANCER

Chang et al. (2009). Chang EL, Wefel JS, Hess KR, et al. Neurocognition in patients with brain metastases treated with radiosurgery or radiosurgery plus whole-brain irradiation: a randomized controlled trial. Lancet Oncol 2009;10:1037—44.

In this study, patients with one to three newly diagnosed brain metastases were randomly assigned to SRS plus WBRT or SRS alone, and learning and memory functions were compared. After 58 patients were recruited (n = 30 in the SRS alone group, n = 28 in the SRS plus WBRT group), the trial was stopped by the data monitoring committee according to early stopping rules because there was a high probability (96%) that patients randomly assigned to receive SRS plus WBRT were significantly more likely to show a decline in learning and memory function (mean posterior probability of decline 52%) at 4 months than patients assigned to receive SRS alone (mean posterior probability of decline 24%).

Kocher et al. (2011). Kocher M, Soffietti R, Abacioglu U, et al. Adjuvant whole-brain radiotherapy versus observation after radiosurgery or surgical resection of one to three cerebral metastases: results of the EORTC 22,952—26,001 study. J Clin Oncol 2011;29(2):134—41.

In this study, 359 patients with one to three BM and controlled primaries were randomized to WBRT or observation arms after neurosurgery or SRS. The OS was not different (10.9 vs. 10.7 months, $P = .89$), but neurologic deaths were more common in

TABLE 7.3   Dose Tolerance Limits for SRS and SBRT

Organs	Fractions (n)	Volume (cc)	Volume (%)	Volume Limit (Gy)	D_{max} Limit (Gy)	References
Brainstem	1	1		10	15	[9]
	1	1		18	8	[9]
	1				23	Traditional
	3				31	[9]
Optic chiasm and nerves	1	0.2	100	15	15a	[10]
	1	0.2		20	13	[11]
	1			20	12	[11]
	1				11	[11]
	1				10+	[9]
	3				19.5	[9]
	3				25	[9]
Cochlea	1				12	[9]
	3				20	[9]
	5				27.5	[9]
Brain	5		100	20		[11]
Lens	1				3	[11]
	2				6	[11]
	3				7	[11]
	5				7	[11]

SRS, stereotactic radiosurgery; *SBRT*, stereotactic body radiotherapy.
a77% probability of neuritis if Dmax >15 Gy; no risk of optic neuritis if Dmax <10 Gy.

observation arm (44% vs. 28%, $P = .002$). The 2-year relapse rates at both the initial sites (surgery: 59% to 27%; $P < .001$; SRS: 31% to 19%; $P = .04$) and at new sites (surgery: 42% vs. 23%, $P = .008$; SRS: 48% vs. 33%, $P = .023$) were reduced by WBRT, as was the need for salvage therapies.

Brennan et al. (2014). Brennan C, Yang TJ, Hilden P, et al. A phase 2 trial of stereotactic radiosurgery boost after surgical resection for brain metastases. Int J Radiat Oncol Biol Phys 2014;88(1):130−6.

In this phase II trial, the role of adjuvant tumor bed SRS in surgically removed BMs was investigated. RPA class I (24%) or II (76%) patients (n = 47) with one or two surgically resected BM were included. Actuarial 1-year infield and brain failure rates were reported to be 22% and 42%, respectively, despite the fact that the rate of pathologically confirmed overall radionecrosis was high (17.5%). Local control was achieved in all patients with <3 cm and deeply located BM, while patients with BMs of >3 cm or superficial dural/pial involvement had the lowest chance for local control, i.e., than 50%.

BrownPD et al. (2015). NCCTG N0574 (Alliance): A phase III randomized trial of whole brain radiation therapy (WBRT) in addition to radiosurgery (SRS) in patients with one–three brain metastases. J Clin Oncol 33(18_suppl) Alliance Trial.

In this trial 213 patients with one to three brain metastases, each <3 cm were randomized to SRS alone or SRS + WBRT. The WBRT dose schedule was 30 Gy in 12 fractions; the SRS dose was 18–22 Gy in the SRS plus WBRT group and 20–24 Gy for SRS alone. The data showed that in the SRS versus SRS + WBRT group the cognitive progression was 62 versus 88 with $P = .002$, 1 year brain control 51% versus 85% (p 0.001) and median survival 10.7 mo versus 7.5 mo (p 0.93). The study concluded that decline in cognitive function was more frequent with the addition of WBRT to SRS. Adjuvant WBRT did not improve OS despite better brain control.

Aoyama H et al. (2015). Stereotactic radiosurgery with or without whole-brain radiotherapy for brain metastases: secondary analysis of the JROSG 99-1 randomized clinical trial. JAMA Oncol July 2015;1(4):457–64.

In this study, secondary analysis of the 88 lung cancer patients (n = 132) based on diagnosis-specific graded prognostic assessment (DS-GPA). The data showed that outcome: significantly better OS was observed with the addition of WBRT + SRS in patients with favorable prognosis. In the GPA 2.5–4.0 group (favorable prognosis pts) WBRT + SRS versus SRS alone, median survival time of 16.7 months versus 10.6 months ($P = .04$). However, no such difference was observed in the unfavorable GPA 0.5–2.0 group ($P = .86$). The 5-year OS was dramatically better in favorable prognosis pts (24% vs. 4%—P value not provided). The study concluded that the important role of WBRT for patients with BMs from NSCLC with a favorable prognosis should be considered.

Yamamoto M et al. (2017). A multi-institutional prospective observational study of stereotactic radiosurgery for patients with multiple brain metastases (JLGK0901 study update): Irradiation-related complications and long-term maintenance of mini-mental state examination scores. Int J Radiat Biol Phys 99(1):31–40. JLGK0901 Trial.

In this study, 1194 patients with 1–10 newly diagnosed brain metastases (largest tumor <10 mL in volume and <3 cm in longest diameter; total cumulative volume <15 mL) and KPS of 70 or higher were prospectively enrolled for observational study. SRS dose at the tumor periphery was 22 Gy for tumor volumes <4 mL, and 20 Gy for tumor volumes 4–10 mL. At median follow-up of 12 months, the data show the following.

		Gr 3–4 Toxicity (%)	
Median OS(m)		12 mo	48 mo
1 tumor	13.9	7	12
2–4 tumors	10.8	8	12
5–10 tumors	10.8	6	13
P value	0.78	0.89	0.38

The study concluded that SRS without WBRT in patients with 5–10 brain metastases is as effective as in patients with two to four brain metastases. Neither mini mental state examination (MMSE) score maintenance nor post-SRS complication incidence differed among groups further supporting noninferiority hypothesis of SRS alone for patients with 5–10 BMs versus 2–4 BMs.

Brown PD et al. (2017). Postoperative stereotactic radiosurgery compared with whole brain radiotherapy for resected metastatic brain disease (NCCTG N107C/CEC 3): a multicenter, randomized, controlled, phase 3 trial. Lancet Oncol;18(8):1049–60. NCCTG N107C Trial.

In this trial, 194 patients with one resected brain metastasis and a resection cavity less than 5 cm were randomly assigned to either postoperative SRS (12–20 Gy single fraction with dose determined by surgical cavity volume) or WBRT (30 Gy in 10 daily fractions or 37.5 Gy in15 fractions of 2.5 Gy). At median follow-up of 11.1 months the data showed for Surg + SRS versus Surg + WBRT, the cognitive progression-free survival was 3.7 months versus 3 months ($P < .0001$), 1 year local control 56 versus 78 (p 0.04), and median OS 12.2% versus 11.6% (p 0.70). The study concluded that decline in cognitive function was more frequent with WBRT than with SRS and there was no different in OS between the treatment groups.

The above data show that with careful patient selection, proper attention to stereotactic radiation technique while respecting the normal tissue tolerances, SRS is a valuable treatment modality for patients who are not suitable for conventional treatments. SRS is effective in brain metastases and other intracranial benign lesions as discussed in this chapter.

References

Ref 1. Barani, et al. Radiation biology of stereotactic radiotherapy: stereotactic and radiosurgery and stereotactic body radiation therapy. New York: Routledge Publishing; 2015. p. 289–314.

Ref 2. Shibamoto, et al. Radiobiology of SBRT: stereotactic body radiation therapy. New York: Springer Publishing; 2015. p. 11–25.

Ref 3. Barani, et al. Stereotactic radiation therapy delivery system: stereotactic and radiosurgery and stereotactic body radiation therapy. New York: Routledge Publishing; 2015. p. 39–89.

Ref 4. *Schell, et al. AAPM report. 54." stereotactic radiosurgery. TG 42 report on stereotactic external beam radiation. American Association of Physicists in Medicine. College PARK: AAPM; 1995.*

Ref 5. *Foster, et al. Stereotactic ablative radiotherapy: treatment planning in radiation therapy. 4th ed. New York: Wolters Kluwer Publishing; 2016. p. 227—43.*

Ref 6. *Shaw LS, et al. Radiosurgery for the treatment of previously irradiated recurrent primary brain tumors and brain metastases: initial report of radiation therapy oncology protocol (90-05). Int J Radiat Oncol Biol Phys 1996;34(3):647—54.*

Ref 7. *Souhami WS, et al. Randomized comparison of stereotactic radiosurgery followed by conventional radiotherapy with carmustine to conventional radiotherapy with carmustine for patients with glioblastoma multiforme: report of Radiation Therapy Oncology Group 93-05 protocol. Int J Radiat Oncol Biol Phys 2004;60(3):853—60.*

Ref 8. *Andrews CS, et al. Whole brain radiation therapy with or without stereotactic radiosurgery boost for patients with one to three brain metastases: phase III results of the RTOG 9508 randomized trial. Lancet 2004;363:1665.*

Ref 9. *Timmerman RD. An overview of hypofractionation and introduction to this issue of seminars in radiation oncology. Semin Radiat Oncol 2008;18(4):215—22.*

Ref 10. *Leber KA, et al. Dose-response tolerance of the visual pathways and cranial nerves of the cavernous sinus to stereotactic radiosurgery. J Neurosurg 1998;88(1):43—50.*

Ref 11. *Grimm J, et al. Dose tolerance limits and dose volume histogram evaluation for stereotactic body radiotherapy. J Appl Clin Med Phys 2011;12(2):3368.*

8

Stereotactic Body Radiation Therapy: Lung Cancers

Because of the success of stereotactic radiosurgery for cranial tumors, the same technique is now applied to extracranial tumors [1]. Appling similar high doses to extracranial tumors such as lung tumors, spinal/paraspinal tumors, and liver tumors up to five fractionations is known as stereotactic body radiation therapy (SBRT). SBRT requires similar strict patient setups and treatment planning processes [12]. SBRT has been shown to be very effective for lung cancer patients and is most commonly used for lung cancer.

SBRT requires stringent patient setups and the following treatment planning processes:

1. High radiation dose delivered in one to five fractions.
2. Nonoverlapping five to nine beams, either coplanar, noncoplanar or multiple arcs with multileaf collimators of leaf width of 5−10 mm.
3. Steep dose falloff immediately outside the target margin.
4. Hot spots are more tolerable within the target.
5. GTV = CTV, PTV= CTV+0.5−1 cm or isotropic margin with 4D CT.
6. Image-guided localization and respiratory gating.

LUNG CANCER

Patients with medically inoperable, untreated non−small cell lung cancer (NSCLC) are expected to die of lung cancer, despite their early detection. Conventional fractionated RT has not provided desired cure rate, as necessary dose escalation is difficult causing lung and other surrounding normal tissue toxicity. As such, SBRT offers an attractive treatment option for these patients [2,3], Fig. 8.1.

However, in addition to all the usual requirements for stereotactic radiosurgery, SBRT has the unique challenge of organ motion for lung cancer patients. Several techniques are used to control such lung tumor motion:

- Abdominal compression
- Voluntary breath hold—voluntary deep inspiration breath hold

Fundamentals of Radiation Oncology
https://doi.org/10.1016/B978-0-12-814128-1.00008-8

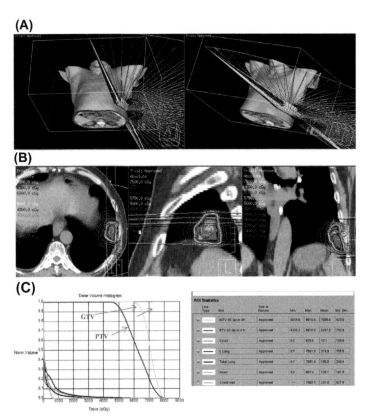

FIGURE 8.1   (A) Stereotactic body radiation therapy (SBRT) delivered by volumetric modulated arc radiotherapy in four fractions. (B) Highly conformal SBRT isodose lines covering the right lung of a medically inoperable non–small cell lung cancer patient. Delivering high dose by covering the PTV between 60% and 90% (typically 80%–85%, isodose line) leads to increased heterogeneous dose increases in the GTV/PTV ratio. (C) Dose volume histogram of the delivered plan of 50 Gy in four fractions with hot isocenter possible, which can also be performed by a simultaneous integrated technique. The DVH demonstrates the difference in homogeneity of SBRT treatments. As a result of covering the PTV with the 60%–90% isodose line, leading to increased heterogeneous dose increases in the GTV/PTV ratio.

- ABC breath hold—active breath hold using an air volume control device
- Respiratory gating system—delivers radiation within a particular portion of the patient's breathing cycle
- Real time tumor tracking—reposition radiation beam dynamically to follow the tumor's changing position

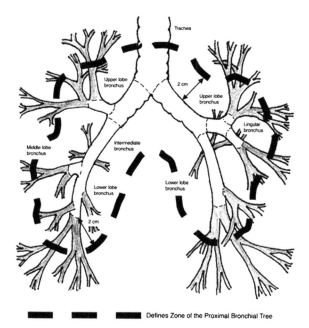

Defines Zone of the Proximal Bronchial Tree

FIGURE 8.2 A schematic diagram of the hilar/pericentral region of the lungs, defining the no-fly zone [5].

The SBRT treatment can be delivered by several techniques and modalities: three-dimensional conformal (3D-CRT; 6 to 12 coplanar or noncoplanar beams), intensity-modulated (IMRT; 6 to 12 coplanar or noncoplanar beams), volumetric modulated arc (VMAT; one to three arcs) or proton radiation therapy.

Treatment of tumors located in close proximity to proximal bronchial tree has caused excessive toxicity near the central airways and created a centrally located "no-fly zone" for SBRT with high fraction per day (20 Gy, 18 Gy after correction) based on (BED10, 151 Gy; BED3, 378 Gy). Consequently, the use of the new definition of "central lesion" published in 2015 by Chang et al. on behalf of the "international study group for lung cancer" as tumor within 2 cm in all directions of any mediastinal critical structure (the brachial plexus/phrenic nerve, bronchial tree, esophagus, major vessels, and heart) is not treated with SBRT [4], as shown in Fig. 8.2.

Image guidance with cone-beam CT (or CT-on-rail). Fiducial tracking at each fraction is mandatory to verify the localization of the target to adjust when necessary.

Dose: 10–18 Gy/fx to 50–54 Gy.

Dose constraints as per Table 8.1.

TABLE 8.1 Organs at Risk Dose Recommendation for 4 and 10 Fractions of Stereotactic Body Radiation Therapy at MDACC [4]

Organs at Risk	50 Gy/4 Fractions	70 Gy/10 Fractions
Total lung	MLD ≤ 6 Gy, V5 ≤ 30%, V10 ≤ 17%, V20 ≤ 12%, V30 ≤ 7%	MLD ≤ 9 Gy, V40 ≤ 7%
Ipsilateral lung	iMLD ≤ 10 Gy, iV10 ≤ 35%, iV20 ≤ 25%, iV30 ≤ 15%	
Trachea	V35 ≤ 1 cm3	V40 ≤ 1 cm3, Dmax < 60 Gy
Bronchial tree	V35 ≤ 1 cm3, Dmax ≤ 38 Gy	V50 < 1 cm3, Dmax < 60 Gy
Hilar major vessels	V40 ≤ 1 cm3, Dmax ≤ 56 Gy	V50 < 1 cm3, Dmax < 75 Gy
Other chest great vessels	V40 ≤ 1 cm3, Dmax ≤ 56 Gy	V50 < 1 cm3, Dmax < 75 Gy
Esophagus	V30 ≤ 1 cm3, Dmax ≤ 35 Gy	V40 ≤ 1 cm3, Dmax ≤ 50 Gy
Heart	V40 ≤ 1 cm3, Dmax ≤ 45 Gy	V45 < 1 cm3, Dmax ≤ 60 Gy
Pericardium	V20 ≤ 5 cm3, Dmax ≤ 45 Gy	
Brachial plexus	V30 ≤ 0.2 cm3, Dmax ≤ 35 Gy	V50 < 0.2 cm3, Dmax < 55 Gy
Spinal cord	V20 ≤ 1 cm3, Dmax ≤ 25 Gy	V35 ≤ 1 cm3, Dmax < 40 Gy
Chest wall	V30 ≤ 30 cm3	V50 ≤ 60 cm3, V40 ≤ 120 cm3, V30 ≤ 250 cm3, Dmax ≤ 82 Gy
Skin	V30 ≤ 50 cm3	V50 ≤ 60 cm3, V40 ≤ 120 cm3, V30 ≤ 250 cm3, Dmax ≤ 82 Gy
Kidney (bilat)	V15 < 35%	V10 < 33% (each)
	V15 < 67% for right kidney, V15 < 35% for both kidneys	

CLINICAL TRIALS FOR STEREOTACTIC BODY RADIATION THERAPY

Onishi H et al. (2007). Hypofractionated stereotactic radiotherapy (HypoFXSRT) for stage I non-small cell lung cancer: updated results of 257 patients in a Japanese multi-institutional study. J Thorac Oncol July 2007;2(7 Suppl. 3):S94−100.

This is a retrospective study of 257 patients, with stage I NSCLC (T1N0 n = 164, T2N0 n = 93), received hypofractionated SBRT, median BED10 = 111 Gy (57−180 Gy), at median F/U 3.2 years the data showed the following:

- Outcome: LF 14%, LF if BED10 < 100 43% versus BED10 > 100 8% (SS)
- 5-year overall survival (OS) 30% versus 71% (SS)
- Operable: 5-year OS if BED10 < 100 30% versus BED10 > 100 71% (SS)
- Toxicity: Grade 3 pulmonary 5%

This study concluded that hypofractionated SBRT is feasible for curative treatment of stage I NSCLC and is superior to conventional RT. Outcomes in operable patients are excellent.

Baumann P et al. (2009). Outcome in a prospective phase II trial of medically inoperable stage I non-small-cell lung cancer patients treated with stereotactic body radiotherapy. Clin Oncol July 10, 2009;27(20):3290−6.

This is a phase II study of 57 patients with medically inoperable stage I NSCLC (T1 70%, T2 30%) treated in Sweden, Norway, and Denmark. The RT dose was SBRT 45 Gy in three fxs prescribed at 67% isodose. The median tumor diameter was 2.5 cm. CTV = GTV + 1−2 mm. PTV = CTV + 5−10 mm. At median F/U 3 years the data showed the following:

- Outcome: 3-year PFS 52%; CSS 88%, OS 60%.
- No difference between T1 and T2.
- Local control 92%, regional relapse 5%, distant metastates 16%.

This study concluded that SBRT is state-of-the-art treatment for medically inoperable stage I NSCLC.

Videtic GM et al. (2009). Intensity-modulated radiotherapy-based stereotactic body radiotherapy for medically inoperable early-stage lung cancer: excellent local control. Int J Radiat Oncol Biol Phys September 16, 2009.

This is a retrospective study of 26 patients with 28 lesions, T1 in 79%, T2 in 21%, no tissue diagnosis in 27%. The RT dose of SBRT IMRT 50 Gy in five fxs with heterogeneity corrected (PTV = ITV + 3−5 mm). At median F/U 2.6 years, the data showed the following:

- Outcome: Actuarial 3-year LC 94%, 3-year OS 52%
- Toxicity: Acute grade 3 dyspnea in one patient (4%) and late grade 2 chest wall pain one patient (4%)

This study concluded SBRT is excellent in local control and in favorable survival.

Fakiris AJ et al. (2009). Stereotactic body radiation therapy for early-stage non-small-cell lung carcinoma: four-year results of a prospective phase II study. Int J Radiat Oncol Biol Phys November 1, 2009;75(3):677–82.

This is a phase II study of 70 medically inoperable patients with cT1 (n = 34) or cT2 (n = 36), diameter < 7 cm, biopsy proven NSCLC. The RT dose was 60–66 Gy to 80% isodose in three fractions. At median F/U 4.2 years, the data showed the following:

- Outcome: 3-year LC 88%, nodal failure 9%, DM 13%. 3-year OS 43%, CSS 82%.
- No difference in outcome between T1 and T2, by tumor volume or by peripheral versus central location.
- Toxicity: Grade 3 + toxicity in peripheral 10% versus central 27% ($P = .09$).

This study concluded that SBRT results in high local control in medically inoperable stage I patients.

Timmerman R et al. (2014). Long-term results of RTOG 0236: a phase II trial of Stereotactic Body Radiation Therapy (SBRT) in the treatment of patients with medically inoperable stage I non-small cell lung cancer. Int J Rad Oncol Biol Phy September 1, 2014;90(1 Suppl.):S30. RTOG 0236.

This is a phase II study of 55 patients with peripheral T1–T2N0 NSCLC, <5 cm diameter, not surgical candidate. The RT dose was SBRT 54 Gy three fxs over 1.5–2 weeks. At median F/U 4 years, the data showed the following:

- Outcome: 5-year local-regional failure rate was 38%. 5-year disseminated failure rate was 31%.
- The rates for disease free and overall survival at 5 years were 26% and 40%, respectively.
- The median overall survival was 4 years.
- Toxicity: Grade 3 in 13%, grade 4 in 4%, and no grade 5.

This study concluded that patients with inoperable NSCLC have high rates of local tumor control and moderate treatment-related morbidity.

Chang J et al. (2015). Stereotactic ablative radiotherapy versus lobectomy for operable stage I non-small-cell lung cancer: a pooled analysis of two randomized trials. Lancet Oncol. June 2015;16(6):630–7.

This is a pooled analysis of two phase III studies, neither of which met accrual goals. This study included 58 patients with operable T1–T2a N0 M0 NSCLC, <4 cm diameter, 1:1 randomization SBRT versus surgery. The RT dose for STARS: SBRT 54 Gy in three fxs peripheral, 50 Gy in four fxs central lesions over 5 days; the RT dose for ROSEL: SBRT 54 Gy in three fxs peripheral (5–8 days), 60 Gy in five fxs central lesions (10–14 days). At median F/U 3.4 years, the data showed the following:

- Outcome: 3-year OS 95% (SBRT) versus 79% (surgery) ($P < .05$)
- Toxicity: SBRT: grade 3 in 10%, no grade 4/5; surgery: grade 3/4 44%; 1 pt. Grade 5

This study concluded that SBRT is better tolerated than surgery and might lead to better OS. As such, SBRT is an option for operable stage I NSCLC.

The RTOG 0618 trial, treating early-stage-operable lung cancer patients with SBRT, at median follow-up of 48.1 months revealed estimated 4-year primary tumor control and local control rate were both 96%, the 4-year estimates of disease-free and overall survival were 57% and 56%, respectively. Median overall survival was 55.2 months [6]. The randomized study by Nyman J et al. [7] of SBRT versus conventional fractionated radiotherapy in medically inoperable stage I NSCLC showed that there was no difference in PFS and OS between SBRT and conventionally treated patients (PFS of 42% vs. 42% and OS of 54% vs. 59%). Therefore, SBRT should be considered the standard treatment for patients with inoperable stage I NSCLC. A recent long-term follow-up on NRG Oncology RTOG 0915 trial [8] of randomized phase II study comparing two stereotactic body radiation therapy schedules (34 Gy vs. 48 Gy) for medically inoperable patients with stage I peripheral NSCLC showed no excess late appearing toxicity in either arm and primary tumor control rates at 5 years were similar by arm (4.1 years vs. 4 years).

The Trans-Tasman phase III CHISEL (NCT01014130; Hypofractionated Radiotherapy—Stereotactic vs. Conventional Radiotherapy for Inoperable Early Stage I Non-small Cell Lung Cancer) trial enrolled patients in a similar scheme of SBRT (54 Gy in three fractions) versus conventional RT (60−66 Gy in 30−33 fractions) to clarify the efficiency and clinical endpoints. All living patients were followed for a minimum of 2 years, the data shows patients randomized to SABR had superior freedom from local failure (HR = 0.29, 95% CI 0.130, 0.662, P = 0.002) and longer overall survival (HR = 0.51, 95% CI 0.51, 0.911, P=0.020). Worst toxicities by arm were: CRT grade 3, 2 patients; SABR grade 4, 1 patient and grade 3, 9 patients [9].

Other ongoing prospective trials are stage I peripheral NSCLC patients such as United Kingdom SABRTooTH study (NCT02629458) to compare SBRT with lobectomy or sublobar resection in patients considered having higher surgical risk of complications; RTOG 3502/POSTLIV study (NCT01753414) to compare radical resection versus SBRT and University of Texas Southwestern STABLE-MATES study (NCT02468024), to compare sublobar resection with SBRT, as well as in both peripheral and central stage I NSCLC patients such as Veterans' Affairs VALOR study (Under IRB review) to compare lobectomy or segmentectomy to SBRT [10].

Recently, Videtic et al. (2017) have released the executive Summary of The American Society for Radiation Oncology (ASTRO) Evidence-Based Guideline on SBRT for early-stage NSCLC [11]. This important summary was based on a systematic literature review on four key questions addressing (1) application of SBRT to operable patients; (2) appropriate use of SBRT in tumors that are centrally located, large, multifocal, or unbiopsied; (3) individual tailoring of SBRT in "high-risk" clinical scenarios, and (4) SBRT as salvage therapy after recurrence. The authors concluded that SBRT now has gained a significant role, especially in treating medically inoperable early-stage NSCLC patients with limited other treatment options.

References

Ref 1. *Kavanagh, et al. Stereotactic body Irradiation: extracranial tumors: clinical radiation Oncology. 4th ed. New York: Elsevier Publishing; 2016. p. 427—31.*

Ref 2. *Nagata Y, Takayama K, Matsuo Y, et al. Clinical outcomes of a phase I/II study of 48 Gy of stereotactic body radiotherapy in 4 fractions for primary lung cancer using a stereotactic body frame. Int J Radiat Oncol Biol Phys Dec 1, 2005;63(5):1427—31.*

Ref 3. *ematsu M, Shioda A, Suda A, et al. Computed tomography-guided frameless stereotactic radiotherapy for stage I non-small cell lung cancer: a 5-year experience. Int J Radiat Oncol Biol Phys 2001;51:666—70.*

Ref 4. *Chang JY, et al. Stereotactic ablative radiation therapy for centrally located early stage or isolated parenchymal recurrences of non-small cell lung cancer: how to fly in a "no fly zone". Int J Radiat Oncol Biol Phys April 1, 2014;88(5):1120—8.*

Ref 5. *Timmerman, et al. Excessive toxicity when treating central tumors in a phase II study of stereotactic body radiation therapy for medically inoperable early-stage lung cancer. J Clin Oncol October 2006;24(no. 30):4833—9.*

Ref 6. *Timmerman, et al. RTOG 0618: Stereotactic body radiation therapy for operable early-stage lung cancer: findings from the NRG oncology RTOG 0618 trial. JAMA Oncol 2018 May 31.*

Ref 7. *Nyman J, et al. SPACE — a randomized study of SBRT vs conventional fractionated radiotherapy in medically inoperable stage I NSCLC. Radiother Oncol 2016;121(1):1—8.*

Ref 8. *Videtic, et al. Long-term follow-up on NRG Oncology RTOG 0915 (NCCTG N0927): a randomized phase 2 study comparing 2 stereotactic body radiation therapy schedules for medically Inoperable patients with stage I peripheral Non-small cell lung cancer. Int J Radiat Oncol Biol October 1, 2017;99(Issue 2):S15—6.*

Ref 9. *Ball DL, et al. (2017). A randomized trial of SABR vs conventional radiotherapy for inoperable stage I non-small cell lung cancer: TROG 09.02 (CHISEL). Presented at: International Association for the Study of Lung Cancer 18th World Conference on Lung Cancer; Yokohama, Japan: October 15-18, 2017. Abstract OA 01.01.*

Ref 10. *Moghanaki D, Chang JY. Is surgery still the optimal treatment for stage I non-small cell lung cancer? Transl Lung Cancer Res 2016;5:183—9.*

Ref 11. *Videtic GMM, et al. Stereotactic body radiation therapy for early-stage non-small cell lung cancer: executive Summary of an ASTRO Evidence-Based Guideline. Practical Radiation Oncology 2017;2017(7):295—301.*

Ref 12. *Benedict SH, et al. Stereotactic body radiation therapy: the report of AAPM Task Group 101. Med Phys 2010;37(8):4078—101.*

Proton Radiation Therapy

Recently, Proton therapy (PT) has emerged as an important tool for cancer treatments. More and more commercially available proton canters are now available for clinical use. This chapter will discuss the rationale, clinical indications, techniques, and toxicity of proton radiotherapy.

PROTON BEAM DEPTH DOSE

Protons are heavy charged particles, have mass, and possess a positive charge, as such interact differently with matter than do photons. Protons do not change direction appreciably while traveling through matter but generally interact with matter by undergoing inelastic collisions with atomic electrons. In this process, they give up a portion of their energy with each collision (without changing direction appreciably). Hence, a monoenergetic proton beam continues to lose its energy while traveling through tissue, and the rate of energy loss increases with decreasing proton energy, resulting in most of the dose deposition occurring at the end of the range in a sharp Bragg peak.

Proton beam absorbed dose beyond the Bragg peak is negligible [1–3]. The depth of the Bragg peak is dependent on the incident proton beam energy. To deliver a uniform dose to a target volume, the proton energy is tuned and varied to superimpose multiple Bragg peaks across the target, resulting in a region of relatively uniform dose called the spread out Bragg peak (SOBP). Proximal to the target, the SOBP delivers less of a dose than that given at the target dose (low entrance dose). Distal to the target, the SOBP delivers negligible dose (minimum exit dose). A single photon beam, on the other hand, delivers a higher dose proximal to the target and lower, but nonnegligible dose distal to the target. Protons therefore have a dosimetric advantage over photons, delivering less integral dose to normal tissues for the same tumor dose. Furthermore, most proton treatment plans require only one to three beams. Proton and photon beam depth dose characteristics are illustrated in Fig. 9.1.

PROTON RELATIVE BIOLOGICAL EFFECTIVENESS

The relative biologic effectiveness (RBE) of protons is similar to megavoltage photons that are used in radiation therapy. The RBE of therapeutic energy protons (up to

Fundamentals of Radiation Oncology
https://doi.org/10.1016/B978-0-12-814128-1.00009-X

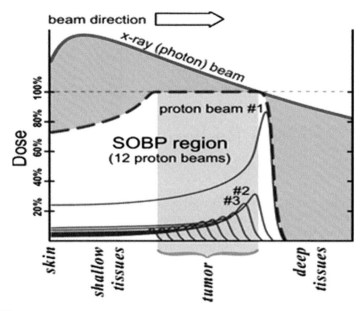

FIGURE 9.1   In a typical treatment plan for proton therapy, the spread out Bragg peak (SOBP, *dashed blue line*) is the therapeutic radiation distribution. The SOBP is the sum of several individual Bragg peaks (*thin blue lines*) at staggered depths. The depth–dose plot of an X-ray beam (*red line*) is provided for comparison. The pink area represents additional doses of X-ray radiotherapy—which can damage normal tissues and cause secondary cancers, especially of the skin. *Ref 4. Reproduced from Wikipedia, the free encyclopedia. Proton therapy, page 1: Wikimedia Foundation, Inc.; 2008.*

250 MeV) is around 1.1; however, the RBE increases from 1.1 to 1.7 in the Bragg peak where slow protons have higher biologic effectiveness [5–8]. Thus, lower doses to normal structures at the entrance and along the protons' pathway and with no exit dose improves the therapeutic ratio of PT compared with photon therapy. Nevertheless, sensitive normal tissues should not be positioned immediately distal to the dose falloff. As small changes in the penetration of the beam resulting from uncertainty, for example, the treatment planning CT, can cause the sensitive structure receiving the full physical dose because of the increased RBE.

BEAM PRODUCTION, DELIVERY, TREATMENT PLANNING, AND QUALITY ASSURANCE

Proton generation: High-voltage electric current is applied to hydrogen gas, stripping electrons from the hydrogen atoms, leaving positively charged proton particles.

Proton acceleration: Protons are accelerated by either a cyclotron or a synchrotron. A cyclotron produces a monoenergetic proton beam, typically 250 MeV. The proton energy of a synchrotron can be selected within a designed range.

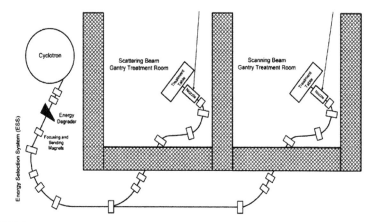

FIGURE 9.2   Proton therapy system with cyclotron, energy selection system, beam line, gantry, and nozzle. Scattering is illustrated in the nozzle on the left and scanning in the nozzle on the right. *Modified from Mendenhall NL, et al. Proton Therapy; July 2, 2016, Posted by admin in Oncology. https://oncohemakey.com/proton-therapy-2.*

Proton beam transport: A series of large bending and focusing magnets along with diagnostic measuring tools guides the proton beam from the cyclotron or synchrotron to the patient treatment rooms, Fig. 9.2.

Proton beam delivery: The pencil-shaped proton beam has to be modified for clinical use by the following techniques: Fig. 9.3.

- Scattering beam technique: The pencil beam passes through a range modulator followed by first and second scatterer then through a compensator to treat the patient. The variable thickness range modulator spins in front of the pencil beam creating a flat top Bragg peak. By using the two scatterers and the compensator, the pencil beam—shaped proton beam is spread laterally for clinical use. The scatterers and the compensator are custom-made for each proton beam.
- Scanning beam technique: Multiple variable strength magnets scan the pencil beam—shaped proton beam laterally to conform to the tumor/target volume. The scanning beam technique does not require patient-specific hardware.

Treatment planning: A CT simulation of the patient is performed for imaging data collection. The CT values are converted to proton stopping power (as opposed to electron densities for photon treatment planning). This is followed by delineation of the target volume. Finally, selection of beam direction and plan optimization is performed. A field patching technique to match multiple beams at the 50% isodose lines laterally and at the distal level produces the desired treatment plan. The planning system designs the aperture and the compensator for each single field. Pencil beam algorithms are used for the dose calculation and the radiation dose unit is cobalt Gray equivalent (CGE).

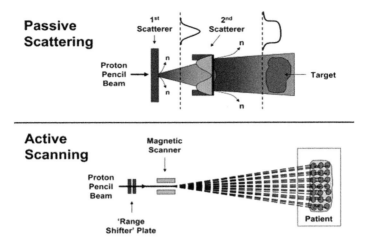

FIGURE 9.3   The protons emerging from a cyclotron or synchrotron form a narrow pencil beam. To cover a treatment field of practical size, the pencil beam must be either scattered by a foil or scanned. Passive scattering is by far the simplest technique but suffers the disadvantage of increased total-body effective dose to the patient. *From Hall EJ. Intensity-modulated radiation therapy, protons, and the risk of second cancers. Int J Radiat Oncol Biol May 1, 2006;65(1):1−7.*

Currently, intensity-modulated proton therapy (IMPT) is in use in the clinical environment. With this technique, Bragg peaks of pencil beams are distributed around the target volume and beam weights are optimized by inverse planning. Finally, several magnets are used to deflect and focus the pencil beams to the target to treat the patient. Using the IMPT technique can dramatically reduce the proton treatment time because of its complexity and labor-intensity in making the 3D compensators.

PT quality assurance: Daily, monthly, and annual quality assurance (QA) for mechanical and X-ray system is needed for the PT machine and the proton radiation beam. QA includes constancy of radiation field dose/MU, distal range, SOBP width and flatness and symmetry, range uniformity check, constancy of output versus gantry angle, gantry mechanical isocentricity check, treatment able translational motion accuracy and mechanical isocentricity checks, snout horizontal motion accuracy check, patient positioning system accuracy check, X-rays, and proton field coincidence check.

In addition, the patient-specific QA procedures, such as MU verification measurement and dosimetric tolerance are usually set at less than 3% difference from calculation. The QA items include, but are not limited to, items such as compensator apertures must match the treatment plan: compensator thickness tolerance <0.5 mm, point dose measurement in phantom for the treatment, depth dose measurement in solid phantoms, 2D dose verification at three to five different depths for each field, QA tolerance for point dose is within 2% or 2 mm of calculation, 2D dose distribution verification, and the tolerance is 90% that of the pixels have the passing gamma with 2% dose or 2 mm distance agreement criteria.

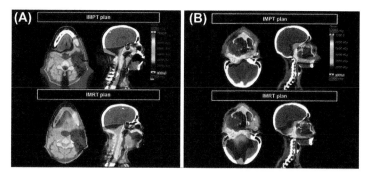

FIGURE 9.4   Comparative dose painting treatment plans using intensity-modulated radiotherapy (IMRT), intensity-modulated proton therapy (IMPT). (A) A 56-year-old woman with T1N1 left-sided nasopharyngeal carcinoma (four nodes in left levels IIa, IIb, III, and Va). (B) A 47-year-old woman with T4N0 adenoid cystic carcinoma of the hard palate (surgery followed by adjuvant radiotherapy). *Ref 11. Modified from Blanchard P, et al. Proton therapy for head and neck cancers. Semin Radiat Oncol January 2018;28(1):53—63.*

CLINICAL EXPERIENCE OF PROTON RADIOTHERAPY

Head and Neck Cancer

PT is well established for paranasal sinus cancer treatments. A metaanalysis from Mayo Clinic reported that PT provides better disease-free survival 72% versus 50%, at 5 years, ($P = 0.045$) and tumor control of 81% versus 64% at the longest follow-up, for PT versus photon treatments, respectively, ($P = 0.011$) [9]. With the development of active scanning PT and the multifield optimization IMPT technique reduces radiation dose compared with photon beam intensity-modulated radiotherapy (IMRT). Frank et al., have demonstrated that gastrostomy tubes decrease by more than 50% with IMPT during the treatment of patients with oropharyngeal cancer [10]. A current ongoing randomized phase II/III clinical trial NCT01893307 is comparing the side effects of 2 radiation treatments for head and neck cancer. The 2 treatments are intensity modulated photon therapy (IMRT) and intensity modulated proton therapy (IMPT). The RT dose is 70 Gy, and chemotherapy is at the discretion of the physician. The primary end point of the trial is rate of grade 3—5 late toxicities. Fig. 9.4 shows photon versus proton treatments for a nasopharyngeal and adenoid cystic carcinoma of patients with hard palate cancer, IMPT significantly reduces radiation dose to the critical normal structures.

Lung Cancer

For medically inoperable early-stage lung cancer patients, stereotactic body radiation therapy (SBRT) is now considered the standard of care. A systematic review by Chi et al., demonstrated that PT was associated with improved overall survival and progression-free survival relative to SBRT for early-stage lung cancer [12]. In several clinical trials, it has been demonstrated that small peripheral tumors could be treated effectively by PT or photons; however, large and central tumors are good candidates

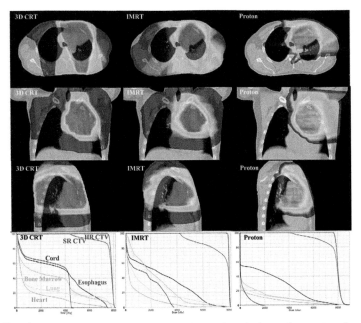

FIGURE 9.5   Typical dose distributions achieved with three-dimensional conformal radiotherapy (3DCRT), intensity-modulated radiotherapy (IMRT), and protons for a patient with stage III non—small cell lung cancer. *Reprinted with permission from Nichols RC, Huh SN, Henderson RH, Mendenhall NP, Flampouri S, Li Z, D'Agostino HJ, Cury JD, Pham DC, Hoppe BS. Proton radiation therapy provides reduced normal lung and bone marrow exposure for patients receiving dose-escalated radiation therapy for unresectable stage III non-small-cell lung cancer: A dosimetric study. Clin Lung Cancer July 2011;12(4):252—7. https:// doi.org/10.1016/j.cllc.2011.03.027. Epub 2011 April 27.*

for PT [13—18]. For locally advanced lung cancers, several trials have shown promising results [19,20]. The first randomized trial comparing passively scattered proton therapy (PSPT) and IMRT did not show a significant difference between the groups [21]. The ongoing clinical trial RTOG 1308 is currently enrolling patients with stage II—IIIB non—small cell lung cancer, which is randomized with respect to image-guided, and motion-managed photon radiotherapy (Arm 1) versus image guided, motion-managed proton radiotherapy (Arm 2), both given with concurrent platinum-based chemotherapy. The primary end of the study is overall survival, and the secondary end point is toxicity, QoL, and cost-effectiveness.

Fig. 9.5 is a comparison between plans for three-dimensional conformal radiotherapy (3DCRT)/IMRT and proton treatments for a lung cancer patient.

Prostate Cancer

A randomized trial by Shipley et al. [22] did not show any differences between photon IMRT and PT; however, PT was only used as a boost in this study. In a more recent study, PT provided superior rectal sparing at low-to-higher doses and bladder sparing

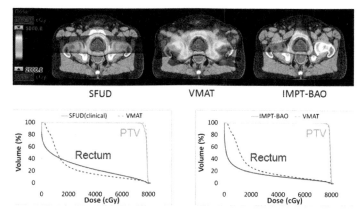

FIGURE 9.6 Comparison of single-field uniform dose, VMAT, and intensity-modulated proton therapy (IMPT) treatment plans for one prostate cancer patient. Here, SFUD represents a two-beam IMPT single-field uniform dose distribution plan. This plan is used to treat patients at our institution. VMAT represents a photon volumetric-modulated arc therapy plan, and IMPT-BAO is a class III—angle IMPT plan, where BAO interprets beam angle optimization. *Chao W et al. Improved beam angle arrangement in intensity modulated proton therapy treatment planning for localized prostate cancer. Cancers (Basel) March 30, 2015;7(2):574—84. https://doi.org/10.3390/cancers7020574.*

at low-to-medium doses compared with sliding window and rapid arc techniques [23]. In addition, the latest trial data report less toxicity with prostate cancer proton treatments [24,25]. A current ongoing phase III clinical trial NCT01617161 (PartiQOL) is comparing Proton Beam or Intensity-Modulated Radiation Therapy in Treating Patients with Low or Low-Intermediate Risk Prostate Cancer. Patients are randomized to either ARM I: IMRT 5 days a week for 9 weeks vs ARM II: PBT 5 days a week for 9 weeks. The primary objective of the trial is to compare the reduction in mean Expanded Prostate Cancer Index Composite (EPIC) bowel scores for men with low or intermediate risk prostate cancer (PCa) treated with PBT versus IMRT at 24 months following radiation. Fig. 9.6 is a comparison between three-field IMPT and volumetric-modulated arc therapy for a prostate cancer patient.

Pediatric Cancer

Modeling studies suggest there is a significant reduction in the risk of second malignancies with PT for pediatric patients [26,27]. Miralbell et al., showed improved dose distribution with PT compared with 3D conformal photon radiation and intensity-modulated photon beam radiation regarding second malignancies [26]. Recently an update from the Pediatric Proton Consortium Registry by Hess CB et al (2018), reported that a total of 1,854 patients have consented and enrolled in the PPCR from October 2012 until September 2017. The most tumors treated are the central nervous system (CNS) tumors comprising 61% of the cohort. The most common CNS histologies are: medulloblastoma (n = 276), ependymoma (n = 214), glioma/astrocytoma (n = 195),

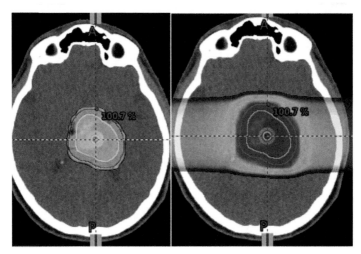

FIGURE 9.7 Pencil-beam scanning proton dose distribution for a 17-year-old patient with an unresectable pilocytic astrocytoma centered on the left thalamus. The teal line denotes the GTV, whereas the red line denotes the CTV (5-mm isotropic margin). The maximum dose point on this slice is 100.7% (54 Gy prescription). Color wash represents 95% isodose line (left) and 10% isodose line (right). *Courtesy of Derek Tsang MD. Radiation Oncology: University of Toronto, Princess Margaret Cancer Centre, Toronto, ON, Canada.*

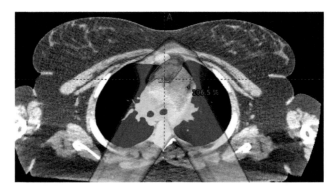

FIGURE 9.8 In this pediatric patient with mediastinal Hodgkin's lymphoma, the target is shown in red and the color wash represents 10% isodoses and higher. Intensity-modulated proton therapy was planned using robust planning, to account for the presence of breathing motion and heterogeneous tissues. The posterior oblique beams are able to spare breast tissue. *Courtesy of Derek Tsang MD. Radiation Oncology: University of Toronto, Princess Margaret Cancer Centre, Toronto, ON, Canada.*

craniopharyngioma (n = 153), and germ cell tumors (n = 108). The most common non-CNS tumors diagnoses are: rhabdomyosarcoma (n = 191), Ewing sarcoma (n = 105), Hodgkin lymphoma (n = 66), and neuroblastoma (n = 55). The median follow-up of the registry is 1.5 years with a range of 0.14 to 4.6 years. The authors concluded that the PPCR's prospective cohort of children irradiated with modern proton therapy has reached critical mass for long-awaited clinical outcomes research through use of the cohort's open access partnership design [28]. As such varius CNS and non-CNS pediatric patients now treated with PT with lower morbidity compared with photon treatment as shown below (Figs. 9.7 and 9.8).

Proton technology is improving and is very promising for the future of radiation therapy. Randomized phase II and III trials with PT are ongoing. In the adult population, cost-effectiveness is still a debate because of the lack of comparative clinical trials. Among the pediatric population, however, PT has established its presence, and it is already standard of treatment for many pediatric cancers.

References

Ref 1. *Mendenhall, et al. Proton therapy: principles and practice of radiation oncology. 6th ed. New York: Lippincott Willimas & Wilkins publishing; 2013. p. 379–92.*

Ref 2. *Levin, et al. Charged particle radiotherapy: clinical radiation oncology. 4th ed. New York: Elsivier publishing; 2016. p. 358–72.*

Ref 3. *Lomax T. Intensity-modulated proton therapy: treatment planning in radiation therapy. 4th ed. Wolters Kluwer Publishing; 2016. p. 150–67.*

Ref 4. *Wikipedia, the free encyclopedia. Proton therapy, page 1. Wikimedia Foundation, Inc; 2008.*

Ref 5. *Paganetti H, Niemierko A, Ancukiewicz M, et al. Relative biological effectiveness (RBE) values for proton beam therapy. Int J Radiat Oncol Biol Phys 2002;53:407–21.*

Ref 6. *Gerweck LE, Kozin SV. Relative biological effectiveness of proton beams in clinical therapy. Radiother Oncol 1999;50:135–42.*

Ref 7. *Britten RA, Nazaryan V, Davis LK, et al. Variations in the RBE for cell killing along the depth-dose profile of a modulated proton therapy beam. Radiat Res 2013;179:21–8.*

Ref 8. *Matsumoto Y, Matsuura T, Wada M, et al. Enhanced radiobiological effects at the distal end of a clinical proton beam: in vitro study. J Radiat Res 2014;55:816–22.*

Ref 9. *Patel SH, Wang Z, Zong WW, et al. Charged particle therapy versus photon therapy for paranasal sinus and nasal cavity malignant disease: a systematic review and meta-analysis. Lancet Oncol 2014;15:1027–38.*

Ref 10. *Frank SJ, Rosenthal DI, Ang K, et al. Gastrostomy tubes decrease by over 50% with intensity modulated proton therapy during the treatment of oropharyngeal cancer patients. A case control study (abstract). Int J Radiat Oncol Biol Phys 2013;87(Suppl 2):S144.*

Ref 11. *Blanchard P, et al. Proton therapy for head and neck cancers. Semin Radiat Oncol January 2018;28(1):53–63.*

Ref 12. *Chi A, Chen H, Wen S, Yan H, Liao Z. Comparison of particle beam therapy and stereotactic body radiotherapy for early stage non-small cell lung cancer: a systematic review and hypothesis-generating meta-analysis. Radiother Oncol 2017;123(3):346—54.*

Ref 13. *Koto M, Takai Y, Ogawa Y, et al. A phase II study on stereotactic body radiotherapy for stage I non-small cell lung cancer. Radiother Oncol 2007;85(3):429—34.*

Ref 14. *Iwata H, Demizu Y, Fujii O, et al. Long term outcome of proton therapy and carbon-ion therapy for large (T2a-T2bN0M0) non-small cell lung cancer. J Thorac Oncol 2013;8(6):726—35.*

Ref 15. *Timmerman R, McGarry R, Yiannoutsos C, et al. Excessive toxicity when treating central tumors in a phase II study of stereotactic body radiation therapy for medically inoperable early-stage lung cancer. J Clin Oncol 2006;24(30):4833—9.*

Ref 16. *Register SP, Zhang X, Mohan R, Chang JY. Proton stereotactic body radiation therapy for clinically challenging cases of centrally and superiorly located stage I non-small-cell lung cancer. Int J Radiat Oncol Biol Phys 2011;80(4):1015—22.*

Ref 17. *Kanemoto A, Okumura T, Ishikawa H, et al. Outcomes and prognostic factors for recurrence after high-dose proton beam therapy for centrally and peripherally located stage I non—small-cell lung cancer. Clin Lung Cancer 2014;15(2):e7—12.*

Ref 18. *Makita C, Nakamura T, Takada A, et al. High-dose proton beam therapy for stage I non—small cell lung cancer: clinical outcomes and prognostic factors. Acta Oncol 2015;54(3):307—14.*

Ref 19. *Oshiro Y, Okumura T, Kurishima K, et al. High-dose concurrent chemo-proton therapy for Stage III NSCLC: preliminary results of a phase II study. J Radiat Res 2014;55(5):959—65.*

Ref 20. *Chang JY, Komaki R, Lu C, et al. Phase 2 study of high-dose proton therapy with concurrent chemotherapy for unresectable stage III non-small cell lung cancer. Cancer 2011;117(20):4707—13.*

Ref 21. *Liao ZX, Lee JJ, Komaki R, et al. Bayesian randomized trial comparing intensity modulated radiation therapy versus PSPT for locally advanced non-small cell lung cancer. J Clin Oncol 2016;34(Suppl. 15):abstr 8500.*

Ref 22. *Shipley WU, Verhey LJ, Munzenrider JE, et al. Advanced prostate cancer: the results of a randomized comparative trial of high dose irradiation boosting with conformal protons compared with conventional dose irradiation using photons alone. Int J Radiat Oncol Biol Phys 1995;32:3—12.*

Ref 23. *Scobiola S, Kittel C, Wismann N, et al. A treatment planning study comparing tomotherapy, volumetric modulated arc therapy, Sliding Window and proton therapy fpr low-risk prostate carcinoma. Radiat Oncol 2016;11(1):128.*

Ref 24. *Mendenhall NP, Li Z, Hoppe BS, et al. Early outcomes from three prospective trials of image-guided proton theray for prostate cancer. Int J Radiat Oncol Biol Phys 2012;82:213—21.*

Ref 25. *Hoppe BS, Nichols RC, Henderson RH, et al. Erectile function, incontinence, and other quality of life outcomes following proton therapy for prostate cancer in men 60 years old and younger. Cancer 2012;118:4619—26.*

Ref 26. *Miralbell R, Lomax A, Cella L, Schneider U. Potential reduction of the incidence of radiation-induced second cancers by using proton beams in the treatment of pediatric tumors. Int J Radiat Oncol Biol Phys 2002;54(3):824–9.*

Ref 27. *Paganetti H, Athar BS, Moteabbed M, et al. Assesment of radiation induced second cancer risks in proton therapy and IMRT for organ inside the primary radiation fields. Phys Med Biol 2012;57(19):6047–61.*

Ref 28. *Hess CB, et al. An Update From the Pediatric Proton Consortium Registry. Front Oncol 2018;8:165.*

Immunotherapy

Immunotherapy has recently become an increasingly critical component in the management of various malignancies based on data from several large prospective studies, which have shown significant clinical benefits. A number of studies are now underway to assess the potential synergism that may exist between these agents alongside traditional chemotherapeutics, surgery, and radiation therapy. Radiation therapy has the potential to enhance the efficacy of immunotherapy agents. This chapter highlights the immunologic principles, and the biologic rationale for the use of immunotherapeutic along with the key immunotherapy studies, which have led to the approval of these agents.

IMMUNE SYSTEM COMPONENTS

Anatomy of the Immune System

Bone marrow contains hematopoietic stem cells and is the site of development of all blood cells except T cells, which are produced by the thymus through positive and negative selection. Lymph nodes are the site of antigen presentation within the lymphatic circulation, whereas the spleen is the site of antigen presentation from the blood.

Cells of the Immune System

The innate immune system: The innate immune system is comprised of dendritic cells, natural killer (NK) cells, macrophages, neutrophils, eosinophils, basophils, and myeloid-derived suppressor cells. It provides immediate defense through nonspecific recognition of foreign pathogens or tumors, but does not provide long-lasting immunity.

The adaptive immune system: The adaptive immune system is made up of CD4 T cells, CD8 T cells, B cells, and regulatory T cells, which provide specific recognition of foreign antigens or tumor-associated antigens by the immune system. It is characterized by an initial weaker response and stronger memory response upon rechallenge. The large variety of T-cell receptors (TCRs) and B-cell receptors occurs through somatic DNA recombination events (VDS recombination) initiated by the RAG gene.

Fundamentals of Radiation Oncology
https://doi.org/10.1016/B978-0-12-814128-1.00010-6

The Immune Synapse

The immune synapse between antigen-presenting cells (APCs) and the adaptive immune cells defines the immunologic response as represented in Fig. 10.1. The immune synapse between the antigen-presenting cells and cognate T cells requires two signals for an effective immune response.

- Signal 1: Presentation of specific peptide antigen by major histocompatibility complex (MHC) on the APCs to the cognate TCR on the T cells.
- Signal 2: The danger signal is provided by APCs to alert the immune system via interaction of costimulatory molecules, suppression of immune checkpoints, and release of proinflammatory cytokines. APCs recognize the danger via pathogen-associated molecular patterns (PAMPs) during foreign pathogen invasion or damage-associated molecular pattern (DAMP), during immunogenic cell death.

Immune checkpoints provide suppressor signals to the T cells during immune recognition, which limit excessive immune responses or autoimmune responses, often used by tumors to suppress antitumor immune responses, and most effective cancer immunotherapy targets these check points using antagonists. Examples of immune checkpoints include programed death 1 (PD-1), cytotoxic T-lymphocyte-associated protein 4 (CTLA-4), Tim3, LAG3.

Costimulatory molecules provide activating signals to the T cells during immune recognition, and some of the newer cancer immunotherapy targets use agonists. Examples of these costimulatory molecules include 4-1BB, Ox40, CD40, CD28, and CD27.

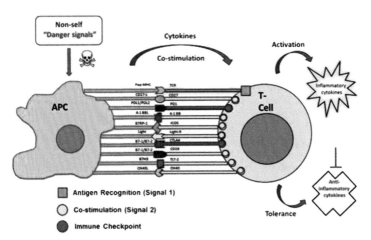

FIGURE 10.1   Immune synapse. A snapshot of an immune synapse between antigen-presenting cell (APC) and effector cell (T cell) during immune priming is depicted. The APC stimulated by the danger signal will present antigen (signal 1) and costimulation (signal 2) via ligand receptor interaction or cytokines. The immune response is restrained by immune checkpoint receptors and antiinflammatory cytokines. *CTLA-4*, cytotoxic T-lymphocyte antigen 4; *MHC*, major histocompatibility complex; *PD-1*, programmed cell death 1. *From Grass GD, Krishna N, Kim S. The immune mechanisms of abscopal effect in radiation therapy. Curr Probl Cancer 2016;40:12; with permission.*

The Immune Tolerance Mechanisms

1. Central tolerance: During T-cell development in the thymus, T-cell precursors undergo positive and negative selection. T-cell precursors with specific rearranged TCRs are positively selected when they recognize self-peptide/MHC presented by thymic cortical epithelium. If the TCR interaction with self-peptide/MHC is too strong, these cells are negatively selected to undergo apoptosis. Negative selection ensures autoimmunity does not occur; however, most T cells that can recognize tumor cells are also deleted during the process.

2. Peripheral tolerance: During immune recognition in the periphery, if signal 2 is insufficient (i.e., absence of CD28 signaling) after initial clonal expansion, then T cells contract and become anergic and are unable to respond, even when rechallenged with specific antigen. However, T-cell anergy can be rescued by IL-2.

3. T-cell exhaustion: T-cell exhaustion occurs in the setting of chronic antigenic stimulation without clearance, characterized by minimal immune response, even with recognition of specific antigen. It was first described in chronic viral infection (HIV) but has been expanded to include exhausted T cells in the setting of cancer. PD-1, LAG3, and Tim3 are prominent molecules mediating T-cell exhaustion.

4. Suppressive tumor microenvironment: Multiple mechanisms suppress immune cells in the tumor microenvironment. Tumors often downregulate MHC I molecules and thus evade immune recognition. Some tumors express immune checkpoint ligands (i.e., PD-L1) to elicit immune suppression. Tumors recruit tolerogenic immune cells (regulatory T cells, MDSCs) to avoid the host immune system.

Cancer Immunotherapy

Generally speaking, cancer immunotherapy is passive or active and is categorized below and in Fig. 10.2.

Passive immunotherapy is transferred from donor source.

- Nonspecific: nonspecifically activated T cells
- Specific: monoclonal antibodies, T cell—adoptive cellular therapy

Active immunotherapy is antigen specific.

- Nonspecific: cytokines, checkpoint inhibitors—CTLA-4, PD-1, PD-L1
- Specific: vaccines—dead tumor cells with adjuvants, dendritic cells with antigens or tumor cells transfected with cytokines or genes.

Vaccine Immunotherapy

Immune system cells are removed from the patient's body, which are then transformed to dendritic cells in the laboratory. These cells are also exposed to antigens (e.g., prostatic acid phosphatase). The dendritic cells are injected back into the patient, which produces an immune response to the cancer. Provenge is an example of a cancer vaccine for prostate cancer.

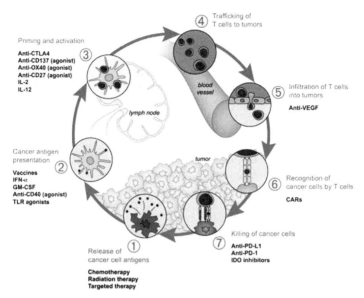

FIGURE 10.2   This figure highlights examples of some of the therapies currently under preclinical or clinical evaluation. Key highlights include that vaccines can primarily promote cycle step 2; anti-CTLA-4 can primarily promote cycle step 3, and anti-PD-L1 or anti-PD-1 antibodies can primarily promote cycle step 7. Although not developed as immunotherapies, chemotherapy, radiation therapy, and targeted therapies can primarily promote cycle step 1 and inhibitors of vascular endothelial growth factor can potentially promote T-cell infiltration into tumors (cycle step 5). Abbreviations are as follows: *GM-CSF*, granulocyte macrophage colony-stimulating factor; *CARs*, chimeric antigen receptors. *From Chen DSI, Mellman I, et al. Oncology meets immunology: the cancer-immunity cycle. Immunity July 25, 2013;39(1):1−10. https://doi.org/10.1016/j.immuni.2013.07.012.*

Antibody Immunotherapy

Monoclonal antibody immunotherapy: Tumor-specific antibodies bind to tumor cells, activating NK cells and CD16 killing tumor cells. Rituxan and Herceptin are monoclonal antibodies effective for non-Hodgkin's lymphoma and breast cancer, respectively.

Tumor-specific antibody is conjugated with chemotherapeutic agent or radionuclide, which then binds to the surface of the tumor cells. Drug-conjugated antibody is internalized by the tumor cell resulting in cell killing. Adcetris and Zevalin (90Y-labeled anti-CD20) are examples of tumor-specific antibodies treating Hodgkin's lymphoma and non−Hodgkin' lymphoma.

Cytokine Immunotherapy

Immune cells produce cytokines that control the growth and activation of immune cells. IFN increases cancer cell antigen presentation, leading to activation of cytotoxic

T cells, which in turn kill tumor cells. IFN is approved to treat renal cell cancers and melanoma. IL2 is another synthetic cytokine that primes and activates T cells and is used to treat renal cell cancer.

Antivascular Endothelial Growth Factor Immunotherapy

Cancer cells produce proangiogenic factors, causing formation of new blood vessels to supply oxygen and nutrients to the tumor. Humanized recombinant monoclonal antibodies are used to target VEGF or prevent VEGF from binding to its receptor or inhibiting tyrosine kinase activation, which prevents neoangiogenesis. Bevacizumab is used to treat ovarian cancer as well as other cancers.

Adoptive T-Cell Immunotherapy

T cells are removed from the patient through apheresis. A specific chimeric antigen receptor is added to the T cells, which are then infused back into the patient, where they recognize and target tumor cells. The CAR-T cell is used for ALL, CLL, and NHL patients.

Checkpoint Inhibitor–Targeted Immunotherapy

The immune system uses checkpoint molecules on certain immune cells needed to activate or inactivate an immune response. Tumor cells can avoid checkpoints and evade the immune system. Several proteins have been identified for use as immunotherapy targets.

- CTLA-4: This protein is induced during T-cell activation and is expressed on regulatory T cells. CTLA-4 checkpoint protein prevents dendritic cells from priming the T cells to recognize tumor cells. Inhibitor drugs blocking this checkpoint protein allows T-cell activation, which then attack the tumor cells. This has an important role in peripheral tolerance by inducing T-cell anergy.
- Programmed cell death-1/programmed cell death ligand 1 (PD-1/PD-L1/2): Binding of the PD-1 ligands, PD-L1, and PD-L2, to the PD-1 receptor found on T cells, inhibits T-cell proliferation and cytokine production. Upregulation of the PD-1 ligands occurs in some tumors and signaling through this pathway can inhibit active T-cell immune surveillance of tumors.

Below are the checkpoint inhibitors that have received FDA approval:

Ipilimumab—Human monoclonal antibody that binds to the CTLA-4, a molecule on T cells that suppresses the immune response. Blockade of CTLA-4 augments T-cell activation and proliferation and stimulates antitumor immune responses.
Pembrolizumab and Nivolumab—monoclonal antibodies that bind to the PD-1 receptor and blocks its interaction with PD-L1 and PD-L2, releasing PD-1 pathway-mediated inhibition of the immune response, including the antitumor immune response.
Atezolizumab—monoclonal antibody that binds to PD-L1, blocking its interactions with both PD-1 and B7-1 receptors. This releases the PD-L1/PD-1-mediated inhibition of the immune response, including activation of the antitumor immune response.

Durvalumab—monoclonal antibody that blocks the interaction of PD-L1 with PD-1 and CD80, thereby releasing the inhibition of immune responses. PD-L1 blocks T-cell function and activation through interaction with PD-1 and CD80.

RADIATION AND IMMUNOTHERAPY

Radiation can induce immunogenic cell death. The specific mode of cell death eliciting the immune response is not fully understood, although the primary mechanism for this is the immune activation by radiation therapy. Mediated by danger-associated molecular patterns (DAMPs) such as calreticulin, HMG-B1, ATP and heat-shock proteins to activate and mature dendritic cells (DCs), which in turn produce antigens and the danger signal to T cells. Activation of the immune system as such from localized radiation can initiate systemic immune effect known as abscopal effect.

Abscopal effect of radiation is the regression of tumor(s) outside the radiation field after local radiation therapy. It is primarily seen in immunogenic tumors (melanoma, Merkel cell carcinoma, lymphoma, and lung cancer) [2, 3]. Figure 10.3 shows an example of an abscopal response in a patient treated for squamous NSCLC with progression on nivolumab followed by palliative radiotherapy with an adjacent disease response.

RT timing: The sequencing of immunotherapy is relation to radiation therapy is under investigation and may be immunotherapy and tumor specific. However, to date many preclinical and clinical studies use immunotherapy after completion of chemoRT. Trials are ongoing to investigate if concurrent immunotherapy can be tolerated with RT and/or chemoRT.

RT dose fractionation: Currently, hypofractionated regimen (21–24 Gy/3fx) is considered most immunogenic based on preclinical studies. Low-dose irradiation also appears to induce immune activation in some studies. High doses (> 20 Gy per fraction) may be less immunogenic because of recruitment of regulatory T cells in preclinical studies.

RT field size, techniques, and treatment sites: Although larger RT field size causes lower lymphocyte counts in treated patients and immune biomarkers may be RT dose dependent, no data is available to indicate that these impacts antitumor response.

Combination radiation and immunotherapy: Numerous radiation and immunotherapy trials are currently ongoing to assess whether radiation therapy can help stimulate the immune response and improve the response rate of various immunotherapy regimens. This is based on preclinical evidence, which suggests combination therapy may enhance immunogenicity [25]. Preclinical evidence suggests a hypofractionated regimen may be optimal to stimulate the immune response over single dose radiation regimens [26]. The potential for a synergistic effect has been demonstrated in a phase I trial of hypofractionated radiation and ipilimumab in 22 metastatic melanoma patients [27] as well as secondary analyses of prospective trials [28, 29]. One prospective study combining 35 Gy in 10 fractions with granulocyte–macrophage colony-stimulating factor in patients with stable or progressive metastatic solid tumors produced responses outside of the irradiated area in 11 of 41 accrued patients (27%) [30]. Recently, combination of RT and targeted PD-1/PD-L1 therapy are being studied in two open phase III trials looking at combination of nivolumab with RT in locally advanced NSCLC (NCT02768558) and glioblastoma (NCT02617589).

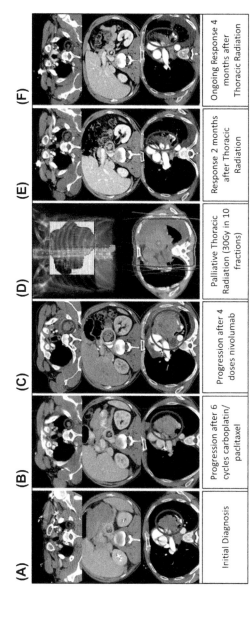

FIGURE 10.3 Axial CT images are shown, corresponding to the timeline showing therapy and disease status. Magenta circles indicate the left apical pleural-based lung mass, teal circles indicate the left retroperitoneal lymph node, and red circles indicate the dominant left anterior perihilar primary lung tumor. Disease response outside of the radiation field is seen after thoracic radiotherapy with decreased left apical lung mass and left retroperitoneal lymph node after palliative thoracic radiotherapy. The response was durable, as shown 2 and 4 months after thoracic radiation. Radiation isodose lines represent total doses of 3000cGy (red), 2000cGy (yellow), and 1000cGy (magenta) (lower panel D). *(From Ref 4, Yuan Z, Fromm A, Ahmed KA, Grass GD, Yang GQ, Oliver DE, Dilling TJ, Antonia SJ, Perez BA. Radiotherapy Rescie of a Nivolumab-Refractory Immune Response in a Patient with a PD-L1 Negative Metastatic Squamous Cell Carcinoma of the Lung. J ThoracOncol 2017;12:e135-6; with permission.)*

SITE-SPECIFIC CANCER IMMUNOTHERAPY

Melanoma

Ipilimumab

Ipilimumab is used for unresectable or metastatic melanoma. Phase III study results revealed a median overall survival (OS) of 10 and 10.1 months with ipilimumab alone and ipilimumab plus gp100 versus 6.4 months with gp100 alone with 1 and 2 year OS rates of 45.6% and 23.5% for ipilimumab alone [6]. In addition, it is approved for stage III melanoma for adjuvant therapy after surgical resection. An improved 5-year recurrence-free survival (RFS) of 41% was noted in the ipilimumab group compared with 30% in placebo group with a 5-year OS of 65% in the ipilimumab group compared with 54% in the placebo group [7].

Nivolumab

Nivolumab is approved for unresectable or metastatic melanoma after treatment with ipilimumab or a BRAF inhibitor, based on data from the phase III CheckMate-037 trial, which confirmed objective responses in 38 (32%) of the first 120 patients in the nivolumab group versus 5 (11%) of 47 patients in the investigator's choice chemotherapy group [8]. Adjuvant nivolumab had an improved RFS of 71% versus 61% in ipilimumab group with a lower rate of grade 3/4 adverse events in a phase III trial of stage IIIB, IIIC, or IV melanoma [9].

Pembrolizumab

Pembrolizumab is approved for unresectable or metastatic melanoma after KEYNOTE-006 revealed improved progression-free survival (PFS), OS, and response rates compared with ipilimumab with lower rates of grade 3 to 5 toxicity [10]. In patients with unresectable stage III or IV melanoma, pembrolizumab (at 10 mg/kg every 2 weeks or every 3 weeks) prolonged OS versus ipilimumab. Two-year survival was 55% in each pembrolizumab group versus 43% in the ipilimumab group.

Ipilimumab in Combination With Nivolumab

Nivolumab and ipilimumab are approved for unresectable or metastatic melanoma in combination based on CheckMate-067. The median OS had not been reached in the nivolumab plus ipilimumab group and was 37.6 months in the nivolumab group, compared with 20 months in the ipilimumab group. The OS rate at 3 years was 58% in the nivolumab plus ipilimumab group and 52% in the nivolumab group compared with 34% in the ipilimumab group [11].

Non—Small Cell Lung Cancer

Pembrolizumab

Pembrolizumab is approved for metastatic, high PD-L1 expressers ($\geq$50% of tumor cells) without EGFR or ALK tumor mutations in the first-line setting. This is based on KEYNOTE-024, which revealed a median PFS of 10 months with pembrolizumab versus 6 months with chemotherapy. A 6-month OS of 80% and 72% were noted with pembrolizumab and chemotherapy, respectively, with longer response durations with pembrolizumab [12]. Second-line therapy in patients with ≥ PD-L1 expression after progression on platinum-based chemotherapy and after KEYNOTE-010 revealed improved OS and toxicity compared with docetaxel [13]. It is approved for first-line therapy in metastatic NSCLC in combination with pemetrexed and carboplatin based on phase II KEYNOTE-021 study [14].

Nivolumab

Indications include metastatic NSCLC with progression on or after platinum-based chemotherapy. Patients with EGFR or ALK tumor aberrations should have progressed on prior therapy for these aberrations before starting nivolumab. This is based on two studies—CheckMate-017 in SCCa and CheckMate-057 in non-SSCa [15,16]. After 40.3 months' minimum follow-up in CheckMate 017 and 057, nivolumab continued to show an OS benefit versus docetaxel: estimated 3-year OS rates were 17% versus 8% in the pooled population with squamous or nonsquamous NSCLC. Nivolumab was generally well tolerated, with no new safety concerns identified [17].

Durvalumab

In a randomized trial (the PACIFIC study) durvalumab after chemoradiotherapy in stage III NSCLC was found to have an improved PFS of approximately 16.8 months versus 5.6 months with placebo. The response rate was higher with durvalumab than with placebo (28% vs. 16.0%), and the median duration of response was longer (73% vs. 47% of patients having an ongoing response at 18 months). The median time to death or distant metastasis was longer with durvalumab than with placebo (23 months vs. 15 months) [18].

Atezolizumab

Atezolizumab is approved for treatment of metastatic NSCLC patients whose disease progressed during or after platinum-containing chemotherapy. Patients with EGFR or ALK genomic tumor aberrations should have disease progression on FDA-approved therapy for these aberrations before receiving atezolizumab. This approval was based on two international, randomized, open-label clinical trials (OAK and POPLAR), which demonstrated consistent results in efficacy and safety for 1137 patients with NSCLC. Compared with docetaxel, treatment with atezolizumab two trials resulted in a 4.2-month and a 2.9-month improvement in OS, respectively [19,20].

Head and Neck Cancer

Nivolumab

Nivolumab is approved for recurrent or metastatic squamous cell cancer (SCC) of the head and neck after progression on or after platinum-based chemotherapy after phase III data revealed improved median OS (7.5 vs. 5 months) with a 13% versus 6% response rate with nivolumab compared with single-agent systemic therapy, respectively. Responses were noted regardless of HPV status and PD-L1 staining [21].

Pembrolizumab

Pembrolizumab is approved for recurrent or metastatic SCCa of the head and neck with disease progression during or after platinum-based chemotherapy with any level of PD-L1 expression ($\geq$1%) based on phase IB KEYNOTE-012 [22]. Overall response to treatment was observed in 18% of patients; patients with HPV+ disease experienced higher response rates compared with HPV disease, 25% versus 14%, respectively. An 18.2% overall response rate was observed in patients enrolled in an ongoing expansion cohort of KEYNOTE-012 (pembrolizumab 200 mg every 3 weeks), irrespective of PD-L1 or HPV status.

Lymphoma

Pembrolizumab

Pembrolizumab is approved for classical refractory or relapsed Hodgkin's lymphoma after three or more lines of prior therapy. The approval is based on data from the nonrandomized, open-label KEYNOTE-087 trial, in which the overall response rate (ORR) with pembrolizumab was 69%, including complete responses (CRs) in 22% and partial responses (PRs) in 47% of patients. The median duration of response was 11 months among 145 patients [23].

Nivolumab

Nivolumab is approved for classical relapsed or progressed disease after autologous stem cell transplant and brentuximab vedotin or three or more lines of systemic therapy based on two studies. The first study enrolled 23 patients and noted an objective response in 20 patients (87%), including 17% with a CR and 70% with a PR. The remaining three patients (13%) had stable disease [24]. The second study enrolled 80 patients and at a median follow-up of 8.9 months, 53 (66%) had achieved an objective response [25].

Renal Cell Carcinoma

Nivolumab and Ipilimumab

Nivolumab and ipilimumab are approved in combination for the treatment of intermediate or high risk, previously untreated advanced renal cell carcinoma. The approvals were based on CheckMate 214 (NCT02231749), a randomized open-label trial. At a median follow-up of 25.2 months in intermediate- and poor-risk patients, the 18-month OS rate was 75% with nivolumab plus ipilimumab and 60% with sunitinib [26].

Hepatocellular Carcinoma

Nivolumab

Nivolumab is approved for patients who have been previously treated with sorafenib. The approval was based on a 154-patient subgroup of CHECKMATE-040 (NCT01658878), a multicenter, open-label trial, conducted in patients with hepatocellular carcinoma (HCC) and Child—Pugh A cirrhosis who progressed on or were intolerant to sorafenib. Patients with active HBV (31%) or HCV (21%) but not those with active coinfection with HBV and HCV or with hepatitis D virus infection as well as patients without active hepatitis virus infection were enrolled. Response was observed in 42 patients (20%), including a CR in three patients; stable disease was observed in 45%, yielding a disease control rate of 64%. Responses occurred within 3 months in 69% of responders. The Kaplan–Meier median duration of response was 9.9 months; 67% of responders had an ongoing response at data cutoff. OS was 83% at 6 months and 74% at 9 months, and median OS was not reached. Progression-free survival was 37% at 6 months and 28% at 9 months [27].

Gastric Cancer

Pembrolizumab

Pembrolizumab is approved for patients with recurrent locally advanced or metastatic, gastric, or gastroesophageal junction adenocarcinoma whose tumors express PD-L1 as determined by an FDA-approved test. Patients must have had disease progression on or after two or more prior systemic therapies, including fluoropyrimidine- and platinum-containing chemotherapy and, if appropriate, HER2/neu-targeted therapy. Approval was based on the results of KEYNOTE 059 (NCT02335411), an open-label, multicenter, noncomparative, multicohort trial that enrolled 259 patients with gastric or gastroesophageal junction adenocarcinoma. Among the 259 patients, 55% (n = 143) had tumors expressing PD-L1 and either microsatellite stable, or undetermined microsatellite instability (MSI) or mismatch repair (MMR) status. The ORR in these patients was 13.3%, including a CR rate of 1.4% and a PR rate of 11.9%. The duration of response among the 19 responding patients ranged from 2.8+ to 19.4+ months. Responses were 6 months or longer in 11 (58%) patients and 12 months or longer in 5 (26%) patients [28].

Colorectal Cancer

Nivolumab

Nivolumab is approved for the treatment of patients of 12 years and older with mismatch repair deficient (dMMR) and microsatellite instability high (MSI-H) metastatic colorectal cancer (CRC) that has progressed after treatment with a fluoropyrimidine, oxaliplatin, and irinotecan. The approval was based on data from Study CA209142 (CHECKMATE 142; NCT02060188), a multicenter, open-label, single-arm study conducted in 53 patients with locally determined dMMR or MSI-H metastatic CRC who had disease progression during, after, or were intolerant to prior treatment with fluoropyrimidine-, oxaliplatin-, and irinotecan-based chemotherapy. This was a subset of the 74 patients who received at least one prior regimen for treatment of metastatic disease containing a fluoropyrimidine with oxaliplatin or irinotecan. The OS rate was 72% at 12 months and 67% at 18 months. The 12-month OS rates were 68% and 81% in groups A and B, respectively, and the 18-month OS rates were 66% and 70%, respectively. The 21 patients with the best overall response of PD who had a reduction in or stabilization of target lesions were more likely to survive at least 12 months [29].

Urothelial Carcinoma

Pembrolizumab

Pembrolizumab is approved for patients with locally advanced or metastatic urothelial carcinoma who have disease progression during or after platinum-containing chemotherapy or within 12 months of neoadjuvant or adjuvant treatment with platinum-containing chemotherapy. FDA also granted accelerated approval to pembrolizumab for patients with locally advanced or metastatic urothelial carcinoma who are not eligible for cisplatin-containing chemotherapy. The regular approval for the second-line indication was based on data from Trial KEYNOTE-045, a multicenter, randomized, active-controlled trial in patients with locally advanced or metastatic urothelial carcinoma with disease progression on or after platinum-containing chemotherapy. The accelerated approval for the first-line indication was based on data from KEYNOTE-052, a single-arm, open-label trial in 370 patients with locally advanced or metastatic urothelial carcinoma who were deemed ineligible for cisplatin-containing chemotherapy. Pembrolizumab produced a response in 24% of all patients, with 78% of responses longer than 6 months at data cutoff. The response rate was 38% in patients with a combined PD-L1 expression score ≥10% [30].

Avelumab

Avelumab is approved for patients with locally advanced or metastatic urothelial carcinoma, whose disease progressed during or after platinum-containing chemotherapy or within 12 months of neoadjuvant or adjuvant platinum-containing chemotherapy. Approval was based on data from an open-label, single-arm, multicenter study that enrolled 242 patients with locally advanced or metastatic urothelial carcinoma whose disease progressed on or after platinum-based therapy or within 12 months of a platinum-containing neoadjuvant or adjuvant chemotherapy regimen. Overall response rate was 13.3% in the 30 patients followed for at least 13 weeks, and 16.1% in those followed for at least 6 months. Median duration of response ranged from 1.4-plus to 17.4-plus months in these two groups but had not been reached in either group. Median time to response was 2 months [31].

Durvalumab

Durvalumab is approved for treatment of patients with locally advanced or metastatic urothelial carcinoma who have disease progression during or after platinum-containing chemotherapy or who have disease progression within 12 months of neoadjuvant or adjuvant treatment with platinum-containing chemotherapy. Median progression-free survival and OS were 1.5 and 18.2 months, respectively; the 1-year OS rate was 55%, as estimated by Kaplan—Meier method [32].

Nivolumab

Approval was based on a single-arm study CHECKMATE 275, treating 270 patients with locally advanced or metastatic urothelial carcinoma, who progressed during or after platinum-containing chemotherapy or progressed within 12 months of neoadjuvant or adjuvant treatment with platinum-containing chemotherapy. Nivolumab produced response in 19.6% of patients, including 28.4%, 23.8%, and 16.1% of those with PD-L1 expression of $\geq$5%, $\geq$1%, and <1%, respectively. The median duration of response was not reached [33].

Merkel Cell Carcinoma

Avelumab

Avelumab is approved for the treatment of patients of 12 years and older with metastatic MCC. Approval was based on data from an open-label, single-arm, multicenter clinical trial (JAVELIN Merkel 200 trial), demonstrating a clinically meaningful and durable ORR. All patients had histologically confirmed metastatic MCC with disease progression on or after chemotherapy administered for metastatic disease. The confirmed objective response rate was 33.0%. An estimated 74% of responses lasted $\geq$1 year, and 72.4% of responses were ongoing at data cutoff. Responses were durable, with the median DOR not yet reached, and PFS was prolonged; 1-year PFS and OS rates were 30% and 52%, respectively. Median OS was 12.9 months [34].

Chimeric Antigen Receptor T-Cell Therapy

YESCARTA (AXICABTAGENE CILOLEUCEL) AND KYMRIAH (TISAGENLECLEUCEL)

CAR-T is a form of adoptive cell transfer (ACT), using the patient's immune cells, in the case of CAR-T, T-cells that are genetically engineered typically through viral vectors or nonintegrating vectors such as plasmids and mRNA to graft a chimeric monoclonal antibody onto the tumor-specific T cell. These cells are then infused back into the patient with or without lymphodepletion or conditioning. Yescarta is approved for use in adult patients with large B-cell lymphoma after at least two other kinds of treatment have failed, including diffuse large B-cell lymphoma (DLBCL), primary mediastinal large B-cell lymphoma, high-grade B-cell lymphoma and DLBCL arising from follicular lymphoma, based on the Zuma-1 trial. The study found 111 patients to have an ORR of 82%. The median duration of response was 8 months overall and had not been achieved for complete responders [35]. Median OS was not reached; 80% of patents remained alive at 6 months.

IMMUNOTHERAPY TOXICITY

Immunotherapy regimens can have a diverse array of side effects that require special consideration both during and after treatment. These agents may have unique toxicities caused by a T-cell response that is hyperactivated against normal tissue. Checkpoint inhibition as well as vaccines and ACT cause more specific T-cell interactions directly with normal tissue causing specific organ damage while cytokines generate more diffuse and nonspecific T-cell toxicities.

Common immunotherapy toxicities are summarized in Table 10.1.

Cancer requires multimodality management. Currently optimal sequencing of immunotherapy with RT, and RT fractionation and dose are still under investigation. However, advancing personalized immunotherapy and incorporation of combinational immunotherapy with traditional therapies such as radiation therapy will improve treatment outcomes for cancer patients in the future.

TABLE 10.1 Immunotherapy causing common toxicities of the body systems.

System	Entities	Symptoms	Comments
Generalized	Flu like	Fatigue, fever, chills, weakness	
Skin	Dermatitis exfoliative, erythema multiforme, Steven Johnson syndrome, alopecia	Skin rash	Onset within few weeks of first treatment, common in anti-CTLA-4 and anti-PD-1 treatments
Eye	Uveitis, Iritis		
Neurology	Autoimmune neuropathy, demyelinating polyneuropathy, myasthenia-like syndrome		
Endocrine	Hypothyroidism, hyperthyroidism, adrenal insufficiency, hypophysitis		Median time of onset 11 weeks, can be fatal
Pulmonary	Pneumonitis, interstitial lung disease		In patients with CTLA-4 and PD-1 combination treatment, can be fatal
Gastrointestinal	Autoimmune hepatitis, colitis, enterocolitis, GI perforation		Hepatitis is worse with ipilimumab with other combination treatments
Renal	Autoimmune nephritis, renal failure		

References

Ref 1. *Grass GD, Krishna N, Kim S. The immune mechanisms of abscopal effect in radiation therapy. Curr Probl Cancer 2016;40:12.*

Ref 2. *Abuodeh Y, Venkat P, Kim S. Systematic review of case reports on the abscopal effect. Curr Probl Cancer 2016;40:25—37.*

Ref 3. *Waxweiler, et al. Biologis and their interaction with radiation: clinical radiation oncology. 4th ed. Philadelphia (PA): Elsevier; 2016. p. 80—92.*

Ref 4. *Yuan Z, Fromm A, Ahmed KA, Grass GD, Yang GQ, Oliver DE, Dilling TJ, Antonia SJ, Perez BA. Radiotherapy rescie of a nivolumab-refractory immune response in a patient with a PD-L1 negative metastatic squamous cell carcinoma of the lung. J Thorac Oncol 2017;12:e135—6.*

Ref 5. *Chen DSI, et al. Oncology meets immunology: the cancer-immunity cycle. Immunity July 25, 2013;39(1):1—10.*

Ref 6. Hodi FS, O'Day SJ, McDermott DF, et al. *Improved survival with ipilimumab in patients with metastatic melanoma.* N Engl J Med 2010;363:711–23.

Ref 7. Eggermont AM, Chiarion-Sileni V, Grob JJ, et al. *Prolonged survival in stage III melanoma with ipilimumab adjuvant therapy.* N Engl J Med 2016;375:1845–55.

Ref 8. Weber JS, D'Angelo SP, Minor D, et al. *Nivolumab versus chemotherapy in patients with advanced melanoma who progressed after anti-CTLA-4 treatment (CheckMate 037): a randomised, controlled, open-label, phase 3 trial.* Lancet Oncol 2015;16:375–84.

Ref 9. Weber J, Mandala M, Del Vecchio M, et al. *Adjuvant nivolumab versus ipilimumab in resected stage III or IV melanoma.* N Engl J Med 2017;377:1824–35.

Ref 10. Robert C, Schachter J, Long GV, et al. *Pembrolizumab versus ipilimumab for advanced melanoma: final overall survival results of a multicentre, randomised, open-label phase 3 study (KEYNOTE-006).* Lancet 21 October 2017;390(10105):1853–62.

Ref 11. Wolchok JD, Chiarion-Sileni V, Gonzalez R, et al. *Overall survival with combined nivolumab and ipilimumab in advanced melanoma.* N Engl J Med 2017;377:1345–56.

Ref 12. Reck M, Rodriguez-Abreu D, Robinson AG, et al. *Pembrolizumab versus chemotherapy for PD-L1-positive non-small-cell lung cancer.* N Engl J Med 2016;375:1823–33.

Ref 13. Herbst RS, Baas P, Kim DW, et al. *Pembrolizumab versus docetaxel for previously treated, PD-L1-positive, advanced non-small-cell lung cancer (KEYNOTE-010): a randomised controlled trial.* Lancet 2016;387:1540–50.

Ref 14. Langer CJ, Gadgeel SM, Borghaei H, et al. *Carboplatin and pemetrexed with or without pembrolizumab for advanced, non-squamous non-small-cell lung cancer: a randomised, phase 2 cohort of the open-label KEYNOTE-021 study.* Lancet Oncol 2016;17:1497–508.

Ref 15. Borghaei H, Paz-Ares L, Horn L, et al. *Nivolumab versus docetaxel in advanced non-squamous non-small-cell lung cancer.* N Engl J Med 2015;373:1627–39.

Ref 16. Brahmer J, Reckamp KL, Baas P, et al. *Nivolumab versus docetaxel in advanced squamous-cell non-small-cell lung cancer.* N Engl J Med 2015;373:123–35.

Ref 17. Vokes EE, et al. *Nivolumab versus docetaxel in previously treated advanced non-small-cell lung cancer (CheckMate 017 and CheckMate 057): 3-year update and outcomes in patients with liver metastases.* Ann Oncol April 1, 2018;29(4):959–65.

Ref 18. Antonia SJ, Villegas A, Daniel D, et al. *Durvalumab after chemoradiotherapy in stage III non-small-cell lung cancer.* N Engl J Med 2017;377:1919–29.

Ref 19. Rittmeyer A, Barlesi F, Waterkamp D, et al. *Atezolizumab versus docetaxel in patients with previously treated non-small-cell lung cancer (OAK): a phase 3, open-label, multicentre randomised controlled trial.* Lancet 2017;389:255–65.

Ref 20. Fehrenbacher L, Spira A, Ballinger M, et al. *Atezolizumab versus docetaxel for patients with previously treated non-small-cell lung cancer (POPLAR): a multicentre, open-label, phase 2 randomised controlled trial.* Lancet 2016;387:1837–46.

Ref 21. Ferris RL, Blumenschein Jr G, Fayette J, et al. *Nivolumab for recurrent squamous-cell carcinoma of the head and neck.* N Engl J Med 2016;375:1856–67.

Ref 22. *Seiwert TY, Burtness B, Mehra R, et al. Safety and clinical activity of pembrolizumab for treatment of recurrent or metastatic squamous cell carcinoma of the head and neck (KEYNOTE-012): an open-label, multicentre, phase 1b trial. Lancet Oncol 2016;17:956—65.*

Ref 23. *Chen R, Zinzani PL, Fanale MA, et al. Phase II study of the efficacy and safety of pembrolizumab for relapsed/refractory classic Hodgkin lymphoma. J Clin Oncol 2017;35:2125—32.*

Ref 24. *Ansell SM, Lesokhin AM, Borrello I, et al. PD-1 blockade with nivolumab in relapsed or refractory Hodgkin's lymphoma. N Engl J Med 2015;372:311—9.*

Ref 25. *Younes A, Santoro A, Shipp M, et al. Nivolumab for classical Hodgkin's lymphoma after failure of both autologous stem-cell transplantation and brentuximab vedotin: a multicentre, multicohort, single-arm phase 2 trial. Lancet Oncol 2016;17:1283—94.*

Ref 26. *Motzer R, et al. Nivolumab plus ipilimumab versus sunitinib in advanced renal-cell carcinoma. N Engl J Med April 5, 2018;2018(378):1277—90.*

Ref 27. *El-Khoueiry AB, Sangro B, Yau T, et al. Nivolumab in patients with advanced hepatocellular carcinoma (CheckMate 040): an open-label, non-comparative, phase 1/2 dose escalation and expansion trial. Lancet 2017;389:2492—502.*

Ref 28. *Fuchs CS, Doi T, Jang RW-J, et al. KEYNOTE-059 cohort 1: efficacy and safety of pembrolizumab (pembro) monotherapy in patients with previously treated advanced gastric cancer. J Clin Oncol 2017;35. abstr 4003.*

Ref 29. *Overman MJ, Bergamo F, McDermott R, et al. Nivolumab in patients with DNA mismatch repair-deficient/microsatellite instability-high (dMMR/MSI-H) metastatic colorectal cancer (mCRC): long-term survival according to prior line of treatment from CheckMate-142. San Francisco (CA): Presented at: 2018 Gastrointestinal Cancers Symposium; January 18—20, 2018. Abstract 554.*

Ref 30. *Balar AV, Castellano D, O'Donnell PH, et al. First-line pembrolizumab in cisplatin-ineligible patients with locally advanced and unresectable or metastatic urothelial cancer (KEYNOTE-052): a multicentre, single-arm, phase 2 study. Lancet Oncol September 26, 2017.*

Ref 31. *Patel MR, Ellerton J, Infante JR, et al. Avelumab in metastatic urothelial carcinoma after platinum failure (JAVELIN Solid Tumor): pooled results from two expansion cohorts of the open-label, phase 1 trial. Lancet Oncol 2018;19:51—64.*

Ref 32. *Powles T, et al. Efficacy and safety of durvalumab in locally advanced or metastatic urothelial carcinoma: updated results from a phase 1/2 open-label study. JAMA Oncol September 14, 2017;3(9):e172411. https://doi.org/10.1001/jamaoncol.2017.2411. Epub 2017 Sep. 14.*

Ref 33. *Sharma P, Retz M, Siefker-Radtke A, et al. Nivolumab in metastatic urothelial carcinoma after platinum therapy (CheckMate 275): a multicentre, single-arm, phase 2 trial. Lancet Oncol 2017;18:312—22.*

Ref 34. *Kaufman HL, Russell J, Hamid O, Bhatia S, Terheyden P, D'Angelo SP, et al. Updated efficacy of avelumab in patients with previously treated metastatic Merkel cell carcinoma after ≥1 year of follow-up: JAVELIN Merkel 200, a phase 2 clinical trial. J Immuno Ther Cancer 2018;6:7.*

Ref 35. *Locke FLNS, Bartlett NL, Lekakis LJ, Miklos D, Jacobson CA, Braunschweig I, Oluwole O, Siddiqi T, Lin Y, Timmerman J, Friedberg JW, Bot A, Rossi J, Navale L, Jiang Y, Aycock J, Elias M, Wiezorek J. Go WY Primary results from ZUMA-1: a pivotal trial of axicabtagene ciloleucel (axicel; KTE-C19) in patients with refractory aggressive non-Hodgkin lymphoma (NHL) [abstract]. In: Proceedings of the American association for cancer research annual meeting 2017; 2017 Apr 1—5, vol. 77. Washington (DC) Philadelphia (PA): AACR; Cancer Res; 2017. Abstract nr CT019.*

Ref 36. *Weichselbaum RR, Liang H, Deng L, Fu YX. Radiotherapy and immunotherapy: a beneficial liaison? Nat Rev Clin Oncol 2017;14:365—79.*

Ref 37. *Dewan MZ, Galloway AE, Kawashima N, et al. Fractionated but not single-dose radiotherapy induces an immune-mediated abscopal effect when combined with anti-CTLA-4 antibody. Clin Cancer Res 2009;15:5379—88.*

Ref 38. *Twyman-Saint Victor C, Rech AJ, Maity A, et al. Radiation and dual checkpoint blockade activate non-redundant immune mechanisms in cancer. Nature 2015;520:373—7.*

Ref 39. *Ahmed KA, Stallworth DG, Kim Y, et al. Clinical outcomes of melanoma brain metastases treated with stereotactic radiation and anti-PD-1 therapy. Ann Oncol 2015.*

Ref 40. *Shaverdian N, Lisberg AE, Bornazyan K, et al. Previous radiotherapy and the clinical activity and toxicity of pembrolizumab in the treatment of non-small-cell lung cancer: a secondary analysis of the KEYNOTE-001 phase 1 trial. Lancet Oncol 2017;18:895—903.*

Ref 41. *Golden EB, Chhabra A, Chachoua A, et al. Local radiotherapy and granulocyte-macrophage colony-stimulating factor to generate abscopal responses in patients with metastatic solid tumours: a proof-of-principle trial. Lancet Oncol 2015;16:795—803.*

11

Radiation and Combined Modality Therapy

Radiation therapy is a highly effective, locoregional treatment modality for many cancers. Recent advances in cancer treatment involve multimodality management, i.e., surgery, chemotherapy, and radiation treatments. Combining any of these three modalities improves cancer cure rates and/or decreases treatment-related side effects. The following is a brief description of the optimization of radiation therapy with surgery and chemotherapy and its application in clinical radiation oncology.

RADIATION THERAPY

The mainstay of radiation is photon therapy. As photons travel through a material, they release atomic orbital electrons along their path. These freed electrons, called primary electrons, cause most of the energy deposition that occurs in therapeutic photon beams. Photon interactions with matter are a two-step process:

- Energy transfer and Kerma: An incident photon interacts with an atomic orbital electron in of the material through some photon interaction mechanism (such as photoelectric, Compton, or pair production). During these interactions, photons will transfer some or all of their kinetic energy to an atomic orbital electron. This orbital electron can then gain enough kinetic energy to leave the atomic orbital and become a primary electron.
- Energy absorption and absorbed dose: The primary electrons that are released in the energy transfer process then interact with other atomic orbital electrons and release ions and excited atoms along irregular tracks. In addition, primary electrons with enough energy may cause secondary tracks of their own called delta rays. The energy from electrons deposited at the site of interaction is the basis of the absorbed dose.

Free electrons released by photons, react with the cells altering the chemical properties of the cell causing biological damage by indirect and/or direct effects:

- Indirect effects occur when a nontarget material, typically H_2O, is ionized and free radicals are produced that diffuse and damage a critical target, such as DNA.

Fundamentals of Radiation Oncology
https://doi.org/10.1016/B978-0-12-814128-1.00011-8

About two-thirds of all biological damage results from the indirect action with low linear energy transfer (LET) photons but decreases to nearly zero with high-LET radiation such as protons and neutrons.

• Direct effects occur when atoms of the critical target, such as DNA, are directly ionized by radiation, causing damage. About one-third of all biological damage results from direct action with low-LET photons but increases to nearly 100% with high-LET radiations.

DNA is the critical target for radiation-induced damages leading to cell killing [1−3]. DNA lesions can be single-strand breaks (SSBs) involving one sugar/phosphate backbone of the DNA molecule. Most of these breaks are effectively repaired with no long-term damage to the cell. The DNA lesions can also be double-strand breaks (DSBs) involving both backbones of the DNA molecule. Half of these breaks are effectively repaired. If the repair does not happen, then damage to the cell may lead to cell death from radiation.

In general, 45−50 Gy of radiation can provide excellent local control for subclinical disease. However, it is clear from Table 11.1 that optimal local control of macroscopic squamous cell cancer and adenocarcinoma requires high doses of radiation up to 100 Gy. Such high dose of radiation would cause significant morbidity for patients and is prohibitive. As such, the goal of radiation therapy is to increase the radio toxicity of the tumor while minimizing the normal tissue complication, otherwise known as

TABLE 11.1 Probability of Cancer Control as a Function of Radiation Dose and Tumor Sizes [4,5]

Dose (Gy)	Squamous Cell Cancer of the Upper Respiratory and Digestive Tracts	Cancer Control (%)	Adenocarcinoma of the Breast	Cancer Control (%)
50 Gy	Subclinical	>90%	Subclinical	>90%
	T1 lesions of nasopharynx	50%		
	2−3 cm neck nodes	50%		
60 Gy	T1 lesions of pharynx and larynx	80%−90%		
	T3, T4 lesions of tonsillar fossa	∼50%		
	1−3 cm neck nodes	∼90%		
	3−5 cm neck nodes	∼70%		
70 Gy	T1 lesions of tonsillar fossa and subglottic larynx	80%−90%	Clinically positive axillary nodes 2.5−3 cm	90%
	T3, T4 lesions of tonsillar fossa	∼80%		
70−80 Gy			2−3 cm primary	65%
			>5 cm primary	30%
80−90 Gy			>5 cm primary	56%
80−100 Gy			>5−15 cm primary	75%

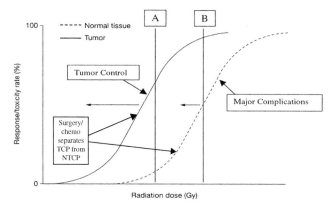

FIGURE 11.1 Therapeutic ratio. Sigmoidal curves of tumor control and complications. Line A shows dose for tumor control with minimum complications; line B shows dose for maximum tumor control with significant complications. *Modified from Lawrence RC, et al. Combined modality treatment of cancer. In: Introduction to clinical radiation oncology. 3rd ed.; 1998. pp. 467−86, Seiwer T, et al. The concurrent chemoradiation paradigm—general principles. Nat Clin Pract Oncol 4:86−100, © 2007 with permission from Wolters Kluwer Health and Perez CA, Brady LW. Biologic basis of radiation therapy: principles and practice of radiation oncology 6th ed.; 2013. pp. 61−88. Baltimore (MD): Lippincott Williams & Wilkins, Coia LR, Moylan DJ. Introduction to clinical radiation oncology. 3rd ed., Fig. 2.4, p. 46, © 1998, with permission.*

therapeutic ratio [3]. As the treatment dose increases, tumor control improves but normal tissue complications also increase. The distance between the two curves shown in Fig. 11.1 is the therapeutic ratio.

Combined modality treatments of radiation with surgery and/or with chemotherapy for cancer treatments can improve the cure and/or optimize the treatment-related side effects. Hence, the rationale for combined modality treatment is to improve the therapeutic ratio of the cancer treatment by separating the tumor control and the major complications curves depicted in Fig. 11.1.

SURGERY COMBINED WITH RADIATION THERAPY

Like radiation therapy, surgery is a locoregional modality. Surgical biopsies not only help to diagnose cancer but also help staging of the cancer. Surgical resection is the mainstay of treatment for most solid cancers. Surgery can be curative or palliative. Post-operative surgical margins are classified as the following:

- R0—no cancer cells seen microscopically at the resection margin
- R1—cancer cells present microscopically at the resection margin
- R2—gross examination by the naked eye shows tumor tissue present at the resection margin

The extent of surgical margin is important as the risk of tumor locoregional recurrence, and eventual distant metastases can be a function of post-op margin status.

Radiation therapy can be combined with surgery preoperatively, intraoperatively, or postoperatively as below:

1. Preoperative radiation—before surgery, the tissue vascularization and oxygenation is intact. Therefore, the cells are more sensitive to radiation therapy, requiring lower doses of radiation. The goals of preoperative radiation treatment can be downsizing the bulky tumor for easier and margin negative resectability and/or minimizing the risk of surgical bed tumor cell implants by decreasing viable tumor cells. Often pre-op RT is combined with chemotherapy as well. Bulky head and neck cancer, esophageal cancer, pancreatic cancer, and soft tissue sarcoma are treated with preoperative radiation.
2. Intraoperative radiation—this is a relatively new technology of delivering a single large dose of radiation therapy directly to the tumor bed during the surgery. This technique allows high dose of radiation delivered directly and precisely to the tumor bed, thus minimizing radiation to the surrounding critical structures as they are displaced from the direct path of the radiation during the intraoperative radiation treatment. Intraoperative radiation technique is used to treat brain cancer, breast cancer, retroperitoneal sarcoma, and pancreatic cancer.
3. Postoperative radiation—many cancers require postoperative radiation treatment. This is because high risk of post-op locoregional recurrences due to multiple lymph node metastases, extra capsular extension of the lymph node metastases, regional lymph nodes at risk of metastases, high-grade tumors, close or positive surgical margins, and gross residual disease. Postoperatively, the vascularization is disrupted, and the tissue may be hypoxic. As such postoperative radiation requires higher dose. Post-op RT can be combined with chemotherapy to better sterilize microscopic and/or treat macroscopic disease. Postoperative radiation treatment is used for high-grade primary or metastatic brain cancer, bulky head and neck cancer, breast cancer as a part of breast conservation management, locally advanced endometrial cancer, and soft tissue sarcoma.

Side Effects of Combined Modality of Radiation and Surgery

In general, combining radiation and surgery can cause delayed wound healing or non-healing, scar tissue formation at the surgical bed and tissue necrosis. For example, post-op RT for primary brain tumor may cause necrosis requiring further neurosurgical intervention, post-op RT for breast cancer may cause upper extremity lymph edema, and post-op RT for endometrial or cervical cancer can cause bowel adhesions, fistula formation, and bowel obstruction. Therefore, proper planning is required when radiation and surgery are combined to minimize side effects. The use of modern techniques of radiation such as Intensity modulated radiation therapy (IMRT) and Image guided radiation therapy (IGRT) decreases high dose of radiation to the surrounding normal tissues, thus minimizing the risk of surgical complications. Postradiation tissues must be carefully operated to minimize large incision size, and proper hemostasis is required. Medications that improve peripheral blood flows such as Pentoxifylline and hyperbaric treatments may improve or reduce the above side effects of combined radiation and surgical treatments.

CHEMOTHERAPY COMBINED WITH RADIATION THERAPY

Combining chemotherapy with radiation therapy is a common practice in cancer management. This improves locoregional and distant control of the cancer. It also improves the therapeutic ratio by the following mechanisms [6]:

1. Spatial cooperation—chemotherapeutic agent and radiation therapy are given separately to different anatomic sites. For example, radiation therapy for locoregional disease and chemotherapy for distant micrometastasic disease.
2. Toxicity independence—chemotherapy and radiation have different side effects thus making combined modality treatment less toxic.
3. Normal tissue protection—drugs with a radioprotective effect of the irradiated normal tissue may allow higher dose of radiation for cancer treatment.
4. Radiosensitivity—with this mechanism, chemotherapy agents enhance cytotoxic effects of the radiation therapy. The mechanisms may include increased radiation damage, inhibition of the DNA repair process, cell cycle interference (cytokinetic cooperation and synchronization), enhanced activity against hypoxic cells and radiotherapy enhancement by preventing repopulation.

Chemotherapy can be combined with radiation therapy sequentially, concurrently, or alternatively as below:

- Sequential treatment: Chemotherapy is followed by radiation therapy, or radiation therapy is followed by chemotherapy. Sequential treatments reduce large tumor mass by the first modality helping increase the efficacy of the second modality to control the disease. In breast cancer and Hodgkin's lymphoma, chemotherapy is followed by radiation therapy.
- Concurrent treatment: Chemotherapy and radiation therapy are given together. Chemotherapy may be given once a week or every 3—4 weeks, whereas radiation therapy is given daily. Concurrent chemotherapy with RT enhances radiosensitivity and treats primary disease and distant disease simultaneously. Many cancer sites use concurrent chemoRT, such as head and neck cancer, lung cancer, esophageal cancer, cervical cancer, and anal cancer.
- Alternating treatment: Chemotherapy and radiation therapy are given on alternating weeks, such as every 1—3 weeks, with no concurrent treatments. This may reduce side effects while allowing delivery of full dose of each modality. Recurrent head and neck cancer treatments use alternating chemotherapy and radiation therapy.

Side Effects of Combined Modality Radiation and Chemotherapy

Chemotherapy given with radiation can increase both acute and late toxicities. This is because combining two cytotoxic treatments causes increase volume of normal cells to be damaged. This is most evident during the concurrent chemoRT. As such combining chemotherapy and radiation may require to reduce chemotherapy dose. Side effects from combining chemotherapy with RT can be increased fatigue, lowering of blood counts, cardiac dysfunction, cognitive dysfunction, and second malignancies. Proper patient selection, such as avoiding combined chemoRT for poor performance status patients or patients with comorbidities, help reduce the side effects. Optimizing the sequence and schedule of the chemotherapy and RT may reduce side effects. Using molecular and genetic analysis of the tumor, such as oncotype Dx®, help avoid chemotherapy for breast cancer patients with lower scores thus avoid toxicities of chemotherapy. Studies are ongoing to test if p16+ oropharyngeal cancer patients can have reduced RT dose thus minimizing RT side effects as well. The use of modern techniques of radiation such as IMRT and IGRT decreases high dose of radiation to the surrounding normal tissues, thus minimizing the risk of chemoRT complications. Also optimizing RT dose fractionation such as hypofractionation, and RT techniques such as employing SRS technique or proton beam therapy can help control the acute and late side effects of the chemoRT treatments.

In addition proper supportive care involving proper nutrition, adequate hydration, anti-nausea, anti-pain and anti-depression management, is essential to minimize and mitigate side effects of the combination of chemotherapy and radiation treatments for cancer patients.

SITE-SPECIFIC CHEMOTHERAPEUTIC AGENTS USED IN COMBINATION WITH RADIOTHERAPY: MECHANISMS OF ACTION AND SIDE EFFECTS. FIG. 11.2

Primary Brain Cancer

- Carmustine (BCNU): Alkylates and cross-links DNA and carbamoylates proteins. Not cell cycle—dependent. Can cross the blood—brain barrier. Other agents of this class include CCNU. Toxicity includes myelosuppression.

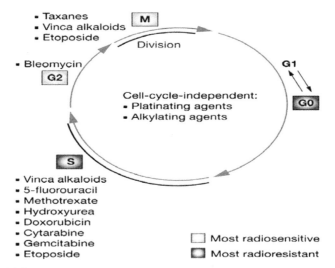

FIGURE 11.2 Chemotherapy agents acting on radiosensitive and radioresistant phases of the cell cycle [7].

- Temozolamide: An oral alkylating agent. Used in gliomas with efficacy related to the methylation state of the MGMT gene (if methylated, temozolamide is more effective). Side effects include neutropenia, anemia, thrombocytopenia, and constipation.

Head and Neck Cancer

- Cisplatin: Binds to DNA causing intra-/interstrand cross-links. Side effects include nephrotoxicity (ATN), ototoxicity, nausea, vomiting, and neurotoxicity (neuropathy).
- Docetaxel: Inhibits microtubule disassembly causing G2/M arrest. Other members of the taxane class include paclitaxel, navelobine, and eribulin. Toxicities include myelosuppression.
- Fluorouracil: Pyrimidine analogue that is metabolized to F-UMP. F-UMP is incorporated into RNA and DNA, inhibiting RNA processing (faulty translation of proteins) and DNA replication blocking cell growth. Also blocks thymidylate synthetase, reducing the availability of TTP (thymidine triphosphate), necessary for DNA synthesis. Toxicities include myelosuppression GI side effects, mucositis, oral ulcers, and diarrhea.

Breast Cancer

- Cyclophosphamide: Nitrogen mustard—alkylating agents which can cause DNA cross-links. Other agents of this class include ifosfamide. Toxicities include hemorrhagic cystitis, myelosuppression, and nausea and vomiting.
- Docetaxel: Inhibits microtubule disassembly causing G2/M arrest. Another member of the taxane class is paclitaxel. Toxicities include myelosuppression.
- Doxorubicin: DNA intercalator, which interacts with topoisomerase II, blocking DNA replication/repair, and RNA and protein synthesis. Also produces free radicals. Side effects include cardiotoxicity (which has memory lasting years such that it and radiation given years after chemotherapy).
- Methotrexate: Inhibitor of DHFR gene, which results in inhibition of purine and thymidylate synthetase inhibition of DNA and RNA synthesis. Can cause stomatitis, leucopenia and nausea.

Lung Cancer

- Carboplatin: Binds to DNA causing intra- and interstrand cross-links. Side effects include nephrotoxicity, ototoxicity, nausea, vomiting, and neurotoxicity.
- Docetaxel: Inhibits microtubule disassembly causing G2/M arrest. Other members of the taxol family include paclitaxel. Toxicities include myelosuppression.
- Etoposide (VP-16): Inhibits topoisomerase II, causing accumulation of SSBs and DSBs. Acts primarily at S/G2. Can cause myelosuppression.

Gastrointestinal Cancer

- Fluorouracil: Pyrimidine analogue that is metabolized to F-UMP. F-UMP, which is incorporated into RNA, inhibits RNA processing and cell growth. Also blocks thymidylate synthetase, reducing the availability of TTP, necessary for DNA synthesis. Capecitabine is an oral 5-FU precursor. Toxicities include myelosuppression and mucositis.
- Gemcitabine: Competes for incorporation into DNA, thus blocking DNA one nucleotide past the drug. Also inhibits ribonucleotide reductase. Kills at S phase and blocks at G1/S. Side effects include anemia, thrombocytopenia, and nausea/vomiting.
- Oxaloplatin: Binds to DNA causing intra/interstrand cross-links. Side effects include nephrotoxicity, ototoxicity, nausea, vomiting, and neurotoxicity.
- Irinotecan (CPT-11): Interacts with topoisomerase I, preventing the relegation of SSB, thus increasing the incidence of DSB. Can cause diarrhea and immunosuppression. Class includes topotecan.
- Mitomycin C: Binds to DNA leading to cross-linking and inhibition of DNA synthesis and function. Mitomycin is cell cycle phase-nonspecific. Side effects include bone marrow damage, lung fibrosis, and renal damage.

Lymphoma

- Bleomycin: Binds DNA and generates free radicals, promoting scission reaction between base pairs. Dose-limiting toxicity is lung fibrosis.
- DTIC (dacarbazine): Inhibits DNA synthesis by its action as a purine analogue and interaction with SH (sulfhydryl) groups. Common side effects include loss of appetite, vomiting, low white blood cell count, and low platelets.
- Doxorubicin: Intercalates into DNA, interacting with topoisomerase II, blocking DNA replication/repair, and RNA and protein synthesis. Also produces free radicals. Side effects include cardiotoxicity.
- Vinblastine: Binds tubulin preventing microtubule formation. Results in M phase arrest. Side effects include peripheral neuropathy and bone marrow suppression.
- Vincristine: Vincristine binds to the microtubular proteins of the mitotic spindle, leading to crystallization of microtubules and mitotic arrest or cell death. Side effects include hair loss, constipation, difficulty walking, headaches, neuropathic pain, lung damage, and/or low blood white cells.

The most significant advancement in cancer treatment in the past 25 years is the recognition that the optimum cancer treatment outcome requires multimodality management involving surgery, chemotherapy, and radiation therapy. With advances in targeted therapy and immunotherapy, incorporation of new multimodality treatments is being implemented. Combined modality therapy increases locoregional control and overall survival for cancer patients and also decreases treatment related side effects.

References

Ref 1. Gunderson LL, Tepper JE. The biologic basis of radiation oncology: clinical radiation oncology. 4th ed. Philadelphia: Elsevier; 2016. p. 2—40.

Ref 2. Hall EJ, Giaccia AJ. Radiobiology for the radiologist. 6th ed. 2006.

Ref 3. Perez CA, Brady LW. Biologic basis of radiation therapy: principles and practice of radiation oncology. 6th ed. Baltimore (MD): Lippincott Williams & Wilkins; 2013. p. 61—88.

Ref 4. Fletcher GH, et al. The interplay of radiocurability and tolerance in the irradiation of human cancer. J Radiol Electrol Med Nucl May 1975;56(5):383—400.

Ref 5. Lawrence RC, et al. Combined modality treatment of cancer. In: Introduction to Clinical Radiation Oncology. 3rd ed. 1998. p. 467—86.

Ref 6. Steel GG, Peckham MJ. Exploitable mechanisms in combined radiotherapy chemotherapy: the concept of additivity. Int J Radiat Oncol Biol Phys 1979;5:85—91.

Ref 7. Tanguy YS. The concurrent chemoradiation paradigm-general principles. Nat Clin Pract Oncol 2007;4(2):86—100.

—

Statistical Considerations in Radiation Oncology

DEFINITION OF STATISTICAL TERMS

Mean and Mode

- The mean (average) is the arithmetic sum of observations, divided by the number of observations.
- The mode is the value that occurs most frequently among a set of numbers. There may be multiple modes in a sample. Bimodal refers to a distribution of data that cluster around two distinct values. Certain cancer incidences, such as craniopharyngiomas, are bimodal with respect to age at onset (i.e., children and older adults).

Sample

Inferential statistics is the process of identifying a representative and manageable group of research subjects to infer quantitative attributes to a larger population. A sample, then, should ideally mirror the research population of interest. A sampling frame is the accessible population for research, which may differ from the idealized population of interest. Bias is likely to contaminate research in which the sampling frame differs substantially from the desired population.

Variance

- Variance is a statistic on the squared unit scale that measures the dispersion of a data set. Small variances indicate predictable, repeatable experiments, whereas large variances indicate scattered, unexpected outcomes with repeated sampling.
- The sample variance is calculated by the following [1]:

$$S^2 = \frac{\sum (X - M)^2}{N - 1}$$

Fundamentals of Radiation Oncology
https://doi.org/10.1016/B978-0-12-814128-1.00012-X

where X is each observation in the sample, M is the mean of the sample, and N is the number of observations in the sample.

Standard Deviation

- Standard deviation is the square root of variance as shown below [1,2].

$$S = \sqrt{\frac{\sum (X - M)^2}{N - 1}}$$

- The standard deviation is on the same unit scale as the sample. Like variance, small standard deviations indicate that the data are repeatable and predictable when the experiment is conducted again.

Confidence Intervals

The confidence interval (CI) is an estimated set of boundaries that likely include the population mean for a specified degree of probability. CIs are generally reported at the 95% level, that is, upon repeated sampling, 95% of the bounds calculated will include the population mean.

CI is calculated by the following [2]:

$$95\% \, CI = M - \left(1.96 \times s \Big/ \sqrt{(N)}\right) \text{ to } M + \left(1.96 \times s \Big/ \sqrt{(N)}\right),$$

where M is the sample mean, $s \big/ \sqrt{(N)}$ is the sample standard deviation divided by the square root of the sample size N. Note that $s \big/ \sqrt{(N)}$ is referred to as the standard error of the mean, abbreviated SEM, often reported as error bounds. It is common to see "M±SEM" in descriptive statistical tables in journal articles.

Null and Alternative Hypotheses

In inferential statistics, sample data are extrapolated to the research population. It is rare to observe an entire population. In practice, assumptions made about the data from populations include how the values are spread and where the observations tend to occur. Samples allow refining assumptions to make them more reasonable. However, to draw conclusions about the population from samples, the scientific method suggests taking an objective approach.

- Hypothesis testing in statistics allows an investigator to decide between two mutually exclusive choices based only on data. By crafting the decision-making as objectively as possible, there is less risk of bias or incorrect conclusions. The two mutually exclusive choices are called the null hypothesis and the alternative hypothesis.

- The null hypothesis is that which would be due to chance alone and assumes that there is no association between experimental outcomes that cannot be explained by pure randomness.
- The alternative hypothesis is that which is unlikely to be due to chance alone. There may be an association between experimental outcomes.

Statistical inference involves specifying and refining these two choices so that they may be applied directly to the outcomes in a given experiment.

p-value

The P-value may be considered as a measure of evidence or likelihood. It is a statistic used for decision-making in inferential statistics. Its utility in interpreting the results of a hypothesis test stems from the idea that it is loosely related to a probability statement about the null hypothesis. The P-value is derived from observed data and assumptions made about the population. If the P-value is small (meaning close to zero), one may conclude that there is evidence suggesting that the null hypothesis is unlikely.

Unfortunately, P-values are often misunderstood and misused. The P-value contains no intrinsic information. For example, consider a population on which two experiments are performed. A large experiment with a small effect size may have the same P-value as a small experiment with a large effect size in the same population. Some investigators have published in peer-reviewed papers the misinterpretation that P-values between 0.05 and 0.20 constitute a "trend," although statements like these have no statistical basis.

Type I (α) and Type II (β) Error

- Type I error occurs when the null hypothesis is true yet rejected.
- Type II error occurs when the null hypothesis is false yet accepted.
- Minimizing the chances of either error is ideal. Large sample sizes and efficient study designs directly reduce type II errors.
- In general, a value of 0.05 is chosen for type I (α) error and a value of 0.2 or less is chosen for type II (β) error.

Power

The power of the study is the probability of rejecting the null hypothesis if indeed false. Power is defined as $1 - \beta$. Biomedical studies with power less than 80% are of questionable regarding statistical significance.

Parametric and Nonparametric Methods

A parametric method refers to the use of statistical models that assume explicitly mathematical properties (such as the shape function, location, and dispersion) of the population of interest. On the other hand, when one uses a nonparametric method, fewer assumptions regarding the population's mathematical structure are made.

A familiar example of a parametric test is the t-test. The t-test analyzes differences between two sample set means. The t-test assumes that the populations have a Gaussian (normal) distribution. The t-test has a nonparametric analog. The Wilcoxon test also analyzes differences in two sample means, but it does not require that the data be sampled from a Gaussian distribution.

Using a parametric test for data that are not sampled from the assumed distribution results in biased tests, and those results (especially the P-value) should be considered questionable or uninterpretable. Despite requiring larger sample sizes to retain the same inferential power as parametric tests, nonparametric tests are more robust and less biased than applying an inappropriate parametric test or method. With the advent of computers, nonparametric methods are gaining popularity in biomedical research and should be considered when such methods are available.

Sensitivity, Specificity, and Predictive Value

The sensitivity is the proportion of patients with the disease who are correctly identified by a diagnostic test. The specificity is the proportion of patients without the disease who are correctly identified by a diagnostic test.

The positive predictive value is the proportion of patients with a positive test result who have the disease. The negative predictive value is the proportion of patients with a negative test result who do not have the disease.

True positives and negatives are determined by an irrefutable standard. Tests with less than or equal to 50% sensitivity are generally not useful because they have the same or less utility than the random flip of a coin. A 2×2 table (Table 12.1) of a diagnostic test result is used to calculate the sensitivity, specificity, and predictive values.

Clinical Trials: Phase I, II, III, IV

Phase I trials use the preclinical (i.e., animal studies) dose estimates. In a phase I trial, the first patients are enrolled with the objective of estimating a tolerable dose that is not overly toxic in humans. A common design for a phase I trial is the "$3 + 3$" dose

TABLE 12.1   A 2×2 Table Showing Definitions of Sensitivity, Specificity, and Predictive Value

Diagnostic Test Result	Disease Present	Disease Absent
Positive	a (true positive)	b
Negative	c	d (true negative)

Sensitivity $= \dfrac{a}{a+c}$

Specificity $= \dfrac{d}{b+d}$

Positive predictive value $= \dfrac{a}{a+b}$

Negative predictive value $= \dfrac{d}{d+c}$

escalation scheme wherein cohorts of three patients are assigned to ever-increasing doses until excessive toxicity is observed. The sample size for a phase I trial is generally less than 20 subjects.

Phase II trials use the dosing scheme derived from the phase I study. A phase II trial assesses the agent's efficacy in humans. Phase II studies may be blinded, comparative, randomized trials, or single-agent open-label trials. Phase II objectives are to assess efficacy in a small number of patients and to prepare for a pivotal trial, if justified. In oncology, it is common to use response rate as an endpoint for phase II trials, particularly for diseases with multiyear expected survival. The sample size for a phase II trial is often between 40 and 100 subjects.

Phase III trials are large, randomized pivotal trials in which a new therapeutic agent is compared with an accepted standard, either alone or in combination. Subjects are randomized to one of the arms, often with randomization depending on their geographic location and their disease characteristics. These trials are generally multicenter studies with endpoints such as overall survival or progression-free survival. Randomization and day-to-day trial administration is handled by a single center or a cooperative group, such as Radiation Therapy Oncology Group (RTOG). The sample size for a phase III trial is often well over 300 subjects. An incomplete list of currently open RTOG trials is given in Table 12.2 [3].

Phase IV trials are used for long-term surveillance of a drug or a device after it has regulatory approval for public use. These trials are also known as postmarking or confirmatory trials. The time period for phase IV trials is for 2 years or more to detect any long-term adverse effects of the drug or the device for its use.

Survival Analysis

- Life table method: This is a table of the proportion of patients surviving over time. This method is useful for data when the exact times of death are not known, although it is rarely used outside of epidemiological research.
- Kaplan—Meier method: This is a plot of the cumulative probability of survival of patients, of which the survival estimates are recalculated whenever there is an event. It accommodates censoring more efficiently and intuitively than the life table method.

Retrospective Chart Reviews

Retrospective chart reviews assemble data from patients who have finished their course of treatment and are useful for quality control and hypothesis-generating studies. They are also useful when a randomized prospective trial is too expensive or not feasible but are prone to selection bias, confounding, and sampling errors. Many investigators do not recognize their results as being sufficient evidence to affect clinical practice.

Metaanalyses

Metaanalyses are formal statistical models for pooling randomized studies to reach a combined effect size. Metaanalyses have an advantage of providing estimates based on large sample sizes but are also prone to selection bias, heterogeneity among studies, and publication bias.

TABLE 12.2   A List of Currently Open RTOG Trials

Study	Name	Status	Phase
0538	CALGB 30610/Endorsed Study: Phase III Comparison of Thoracic Radiotherapy Regimens in Patients with Limited Small Cell Lung Cancer Also Receiving Cisplatin and Etoposide	Open	III
0631	Phase II/III Study of Image-Guided Radiosurgery/SBRT for Localized Spine Metastasis—RTOG CCOP Study	Open	II/III
0724	Phase III Randomized Study of Concurrent Chemotherapy and Pelvic Radiation Therapy with or without Adjuvant Chemotherapy in High-Risk Patients with Early-Stage Cervical Carcinoma Following Radical Hysterectomy	Open	III
0848	A Phase IIR and A Phase III Trial Evaluating Both Erlotinib (Ph IIR) And Chemoradiation (Ph III) As Adjuvant Treatment For Patients With Resected Head Of Pancreas Adenocarcinoma	Open	II/III
0920	A Phase III Study of Postoperative Radiation Therapy (IMRT) +/− Cetuximab for Locally-Advanced Resected Head and Neck Cancer	Open	III
0926	A Phase II Protocol for Patients with Stage T1 Bladder Cancer to Evaluate Selective Bladder Preserving Treatment by Radiation Therapy Concurrent with Radiosensitizing Chemotherapy Following a Thorough Transurethral Surgical Re-Staging	Open	II
0924	Androgen Deprivation Therapy and High Dose Radiotherapy With or Without Whole-Pelvic Radiotherapy in Unfavorable Intermediate or Favorable High Risk Prostate Cancer: A Phase III Randomized Trial	Open	III
0973	GOG-0238/Endorsed Study: "A Randomized Trial of Pelvic Irradiation With or Without Concurrent Weekly Cisplatin in Patients With Pelvic-Only Recurrence of Carcinoma of the Uterine Corpus"	Open	II R
0974	NSABP B-43/Endorsed Study: "A Phase III Clinical Trial Comparing Trastuzumab Given Concurrently with Radiation Therapy and Radiation Therapy Alone for Women with HER2-Positive Ductal Carcinoma In Situ Resected by Lumpectomy"	Open	III
1008	A Randomized Phase II/Phase III Study of Adjuvant Concurrent Radiation and Chemotherapy versus Radiation Alone in Resected High-Risk Malignant Salivary Gland Tumors	Open	II R
1071	NCCTG N0577/Endorsed Study: Phase III Intergroup Study of Radiotherapy versus Temozolomide Alone versus Radiotherapy with Concomitant and Adjuvant Temozolomide for Patients with 1p/19q Codeleted Anaplastic Glioma	Open	III
1073	GOG-0258/Endorsed Study: "A Randomized Phase III Trial of Cisplatin and Tumor Volume Directed Irradiation Followed by Carboplatin and Paclitaxel vs. Carboplatin and Paclitaxel for Optimally Debulked, Advanced Endometrial Carcinoma"	Open	III

TABLE 12.2   A List of Currently Open RTOG Trials—cont'd

Study	Name	Status	Phase
1112	Randomized Phase III Study of Sorafenib versus Stereotactic Body Radiation Therapy followed by Sorafenib in Hepatocellular Carcinoma	Open	III
1119	Phase II Randomized Study of Whole Brain Radiotherapy/ Stereotactic Radiosurgery in Combination With Concurrent Lapatinib in Patients With Brain Metastasis From HER2-Positive Breast Cancer: A Collaborative Study of RTOG and KROG	Open	II R
1171	GOG-0263/Endorsed Study: "Randomized Phase III Clinical Trial of Adjuvant Radiation Versus Chemoradiation in Intermediate Risk, Stage I/IIA Cervical Cancer Treated With Initial Radical Hysterectomy and Pelvic Lymphadenectomy"	Open	III
1172	COG AEWS1031/Endorsed Study: "A Phase III Randomized Trial of Adding Vincristine-topotecan-cyclophosphamide to Standard Chemotherapy in Initial Treatment of Non-metastatic Ewing Sarcoma"	Open	III
1173	ECOG E2108/Endorsed Study: "A Randomized Phase III Trial of the Value of Early Local Therapy for the Intact Primary Tumor in Patients with Metastatic Breast Cancer"	Open	III
1175	CALGB 80803/Endorsed Study: Randomized Phase II Trial of PET Scan-Directed Combined Modality Therapy in Esophageal Cancer	Open	II R
1270	NCCTG N107C/Endorsed Study: A Phase III Trial of Post-Surgical Stereotactic Radiosurgery (SRS) Compared With Whole Brain Radiotherapy (WBRT) for Resected Metastatic Brain Disease	Open	III
1271	N1048/Endorsed Study: A Phase II/III trial of Neoadjuvant FOLFOX, with Selective Use of Combined Modality Chemoradiation versus Preoperative Combined Modality Chemoradiation for Locally Advanced Rectal Cancer Patients Undergoing Low Anterior Resection with Total Mesorectal Excision	Open	II/III
1272	NSABP B-47/Endorsed Study: A Randomized Phase III Trial of Adjuvant Therapy Comparing Chemotherapy Alone (Six Cycles of Docetaxel Plus Cyclophosphamide or Four Cycles of Doxorubicin Plus Cyclophosphamide Followed by Weekly Paclitaxel) to Chemotherapy Plus Trastuzumab in Women with Node-Positive or High-Risk Node-Negative HER2-Low Invasive Breast Cancer	Open	III
1304	NSABP B-51/Endorsed Study: A Randomized Phase III Clinical Trial Evaluating Post-Mastectomy Chestwall and Regional Nodal XRT and Post-Lumpectomy Regional Nodal XRT in Patients with Positive Axillary Nodes Before Neoadjuvant Chemotherapy who Convert to Pathologically Negative Axillary Nodes After Neoadjuvant Chemotherapy	Open	III

(Continued)

TABLE 12.2 A List of Currently Open RTOG Trials—cont'd

Study	Name	Status	Phase
HN001	Randomized Phase II and Phase III Studies of Individualized Treatment for Nasopharyngeal Carcinoma Based on Biomarker Epstein Barr Virus (EBV) Deoxyribonucleic Acid (DNA)	Open	II/III
1306	A Randomized Phase II Study of Individualized Combined Modality Therapy for Stage III Non-Small Cell Lung Cancer (NSCLC)	Open	II R
1308	Phase III Randomized Trial Comparing Overall Survival After Photon Versus Proton Chemoradiotherapy for Inoperable Stage II-IIIB NSCLC	Open	III
BR001	A Phase 1 Study of Stereotactic Body Radiotherapy (SBRT) for the Treatment of Multiple Metastases	Open	I
GI001	Randomized Phase III Study of Focal Radiation Therapy for Unresectable, Localized Intrahepatic Cholangiocarcinoma	Open	III
BN002	Phase I Study of Ipilimumab, Nivolumab, and the Combination in Patients With Newly Diagnosed Glioblastoma	Open	I
BN001	Randomized Phase II Trial of Hypofractionated Dose-Escalated Photon IMRT or Proton Beam Therapy Versus Conventional Photon Irradiation With Concomitant and Adjuvant Temozolomide in Patients With Newly Diagnosed Glioblastoma	Open	II R
1470	Alliance A071101/Endorsed Study: A Phase II Randomized Trial Comparing the Efficacy of Heat Shock Protein-Peptide Complex-96 (HSPPC-96) (NSC #725085, ALLIANCE IND# 15380) Vaccine Given With Bevacizumab Versus Bevacizumab Alone in the Treatment of Surgically Resective Recurrent Glioblastoma Multiforme (GBM)	Open	II R
1471	SWOG S1400/Endorsed Study: Phase II/III Biomarker-Driven Master Protocol for Second Line Therapy of Squamous Cell Lung Cancer	Open	II/III

MODEL FITTING

Significance and Tests of Significance

In fitting a model to data, not only are the parameter values estimated, but it is also important to determine if the parameters should be included in the model at all. This is accomplished by testing the hypothesis that, for the parameter β, $\beta = 0$ (vs. $\beta \neq 0$). This tests whether β contributes additional reduction in predictive utility owing to its presence in the model. Based on the estimated value of β and its variance, it is relatively straightforward to calculate the probability that the true value of β lays within a given range. If $1 - \alpha$ is the amount of assurance or "confidence," as expressed as a probability, that the β is in a certain range that does not include zero, then the probability that the true value of β is zero is less than α, and the above hypothesis is rejected with a confidence $1 - \alpha$. The shorthand for this is usually written β ($p < \alpha$). Very small values of p are not particularly useful because they are very sensitive to the assumed distribution of the parameter. The convention for statistical significance has traditionally been $\alpha = 5\%$ or 0.05. This is the cutoff generally used by regulatory agencies, and the 0.05 cutoff appears in the International Conference on Harmonization E9 [4]: Statistical Principles for Clinical Trials document, which governs evidence presented for clinical treatment approvals.

In model validation, tests of significance go in the opposite direction, that is, a good fit is not indicated by small P-values. In this case, the P-value is a measure of the probability of obtaining the actual data randomly given the correctness of the model. Thus a small P-value indicates that the model fits the data too well to be random.

Survival Analysis and Its Pitfalls

With statistical software being widely available, it is often possible to apply a procedure to data for which the procedure is totally inappropriate. It is not the misuse that is the ultimate problem, but rather the erroneous conclusions drawn from this misuse and the potential application of these conclusions to clinical decision-making.

- Survival analysis curves are used as an indication of the response to treatment. The simplest version of survival analysis is crude survival. A number of patients are identified as the cohort of interest at a time t = 0. At some later time, the number remaining alive is determined and the crude survival is simply the ratio of the number surviving divided by the initial number. Two values of crude survival can be compared as ratios using the chi-squared statistic. Although this may be a legitimate method to compare the two ratios, the comparison itself may be irrelevant if a significant number of patients were lost to follow up, removed from the study, died of complications of treatment, or died of causes unrelated to the disease being investigated. The conclusions from this survival comparison are misleading because of the bias inherent in the data.
- Because patients are put on studies throughout the study period and because they may leave the study for many reasons other than dying of disease, it is necessary to account for the effects of less-than-complete follow-up when trying to describe the survival experience of the study cohort.
- Assume that for each patient, one can identify a time, t_i, which is either the time of death from the disease being studied (the failure time) or the last time the patient was known to be alive. In the latter case, one may include the following situations: the last time the patient was seen or contacted or the patient died of intercurrent disease or some other unrelated events. These patients are said to be censored at time t_i. There are many possible reasons for censoring, but mathematically they all have the same effect. The most common method of estimating the survival function for a patient population is the Kaplan—Meier or product limit method. Patients are ordered by their survival (failure or censoring) times. Intervals are defined by the failure times only. Thus the i th interval will occur between the time t_{i-1}, when patient i−1 failed, to t_i when patient i failed. If the survival at time t_{i-1} was S_{i-1}, then the survival at time t_i is shown as below:

$$\text{Survival time at time } t_i \ = \ S_i \times (N_i - d_i)/N_i,$$

where N_i denotes the number of patients alive just before time t_i and d_i is the number whose failure time is t_i.

The number of patients who are censored between failure times does not directly appear in the calculation, except that these censored patients serve to reduce N from one interval to the next. It is sufficient to understand that any failure will cause the survival curve to decrement parallel to the y-axis. The probability of surviving to any given time is thus the product of the probabilities of surviving all preceding time intervals.

Death from disease is not always the failure event. Other events that can define failure are death from any cause, recurrence of disease, occurrence of metastases, local recurrence, etc. Table 12.3 shows the failure event and the name for the survival associated with that event. Sometimes the failure event can be complicated to define. Consider the use of biochemical failure as a surrogate for recurrence in prostate cancer. The American Society for Therapeutic Radiology and Oncology (ASTRO) definition of biochemical failure is three consecutive rises in prostate-specific antigen (PSA) with the time of failure defined as the midpoint between the last nonrising PSA and the first rise. No matter how one defines failure time for recurrence, the patient who recurs has never been free of disease, and in that sense, the treatment has failed.

To compare the survival curves for two (or more) groups, the groups must be appropriately similar. Furthermore, within a single group, the patients either fail or are censored. The patients who are censored must have the same expectation

TABLE 12.3 Common Definitions of Time-To-Event—Related Outcomes

	Failure Occurs	Censoring Occurs
Overall survival	Death from any cause	Alive at last contact
Disease-specific survival	Death from disease	Death unrelated to the disease or alive at last contact[a]
Recurrence-free survival, NED survival, disease-free survival	First evidence of recurrence, or death from disease if recurrence is not documented	Death unrelated to the disease or alive and progression-free at last contact
Local recurrence-free failure rate	Local recurrence	Death unrelated to the disease or alive and free of local recurrence at last contact
Event-free failure rate	First evidence of "event" of interest, however, defined	Death unrelated to the event or alive with no "event" at last contact

NED, No evidence of disease.
[a]*Often, cause of death is completely unknown, as in the Social Security Death Index. In these cases, death may be treated either as an event or as a censoring event. The issue is controversial.*

of failure as the patients who actually fail. In other words, the patient who is censored at time t must have the same probability of failing as the patient who is followed well beyond time t. Censoring must be a random event, and not one that is correlated in any way with the outcome. If this assumption fails, there may be a statistical bias and hence the conclusions from inferences may be spurious.

LOGISTIC REGRESSION AND ITS PITFALLS

In radiation oncology, one often wishes to assess the effects of various factors on the outcome of a binary event where time is not an explicit variable. The most popular method for such an assessment is multiple logistic regression.

- In this case the probability P of the event is given by

$$P = \frac{\exp(\beta_0 + \beta_1 X_1 + \beta_2 x_2 ...)}{1 + \exp(\beta_0 + \beta_1 x_1 + \beta_2 x_2 ...)}$$

where $(x_1, x_2, ...)$ is a vector of parameters putatively related to the event and $(\beta_0, \beta_1, \beta_2, ...)$ is a vector of coefficients. The values of x_i can be continuous or discrete. For the case where x is a continuous variable with values from $-\infty$ to ∞, $P(x)$ is a sigmoid function in x.

- If we consider the case where variable x_j takes on only two values, it is possible without loss of generality to assign these values 0 and 1. It is a straightforward exercise to show that

$$\exp(\beta_j) = \frac{P(x_j = 1)/[1 - P(x_j = 1)]}{P(x_j = 0)/[1 - P(x_j = 0)]}.$$

$P/(1 - P)$ is the probability of occurrence divided by the probability of nonoccurrence or the odds. The expression on the right in equation is the odds ratio for $x_j = 1$ compared with $x_j = 0$. For small values of P, the odds ratio is approximately equal to the relative risk, and like relative risk, odds ratios significantly different from unity indicate that $x_j = 1$ is significantly associated with the event. Thus, logistic regression may be used to determine whether the presence of a condition ($x_j = 1$) significantly increases the likelihood of the occurrence of the event.

- For radiation oncology, a typical application would be where a number of discrete variables are assumed to be associated with a binary event. For example, one may be investigating the occurrence of interstitial pneumonitis (IP) in a large cohort of patients undergoing total body irradiation (TBI) as part of the conditioning regimen in hematopoietic stem cell transplant (HCT). Potential variables might include the age of the patient, the dose rate, the type of transplant, etc. These variables could be dichotomized as follows: pediatric ($x_j = 1$) versus adult ($x_1 = 0$); 10 cGy/min or less ($x_2 = 1$) versus greater than 10 cGy/min ($x_2 = 0$); autologous ($x_3 = 1$) versus allogeneic ($x_3 = 0$). Once the analysis was complete, e^{β_j} would give the odds ratio, i.e., it would approximate the relative risk, for pediatric patients, low dose rate, and autologous transplants for $i = 1$, 2, or 3, respectively.

- As stated above, logistic regression should be used on data that are time independent. However, outcome data generally are time dependent. This problem is usually obviated by including in the analysis only patients who survive a certain minimum time and evaluating patients for the endpoint at that minimum time. Thus in the example, one could include only patients who survive 12 months posttransplant and ignore any cases of IP that occur after 12 months. For acute effects, this treatment of the data is not necessary.

- The potential pitfalls of multiple logistic regressions are many. The first issue that the investigator should address is whether the model fits the data. This is a parametric analysis, in which there is a mathematical model being deployed and there are underlying assumptions about the distributions of the parameters in the model. Thus, there are normative procedures for examining how well the model fits (describes) the data [4]. In other words, before the investigator starts thinking about what the odds ratios for the variables in the model mean, she or he should first consider whether the model fits the data. If not, further efforts would be a waste of time until the fit is examined further. Consultation with a statistician is important throughout any statistical analysis of clinical data, but it is especially important when it comes to interpretation of goodness-of-fit statistics and diagnostics.

- On a very basic level, an error that may occur either by accident or by manipulation is the defining of dichotomous covariates. This is often trivial, as in the case of sex or other unambiguous and naturally dichotomous variables. However, searching for just the right cut point at which dichotomizing a continuous variable is potentially problematic. Also, one should keep in mind that the odds ratio will apply to the group for which $x = 1$ compared with the group for which $x = 0$. In other words, each group is compared relative to a single standard group, often referred to as the "base-line" group. Therefore, grouping is important but often unstated in the literature. In one example, one has seen a relative risk reported for second malignancies after TBI. However, the $x = 0$ group was not the group who underwent HCT without TBI but a sibling control group that did not have cancer at all. Clearly this does not speak to the added risk associated with TBI in an HCT setting.

- Another potential pitfall is the application of logistic regression to a population that is either too small itself or, more likely, that has too few events. Typically, statisticians will quote that there should be approximately 10 events for every parameter that is being estimated. This is an ideal that may not always be achievable, but one should avoid overparameterizing the analysis.

In that vain, a reader of the literature should be on the lookout for hidden parameters. In many radiation oncology papers, biological effects are handled by what the authors may feel are standard models, with what they state are reasonable parameters.

For example, a biologically effective dose, Deq, may be used to account for fractionation effects using a "standard" α/β ratio for the linear-quadratic model. Then this dose along with other parameters may be included in the logistic regression. Just because the parameters in the model used to determine the biologically effective dose are simply stated and not determined by the statistical procedure does not mean that they do not count as statistical variates.

One should also consider whether an explanatory parameter is time dependent, that is, whether its value may change over time if measured repeatedly. For example, new diagnostic techniques may be introduced that allow for better staging of patients. If stage is significantly related to outcome, then one may experience the "Will Rogers effect" in the analysis of the data. For example, consider patients on the borderline between stage II and stage III of some hypothetical disease. Those patients with slightly more disease, who were previously categorized as stage II, may with better diagnostic tests begin to be categorized as stage III. Presumably, these would have been among the poorer performing stage II patients, but among the better performing stage III patients. Thus by moving these patients from stage II to stage III based on the better diagnostic test, the survival for both stages would appear to improve even though no overall change actually occurs.

Among the factors that can lead to poor estimates of the coefficients or erroneous confidence limits is "confounding." The relationship between a variable and the outcome is confounded when that variable is correlated with both the outcome and another variable. For example, if we also included in our example of IP analysis a variable for whether the patient exhibited acute growth versus host disease (GVHD), confounding could occur because GVHD is correlated with the type of transplant and possibly with the outcome (IP) as well.

One should be attentive to any error or warning messages that appear when fitting logistic regression models. Logistic regression maximum likelihood estimates are dependent on the Newton–Raphson iterative gradient ascent method. However, this estimation method fails when categorical independent variables have too few observations in any group, either if there is an excessive amount of missing data or if the model is overparameterized. In these cases, many current software packages will report a warning that the logistic regression "failed to converge" or that the estimates are "unstable." This means that the model should be refitted with fewer explanatory factors or after groups with small numbers of observations are dropped or combined.

PROPORTIONAL HAZARDS AND THEIR PITFALLS

A further topic in survival analysis that combines the multivariate aspect of logistic regression with data whose outcome statistic is a failure time is the proportional hazards model.

- This is also frequently termed Cox regression. The hazard function, h(t), is the instantaneous or age-specific failure rate. If F(t) denotes the survival function, then

$$h(t) = \frac{\dfrac{dF(t)}{dt}}{F(t)}.$$

It gives the probability of failing at time t, given that failure has not occurred before time t. In the proportional hazards model, it is assumed that the hazard function can be separated into a baseline hazard function $h_0(t)$, depending only on t and a link function ψ, which depends on observable covariates, but not t. Thus $\psi = \psi(\beta_0 + \beta_1 x_1 + ...)$, and

$$h(t) = h_0(t)\psi(\beta, x)$$

The most commonly used form of ψ is the exponential $\psi = \exp(\beta_0 + \beta_1 x_1 + \cdots)$, which makes $\exp(\beta_i)$ the hazard ratio, that is, the ratio of the hazard function for $x_i = 1$ compared with $x_i = 0$.

- The same pitfalls exist for proportional hazards analysis as for logistic regression. In addition, the assumption of proportionality of hazards may not apply, in which case, the analysis is not valid.
- The most straightforward way of inspecting the assumption of proportionality is to compare the Kaplan—Meier curves. If the curves are parallel and do not cross, that is evidence that the proportional hazards assumptions hold. However, if the curves cross or do not follow an exponential decay function, this indicates that the Cox model's assumptions do not hold and therefore the parameter estimates are likely biased (Fig. 12.1).
- There are also formal hypothesis tests for the proportional hazards assumption, but these complex tests are best left to a statistician.

A statistician may also suggest alternative models to the Cox model when the proportional hazards assumptions are not met.

- It may be known or reasonably suspected that patients having different values of the variables being investigated will be likely to have different outcomes. The most obvious example is in the comparison of two different treatment arms. It is reasonable to suspect that outcomes for different treatments will be different and therefore patients should be randomly allocated to the two arms. However, even within the context of a randomized clinical trial, it is quite easy to achieve a nonrandom allocation.
  1. First, patients who are offered participation in the trial may be somehow different from patients who are not offered participation.
  2. Also, patients who select participation may be different from those who decline. Either of these situations may be called "selection bias."
  3. Even with a randomized cohort, biases may still occur because of confounding. Confounding variables may exist in the data. That is, there may be factors that are related to outcome but are not evenly distributed between treatment arms.

If these factors are unsuspected and not included in the analysis, biased results will certainly occur. Even if they are examined, random fluctuations may make it appear that a variable correlated with the confounding factor is more significant variable and the confounding factor may not be identified by statistically fitting the algorithms as the truly significant variable.

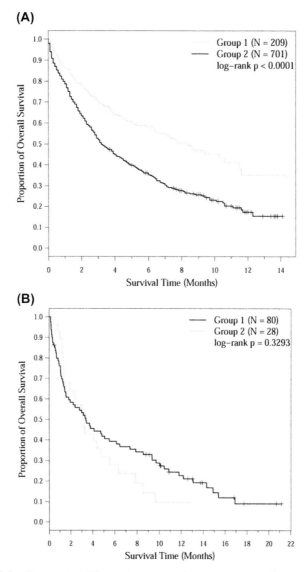

FIGURE 12.1 Proportional hazards assumptions are met on the survival curve in (A) but not met on the survival curve in (B).

RETROSPECTIVE STUDIES AND THEIR PITFALLS

If the above problems exist for properly randomized data, it is easy to see why nonrandom, retrospectively collected data are viewed with such a jaundiced eye. Confounding, false correlations, and selection bias may invalidate all conclusions drawn from the data. A classic example is the survival analysis of prostate cancer patients by treatment—radiation versus surgery. Because of the possibility of incomplete resection of the tumor, most urological surgeons agree that it is inappropriate to operate on patients with advanced disease. These patients, poorer performers, would then receive radiation. In addition, only those patients considered surgical candidates would undergo surgery. Clearly, a nonbiased analysis is not possible in these data.

METAANALYSIS AND ITS PITFALLS

When one is faced with many randomized trials testing the same hypotheses, a natural instinct is to combine all of the studies to determine their "bottom line." The field of metaanalysis formalizes the analyses of combining statistics reported in randomized studies. There are many philosophies regarding when it is appropriate to combine studies. Another consideration is whether studies are too qualitatively or quantitatively heterogeneous for a metaanalysis; the consequence of combining heterogeneous studies is that the results are not easily interpretable, or worse, misleading. For example, if a study reports a result in pediatric patients but the hypothesis of the metaanalysis concerns adults only, it is difficult to justify using a pediatric effect size statistic in a metaanalysis in adult trials.

- One difficulty with metaanalysis is that the raw data are rarely available and so metaanalyses are performed on summary statistics. In this case, the investigator must decide which statistics and which assumptions are most appropriate for measuring the intended effect size. An example of this dilemma is whether it is appropriate to combine eight studies, which report the raw odds ratio from a case–control design with the odds ratio of a logistic regression, adjusted for multiple factors. These two types of odds ratio statistics have a similar interpretation, but they are not reasonably combinable in a formal metaanalysis.
- Another difficulty with metaanalysis is selection bias. However, a certain type of selection bias is unique to metaanalysis. If journals tend to publish significant (positive) studies, and an investigator uses the literature to search for studies in a metaanalysis, there is an implicit selection effect that tends to bias the results of the metaanalysis toward significance. This is called "publication bias" and is often difficult to quantify [5].

Metaanalyses that do not consider problems with study heterogeneity and publication bias do not provide evidence of an objective test of hypotheses.

Testing hypotheses appropriately is an integral part of applying the scientific method to radiation oncology data. When clinical decision-making is dependent on poorly designed studies or biased analyses, patients may receive suboptimal treatment and the clinical literature may become muddled. Clinicians should collaborate with experienced investigators and statisticians to avoid these errors. The investment of time into understanding these potential problems and the thoughtful application of these statistical methods will result in improved quality in radiation oncology research.

References

Ref 1. *Petrie A, Sabin C. Medical statistics at a glance. 2nd ed. Cambridge (MA): Blackwell Scientific Publishers Inc.; 2005.*

Ref 2. *Harris M, Taylor G. Medical statistics made easy. 2nd ed. Bloxham, Oxfordshire (UK): Scion Publishing; 2008.*

Ref 3. *International Conference on Harmonisation. Statistical principles for clinical trials (ICH E9). Stat Med 1999;18(15):1905–42.*

Ref 4. *Hosmer DW, Lemeshow S. Applied logistic regression (Wiley Series in probability and statistics). 2nd ed. New York: John Wiley & Sons, Inc.; 2000.*

Ref 5. *Givens GH, Smith DD, Tweedie RL. Publication bias in meta- analysis: a Bayesian data-augmentation approach to account for issues exemplified in the passive smoking debate (with discussion). Stat Sci 1997;12(4):221–50.*

PART III

CLINICAL RADIATION ONCOLOGY

Skin Cancers

NONMELANOMA

The estimated annual incidence of skin cancer in the United States is > 5.4 million with 3.3 million patients and estimated 2000 deaths in 2018.

Nonmelanoma skin cancers include basal cell (BCC) and squamous cell carcinomas (SCCa), with BCC being the most common and SCCa more likely to spread to local and regional lymph nodes (LNs) although uncommon.

Skin cancer drains from the posterior scalp to the occipital nodes, from the parietal area to the posterior auricular, temporal area/eyelids to the parotid LN, and from the face and lips to the submandibular and parotid nodes.

Workup

Risk Factors
- Fair skin, blonde or red hair, blue eyes, exposure to sun and UV light—90% of nonmelanoma skin cancer
- Exposure to chemicals such as arsenic
- Immunosuppression from organ transplantation (mostly SCCa)
- Site of prior radiation therapy or chronic scarring, and history of indoor tanning

Symptoms and Signs
- New growth or sore that does not heal or change in old growth, such as crusting, bleeding, size increase.
- Complete skin exam: surface characteristics and extent of tumor carefully palpated, regional LN, CNS, and head and neck region are carefully examined

Investigation
- Biopsy: should include deep reticular dermis, fine needle aspiration or open biopsy of any palpable or imaging positive LN.
- CT, MRI or PET/CT for extensive skin lesion suspected to have LN or perineural involvement.

Fundamentals of Radiation Oncology
https://doi.org/10.1016/B978-0-12-814128-1.00013-1

TNM Staging (Nonmelanoma)

T1	Tumor 2 cm or less in greatest dimension
T2	Tumor greater than 2 cm, but less than 4 cm in greatest dimension
T3	Tumor 4 cm or larger in maximum dimension, minor bone erosion, perineural, or deep invasion[a]
T4	Tumor with gross cortical bone/marrow, skull base and/or skull base foramen invasion

[a]*Deep invasion is defined as invasion beyond the subcutaneous fat or >6 mm; perineural invasion for T3 classification is defined as tumor cells within the nerve sheath of a nerve lying deeper than the dermis or measuring >0.1 mm in caliber, or presenting with clinical or radiographic involvement of named nerves without skull base invasion or transgression.*

N0	No regional lymph node metastasis
N1	Metastasis in a single ipsilateral lymph node (<3 cm greatest dimension) and ENE (−)
N2	Metastasis in a single ipsilateral lymph node [> 3 cm, < 6 cm in greatest dimension and ENE (−)] or metastases in multiple ipsilateral lymph nodes [none > 6 cm in greatest dimension and ENE (−)] or in bilateral or contralateral lymph nodes [none > 6 cm in greatest dimension and ENE (−)]
N3	Metastasis in a lymph node > 6 cm in greatest dimension and ENE (−); or metastases in in any nodes and clinically overt ENE [ENE (+)]
M0	No distant metastasis (no pathologic M0; use clinical M to complete stage group)
M1	Distant metastasis

Stage Grouping

Stage I	T1	N0	M0
Stage II	T2	N0	M0
Stage III	T1	N1	M0
	T2	N1	M0
	T3	N0, 1	M0
Stage IV	T1,2,3	N2	M0
	T Any	N3	M0

| T4 | N Any | M0 |
| T Any | N Any | M1 |

cSCC, cutaneous squamous cell carcinoma; M, (distant metastasis); N, (regional lymph nodes); TNM, T (tumor).

Used with permission of the American Joint Committee on Cancer (AJCC), Chicago, Illinois. The original source for this material is the A JCC Cancer Staging Manual, Eighth Edition (2017) published by Springer Science Business Media LLC, www.springer.com.

Treatment

- **T1, T2 operable**—wide local excision with >4 mm margin, Mohs microsurgery. Post-op RT indicated for high-risk features such as depth >6 mm, PNI or large nerve involvement, and positive margins.
- **T1, T2 inoperable**—definitive RT [1,2,3,4]
- **LN positive**—node dissection. Post-op RT for multiple metastatic LNs, ECE. Consider concurrent chemoRT with CDDP± 5FU.
- **LN positive, inoperable disease**—definitive RT ± concurrent chemo.
- Very superficial skin cancer—photodynamic therapy, imiquimod or 5FU applied topically
- **For small superficial <2 cm BCC, well-differentiated SCCa**—cryotherapy or curettage/electrodessication can be considered.

RT Technique

- CT simulation for head and neck area skin cancers, whereas other sites can be clinically simulated on the treatment table.
- With electron beams, for tumor size <2 cm, the lateral margin is 1—1.5 cm; for >2 cm tumors, lateral margin is 1.5—2 cm.
- Electron beam energy to include deep margin of the tumor by at least 90% isodose line. Electron beam treatment requires bolus to achieve adequate surface dose.
- Secondary skin collimation with lead shielding is used to obtain tighter lateral margins close to critical structures such as orbit for a nose/eyelid/canthi tumor. The thickness of the lead in mm for electron block is given by energy MeV divided by 2 . Always use a wax-coated lead shield at the electron beam exit site.

Doses

- RT dose for lesions of 2 cm or less of the ear/nose/eyelid/canthi is 200 cGy/fx to 60—64 Gy or 250 cGy/fx to 50 Gy.
- Lesions of 2—5 cm, the dose is 200 cGy/fx to 60—70 Gy or 300 cGy/fx to 45 Gy; for lesions of 5 cm or more, the dose is 200 cGy/fx to 66—70 Gy.
- Post-op adjuvant radiation dose is 200 cGy/fx to 60 Gy or 250 cGy/fx to 50 Gy.

Note: 1. Treating eyelid, use a lead shield with wax coating to prevent backscatter. 2. When treating over cartilage as over an ear, use daily dose <300 cGy/fx. 3. Delay RT over a skin graft until it has fully healed (typically 6—8 weeks post-op). 4. Careful treating below the elbow and knee, as healing is poor after RT due to decrease or poor blood supply and constant trauma when walking.

Outcome

Basal cell cancer: Five-year local control for tumor <1 cm is 97%; for tumor 1—5 cm, 87%.

Squamous cell cancer: Five-year local control for tumor <1 cm is 91%, for tumor 1—5 cm, 76%.

Complications

- Hyperpigmentation, scarring of the skin, hair loss at treatment site, telangiectasia, and necrosis of the bone/cartilage.

Follow-Up

- Every 6 months for the first year; every 12 months thereafter.
- Skin exam every 12 months.

MELANOMA

The estimated annual incidence in the United States is 91, 270 with 9320 estimated deaths in 2018.

Melanomas arise from melanocytes. There are mainly four types: superficial spreading, lentigo malignant, nodular, and acral lentiginous. It has been noted that regional lymph node involvement is a function of the depth of invasion by the melanoma tumor into the skin, as below.

Clark's Level	Breslow Thickness (mm)	Risk of Nodal Metastasis (%)
I—II	<0.75	0—5
III	0.76—1.5	15
IV	1.6—4	35
V	>4	50

Data modified from Balch CM. Surgical management of regional lymph nodes in cutaneous melanoma. J Am Acad Dermatol 1980;3(5):511—24.

Workup

Risk Factors
- Number of moles, clinical atypical moles
- Prior and family melanoma history
- Exposure to sun and sunburns

Symptoms and Signs

- Complete skin examination (A, B, C, D, E): asymmetry, border irregularity, color variation, diameter of skin lesion, evolution (change), and examination of the regional LNs.

Investigations

- CBC, LDH, liver function test (LFT) (optional)
- Biopsy of any suspicious pigmented lesion, sentinel LN biopsy as indicated
- Chest X-ray, CT/PET/MRI if clinically indicated

TNM Staging (Melanoma)

T1	Melanomas $\leq$ 1.0 mm in thickness
T1a	without ulceration < 0.8 mm
T1b	with ulceration < 0.8 mm; 0.8–1 mm with or without ulceration
T2	Melanomas > 1.0–2.0 mm
T2a	without ulceration
T2b	with ulceration
T3	Melanomas >2.0–4.0 mm
T3a	without ulceration
T3b	with ulceration
T4	Melanomas >4.0 mm T4a without ulceration T4b with ulceration
N0	No regional lymph node metastasis
N1	Single node or in transit, satellite, and/or microsatellite metastases with no tumor-involved nodes
N2	2–3 nodes or in transit, satellite, and/or microsatellite metastases with one tumor-involved node
N3	4 or more metastatic nodes, or in transit, satellite, and/or microsatellite metastases with two or more tumor-involved nodes or matted nodes with or without in transit satellite(s) and/or microsatellites metastases.
M0	No distant metastasis (no pathologic M0; use clinical M to complete stage group)
M1a	Metastases to skin, subcutaneous tissues or distant lymph nodes
M1b	Metastases to lung
M1c	Metastases to all other visceral sites or distant metastases to any site
M1d	Metastases to CNS

Stage Grouping

Stage IA	T1a	N0	M0
Stage IB	T1b,2a	N0	M0
Stage IIA	T2b,3a	N0	M0
Stage IIB	T3b,4a	N0	M0
Stage IIC	T4b	N0	M0
Stage III	Any T	N1-3	M0
Stage IV	Any T	Any N	M1

LDH, L-lactate dehydrogenase; *M*, (distant metastasis); *N*, (regional lymph nodes); *TNM*, T (tumor).
Used with permission of the American Joint Committee on Cancer (AJCC), Chicago, Illinois. The original source for this material is the A JCC Cancer Staging Manual, Eighth Edition (2017) published by Springer Science Business Media LLC, www.springer.com.

Treatment

Stage I, II:
- Wide local excision with resection margin of 1–2 cm and sentinel lymph node biopsy for >1 mm thickness tumor. Post-op RT is considered for [1] close margin and no re-resection, [2] one or more positive LNs depending on the primary site, [3] extracapsular nodal extension, or [4] gross residual disease after wide local excision [5, 7]
- Adjuvant interferon alpha has been shown to increase disease-free survival but not overall survival [6]

Stage III:
- Wide local excision and SNL dissection and post-op RT is recommended.
- Immunotherapy with nivolumab or high-dose ipilimumab [8, 9, 11] is recommended.
- Targeted treatment with dabrafenib plus trametinib is recommended for patients with BRAF V600 mutation [12].
- Intralesion injection with T-VEC [10] for satellite or in transit lesions is recommended.
- Adjuvant interferon alpha has been shown to increase disease-free survival but not overall survival.

Stage IV:
- Palliative RT for brain, lung, and bone metastases is recommended.
- Immunotherapy or targeted therapy is recommended as above.
- Intralesion injection with T-VEC for satellite or in transit lesions.

RT Technique

CT simulation for head and neck area sites, other sites set up varies accordingly, such as axilla arms akimbo or above head. Skin bolus is needed.

Volumes

Definitive RT
GTV = gross disease
CTV = GTV+2 cm
PTV = CTV+0.5 cm
Adjuvant RT
CTV = tumor bed+2 cm
PTV = CTV+0.5 cm

Elective Nodal Regions for Primary Tumor Location

Target is ipsilateral draining lymphatics of cervical region includes level I–V and supra-clavicular LN, axilla includes level I–III and supraclavicular LN, and inguinal area includes confirmed nodal disease and external iliac LN, depending on the primary site.

Doses

Definitive RT: 200 cGy/fx to 64–70 Gy or 200–250 cGy/fx to 50–60 Gy.
Post-op RT: 200 cGy/fx to 60–66 Gy or 240 cGy/fx to 48 Gy.
Hypofractionated RT: 600 cGy/fx twice weekly to 30–35 Gy.
Palliative RT: 300 cGy/fx to 30 Gy or bone lesions can be treated with 600 cGy/fx to 30 Gy with two fxs per week.
NOTE: When using hypofractionated RT, dose prescription is to dmax, not to volume, and normal critical structures (brain, spinal cord, brachial plexus, and bowel) are not to exceed 24 Gy.

Outcome

Five-year survival for Clark's levels I, II, III, and IV are 90, 85, 70%, and 20%, respectively.

Complications

- Scarring of the skin
- Hair loss at treatment site, telangiectasia
- Lymphedema after regional nodal irradiation
- Necrosis of the bone/cartilage

Follow-Up

- Every 3 months for the first year, 6 months for the second year, and 12 months thereafter
- CBC, LFTs, LDH, and chest X-ray annually
- Imaging of the primary site as indicated

MERKEL CELL CANCER

Merkel cell cancer of the skin is a rare of neuroendocrine cell of origin malignancy. The most common sites are the head and neck and extremities.

Workup

Risk factors
- Fair skin, older age men, sun exposure
- Immunosuppression, organ transplant
- HIV, human polyomavirus

Symptoms and signs

As nonmelanoma and melanoma skin cancer

Investigation

As nonmelanoma and melanoma skin cancer

TNM Staging (Merkel Cell)

T0	No evidence of primary tumor
T1	Less than or equal to 2 cm maximum tumor dimension
T2	Greater than 2 cm but not more than 5 cm maximum tumor dimension
T3	Greater than 5 cm maximum tumor dimension
T4	Primary tumor invades bone, muscle, fascia, or cartilage

N0	No regional lymph node metastasis
N1	Metastasis in regional lymph node(s)*
N2	In transit metastasis without lymph node metastasis**
N3	In transit metastasis with lymph node metastasis**

Clinical detection of nodal disease may be via inspection, palpation, and/or imaging.
** *In transit metastasis: a tumor distinct from the primary lesion and located either (1) between the primary lesion and the draining regional lymph nodes or (2) distal to the primary lesion.*

M0	No distant metastasis
M1	Metastasis beyond regional lymph nodes
M1a	Metastasis to skin, subcutaneous tissues, or distant lymph nodes
M1b	Metastasis to lung
M1c	Metastasis to all other visceral sites

Stage Grouping

Stage I	T1	N0	M0
Stage IIA	T2/T3	N0	M0
Stage IIB	T4	N0	M0
Stage III	T0-4	N1-3	M0
Stage IV	T0-4 Any	N	M1

Used with permission of the American Joint Committee on Cancer (AJCC), Chicago, Illinois. The original source for this material is the A JCC Cancer Staging Manual, Eighth Edition (2017) published by Springer Science Business Media LLC, www.springer.com.

Treatment

- **T1, T2 operable**—wide local excision with 1–2 cm margin, Mohs microsurgery with SLN biopsy. Post-op RT indicated to primary site for high-risk features such as close/positive margins, more than 1–2 cm tumor, LVI.
- **T1, T2 inoperable**—definitive RT.
- **LN negative**—consider elective RT.
- **LN positive**—node dissection. Post-op RT for multiple metastatic LNs, ECE; consider concurrent chemoRT with CDDP ± etoposide.
- **M1**—chemotherapy CDDP or carboplatin ± etoposide; consider PD1/PD-L1 inhibitor atezolizumab or pembrolizumab.

RT Technique

- CT simulation for head and neck area skin cancers, whereas other sites can be clinically simulated on the treatment table.
- With electron beams, for head and neck sites >2 cm margin, for other sites 3–5 cm margin. Electron beam energy to include deep margin of the tumor by at least 90% isodose line. Electron beam treatment requires bolus to achieve adequate surface dose.
- Volumes: definitive GTV = gross disease, CTV = GTV + 3–5 cm, PTV = CTV + 0.5 cm; Post-op CTV = tumor bed + 2–3 cm, PTV = CTV + 0.5 cm.
- Elective nodal RT depending on the primary site: Head and neck primary cervical level I–IV and supraclavicular; lower extremity primary inguinal area (external iliac if positive inguinal LN).

Doses

Definitive 200 cGy/fx to 60–66 Gy
    Post-op 200 cGy/fx to 46–56 Gy (negative margin); 56–60 Gy (positive margin)
    Nodal 200 cGy/fx to 46–50 Gy (elective); 46–50 Gy (post-op negative); 50–60 (post-op multiple positive LNs, ECE)

Outcome

Five-year LC All 91%, 5-year OS stage I–IIA 48%, stage III 27%*

Complications

As nonmelanoma and melanoma skin cancer

Follow-up

As melanoma skin cancer

ANNOTATED BIBLIOGRAPHY

NON-MELANOMA SKIN CANCER

Ref 1. Hernández-Machin et al. (2007). Office-based radiation therapy for cutaneous carcinoma: Evaluation of 710 treatments. *Int J Dermatol*;46(5):453–9.

In this study, 710 patients with primary BCC and SCCa irradiated were analyzed for recurrence rates.

Tumor Type	5 years Cure (%)	15 years Cure (%)
BCC	94	85
SCCa	93	79

This study showed that radiation treatment is effective for BCC and SCCa and can usually be considered as a first option.

Ref 2. Balamucki CJ et al. (2012). Skin carcinoma of the head and neck with perineural invasion. *Am J Otolaryngol*;33(4):447–54.

In this study, 216 patients cutaneous with SCCa and BCC of the head and neck with perineural invasion analyzed who received RT alone, pre-op, or post-op. The median follow-up results at 6 years were as follows:

	LC (%)	CSS (%)	OS (%)
Incidental PNI	80	73	55
Clinical PNI	54	64	54

*Mendenhall WM et al (2018). 'Management of cutaneous Merkel cell carcinoma'. Journal Acta Oncologica Volume 57, 320-323.

The study concluded that RT plays a critical role in the treatment of this disease. Clinical PNI should be adequately irradiated to include the nerves to the skull base.

Ref 3. Cognetta AB et al. (2012). Superficial X-ray in the treatment of basal and squamous cell carcinomas: a viable option in select patients. *J Am Acad Dermatol*;67(6):1235–41.

In this retrospective study, 712 BCC and 994 SCCa skin cancer patients were treated with superficial X-rays. The recurrence rates at 5 years were as follows:

	Recurrence Rate (%)
BCC	4.2
SCC	5.8
All	5

The study concluded that superficial X-ray therapy remains a viable nonsurgical option for the treatment of primary BCC and SCCa in patients where surgical intervention is declined, unadvisable, or potentially associated with significant cosmetic or functional limitations.

Ref 4. Grossi MD (2016). Head and neck non-melanoma skin cancer treated by superficial X-ray therapy: an analysis of 1021 cases. *PLoS One*;11(17).

In this study, 597 patients with 720 BCC lesions, 242 SCCa lesions, and 59 SCCa in situ lesions treated with superficial X-rays were retrospectively analyzed. All patients were node negative and distant metastasis negative. At median follow-up of 44 months, the data shows the following:

	10-Year Local Control (%)
BCC	94
SCCa	87
P value	0.03

Superficial X-ray treatment for nonmelanoma skin cancer of the head and neck achieves excellent local control and should be recommended in the disease's management.

MELANOMA SKIN CANCER

Ref 5. Ballo et al. (2006). Combined-modality therapy for patients with regional nodal metastases. *Int J Radiat Oncol Biol Phys*;64(1):106–13.

In this study, 466 patients with nodal metastases from melanoma were managed with lymphadenectomy and radiation with or without systemic therapy. Adjuvant radiation therapy was given 600 cGy per fraction twice weekly to 30 Gy. Results at 5 years are given below.

Regional Control Rate	*89%*
Disease-specific survival	*49%*
Patients treated to axilla, lymphedema	*20%*
Patients treated to inguinal, lymphedema	*27%*

This retrospective study showed that melanoma patients receiving combined modality treatment achieved superior regional control to historical nodal dissection alone. One-third of the patients developed lymphedema when treated to axillary or inguinal region.

Ref 6. Garbe et al. (2008). Adjuvant low-dose interferon {alpha}2a with or without dacarbazine compared with surgery alone: a prospective-randomized phase III DeCOG trial in melanoma patients with regional lymph node metastasis. *Ann Oncol*;19(6):1195–201. DeCOG Trial.

In this study, 444 patients with melanoma who had received a complete LN dissection for pathologically proven regional node involvement were randomized to receive either 3 MU subcutaneous of interferon alpha2a 3X a week for 2 years or combined treatment with the same doses of interferon alpha2a plus dacarbazine (DTIC) 850 mg/m² every 4–8 weeks for 2 years or to observation alone. Treatment was discontinued at first sign of relapse. Results at 4 years were as follows:

	DFS (%)	*OS (%)*
Surg alone	*27*	*42*
Surg + IFN 2a	*39 ss*	*59 ss*
Surg + IFN 2a + DTIC	*29*	*45*

This study showed that 3 MU interferon alpha 2a given subcutaneous three X a week significantly improved DFS and OS inpatients with melanoma that had spread to the regional LNs, while adding chemotherapy DTIC reversed the beneficial effect of adjuvant interferon alpha 2a therapy.

Ref 7. Henderson et al. (2015). Adjuvant lymph-node field radiotherapy versus observation only in patients with melanoma at high risk of further lymph-node field relapse after lymphadenectomy (ANZMTG 01.02/TROG 02.01): 6-year follow up of a phase 3, randomized controlled trial. *Lancet Oncol*;16(9):1049–60. ANZMTG/TROG Trial.

In this study, 250 patients with isolated regional recurrence of melanoma considered to be at high risk of further regional recurrence after lymphadenectomy were randomized to observation or regional nodal basin RT. Adjuvant radiotherapy was given 240 cGy per fraction to 48 Gy. Eligible patients included ≥1 parotid, ≥ 2 cervical or axillary or ≥3 groin nodes or extra nodal spread of tumor or maximum metastatic node diameter >3 cm in neck or axilla or ≥4 cm in the groin. Results at median follow-up of 73 months are as follows.

	LR (%)	*OS (%)*
Surgery alone	*36*	*no*
Surgery + post-op RT	*21*	*difference*
P *value*	*0.023*	*0.51*

The study showed that adjuvant RT improved regional control in melanoma patients at high risk of regional relapse after lymphadenectomy.

Ref 8. Robert C et al. (2015). Nivolumab in previously untreated melanoma without BRAF mutation. *N Eng J Med* 22;372(4):320−30.

In this study, 418 previously untreated patients with metastatic melanoma without a BRAF mutation were randomly assigned nivolumab at a dose of 3 mg/kg every 2 weeks and dacarbazine-matched placebo every 3 weeks versus dacarbazine at a dose of 1000 mg/m^2 body surface area every 3 weeks and nivolumab-matched placebo every 2 weeks. At 1 year, overall survival reported was as follows:

	PFS	*OS (%)*
Darbazine group	*2.2*	*42.1*
Nivolumab group	*5.1*	*72.9*
P *value*	*<0.001*	*<0.001*

This study showed that nivolumab was associated with significant improvements in PFS and OS compared with dacarbazine, among previously untreated patients who had metastatic melanoma without BRAF mutation.

Ref 9. Eggermont et al. (2015). Adjuvant ipilimumab versus placebo after complete resection of high risk stage III melanoma (EORTC 18,071): a randomized, double-blind phase 3 trial. *Lancet Oncol*;16:522−30. EORTC 18,071 Trial.

In this study, 951 patients with stage III cutaneous melanoma with adequate resection of LNs who had not received previous systemic therapy were randomly assigned 1:1 to receive ipilimumab 10 mg/kg or placebo every 3 weeks × four doses, then every 3 months up to 3 years. At a median follow-up of 2.74 years the data showed the following:

	3-Year RFS (%)
Placebo	34.8
Ipilimumab	46.5
P value	0.0013

This study noted that adjuvant ipilimumab improved RFS for patients with completely resected stage III high-risk melanoma.

Ref 10. Andtbacka RHI et al. (2015). Talimogene laherparepvec improves durable response rate in patients with advanced Melanoma. *J Clin Oncol* September 2015;33(25):2780—88.

In this trial, 463 patients with stage IIIB—IV injectable melanoma that was not surgically resectable were randomly assigned at a two-to-one ratio to intralesional T-VEC or subcutaneous GM-CSF. The data showed the following:

	Durable Response (%)	Overall Response Rate (%)	Median Overall Survival (m)
GM-CSF	2.1	5.7	18.9
T-VEC	16.3	26.4	23.3
P value	<0.001	—	0.51

The study concluded that T-VEC was well tolerated, resulting in a higher durable response rate and longer median OS, particularly in untreated patients or those with stage IIIB, IIIC, or IVM1a disease.

Ref 11. Wolchok JD et al. (2017). Overall survival with combined Nivolumab and Ipilimumab in advanced Melanoma. *N Engl J Med* 2017;377:1345—56.

In this study, 945 previously untreated patients with unresectable stage III or IV melanoma were randomly assigned 1:1:1 ratio, to receive nivolumab at a dose of 1 mg/kg of body weight plus ipilimumab at a dose of 3 mg/kg every 3 weeks for four doses, followed by nivolumab at a dose of 3 mg/kg every 2 weeks; nivolumab at a dose of 3 mg/kg every 2 weeks plus placebo; or ipilimumab at a dose of 3 mg/kg every 3 weeks for four doses plus placebo, until progression, the occurrence of unacceptable toxic effects or withdrawal of consent. The data at median follow-up of 36 months are given below.

	3-Year *PFS (%)*	*3-Year* *OS (%)*	*Grade 3/4* *Toxicity*
Ipilimumab	*10*	*34*	*28*
Nivolumab	*32*	*52*	*21*
Nivolumab + ipilimumab	*39*	*58*	*59*
P *value*	*<0.001*	*<0.001*	

This study showed that among previously untreated patients with advanced melanoma, nivolumab alone or combined with ipilimumab resulted in significantly longer overall survival than ipilimumab alone.

Ref 12. Long GV et al. (2017). Dabrafenib plus trametinib versus dabrafenib monotherapy in patients with metastatic BRAF V600E/K-mutant melanoma: long-term survival and safety analysis of a phase 3 study. *Ann Oncol* July 2017;28(7):1631–39.

In this trial, 423 patients previously untreated with BRAF V600E/K-mutant unresectable stage IIIC or stage IV melanoma were randomized to receive dabrafenib (150 mg twice daily) plus trametinib (2 mg once daily) or dabrafenib plus placebo. At follow-up of 36 months the data were as follows:

	3-Year *PFS (%)*	*3-Year* *OS (%)*
Dabrafenib	*12*	*32*
Dabrafenib + trametinib	*22 ss*	*44 ss*

The study concluded that durable (≥3 years) survival is achievable with dabrafenib plus trametinib in patients with BRAF V600-mutant metastatic melanoma.

Primary Brain Cancers

The estimated annual incidence in the United States of primary brain cancer is 23,880 with an estimated 16,830 deaths in 2018.

Primary brain cancer incidence peaks in childhood and again after the age of 60 and has been increasing. The major brain sites are the cerebrum, diencephalon, brainstem, and cerebellum. The brain and spinal cord together form the central nervous system (CNS). CNS tumors are locally invasive even though cerebrospinal fluid (CSF) dissemination and drop metastases can occur along the spine; they are uncommon. Extra neuraxial metastases are extremely rare.

Workup

Risk Factors
- Neurofibromatosis
  - NF1: astrocytoma, optic glioma, and malignant peripheral nerve sheath tumors
  - NF2: meningioma, vestibular schwannoma, other cranial nerve schwannomas
- Von Hippel—Lindau disease: hemangioblastoma
- Tuberous sclerosis: subependymal giant cell astrocytoma
- Turcot's syndrome: medulloblastoma, glioblastoma
- Li-Fraumeni syndrome: glioma
- Multiple endocrine neoplasia type 1: pituitary tumor
- Ionizing radiation: meningioma and high-grade glioma

Symptoms and Signs
- Seizures, headache, nausea, vomiting, blurred vision, diplopia, weakness, ataxia, memory loss, change in personality, and language/speech difficulties (dysarthria)
- Enlarged head size in children (cephalomegaly)

Investigations
- CBC with routine chemistry, CSF cytology helpful in medulloblastoma, ependymoma (EP), choroid plexus tumors, and pineal and suprasellar tumors (including germinoma)
- Stereotactic biopsy

Fundamentals of Radiation Oncology
https://doi.org/10.1016/B978-0-12-814128-1.00014-3

- Molecular testing by tumor type (IDH, 1p/19q codeletion and/or ATRX for oligodendrogliomas, BRAF for pilocytic astrocytomas (PAs), BRAF V600E for pleomorphic xanthoastrocytomas, MGMT methylation and IDH1 status for gliomas, H3 K27M for diffuse midline gliomas or brainstem gliomas)
- MRI with and without gadolinium contrast; MRA may be necessary before surgery

LOW-GRADE GLIOMA (WHO GRADE I–II)

The World Health Organization (WHO) 2016 classification divides low-grade gliomas into the following two grades:

- Grade I (PA, subependymal giant cell astrocytoma, sub-EP, and ganglioglioma)
- Grade II (oligodendroglioma [IDH-mutant and 1p/19q codeleted], diffuse astrocytoma [IDH-mutant], central neurocytoma, pleomorphic xanthoastrocytoma)

PAs are well-demarcated tumors that frequently have a solid enhancing and cystic component. In the cerebellum, PAs are usually located laterally and are avidly enhanced on contrast-enhanced MRIs. Diffuse astrocytomas are typically located midline and can have a solid-enhancing, cystic component. Non-PAs are considered less-favorable tumors; they lack contrast enhancement on CT/MRI and have a predominantly hyperintense component on T_2 FLAIR sequences.

The classic negative clinicopathologic factors associated with poor prognosis in adult patients include age ≥ 40, astrocytoma histology, size ≥ 6 cm, tumor crossing midline, and preoperative neurologic deficit. More recently discovered molecular risk factors associated with poorer prognosis include IDH1-wildtype or 1p/19q-intact tumors.

Treatment

- Maximal safe resection using image-guided surgery.
- **Children:**
  - PA observation after gross total resection (GTR) and subtotal resection (STR).
  - Progressive low-grade glioma after observation or after initial surgery, consider repeat surgery, chemotherapy (carboplatin and/or vincristine; weekly administration of single-agent vinblastine), targeted agents in case of BRAF V600E mutation or RT.
  - Non-PA with good performance status, maximal safe resection followed by observation.
- **Adults:**
  - PA observation after GTR and STR.
  - Non-PA with higher risk features (age ≥ 40, STR or IDH-wildtype) consider RT and adjuvant chemotherapy with patients receive chemotherapy (PCV) every 8 weeks × 6 cycles ($60 \, mg/m^2$ procarbazine, $110 \, mg/m^2$ CCNU[1], $1.4 \, mg/m^2$ vincristine) [1, 2].

---

[1]1-(2-chloroethyl)-3-cyclohexyl-1-nitrosourea.

- Non-PA with high-risk or progressive low-grade glioma after initial surgery may also receive RT and concurrent temozolomide. Temozolomide ($75 \text{ mg}/\text{m}^2$) is orally administered daily during radiation followed by $150 \text{ mg}/\text{m}^2$ for 5 days every 4 weeks for 6 months [3].

Radiation Therapy Technique

3D Technique

Patient is supine, with face mask on for immobilization and CT simulation, 3D conformal radiation therapy (3D-CRT) with MRI fusion, 6-MV photons, noncoplanar, multiple four to five fields. Maintaining a 3-cm margin around the CT volume or a 2-cm margin around the T2-weighted MRI edema volume, whichever is larger is recommended (Fig. 14.1).

IMRT/Proton Technique

Patient is supine, with face mask for immobilization, CT simulation, and MRI fusion. 6-MV photon intensity-modulated radiation therapy (IMRT) or proton therapy (Fig. 14.2) should be used, if available.

Volumes

GTV = surgical bed + T1 gross enhancing disease + T2 FLAIR intensity.
CTV = GTV+0.5–1 cm, or greater in selected patients to include regions at risk of disease spread, respecting natural barriers.
PTV = CTV+ 0.3–0.5 cm.

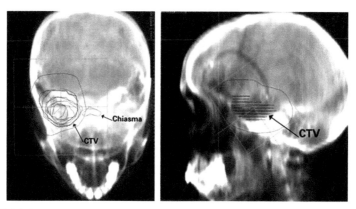

FIGURE 14.1 Digitally reconstructed radiograph (DRR) of a low-grade glioma, 3D anterior oblique and lateral oblique fields showing a 2–3 cm margin around the target volume with sparing of the critical structure, optic chiasm.

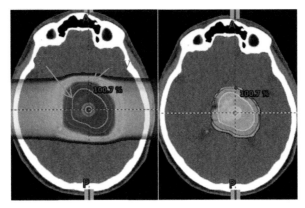

FIGURE 14.2   Pencil-beam scanning proton dose distribution for a 17-year-old patient with an unresectable pilocytic astrocytoma centered on the left thalamus. The teal line denotes the GTV, whereas the red line denotes the CTV (5 mm isotropic margin). The maximum dose point on this slice is 100.7% (54 Gy prescription). Color wash represents 10% isodose line (left) and 95% isodose line (right).

Doses

Low risk
PTV = 180 cGy/fx to 45−54 Gy.
High risk
PTV = 180 cGy/fx to 54 Gy.

Outcome

The 10-year overall survival (OS) of PA is >90%. For non-PA, the disease-free survival is 40% and the OS is 60%. Furthermore, a majority of low-grade gliomas (treated with surgery alone, chemotherapy, and/or radiation), particularly those with unfavorable features, progress over time to higher-grade lesions such as an anaplastic astrocytoma (grade III) or glioblastoma (grade IV). Oligodendrogliomas, proven by the presence of IDH mutation and 1p/19q codeletion, have better outcomes than astrocytoma histology.

Complications

- Fatigue, skin reactions: erythema, dryness, hair loss, nausea, vomiting, headaches, otitis externa/media, hearing loss, and cataracts
- Temporary somnolence
- Optic neuropathy
- Hypopituitarism
- Neuropsychological disorder and neurocognitive decline
- Leukoencephalopathy and vasculopathy

Follow-Up

Brain MRI and clinical assessment every 3−6 months for the first 5 years; thereafter every 12 months.

HIGH-GRADE GLIOMA (ANAPLASTIC ASTROCYTOMA GRADE III/GLIOBLASTOMA GRADE IV)

The WHO 2016 classification divides high-grade gliomas into the following types:

- Anaplastic oligodendroglioma IDH-mutant and 1p/19q codeleted
- Anaplastic astrocytoma IDH-mutant and 1p/19q noncodeleted
- Glioblastoma IDH-wildtype (formerly called glioblastoma multiforme [GBM])
- Gliosarcoma

On imaging studies, high-grade gliomas show ringlike or nodular enhancement in contrast CT or with central necrosis and irregular borders in MRI. Almost half of the patients with glioblastoma will have microscopic extension of the tumor >2 cm beyond the T2-weighted MRI abnormality.

Treatment

- Maximal safe resection using image-guided surgery.
- Post-op radiation therapy (RT) is recommended in all patients.
- **Anaplastic oligodendroglioma:** PCV before or after RT [6, 7, 8].
- **Anaplastic astrocytoma:** Concurrent temozolomide with RT, followed by adjuvant temozolomide [10, 11].
- **Glioblastoma:**
  - Concurrent temozolomide with post-op RT, followed by 6 months of adjuvant temozolomide. Temozolomide dose is 75 mg/m^2 orally, daily during radiation followed by 150–200 mg/m^2 × 5 days every 4 weeks for 6 months [5, 6].
  - Some institutions offer adjuvant tumor-treating fields (TTFs) for patients concurrently with adjuvant temozolomide after RT [12].
  - Consider hypofractionated RT with or without temozolomide for patients with poor prognostic factors: age ≥70 years or poor performance status (KPS ≤60) [4, 9].

Radiation Therapy Technique

Patient is supine, with face mask on, CT and MRI simulation, 3D-CRT or IMRT with post-op day 1 MRI fusion. An initial plan for PTV1 is treated, followed by a boost plan for PTV2. See Figs. 14.3 and 14.4.

Volumes

GTV1 = resection cavity + T1 gross enhancing disease + T2 FLAIR intensity.
CTV1 = GTV1 + 2 cm margin, respecting natural barriers.
GTV2 = resection cavity + T1 gross enhancing disease.
CTV2 = GTV2 + 2 cm margin, respecting natural barriers.
PTV = CTV + 0.3–0.5 cm margin.

Doses

PTV1 = 180–200 cGy/fx to 45–46 Gy.
PTV2 = 180–200 cGy/fx to 14–14.4 Gy.
Hypofractionated RT

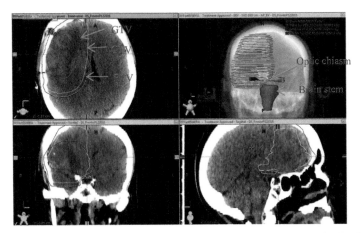

FIGURE 14.3 CT images showing target volumes GTV, CTV, and PTV based on post-op contrast MRI of a patient with glioblastoma multiforme. Critical structures, optic chiasm, optic nerves, and brainstem are delineated.

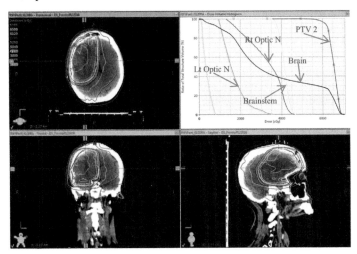

FIGURE 14.4 CT images of two-arc VMAT treatment plan of a patient with glioblastoma multiforme illustrating isodose lines conforming to PTV and DVH showing 95% coverage of the PTV, and all normal critical structures are within dose constraints. A dose of 46 Gy to PTV1 and 60 Gy to PTV2 is prescribed.

267 cGy/fx to 40.05 Gy with or without temozolomide.
500 cGy/fx to 25 Gy without temozolomide.

Constraints

Brain = V60 to <30%, V50 to <60%.
Brainstem = <54 (QUANTEC); <60 Gy (RTOG 0825).

Retina = 50 Gy (RTOG 0825).
Optic nerve = <50–55 Gy (RTOG 0825).
Optic chiasm = <50–55 Gy.
Lens = <7 Gy (RTOG 0825).
Lacrimal gland = mean < 25 Gy.
Pituitary gland = 30 Gy.
Cochlea = mean dose ≤45 Gy.

Outcome

The median survivals for glioblastoma and anaplastic astrocytoma are 11–21 and 36 months, respectively. Median survival for anaplastic oligodendroglioma, especially those with 1p/19q codeletion, is greater than 10 years.

Complications

Same as for low-grade glioma.

Follow-Up

Same as for low-grade glioma.

BRAINSTEM GLIOMA

Brainstem gliomas are most commonly diffusely infiltrating and intrinsic to the organ. They are clinically diagnosed and termed diffuse intrinsic pontine gliomas (DIPGs). There also exist some dorsally exophytic brainstem gliomas (DEBSGs) which are exophytic and more indolent; these tumors possess low-grade histology and are slow-growing.

The remainder of this discussion will focus on DIPG. DIPG is a clinical diagnosis. Classical criteria include the following:

- Symptom onset ≤6 weeks
- Long-tract signs (hemiparesis and/or hyperreflexia)
- Characteristic expansile, intrinsic lesion of brainstem on MRI

Midbrain lesions can cause	CN III, IV, V deficits.
Pontine lesions can cause	CN VI, VII deficits.
Medullary lesions can cause	CN IX, X, XI, XII deficits.

DIPG commonly affects children aged 5–7 years. Brainstem gliomas can be biopsied with a stereotactic technique; however, clinical symptoms and MRI alone can be used for diagnosis and treatment. Biopsies are not required and not traditionally performed because of the eloquent regions that are involved but are being performed more frequently to obtain tissue confirmation for molecular profiling.

The WHO 2016 classification describes a pathologic entity, diffuse midline glioma, H3 K27M—mutant (WHO grade IV). Approximately, 85% of DIPGs are also diffuse midline gliomas with an H3 K27M mutation. However, not all diffuse midline gliomas are located in the brainstem, and not all DIPGs have an H3 K27M mutation that makes them diffuse midline gliomas.

Treatment

- For focal tumors, a stereotactic biopsy can be attempted. Surgery for focal low-grade tumors may be indicated if feasible, followed by post-op RT.
- **DIPG:** Definitive RT. Hypofractionated RT may be considered [13].
- **DEBSG:** For dorsal exophytic lesions, surgery is the primary treatment. Post-op RT is given only if tumor progression is noted. Chemotherapy is not indicated. Hypofractionated RT for reirradiation can be considered.

Radiation Therapy Technique

Patient is supine, with face mask on, CT simulation, 6-MV photon, and 3D-CRT or IMRT with MRI fusion. The tumor should be viewed on sagittal MRI to ensure the entire craniocaudal extent of disease is included.

Volumes

GTV = all T2 FLAIR hyperintensity.
CTV = GTV+1 cm, respecting the natural barriers.
PTV = CTV+0.5 cm.

Doses

PTV = 180 cGy/fx to 54 Gy
Hypofractionated, PTV = 300 cGy/fx to 39 Gy.

Outcome

- Median survival is 8 months.
- Two-year OS is less than 10%.

Complications

Same as for low-grade glioma.

Follow-Up

Same as for low-grade glioma.

OPTIC GLIOMA

Optic gliomas are more common in younger children and in those with neurofibromatosis type 1. These tumors commonly involve the chiasm and often have significant invasion of the hypothalamus. In general, the lesions are small and homogenously enhancing in imaging studies, but these lesions often have occult extension along the optic nerves and optic radiations in the form of subtle T2 hyperintensity on MRI. Biopsy of the tumor is not required, although histologic confirmation is sometimes performed to test for BRAF mutations.

Treatment

- Surgery is recommended for unilateral optic nerve tumors.
- Consider use of chemotherapy to delay RT for young children.
- Definitive RT is an option for older children (age >10).
- RT is indicated in any patient with progressive disease on imaging studies or significant visual or neurologic deficits at presentation.

Radiation Therapy Technique

Localized lesions may be treated with IMRT or proton therapy. The recommended radiation dose is 180 cGy/fx to 54 Gy, with a strict limit on hot spots in organs at risk. Observation or chemotherapy is recommended in young children to delay radiation-related late toxicities.

Outcome

Vision improves in 80% of patients. Five-year disease-free survival is 80%–100%.

Complications

- Hair loss, skin redness, cataract formation, radiation-induced optic neuropathy.
- Neurocognitive decline, pituitary insufficiency, vasculopathy, and stroke.
- Moyamoya syndrome: stenosis of vessels in the circle of Willis leading to incomplete brain perfusion.
- Increased incidence of second neoplasms among those with neurofibromatosis type 1 (especially malignant peripheral nerve sheath tumors).

Follow-Up

Same as for low-grade glioma.

EPENDYMOMA

EPs are intraaxial tumors that arise from the lining of the lateral, third or fourth ventricles. EPs are most commonly located in the posterior fossa, whereas supratentorial sites are less common. Intracranial EPs are typically WHO grade II (classical) or grade III (anaplastic), whereas spinal EPs are typically WHO grade I (myxopapillary). Perivascular pseudorosette formation is characteristic of EPs. This section will focus on intracranial EP.

Molecular profiling of EPs has revealed several subgroups with unique clinicopathologic characteristics:

- Supratentorial: C11orf95-RELA fusion (poorer prognosis); YAP1 fusion (better prognosis)
- Infratentorial: Group A (poorer prognosis; younger patients); group B (better prognosis; older patients)

Ependymoblastomas are no longer considered part of the spectrum of EPs but are classified as embryonal tumor with multilayered rosettes, C19MC-altered (WHO grade IV).

Treatment

- **Supratentorial:** Maximal safe resection followed by post-op RT is recommended [14, 15]. For patients with GTRs, observations may be considered but with an increased chance of recurrence.
- **Infratentorial:** Maximal safe resection followed by post-op RT is recommended.
- **Metastatic:** Surgery, craniospinal irradiation (CSI), and boost radiotherapy to sites of metastatic and resected disease are recommended.
- The role of chemotherapy in this disease is uncertain and is under investigation. Patients with residual tumor after surgery may be treated with chemotherapy (VCR, CDDP,[2] and either etoposide or cyclophosphamide) followed by second-look surgery and focal RT.
- Children under the age of 3 may be treated with CRT.
- Very young infants may be treated with multiagent chemotherapy and deferred radiation until older.

Radiation Therapy Technique

Patient is supine, with face mask on, CT and MRI simulation, and photons treated with IMRT or proton therapy (note institutional series indicating increased risk of brainstem necrosis from proton therapy). Post-op MRI should be obtained within 24—72 h after surgery.

Volumes

GTV1 = tumor bed + T1 residual disease (if present).
CTV1 = GTV1 + anatomic areas that are touched by preoperative tumor should be included in GTV1 + 1—2 cm, respecting the natural barriers.
GTV2 = options include excluding volume of GTV caudal to foramen magnum (to exclude cervical spinal cord) and excluding optic chiasm.
CTV2 = GTV2 (no expansion).
PTV = CTV+0.3—0.5 cm.

Doses

For individuals of age <18 months: PTV1 is treated 180 cGy/fx to 54 Gy.
For individuals of age ≥18 months: PTV1 is treated 180 cGy/fx to 54 Gy followed by a boost to PTV2 to a total dose of 59.4 Gy.
Craniospinal: whole brain and spine are treated 180 cGy/fx to 36 Gy.
Spinal gross disease may be treated 180 cGy/fx to 45—54 Gy.

---

[2]Cisplatin.

Outcome

The 7-year OS rate for all patients is 80%—90% [14].

Complications

Same as for low-grade glioma but includes brainstem and spinal cord necrosis and optic neuropathy.

Follow-Up

- Brain MRI every 3—4 months for 1 year, every 4—6 months for 2 year, then every 6—12 months for 5—10 years.
- Spine MRI at years 1 and 2.

MENINGIOMA

Meningioma is an extra axial tumor that originates from the meninges. Common locations are in the convexity of the brain, the sphenoid wing, and cerebellopontine angle. On imaging studies, intense homogeneous enhancement is evident as well as a dural tail. These tumors can cause seizures and focal neurologic deficits due to the mass effect from the tumor.

Most meningiomas are benign (WHO grade I), atypical (WHO grade II), or malignant (WHO grade III) meningiomas. Malignant meningiomas are identified by pathologic evaluation (brain invasion, anaplasia, mitosis); these tumors are clinically more aggressive (rapid growth, frequent recurrences, invasiveness).

Treatment

- Small, incidentally detected meningioma may be observed with serial MRI.
- Maximal safe resection is recommended if possible, particularly for tumors not involving the skull base or intracerebral vasculature.
- Post-op observation and RT [16]:
    Grade I—observation
    Grade II—GTR: observation or adjuvant RT; STR: adjuvant RT
    Grade III—adjuvant RT
- Unresectable tumors: Definitive RT, either fractionated or radiosurgery, with curative intent.
- Symptomatic patients: Consider RT.

Radiation Therapy Technique

Patient is supine, with thermoplastic face mask, CT simulation, and with MR simulation if available. 1—3 mm CT slices if treating with stereotactic radiosurgery (SRS). Intravenous CT contrast and/or MR contrast helpful to delineate tumor. 6-MV photons and IMRT planning.

Volumes

GTV = enhancing tumor and tumor bed ± dural tail (controversial: T2-weighted sequence can help distinguish vasculature from dural tail with nodular enhancements).

Grade I CTV = GTV.

Grade II CTV = GTV + 1–2 cm (or per NRG BN003 0.5–1 cm) respecting natural barrier.

Grade III CTV = GTV + 2–3 cm, respecting natural barrier.

PTV = CTV + 0.3–0.5 cm.

Doses

Grade I: PTV = 180 cGy/fx to 45–54 Gy.

Grade II: PTV = 180 cGy/fx to 54–59.4 Gy.

Grade III: PTV = 200 cGy/fx to 60 Gy.

Grade I: SRS single fraction to 12–16 Gy.

Outcome

See summary table in ref 13a for results of RTOG 0539.

Complications

Same as for low-grade glioma.

Follow-Up

- Grade I/II or unresected: MRI at 3, 6, and 12 months, then every 6–12 months for 5 years, then annually.
- Grade III: More frequent imaging may be required.

MEDULLOBLASTOMA

Medulloblastoma is an embryonal tumor most frequently located in the fourth ventricle. It is the most common infratentorial tumor of childhood. It is a WHO grade IV tumor. Occult metastatic dissemination is common; thus, the mainstay of treatment involves surgery followed by CSI and chemotherapy.

Histology consists of small, round, blue cells. Molecular subclassification of medulloblastoma has revealed four major subgroups:

- WNT-activated: They express nuclear beta-catenin and classically have monosomy 6.
- SHH-activated: These are often described as desmoplastic or nodular, with lateralized tumor primaries in the posterior fossa.
- Non-WNT/non-SHH: These are subdivided into group 3 or group 4 tumors. Group 3 tumors have poorer prognosis.

Additional negative prognostic factors include the presence of p53 mutation and MYC amplification. These molecular features are used, along with classical risk factors (discussed under Staging), to guide therapy on contemporary treatment protocols.

Gorlin syndrome is associated with medulloblastoma. Because of the risk of secondary basal cell carcinomas after RT, radiation is avoided for these patients.

Workup

Symptoms and Signs
- Nausea/vomiting, headaches.
- Cranial nerve palsy, hydrocephalus, cerebellar ataxia.
- Leptomeningeal spread: evidence of spinal and/or CSF metastasis at diagnosis in one-third of the patients.

Investigations
- CBC, Chemistry with liver and renal function.
- Audiologic, endocrinologic, and neuropsychological assessment.
- Pre-op MRI with contrast and MRI brain <48 h postoperatively.
- CSF cytology and MR spine ≥14 days post surgery.

Staging

Use the Chang-Harisiadis method (Langston modification) for staging.

Stage	Description
T1	Tumor <3 cm (no brainstem invasion).
T2	Tumor >3 cm (no brainstem invasion).
T3a	Tumor with extension into the aqueduct of Sylvius and/or into the foramen of Luschka.
T3b	Tumor with extension into the brainstem.
T4	Tumor with extension up past the third ventricle or down past the foramen magnum to the upper cord.
M0	Cerebrospinal fluid (CSF) negative, MRI negative.
M1	Microscopic CSF positive, MRI negative.
M2	Gross nodular seedings demonstrated in the cerebellar or cerebral subarachnoid spaces or in the lateral or third ventricles, MRI positive.
M3	Extra cranial metastatic, gross nodular seeding in spinal subarachnoid spaces.
M4	Metastasizes outside the cerebrospinal space.

Note: M1 exists only if the CSF is from the spine or lateral (not fourth) ventricle.
Contiguous extension of the primary through the tentorial notch does not constitute M2.
Classic clinicopathologic factors for risk stratification are as follows:

Standard risk: M0, <1.5 cm^2 residual disease on axial MR, not anaplastic/large cell[a]

High risk: M1 or greater, >1.5 cm^2 residual disease on axial MR, age <3[b]

[a]*Anaplastic tumors were eligible for treatment on the "other-than-average-risk" COG ACNS0332 protocol.*
[b]*Sometimes classified as high risk because of the inability to use CSI.*

Treatment

- Treatment for hydrocephalus is surgical resection of the primary tumor mass. Sometimes, a ventriculoperitoneal shunt is also needed.
- **Standard risk, age >3 years**—maximum safe resection followed by CSI and PF resection cavity boost. Some protocols give concurrent chemotherapy (vincristine) with radiation, followed with adjuvant chemotherapy VCR/CDDP/CCNU × 1 - year [19].
- **High risk**—maximum safe resection followed by CSI and entire PF boost and boost to M+ sites. Some protocols give concurrent chemotherapy (vincristine) with radiation, followed with adjuvant chemotherapy VCR/CDDP/CCNU ×1 year [17, 18].
- **High risk, age <3 years**—RT is deferred for young children of less than 3 years of age using chemotherapy.

Radiation Therapy Technique

3D Technique: Craniospinal

The patient is positioned with arms by side, chin extended, either supine or prone.

- A supine technique is safer and more reproducible for airway control during anesthesia and is more reproducible but requires use of a BB at the anterior neck to visualize the cranial/spine junction on portal imaging.
- A prone technique allows facile visualization of field junctions.

Borders: PA spine field is set up with the superior border at C5/C7 and the inferior border at bottom of S3 (at least 1 cm below the thecal sac, as seen on sagittal CT or T2-weighted MRI). Lateral borders along the spine should include entire vertebral body with a 1-cm margin to field edge. Lateral borders by the sacrum should include sacral foramina bilaterally. For treatment setup requiring two spine fields, a skin surface gap is calculated to avoid field overlap at the spinal cord and excess dosing. This gap is calculated as

$$ \text{Gap} = \frac{1}{2}\text{dx}\left(\frac{L1}{SSD1} + \frac{L2}{SSD2}\right), $$

where d = depth at spinal cord L1 and L2 = lengths of first and second spinal fields, respectively.

All spinal and cranial junctions are shifted 0.5 cm weekly to avoid overdosing due to setup error ("feathering").

Borders: whole brain and upper cervical spine are treated with parallel-opposed lateral fields with the isocenter placed at the canthi, to provide an anterior half-beam block for eye protection. Field **borders** for the cranial fields are as follows:

- In the brain: Superior, anterior, and posterior borders should flash the scalp.
- In the face and neck: Inferior border is at C5/C7. MLC shielding should cover with the cribiform plate and temporal fossa with a 1-cm margin. Attempt to

shield lenses while treating the posterior globe and cribiform plate. Anterior border in the neck should be at or 1 cm anterior to the cervical vertebral bodies.

The brain-field collimator is angled to match the divergence of field of posterior spine field; the collimator angle is calculated by $\arctan^{-1}\left(\frac{1/2L1}{SSD1}\right)$. The divergence of the lateral brain field into the spine field is taken into account by angling the couch toward the gantry head, $\arctan^{-1}\left(\frac{1/2L1}{SSD1}\right)$. Finally, the gantry is angled 4–5 degrees to superimpose BBs to spare lens. A skin surface gap is calculated for the inferior border.

The posterior fossa is boosted after completion of craniospinal radiation. The posterior fossa is best visualized on sagittal MRI but may be estimated based on bony anatomy. Superior **border** is midway between foramen magnum and vertex plus 1 cm; inferior border is bottom of C2; anterior border is posterior clinoid, and posterior border is flash. Alternatively, pre-op tumor volume with margin can be used to treat conformal posterior fossa boost.

IMRT/Proton Technique: Craniospinal

Proton CSI has the benefit of reducing exit dose from the PA spine field to the thorax, mediastinum, abdomen, and upper pelvis. Two posterior oblique fields are used for the cranium, and one or two PA fields are used for the spine.

Volumes

GTV1 = any residual disease.
CTV1 = GTV + craniospinal axis.
For the boost phase of treatment, IMRT or proton therapy may be used.
GTV2 = tumor bed and any residual disease.
CTV2 = GTV2+0.5–1.5 cm (for high-risk patients boost entire posterior fossa).
PTV = CTV+0.3–0.5 cm.

Craniospinal Axis Volume

Entire brain, including the internal auditory canals, cribiform plate, dorsum sellae bone, optic canals bilaterally, and most of the optic nerve, entire spinal canal, and nerve roots on slices with foramina is present. Attention should be paid to include sacral nerve roots within the sacrum. The caudal extent of the CTV is 1 cm inferior to the thecal sac.

Doses

NOTE: Children who have not yet attained skeletal maturity (age <13 or determined using bone age X-rays) may need treatment to their vertebral bodies to ensure homogeneous axial skeletal growth. The vertebral bodies, excluding transverse processes, are treated to 18–24 Gy.

Standard risk—CSI 180 cGy/fx to 23.4–30.6 Gy followed by tumor bed boost to 54–55.8 Gy.

High risk—CSI 180 cGy/fx to 36–39.6 Gy followed by tumor bed boost to 54–55.8 Gy. Consider posterior fossa boost for involvement of Foramen of Luschka or fourth ventricular nodularity.

Outcome

Five-year disease-free survival for low-risk disease is 60%—90%; for high-risk disease, 50%—85%.

Complications

- Alopecia (usually temporary), dermatitis, esophagitis, cataract, and vasculopathy
- Posterior fossa syndrome occurs in 10%—15% of patients post-op (swallowing dysfunction, ataxia, mutism, and emotional lability)
- Speech and memory deficit
- Neurocognitive decline, microcephaly, hearing loss
- Hypothyroidism, decreased growth hormone (GH) causing decreased growth, central hypogonadism, transient azoospermia, and amenorrhea
- Second neoplasms
- Radionecrosis of the brain

Follow-Up

Brain and spinal MRI every 3 months for 2 years, every 6—12 months for 5—10 years

PITUITARY ADENOMA

Pituitary adenomas are classified as either microadenomas (<10 mm in size) or macro-adenomas (>10 mm in size). In addition, they can be

- chromophobic—inactive or secreting prolactin
- acidophilic-secreting GH
- basophilic-secreting ACTH (adrenocorticotropic hormone)
- TSH-secreting

Workup

Symptoms and Signs
- Headaches, visual defects (bitemporal hemianopsia is classic), cranial nerve deficits (may indicate cavernous sinus involvement), and hypopituitarism (in nonfunctional type of adenoma)
- Excess hormones (in functional type of adenoma)
- Prolactin-secreting: gynecomastia/galactorrhea, impotence, and infertility
- ACTH-secreting: acromegaly, Cushing's disease, and Nelson's syndrome
- GH-secreting: acromegaly

Investigations
- Endocrine evaluation
- Ophthalmologic evaluation
- MRI/CT of sella
- Skeletal survey (for acromegaly)

Treatment

- For prolactinomas with prolactin 500 mg/mL, medically manage with dopamine agonists (bromocriptine, cabergoline). If there is no response by 4—6 weeks, then transsphenoidal surgery (TSS), followed by further medical management. If prolactin is < 500 mg/mL, then initial TSS may be curative.
- For acromegaly (GH-secreting tumor) and Cushing's disease (ACTH-secreting tumor), TSS is the preferred option. In addition, nonfunctional tumors those are symptomatic, progressive, or in younger patients, are often treated with TSS.
- For completely resected microadenoma, tumors with normalized hormonal level, observation only. With gross residual disease but normal hormonal level, patients may be closely observed.
- Individuals with a high MIB-1 labelling index (or Ki-67) may be considered for adjuvant RT to reduce the risk of recurrence.
- RT is indicated for all pituitary macroadenomas with persistently elevated hormonal levels.
- RT is also recommended for nonsurgical patients or for patients with recurrent tumors.

Radiation Therapy Technique

Options include 3D-CRT with three-field technique (bilateral wedge and vertex fields), IMRT, or SRS. SRS is appropriate for small, well-demarcated tumors away from optic structures (>3 mm separation).

3D Three-Field Technique

Patient is set up in the supine position with the chin tucked and head immobilized with a face mask. Two lateral opposed fields are placed. The vertex field is placed with the couch rotated 90 degrees (Fig. 14.5).

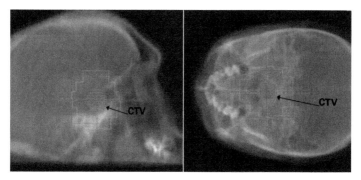

FIGURE 14.5   Digitally reconstructed radiograph (DRR) of a pituitary adenoma, a right lateral field and the vertex field for the 3-field technique.

IMRT/Stereotactic Radiosurgery

Patient is supine, with face mask on for immobilization, CT, and MRI simulation. 6-MV photon IMRT, multiple coplanar and/or nonplanar beams may be used. IGRT is needed. SRS is not recommended for tumors near optic nerves or with cavernous sinus involvement or tumor volume size ≤3–4 cm.

Volumes

GTV = tumor bed and residual disease.
CTV = GTV+ and at-risk regions.
PTV = CTV+0.5 cm (0–1 mm if treating with SRS).

Doses

3D or IMRT:
Nonfunctioning tumor: 180 cGy/fx to 45–50.4 Gy.
Functioning tumors: 180 cGy/fx 50.4–54 Gy.
SRS:
Nonfunctioning tumor: 12–20 Gy to 50% isodose line.
Functioning tumor: 15–30 Gy to 50% isodose line.
Optic chiasm dose <8 Gy.

Outcome

TSS can cure microadenomas up to 90% and macroadenomas up to 50%. With surgery and radiation treatment, the local control rate is up to 90%.

Complications

- Hypopituitarism, vasculopathy
- Brain necrosis
- Second cancer
- Optic neuropathy, chiasm, and optic nerve damage can be minimized if the maximum tumor dose is kept to 50 Gy or less and if the fraction size is kept to 180 cGy or less. For stereotactic radiosurgery, the risk of optic neuropathy is reduced if the dose to optic structures is <8 Gy.

Follow-Up

- Brain MRI every 6 months for first year, then annually.
- Consider MR angiography to screen for vasculopathy.
- Thyroid, adrenal, and gonadal function testing every 6 months for first year, then annually.
- Ophthalmologic evaluation annually.

CRANIOPHARYNGIOMA

Craniopharyngiomas are benign neoplasms arising from Rathke's pouch in the sellar or suprasellar region. Although classified as benign, they can be locally recurrent and cause substantial morbidity. The peak age is 5–14 years.

On CT, calcifications are common and are useful for target delineation. On MRI, these tumors contain cystic and solid components. Histologically, the cysts contain cholesterol crystals in a fluid resembling "crankcase oil." The adamantinomatous histologic subtype is most common, especially in children. Papillary tumors appear in adults and may harbor a BRAF V600E mutation.

Workup

Symptoms and Signs
- Headache, visual defects (bitemporal hemianopsia is classic), cranial nerve deficits, and nausea/vomiting (from hydrocephalus)
- Hypopituitarism, especially growth retardation
- Precocious puberty

Investigations
- Endocrine evaluation, ophthalmologic evaluation, neuropsychological evaluation
- MRI/CT of the brain, including CISS MR sequences MR angiogram

Treatment

- Maximal safe resection while avoiding neurologic deficits is most appropriate. Cystic fenestration may help reduce the possibility of cystic regrowth.
- Adjuvant RT is indicated for STR or recurrent disease after initial surgery [20].
- For persistent cystic growth, intracystic therapy (interferon alpha, bleomycin, or radioisotopes [phosphorus-32 or yttrium-90]) may be considered.

Radiation Therapy Technique

IMRT Technique
Patient is supine, with face mask on for immobilization, CT, and MRI simulation. Any MRIs preceding simulation date should be fused and used to guide target delineation. For 6-MV photon IMRT, multiple coplanar and/or nonplanar beams may be used.

Proton Therapy
Simulation and target delineation procedures are similar to those of IMRT. Field arrangement is typically two opposed lateral or inferiorly angled beams to avoid the mastoid air cells. See Fig. 14.6.

Volumes
GTV = tumor bed and residual solid or cystic components on MRI, as well as tumor-related calcifications on CT.

CTV = GTV + 0.5—1 cm and at-risk regions, confined to anatomic barriers. At-risk regions are defined with the assistance of imaging before RT, including preoperative images.

PTV = CTV + 0.3—0.5 cm.

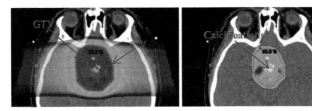

FIGURE 14.6   Volumes and pencil-beam scanning proton dose-distribution for a pediatric patient with craniopharyngioma. Note the prominent calcifications in the target. The *blue line* represents GTV; the red line represents CTV. **Left** color wash represents 10% isodose line and higher. **Right** color wash represents 95% isodose line and higher.

Doses

PTV = 180 cGy/fx to 54 Gy.

Outcome

Five-year progression-free survival (PFS) is >85%. 10-year PFS and OS are 77% and 83%, respectively.

Complications

- Hypopituitarism (especially diabetes insipidus as a postsurgical complication)
- Hypothalamic obesity (postsurgical complication)
- Cystic growth after RT (may require Ommaya tap or shunt placement)
- Sleep and psychological disturbance, vasculopathy and stroke, neurocognitive decline, optic neuropathy
- Second cancer, brain necrosis

Follow-Up

- Brain MRI every 3 months for first year, every 6 months through fifth year, then annually.
- Consider MR angiography to screen for vasculopathy.
- Close endocrinology and ophthalmologic follow-up.

ANNOTATED BIBLIOGRAPHY

LOW-GRADE GLIOMA

Ref 1. van den Bent et al. (2005). Long-term efficacy of early versus delayed radiotherapy for low-grade astrocytoma and oligodendroglioma in adults: the EORTC 22845 randomised trial. *Lanncet*;366(9490):985–90. EORTC 22845 Trial.

In this study, 311 patients with supratentorial low-grade gliomas were randomized after neurosurgery to observation versus post-op RT of 54 Gy in 6 weeks. After recurrence, the same RT was given to the control arm. With a 55-month median follow-up, the results at 5 years were as follows:

Variant	Median Progression-Free Survival (Year)	Median Survival (Year)
Initial RT arm	5.3	7.4
Delayed RT arm	3.4	7.2
P-value	0.00001	0.872

The study suggests that immediate post-op RT at a dose of 54 Gy improves the period without progression but does not affect the OS of low-grade glioma patients.

Ref 2. Buckner JC et al. (2016). Radiation plus Procarbazine, CCNU, and Vincristine in Low-Grade Glioma. N Eng J Med;374:1344–55. RTOG 9802 Trial.

In this study, 251 patients of age <40 years with STR/biopsy, of age >40 with any extent of resection, supratentorial WHO grade II astrocytoma, oligoastrocytoma, or oligodendroglioma were enrolled. Patients were randomized to RT alone (54 Gy/30 fx) or RT followed by six cycles of standard dose PCV. The results at median follow-up of 11.9 years yielded the following data at the 10-year time point:

	Progression-Free Survival (%)	Overall Survival (%)
RT alone	21	40
RT + PCV	51	60
P-value	<0.001	0.003

This study led to a new standard-of-care for low-grade glioma patients receiving RT, consisting of RT followed by adjuvant PCV chemotherapy.

Ref 3. Baumert et al. (2016). Temozolomide chemotherapy versus radiotherapy in high-risk low-grade glioma (EORTC 22033–26033): a randomised, open-label, phase 3 intergroup study. Lancet Oncol;17(11):1521–32. EORTC 22,033 Trial.

In this study, 707 patients with WHO grade II gliomas and at least one high-risk feature (age >40, progression, tumor size >5 cm, crossing midline, or neurologic symptoms) were assigned to RT (50.4 Gy in 28 fx) or dose-dense oral temozolomide (75 mg/mg^2 once daily *for 21 days, every 28 days, for up to 12 cycles). Median follow-up was 48 months. Results were as follows:*

	Median Progression-Free Survival (Months)
RT	*46*
Temozolomide	*39*
P-value	*0.22*

Those with IDH-mutated tumors without 1p/19q codeletion had longer progression-free survival with RT than temozolomide (hazard ratio 1.86, P = .0043), whereas there were no differences between treatment arms among those with IDH-mutated and codeleted tumors and IDH-wildtype tumors.

HIGH-GRADE GLIOMA

Radiation Therapy

Ref 4. Roa et al. (2015). International atomic energy agency randomized phase III study of radiation therapy in elderly and/or frail patients with newly diagnosed glioblastoma multiforme. *J Clin Oncol*;33(35):4145−50. IAEA Trial.
    In this study, 98 patients with glioblastoma who were frail (KPS 50%−70% and age ≥50) or elderly (age ≥65) or elderly and frail were assigned to RT alone, 25 Gy in five daily fractions for more than 1 week or 40 Gy in 15 fractions for more than 3 weeks. Short-course RT was noninferior. Results follow.

	Median Overall Survival (Months)
25 Gy RT	*7.9*
40 Gy RT	*6.4*
P-value	*0.99*

This study showed noninferiority of short-course RT compared with 40 Gy in 15 fractions, in a frail and/or elderly population.

Chemotherapy

Ref 5. Stupp et al. (2009). Effects of radiotherapy with concomitant and adjuvant temozolomide versus radiotherapy alone on survival in a glioblastoma in a randomized phase III study: 5-year analysis of the EORTC-NCIC trial. *Lancet Oncol*;10(5):434−35. EORTC 26,981.

In this study, 573 patients with newly diagnosed histologically confirmed glioblastoma were randomized between radiotherapy versus radiotherapy plus temozolomide, given concomitantly with and after radiotherapy. Radiotherapy was given 2 Gy per fraction to a total dose of 60 Gy in 6 weeks. Temozolomide was given 75 mg/m² daily, 7 days a week from the first to the last day of radiotherapy, followed by six cycles of adjuvant temozolomide 150–200 mg/m² for 5 days during each 28-day cycle. Results at 5 years showed the following:

	Overall Survival (%)
Radiotherapy alone	1.9
Radiotherapy + temozolomide	9.8
P-value	<0.0001

This study showed that the addition of temozolomide to radiotherapy for glioblastoma patients resulted in a survival benefit.

Ref 6. Cairncross et al. (2013). Phase III trial of chemoradiotherapy for anaplastic oligodendroglioma: long-term results of RTOG 9402." *J Clin Oncol;*31(3):337–43. RTOG 9402 Trial.

In this study, 291 patients with anaplastic oligodendrogliomas and anaplastic oligoastrocytoma were randomized between post-op RT alone versus PCV + RT (in that order). RT dose was 180 cGy to 59.4 Gy. Long-term follow-up of the study revealed the following:

	Median Overall Survival (Years)	P-Value
ALL PATIENTS		
RT	4.7	0.1
PCV → RT	4.6	
1p/19q codeleted		
RT	7.3	<0.001
PCV → RT	14.7	
1p/19q-intact		
RT	2.7	0.39
PCV → RT	2.6	

In the entire cohort of patients with anaplastic oligodendroglioma and oligoastrocytoma, PCV plus RT did not prolong survival. However, a subgroup analysis revealed a benefit to PCV preceding RT among those tumors with a 1p/19q codeletion.

Ref 7. van den Bent et al. (2013). Adjuvant procarbazine, lomustine, and vincristine chemotherapy in newly diagnosed anaplastic oligodendroglioma: long-term follow-up of EORTC brain tumor group study 26,951. *J Clin Oncol*;31(3):344–50. EORTC 26,951 Trial.

This study was very similar to RTOG 9402 (above); however, PCV was given adjuvant to radiotherapy, 368 patients with anaplastic oligodendrogliomas were treated with 59.4 Gy RT followed by observation or PCV for six cycles. After a median follow-up of 140 months, the following results were found:

	Median Survival (Months)
Radiotherapy alone	*30.6*
Radiotherapy + PCV	*42.3*
P-value	*0.018*

In those with 1p/19q codeletion, there was greater benefit from adjuvant PCV (median OS was not reached in those receiving PCV compared with 112 months in the RT-alone group).

Ref 8. Wick W et al. (2016). Long term analysis of the NOA-04 randomized phase III trial of sequential radiochemotherapy of anaplastic glioma with PCV or temozolomide. *Neuro Oncol*;18(11):1529–37. NOA 04 Trial.

In this trial, 318 patients with glioma WHO grade III AA, AO, AOA were randomized to RT alone (arm A), PCV (arm B1), or TMZ (arm B2). RT was given GTV+2 cm to 59.6–60 Gy. Progression after RT, chemo is given; progression after chemo, RT is given. At 9.5 years, the data show the following:

	Median Tumor-Treating Field (Years)	*Progression-Free Survival (Years)*	*Overall Survival (Years)*
Arm A	*4.6*	*2.5*	*8*
Arm B1/B2	*4.4*	*2.7*	*6.5*
	ns	*ns*	*ns*

No difference RT first versus chemo first.
No difference PCV versus TMZ.
AA worse than AO, but AO same as mixed AOA.
IDH mutant/codel better OS.
IDH mutant/no codel/IDH wt worse OS.

This study showed that monochemotherapy was not better than primary RT. For 1p/19q codeleted, the study supports sequential chemoradiotherapy per RTOG 9402, 9802 and EORTC 26,951.

Ref 9. Perry et al. (2017). Short-course radiation plus Temozolomide in elderly patients with glioblastoma. *N Engl J Med*;376:1027—37. EORTC 26062/CCTG CE.6/TROG 08.02 Trial.

In this study, 562 patients aged ≥65 years with newly diagnosed glioblastoma were assigned to receive hypofractionated RT alone or RT with concurrent and adjuvant temozolomide. The RT was 40 Gy in 15 fractions. This study also incorporated analysis by MGMT methylation status in a subset of patients with available molecular information.

	Median Overall Survival (Months)
Radiotherapy alone	7.6
Radiotherapy + temozolomide	9.3
P-value	<0.001

Overall, in the entire cohort, use of temozolomide in an elderly population receiving hypofractionated RT led to an improvement in OS.

Ref 10. Van den Bent MJ et al. (2017): Interim results from CANTON trial (EORTC study 26053-22054) of treatment with concurrent and adjuvant temozolomide for 1p/19q non-co-deleted anaplastic glioma: a phase 3, randomized, open-label intergroup study. *Lancet*, published 08 August, 2017. CANTON Trial.

In this trial, 747 patients with 2 × 2 factorial design with noncodeleted anaplastic glioma with WHO PS 0—2, were randomized to RT 59. 4 Gy alone or with adjuvant temozolomide (Twelve 4-week cycle of 150—200 mg/m² temozolomide given on days 1—5); or to receive RT with concurrent temozolomide 75 mg/m² per day with or without adjuvant temozolomide. The data follow.

	5-Year Overall Survival (%)	Hematologic Grade 3—4 (%)
RT alone	44.1	
RT + adjuvant temozolomide	55.9	12%
	ss	

This study demonstrated that adjuvant temozolomide was associated with a significant survival benefit in patients with newly diagnosed noncodeleted anaplastic glioma.

Ref 11. Chang et al. (2017). Phase III randomized study of radiation and temozolomide versus radiation and nitrosourea therapy for anaplastic astrocytoma: results of NRG Oncology RTOG 9813. *Neuro-Oncology;*19(2):252–58. RTOG 9813 Trial.

In this study, 196 patients with histologically confirmed anaplastic astrocytoma were randomly assigned 1:1 to receive RT and temozolomide or RT and a nitrosourea. Median follow-up was 10.1 years. Results were as follows:

	Median Overall Survival (Years)
Radiotherapy + TMZ	3.9
Radiotherapy + NU	3.8
P-value	0.36

RT + TMZ did not improve survival over RT + nitrosourea. Those receiving temozolomide experienced fewer grade ≥3 toxicities.

Re 12. Stupp et al. (2017). Effects of tumor-treating fields plus maintenance Temozolomide versus maintenance Temozolomide alone on survival in patients with Glioblastoma. *JAMA;*318(23):2306–16.

In this study, 695 patients with GBM whose tumors were resected or biopsied and had concomitant radiochemotherapy with temozolomide were randomized 2:1 to receive maintenance treatment with TTFs and temozolomide or temozolomide alone. The TTFs, consisting of low-intensity, 200-kHz frequency, alternating electric fields, were delivered (>18 h/d) via four transducer arrays on the shaved scalp and connected to a portable device. Temozolomide was administered to both groups (150–200 mg/m^2) for 5 days per 28-day cycle (6–12 cycles). The data follow.

	Median Overall Survival (Months)
RT/Tmz + Temozolomide alone	16
RT/Tmz + Temozolomide + TTF	20.9
P-value	0.001

The study concluded that with GBM patients who had received standard chemoRT, the addition of TTF to maintain temozolomide improved OS.

BRAINSTEM GLIOMAS

Re 13. Zaghloul et al. (2014). Hypofractionated conformal radiotherapy for pediatric diffuse intrinsic pontine glioma (DIPG): A randomized clinical trial. *Radiother Oncol;*111:35–40.

In this small randomized controlled trial, 71 children with DIPG were randomized to two RT fractionation schedules: 39 Gy in 13 fractions versus 54 Gy in 30 fractions. The results were as follows:

Treatment	Median Survival	1-Year Survival (%)
39 Gy in 13 fx	7.8 months	36
54 Gy in 30 fx	9.5 months	26
P-value	0.59	

Although the hypofractionated arm did not meet the prespecified noninferiority margin, both arms had comparable survival.

EPENDYMOMA

Ref 14. Merchant et al. (2009). Conformal radiotherapy after surgery for paediatric ependymoma: a prospective study. *Lancet Oncol*;10:258–66.

In this study, 153 young children and infants were treated with surgery and conformal radiotherapy for localized EP. 51% of children were aged <3 years. Individuals aged <18 months received 54 Gy in 30 fractions; all other children received 59.4 Gy in 33 fractions. The CTV was a 10-mm expansion on the GTV. The median follow-up was 5.3 years. The 7-year results for all patients are as follows:

Treatment	Local Control (%)	Overall Survival (%)
Post-op radiation therapy	87	81

This study established a role of post-op focal radiation for children (<3 years) with intracranial EP.

Ref 15. Merchant TE et al. (2015). A phase II trial of conformal radiation therapy for pediatric patients with localized ependymoma, chemotherapy prior to second surgery for incompletely resected ependymoma and observation for completely resected, differentiated, supratentorial ependymoma. *Int J Rad Oncol Bio Phys* November 1, 2015;93(3):Supp S1. ACNS0121 Trial.

In this trial, 378 patients with WHO grade II, supratentorial EP after microscopically complete (GTR1) resection (stratum 1), administer chemotherapy with optional second surgery before CRT for patients with STR at the time of protocol enrollment (stratum 2) and immediate post-op CRT for patients after near-total (NTR defined as <5 mm residual thickness) or macroscopic gross-total (GTR2) resection (stratum 3) and WHO grade III, supratentorial or any grade, infratentorial after GTR1 (stratum 4). Stratum two patients were treated with pre-CRT chemotherapy—two 3 week cycles of vincristine, carboplatin, and cyclophosphamide (cycle 1) and etoposide (cycle 2); second surgery before CRT was optional. Stratum 3 and 4 received *post-op CRT. Radiation was administered using a 1.0 cm clinical target volume margin. The cumulative total dose was 59.4 Gy except for age <18 months after GTR. The data follow.*

	5-Year Event-Free Survival (%)		5-Year Overall Survival (%)	
	All pt	*Stratum 3/4*	*All pt*	*Stratum 3/4*
<3 years	57	63	85	87
≥3 years	65	71	83	85

The study concluded that the outcome for patients with EP treated with immediate post-op RT appears to be favorable, consistent with single institution benchmarks, and associated with the known prognostic factors of extent of resection and tumor grade.

MENINGIOMA

Ref 16. Rogers et al. (2016). Low-risk meningioma: initial outcomes from NRG oncology/RTOG 0539. ASTRO abstract 2016. *Int J Rad Oncol Biol Phys*;96(5):939–40. RTOG 0539 Trial.

    Rogers L et al. (2017). Intermediate-risk meningioma: initial outcomes from NRG oncology RTOG 0539. J Neurosurg October 2017;6:1–13.

    Rogers L et al. (2017). High-risk meningioma: initial outcomes from NRG oncology/RTOG-0539. Neuro-Oncology November 6, 2017;19(suppl_6):vi133.

    NRG Oncology/RTOG 0539 was a prospective phase II study that had three treatment groups, based on risk classification. The primary endpoint for all strata was 3-year PFS.

	Low-Risk	*Intermediate-Risk*	*High-Risk*
Eligibility	*Any G1*	*G2 GTR, recurrent G1*	*Any G3, recurrent G2, G2 STR*
Evaluable patients	*63*	*48*	*51*
Median follow-up (years)	*n/a*	*3.7*	*4*
Treatment	*Observation*	*54 Gy/30*	*60 Gy/30*
3 y PFS	*91.8%*	*93.8%*	*58.8%*
3 y LC	*93.5%*	*95.9%*	*68.9%*
3 y OS	*98.4%*	*96.0%*	*78.6%*

Low-risk: observation after GTR is appropriate, but those with STR may potentially benefit from RT. Intermediate-risk: post-op RT was effective for completely resected grade II tumors and recurrent grade I tumors. High-risk: 3 y PFS was comparable to literature estimates.

MEDULLOBLASTOMA

Ref 17. Packer et al. (2006). Phase III study of craniospinal radiation therapy followed by adjuvant chemotherapy for newly diagnosed average-risk medulloblastoma. *J Clin Oncol* 24(25):4204–08.

In this study, 421 standard-risk patients between 3 and 21 years of age with nondisseminated medulloblastoma were randomized to reduced-dose RT (23.4 Gy CSI + 55.8 Gy to posterior fossa) and concurrent vincristine, and randomized to either (1) CCNU, cisplatin, and vincristine or (2) cyclophosphamide, cisplatin, and vincristine. The results at median follow-up at 5 years showed the following:

	Event-Free Survival (%)	Overall Survival (%)
Concurrent chemoRT + CCNU/Cis/Vincristine	82	87
Concurrent chemoRT + Cyclo/Cis/Vincristine	80 ns	85 ns

The main significance of this study was that reduced-dose CSI can be combined with CCNU/Cis/Vincristine and Cyclo/Cis/Vincristine to avoid toxicities of higher dose RT in standard-risk patients.

Ref 18. Gajjar et al. (2006). Risk-adapted craniospinal radiotherapy followed by high-dose chemotherapy and stem-cell rescue in children with newly diagnosed medulloblastoma (St Jude Medulloblastoma-96): Long-term results from a prospective, multicentre trial. *Lancet Oncol;*7(10):813–20.

In this study, 134 patients aged 3–21 with newly diagnosed medulloblastoma after resection were classified as having average-risk medulloblastoma (<1.5 cm² residual tumor and no metastatic disease) or high-risk medulloblastoma (>1.5 cm² residual disease or metastatic disease localized to neuraxis). All patients received risk-adapted radiotherapy (CSI 23.4 Gy/posterior fossa boost 36 Gy/primary bed boost 55.8 Gy for average-risk disease and CSI 36.0–39.6 Gy/ primary bed boost 55.8 Gy for high-risk disease) followed by four cycles of cyclophosphamide-based, dose-intensive chemotherapy with autologous stem cell rescue after each cycle. The 5-year result follows.

	Event-Free Survival (%)	Overall Survival (%)
Average-risk medulloblastoma	83	85
High-risk medulloblastoma	70	70
P-value	0.046	0.04

The study revealed that risk-adapted radiotherapy followed by a schedule of dose-intensive chemotherapy can be used to improve the outcome of patients with high-risk medulloblastoma.

Ref 19. Michaleski J et al. (2016). Results of COG ACNS0331: A phase III trial of involved-field radiotherapy (IFRT) and low dose craniospinal irradiation (LD-CSI) with chemotherapy in average-risk medulloblastoma: a report from the children's oncology group. *ACNS0331 Trial.*

In this study, 549 children with A-R medulloblastoma without excessive residual disease or anaplasia were randomized to posterior fossa radiotherapy (PFRT) or IFRT. Conventional therapy for A-R medulloblastoma is standard dose CSI (SD-CSI) to 23.4 Gy and PFRT to 54 Gy with cisplatin-/cyclophosphamide-based chemotherapy. This trial tests whether a 5.4 Gy reduction in the CSI dose (18 Gy, LD-CSI) in patients 3–7 years of and a reduction in boost volume (IFRT) in patients of 3–21 years of age receiving chemotherapy results in non-inferior event-free survival or OS. At median follow-up of 6.6 years the data showed the following:

	5-Year (%) Event-Free Survival	5-Year (%) Overall Survival
PFRT	80.8	85.2
IFRT	82.2	84.1
SD-CSI	82.6	85.9
LD-CSI	72.1	78.1

This study concluded that for patients with average-risk medulloblastoma, radiation boost volume to the primary site can be reduced. However, decreasing CSI dose to 18 Gy may increase risk of recurrence and is not recommended.

CRANIOPHARYNGIOMA

Ref 20. Merchant et al. (2013). Disease control after reduced volume conformal and intensity modulated radiation therapy for childhood craniopharyngioma. *Int J Rad Oncol Biol Phys* 85(4):e187–92.

This was a prospective study of 88 patients with craniopharyngioma treated with 54 Gy in 30 fractions post-op photon RT. Those who received a CTV of 5 mm versus 10 mm were compared.

	Progression-Free Survival (%)	P-Value
CTV margin ≤5 mm	96	0.64
CTV margin >5 mm	88	

There was no difference in PFS by CTV margin size. The study also found an association between the number of weekly, noncontrast MR examinations and disease progression. Those who had three or fewer on-treatment MRI studies had a >15% progression rate, whereas those who had four or more MRI studies had a progression rate of <3% (trend test, P = .04).

15

Head and Neck Cancers

The major sites of head and neck cancers are the nasopharynx, oropharynx, hypopharynx, and larynx. The larynx is subdivided into the supraglottis, glottis, and subglottis. Their borders (superiorly to inferiorly) are as follows:

Nasopharynx	Anterior-superiorly from posterior choana, inferiorly to the superior surface of the soft palate.
Oropharynx	Superiorly from the inferior surface of the soft palate, inferiorly to the inferior border of the hyoid bone.
Hypopharynx	Superiorly from the inferior border of the hyoid bone, inferiorly to the inferior border of cricoid cartilage.
Supraglottis	Superiorly from the tip of the epiglottis, inferiorly to a horizontal plane passing through the apex of the ventricle.
Glottis	Superiorly from the lateral margin of the ventricle extending 1 cm inferiorly.
Subglottis	Superiorly from the lower boundary of the glottis, inferiorly to the lower margin of the cricoid.

HEAD AND NECK LYMPH NODE BORDERS*

Level 1a submental nodes: Superiorly mylohyoid m. and caudal edge of the mandible, inferiorly platysma m. and mid-hyoid bone, anteriorly symphysis menti, posteriorly body of hyoid bone, and laterally medial edge of the anterior belly of digastric m. (Fig 15.1).

    Level Ib submandibular nodes: Superiorly cranial edge of the submandibular gland, inferiorly caudal edge of hyoid bone or inferior edge of submandibular gland (whichever is lower), anteriorly symphysis menti, posteriorly posterior edge of the

Fundamentals of Radiation Oncology
https://doi.org/10.1016/B978-0-12-814128-1.00015-5

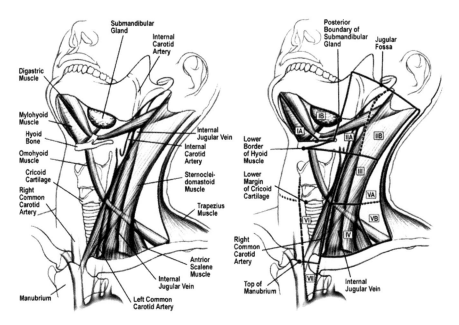

FIGURE 15.1   Diagram of the neck as seen from the left anterior view. Left, the pertinent anatomy that relates to the nodal classification. Right, an outline of the levels of the classification. *Reproduced from Som PM, Curtin HD, Mancuso AA. An imaging based classification for the cervical nodes designed as an adjunct to recent clinically based nodal classifications. Arch Otolaryngol—Head Neck Surg 1999;125:388—96.*

submandibular gland, laterally Medial aspect of the mandible, and medially lateral edge of anterior belly of digastric m.

Level II upper jugular nodes: Superiorly caudal edge of the lateral process of C1, inferiorly caudal edge of the body of the hyoid bone, anteriorly posterior edge of the submandibular gland/posterior edge of posterior belly of digastric m., posteriorly posterior edge of sternocleidomastoid m., laterally medial surface of SCM/platysma m./parotid gland/posterior belly of digastric m., and medially medial edge of internal carotid artery/scalenus m.

Level III middle jugular nodes: Superiorly caudal edge of the body of the hyoid bone, inferiorly caudal edge of cricoid cartilage, anteriorly anterior edge of SCM/posterior third of thyrohyoid m., posteriorly posterior edge of SCM, laterally medial surface of SCM, and medially medial edge of common carotid artery/scalenus m.

Level IV lower jugular nodes: Superiorly caudal edge of cricoid cartilage, inferiorly 2 cm cranial to sternocleidomastoid joint (N−) or sternocleidomastoid joint (N+), anteriorly posterolateral edge of SCM, posteriorly anterior edge of paraspinal m., laterally lateral edge of SCM, and medially medial edge of common carotid artery/lateral edge of thyroid gland.

Level V posterior neck nodes: Superiorly cranial base, inferiorly transverse cervical vessels/cranial borders of clavicle, anteriorly posterior edge of SCM, posteriorly anterior edge of trapezius m., laterally platysma m., and medially paraspinal m.

Retropharyngeal nodes: Superiorly base of skull (BOS), inferiorly cranial edge of the hyoid bone, anteriorly levator veli palatine, posteriorly prevertebral m., laterally medial edge of vessel bundle, and medially midline.

*Data from:

1. *Chao KSC et al. (2002). Determination and delineation of nodal target volumes for head-and-neck cancer based on patterns of failure in patients receiving definitive and postoperative IMRT. Int J Radiat Oncol Biol Phys August 1, 2002;53(5):1174−84.*
2. *Gregoria V, et al. (2014). Delineation of the neck node levels for head and neck tumors: a 2013 update. DAHANCA, EORTC, HKNPCSG, NCIC CTG, NCRI, RTOG, TROG consensus guidelines. Radiother Oncol January 2014;110(1):172−81. https://doi.org/10.1016/j.radonc.2013.10.010. Epub 2013 Oct 31.*

LYMPH NODE RISK

Tumor Site: Lymph Nodess at Risk[a]	Ipsilateral (%)	Contralateral (%)
Nasopharynx: upper postcervical, superior deep jugular, subdigastric	80	40
BOT: subdigastric, superior deep jugular, submandibular	75	40
Tonsil fossa: subdigastric, sup deep jugular, mid-jugular	75	10
Hypopharynx: subdigastric, mid-jugular, low jugular	75	10
Supraglottis: subdigastric, mid-jugular, low jugular	55	15
Soft palate: subdigastric, mid-jugular	40	15
Tonsilar pillar: subdigastric, submandibular	40	5
Oral tongue: subdigastric, mid-jugular, submandibular	35	5
Floor of mouth: subdigastric, submandibular	25	<5
Glottis T1	0	
T2	<5	
T3−4	25	

(Continued)

Tumor Site: Lymph Nodess at Risk[a]	Ipsilateral (%)	Contralateral (%)
Lip commissure	20	
Lip: submental, submandible, subdigastric, parotid, buccinator	10	
Subglottis	10	

[a]Data from: Lindberg R. Distribution of cervical lymph node metastases from squamous cell carcinoma of the upper respiratory and digestive t racts. Cancer 1972;29(6):1446–9; Mendenhall WM, Million RR, Cassisi NJ. Elective neck irradiation in squamous-cell carcinoma of the head and neck. Head Neck Surg 1980;3(1):15–20.

ORAL CAVITY CANCER

The estimated total incidence in the United States for oral cavity and pharynx cancer is 51,540 with a total of 10,030 estimated deaths in 2018.

The oral cavity consists of the lips, buccal mucosa, upper alveolar ridge, lower alveolar ridge, retromolar trigone (small triangular surface posterior to last molar, overlying the ascending ramus), floor of mouth (FOM), hard palate, and the anterior two-thirds of the tongue.

Workup

Risk Factors

Poor oral hygiene, tobacco, alcohol, and middle age (male).

Symptoms and Signs
- Sore mouth, bleeding and painful mass in mouth, difficulty with eating or swallowing, voice hoarseness (dysphonia), earache (otalgia), ear fullness, trismus
- Physical exam should include skin, scalp, lymph nodes, HEENT, and CNS

Investigations
- CBC, chemistry with liver/renal function
- Indirect and direct laryngoscopy
- Tissue diagnosis (punch biopsy, FNA, core biopsy, open biopsy)
- CT or MRI of neck with contrast chest X-ray and consider PET scan
- Exam under anesthesia and endoscopic exam
- Dental consult: Stannous fluoride trays (0.4%) starting within 1 month of completion of treatment
- Speech and swallowing evaluation as indicated

TNM Staging (Oral Cavity)

T1	Tumor ≤2 cm, ≤5 mm depth of invasion (DOI).
T2	Tumor ≤2 cm, DOI >5 mm and ≤10 mm or tumor >2 cm but ≤4 cm and ≤10 mm DOI.
T3	Tumor ≥4 cm or any tumor >10 mm DOI.
T4a	Moderately advanced local disease. Lip: Tumor invades through cortical bone, inferior alveolar nerve, floor of mouth, or skin of face, i.e., chin or nose (oral cavity). Tumor invades adjacent structures only (e.g., through cortical bone, [mandible or maxilla] into deep [extrinsic] muscle of tongue [genioglossus, hyoglossus, palatoglossus, and styloglossus], maxillary sinus, and facial skin)
T4b	Very advanced local disease. Tumor invades masticator space, pterygoid plates, or skull base and/or encases internal carotid artery.

Superficial erosion of bone/tooth socket by gingival primary is insufficient T4 tumor classification.

N0	No regional lymph node metastasis.
N1	Metastasis in a single ipsilateral lymph node, 3 cm or less in greatest dimension and ENE (−)
N2	Metastasis in a single ipsilateral lymph node, more than 3 cm but not more than 6 cm in greatest dimension and ENE(−) (N2a); or in multiple ipsilateral lymph nodes, none more than 6 cm in greatest dimension and ENE (−) (N2b); or in bilateral or contralateral lymph nodes, none more than 6 cm in greatest dimension and ENE (−) (N2c)
N3	Metastasis in a lymph node more than 6 cm in greatest dimension and ENE (−) (N3a); or metastases in any node (s) and clinically overt ENE (+) (N3b)
M0	No distant metastasis (no pathologic M0; use clinical M to complete stage group)
M1	Distant metastasis

Stage Grouping

Stage I	T1	N0	M0
Stage II	T2	N0	M0
Stage III	T1,2	N1	M0
	T3	N0, 1	M0
Stage IVA	T1, 2, 3	N2	M0
	T4a	N0, 1, 2	M0
Stage IVB	Any T	N3	M0
	T4b	Any N	M0
Stage IVC	Any T	Any N	M1

M, distant metastasis; N, regional lymph nodes; TNM, T (tumor).
Used with permission of the American Joint Committee on Cancer (AJCC), Chicago, Illinois. The original source for this material is the AJCC Cancer Staging Manual, Eighth Edition (2017) published by Springer Science Business Media LLC, www.springer.com.

Treatment

- **Stage I, II**—Surgery with upfront supraomohyoid (levels I—III) or selective neck dissection [3]. SLN biopsy can be considered. Post-op RT is indicated if positive margin, PNI, LVI, depth of invasion >4 mm or positive lymph node (LN) (consider).
- **Stage III, IVB**—Resection and ipsilateral or bilateral selective (when tumor passes midline) versus comprehensive neck dissection.
- **Post-op**—RT for lesions with pT3-4, close margin, PNI, LVI [1,2]. ChemoRT for positive margin, ENE, residual gross disease.
- **Unresectable**—Concurrent chemoRT or chemo followed by RT or RT alone.

RT Technique
3D Technique

LIP
- Electron beams are used with a waxed lead shield to protect the gum/mandible. Use 6—9 Mev electrons. A bolus is used and the dose is prescribed to the 80%—90% isodose line, treated with an enface field with 2-cm margin. Dose is 200 cGy/fx to 60—66 Gy. For advanced lesions; total tumor dose is 66—70 Gy.
- Postoperatively first echelon lymph nodes will be treated with **borders** superiorly to abut the level of the hard palate, lower border at thyroid notch, flashing anteriorly and posterior border is at the back of the vertebral body. The initial fields are taken to 45—50 Gy, then cone down to half the oral cavity to 54 Gy and then boost the primary site to 60 Gy.

ORAL TONGUE/FLOOR OF MOUTH

- T1 patients are treated with opposed lateral beams. Patients are supine, face mask on, arms strapped down, IV contrast in, tongue blade in with CT simulation.
- **Borders:** The anterior border is in front of the mandible (lower lip excluded); the posterior border for node negative is behind the vertebral body, for node positive, behind the spinous process; the superior border is 2 cm above the tongue; the inferior border is at the thyroid notch. T2—T3 patients are treated with opposed laterals and low anterior neck (LAN) fields. The LAN field borders are superior border at bottom of upper neck field; the inferior border is at the bottom of the clavicle and lateral borders are outside the first ribs. Isocentric technique is used.
- RT dose is to 70 Gy if primary RT is used. Post-op RT to primary site to 60 Gy; if positive margin, to 66 Gy; if positive gross disease, to 70 Gy. Offcord at 40 Gy, with larynx and cheater blocks in place. A superolateral block is placed in node negative patients to exclude part of the oral cavity, the mandible and the parotid gland. Boost with 1—2 cm margin.

BUCCAL MUCOSA

- For T1-2N0, use ipsilateral mixed beam (4:1 electrons:photons) covering the primary with margin plus first echelon nodes (electron field is 1 cm larger than photon).
- Use an intraoral shield to protect gum/mandible.
- For T1-2N1, use anterior/posterior (AP)/lateral wedged pair with asymmetric jaw technique and also treat LAN. **Borders:** For lateral field, superior border is 2 cm above the primary; inferior border is at the thyroid notch; anterior border has a 2-cm margin on primary; posterior border is at the back of the vertebral body. Prescribe 50 Gy to initial field and LAN, then boost primary with electrons or smaller wedged pair field to 66—70 Gy.

GINGIVA, HARD PALATE, AND RETROMOLAR TRIGONE

- Gingiva **Borders:** AP and lateral fields are similar to buccal mucosa but include the entire hemimandible and superiorly include the temporomandibular joint and pterygoid plate.
- Hard Palate/Retromolar Trigone **Borders:** Opposed laterals using a 3-cm margin superiorly including pterygoid plate and inferiorly on the hard palate. Anteriorly, the border is placed at the premaxillary process, and posteriorly to the uvula.
- Use a bite block to depress the tongue out of the field.
- Treat this field to 60 Gy, then boost with a smaller photon field putting 1—2 cm margin on the target volume for a total dose of 70 Gy.
- Postoperatively treat to 50 Gy followed by a boost to 60—66 Gy.
- For small superficial node-negative patients, lymph nodes are not treated, treat LNs in node-positive patients. Posterior and inferior field borders would be similar to other OC lesions.

IMRT Technique

Patients are supine, face mask on, arms strapped down, IV contrast in, tongue blade in if indicated, and patients are CT simulated. PET/CT and MR fusion are recommended if available for delineation of gross disease. 6 MV photons, 9 equally spaced IMRT beams, or 2 arcs for VMAT planning.

Volumes

GTV = gross disease + enlarged LNs, as seen on CT, MRI, or PET scans
CTV1 = GTV + subclinical disease around GTV + ipsilateral and contralateral at risk LNs + 0.5−1 cm around primary and 0.3−0.5 cm around LNs, respecting tissue boundaries
CTV2 = GTV + subclinical disease around GTV + ipsilateral at risk LNs + 0.5−1 cm around primary and 0.3−0.5 cm around LNs, respecting tissue boundaries
CTV3 = GTV + 0.5−1 cm around primary and 0.3−0.5 cm around LNs, respecting tissue boundaries
PTV= CTV + 0.3−0.5 cm

Subclinical disease around GTV is based on primary site and typically includes the entire postoperative bed and adjacent tissues at risk.

Ipsilateral and/or contralateral at risk LNs are based on primary site: Submental (level Ia), submandibular (level Ib), internal jugular (level II, III, IV), posterior neck (level V), and retropharyngeal LNs can be included at the discretion of the treating physician.

Doses

STANDARD FRACTION

PTV1 = 200 cGy/fx to 50−54 Gy
PTV2 = 200 cGy/fx to 60−66 Gy (66 Gy suggested in areas of ECE or margin positivity)
PTV3 = 200 cGy/fx to 70 Gy, post-op to 60 Gy, positive margin to 66 Gy

HYPERFRACTIONATION RT

1.2 Gy/fx bid to 81.6 Gy

CONCOMITANT BOOST

Large field 1.8 Gy/fx, boost dose 1.2 Gy/fx for last 12 days as second daily fraction to 72 Gy

Outcomes

Lip/oral cavity: Local controls for T1, 92%; T2, 87%; T3, 75%.
Oral tongue/FOM: Local controls are oral tongue: T1, 90%; T2, 80%; T3, 60%; T4, 30%. FOM: T1, 85%; T2, 70%; T3, 50%; T4, 30%.
Buccal mucosa: Local control rates: T1/2, 80%; T3, 40%.
Gingiva: Local control rates: T1, 70%; T2, 60%; T3, 20%; T4, 0%.
Hard palate: Local control rates: T1, 100%; T2, 75%; T3, 50%; T4, 0%.

Complications

Skin erythema, swelling of the gum and the lips, sore mouth, dry mouth, trismus, dysgeusia, dysphagia, odynophagia, weight loss, dental caries, and bone damage (osteoradionecrosis).

Follow-Up

- Every 1–3 months for the first year, every 4 months for the second year, then every 6 months for years 3–5
- Posttreatment PETCT
- Chest X-ray or CT of chest as indicated
- TSH every 12 months
- Hearing, speech, and swallowing evaluation as indicated

NASOPHARYNGEAL CANCER

Painless neck mass is the presenting complaint in many nasopharyngeal cancer patients. Most often, they present with junctional nodes at the tip of the mastoid bone. The lymphatic drainage of the nasopharynx also includes the retropharyngeal nodes, the uppermost of which is the node of Rouvière at C1 level. Tumors can spread through the foramen lacerum, which lies within the roof of the nasopharynx and communicates with the middle cranial fossa. One-fourth of patients with nasopharyngeal cancer can present with cranial nerve V and VI palsies.

Workup

Risk Factors
- Smoking and alcohol
- Dust and wood fire smoke, salted and smoked fish
- Epstein–Barr virus (EBV)

Symptoms and Signs
- Nasal stuffiness/discharge/epistaxis, nasal voice, otalgia and unilateral hearing loss from middle ear effusion, swallowing difficulty/sore throat, and trismus
- Other syndromes
  - **Petrosphenoid syndrome of Jacob.** Tumor extension through the foramen lacerum or other foramina to the cavernous sinus involving CN III–VI can result in ptosis and ophthalmoplegia, facial pain, and numbness.
  - **Retropharyngeal space/retroparotidian syndrome of Villaret/parapharyngeal syndrome.** Spread of the tumor through the fossa of Rosenmüller, or nodal disease in the parapharyngeal space can involve CN IX–XII, causing altered taste, difficulty swallowing, paralysis of the neck muscles and the tongue.
  - **Trotter's triad.** Patients present with decreased movement of the soft palate, mandibular neuralgia, and hearing loss.

Investigations
- Same as for oral cavity
- CT and/or MRI scans with contrast from the BOS to the bottom of the clavicle, PET/CT scan.

TNM Staging (Nasopharynx)

T1   Tumor confined to the nasopharynx or extends to oropharynx and/or nasal cavity without parapharyngeal extension[a]

T2   Tumor with parapharyngeal extension[a]

T3   Tumor involves bony structures of skull base and/or paranasal sinuses

T4   Tumor with intracranial extension and/or involvement of involvement of cranial nerves, hypopharynx, orbit, or with extension to the infratemporal fossa/masticator space

[a]*Parapharyngeal extension denotes posterolateral infiltration of tumor.*

N0   No regional lymph node metastasis

N1   Unilateral metastasis in lymph node(s), 6 cm or less in greatest dimension, above the caudal border of cricoid cartilage, and/or unilateral or bilateral, retropharyngeal lymph nodes, 6 cm or less, in greatest dimension[a]

N2   Bilateral metastasis in lymph node(s), 6 cm or less in greatest dimension and above the caudal border of cricoid cartilage[a]

N3   Metastasis in lymph node(s)[a] >6 cm and/or extended below the cricoid cartilage

M0   No distant metastasis (no pathologic M0; use clinical M to complete stage group)

M1   Distant metastasis

[a]*Midline nodes are considered ipsilateral nodes.*

Stage Grouping

Stage I	T1	N0	M0
Stage II	T1	N1	M0
	T2	N0, 1	M0
Stage III	T1,2	N2	M0
	T3	N0, 1, 2	M0
Stage IVA	T4	N0, 1, 2	M0
	Any T	N3	M0
Stage IVB	Any T	Any N	M1

M, distant metastasis; *N*, regional lymph nodes; *TNM*, T tumor.
Used with permission of the American Joint Committee on Cancer (AJCC), Chicago, Illinois. The original source for this material is the AJCC Cancer Staging Manual, Eighth Edition (2017) published by Springer Science Business Media LLC, www.springer.com.

Treatment

- **Stage I**—definitive RT
- **Stage II/IVB**—concurrent chemoRT followed by adjuvant chemotherapy. Concurrent chemotherapy CDDP 100 mg/m² every 3 weeks X3 cycles, adjuvant chemotherapy CDDP 80 mg/m², and 5FU 1000 mg/m² X3 cycles [8–11].
- Patients receiving concurrent chemoRT, with complete response of the primary tumor but residual disease of the neck, should receive neck dissection.
- **Stage IVB** with distant metastasis should receive combination chemotherapy. If response is CR, definitive radiation therapy to the primary site and to the neck region can be considered.

RT Technique

3D Technique

- Patient is supine, neck normal, arms by side and strapped to pull shoulder, face mask on, IV contrast in, and patient CT simulated. Three fields with opposed laterals and LAN, isocentric technique.
- **Borders:** Superior for T1/T2 lesions includes sphenoid sinus, cavernous sinus, BOS with half pituitary. T3/T4 lesions and with BOS involvement, the superior border is elevated to cover all of pituitary; inferior above the thyroid notch; anterior includes posterior, 2 cm of nasal cavity, posterior one-third of maxillary sinus, and posterior one-fourth of orbit; posterior behind the spinous process, or 2 cm beyond palpable lymph nodes (Fig. 15.2).

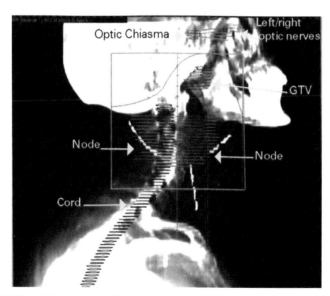

FIGURE 15.2 DRR for nasopharyngeal cancer, 3D right lateral field, showing superior border covering base of the skull and inferior border above the thyroid notch.

- Treat with opposed laterals for initial 40 Gy and then boost posterior neck to 50 Gy; take offcord neck to 50 Gy. Come off optic nerves/chiasm by 50 Gy. The final dose of 70 Gy is boosted with high-energy photons (10—15 MV). Boost with a 1—2 cm margin.

IMRT Technique

Patient is supine, neck normal, arms by side and strapped to pull shoulder, bite block should be utilized, face mask on, IV contrast in, patient CT simulated. Fuse PETCT and MRI (if available) with planning CT. 6 MV photon (9 equally spaced coplanar IMRT beams or 2 arcs for VMAT treatment plan) Figs. 15.3 and 15.4.

Volumes

GTV = gross disease + enlarged LNs as seen on CT, MRI or PET scans
CTV1 = GTV + subclinical disease around GTV + ipsilateral and contralateral at risk LNs + 0.5—1 cm around primary and 0.3—0.5 cm around LNs, respecting tissue boundaries.

CTV2 = GTV + subclinical disease around GTV + ipsilateral at risk LNs + 0.5—1 cm around primary and 0.3—0.5 cm around LNs, respecting tissue boundaries.

CTV3 = GTV + 0.5—1 cm around primary and 0.3—0.5 cm around LNs, respecting tissue boundaries.

PTV = CTV + 0.3—0.5 cm.

Subclinical disease around GTV: Entire nasopharynx, clivus, skull base, pterygoid fossa, parapharyngeal space, inferior sphenoid sinus, posterior third of the nasal cavity, and maxillary sinus.

Ipsilateral and contralateral at risk LNs: Retropharyngeal, submandibular (level Ib), internal jugular (level II, III, IV), and posterior neck (level V).

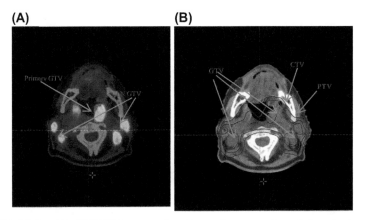

FIGURE 15.3 (A) PETCT images showing primary and nodal metastases for a nasopharyngeal cancer patient. (B) Target volumes GTV, CTV, PTV based on PETCT scan fusion with planning CT scan.

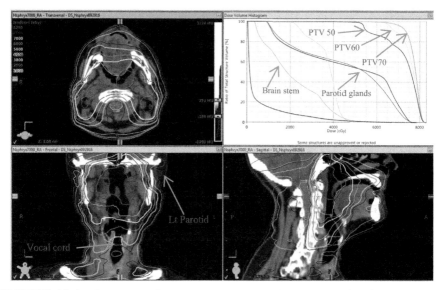

FIGURE 15.4 CT images showing two arcs VMAT treatment plan for a nasopharyngeal cancer patient illustrating isodose lines conforming PTV and DVH showing 95% PTV coverage and parotid gland did not meet constraints. The low neck is treated with VMAT with an extended field approach, eliminating the need for field matching. A dose of 50, 60, and 70 Gy is prescribed to the PTVs.

Doses

PTV1 = 200 cGy/fx to 50 Gy
PTV2 = 200 cGy/fx to 60 Gy
PTV3 = 200 cGy/fx to 70 Gy

Constraints

Brain = V60 < 30% Temporal lobes = <60 Gy Brainstem = <54 Gy Retina = 45 Gy
Optic nerve = 50–55 Gy Optic chiasm = 50–55 Gy Pituitary = 30 Gy
Lens = <10 Gy
Middle ear = mean dose <45 Gy
Spinal cord = 45–50 Gy
Parotid gland = unilateral, mean dose: 20 Gy; bilateral mean dose: 25 Gy
   Submandibular glands = mean dose <39 Gy
   Mandible = 70 Gy
   Lips and oral cavity = 30 Gy
   Glottic larynx = V50 < 27%; mean dose <44 Gy

Outcome

Five-year disease-free survival is 65%, and overall survival is 80%.

Complications

- Skin erythema, swelling of the gum and lips, sore mouth, dry mouth, loss of taste, dysphagia, odynophagia, weight loss and bone damage, nasal dryness
- Ototoxicity
- Temporal lobe necrosis

Follow-Up

- Every 1–3 months for the first year, every 4 months for the second year, and every 6 months for 3 to 5 years
- Posttreatment PETCT at 3 months
- Chest X-ray or CT/MRI as indicated
- TSH (thyroid-stimulating hormone) every 12 months
- Hearing, speech, and swallowing evaluation as indicated

OROPHARYNGEAL AND HYPOPHARYNGEAL CANCERS

The oropharynx consists of the base of the tongue, tonsillar area (anterior and posterior tonsillar pillars, tonsil), uvula, and soft palate. The oropharynx is divided into the oropharynx proper and the faucial arch. The faucial arch is the junction between the oral cavity and the laryngopharynx.

The hypopharynx has three subsites:

- Pyriform sinus (PS): Superior edge is at the level of the hyoid or vallecular and the apex is at C-6 (mid-cricoid level).
- Posterior pharyngeal wall: Extends from the level of the vallecula to the level of the cricoarytenoid joints.
- Postcricoid region: Division between the larynx and posterior pharyngeal wall.

(**Note:** Hypopharyngeal cancer pain is referred via CN X [nerve of Arnold] to the back of the pinna/posterior wall of the external auditory canal.) (**Note:** Pharyngeal wall cancer commonly involves the retropharyngeal LN.)

Workup

Risk Factors
- Tobacco and alcohol, these are synergistic in nature
- Human papillomavirus 16 (HPV 16)
- HPV oropharynx cancer is now established as an independent risk factor. HPV+ patients have a better survival rate as opposed to HPV−patients

Symptoms and Signs
- Same as for oral cavity cancer
- BOT cancer pain is referred via CN IX (glossopharyngeal and nerve of Jacobson) to the tympanic membrane

Investigations
- Same as for oral cavity cancer
- HPV status via p16 testing or HPV ISH

TNM Staging (Oropharynx HPV +)

T1	Tumor 2 cm or less in greatest dimension
T2	Tumor greater than 2 cm but not 4 cm in greatest dimension
T3	Tumor more than 4 cm in greatest dimension or extension to lingual surface of epiglottis
T4	Moderately advanced local disease. Tumor invades the larynx, extrinsic muscle of tongue, medial pterygoid, hard palate, or mandible[a]

[a]Mucosal extension to lingual surface of epiglottis from primary tumors of the base of the tongue and vallecular. Does not constitute invasion of larynx.

N0	No regional lymph node metastasis
N1	Metastasis in a single ipsilateral lymph node, 6 cm or less in greatest dimension
N2	Metastasis in bilateral or contralateral lymph nodes, none more than 6 cm in greatest dimension
N3	Metastasis in a lymph node more than 6 cm in greatest dimension
M0	No distant metastasis (no pathologic M0; use clinical M to complete stage group)
M1	Distant metastasis

Stage Grouping

Stage I	T1, T2	N0, 1	M0
Stage II	T1, 2	N2	M0
	T3	N0, 1, 2	M0
Stage III	T1, 2, 3, 4	N3	M0
	T4	N0, 1, 2, 3	M0
Stage IV	Any T	Any N	M1

M, distant metastasis; N, regional lymph nodes; TNM, T (tumor).
Used with permission of the American Joint Committee on Cancer (AJCC), Chicago, Illinois. The original source for this material is the AJCC Cancer Staging Manual, Eighth Edition (2017) published by Springer Science Business Media LLC, www.springer.com.

TNM Staging (Oropharynx HPV and Hypopharynx)

T1   Tumor 2 cm or less in greatest dimension

T2   Tumor greater than 2 cm but not 4 cm in greatest dimension

T3   Tumor more than 4 cm in greatest dimension or extension to lingual surface of epiglottis

T4a   Moderately advanced local disease; tumor invades the larynx, extrinsic muscle of tongue, medial pterygoid, hard palate or mandible[a]

T4b   Very advanced local disease; tumor invades lateral pterygoid muscle, pterygoid plates, lateral nasopharynx, or skull base or encases carotid artery

[a]*Mucosal extension to lingual surface of epiglottis from primary tumors of the base of the tongue and vallecular. Does not constitute invasion of larynx.*

N0   No regional lymph node metastasis

N1   Metastasis in a single ipsilateral lymph node, 3 cm or less in greatest dimension and ENE (−)

N2   Metastasis in a single ipsilateral lymph node, greater than 3 cm but not 6 cm in greatest dimension and ENE (−), or in multiple ipsilateral lymph nodes, none more than 6 cm in greatest dimension and ENE (−) or in bilateral or contralateral lymph nodes, none more than 6 cm in greatest dimension and ENE (−)

N3   Metastasis in a lymph node more than 6 cm in greatest dimension and ENE (−) or lymph node metastases with overt ENE (+)

M0   No distant metastasis (no pathologic M0; use clinical M to complete stage group)

M1   Distant metastasis

Stage Grouping

Stage I	T1	N0	M0
Stage II	T2	N0	M0
Stage III	T1,2	N1	M0
	T3	N0, 1	M0
Stage IVA	T1, 2, 3	N2	M0
	T4a	N0, 1, 2	M0

Stage IVB	T4b	Any N	M0
	Any T	N3	M0
Stage IVC	Any T	Any N	M1

M, distant metastasis; *N*, regional lymph nodes; *TNM*, T (tumor).
Used with permission of the American Joint Committee on Cancer (AJCC), Chicago, Illinois. The original source for this material is the AJCC Cancer Staging Manual, Eighth Edition (2017) published by Springer Science Business Media LLC, www.springer.com.

Treatment

Oropharyngeal Cancer

- **Stages 1, II**—Definitive RT, for well-lateralized lesions treat ipsilateral neck, for central lesions treat bilateral neck with RT.
  - Surgical resection can also be considered, ideally with a transoral robotic approach.
  - Tonsil surgery involves tonsillectomy and partial mandibulectomy. For early-stage BOT lesions, surgery involves partial glossectomy, supraglottic laryngectomy or partial laryngopharyngectomy, and ipsilateral neck dissection.
- **Stage III, IVB**—Concurrent chemoRT [8,14].
- Post-op RT for close margin, multiple positive LNs, PNI, LVI. Concurrent chemoRT for high-risk patients with positive margin, ECE, or gross residual disease [11].
- For patients receiving concurrent chemoRT, chemo is CDDP 100 mg/m^2 every 3 weeks X3 cycles [14].
- Alternatively, induction chemotherapy with triplet docetaxel, cisplatin, and 5FU (TPF) followed by concurrent chemoRT with weekly carboplatin can also be considered, particularly in high risk cases (impending airway compromise, large disease burden/low lying lymph nodes) [8,9].
- If patient is unable to tolerate chemotherapy, then RT with cetuximab can be considered. Cetuximab at an initial dose of 400 mg/m^2 of body surface area (BSA), followed by 250 mg/m^2 weekly with RT [10,14].
- However, if patient is unable to tolerate chemotherapy or cetuximab, then RT alone can be considered, ideally with an altered fractionations (120 cGy b.i.d. to 81.6 Gy or 200 cGy daily 6 fx/week) is considered [12,13].
- Patients receiving concurrent chemoRT, with primary complete response but residual neck disease, should receive neck dissection, although PET/CT can be utilized in follow-up to assess and follow areas of residual hypermetabolism which can resolve over the course of months.
- In general, treat regional nodes and bilateral low neck, bilateral II—IV and bilateral retropharyngeal LNs. Levels IB and V can be treated at the discretion of the treating physician. For tonsillar lesions, treatment of pterygoid plates to cover subclinical disease is necessary.

Hypopharyngeal Cancer

- Stage I/II—Organ preserving definitive RT or surgery involving partial laryngo-pharyngectomy and ipsilateral or bilateral selective neck dissection.
- Stage III/IV—Concurrent chemoRT or induction chemotherapy followed by RT for complete response; concurrent chemoRT for partial response [5–18].
  - Alternatively, surgery involving partial laryngopharyngectomy or pharygolaryngectomy
- Post-op chemoRT for high-risk patients with positive margins, ECE, or gross residual disease are recommended.
- Concurrent chemoRT therapy is CDDP 100 mg/m^2 every 3 weeks X3 cycles. Induction chemotherapy with CDDP 100 mg/m^2 IV bolus and 5FU 100 mg/m^2 over 5 days X3 cycles followed by concurrent chemoRT.
  - For patients with treatment failure, salvage laryngectomy is recommended.

RT Technique

3D Technique
Oropharyngeal Cancer

Patient is supine, face mask on, neck extended, arms pulled down with straps, IV (intravenous) contrast in, wire any lymph nodes, patient CT simulated. Treat patients with three fields, with opposed laterals and LAN, with either an isocentric technique or a separate upper neck and supraclavicular fields as shown in Fig. 15.5.

Borders: Anterior 2-cm margin or 2-cm anterior to the mandibular ramus, posterior behind spinous process, superior at the base of sphenoid (cover retropharyngeal lymph node at C1), include pterygoid plate (two to three cm superior to mastoid process), inferior thyroid notch (above larynx), offcord at 40 Gy, with larynx/cheater block; continue boost treatment to final dose of 66–70 Gy, as indicated. Boost with a 1–2 cm margin. Posterior neck gets treated with electron field to doses of 50–70 Gy as indicated.

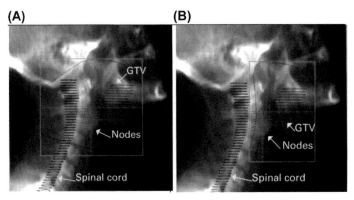

(A)　　　　　　**(B)**

GTV

Nodes

Spinal cord

GTV

Nodes

Spinal cord

FIGURE 15.5 (A) DRR for BOT cancer. 3D right lateral field, showing superior border at the base of the sphenoid, inferior border at the thyroid notch, anterior border with a 2-cm margin on GTV and the posterior border behind the spinous process. (B) DRR for BOT cancer, 3-D right lateral offcord photon field.

Hypopharyngeal Cancer

- Patient is supine, neck normal extension, arms by side, strapped to pull shoulders down, face mask on, IV contrast in. Patient is CT simulated for three fields with opposed laterals, isocentric technique (Fig. 15.6).
- **Borders:** Superior is 2—3 cm above mastoid (includes pterygoid plate); inferior is below cricoid (low as possible); anterior is spare skin (do not flash if possible); posterior is behind spinous process.
- Offcord at 40 Gy, no larynx or cord block on laterals. Boost with a 1—2 cm margin (Fig. 15.5).
- Treat neck as before.
- Feather match line if tumor/lymph node close to cord block; boost stoma if sub-glottic extension or emergency tracheostomy to 60 Gy with electrons.
  - RT dose is 200 cGy/Fx to 70—74 Gy. Post-op RT to primary is 60 Gy; if positive margin to 66 Gy; if residual gross disease to 70 Gy.

The anterior supraclavicular field is always matched on the upper neck fields, while the cheater block is placed on the lateral fields. For cone downs, a half beam block is recommended to exclude the spinal cord from high-dose radiation.

IMRT Technique for Oropharyngeal and Hypopharyngeal Cancer

Patient is supine, face mask on, arms strapped down, IV contrast in, tongue blade in if indicated, patient CT simulated, fuse PET CT and MRI if available. 6 MV photons, 9 equally spaced IMRT beams or 2 arcs for VMAT planning, Figs. 15.7 and 15.8.

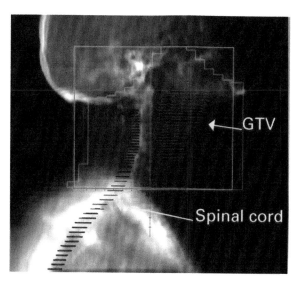

FIGURE 15.6 DRR for hypopharyngeal cancer, 3-D right lateral field, showing superior border above mastoid and inferior border below cricoid as low as possible.

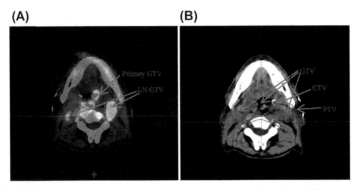

FIGURE 15.7   (A) PETCT images showing primary tonsil and nodal metastases for a right tonsil cancer patient. (B) Target volumes GTV, CTV, PTV and critical structures based on PETCT scan fusion.

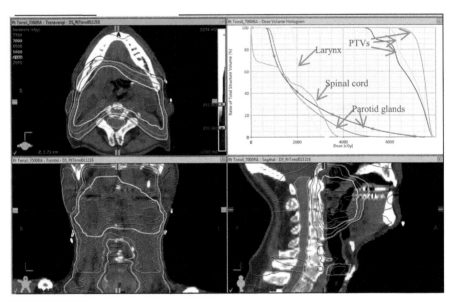

FIGURE 15.8   CT images showing two arcs VMAT treatment plan for a right tonsil cancer patient, illustrating isodose lines conforming to PTV, and DVH shows 95% PTV coverage and meets all constraints. The LAN neck field is treated with VMAT eliminating need for matching. A dose of 50, 60, and 70 Gy is prescribed to the PTV volumes.

Volumes

GTV = gross disease + enlarged LNs, as seen on CT, MRI, or PET scans

CTV1 = GTV + subclinical disease around GTV + ipsilateral and contralateral at risk LNs + 0.5–1 cm around primary and 0.3–0.5 cm around LNs, respecting tissue boundaries

CTV2 = GTV + subclinical disease around GTV + ipsilateral at risk LNs + 0.5–1 cm around primary and 0.3–0.5 cm around LNs, respecting tissue boundaries

CTV3 = GTV + 0.5–1 cm around primary and 0.3–0.5 cm around LNs, respecting tissue boundaries

PTV = CTV + 0.3–0.5 cm

Subclinical Disease Around GTV

Tonsil: glossotonsillar sulcus, parapharyngeal space, pterygomandibular raphe (common pattern of spread into retromolar trigone), adjacent soft palate, and pterygoid plates.

BOT: Entire base of tongue, glossotonsillar sulcus, mucosal margin, vallecula, and preepiglottic space.

Post Pharyngeal Wall: Mucosal Margin

Ipsilateral and contralateral at risk LN: submandibular (level Ib) at physician's discretion, internal jugular (level II, III, and IV), posterior neck (level V) at physician's discretion, and retropharyngeal LNs.

Doses

STANDARD FRACTION

PTV1 = 200 cGy/fx to 50–54 Gy

PTV2 = 200 cGy/fx to 60–66 Gy (66 Gy suggested in areas of ECE or margin positivity)

PTV3 = 200 cGy/fx to 70 Gy, post-op to 60 Gy, positive margin to 66 Gy

HYPERFRACTIONATION RT

1.2 Gy/fx bid to 81.6 Gy

CONCOMITANT BOOST

Large field 1.8 Gy/fx, boost 1.2 Gy/fx for last 12 days as second daily fraction to 72 Gy.

Note: While HPV + oropharynx cancer can respond more readily to standard chemoradiation, currently, dose de-escalation should not be attempted outside of clinical trials.

Constraints

Brainstem = <54 Gy, retina = 45 Gy

Optic nerve = 50–55 Gy, optic chiasm = 50–55 Gy, lens = 10 Gy or less

Middle ear = mean dose <45 Gy

Spinal cord = 45–50 Gy
Parotid gland = unilateral, mean dose <20 Gy; bilateral, mean dose <25 Gy
Submandibular glands: mean dose <39 Gy
Mandible = 70 Gy
Lips and oral cavity = 30 Gy
Glottic larynx = V50 < 27%; mean dose <44 Gy

Outcome

Tonsil: Local control rates: T1, 85%; T2, 75%; T3, 70%; T4, 45%.
  BOT: Local control rates: T1, 85%; T2, 75%; T3, 70%; T4, 45%.
  Hypopharynx: Local control is T1, 70%; T2, 70%; T3, 35%; T4, 30%.

Complications

- Skin erythema, swelling of the gum and the lips, sore mouth, dry mouth, loss of taste, dysphagia, odynophagia, weight loss, and bone damage
- Ototoxicity
- Temporal lobe necrosis

Follow-Up

- Every 1–3 months for the first year, every 4 months for the second year, then every 6 months for the third through fifth year
- Posttreatment PETCT at 3 months
- Chest X-ray or CT/MRI chest as indicated
- TSH every 12 months
- Hearing, speech, and swallowing evaluation as indicated

LARYNGEAL CANCER

The estimated total incidence in the United Science for larynx cancer is 13,150 with 3710 total estimated deaths in 2018.
  Subsites of the larynx include:

- Supraglottic larynx (SGL): Epiglottis, aryepiglottic (AE) folds including arytenoids, false cord and ventricles; lower boundary is the horizontal plane passing through apex of ventricle.
- Glottis: True vocal cords (TVC) and anterior/posterior commissures; lower boundary of the glottis is horizontal plane 1 cm below apex of ventricle by American Joint Committee on Cancer (AJCC) definition or 5 mm below the free margin of vocal cord by Rodney Million's definition.
- Subglottic larynx: region extending from lower boundary of glottis to lower margin of cricoid cartilage. Glottic/subglottic border is 1 cm inferior to the apex of the ventricle.

Workup

Risk Factors
Tobacco, marijuana, alcohol (?)

Symptoms and Signs
- Weight loss, sore throat, dysphagia, odynophagia, hoarseness, and otalgia. Laryngeal cancer pain is referred via CN X (nerve of Arnold) to the posterior ear canal and back of pinna and difficulty in swallowing, phonation, hearing, and hemoptysis
- Physical exam of lymph nodes, HEENT and CNS. Laryngeal click is negative in advanced laryngeal cancer.
- Indirect or direct laryngoscopy may show fullness of the preepiglottic space or ulceration of the infrahyoid epiglottis, indicating preepiglottic invasion. Indirect or direct laryngoscopy may show fixed vocal cord.

Note: Fixation of the cord may be due to destruction of the cricothyroid muscle (extrinsic muscle), involvement of the criocoarytenoid joint or muscle or involvement of the recurrent laryngeal nerve (intrinsic muscle), mass effect from the tumor.

Investigations
Same as for oral cavity.

TNM Staging (Larynx)
Supraglottis

T1	Tumor limited to one subsite of supraglottis with normal vocal cord mobility
T2	Tumor invades mucosa of more than one adjacent subsite of supraglottis, glottis or region outside the supraglottis (e.g., mucosa at base of tongue, vallecula, medial wall of pyriform sinus) without fixation of the larynx
T3	Tumor limited to larynx with vocal cord fixation and/or invades any of the following: postcricoid area, preepiglottic space, paraglottic space, and/or inner cortex of thyroid cartilage
T4a	Moderately advanced local disease and tumor invades through the thyroid cartilage and/or invades tissues beyond the larynx (e.g., trachea, soft tissues of neck including deep extrinsic muscle of the tongue, strap muscles, thyroid, or esophagus)
T4b	Very advanced local disease and tumor invades prevertebral space, encases carotid artery, or invades mediastinal structures

Glottis

T1	Tumor limited to the vocal cord(s) (may involve anterior or posterior commissure) with normal mobility
T2	Tumor extends to supraglottis, subglottis, and impairs vocal cord mobility.
T3	Tumor limited to the larynx with vocal cord fixation and/or invades paraglottic space, and/or inner cortex of the thyroid cartilage
T4a	Moderately advanced local disease and tumor invades tissues beyond the larynx (e.g., trachea, soft tissues of neck including deep extrinsic muscle of the tongue, strap muscles, thyroid, or esophagus) through the outer cortex of the thyroid cartilage
T4b	Very advanced local disease. Tumor invades prevertebral space, encases carotid artery or invades mediastinal structures

Subglottis

T1	Tumor limited to the subglottis
T2	Tumor extends to vocal cord(s) with normal or impaired mobility
T3	Tumor limited to larynx with vocal cord fixation
T4a	Moderately advanced local disease; tumor invades cricoid or thyroid cartilage and/or invades tissues beyond the larynx (e.g., trachea, soft tissues of neck including deep extrinsic muscles of the tongue, strap muscles, thyroid, and/or esophagus)
T4b	Very advanced local disease; tumor invades prevertebral space, encases carotid artery, or invades mediastinal structures
N0	No regional lymph node metastasis
N1	Metastasis in a single ipsilateral lymph node, 3 cm or less in greatest dimension and ENE (−)
N2	Metastasis in a single ipsilateral lymph node, more than 3 cm but not more than 6 cm in greatest dimension and ENE (−), or in multiple ipsilateral lymph nodes, none more than 6 cm in greatest dimension and ENE (−) or in bilateral or contralateral lymph nodes, none more than 6 cm in greatest dimension
N3	Metastasis in a lymph node more than 6 cm in greatest dimension and ENE (−) or metastases in any lymph nodes with overt ENE (+)
M0	No distant metastasis (no pathologic M0; use clinical M to complete stage group)
M1	Distant metastasis

Stage Grouping

Stage I	T1	N0	M0
Stage II	T2	N0	M0
Stage III	T1, 2	N1	M0
	T3	N0, 1	M0
Stage IVA	T1, 2, 3	N2	M0
	T4a	N0, 1, 2	M0
Stage IVB	T4b	Any N	M0
	Any T	N3	M0
Stage IVC	Any T	Any N	M1

M, distant metastasis; *N*, regional lymph nodes; *TNM*, T (tumor).
*Used with permission of the American Joint Committee on Cancer (AJCC), Chicago, Illinois. The
original source for this material is the AJCC Cancer Staging Manual, Eighth Edition (2017) published
by Springer Science Business Media LLC, www.springer.com.*

Treatment
Supraglottic Cancer
- **Stage I/II**—Definitive RT or surgery is partial supraglottic laryngectomy and se-
  lective neck dissection.
- **Stage III/IV**—Concurrent ChemoRT [15–18]. Concurrent chemo is CDDP
  100 mg/m^2 every 3 weeks X3 cycles.
  - Post-op—RT for close margin, PNI/LVI; chemoRT for margin positive, ECE or
    gross residual disease.
  - Post-RT if residual tumor—Salvage surgery and neck dissection.

Glottic Cancer

Stage CIS

Endoscopic resection or definitive RT.

Stage T1/T2

Definitive RT or surgery is partial laryngectomy.

Stage T3
- Concurrent chemoRT. Concurrent chemotherapy CDDP 100 mg/m^2 every 3 weeks
  X3 cycles. If patient is unable to tolerate chemotherapy, then RT with cetuximab
  can be considered. RT dose is the same; cetuximab at an initial dose of 400 mg/
  m^2 of BSA, followed by 250 mg/m^2 weekly with RT.
- Induction chemotherapy is an option followed by RT only for complete response,
  or chemoRT for partial response or surgery for less than partial response.

Stage T4
- Total laryngectomy with ipsilateral thyroidectomy and unilateral or bilateral neck dissection.
- Post-op RT as indicated: (1) subglottic extension, (2) cartilage invasion, PNI, LVI, (3) extension to the neck, and (4) multiple positive nodes. Concurrent chemoRT is recommended for high-risk patients with positive margin, ECE, gross residual.
- Post-RT, if residual tumor—salvage surgery and neck dissection is indicated.

RT Technique

3D Technique
SUPRAGLOTTIC CANCER

Patient is supine, neck normal position, face mask on, IV contrast in, arms strapped to pull shoulders down with CT simulation. **Borders:** superior for node negative, 2 cm above the angle of mandible (the hyoid and epiglottis included); for nodes positive, 2 cm above mastoid tip; inferior below cricoid as low as possible; anterior flash 2 cm; posterior for node negative behind the mastoid process, for node positive behind spinous process. Cheater block is placed on the lateral fields for positive patients. Boost with a 1–2 cm margin. All get elective LAN to 3 cm depth. RT alone doses are 66 Gy for T1, 70 Gy for T2, and 81.6 Gy b.i.d. RT for T3. Post-op dose of 60 Gy is the same as for glottic cancer.

GLOTTIC CANCER
- **Borders** for T1 and small T2 lesions are superior, top of thyroid ala; inferior, bottom of cricoid; anterior, flash 2 cm; posterior, anterior to vertebral body; collimate the field (Figs. 15.9 and 15.10).
- **Borders** for large T2 lesions are superior, 2 cm above supraglottic extension of the tumor; inferior, 2 cm below infraglottic extension of tumor; anterior, flash 2 cm; posterior mid-vertebral body.

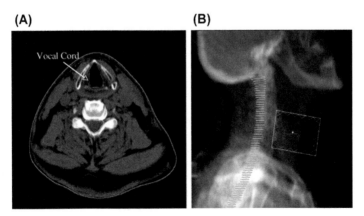

(A)   **(B)**

FIGURE 15.9   (A) Axial image of planning CT showing outline of the vocal cord and spinal cord. (B) A 3D right lateral DRR of a T1 tumor patient showing the vocal cord and the treatment field. The superior border at the top of the thyroid and the inferior border at the bottom of the cricoid. The anterior border is flashing the skin and the posterior border is anterior to the vertebral body.

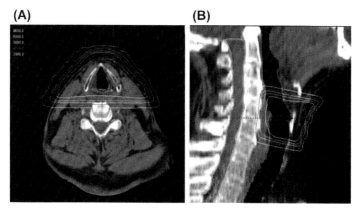

FIGURE 15.10   (A) Dose distribution of an opposed lateral beam 3D CRT treatment plan axial and (B) sagittal views for a T1 vocal cord cancer patient. Isodose lines are showing outside the skin margin due to the bolus effect. A dose of 66 Gy is prescribed to the vocal cord tumor.

- **Borders** for T3/T4 lesions are superior, for node negative 2 cm above angle of mandible to treat JD nodes; for node positive, 2 cm above mastoid tip; inferior, bottom of cricoid cartilage; anterior, flash 2 cm; posterior, behind spinous process.
- RT dose for CIS and T1 is 225 cGy/fx to 63 Gy, and for T3—4 is 70 Gy. Offcord at 40 Gy; cord block on laterals; feather match line if tumor/lymph node is close to cord block; bolus as needed; wedge used; boost stoma if needed; RT neck as before. Boost with a 1—2 cm margin.

IMRT TECHNIQUE FOR SUPRAGLOTTIC AND GLOTTIC CANCER

Patients are supine, face mask on, arms strapped down, IV contrast in, tongue blade in if indicated, and patients are CT simulated. Use 9 equally spaced coplanar 6-MV photon beams for planning. Alternatively 2 arcs for VMAT planning are used.

Volumes

GTV = gross disease + enlarged LNs, as seen on CT, MRI, or PET scans

   CTV1 = GTV + subclinical disease around GTV + ipsilateral and contralateral at risk LNs + 0.5—1 cm around primary and 0.3—0.5 cm around LNs, respecting tissue boundaries

   CTV2 = GTV + subclinical disease around GTV + ipsilateral at risk LNs + 0.5—1 cm around primary and 0.3—0.5 cm around LNs, respecting tissue boundaries

   CTV3 = GTV + 0.5—1 cm around primary and 0.3—0.5 cm around LNs, respecting tissue boundaries

   PTV = CTV + 0.3—0.5 cm (0.5—1 cm around larynx for intrafraction motion).

Subclinical Disease Around GTV

Hypopharynx: Entire subsite of hypopharynx, adjacent soft tissue and fat, entire larynx.
   Larynx: Entire larynx.

Ipsilateral and Contralateral at Risk LNs

Hypopharynx: Retropharyngeal, internal jugular (level II, III, IV), ipsilateral submandibular (level IB), and posterior neck (level V)

Larynx: Internal jugular (level II, III, IV), ipsilateral submandibular (level IB). The posterior neck (level V) can be treated at the discretion of the physician. If subglottic extension is present then level VI LN can be treated as well.

Dose

STANDARD FRACTION

CIS and T1, T2 glottic—225 cGy/fx to 63 Gy (65.25 Gy for T2)

T1—T4—200 cGy/fx to 66—70 Gy, post-op to 60 Gy, positive margin to 66 Gy

HYPERFRACTIONATION RT

1.2 Gy/fx bid to 81.6 Gy

CONCOMITANT BOOST

Large field 1.8 Gy/fx, boost 1.2 Gy/fx for last 12 days as second daily fraction to 72 Gy

Outcome

Supraglottic: Local control rates: T1, 90%; T2, 80%; T3, 60%; T4, 30%.

Glottic: Local control rates: T1, 90%; T2, 80%; T3, 50%; T4, 40% with either surgery or RT.

Complications

- Skin erythema, swelling of the gum and lips, sore mouth, dry mouth, loss of taste, dysphagia, odynophagia, voice hoarseness, and weight loss
- Under chin soft tissue fibrosis, swallowing dysfunction, dental carries, osteoradionecrosis, hypopituitarism.

Follow-Up

- Every 1—3 months for the first year, every 4 months for the second year then every 6 months for 3 to 5 years
- Posttreatment PETCT in 3 months
- Chest X-ray or CT/MRI chest as indicated
- TSH every 12 months
- Hearing, speech, and swallowing evaluation as indicated

NASAL CAVITY AND PARANASAL SINUSES

The maxillary sinus extends below and above the floor of the nasal cavity and infraorbital rim, respectively. Lymph node involvement typically occurs only after tumor extension into the nasopharynx, oropharynx, or oral cavity. Lymph nodes are typically only treated for locally advanced disease.

Workup

Symptoms and Signs
- Often asymptomatic, nasal congestion
- Advanced tumor may cause pain and unilateral bleeding

Investigations
- CBC, chemistry with liver/renal function
- Indirect and direct laryngoscopy
- Tissue diagnosis, need biopsy or preferred transnasal route
- Head and CT scans with contrast or MRI and chest X-ray
- Dental consult: Stannous fluoride (0.4%) trays every HS 35 min starting within 1 month of treatment completion.

TNM Staging (Maxillary Sinus)

T1 Tumor limited to maxillary sinus mucosa without bone damage

T2 Tumor causing bone erosion or destruction including extension into the hard palate and/or middle nasal meatus, except extension to posterior wall of maxillary sinus and pterygoid plates

T3 Tumor invades any of the following: bone of the posterior wall of maxillary sinus, subcutaneous tissues, floor or medial wall of orbit, pterygoid fossa, and ethmoid sinuses

T4a Moderately advanced local disease; tumor invades anterior orbital contents, skin of cheek, pterygoid plates, infratemporal fossa, cribriform plate, sphenoid, or frontal sinuses

T4b Very advanced local disease; tumor invades any of the following: orbital apex, dura, brain, middle cranial fossa, cranial nerves other than maxillary division of trigeminal nerve (V2), nasopharynx, or clivus

N0 No regional lymph node metastasis

N1 Metastasis in a single ipsilateral lymph node, 3 cm or less in greatest dimension and ENE (−)

N2 Metastasis in a single ipsilateral lymph node, more than 3 cm but not more than 6 cm in greatest dimension and ENE (−), or in multiple ipsilateral, bilateral, or contralateral lymph nodes lymph nodes, none more than 6 cm in greatest dimension and ENE (−)

N3 Metastasis in a lymph node more than 6 cm in greatest dimension and ENE (−) or metastases in any node with clinically overt ENE (+)

M0 No distant metastasis (no pathologic M0; use clinical M to complete stage group)

M1 Distant metastasis

Stage Grouping

Stage I	T1	N0	M0
Stage II	T2	N0	M0
Stage III	T1, 2	N1	M0
	T3	N0, 1	M0
Stage IVA	T1, 2, 3	N2	M0
	T4a	N0, 1, 2	M0
Stage IVB	T4b	Any N	M0
	Any T	N3	M0
Stage IVC	Any T	Any N	M1

M, distant metastasis; N, regional lymph nodes; TNM, T (tumor).
Used with permission of the American Joint Committee on Cancer (AJCC), Chicago, Illinois. The original source for this material is the AJCC Cancer Staging Manual, Eighth Edition (2017) published by Springer Science Business Media LLC, www.springer.com.

Treatment

Maxillary Sinus
- Surgery for all resectable lesions.
- Post-op—RT for adenoid cystic pathology, positive PNI/LVI invasion, or close/positive surgical margin.
- Extension to the BOS, nasopharynx, or sphenoid, or unresectable, then treat with definitive RT or concurrent chemoRT.
- Lymph nodes are not routinely treated, unless there is locally advanced disease including gross lymph node involvement.

Nasal Cavity and Ethmoids
- Surgery followed by post-op RT for all.
- Unresectable, then definitive RT or chemoRT is recommended.
- Lymph nodes are not routinely treated, unless there is locally advanced disease including gross lymph node involvement.

RT Technique

3D Technique
Maxillary sinus and nasal cavity, ethmoids techniques are similar. These are usually treated with an anterior field and one or more wedged lateral fields posteriorly angled or with iso-center at the canthus.

- **Borders:** The anterior field extends across the midline to include the contralateral medial limbus. The superior margin includes the cribriform plates and all or part of the frontal sinus. The inferior margin usually includes the lip commissure. The lateral border includes all the ipsilateral sinus or flash if the infratemporal fossa is involved, contralateral 1.5 cm across the midline. Use a tongue blade to displace the tongue out of the field. Pack surgical defects with a water balloon.
- **Borders:** The lateral field anteriorly is at the bony canthus and posteriorly includes the pterygoids or clivus. Superior and inferior margins as above.
- The initial field is taken to 45–50 Gy and then cone down for the remainder of the dose to 60–70 Gy. Postoperative RT dose is 60 Gy to negative margins and 70 Gy for definitive cases, or for definitive treatment 120 cGy b.i.d. to 74.4–76.8 Gy. All critical structures, such as contralateral eye, optic nerve, optic chiasm, lacrimal apparatus, spinal cord, and retina, need appropriate dose constraints.

IMRT Technique

Patients are supine, face mask on, arms strapped down, IV contrast in, and CT simulated; fuse PETCT, MR fusion can be helpful to assess the extent of gross disease and differentiate tumor from secretions, 6 MV photons, 9 equally spaced coplanar IMRT beams or 2 arcs for VMAT planning.

Volumes

GTV = none postoperatively or gross disease + enlarged lymph nodes (LNs), as seen on CT, MRI or PET scans

CTV1 = tumor bed or GTV + subclinical disease around tumor bed or GTV + ipsilateral and contralateral at risk LNs + 0.5–1 cm around the primary and 0.3–0.5 cm around the LNs, respecting tissue boundaries

CTV2 = tumor bed or GTV + subclinical disease around tumor bed or GTV + ipsilateral at risk LNs + 0.5–1 cm around the primary and 0.3–0.5 cm around the LNs, respecting tissue boundaries

CTV3 = tumor bed or GTV + 0.5–1 cm around the primary and 0.3–0.5 cm around the LNs, respecting tissue boundaries

PTV = CTV + 0.3–0.5 cm

Subclinical Disease Around Tumor Bed or GTV

Nasal cavity, maxillary sinus: entire subsite.

Ethmoid sinus: entire subsite and cribriform plate.

Adenoid cystic or PNI: entire subsite and facial nerve to skull base.

HG SCCa, maxillary sinus, nasopharyngeal involvement at risk LNs: Submandibular (level Ib), internal jugular (level II, III, and IV), posterior neck (level V), and retropharyngeal LNs.

Dose

STANDARD FRACTION

PTV1 = 200 cGy/fx to 50 Gy

PTV2 = 200 cGy/fx to 60 Gy (post-op tumor bed)

PTV3 = 200 cGy/fx to 66 (positive margin or ECE), 70 Gy (gross disease)

HYPERFRACTIONATION RT

1.2 Gy/fx bid to 81.6 Gy

CONCOMITANT BOOST

Large field 1.8 Gy/fx, boost 1.2 Gy/fx for last 12 days as second daily fraction to 72 Gy.

Outcome

Five-year survival rates are T1/T2, 60%–70% and T3/4, 30%–40%.

Complications

Erythema of the skin, nasal dryness, dry mouth, dry eye, cataracts, chronic sinusitis, choanal stenosis, and osteoradionecrosis.

Follow-Up

- Every 1–3 months for the first year, every 4 months for the second year, every 6 months for years 3–5.
- CT with contrast or MRI of the head and neck at 3 months and annually thereafter.
- CXR or CT chest as indicated.
- TSH every 12 months.

PAROTID GLAND

The parotid gland is one of the major salivary glands. It lies between the zygomatic bone superiorly and the hyoid bone inferiorly; anterior is the second molar, posteriorly is the mastoid tip. These tumors can be benign pleomorphic adenomas or malignant tumors. Malignant tumors can be low-grade mucoepidermoid and acinic cell tumors or high-grade mucoepidermoid or adenoid cystic tumors.

Workup

Risk Factors
- Low intake of vitamins A and C
- Radiation exposure
- Increased risk associated with female breast cancer

Symptoms and Signs
- A small number of patients may present with dysphagia, sore throat, earaches, and headaches secondary to other structure involvement by the tumor.
- Painless mass, fixed ulcer through skin, facial nerve involvement in 25% causing paralysis.
- Patients may present with parotid, submandibular, or upper and mid-cervical LN involvement.

Investigations
- Indirect and direct laryngoscopy
- Tissue diagnosis, fine needle aspiration, or open biopsy
- Head and CT scans with contrast or MRI scan, chest X-ray
- Dental consult: (0.4%) stannous fluoride trays every HS 35 min starting within 1 month of completion of treatment

TNM Staging (Parotid Gland)

T1	Tumor 2 cm or less in greatest dimension without extraparenchymal extension[a]
T2	Tumor more than 2 cm but not 4 cm in greatest dimension without extraparenchymal extension[a]
T3	Tumor more than 4 cm and/or having extraparenchymal extension[a]
T4a	Moderately advanced disease; tumor invades skin, mandible, ear canal, and/or facial nerve
T4b	Very advanced disease; tumor invades skull base and/or pterygoid plates and/or encases carotid artery

[a]Extraparenchymal extension is clinical or macroscopic evidence of invasion of soft tissues. Microscopic evidence alone does not constitute extraparenchymal extension for classification purposes.

N0	No regional lymph node metastasis
N1	Metastasis in a single ipsilateral lymph node, 3 cm or less in greatest dimension and ENE (−)
N2	Metastasis in a single ipsilateral lymph node, more than 3 cm but not 6 cm in greatest dimension and ENE (−), or in multiple ipsilateral lymph nodes, none more than 6 cm in greatest dimension and ENE (−) or in bilateral or contralateral lymph nodes, none more than 6 cm in greatest dimension and ENE (−)
N3	Metastasis in a lymph node more than 6 cm in greatest dimension and ENE (−) or metastases in any nodes with clinically overt ENE (+)
M0	No distant metastasis (no pathologic M0; use clinical M to complete stage group)
M1	Distant metastasis

Used with permission of the American Joint Committee on Cancer (AJCC), Chicago, Illinois. The original source for this material is the AJCC Cancer Staging Manual, Eighth Edition (2017) published by Springer Science Business Media LLC, www.springer.com.

Stage Grouping

Stage I	T1	N0	M0
Stage II	T2	N0	M0
Stage III	T1, 2, 3	N1	M0
	T3	N0,1	M0
Stage IVA	T1, 2, 3	N2	M0
	T4a	N0, 1, 2	M0
Stage IVB	T4b	Any N	M0
	Any T	N3	M0
Stage IVC	Any T	Any N	M1

M, distant metastasis; N, regional lymph nodes; TNM, T (tumor).
Used with permission of the American Joint Committee on Cancer (AJCC), Chicago, Illinois. The original source for this material is the AJCC Cancer Staging Manual, Eighth Edition (2017) published by Springer Science Business Media LLC, www.springer.com.

Treatment

Benign Tumors
Usually treated with superficial parotidectomy followed by observation. However, definitive RT can be considered for large or recurrent tumors. Post-op RT can be considered after resection for PNI, positive margins.

Malignant Tumors
- Treatment is complete surgical resection of the parotid gland, neck dissection if node positive, and possible temporal bone resection.
- Post-op RT for adenoid cystic tumors, all high-grade tumors, close or positive margins, PNI, LVI, regional LN metastases, pT3-4 tumors, and recurrent tumors. Alternatively, concurrent chemoRT can be considered.

RT Technique

3D Technique
- A single direct field using 10–18 MeV electrons is the simplest setup.
- However, a mixed beam of 4:1 electrons:photons can be used. A wedge pair technique using photon beams is another option.
- For high-grade tumors with positive lymph nodes, an ipsilateral LAN can be added.
- If there is perineural invasion or the tumor is adenoid cystic, then the facial nerve must be covered from the stylomastoid foramen to the base of the skull. Ipsilateral superior and inferior wedge pair with photons to eliminate exit through the contralateral eye can be used when facial nerve is treated.

- **Borders:** Superior is at the zygomatic arch (bisecting the sphenoid); inferior is at top of thyroid cartilage; anterior is up to second molar or 2 cm in front of mandibular ramus; posterior is behind mastoid process.
- RT dose post-op is 60 Gy, positive margin is to 66 Gy, residual gross disease is to 70 Gy. Ipsilateral neck field, if treated, is treated to 50 Gy.

IMRT Technique

Patients are supine, face mask on, arms strapped down, IV contrast in, and CT simulated, fuse PETCT, MR fusion can be helpful in the definitive setting, 6 MV photons, 9 equally spaced coplanar IMRT beams or 2 arcs for VMAT planning.

Volumes

GTV = none in postoperatively or gross disease + enlarged lymph nodes (LNs), as seen on CT, MRI, or PET scans

CTV1 = tumor bed or GTV + subclinical disease around tumor bed or GTV + ipsilateral and contralateral at risk LNs + 0.5–1 cm around primary and 0.3–0.5 cm around LNs, respecting tissue boundaries

CTV2 = tumor bed or GTV + subclinical disease around tumor bed or GTV + ipsilateral at risk LNs + 0.5–1 cm around primary and 0.3–0.5 cm around LNs, respecting tissue boundaries

CTV3 = tumor bed or GTV + 0.5–1 cm around primary and 0.3–0.5 cm around LNs, respecting tissue boundaries

PTV = CTV + 0.3–0.5 cm

Subclinical disease around tumor bed or GTV

Parotid gland: Entire parotid gland, if adenoid cystic or PNI then facial nerve track to BOS.

Submandibular gland: Entire submandibular gland, if adenoid cystic or PNI cover lingual or hypoglossal nerve track.

HG SCCa, maxillary sinus and/or nasopharyngeal involvement at risk LNs: Submandibular (level Ib), internal jugular (level II, III, and IV).

Dose

PTV1 = 200 cGy/fx to 50 Gy
PTV2 = 200 cGy/fx to 60 Gy (post-op tumor bed)
PTV3 = 200 cGy/fx to 66 (positive margin), 70 Gy (gross disease)

Outcome

Local control is 75%; overall survival is 70%.

Complications

Erythema of the skin, sore mouth, dry mouth, loss of taste, weight loss, trismus, and bone damage.

Follow-Up

- Every 1–3 months for the first year, every 4 months for the second year, and every 6 months for 3–5 years
- CT with contrast or MRI of the head and neck at 3 months and annually thereafter
- Chest X-ray or CT chest as indicated
- TSH every 12 months, if neck is irradiated

UNKNOWN PRIMARY

Patients presenting with upper neck nodes with unknown primary have a better prognosis compared with lower neck node presentation. Most are SCCa or poorly differentiated cancer. However, unknown primary tumors below the clavicle can present as adenocarcinoma.

Workup

Risk Factors
- Tobacco, alcohol, HPV, EBV, dust and wood fire smoke, salted and smoked fish

Symptoms and Signs
- Cough, hemoptysis, family history of gastric cancer in Japanese patients, and nasopharynx cancer in Chinese patients.
- Careful head and neck exam, skin exam, palpation of thyroid, breast, lymph nodes, liver, prostate, and testes.

Investigations
- FNA of the neck mass, however, if nondiagnostic, then core biopsy or open biopsy is indicated.
- Assessment of p16/HPV and EBV status.
- Further specific workup is recommended as per the tissue diagnosis, such as thyroid functions and scan for thyroid cancer diagnosis or workup for lymphoma for diagnosis.
- CT or MRI scans of head and neck, CT scan chest/abdomen/pelvis, PET scan before biopsy is done.
- Direct laryngoscopy (DL)/examination under anesthesia (EUA)/blind biopsies of NP, BOT, and pyriform sinuses, and any abnormalities on imaging or DL, tonsillectomy.

Treatment

- **Stage TxcN1** – surgery is selective neck dissection of the level I through V based on the involved neck node. Post-op pN1 with no ECE observation is recommended.

- **Stage TxN2-3** − definitive chemoRT. Mucosal sites and neck treated based on involved neck node (s). Chemo is CDDP 40 mg/m^2 weekly or 100 mg/m^2 q21 days x3 cycles
- **Post op RT** − TxpN1 with ECE or TxpN2-3 with no ECE. RT is bilateral wide field encompassing mucosal sites of NP, OP and entire neck (OC is not treated, consider HP, SGL, GL treated if level II/III LN).
- **Post op chemoRT** − ECE, positive margin or gross residual disease. RT and chemo as above.

Note: As alternative to comprehensive mucosal therapy, one may direct therapy to the most likely site of recurrence which may include unilateral mucosal and neck coverage only, particularly in the context of EBV + (nasopharynx) and HPV+ (oropharynx) disease.

RT Technique

3D Technique

Patient is supine, face mask on, arms strapped to pull shoulder down, IV contrast in, wire scar, and lymph nodes with CT simulation. Treat patient with three fields, with opposed laterals and LAN. Lateral field **borders**: superior includes nasopharynx and cranial base, inferior at thyroid notch; anterior includes two-thirds of tongue and half of mandible; posterior is behind C2 spinous process. LAN field borders are superior border at bottom of upper neck fields, inferior border at the bottom of clavicle, and lateral borders outside the first ribs. The initial field is taken to 45−50 Gy and then cone down for the remainder of the dose to 60−70 Gy. Postoperative RT dose is 60 Gy to negative margins and 70 Gy for definitive cases. Posterior neck fields treated with electron to 50−70 Gy as indicated.

IMRT Technique

Patients are supine, face mask on, arms strapped down, IV contrast in, with CT simulation, 9 equally spaced coplanar 6-MV photon beams for planning. Alternatively 2 arcs for VMAT planning are used.

Volumes

GTV = none in postoperative or gross disease + enlarged lymph nodes (LNs), as seen on CT, MRI, or PET scans

CTV1 = tumor bed or GTV + mucosal site(s) based on involved neck node(s) + ipsilateral and contralateral at risk LNs + 0.5−1 cm around primary and 0.3−0.5 cm around LN, respecting tissue boundaries

CTV2 = tumor bed or GTV + (consider mucosal site(s) based on involved neck node(s) and HPV − status) + ipsilateral at risk LN + 0.5−1 cm around primary and 0.3−0.5 cm around LN, respecting tissue boundaries

CTV3 = tumor bed or GTV + 0.5−1 cm around primary and 0.3−0.5 cm around LN, respecting tissue boundaries.

PTV = CTV + 0.3−0.5 cm.

Subclinical disease around tumor bed or GTV:

LN Positive	Mucosal Site Treated With RT
Level II (high jugular)	NP, OP
Level II/III (high/mid-jugular)	NP, OP, HP, SGL, GL
Level III (mid-jugular)	OP, HP, SGL, GL (NP may be excluded)
Level IV (inferior jugular)	HP, SGL, GL
Level V (Post cervical triangle)	NP, skin
Level IB (submandibular)	LND and observation
Preauricular	Parotidectomy + RT, RT alone (likely skin origin)

At risk LNs: Submandibular (level Ib), internal jugular (level II, III, IV), posterior neck (level V), and retropharyngeal LNs.

Dose

PTV1 = 200 cGy/fx to 50 Gy
  PTV2 = 200 cGy/fx to 60 Gy
  PTV3 = 200 cGy/fx to 66 (positive margin), 70 Gy (gross disease)

Complications

Skin erythema, sore mouth, dry mouth, loss of taste, weight loss, hypothyroidism, dysphagia, odynophagia, and bone damage, damage to the bone.

Follow-Up

- Every 1–3 months for the first year, every 4 months for the second year and every 6 months for 3–5 years
- CT scan with contrast or MRI of the head and neck at 3 months and annually thereafter
- Chest X-ray or CT chest as indicated
- TSH every 12 months

ANNOTATED BIBLIOGRAPHY

ORAL CAVITY SITE

Ref 1. Bernier et al. (2004). Postoperative irradiation with or without concomitant chemotherapy for locally advanced head and neck cancer. *N Engl J Med*; 350(19):1945–52. EORTC 22913 Trial.
  In this study, 334 patients with stage III, IV head and neck cancers after undergoing surgery, were randomized to receive radiotherapy alone (66 Gy over a period of 6 1/2 weeks) versus receiving the same radiotherapy regimen combined with 100 mg of cisplatin per square meter of body surface area on days 1, 22, and 43 of the radiotherapy regimen. After a median follow-up of 60 months the results are given below.

	LRC (%)	PFS (%)	OS (%)	Gr 3/4 Toxicity (%)
Surgery + RT	69	36	40	21
Surgery + chemoRT	82	47	53	41
P-value	.007	.04	.02	.001

This study revealed that locally advanced head and neck cancer patients receiving post-op concurrent chemoRT had improved PFS and OS compared with post-op RT alone.

Ref 2. Cooper et al. (2012). Long-term follow up of the RTOG 9501/intergroup phase III trial: postoperative concurrent radiation therapy and chemotherapy in high-risk squamous cell carcinoma of the head and neck. *Int J Radiat Oncol Biol Phys*; 84(5):1198–205. RTOG 9501 Trial.

In this study, 459 patients with resected high-risk head and neck cancer of the oral cavity, oropharynx, larynx, and hypopharynx were randomized to receive post-op radiotherapy alone (60–66 Gy in 30–33 fractions over a period of 6–6.6 weeks) versus receiving the identical treatment plus concurrent cisplatin (100 mg per square meter of body surface area intravenously on days 1, 22, and 43). High risk was defined as patients with two LNs + ECE, + margin. Results for 10 years are given below.

	LRF (%)	DFS (%)	OS (%)	Gr 3/4 Toxicity (%)
Surgery + RT	28.8	19.1	27	34
Surgery + chemoRT	22.3	20.1	29.1	77
P-value	.1	.25	.31	<.001

This study revealed that there were no significant differences in outcome. However, analysis of the subgroup of patients who had either microscopically involved resection margins and/or extracapsular spread of disease showed improved LRC, DFS, and OS with concurrent chemoRT.

Ref 3. D Cruz AK et al. (2015). Elective versus therapeutic neck dissection in node-negative oral cancer. *N Eng J Med*; 373:521–9.

In this trial, 596 patients with lateralized stage T1 or T2 oral SCCa of the oral cavity were randomized to elective node dissection (ipsilateral neck dissection at the time of the primary surgery) versus therapeutic node dissection (watchful waiting followed by neck dissection for nodal relapse). All patients who had positive nodes, a primary tumor depth of invasion of 10 mm or more, or a positive resection margin received adjuvant radiation. In patients with node-negative disease with a depth of invasion less than 10 mm, the decision to administer adjuvant radiation was individualized on the basis of the presence or absence of high-grade or perineural invasion or lymphovascular embolization. When two of these factors were present, adjuvant radiation was administered. Data from median follow-up of 39 months are given below.

	3 yr	
	DFS (%)	OS (%)
Therapeutic dissection	45.9	67.5
Elective dissection	69.5	80
P *value*	<.001	.01

This study revealed patients with early-stage oral cavity SCCa, elective neck dissection resulted in higher rates of DFS and OS than therapeutic neck dissection.

NASOPHARYNX SITE

Ref 4. Al-Sarraf et al. (1998). Chemoradiotherapy versus radiotherapy in patients with advanced nasopharyngeal cancer: Phase III randomized Intergroup study 0099. *J Clin Oncol*; 16(4):1310−7 (Intergroup 0099).

In this study, 146 patients were randomized between RT alone and RT with concurrent chemotherapy. RT was given 180−200 cGy 70 Gy to primary tumor with 2 cm margin, N0 50 Gy, lymph node: S2 cm 66 Gy, lymph node >2 cm 70 Gy. Chemotherapy CDDP (100 mg/m² every 3 weeks, days 1, 22, 43) followed by CDDP (80 mg/m² days 71, 99, 127) and 5FU (1000 mg/m² for 96 h) for X3 cycles 4 weeks after completing RT. Results at 3 years were as follows.

	Disease free Survival (%)	Overall Survival (%)
RT alone	24	47
RT + chemo	64	78

This study showed that chemoRT is superior to RT alone for patients with LANPC.

Ref 5. Sun Y et al. (2016): Induction chemotherapy plus concurrent chemotherapy versus concurrent chemotherapy alone in locoregionally advanced nasopharyngeal carcinoma: a phase 3, multicenter, randomised controlled trial. *The Lancet*; 17(11):1509−20.

In this trial, 241 patients with stage III−IVB (except T3-4N0) nasopharyngeal carcinoma were randomly assigned to receive induction chemotherapy plus concurrent chemoradiotherapy or concurrent chemoradiotherapy alone (3 cycles of 100 mg/m² CDDP every 3 weeks, concurrently with IMRT). Induction chemotherapy was three cycles of IV docetaxel (60 mg/m² per day on day 1), IV CDDP (60 mg/m² on day 1), and continuous IV 5FU (600 mg/m² per day from day 1 to day 5) every 3 weeks before concurrent chemotherapy. Median 45 day follow-up data are given below.

	3 year FFS (%)	Neutropenia Grade 3−4	Leucopenia Grade 3−4
ChemoRT	72	7	17
TPF + chemoRT	80	42	41
P value	.034	−	−

This study clearly shows that addition of TPF induction chemotherapy to concurrent chemotherapy significantly improved FFS in locoregionally advanced nasopharyngeal cancer with acceptable toxicity.

Ref 6. Lee et al. (2017). A multicenter, phase 3, randomized trial of concurrent chemotherapy plus adjuvant chemotherapy versus radiotherapy alone in patients with regionally advanced nasopharyngeal carcinoma: 10-year outcomes for efficacy and toxicity. *Cancer*; 123(21):4147−57. Intergroup 0099.

In this study, 348 patients with nonkeratinizing nasopharyngeal carcinoma staged T1-4N2-3M0 were randomly assigned to RT or to CRT using cisplatin (100 mg/m²) every 3 weeks for three cycles in concurrence with radiotherapy, followed by cisplatin (80 mg/m²) plus fluorouracil (1000 mg per m²) per day for 4 days) every 4 weeks for three cycles. Results at 10 years were:

	Failure-free Rate (%)	Progression-free Survival (%)	Locoregional Control (%)	Overall Survival (%)	Late Toxicity (%)
RT	50	42	74	49	47
CRT	62	56	87	62	52
P-value	.01	.006	.03	.047	.20

This study showed that CRT can significantly improve OS long term without excessive late toxicities for patients with regionally advanced NPC.

Ref 7. Chen L et al. (2017): Adjuvant chemotherapy in patients with locoregionally advanced nasopharyngeal carcinoma: Long-term results of a phase 3 multicentre randomised controlled trial. *Eur J Cancer*; 75:150−8.

In this trial, 251 patients with stage III—IVB (except T3-4N0) were randomly assigned to receive CCRT plus AC or CCRT only. Patients in both groups received CDDP 40 mg/m² *weekly up to 7 weeks concurrently with RT. The CCRT plus AC subsequently received adjuvant CDDP 80 mg/m² and 5FU 800 mg/m²/d for 120 h every 4 weeks for three cycles. At median follow-up of 68.4 months, the data showed the following:*

	5 year FFS (%)
ChemoRT + chemo	75
ChemoRT	71
P value	0.45

This study confirmed that adjuvant CDDP and 5FU failed to demonstrate significant survival benefit after CCRT in locoregionally advanced NPC.

OROPHARYNX SITE

Ref 8. Denis et al. (2004). Final results of the 94-01 French Head and Neck Oncology and Radiotherapy Group randomized trial comparing radiotherapy alone with concomitant radiochemotherapy in advanced-stage oropharynx carcinoma. *J Clin Oncol;* 22(1):69—76 (GORTEC 9401).

In this study, 226 patients with advanced stage III, IV oropharyngeal cancer (tonsillar, base of tongue, soft palate, posterior wall) were randomized to RT alone versus RT with concomitant chemo. RT was given using a three-field technique of 200 cGy to 70 Gy to the primary tumor and involved lymph nodes in both arms. If there were no palpable lymph nodes, 44 Gy was delivered in the lower part of the neck and in the spinal lymph nodes and 56 Gy was delivered in the cervical areas adjacent to an involved lymph node area. Lateral fields were prescribed at midplane, and supraclavicular field was prescribed at 3 cm. Chemotherapy consisted of carboplatin 70 mg/m²/d X4 days and 5FU 600 mg/m²/d CVI X3 cycles during the period of first, fourth, and seventh weeks of RT. Results at 5 years are given below.

	Median Survival (months)	Local Control (%)	Disease-Free Survival	(Overall Survival) (%)	Gr 3/4 Mucositis (%)	Late Toxicity (%)
RT	15	27	15	(31)	36	4
RT + Chemo	29	53	30	(51) 3 year	67	8
		ss	ss	ss		

The statistically significant improvement of overall survival that obtained supports the further use of concomitant chemotherapy as an adjunct to RT in the management of advanced cancer of the oropharynx.

Ref 9. Posner et al. (2007). Cisplatin and fluorouracil alone or with docetaxel in head and neck cancer. *N Engl J Med*; 357:1705−15.

In this study, 501 patients with stage III or IV disease and no distant metastases or tumors considered to be unresectable and who were candidates for organ preservation were randomized to receive either docetaxel plus cisplatin and fluorouracil (TPF) or cisplatin and fluorouracil (PF) induction chemotherapy, followed by chemoradiotherapy to 70−74 Gy with weekly carbo-platin therapy. The results at 3 years are given below.

	Median Survival (months)	Overall Survival (%)
PF + chemoRT	30	48
TPF + chemoRT	71	62
P-value	.006	.006

The study showed that patients with squamous cell carcinoma of the head and neck who received docetaxel plus cisplatin and fluorouracil induction chemotherapy plus chemoradio-therapy had a very significantly longer survival than did patients who received cisplatin and fluorouracil induction chemotherapy plus chemoradiotherapy.

Ref 10. Bonner et al. (2010). Radiotherapy plus cetuximab for locoregionally advanced head and neck cancer: 5-year survival data from a phase 3 randomised trial, and relation between cetuximab-induced rash and survival. *Lancet Oncol*; 11(1):21−8.

In this study, 424 patients with locoregionally advanced head and neck system cancer were randomized to high-dose RT alone versus high-dose RT + cetuximab. Cetuximab was given at an initial dose of 400 mg/m^2 followed by 250 mg/m^2 weekly for the duration of the radiation therapy.

With a median follow-up of 5 years, the results showed:

	Median Survival (m)	OS (%)
RT alone	29.3	36.4
RT + cetuximab	49 ss	45.6 ss

This study showed that RT + cetuximab improved overall survival in locally advanced head and neck cancer patients, confirming cetuximab plus radiotherapy is an important treatment option for this group of patients.

Ref 11. Harari PM et al. (2014): Postoperative chemoradiotherapy and cetuximab for high-risk squamous cell carcinoma of the Head and Neck: Radiation Therapy Oncology Group RTOG-0234. *J Clin Oncol* August; 32(23):2486–95. RTOG 0234 Trial.

In this trial, 238 patients with stage III and IV SCCHN with gross total resection showing positive margins and/or extracapsular nodal extension and/or two or more nodal metastases randomized to 60 Gy RT with cetuximab once per week plus either cisplatin 30 mg/m^2 or docetaxel 15 mg/m^2 once per week. The median follow-up data of 4.4 years follows.

	2 year DFS (%)	2 year OS (%)	Grade 3–4 myelosuppression (%)	Mucositis(%)
Post-op RT + cetuximab Cisplatin arm	57	69	28	56
Post-op RT + cetuximab Docetaxel arm	66	79	14	54

This study revealed that the delivery of postoperative chemoradiotherapy and cetuximab to patients with SCCHN is feasible and tolerated with predictable toxicity. The docetaxel regimen shows favorable outcome with improved DFS and OS.

Ref 12. Beitler et al. (2014). Final results of local-regional control and late toxicity of RTOG 9003: a randomized trial of altered fractionation radiation for locally advanced head and neck cancer. *Int J Radiat Oncol Biol Phys*; 89(1):13,020. RTOG 9003 Trial.

In this study, 1073 patients with stage II BOT, HP, stage III/IV OC, OP, SGL (supraglottic laryngectomy) were randomly assigned to
200 cGy to 70 Gy (conventional)
120 cGy to 81.6 Gy (true HFx, UF)
160 BID to 67.2 Gy with 2-week break after 38.4 Gy (accel fraction, MGH)
Concomitant boost 180 cGy X 30 = to 54 Gy, large field.
150 cGy X 12 = to 18 Gy, tumor only in last 2 weeks.
Total = to 72 Gy (accel fraction, MDAH) At 5 years the data Showed

	LR (%)	DFS (%)	OS (%)	Toxicity Gr 3/4 (%) Acute	Late
SFx	59.1	21.2	29.5	35	27
HFx	51.2	31.7 ss	37.1 ss	55	27
AFx-s	57.8	26.6	30.8	52	27
AFx-c	51.7	28.9	33.5	59	37

This study showed that at 5 years only HFx improved LRC and OS for patients with locally advanced SCCa without increasing late toxicity.

Ref 13. Nguyen-Tan et al. (2014). Randomized phase III trial to test accelerated versus standard fractionation in combination with concurrent cisplatin for head and neck carcinomas in Radiation Therapy Group 0129 Trial: Long-term report of efficacy and toxicity. *J Clin Oncol* December; 32(34):3858—67. RTOG 0129 Trial.

In this trial, 721 patients with stage III and IV carcinoma of the oral cavity, oropharynx, hypopharynx, or larynx were randomized to standard fraction RT to 70 Gy in 35 fxs versus accelerated fractionation RT to 72 Gy in 42 fractions. CDDP doses were 100 mg/m² once every 3 weeks for three cycles (standard) or two cycles (accelerated). Median follow-up data of 7.9 are given below.

	PFS (%)	OS (%)	Acute/Late Toxicity Gr 3—5(%)		OS (%)
SFx	42	48	No	p16 pos	70.9
AFx	41	48	Diff	p16 neg	30.1
P value	.52	.37	na		.001

This study showed that when combined with CDDP, AFx RT neither improved outcome nor increased late toxicity in patients with locally advanced head and neck cancers. Long-term survival rates in p16 positive patients with oropharyngeal cancer are better.

Ref 14. Trotti et al. (2018). NRG-RTOG 1016: Phase III Trial Comparing Radiation/Cetuximab to Radiation/Cisplatin in HPV-Related Cancer of the Oropharynx. Presented at ASTRO 60th Annual Meeting, San Antonio, TX, October 22, 2018. RTOG 1016 Trial.

In this study 805 patients with locoregionally advanced HPV-related oropharynx cancer were randomly assigned (1:1) to two cycles of cisplatin chemotherapy (100 mg/m²) every three weeks plus radiation therapy, or the same radiation therapy with weekly cetuximab treatments. RT dose was given accelerated IMRT 70 Gy in 6 weeks. The data shows at 5 years

	LRF (%)	PFS (%)	OS (%)
Cetuximab	17	67	78
Cisplatin	10	78	85
p value	<0.001	<0.001	0.02

This study revealed that cisplatin had better LRC, PFS and OS compared to cetuximab for HPV related locally advanced OP cancer.

HYPOPHARYNX AND LARYNX SITE

Ref 15. Yamazaki et al. (2006). Radiotherapy for early glottic carcinoma (T1N0M0): Results of prospective randomized study of radiation fraction size and overall treatment time. *Int J Radiat Oncol Biol Phys*; 64(1):77–82.

In this study, 180 patients with T1N0M0 glottic cancer were randomized to either RT fraction 2 Gy to 60–66 Gy versus 2.25 Gy to 56.25–63 Gy. The results at 5 years are below.

	LC (%)	Cause-specific Survival (%)	Toxicity
2 Gy/fraction	77	97	No
2.25 Gy/fraction	92	100	Difference
P-value	0.004	NS	

This study showed that 2.25 Gy/fraction resulted in improved tumor control for T1 glottic cancer and there were no differences in the incidence or severity of acute reactions or late effects compared with the 2 Gy/fraction dose.

Ref 16. Lefebvre et al. (2012). Laryngeal preservation with induction chemotherapy for hypopharyngeal squamous cell carcinoma: 10-year results of EORTC 24891. *Annal of Oncology*; 23(10):2708–14. EORTC 24891 Trial.

In this study, 194 patients with stage II, III, IV SCCa of the pyriform sinus/hypopharynx were randomized to surgery followed by post-op RT versus induction CDDP/FU followed by RT. RT given was 200 cGy to 70 Gy in definitive RT after chemotherapy, and post-op given to 64 Gy. Spinal cord dose was kept below 40 Gy. Chemotherapy with CDDP 100 mg/m^2 IV bolus and 5FU 1000 mg/m^2 infusion over 5 days X3 cycles. Patients with complete response after X3 cycles received definitive RT; others with partial response were salvaged with surgery. Results at 10.5 years were as follow:

	Disease-Free Survival (%)	Overall Survival (%)	Larynx Preservation (%)
Surgery + RT	8.5	14	—
Chemo + RT	11	13	9 (of the total population)

This study demonstrated that induction chemotherapy followed by definitive RT is a safe alternative to laryngopharyngectomy for patients with resectable hypopharyngeal cancers achieving complete response to induction CT.

Ref 17. Forastiere et al. (2013). Long-term results of RTO G 9 1 - 1 1: a comparison of three nonsurgical strategies to preserve the larynx in patients with locally advanced larynx cancer. *J Clin Oncol*; 31(7):745—52. RTOG 9111 Trial.

In this study, 547 patients with stage III/IV potentially resectable cancers of the larynx were randomized to receive (a) induction CDDP 100 mg/m^2 and 5FU 1000 mg/m^2 X120 h X3 cycles followed by RT in responding patients, (b) concurrent CDDP 100 mg/m^2 days 1, 22, 43 and RT, or (c) RT alone. RT was given 200 cGy to 70 Gy in 7 weeks. The results at 10.8 years showed the following:

	LC (%)	OS (%)	Organ (%) Preservation
RT alone	*50*	*31*	*63*
Ind CDDP+5FU + RT	*53*	*38*	*67*
Conc CDDP + RT	*69*	*27*	*81*
P *value*	*.02*	*.08*	*.005*

This study showed that RT with concurrent administration of cisplatin is superior to induction chemotherapy followed by RT or RT alone for locoregional control and for laryngeal preservation. There is no significant difference in overall survival.

Ref 18. Janoray et al. (2015): Long term results of a multicenter randomized phase III trial of induction chemotherapy with cisplatin, 5-fluorouracil, +/− docetaxel for larynx preservation. *J Natl Cancer Inst* 16;108(4). GORTEC 2000-01 Trial.

In this study, 213 patients with untreated stage III or IV larynx or hypopharynx SCCa who required total laryngectomy were randomly assigned to three cycles of induction chemotherapy with either TPF of PF followed by RT for responders. The results at 10 years showed that:

	Larynx Preservation (%)	DFS/OS (%)
PF + RT	*46*	*No*
TPF + RT	*70*	*Diff*
P *values*	*.01*	

Long-term follow-up confirms that induction chemotherapy with TPF followed by RT increased larynx preservation compared with PF followed by RT.

Unknown Primary Site

Ref 19. Hu KS et al. (2017). Five-year outcomes of an oropharynx-directed treatment approach for unknown primary of the head and neck. *Oral Oncol*; 70:14—22.

In this retrospective study, 60 patients with SCCa of unknown primary treated with RT directed to the laryngopharynx and bilateral neck. RT with 1.8—2 Gy per fraction to a total dose of 70, 63, 60, and 54 Gy was given to gross disease, high-risk ipsilateral involved neck, oropharynx, and low risk neck (uninvolved neck, lateral retropharyngeal nodes, and bilateral low neck), respectively. Patients with more advanced disease and with lymph nodes that demonstrated partial response (e.g., bulky N2 [4—6 cm in size] and or N3) were planned to undergo neck dissection 2—3 months after completion of RT. Fifty-six percent of the patients underwent concurrent chemoradiotherapy (CCRT) with cisplatin (90%), carboplatin (5%), or cetuximab (5%). Carboplatin or cetuximab were prescribed as a replacement for cisplatin in patients with poor performance status or renal impairment. Median 54-month follow-up data follow.

- *The 5 year rates of regional control and primary emergence were 90% and 10%, respectively.*
- *The 5 year rates of distant metastasis and overall survival were 20% and 79%, respectively.*
- *The 5 year rate of primary emergence in a nonoropharynx site was 3%.*

This study noted that this is the first demonstration that an oropharynx-directed approach yields low rates of primary emergence in SCCa of unknown primary with excellent outcomes.

16

Breast Cancers

The estimated incidence of breast cancer in the United States is 268,670 with estimated 41,400 deaths in 2018.

Anatomically, the breast lies between the second and sixth ribs superiorly and inferiorly and between the midline and the axillary line. Level I, II, and III axillary lymph nodes (LNs) lie laterally, behind, and medial to the pectoralis minor muscle, respectively. The interpectoral nodes (rotter nodes) lie in between the pectoralis minor and pectoralis major muscles. The internal mammary LNs lie in the first three intercostal spaces adjacent to the sternum (Fig. 16.1).

RTOG BREAST AND LN VOLUME GUIDELINES[1]

Breast borders: superior, clinical reference + second rib insertion; inferior, clinical reference + loss of CT apparent breast; anterior, skin; posterior, excluded pectoralis m., chest wall, ribs; medial, sternal—rib junction; lateral, clinical reference + midaxillary line typically excluded latissimus dorsi m. (Fig. 16.1).

Chest wall borders: superior, caudal border of the clavicular head; inferior, clinical reference + loss of CT apparent contralateral breast; anterior, skin; posterior, rib—pleural interface; included pectoralis m., chest wall, ribs; medial, sternal—rib junction; lateral, clinical reference + midaxillary line typically excluded latissimus dorsi m.

Axilla level I borders: superior, axillary vessels cross-lateral edge of pec minor m.; inferior, pec major m. insert into ribs; anterior, plane defined by anterior surface of pec major m. and latissimus dorsi m.; posterior, anterior surface of subscapularis m.; medial, lateral border of pec minor m.; lateral, medial border of latissimus dorsi m.

Axilla level II borders: superior, axillary vessels cross-medial edge of pec minor m.; inferior, axillary vessels cross-lateral edge of pec minor m.; anterior, anterior surface of pec minor m.; posterior, ribs and intercostal m.; medial, medial border of pec minor m.; lateral, lateral border of pec minor m.

[1]White, et al. Breast cancer atlas for radiation therapy planning: consensus definitions. www.rtog.org/CoreLab/ContouringAtlases/BreastCancerAtlas.aspx.

Fundamentals of Radiation Oncology
https://doi.org/10.1016/B978-0-12-814128-1.00016-7

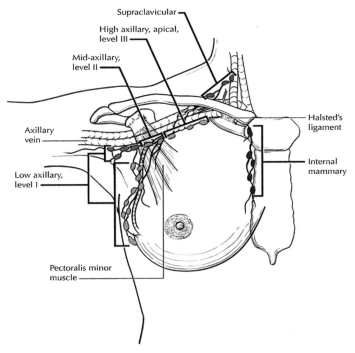

FIGURE 16.1   Schematic of the breast and regional lymph nodes. *Reproduced from the AJCC Cancer Staging Manual, 8th ed. (2017) published by Springer New York, Inc., Fig. 4 8-2, pp. 596.*

Axilla level III borders: superior, pec minor m. insert on coracoid; inferior, axillary vessels cross-medial edge of pec minor m.; anterior, posterior surface of pec major m.; posterior, ribs and intercostal m.; medial, thoracic inlet; lateral, medial border of pec minor m.

Supraclavicular borders: superior, caudal to coracoid cartilage; inferior, junction of brachiocephaxillary vn./caudal edge clavicular head; anterior, sternocleidomastoid m.; posterior, anterior aspect of the scalene m.; medial, excluded thyroid and trachea; lateral, cranial: lateral edge of SCM m. caudal: junction first rib and clavicle.

Internal mammary borders: superior, superior aspect of the medial first rib; inferior, cranial aspect of the fourth rib.

Breast lesions can be noninvasive (in situ) or invasive. Ductal carcinoma in situ (DCIS) is a precursor of invasive breast cancer and often has a low incidence of contralateral breast cancer. Invasive tumors with an extensive intraductal component (EIC) are defined as tumors with 25% or more of the primary lesion being DCIS, which is located next to the focus of the invasive cancer. EIC is no longer believed to be a contraindication to breast conservation therapy (BCT) as long as negative margins are obtained.

RISK FOR AXILLARY NODES

Risk by Tumor Size (cm)	LN Risk by % Positive Nodes
<0.5	5
0.6–1.0	10
1.0–2.0	25
2.0–5.0	35

Data from Recht A, Gray R, Davidson NE, Fowble BL, Solin LJ, Cummings FJ, Falkson G, Falkson HC, Taylor SG 4th, Tormey DC. Locoregional failure after 10 years after mastectomy and adjuvant chemotherapy with or without tamoxifen without irradiation: experience of the Eastern Cooperative Oncology Group. J Clin Oncol 1999;17(6):1689–700 (ECOG).

Workup

Risk Factors
- Age, female gender, history of prior breast cancer, early menarche, late menopause, family history (of first-degree relative)
- Genetic hereditary is noted in 5%–10% of breast cancers
- Obesity (excess estrogen), alcohol use
- Current hormone treatment—especially progesterone and estrogen combination
- Prior radiation therapy (RT) exposure to chest

The lifetime risk of developing breast cancer is 12% (1 in 8) and the risk of dying from breast cancer is 4% (1 in 28).

Symptoms and Signs
- Palpable breast mass or LN, nipple discharge (malignant discharges can be serious or bloody; however, the most common cause of nipple discharge is benign papilloma)
- Skin edema (peau d'orange), ulceration or erythema, nipple retraction, organomegaly, and bone pain (late stage)
- Physical examination includes breast exam in sitting and supine position and LN examination (cervical, supraclavicular, infraclavicular, axillary, and internal mammary regions)

Investigations
- Labs: routine CBC, chemistry with liver and renal functions
- Consider pregnancy testing if indicated
- Diagnostic mammogram (shows asymmetry, clustered microcalcification, stellate mass, and architectural distortion)
  - Spot compression views for masses
  - Magnification views for calcifications

- Ultrasound of breast for solid lesions and LN basins (internal mammary for central lesions)
- Tissue diagnosis:
  - Fine needle aspiration (FNA)
  - Tru-cut biopsy
  - Vacuum-assisted biopsy—via sonography, MRI, or stereotactic-guided procedure
- Intra-op specimen radiograph—assesses removal and margin around the lesion after definitive surgery, gross examination, and frozen section examination during surgery
- Review of the path specimen: size, grade, margin, estrogen receptor (ER)/progesterone receptor (PR)/Her2neu status
- Breast MRI is recommended if patient is symptomatic or for women with dense breasts and lobular histology, prior RT, and genetic mutations; CT chest, abdomen, and pelvis. Bone scan recommended for stage III—IV or earlier stages with concerning symptoms
- PET scan if equivocal findings on other imaging
- Offer genetic counseling with comprehensive breast genetic panel including BRCA 1 and 2 in patients meeting the criteria per NCCN guidelines
- Oncotype Dx DCIS score analyzes the activity of 12 genes. For recurrence score <39, the benefit of RT is small. For scores between 39 and 54, it is unclear whether the benefits of RT outweigh the side effects, and for scores >54, the benefits of RT are greater than the side effects
- Oncotype Dx for early-stage ER+, LN−, invasive breast cancer is a diagnostic test that analyzes a panel of 21 genes within a breast tumor to determine a recurrence score between 0 and 100 that predicts a recurrence risk within the next 10 years. Scores of 0—17 indicate low risk with small benefit of chemotherapy, scores of 18—30 are intermediate risk and it is unclear whether the benefit of chemo outweighs the side effects, whereas scores >30 indicate high risk and the benefits of chemo are greater than the side effects. Patients with score <11 may be treated with hormone modulation alone.

TNM STAGING (BREAST CANCER)

Tis (DCIS)	Ductal carcinoma in situ
T1	Tumor <20 mm in greatest dimension
T1mi	Tumor <1 mm in greatest dimension
T2	Tumor >20 mm but <50 mm in greatest dimension
T3	Tumor >50 mm in greatest dimension

T4	Tumor of any size with direct extension to the chest wall and/or to the skin (ulceration or skin nodules)[a]
T4a	Extension to the chest wall, not including only pectoralis muscle adherence/invasion
T4b	Ulceration and/or ipsilateral satellite nodules and/or edema (including peau d'orange) of the skin which do not meet the criteria for inflammatory carcinoma
T4c	Both T4a and T4b
T4d	Inflammatory carcinoma[b]

[a]*Invasion of the dermis alone does not qualify as T4.*
[b]*Inflammatory carcinoma is restricted to cases with typical skin changes involving a third or more of the skin of the breast. Although the histologic presence of carcinoma invading dermal lymphatics is supportive of the diagnosis, it is not required, nor is dermal lymphatic invasion without typical clinical findings sufficient for a diagnosis of inflammatory breast cancer.*

cN0	No regional lymph node metastases
pN0	No regional lymph node metastasis identified or isolated tumor cells (ITCs) only
pN0(i+)	Malignant cells in regional lymph node(s) are no greater than 0.2 mm (detected by hematoxylin and eosin stain [H&E] or immunohistochemistry [IHC] including ITCs)
pN0(mol+)	Positive molecular findings (reverse transcription polymerase chain reaction [RT-PCR]), but no regional lymph node metastases detected by histology or IHC
cN1	Metastases to movable ipsilateral level I, II axillary lymph node(s)
cN1mi	Micrometastases (greater than 0.2 mm and/or more than 200 cells, with none greater than 2.0 mm)
pN1mi	Micrometastases (approximately 200 cells, greater than 0.2 mm, but none greater than 2.0 mm)
pN1a	Metastases in one to three axillary lymph nodes, with at least one metastasis greater than 2.0 mm
pN1b	Metastases in ipsilateral internal mammary sentinel nodes (excluding ITCs)
pN1c	pN1a and pN1b combined
cN2a	Metastasis to ipsilateral levels I and II axillary lymph nodes fixed to one another (matted) or to other structures
cN2b	Metastasis only in ipsilateral internal mammary nodes, and in absence of clinically evident axillary node metastases
pN2a	Metastases in four to nine axillary lymph nodes (at least one tumor deposit greater than 2.0 mm)

(Continued)

pN2b	Metastasis only in clinically detected internal mammary nodes with or without microscopic confirmation; with pathologically negative axillary nodes
cN3a	Metastasis to ipsilateral infraclavicular lymph node(s)
cN3b	Metastasis to ipsilateral internal mammary lymph node(s) and axillary lymph node(s)
cN3c	Metastasis in ipsilateral supraclavicular lymph node(s)
pN3a	Metastases in 10 or more axillary lymph nodes (at least one tumor deposit greater than 2.0 mm); or metastases to the infraclavicular (level III axillary lymph) nodes
pN3b	pN1a or pN2a in the presence of cN2b (positive internal mammary nodes by imaging) or pN2a in the presence of pN1b
pN3c	Metastases in ipsilateral supraclavicular lymph nodes

Clinically detected is defined as detected by imaging studies (excluding lymphoscintigraphy) or by clinical examination and having characteristics highly suspicious for malignancy or a presumed pathologic macrometastasis based on fine needle aspiration biopsy with cytologic examination.

M0	No clinical or radiographic evidence of distant metastases (no pathologic M 0; use clinical M to complete stage group)
cM0(i+)	No clinical or radiographic evidence of distant metastases, but deposits of molecularly or microscopically detected tumor cells that are no larger than 0.2 mm present in circulating blood, bone marrow, or other nonregional nodal tissue in patients without symptoms or signs of metastases
M1	Distant detectable metastases as determined by classic clinical and radiographic means and/or histologically proven larger than 0.2 mm

Stage 0	Tis	N0	M0
Stage IA	T1[a]	N0	M0
Stage IB	T0,1[a]	N1mi	M0
Stage IIA	T0,1[a]	N1[b]	M0
	T2	N0	M0
Stage IIB	T2	N1	M0
	T3	N0	M0
Stage IIIA	T0,1[a],2	N2	M0
	T3	N1,2	M0
Stage IIIB	T4	N0,1,2	M0

| Stage IIIC | Any T | N3 | M0 |
| Stage IV | Any T | Any N | M1 |

M, distant metastasis; *N*, regional lymph nodes; *TNM*, T (tumor).
Note: In addition to Anatomic Stage Groups, Prognostic Stage Groups is added to the new AJCC Eighth edition—incorporating tumor grade, ER, PR, HER2 status, and inclusion of multigene panels as stage modifiers when available.
AJCC has incorporated Genomic Assays, such as when Oncotype DX recurrence score is <11, the anatomic stages IB, IIA, IIB, and IIIA are all classified as IA.
An AJCC-approved App is available—TNM8 Breast Cancer Calculator for staging and grouping.
[a]*T1 includes T1mi.*
[b]*T0 and T1 tumors with nodal micrometastases only are excluded from Stage IIA and are classified Stage IB.*
Used with permission of the American Joint Committee on Cancer (AJCC), Chicago, Illinois. The original source for this material is the AJCC Cancer Staging Manual, Eighth Edition (2017), published by Springer Science Business Media LLC, www.springer.com.

NONINVASIVE BREAST CANCER (DCIS)

Treatment

BCT with lumpectomy without SLN dissection with 2 mm or greater margin is followed by post-op RT to WB and TB boost [1–5].

- Consider omission of RT in patients >50 years with grade 1–2, no necrosis, <2.5 cm in size, >2 mm surgical margin, and ER+ with planned Tamoxifen or AI therapy.
- Consider omission of boost in patients >50 years with screening detected DCIS, size <2.5 cm, grade 1–2, and surgical margins >3 mm.

Alternatively, simple mastectomy with SLN biopsy followed by reconstruction is an option. In addition, patients contraindicated for breast conservation may also undergo simple mastectomy.

Systemic therapy with tamoxifen 20 mg daily or, for post menopausal women, anastrozole 1 mg daily × 5 years for patients with ER positive DCIS reduces the risk of future invasive and noninvasive breast cancer [6–8].

Outcome

Local failure for DCIS treated with breast-conserving therapy (lumpectomy + radiation) is 12%; overall survival is 98%.

Note: Outcome and prognostic grouping has become complicated in breast cancer in light of pathologic versus clinical receptor subtypes, oncotype, and molecular classifications in addition to TNM. Readers are directed to annotated bibliography at the end of the chapter.

EARLY-STAGE BREAST CANCER (STAGE I AND II)

Postlumpectomy Radiation Therapy

Candidates for Breast Conservation Therapy
- Primary tumor less than 5 cm (T1–2)
- Clinically N0–1
- No gross multifocal/diffuse calcification
- Margins negative if EIC

Contraindications for Breast Conservation Therapy
- Larger tumor relative to breast size (relative)
- Multicentric disease (relative)
- Scleroderma, lupus (relative)
- Diffuse microcalcifications
- Persistently positive surgical margin
- Locally advanced or inflammatory breast cancer
- Pregnancy
- Prior RT (high dose) to chest wall

Treatment

Lumpectomy with negative margin and SLN biopsy is followed by post-op RT to WB and TB boost [9–11,15].

- Clinically node-negative patients with one to two pathologically positive SLNs do not need full axillary dissection [17]. Depending on risk factors, offer whole breast RT and regional nodal irradiation [12–14].
- Candidates for post-lumpectomy regional RT:
    1. Negative axillary LN—consider regional nodal RT
    2. 1–3 axillary LNs positive—strongly consider regional nodal RT
    3. 4 or more axillary LNs positive—regional nodal RT.
- Hypofractionated RT is indicated for intact breast treatment only [11].
- Female patients 70 years or older with pathologically negative LNs, primary tumor size <3 cm, negative margins, and ER positive can be considered for lumpectomy and tamoxifen or an aromatase inhibitor and omit post-op RT [16].

Chemotherapy is indicted for high-risk node-negative tumors (T2 or greater, high tumor grade, or patients with a high-risk genetic signature) and most patients with node-positive disease. In general, chemotherapy is given before RT. A dose-dense schedule of Adriamycin, Cytoxan (AC), Adriamycin 60 mg/m^2 with cyclophosphamide 600mg/m^2 given q 2 × 4 followed by paclitaxel 175 mg/m^2 q 2 weeks × 4 (or paclitaxel 80mg/m^2/week × 12) is optimal (18, 19, 20, 21, and 22). AC can also be given at q 3 week × 4 schedule if concerns regarding tolerance or toxicity are present in older patients, followed by T weekly × 12. A three-drug regimen of Taxotere (docetaxel), Adriamycin, and Cytoxan (TAC) 75/50/500 mg/m^2 can be used but is associated with increased myelosuppression and needs growth factors.

- For more aggressive disease (triple-negative ER/PR/H2N negative) not treated with neoadjuvant chemotherapy or positive nodes patients can be considered for dose-dense AC 60/600 mg/m^2 every 2 weeks ×4 cycles followed by Taxol 175 mg/m^2 every 3 weeks ×3 cycles. To avoid Adriamycin cardiotoxicity, patients can be considered for docetaxel and/or Cytoxan 75/600 mg/m^2 every 3 weeks ×4 cycles.
- Preoperative chemotherapy should be considered for large ER-positive tumors in patients who would be BCT candidates. AC × 4 dose-dense followed by a taxane or TAC × 6 are appropriate.
- Patients with TN breast cancer should be considered for neoadjuvant chemotherapy; at present, the role of adding carboplatinum in this setting is unclear.
- In ER-positive premenopausal patients, chemotherapy is followed by tamoxifen 20 mg orally daily ×5−10 years; in postmenopausal women, an aromatase inhibitor ×10 years is preferred [23,24].
- Trastuzumab 6 mg/kg every 3 weeks should be offered to H2N-positive patients (IHC 3+ or overamplification by FISH). For AC followed by taxane, Trastuzumab may be given concurrently with taxane but not AC. Patients may also receive Trastuzumab following chemotherapy during RT, continuing for 1 year [25].
- In neoadjuvant setting consider Pertuzumab for patients receiving Trastuzumab (26).

Outcome

Local failure is 10%; overall survival is 60%−80%.

Note: Outcome and prognostic grouping has become complicated in breast cancer in light of pathologic versus clinical, receptor subtypes, oncotype, and molecular classifications in addition to TNM. Readers are directed to annotated bibliography at the end of the chapter.

POSTMASTECTOMY RADIATION THERAPY

Candidates for PMRT

1. T3—consider PMRT or T4 disease—PMRT
   a. T1−2 with 1−3 positive LNs—strongly consider PMRT
   b. T3N0—controversial PMRT
2. Four or more positive LNs—PMRT
3. Positive supraclavicular, infraclavicular, or IMC disease—PMRT
4. Close (<1 mm)—consider PMRT or positive margins—strongly consider PMRT
5. Recurrent disease—PMRT

Indications Regional LN RT

- Supraclavicular LN—Four or more positive axilla LN, 1−3 axilla LN (consider), no axilla staging or no ALND after positive SLN (consider), inflammatory breast cancer, positive response after neoadjuvant chemotherapy (consider)
- PAB—Patients with large AP separation, needing appropriate coverage of the level II−III axilla

- High nodal burden, SLN dissection alone or inadequate nodal dissection, locally advanced disease, or unresectable after chemotherapy
- IMN—Clinically/pathologically IMN, large axillary nodal burden, medial breast cancer (consider)

Treatment

- Tumors more than 5 cm, close or positive margins—consider postmastectomy chest wall RT [27,28,30]. Patients with >4 positive LNs are recommended to receive post-op RT to the chest wall supraclavicular, infraclavicular, axilla bed at risk, and internal mammary LNs. However, in patients with one to three positive LNs, postmastectomy RT to chest wall and to the supraclavicular, infraclavicular, axilla bed at risk, and internal mammary LNs is strongly considered.
- Systemic therapy is adriamycin, cytoxan 60/600 mg/m^2 every 3 weeks ×4 cycles; if premenopausal and LN positive also, Taxol 175 mg/m^2 every 3 weeks ×3 cycles. Alternatively, dose dense AC followed by taxane or docetaxel/cytoxan regimens can also be considered.
- Tamoxifen 20 mg orally, daily ×5–10 years if premenopausal; aromatase inhibitor ×10 years if postmenopausal [29].
- Trastuzumab should be offered to H2N-positive patients by FISH [25].
- In neoadjuvant setting, consider pertuzumab for patients receiving trastuzumab [26].

Outcome

Local failure is 9%; overall survival is 54%.

Note: Outcome and prognostic grouping has become complicated in breast cancer in light of pathologic versus clinical, receptor subtypes, oncotype, and molecular classifications in addition to TNM. Readers are directed to annotated bibliography at the end of the chapter.

LOCALLY ADVANCED BREAST CANCER

LABCs are T3 disease with positive LN, greater than one-third edema of the breast, ulceration of the skin, satellite lesions; supraclavicular, IMC LN metastasis, and fixed axillary LNs (N2, N3); direct chest wall or skin involvement (T4a, T4b); and inflammatory breast cancer (T4d).

Treatment

- Pre-op chemotherapy followed by lumpectomy and surgical axilla staging or mastectomy (lumpectomy is contraindicated in inflammatory breast cancer). Patients receive post-op RT to breast/chest wall and regional lymphatics (patients with T3N0 are controversial for post-op RT). IMC LNs should receive RT if clinically involved. Otherwise, IMC LN treatment is controversial.
- Pre-op chemotherapy is with AC 60/600 mg/m^2 every 3 weeks ×4 cycles followed by Taxol 175 mg/m^2 every 3 weeks ×4 cycles or if tolerated by patients,

then dose dense AC 60/600 mg/m^2 every 2 weeks ×4 cycles followed by Taxotere 25 mg/m^2 weekly ×12 cycles [31] or Paclitaxel 80mg/m^2/week × 12 weeks.

- If not operable after chemotherapy, then RT to whole breast followed by reevaluation for operability, then RT is continued to full dose if not operable.
- Maintenance chemotherapy is considered for these patients.
- ER/PR-positive patients also receive Tamoxifen if premenopausal, or aromatase inhibitor if postmenopausal.
- Trastuzumab should be offered to H2N-positive patients by FISH [25].
- In the neoadjuvant setting, consider pertuzumab for patients receiving trastuzumab [26].

Outcome

Overall 5-year survival with stage IIIA is 60%; with stage IIIB is 50%.

Note: Outcome and prognostic grouping has become complicated in breast cancer in light of pathologic versus clinical, receptor subtypes, oncotype, and molecular classifications in addition to TNM. Readers are directed to annotated bibliography at the end of the chapter.

RECURRENT BREAST CANCER

Multiple factors are related to the risk of locoregional/distant failure. They include initial size of the tumor, number of positive LNs, hormonal receptor status, type of surgical procedure(s), and the use of adjuvant treatments. For mastectomy patients, the chest wall is the most common site of failure followed by the supraclavicular LN area.

Treatment

- Recurrence after lumpectomy and RT: recommended treatment is mastectomy axilla LN staging. Postoperatively, chemotherapy can be considered. Further RT is typically not administered although reirradiation may be considered for select cases with very high risk factors for locoregional recurrence.
- Chest wall recurrence after mastectomy: surgery followed by RT to chest wall and regional lymphatics if not previously irradiated. Consider preop or postop chemotherapy.
- Supraclavicular recurrence: recommend chemotherapy followed by RT to brachial plexus tolerance.
- Isolated axillary recurrence: recommend chemotherapy followed by axillary dissection and RT to chest wall, supraclavicular area, and IMNs. Dose to the axilla should be determined based on risk of residual axillary disease [positive extranodal extension (ENE), >10 LN removed, positive matted nodes].
- Postoperatively, chemotherapy should be considered as patients are at high risk of distant failure [32].
- ER/PR-positive patients are recommended to undergo ovarian ablation or suppression with LHRH (luteinizing hormone–releasing hormone) agonist such as goserelin and/or endocrine treatment with tamoxifen or aromatase inhibitor.
- Trastuzumab and pertuzumab are given to Her2neu-positive patients.

Outcome

Local failure is 15% with 40% 5-year overall survival.

Note: Outcome and prognostic grouping has become complicated in breast cancer in light of pathologic versus clinical, receptor subtypes, oncotype, and molecular classifications in addition to TNM. Readers are directed to annotated bibliography at the end of the chapter.

RT Technique

3-D Technique

Tangents Alone for Intact Breast

Patient is supine, ipsilateral arm above head, on an angled breast board or on a Vac-Lok cradle, face moved away from ipsilateral breast. Lumpectomy bed scar is delineated with wire. Patient is CT simulated. **Borders:** superior is 1–2 cm above palpable breast tissue; inferior is 2 cm below inframammary fold; medial at midline; lateral at mid–post-axillary line. Patient is virtually simulated with isocentric tangents with a nondivergent deep edge; medial tangent is simulated first, encompassing all of breast, and posterior edge of beam going through medial and lateral borders, making sure there is <2–3 cm lung in field. Flash 2 cm anteriorly; rotate collimator to parallel chest wall. Oppose medial tangent and rotate gantry angle to make lateral tangent coplanar beam to minimize heart dose. Alternatively, heart block may be used. Wedges or field-in-field technique is used to improve dose homogeneity and limit hot spots (<10% with conventional fractionation or <5%–7% with hypofractionated radiotherapy).

Tumor bed is outlined in breast tissue for boost with 1–2 cm margin. The boost can be electrons or photons. For electron boost, enface beam with an energy selected based on the depth of the tumor bed, allowing 90% isodose line encompassing the target. For photon boost, wedged pair or multiple fields including noncoplanar beams may be used to increase conformality and to ensure 95% isodose line covering the boost PTV. Total lung, ipsilateral lung, heart, and contralateral breast dose need to be monitored.

Tangents Matching With Supraclavicular Area for Intact Breast/Chest Wall

Following CT simulation, the data are transferred to the treatment planning computer, where virtual simulation is conducted.

- **Supraclavicular field borders** (Fig. 16.2): superior at thyroid groove, inferior at 0.5 cm superior to bottom of clavicular head, half beam block, medial at midline, lateral medial to humeral head, blocking acromioclavicular joint. Gantry angled 12°–15° away from spinal cord; block cord medially.
- **Tangent field borders**: superior border to above the supraclavicular half-beam blocked central axis, inferior border 2 cm below inframammary fold (contralateral inframammary fold for chest wall), medial at midline, lateral at mid–post-axillary line. All borders are wired and gantry is rotated medially until encompassing entire breast (or chest wall); posterior edge of the beam goes through medial/lateral borders, <2–3 cm of lung, flash 2 cm anteriorly to allow for breast swelling during treatment. Collimator rotated to parallel chest wall. Table is kicked away

(A)   **(B)**

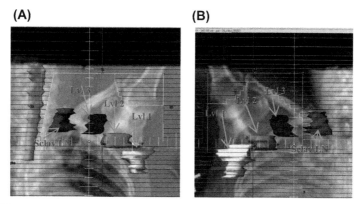

FIGURE 16.2 (A) Breast patient DRR for 3-D left supraclavicular field, showing inferior border at the bottom of the clavicle with half-beam block. Medially, spinal cord is blocked, and laterally the humeral head and the acromioclavicular joint are blocked. The gantry angle is 10° to 15° away from the spinal cord. This field is treating CT-outlined supraclavicular, level 3 and level 2 LNs. (B) DRR for the posterior axillary boost (PAB), showing superior border bisecting the clavicle, inferior border matching the supraclavicular central axis. Medially 2 cm of lung is in the field and laterally blocking the humeral head. This field is treating CT outlined level 3 and level 2 LNs.

from gantry until divergence into supraclavicular eliminated. Block is drawn at the superior part of the tangent to match the supraclavicular. Beams opposed and add 3°–4° to the gantry angle to make lateral tangent coplanar. Alternatively, half beam block matching superior border of tangent fields and inferior border of supraclavicular/axillary apex field can be used.
- Tumor bed is outlined in breast tissue for boost. If boosting with electrons, a 1.5 cm border on tumor bed is usually sufficient. Alternatively, minitangents or wedged pair photon boost may be utilized.
- For chest wall treatment, use 5–10 mm bolus every other day. Bolus thickness depends on the photon energy.

Supraclavicular dose is specified at 3 cm depth or to CT-outlined nodal bed (Fig. 16.2). Dose is specified on the central axis line perpendicular to posterior border of tangents at lung/chest wall interface. Hot spots are <10% for conventional fractionation and <5%–7% for hypofractionation. Wedges or field-in-field technique is used as needed per treatment plan.

(**Note:** Review of the CT dosimetry to ensure adequate coverage of area at risk is critical. Modify calculation point as needed to cover anatomy at risk.)

Posterior Axillary Boost

Set up supraclavicular and rotate gantry to posterior. **Borders for PAB**: superior bisects clavicle, 2 cm inferior at supraclavicular half-beam blocked central axis, medial include 2 cm of lung; lateral bisects humeral head. Alternatively, using CT simulation, the volume at risk can be contoured and coverage can be achieved with adequate homogeneity using field-in-field technique in combination with higher-energy photons or alternative prescriptions. CT data should be used to ensure that the volume at risk achieves adequate dose (Fig. 16.2B).

Internal Mammary Chain

A combination of electron and photon therapy is used to treat the IMN chain. **Borders for electron field**: superior at supraclavicular central axis; inferior at 2 cm below contralateral inframammary fold; medial at 2−3 cm past ML (verify coverage of IMC); lateral matching 1 cm inside the medial entry edge of photon tangents treating chest wall, block laterally. **Borders for photon (partially deep tangent) field**: superior/inferior same as electron; medial is lateral margin of electron field; lateral flash chest wall and skin. Cover first three intercostal spaces or first six intercostal spaces if IMC LN is positive.

   Note: Alternatively, a photon field with a partially wide tangent may be used to cover the IMC.

Scar Line Boost (Postmastectomy)

Borders: 2 cm margin around the scar line; alternatively, MD Anderson technique is 5 cm superior and 5 cm inferior to scar and approximately 1.5 cm to medial and lateral aspect of scar, excluding areas of moist desquamation can be used. Bolus 5 mm used every day for scar boost.

IMRT Technique

Tangents Alone for Intact Breast

Patient is supine, ipsilateral arm above head, on an angled breast board or on a Vac-Lok cradle, chin up, and face moved away from ipsilateral breast. The patient is CT simulated, daily X-ray imaging to match external fiducial markers is needed, and respiratory motion management is recommended (Figs. 16.2−16.4).

- Initial treatment is 6−18 MV, coplanar, two sets of medial and lateral tangent fields covering the CT defined breast PTV and passing through the medial and the lateral margins, minimizing heart and lung within field, while optimizing dose to breast tissue. One set of tangents is open fields with nondivergent posterior edge, no wedge, and with 2−3 cm flash on the breast skin surface. The other set of tangents is inverse planned IMRT fields. The relative weights of the doses delivered from open versus the IMRT fields are 70%−80% versus 20%−30%. The lumpectomy bed with 1−2 cm margin is treated with four to five inverse planned IMRT fields.
- A 3-D supraclavicular field and PAB can be added to the tangent fields above the clavicular head level, when indicated, as above. Alternatively, CT-outlined LN areas can be drawn and covered with the fields as well.

Volumes

GTV = None (after lumpectomy)

   CTV1 = The palpable whole breast as outlined by the skin wire + 1.5 cm margins superiorly and inferiorly, and modified to exclude 0.5 cm near the skin of the breast, and pectoralis muscle and chest wall are excluded + draining LNs.

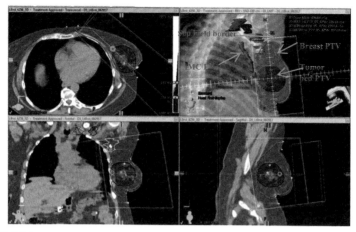

FIGURE 16.3   Left breast cancer planning CT scan showing beam's-eye view of the medial tangent field showing coverage of the level 1 axillary LNs (yellow color), the breast, and tumor bed PTVs.

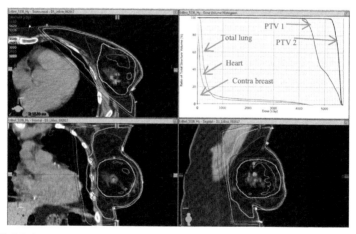

FIGURE 16.4   Left breast planning CT images show isodose lines and DVH for a hybrid breast plan combination of open tangents and inverse plan tangents followed by inverse plan tumor bed boost showing homogeneous dose distribution with hot spots of less than 7%, heart and lung dose is v20 = 5%, respectively. PTV1 dose is 50.4 Gy and PTV2 dose is 61.2 Gy.

CTV2 = Lumpectomy bed and any surgical clips + 1–2 cm margins respecting the CTV1 anteriorly and posteriorly; pectoralis muscle and chest wall are excluded.
PTV = CTV + 0.5 cm.

Doses

CONVENTIONAL DOSES

PTV1 (breast/chest wall) = 180–200 cGy/fx to 50–50.4 Gy.
PTV2 (lumpectomy bed/scar line) = 180–200 cGy to 59.5–60 Gy for DCIS; 60–61.2 Gy for invasive cancer; 59.4–60 Gy for MRM scar line; margin close/positive = 66–66.6 Gy; gross disease 70 Gy.
Supraclavicular = 180–200 cGy to 45–50 Gy, when indicated.
Axilla and IMC = 180 cGy to 45 Gy, when indicated.

HYPOFRACTIONATION DOSES

PTV1 (breast) = 266 cGy/fx to 42.56 Gy.
PTV2 (lumpectomy bed) = 180 cGy/fx to 53.36 Gy or 200–250 cGy to 52.56 Gy; margin close/positive 180 cGy to 58.76 Gy or 200–250 cGy to 55.06 Gy.

Hypofractionated RT ASTRO guidelines (2018):[2]
Age—Any.
Stage—Any, provided intent is to treat the whole breast without an additional field to cover the regional LNs.
Chemotherapy—Any Chemotherapy
Dose homogeneity—Volume of breast tissue receiving >105% of the prescription dose should be minimized regardless of dose fractionation.
Note: *Hypofractionated RT is not recommended per ASTRO guidelines for post-op chest wall and regional nodal irradiation.*

Constraints

Hot spot <5%–7%
Ipsilateral lung = V20 to <15%–20% (whole breast), V20 to <35% (comprehensive nodal)
Contralateral lung = V5to <10%, V10 to <5%
Total lung = V20 to <10%, mean dose <13 Gy
Heart = mean dose < 2 Gy (whole breast), <4 Gy (chest wall)
Contralateral breast = V3<10%
Spinal cord = 45–50 Gy (if treating supraclavicular field)

Complications of Treatment

- Skin changes including redness, dryness, fibrosis, and darkening, sore throat
- Inflammation of the lung with dry cough (radiation pneumonitis), 6 weeks after treatment

---

[2]From Smith BD, et al. Radiation therapy for the whole breast: Executive summary of an American Society for Radiation Oncology (ASTRO) evidence-based guideline. 2018. www.practicalradonc.org/article/S1879-8500(18)30051-1/pdf.

- Lymphedema of the breast and the ipsilateral arm
- Ipsilateral chest wall rib fracture
- Second malignancy
- Cardiotoxicity

Follow-Up

- Every 3—6 months for the first year, every 6—12 months for the second to the fifth year
- New baseline mammogram of the treated breast at 6 months, and thereafter every 12 months bilaterally
- Pelvic exam and pap smear every 12 months for patients on tamoxifen with intact uterus
- Assessment of bone density annually for patients on aromatase inhibitor such as anastrozole

ANNOTATED BIBLIOGRAPHY

NONINVASIVE BREAST CANCER (DCIS)

Adjuvant Radiation Therapy

Ref 1. Early Breast Cancer Trialists' Collaborative Group (EBCTCG); Correa et al. (2010). Overview of the randomized trials of radiotherapy in ductal carcinoma in situ of the breast. *J Natl Cancer Inst Monogr* 2010;2010(41):162—77. EBCTCG Study.

In this study, 3729 women with DCIS individual patient data were analyzed from all four of the randomized trials that began before 1995, which compared adjuvant radiotherapy with no radiotherapy following breast-conserving surgery. The data follow.

	\multicolumn{4}{c}{*10-year Ipsilateral Recurrence Risk (%)*}			
	Total	*Age <50*	*Age >50*	*Margin negative Low Grade*
No RT	28	29	27	30
RT	12	18	10	12
P *value*	*<.001*	*<.0001*	*<.001*	*<.003*

The data showed that the RT reduced the absolute 10-year risk of any ipsilateral breast event by 15.2%, and it was effective regardless of the age at diagnosis, extent of breast-conserving surgery, use of tamoxifen, method of DCIS detection, margin status, focality, grade, comedonecrosis, architecture, or tumor size. Even for women with negative margins and small low-grade tumors, the absolute reduction in the 10-year risk of ipsilateral breast events was 18.0%.

16. BREAST CANCERS

Ref 2. Wapnir et al. (2011). Long-term outcomes of invasive ipsilateral breast tumor recurrences after lumpectomy in NSABP B-17 and B-24 randomized clinical trials for DCIS. *J Nat Cancer Inst* 16;103(6):478−88. B 17/B 24 Trial.

In this study, patients with localized DCIS were randomized to lumpectomy versus lumpectomy + RT (B-17, 813 women) and lumpectomy + RT + placebo versus lumpectomy + RT + tamoxifen (B-24, 1799 women). All patients had negative margins; axillary dissection was obligatory at the onset of the study but subsequently became optional. RT was given, 50 Gy to the whole breast. 90% of the cancers were mammographically detected, and 90% had less than 1-cm tumor size. Results at a median follow-up of 207 months are given below:

	15-year Cumulative Incidence		
	Ipsilateral (%) Recurrence	Contralateral (%) Cancer	Breast (%) Cancer Death
B-17			
Lumpectomy	19	10	3
Lump + RT	9	10	5
B-24			
Lump + RT + plcb	10	11	3
Lump + RT + Tam	8	7	2
P value	0.25	<.001	

These trials showed that radiation and tamoxifen reduced ipsilateral breast tumor recurrence, and long-term prognosis remained excellent after breast-conserving surgery for DCIS.

Ref 3. Donker M et al. (2013). Breast-conserving treatment with or without radiotherapy in ductal carcinoma in situ: 15 year recurrence rates and outcome after a recurrence, from the EORTC 10853 randomized phase III trial. *J Clin Oncol* 2013;31(32):4054−9. EROTC 10853 Trial.

In this trial, 1010 women with complete LE of DCIS less than 5 cm were randomly assigned to no further treatment or RT. The RT dose was 50 Gy to the whole breast, no boost was advised. The use of tamoxifen was not specified in the protocol. At a median follow-up of 15.8 years, results follow:

	LR (%) Free	CSS (%)	OS (%)
Excision	69	No	No
Excision + RT	82	Difference	Difference
P value	<.001		

This study concluded that after 15 years, one in three nonirradiated women developed an LR after LE for DCIS. RT reduced this risk by a factor of 2.

Ref 4. Warnberg et al. (2014). Effect of radiotherapy after breast-conserving surgery for ductal carcinoma in situ: 20 years follow-up in the randomized SweDCIS Trial. *J Clin Oncol* 2014; 32(32):3613—8. SweDCIS Trial.

In this study, 1046 women with DCIS after BCS were randomly assigned to no RT versus RT. RT dose was 200 cGy to 50 Gy. At a median follow-up of 204 months, the results were as tabulated below:

	IBE Cumulative Risk (%)	CSD	OS
No RT	32	4.2	27
RT	20	4.1	22
P value	<.001	ns	ns

The trial showed a decrease of 12% of absolute local recurrence risk in women with DCIS who received post-op RT.

Ref 5. McCormick B et al. (2018). Randomized Trial Evaluating Radiation following Surgical Excision for "Good Risk" DCIS: 12 Year Report from NRG/RTOG 9804. Presented at ASTRO 60th Annual Meeting, San Antonio, TX, October 21, 2018. RTOG 9804 Trial.

In this trial, 636 women with mammographically detected low- or intermediate-grade DCIS, measuring less than 2.5 cm with margins >3 mm, compared RT with observation after surgery. Tamoxifen use was optional. At a median follow-up of 7.17 years, the data showed the following:

	Local Failure (%)	Invasive LR (%)	Gr 1/2 Toxicity (%)	Gr 2/3 Toxicity (%)
No RT	11.4	5.8	29	4.1
RT	2.8	1.5	74.3	4.1
p value	0.0001	0.02	-	-

In this good risk subset of patients with DCIS, the addition of whole breast radiation following breast conservation surgery significantly reduced the risk of any local recurrence and of invasive local recurrence.

Adjuvant Hormone Therapy for DCIS

Ref 6. Fisher et al. (2007). Pathologic variables predictive of breast events in patients with ductal carcinoma in situ. *Am J Clin Pathol* 2007;128(1):86—91. B-24 Trial.

In this study, 1804 patients with localized and multifocal DCIS with positive margins were randomized to lumpectomy + RT + placebo, versus lumpectomy + RT + tamoxifen. RT was given, 50 Gy to the whole breast; tamoxifen 20 mg daily for 5 years. Results at 10.5 years were as follows:

Treatment	Ipsilateral Breast Tumor Recurrence (%)	Contralateral Breast Tumor Recurrence (%)	Distant Metastasis/ Overall Survival
Lump + RT + placebo	14.7 (invasive 50)	5.4	No
Lump + RT + tamoxifen	11 (invasive 44)	4.5	Difference

The combination of lumpectomy, RT, and tamoxifen was effective in the prevention of invasive cancer.

Ref 7. Cuzick et al. (2011). Effect of tamoxifen and radiotherapy in women with locally excised ductal carcinoma in situ: long term results from the UK/ANZ DCIS trial. *Lancet Oncol* 2011;12(1):21—9. UK/ANZ Trial.

In this trial, 1701 women with completely locally excised DCIS were recruited into a randomized 2 × 2 factorial trial of radiotherapy, tamoxifen, or both. The recommended dose of RT was 200 cGy/fx to 50 Gy/fx, and tamoxifen was prescribed at a dose of 20 mg daily for 5 years. After a median follow-up of 12.7 years, the data were as given below:

	Ipsilateral Events (%)	Contralateral Events (%)
No adjuvant therapy	16	2
Tam alone	11	1
RT alone	5	1
Tam + RT	3	1
P value	<.0001	<.0001

This updated analysis confirms the long-term beneficial effect of radiotherapy and reports a benefit for tamoxifen in reducing local and contralateral new breast events for women with DCIS treated by complete local excision.

Ref 8. Margolese RG (2016). Anastrozole versus tamoxifen in postmenopausal women with ductal carcinoma in situ undergoing lumpectomy plus radiotherapy (NSABP B-35): a randomized, double-blind, phase 3 clinical trial. *Lancet* 2016;387(10021):849–56. B-35.

In this trial, 3104 postmenopausal women with hormone-positive DCIS treated with lumpectomy with clear resection margins and whole-breast RT were randomized to receive either tamoxifen 20 mg/d or oral anastrozole 1 mg/d for 5 years. At a median follow-up of 9 years, the data showed the following:

Breast Cancer-free	Interval Events (%)
Tamoxifen group	122
Anastrozole group	90
P value	.0234

This study showed that compared with tamoxifen, anastrozole treatment provided a significant improvement in breast cancer-free interval, mainly in women younger than 60 years of age.

EARLY-STAGE BREAST CANCER

Adjuvant Radiation Therapy

Ref 9. Darby et al. (2011). Effects of radiotherapy after breast-conserving surgery on 10-year recurrence and 15-year breast cancer death: meta-analysis of individual patient data for 10,801 women in 17 randomised trials. *Lancet* 2011;378(9804):1707–16. EBCTCG Study.

In this study, a collaborative metaanalysis of individual patient data for 10,801 women in 17 randomized trials of radiotherapy versus no radiotherapy after breast-conserving surgery were analyzed. The results showed.

	Any First (%) Recurrence	Breast Cancer (%) Mortality	Any (%) Death
BCS	35	25	37
BCS + RT	19	21	34
P value	<.00001	.00005	.03

This study showed that after breast-conserving surgery, radiotherapy to the conserved breast halves the rate at which the disease recurs and reduces death by about a sixth.

Ref 10. Mukesh MB et al. (2013). Randomized controlled trial of intensity-modulated radiotherapy for early breast cancer: 5 year results confirm superior overall cosmesis. *J Clin Oncol* 2013; 31(36):4488—95.

In this study, 815 breast cancer patients with inhomogeneous plans (>2 cubic cm receiving 107% of prescribed dose: 40 Gy in 15 fractions over 3 weeks) were randomly assigned to standard RT or replanned with simple forward plan FIF IMRT. Breast tissue toxicities were assessed at 5 years using photographic assessment (overall cosmesis and breast shrinkage compared with baseline pre-RT photographs) and clinical assessment (telangiectasia, induration, edema, and pigmentation). The results at 5 years showed.

	Skin Telangiectasia Odd Ratio	Overall Cosmesis Odds Ratio
Standard RT	—	—
IMRT	0.57	0.65
P value	.31	.38

The study showed that improved dose homogeneity with simple IMRT reduces the risk of skin telangiectasia and improves overall cosmesis.

Ref 11. Haviland JS et al. (2013). The UK standardization of breast radiotherapy (START) trials of radiotherapy hypofractionation for treatment of early breast cancer: 10 year follow-up results of two randomized controlled trials. *Lancet Oncol* 2013;14(11):1986—94. START A, B Trial.

In these trials, women with completely excised invasive breast cancer (pT1-3a, pN0-1, M0) were randomly assigned after breast surgery to 50 Gy in 25 fractions versus 41.6 Gy or 39 Gy in 13 fractions in START A (2236 women) or 40 Gy in 15 fractions in START B (2215 women). The results at a median follow-up of 9.3/9.9 years showed the following:

Tissue Effects	LRR (%)	Late Normal (%) Tissue Effects
START A		
50 Gy group	7.4	No
41.6 Gy group	6.3 ns	Difference
START B		
50 Gy group	5.5	
40 Gy group	4.3 ns	Less common

The long-term data from these trials confirmed that appropriately dosed hypofractionated RT is safe and effective for patients with early breast cancer.

Ref 12. Donker M et al. (2014). Radiotherapy or surgery of the axilla after a positive sentinel node in breast cancer (EORTC 10,981—22,023) AMAROS): a randomized, multicenter, open-label, phase 3 non-inferiorty trial. *Lancet Oncol* 2015;15(12):1303—10. AMAROS Trial.

In this trial, 4823 patients with T1—2 primary breast cancer and no palpable lymphadenopathy were randomized to receive either axillary LN dissection or axillary radiotherapy in case of a positive SLN. At a median follow-up of 6.1 years, the data showed the following:

	5-year axillary (%) Recurrence	DFS (%)	OS (%)	Clinical (%) Lymphedema
ALND	0.54	87	94	23
AxRT	1.03	83	94	11
P *value*	—	—	—	<.0001

This study showed that axillary LN dissection and axillary radiotherapy after a positive sentinel node provide excellent and comparable axillary control for patients with T1—2 primary breast cancer and no palpable lymphadenopathy. Axillary RT results in significantly less morbidity.

Ref 13. Whelan TJ et al. (2015). Regional nodal irradiation in Early-stage breast cancer. *N Eng J Med* 2015;373(4):307—16. MA.20 Trial.

In this trial, 1832 patients with node-positive or high-risk node-negative (>5 cm or >2 cm and <10 nodes removed and gr 3 or LVI positive or ER negative) breast cancer are treated with breast-conserving surgery and adjuvant systemic therapy randomized to either whole-breast RT plus regional nodal RT (including IMC, Sclav, axilla) or whole-breast RT alone, RT dose 200 cGy/fx to 50 Gy to whole breast, boost dose 10—16 Gy, regional LNs 45—50 Gy. At a median follow-up of 10 years, results were as follows:

	LRR (%)	DFS (%)	OS (%)
No nodal RT	6.8	77	81.8
Nodal RT	4.3	82	82.8
P *value*	.009	.01	.38

This study showed that for women with node-positive or high-risk node-negative breast cancer, the addition of regional nodal RT to whole-breast RT did not improve OS but reduced the rate of breast cancer recurrence.

Ref 14. Poormans PM et al. (2015). Internal mammary and medial supraclavicular irradiation in breast cancer. *N Eng J Med* 2015;373:317—27. EORTC 22922 Trial.

In this trial, 4004 patients with centrally or medially located primary tumor, irrespective of axillary involvement, or an externally located tumor with axillary involvement, were randomized to either whole-breast or thoracic wall RT in addition to regional nodal RT (IM and Sclav) or whole-breast or thoracic wall RT alone. At a median follow-up of 10.9 years, the data showed the following:

	DDFS (%)	DFS (%)	OS (%)
No nodal RT	75	69.1	80.7
Nodal RT	78	72.1	82.3
P value	.02	.04	.06

The study analysis showed that for patients with early-stage breast cancer, irradiation of the regional nodes had a marginal effect on OS; however, DDFS and DFS were improved statistically.

Ref 15. Bartelink et al. (2015). Whole breast irradiation with or without a boost for patients treated with breast-conserving surgery for early breast cancer: 20 year follow-up of a randomized phase 3 trial. *Lancet Oncol* 2015;16(1):47–56. EORTC Trial.

In this study, 5318 breast cancer patients T1-2, N0-1 with microscopically complete excision followed by whole-breast irradiation of 50 Gy were randomly assigned to receive either a boost dose of 16 Gy (2661 patients) or no boost dose (2657 patients). At a median 17.2-year follow-up, data were as given below:

	Ipsilateral Breast (%) Tumor Recurrence	OS (%)	Fibrosis (%) Severe
No boost	16.4	61	1.8
Boost	12	59	5.2
P value	<.0001	.323	<.0001

This study showed that RT boost after whole-breast RT had no effect on long-term overall survival but improved local control, with the largest absolute benefit in young patients, although it increased the risk of moderate to severe fibrosis.

Ref 16. Kunkler IH et al. (2015). Breast-conserving surgery with or without irradiation in women aged 65 years or older with early breast cancer (PRIME II): a randomized controlled trial. *Lancet Oncol* 2015;16(3):266–73. PRIME II Trial.

In this trial, 1326 women aged 65 years or older with low-risk early-stage breast cancer (hormone receptor positive, axillary node negative, T1-2 up to 3 cm, clear margins, grade 3 tumor histology or LVI, but not both), who had breast-conserving surgery and were receiving adjuvant endocrine treatment, were randomly assigned to whole-breast RT (40—50 Gy in 15—25 fractions) or no RT. At a median follow-up of 5 years, the results were as given below:

	Ipsilateral Breast (%) Tumor	DM (%)	OS (%)
RT + HTx	1.3	0.3	94.2
No RT + HTx	4.1	1	93.8
P value	.001	ns	ns

The study showed that postoperative whole-breast RT following breast-conserving surgery and adjuvant endocrine treatment resulted in a significant but modest reduction in local recurrence for women aged 65 years and above with early-stage breast cancer.

Ref 17. Giuliano AE et al. (2017). Effect of axillary dissections versus no axillary dissection on 10-year overall survival among women with invasive breast cancer and sentinel node metastasis: The ACOSOG Z0011 (Alliance) Randomized clinical trial. *JAMA* 2017;318(10):91—926. Z 11 Trial.

In this trial, 891 women with clinical T1 or T2 invasive breast cancer, no palpable axillary adenopathy, underwent lumpectomy/SLND. Those with one or two SLN metastases were randomized to undergo ALND or no further axillary treatment. Those randomized to ALND underwent dissection of 10 or more nodes. All patients received whole-breast irradiation (45—50 Gy, in fractions of 1.8—2.0 Gy/d, 5 d/week) delivered via tangential fields with a coplanar border. Systemic therapy was at the discretion of the treating physician. At a median follow-up of 9.3 years, the data showed the following:

	10-year DFS (%)	10-year OS (%)
ALND group	78	83
SLND group	82	86
P value	.30	.32

This study showed that the routine use of ALND in this patient population is not supported based on 10 years outcome.

Adjuvant Chemotherapy

Ref 18. Mamounas et al. (2005). Paclitaxel after doxorubicin plus cyclophosphamide as adjuvant chemotherapy for node-positive breast cancer: Results from NSABP B-28. *J Clin Oncol* 2005;23(16):3686—96. NSABP B-28.

In this study, 3060 patients were randomly assigned (AC, 1529; AC followed by PTX [AC → PTX], 1531). Patients >50 years old and those younger than 50 with ER- or PR-positive tumors also received tamoxifen for 5 years, starting with the first dose of AC. Postlumpectomy radiotherapy was mandated. Postmastectomy or regional radiotherapy was prohibited. At a median follow-up of 64.6 months, the results were as given below:

	Disease-free Survival (%)	Overall Survival (%)
AC ×4	72	85
AC ×4 + paclitaxel	76	85
P value	.006	.46

The study showed that the addition of PTX to AC resulted in significant improvement in DFS but no significant improvement in OS with acceptable toxicity. No significant interaction between treatment effect and receptor status or tamoxifen administration was observed.

Ref 19. Rastogi et al. (2008). Preoperative chemotherapy: Updates of National Surgical Adjuvant Breast and Bowel Project Protocols B-18 and B-27. *J Clin Oncol* 2008;26(16):2793. B-18.

In this study, 1500 patients with T1-3N0-1 were randomized to pre-op chemotherapy AC ×4 + surgery + RT versus post-op chemotherapy surgery + AC ×4 + RT. Chemotherapy was 60/600 mg/m² every 3 weeks. Results at 16 years were as follows:

	pCR (%)	BCT (%)	Disease-Free Survival (%)	Overall Survival (%)
AC ×4 + surgery + RT	13	68	42	55
Surgery + AC ×4 + RT	—	60	39	55

Pre-op chemotherapy was as effective as, but not more effective than, post-op chemotherapy.

Ref 20. Sparano JA et al. (2015). Long-term follow-up of the E1199 phase III trial evaluating the role of Taxane and schedule in operable breast cancer. *J Clin Oncol* July 2015;33(21):2353–60. E1199 Trial.

In this trial, 4954 patients with stage II or III breast cancer were treated with 4 cycles of doxorubicin plus cyclophosphamide and randomly assigned to receive paclitaxel or docetaxel every 3 weeks for 4 doses weekly for 12 doses using 2 × 2 factorial design. At a median follow-up of 12.1 years, the following data were obtained:

	10-year DFS (%)	10-year OS (%)
AC ×4, T q3wks ×4	65.5	72.7
AC ×4, P q3wks ×4	70.7	77.7
AC ×4, T q3wks ×12	71.9	78.5
AC ×4, P q3wks ×12	67.1	75.9
P value	.011	.019

The analysis of this study showed that improved outcomes initially observed for weekly pacli-taxel were qualitatively similar but quantitatively less pronounced with longer follow-up.

Ref 21. Mackey JR et al. (2016). Long-term outcomes after adjuvant treatment of sequential versus combination docetaxel with doxorubicin and cyclophosphamide in node-positive breast cancer: BCIRG-005 randomized trial. *Ann Oncol* 2016;27(6):1041−7. BCIRG 005 Trial.

In this trial, 3298 women with node-positive, HER2 nonamplified breast cancer were random-ized to doxorubicin and cyclophosphamide every 3 weeks for four cycles followed by docetaxel (AC, T) every 3 weeks for four cycles or docetaxel, doxorubicin, and cyclophosphamide (TAC) every 3 weeks for six cycles. The patients received standard RT and endocrine therapy. Ten-year follow-up follow.

	10-year DFS (%)	OS (%)
AC, T	66.5	79.9
TAC	66.3	78.9
P value	.749	.506

Data analysis confirmed that the efficacy of TAC was not superior to AC, T in women with node-positive early breast cancer.

Ref 22. Early breast cancer trialist's collaborative group (EBCTCG) (2017). Long-term outcomes for neoadjuvant versus adjuvant chemotherapy in early breast cancer: meta-analysis of individual patient data from ten randomized trials. *Lancet Oncol* published 11 December 2017. EBCTCG Study.

In this study, individual data for 4756 women in 10 randomized trials for early breast cancer compared NACT with same chemotherapy given postoperatively. Most chemotherapy was anthracycline based. At a median follow-up of 9 years, the results were as follows:

	15-year Rates			
	Local (%) Recurrence	*Distant (%) Recurrence*	*Breast (%) Cancer Death*	*Any Death*
Post-op	*15.9*	*38*	*33.7*	*41.2*
NACT	*21.4*	*38.2*	*34.4*	*40.9*
P value	*.0001*	*.66*	*.31*	*.45*

The data from this study showed that NACT leads to higher rates of breast-conserving therapy compared with adjuvant chemotherapy, but without decreasing the distant recurrence, breast cancer–specific survival, and overall survival.

Adjuvant Hormonal Therapy

Ref 23. Fisher et al. (2007). Pathobiology of small invasive breast cancers without metastases (T1a/b, N0, M0): National Surgical Adjuvant Breast and Bowel Project (NSABP) protocol B-21. *Cancer* 2007;110(9):1929–36. B21 Trial.

In this study, 1009 patients with node-negative invasive breast cancer of 1 cm or less, treated with lumpectomy and ALND, were randomized to tamoxifen alone, versus RT alone, versus tamoxifen + RT. Average follow-up time was 14 years, and the results were as follows:

	Ipsilateral Breast Tumor (%) Recurrence Free	*DFS (%)*	*OS (%)*
Tam only	*80.5*	*61.5*	*87.2*
RT + placebo	*89.2*	*60.6*	*82.1*
RT + Tam	*89.8*	*56.0*	*77.8*
P value	*ss*	*ns*	*ns*

The combination of tamoxifen + RT was significantly more effective than either tamoxifen or RT alone in reducing IBTR. There was no significant difference in DFS and OS.

Ref 24. Hughes et al. (2013). Lumpectomy plus tamoxifen with or without irradiation in women age 70 or older with early breast cancer: long-term follow-up of CALGB 9343. *J Clin Oncol* 2013;31(19):2382–7. CALGB 9343 Trial.

In this study, 636 female patients who were 70 years of age or older and who had clinical stage I, ER-positive breast cancer were randomized between lumpectomy + RT + tamoxifen versus lumpectomy + tamoxifen, RT dose to whole-breast 45 Gy and boost 14 Gy. Results at 12.6 are given below.

	Locoregional (%) Recurrence Free	DM Free Survival	10-year OS (%)
Tam	90	95	66
RT + Tam	98	95	67
P value	<.001	—	—

This study showed that RT + Tam results in an absolute reduction of 8% in ipsilateral breast tumor recurrence. However, omitting RT in patients of 70 years or older with early-stage, clinically negative LN, and ER-positive breast cancer caused no difference in disease-free survival or overall survival.

Ref 25. Perez et al. (2014). Trastuzumab plus adjuvant chemotherapy for human epidermal growth factor receptor2 positive breast cancer: planned joint analysis of overall survival from NASBP B-31 and NCCTG N9831. *J Clin Oncol* 2014;32(33):3744–52. B 31/N9831 Trial.

In this study, the combined results of 3676 women with surgically removed HER2-positive breast cancers from two trials (NSAB-3 and NCCTG 9831) compared adjuvant chemotherapy with or without concurrent trastuzumab. Postresection chemotherapy was given doxorubicin and cyclophosphamide followed by paclitaxel versus same regimen chemotherapy +52 weeks of trastuzumab given concomitantly with paclitaxel. Results at a median follow-up of 8.4 years showed the following:

	10-year	
	DFS (%)	OS (%)
Chemotherapy	62.2	75.2
Chemotherapy + trastuzumab	73.7	84
P value	<.001	<.001

The addition of trastuzumab to paclitaxel after doxorubicin and cyclophosphamide in early-stage HER2-positive breast cancer results in substantial and durable improvement in survival as a result of a sustained marked reduction in cancer recurrence.

Ref 26. Von Minckwitz G et al. (2017). Adjuvant Pertuzumab and Trastuzumab in early HER2_positive breast cancer. *N Engl J Med* 2017;377(2):122–31. APHINITY Trial.

In this trial, 4805 women with node-positive or high-risk node-negative HER2-positive, operable breast cancer were randomized either to pertuzumab or placebo added to standard adjuvant chemotherapy plus 1 year of treatment with trastuzumab. The data are given below.

	3-year DFS (%)	3-year DFS LN positive	3-year DFS LN Negative	Diarrhea gr > 3
Trastuzumab	93.2	90	98.4	3.7
Trastuzumab+ pertuzumab	94.1	92	97.5	9.8
P value	—	.02	.64	

These results showed that pertuzumab significantly improved the rates of invasive disease-free survival among patients with HER2-positive, operable breast cancer when it was added to trastuzumab and chemotherapy.

POSTMASTECTOMY RADIATION THERAPY

Ref 27. Ragaz et al. (2005). Locoregional radiation therapy in patients with high-risk breast cancer receiving adjuvant chemotherapy: 20-year results of the British Columbia randomized trial. *J Natl Cancer Inst* 2005;97(2):116—26.

In this study, 318 patients with tumor <5 cm, who are node-positive and premenopausal, were randomized after modified radical mastectomy to CMF ×6 (or 12) versus CMF + five-field RT. RT (all Co-60) was 235 cGy to 37.5 Gy to the chest wall and 35 Gy to SC, axilla, and internal mammary node (en face at d = 3 cm) between the fourth and fifth cycles of chemotherapy. Chemotherapy given was cyclophosphamide 600 mg/m^2, methotrexate 40 mg/m^2, 5FU 600 mg/m^2. A second randomization was done in 68 patients with ER-positive tumors to ± RT for ovarian ablation (400 cGy ×5). Median follow-up at 20 years had the following results:

Treatment	Local Relapse (%)	Distant Metastasis (%)	Overall Survival (%)	Cardiac Deaths (%)
Surg + CMF ×6	39	69	37	0.6
Surg + CMF ×6 + RT	13 ss	52 ss	47 ss	1.8

For patients with high-risk breast cancer treated with modified radical mastectomy, treatment with RT and adjuvant chemotherapy leads to better local control and survival outcomes as opposed to chemotherapy alone, with acceptable long-term toxicity.

Ref 28. Danish Breast Cancer Cooperative Group; Nielsen et al. (2006). Study of failure pattern among high-risk breast cancer patients with or without postmastectomy radiotherapy in addition to adjuvant systemic therapy: Long-term results from t he Danish Breast Cancer Cooperative Group DBCC 82 b and c randomized studies. *J Clin Oncol* 2006;24(15):2268—75.

In this study, 1708 breast cancer (ductal, lobular, medullary) patients with $> T3$ (>5 cm), who are node-positive and premenopausal, postmastectomy (TM), were randomized to CMF $\times 9$ versus CMF $\times 8 + RT$ (given after first cycle). RT was given to five fields, 200 cGy to 50 Gy with electrons to chest wall and internal mammary node (upper four interspaces) and photons to the SC and PAB; cyclophosphamide 600 mg/m^2, methotrexate 40 mg/m^2, 5FU 600 mg/m^2 every 4 weeks. Median follow-up at 18 years had the following results:

Treatment	Local Relapse (%)	Distant Metastasis (%)	Disease-Free Survival (%)	Overall Survival (%)
Surg + CMF $\times 9$	32 (49)	58 (64)	34	45
Surg + CMF $\times 8 + RT$	9(14)	43(53)	48	54

Postmastectomy RT decreased local relapses and distant metastasis and increased disease-free survival and overall survival.

Ref 29. Cuzick et al. (2010). Effect of anastrozole and tamoxifen as adjuvant treatment for early-stage breast cancer: 10-year analysis of the ATAC trial. *Lancet Oncol* 2010;11(12):1135—41. ATAC Trial.

In this study, 9366 postmenopausal women with early-stage breast cancer were randomly assigned (1:1:1) to receive active anastrozole plus tamoxifen placebo, active tamoxifen plus anastrozole placebo, or active anastrozole plus active tamoxifen. Anastrozole was given as 1 mg and tamoxifen as 20 mg daily oral tablets for 5 years. The 10-year updated results for the tamoxifen and anastrozole monotherapy for hormone receptor—positive patient groups are as follows:

	Local Recurrence (%)	Distant Recurrence (%)	Contralateral Breast Cancer (%)
Tamoxifen	24	17.7	4.9
Anastrozole	19.7	15.1	3.2
P-value	.03	.002	.003

The data from this study confirm the long-term superior efficacy and safety of anastrozole over tamoxifen as initial adjuvant therapy for postmenopausal women with hormone-sensitive early breast cancer.

Ref 30. Early Breast Cancer Trialist's Collaborative Group (EBCTCG) (2014). Effect of radiotherapy after mastectomy and axillary surgery on 10-year recurrences and 20-year breast cancer mortality: metaanalysis of individual patient data for 8135 women in 22 randomized trials. *The Lancet* 2014;383(9935):2127—35. EBCTCG Study.

In this study, individual data for 8135 women were randomly assigned to treatment groups in 22 trials of radiotherapy to the chest wall and regional LNs after mastectomy and axillary *surgery versus the same surgery but without radiotherapy. RT included chest wall, supraclavicular or axillary fossa (or both), and internal mammary chain. Chemotherapy was usually given CMF. At a median follow-up of 9.4 years, the results were as follows:*

	LRR (%)		Any Recurrence (%)		Breast Cancer Death (%)	
	1–3 LNs	*>4 LNs*	*1–3*	*>4 LNs*	*1–3 LNs*	*>4 LNs*
No RT	20.3	32	45.7	75.1	50.2	80
RT	3.8	13	34.2	66.3	43.3	70.1
P value	.00001		.00006		.01	

The study showed that after mastectomy and axillary dissection, RT reduced both recurrence and breast cancer mortality in the women with one to three positive LNs in these trials, even when systemic therapy was given.

LOCALLY ADVANCED BREAST CANCER

Ref 31. van Nes et al. (2009). Preoperative chemotherapy is safe in early breast cancer, even after 10 years of follow-up; clinical and translational results from the EORTC trial 10902. *Breast Cancer Res Treat* 2009;115(1):101–13. EORTC 10902 Trial.

In this study, 698 patients with T1c, T2, T3, T4b, N0-1, and M0 breast cancer were randomly assigned to receive surgery in combination with either preoperative or postoperative chemotherapy. Surgery consisted of modified radical mastectomy or BCT (lumpectomy plus axillary dissection and irradiation of the whole breast). Additionally, radiotherapy was indicated in all cases where surgery was not considered to be radical. Chemotherapy consisted of four cycles of preoperative fluorouracil 600 mg/m^2, epirubicin 60 mg/m^2, and cyclophosphamide 600 mg/m^2 (FEC) administered intravenous, at 3-week intervals. Patients who were >50 years of age were considered to be postmenopausal and received tamoxifen 20 mg daily for at least 2 years, regardless of the ER. With a median follow-up of 10 years, the study yielded the following results.

	Breast Conservation Therapy (%)	Disease-Free Survival (%)	Overall Survival (%)
Pre-op chemo	35	48	64
Post-op chemo	22	50	66
P-value		.30	.54

This study revealed that the preoperative chemotherapy does not result in a difference in OS or DFS compared with postoperative chemotherapy in patients with early breast cancer. Moreover, it increases BCT rates with no significant increase of local relapses.

LOCALLY RECURRENT BREAST CANCER

Ref 32. Aebi S et al. (2014). Chemotherapy for isolated locoregional recurrence of breast cancer (CALOR): a randomized trial. *Lancet Oncol* 2014;15(2):156−63.

In this trial, 162 patients with histologically proven and completely excised isolated locoregional recurrences after unilateral breast cancer who had undergone a mastectomy or lumpectomy with clear surgical margins were randomized to multidrug chemotherapy ×4 cycles or no chemotherapy. Patients with ER-positive received adjuvant endocrine therapy, RT was mandated for patients with microscopically involved surgical margins, and anti-HER2 therapy was optional. At a median follow-up of 4.9 years, the results were as follows:

	DFS (%)	*Adverse Effect (%)*
No chemotherapy	*57*	*—*
Chemotherapy	*69*	*15*
P *value*	*.046*	

This study indicates that adjuvant chemotherapy should be given to patients with completely resected isolated locoregional recurrence breast cancer, especially if the recurrence is ER receptor negative.

17

Thoracic Cancers

The estimated incidence of lung cancer in the United States is 234,030 with estimated 154,050 deaths in 2018.

Approximately 85% of all lung cancers are non–small-cell lung cancers (NSCLCs) and include adenocarcinoma, squamous cell cancer, and large-cell cancer. Fifteen percent are small-cell lung cancers (SCLCs). The incidence of adenocarcinoma has recently increased and has a tendency to arise peripherally as opposed to SCLC and squamous cell carcinomas, which typically arise centrally.

Lung cancers generally metastasize early (57%) but tend to spread locoregionally. There is a high incidence of lymph node metastases at the time of diagnosis (22%). Lower-lobe lung lymphatics drain to the posterior mediastinum and ultimately to the subcarinal lymph node. The right upper lobe (RUL) drains toward the superior mediastinum; the left upper lobe (LUL) drains to the anterior mediastinum and in one-third of the cases to the superior mediastinum. Ultimately, all drain to the right lymphatic and left thoracic ducts (Fig. 17.1).

NON–SMALL-CELL LUNG CANCER

Workup

Risk Factors
- Cigarette smoke—heavy smokers have 20 times more risk of lung cancer than nonsmokers; about 80%–90% of lung cancers are attributed to tobacco smoke
- Exposure to environmental carcinogens (radon, asbestos, coal tar fumes, nickel, chromium, arsenic, and radioactive materials)

Symptoms and Signs
- Cough, dyspnea, chest pain, hemoptysis, dysphagia, hoarseness (vocal cord paralysis), weight loss, and weakness/anorexia/malaise
- SVC (superior vena cava) syndrome consists of shortness of breath, cough, and face or neck swelling

Fundamentals of Radiation Oncology
https://doi.org/10.1016/B978-0-12-814128-1.00017-9

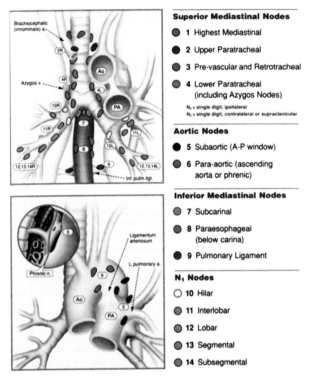

FIGURE 17.1 The Mountain–Dresler modification of the pulmonary and mediastinal lymph node map originally proposed by the American Thoracic Society. *Reproduced from Rusch, et al. The IASLC lung cancer staging project: a proposal for a new international lymph node map in the forthcoming seventh edition of the TNM classification for lung cancer. J of Thorac Oncol May 2009; 4(5):568–77.*

- Other syndromes:
  - **Superior sulcus tumor (Pancoast) syndrome,** lower brachial plexopathy, Horner syndrome, and shoulder/ulnar distribution pain
  - **Horner syndrome** consists of ipsilateral enophthalmos, ptosis, miosis, anhidrosis, hoarseness resulting from laryngeal node involvement
  - **Paraneoplastic syndromes** associated with adenocarcinoma consisting of anorexic cachexia, hypercalcemia, hypertrophic pulmonary osteoarthropathy symptoms of bone/joint pain (secondary to PTHRP), and clubbing of the digits
- Physical examination: attention to any enlarged lymph nodes, lung-atelectasis, effusion, bony tenderness, and neurologic findings

Investigations
- CBC and chemistry with liver/renal function
- Tissue diagnosis
- Sputum cytology diagnoses: lesions more central than peripheral

- For central lesions, bronchoscopic exam with biopsy
- For peripheral lesions, CT-guided needle biopsy
- For pleural effusions, thoracoscopy and thoracentesis
- Cervical mediastinoscopy or endobronchial ultrasound-guided transbronchial needle aspiration (EBUS-TBNA) is recommended before definite local therapy (resection or radiation) to assess paratracheal nodes (levels 2, 4), subcarinal (level 7), and hilar nodes (level 10). Anterior mediastinotomy may be required to assess AP window and para-aortic nodes (levels 5, 6).
- Pulmonary function test (PFT), patients usually accepted for RT if: FEV1 >800 mL, FEV1/FVC >50%, DLCO >60% predicted.
- PET scan, bone scan, and CT abdo/pelvis if PET is unavailable, brain MRI/CT scan (if symptomatic stage I/II/III/IV disease)

Screening
- National Lung Screening Trial (NLST): Use of low dose CT versus CXR for screening. Low dose CT: Average effective dose is 1.5 mSv
- Screening showed lung cancer—specific mortality relative reduction of 20% and reduction of death from any cause by 6.7%

TNM Staging (Lung)

Tx	Primary tumor cannot be assessed or proven by the presence of malignant cells in sputum or bronchial washings but not visualized by imaging or bronchoscopy
T0	No evidence of primary tumor
Tis	Carcinoma in situ
T1	Tumor ≤3 cm in greatest dimension surrounded by lung or visceral pleura without bronchoscopic evidence of invasion, more proximal than the lobar bronchus
T1a(mi)	Minimally invasive adenocarcinoma
T1a	Tumor ≤1 cm in greatest dimension
T1b	Tumor >1 cm but ≤2 cm in greatest dimension
T1c	Tumor >2 cm but ≤3 cm in greatest dimension
T2	Tumor >3 cm but ≤5 cm or having any of the following features: • Involves main bronchus regardless of distance from carina, but without its involvement • Invades visceral pleura • Associated with atelectasis or obstructive pneumonitis extending to hilar region, involving part or all of the lung
T2a	Tumor >3 cm but ≤4 cm in greatest dimension
T2b	Tumor >4 cm but ≤5 cm in greatest dimension

(Continued)

T3 Tumor >5 cm but ≤7 cm or associated with separate tumor nodule(s) in the same lobe as primary tumor or directly invades chest wall (including parietal pleura and superior sulcus tumors), phrenic nerve, and parietal pericardium

T4 Tumor >7 cm in greatest dimension or with separate tumor nodule(s) in a different ipsilateral lobe than that of the primary tumor or invades any of the following structures: diaphragm, mediastinum, heart, great vessels, trachea, recurrent laryngeal nerve, esophagus, vertebral body, and carina

N0 No regional lymph node metastasis

N1 Metastasis in ipsilateral peribronchial and/or ipsilateral hilar lymph nodes and intrapulmonary nodes, including involvement by direct extension

N2 Metastasis in ipsilateral mediastinal and/or subcarinal lymph node(s)

N3 Metastasis in contralateral mediastinal, contralateral hilar, ipsilateral, or contralateral scalene, or supraclavicular lymph node(s)

M0 No distant metastasis

M1 Distant metastasis present

M1a Separate tumor nodule(s) in contralateral lobe; tumor with pleural or pericardial nodule(s) or malignant pleural or pericardial effusion

M1b Single extrathoracic metastasis

M1c Multiple extrathoracic metastases in one or more organs

Stage Grouping

Occult carcinoma	Tx	N0	M0
Stage 0	Tis	N0	M0
Stage IA1	T1a(mi), 1a	N0	M0
Stage IA2	T1b	N0	M0
Stage IA3	T1c	N0	M0
Stage IB	T2a	N0	M0
Stage IIA	T2b	N0	M0
Stage IIB	T1a, b, c	N1	M0
	T2a, b, c	N1	M0
	T3	N0	M0

Stage IIIA	T1a, b, c	N2	M0
	T2a, b	N2	M0
	T3	N1	M0
	T4	N0, 1	M0
Stage IIIB	T1a, b, c	N3	M0
	T2a, b	N3	M0
	T3, 4	N2	M0
Stage IIIC	T3, 4	N3	M0
Stage IVA	Any T	Any N	M1a, 1b
Stage IVB	Any T	Any N	M1c

TNM, T (tumor), N (regional lymph nodes), and M (distant metastasis). Used with permission of the American Joint Committee on Cancer (AJCC), Chicago, Illinois. The original source for this material is the AJCC Cancer Staging Manual, Eight Edition (2017) published by Springer Science Business Media LLC, www.springer.com.

Treatment

Stages IA and 1B

Lobectomy and mediastinal lymph node dissection are recommended. Wedge resection only if pulmonary function is compromised. Patients with positive surgical margins can have reresection. Otherwise post-op RT and may consider concurrent chemotherapy for stage IB patients [1−3].

Stages IIA and IIB

Lobectomy and mediastinal lymph node dissection are recommended. Adjuvant cisplatin-based chemotherapy is recommended for patients who are medically able to tolerate chemotherapy. Post-op chemoRT is recommended when the patient has undergone inadequate mediastinal lymph node dissection, or surgical margins are close or positive and the patient is unable to undergo a reresection.

Stage III

RESECTED

These are patients found to have incidental pN2 disease at the time of surgery. Recommendation is to treat with RT to the bronchial stump and mediastinum postoperatively. In addition, adjuvant chemotherapy is recommended for resected stage III NSCLC patients [4,5].

RESECTABLE

These are patients with clinical N2 disease.

- Induction chemotherapy followed by surgical resection is a treatment option. CDDP 100 mg/m^2 IV day 1, etoposide 100 mg/m^2 IV days 1−3 every 4 weeks × 4 cycles is recommended. Other platinum-based chemotherapy regimens may also be used. These patients should be offered postoperative radiation therapy to the surgical bed and involved mediastinal nodes.

- Neoadjuvant chemoRT is another option with CDDP 50 mg/m^2 IV days 1, 8, etoposide 50 mg/m^2 IV days 1–5 every 4 weeks × 2 cycles is recommended, but other platinum-based chemotherapy regimens may also be used [6–9].
  - Restaging studies are evaluated 4 weeks after chemoRT. A lobectomy is preferred over pneumonectomy. If resected, then patients are advised to receive adjuvant chemotherapy with two additional cycles of CDDP/VP-16.
  - If unresectable after neoadjuvant therapy, then complete chemoradiation to full RT dose is recommended.
- Immunotherapy with durvalumab following chemoRT is recommended for up to 1 year for unresectable patients [14].

UNRESECTABLE
- These are patients with clinical T4, bulky N2, or multiple N2 disease. Treatment is concurrent chemoRT. Chemotherapy regimens may vary but are usually platinum-based, such as CDDP 50 mg/m^2 IV days 1, 8, etoposide 50 mg/m^2 IV days 1–5 every 4 weeks × 2 cycles [10–13].
- Immunotherapy with durvalumab following chemoRT is recommended for up to 1 year [14].
- Patients with poor performance status or impaired pulmonary function can be considered for RT alone or sequential CDDP-based chemotherapy followed by RT.

Pleural or Pericardial Effusion
- Thoracentesis or pericardiocentesis.
- If cytology is negative, treat definitively as above; otherwise therapeutic tap/drain and treat as stage IV.

Stage IV
- Chemotherapy is followed by consolidative RT [15]
- Oligometastatic disease—consider SBRT [15]
- Ipsilateral lung separate nodule—surgery followed by chemotherapy
- Contralateral lung solitary nodule—treat as two separate primary lung tumors. Multiple lung lesions—consider local therapy with RT or palliative chemotherapy
- Solitary brain lesion—resection is recommended, followed by whole brain or stereotactic radiosurgery
- Systemic therapy (first line):
  - EGFR mutant — osimertinib (exon 19 deletions or exon 21 L858 mutations), gefitinib, erlotinib, afatinib
  - ALK mutant — crizotinib, ceritinib, alectinib
  - NSCLC WT —
    - Non-squamous cell, ECOG 0-1, pembrolizumab with pemetrexed and platinum-based drug. If PD-L1 >/= 50 %, pembrolizumab mono therapy (or as above).
    - NSCLC, squamous cell; PD-L1 < 50 %, platinum doublet. If PD-L1/= 50 %, pembrolizumab.

SUPERIOR SULCUS TUMORS

- Induction chemoRT including the ipsilateral supraclavicular fossa; chemo is CDDP 50 mg/m^2 IV days 1, 8, etoposide 50 mg/m^2 IV days 1–5 every 4 weeks × 2 cycles, or alternative platinum-based chemotherapy. Surgery is lobectomy if positive margin, then post-op RT followed by further chemotherapy [16].
- If unresectable, then definitive concurrent chemoRT and chemo × 1 cycle are recommended.
- Immunotherapy with durvalumab after completion of chemoRT is recommended [14].

MEDICALLY INOPERABLE NSCLC

- Stereotactic body radiation therapy (SBRT) is the standard of care for medically inoperable early-stage NSCLC. When using SBRT, special attention must be given to normal critical structures. Lower dose/fraction is recommended for central tumors [17–20].
- Another treatment option is to use a small RT field of gross target volume (GTV) plus 1 cm margin. Node-positive individualized treatment is based on amount of lung in the field; treating asymptomatic mediastinum is not recommended.

Outcome

Stage	MS (Months)	2-Year OS (%)	5-Year OS (%)
IA1	NR	97	92
IA2	NR	94	83
IA3	NR	90	77
IB	NR	87	68
IIA	NR	79	60
IIB	66.0	72	53
IIIA	29.3	55	36
IIIB	19.0	44	26
IIIC	12.6	24	13
IVA	11.5	23	10
IVB	6.0	10	0

Data from: Goldstarw P, et al. The IASLC lung cancer staging project: proposals for revision of the TNM stage groupings in the forthcoming (eighth) edition of the TNM classification for lung cancer. J Thorac Oncol January 2016; 11(1):39–51.

Stage I operable—SBRT: 2-year OS 84%
Stage I inoperable—SBRT: 3-year OS 55%
Stage III—ChemoRT: 2-year OS 58%, 5-year OS 32%

SMALL-CELL LUNG CANCER

Workup

Symptoms and Signs
- Cough, shortness of breath (SOB), weight loss, lack of energy, mediastinal, and systemic dissemination; these tumors typically present as central bulky tumors.
- More likely to present with paraneoplastic syndromes.
- **Lambert—Eaton myasthenic syndrome**: Autoimmune disorder of the neuromuscular junction transmission, prevalence in SCLC ~3%. Unlike myasthenia gravis, fatigue/weakness improves with later use in the day.
- **Syndrome of inappropriate antidiuretic hormone (SIADH):** Normovolemic hyponatremia, ectopic production by tumor.
- **Adrenocorticotropic hormone (ACTH) syndrome**: Cushing syndrome via ectopic production.

Investigations
- Same as for NSCLC, in addition to:
  - CT/MRI brain (30% of patients become positive during overall disease course).
  - Thoracentesis or thoracoscopy for pleural effusion is recommended.

Staging

- **Limited stage:** tumor confined to one hemithorax and regional nodes and can be safely encompassed in a reasonable RT portal. Presently, one-third of patients have limited stage disease.
- **Extensive stage** is disease beyond the ipsilateral hemithorax, including malignant pleural or pericardial effusions. Two-thirds of patients present with extensive stage disease.

Treatment

Limited Stage
- Stage I—lobectomy followed by chemotherapy. If node positive, then sequential or concurrent chemo and mediastinal RT [21].
- Stage II, III—concurrent chemoRT. Chemo CDDP 60 mg/m^2 day 1, etoposide 120 mg/m^2 days 1—3 every 3 weeks ×4—6 cycles [22—24].
- All patients to receive PCI [25]. PCI is given after chemotherapy is completed to minimize neurological toxicity. Restaging scans 4—6 weeks after initial treatment.

Extensive Stage
- Combination chemotherapy CDDP based x4-6 cycles.
- Consolidated RT reserved for patients with good response to chemotherapy [26].

- Patients with partial or complete response after chemotherapy ± RT may receive PCI [25].
- Alternatively, close observation with MRI of brain every 3 month and WBRT as indicated can also be considered [27].

Outcome

For limited-stage disease, 5-year overall survival rate is 25%. For extensive-stage disease, median survival without treatment is about 1–2 months; with chemotherapy, median survival is about 9–12 months.

THYMOMA

Thymoma can be lymphocytic, epithelial, or mixed. Only one-third of all thymomas are invasive. Thymomas are associated with the red cell aplasia and myasthenia gravis (MG) in 5%–15% of the cases. Thymomas are staged surgically.

Staging

TNM Staging

T1a	Encapsulated or unencapsulated, with or without extension into mediastinal fat
T1b	Extension into mediastinal pleura
T2	Involvement of pericardium
T3	Involvement of lung, brachiocephalic vein, superior vena cava, chest wall, phrenic nerve, hilar (extrapericardial), and pulmonary vessels
T4	Involvement of aorta, aortic arch, main pulmonary artery, myocardium, trachea, or esophagus
N0	No nodal involvement
N1	Anterior (perithymic) nodes
N2	Deep intrathoracic or cervical nodes
M0	No metastatic pleural, pericardial, or distant sites
M1a	Separate pleural or pericardial nodule(s)
M1b	Pulmonary intraparenchymal nodule or distant organ metastasis

Stage Grouping

Stage	T	N	M
I	T1	N0	M0
II	T2	N0	M0
IIIa	T3	N0	M0
IIIb	T4	N0	M0
IVa	Any T	N1	M0
	Any T	N0,1	M1a
IVb	Any T	N2	M0, M1a
	Any T	Any N	M1b

Used with permission of the American Joint Committee on Cancer (AJCC), Chicago, Illinois. The original source for this material is the AJCC Cancer Staging Manual, Eight Edition (2017) published by Springer Science Business Media LLC, www.springer.com.

Treatment

- Surgical resection is the primary treatment. Post-op RT is indicated for high-risk completely resected thymomas including positive margins, WHO Class B3, thymic carcinomas.
  - **Stage I**—post-op observation
  - **Stage II high risk**—consider post-op RT
  - **Stage III**—recommend post-op RT
- Post-op RT dose is 180–200 cGy/fx to 45–54 Gy in high-risk R0 or R1 resection cases and 60–66 Gy in R2 resections that cannot be further resected. Consider concurrent chemotherapy for R2 disease.
- Unresectable disease should receive neoadjuvant chemo with CDDP followed by surgery and post-op RT.
- For patients who develop thymic carcinoma, CAP chemotherapy followed by surgery and consider post-op RT.

Outcome

For all patients, overall 5-year survival is 74% and 89% for those receiving total resection.

MALIGNANT MESOTHELIOMA

Malignant mesotheliomas are rare aggressive cancers affecting the mesothelial layer including the pleura, peritoneum, pericardium, and tunica vaginalis. They can be epithelial (50%), sarcomatoid (10%), or mixed (40%) histologies. The sarcomatoid histology has the worst prognosis.

Workup

Risk Factors
- Asbestos exposure is the greatest risk factor with a latency period of 20–30 years. Amosite and crocidolite asbestos pose the highest risk
- Affects 4.5 times as many males, like related to asbestos exposure
- Radiation exposure

Symptoms and Signs
- Unilateral chest wall pain, dyspnea. Pleural/pericardial effusion, cough, shortness of breath (SOB), and weight loss
- Regional lymphatic spread

Investigations
- Same as for lung cancers
- Thoracentesis or thoracoscopy/pleuroscopy for pleural effusion
- Biopsy is necessary to distinguish between epithelial and sarcomatoid histology, but definitive diagnosis is difficult with cytology alone. IHC—pankeratin, calretinin, WT-1

Staging

TNM Staging

Tx Primary tumor cannot be assessed

T0 No evidence of primary tumor

T1 Tumor limited to the ipsilateral parietal ±, visceral ±, mediastinal ±, and diaphragmatic pleura

T2 Tumor involving each of the ipsilateral pleural surfaces listed above with at least one of the following features:

- Involvement of diaphragmatic muscle
- Extension of tumor from visceral pleura into the underlying pulmonary parenchyma

T3 Locally advanced, but potentially resectable tumor involving all four of the ipsilateral pleural surfaces with at least one of the following features:

- Involvement of the endothoracic fascia
- Extension into the mediastinal fat
- Solitary, completely resectable focus of tumor extending into the soft tissues of the chest wall
- Nontransmural involvement of the pericardium

(Continued)

T4 Locally advanced, but technically unresectable tumor involving all of the ipsilateral pleural surfaces with at least one of the following features:

- Diffuse extension or multifocal masses of tumor in the chest wall, with or without associated rib destruction
- Direct transdiaphragmatic extension of tumor to the peritoneum
- Direct extension of tumor to the contralateral pleura
- Direct extension of tumor to mediastinal organs
- Direct extension of tumor into the spine
- Tumor extending through to the internal surface of the pericardium with or without a pericardial effusion or tumor involving the myocardium

Nx Regional lymph nodes cannot be assessed

N0 No regional lymph node metastases

N1 Metastases in the ipsilateral bronchopulmonary, hilar, or mediastinal (including the internal mammary, peridiaphragmatic, pericardial fat pad, or intercostal) lymph nodes

N2 Metastases in the contralateral mediastinal, ipsilateral, or contralateral supraclavicular lymph nodes

M0 No distant metastasis

M1 Distant metastasis present

Group Staging

Stage 1A	T1	N0	M0
Stage IB	T2, 3	N0	M0
Stage II	T1, 2	N1	M0
Stage IIIA	T3	N1	M0
Stage IIIB	T1, 2, 3	N2	M0
	T4	Any N	M0
Stage IV	Any T	Any N	M1

Used with permission of the American Joint Committee on Cancer (AJCC), Chicago, Illinois. The original source for this material is the AJCC Cancer Staging Manual, Eight Edition (2017) published by Springer Science Business Media LLC, www.springer.com.

Treatment

- Stage I–III, epithelial, resectable—chemotherapy followed by pleurectomy/ decortication or extrapleural pneumonectomy (EPP) followed by RT. EPP is an extensive surgery involving removal of the lung, pleura, pericardium, and most of the hemidiaphragm, often requiring a GOR-TEX patch.

- Stage I–III, sarcomatoid, unresectable—chemotherapy and palliative radiotherapy as necessary.
- Chemotherapy is pemetrexed and CDDP or carboplatin.
- Post-EPP RT to hemithorax, dose for negative margins is 180–200 cGy/fx to 50–54 Gy; for positive margin/gross disease 54–60 Gy.

Outcomes

Malignant mesothelioma has a poor prognosis overall with high rates of recurrence, most commonly in the contralateral, pleura, and lymph nodes. Reported median survival for trimodality therapy (EPP, chemo, adjuvant hemithorax RT) has been variable (13–24 months). Perioperative mortality is also variable with most surgical series reporting 5%–10% rates. Historically, natural history without treatment is <12 months with sarcomatoid histology generally carrying a worse prognosis.

RT Technique

Patient is supine, both arms above head, IV contrast as necessary to better delineate mediastinal structures, on Vac-Lok; patient is CT simulated. Consider bolus for treating supraclavicular lymphadenopathy invading through skin. Use 6 MV photons, 3DCRT (Figs. 17.2, 17.3 and 17.4) or nine-field IMRT or two-arc VMAT technique (Figs. 17.5, 17.6 and 17.7).

Respiratory motion management is needed: active breath hold, gating, abdominal compression and the use of 4D CT scans to delineate an ITV. Routine cone beam computed tomography (CBCT) to verify target placement is recommended.

(A)   **(B)**

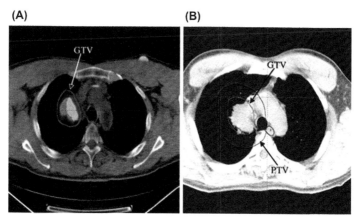

FIGURE 17.2 A PET-CT image shows the right lung tumor (A), which is fused to the planning CT scan to delineate the GVT and the PTV (B). Proper window and level settings help to identify lung tumor edges (B).

(A)   **(B)**

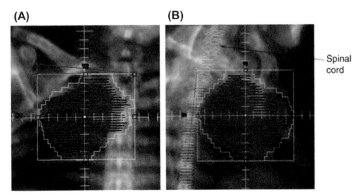

Spinal
cord

FIGURE 17.3 DRR for locally advanced lung cancer patient, showing 0.5 cm margin around the lung tumor PTV not including the ipsilateral supraclavicular in 3-D AP view (A). The spinal cord is blocked in the oblique beam (B).

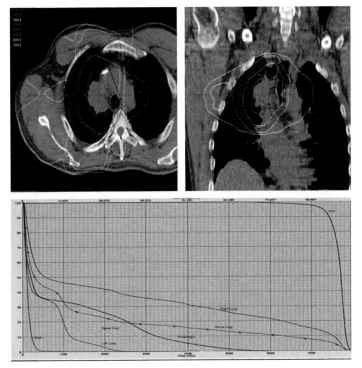

FIGURE 17.4 Upper panel showing locally advanced NSCLC 3D CRT plan isodose lines conforming to PTV and lower panel showing DVH of PTV receiving 95% of the prescribed dose and all the critical normal structures within dose constraints. A dose of 70 Gy is prescribed to the PTV.

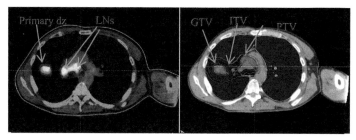

FIGURE 17.5   PETCT scan showing right lung primary tumor, right hilar, and subcarinal LNs is fused with the planning CT scan to delineate GTV, CTV, ITV, and PTV.

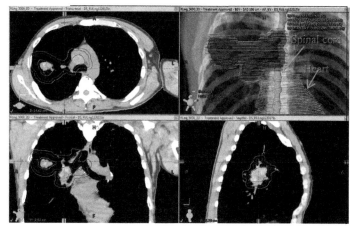

FIGURE 17.6   CT images show PET positive right lung primary and right hilum LN adenocarcinoma. Target volumes GTV, CTV, ITV, and PTV drawn based on PET fusion.

3D Technique

- For 3D CRT, use initial AP/PA followed by off cord planning. Whole mediastinal RT is not recommended; however, if mediastinum is treated, then **borders**: superiorly bottom of clavicle (include ipsilateral supraclavicular fossa if upper lobe involvement), inferiorly 5 cm below carina or 3 cm below tumor, medially 2 cm from contralateral vertebral body, and laterally 2 cm from the tumor. Treat AP/PA 200 cGy/fx to 40−44 Gy, and off cord obliques and/or laterals to 60−70 Gy for NSCLC, and 60−66 Gy for SCLC (or 45 Gy in 30 BID).
- For initial multiple conformal coplanar or noncoplanar beam arrangements, use PTV and dose−volume constraints to prepare plan.
- Elective nodal irradiation is generally not recommended without mediastinal staging by EBUS when mediastinal nodes on PET/CT are concerning. In the

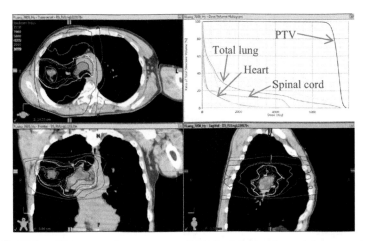

FIGURE 17.7   CT images shows two-arc VMAT planning for a right upper lung and right hilar LN-positive adenocarcinoma patient. The total prescription dose is 70 Gy. Isodose lines conform to PTV and all critical structure constraints are met.

absence of EBUS, however, one can consider including the ipsilateral subclinical lymph nodes in the CTV1 for the initial 46–50 Gy (Figs. 17.1, 17.2 and 17.3).

IMRT/SBRT Technique

Volumes

Stage I SBRT

GTV = Gross primary tumor
CTV = GTV, inspiratory and expiratory
ITV = CTV inspiratory + CTV expiratory
PTV = ITV + 0.5 cm margin

Locally Advanced

GTV = Gross primary tumor and involved LNs as seen on imaging or pathologically determined
CTV = GTV + 0.8–1.5 cm margin accounting for anatomical boundaries, inspiratory and expiratory
ITV = CTV inspiratory + CTV expiratory
PTV = ITV + 0.5 cm margin*
*PTV 1–1.5 cm margin to account for respiration if motion management is not utilized

Postoperative for R0, pN2

GTV = none
CTV = pathologically involved stations ± associated stations by LungART protocol, inspiration and expiration
ITV = CTV inspiratory + CTV expiratory
PTV = ITV + 0.5 cm margin

Doses

NSCLC

Pre-op RT: 180–200 cGy/fx to 45–54 Gy

Concurrent chemoRT: 200 cGy/fx to 60–70 Gy

Post-op RT: negative margin 180–200 cGy/fx to 50–50.4 Gy, positive margin 54–60 Gy, gross residual disease 60–70 Gy

SBRT: 10–18 Gy/fx to 48–60 Gy (treat every other day)

SCLC

Limited stage: 200 cGy/fx to 60–66 Gy QD (150 cGy/fx b.i.d to 45 Gy)

Extensive stage: consolidative thoracic RT 200–300 cGy/fx to 30–45 Gy

PCI: 250 cGy/fx–25 Gy

Constraints

Lung	V20 < 30%–35%, mean lung dose (MLD) <20 Gy, V5 < 65%,
Heart	V30 < 46%, mean dose <26 Gy
Esophagus	V50 < 40%, mean dose <34 Gy
Liver	Mean dose <30–32 Gy
Kidney	V20 < 32%, mean dose <15–18 Gy
Spinal cord	Max dose <50 Gy
Brachial plexus	<66 Gy
Pacemaker	≤2 Gy (relocate out of the direct RT field)
SBRT	see SBRT Chapter 8

Complications

- Skin reactions including redness, irritation, hair loss, skin pigmentation, swallowing difficulty, sore throat, esophagitis, weight loss, and fatigue
- Radiation pneumonitis causing dry cough, low-grade fever, and shortness of breath
- Cardiac sequelae—such as pericardial effusion, constrictive pericarditis, cardiomyopathy
- Neurological side effects from PCI seem to cause diffuse degenerative encephalopathy affecting higher cortical functions particularly impacting short-term memory

Follow-up

- Every 3–6 months for the first 3 years, every 6 months for the fourth and fifth year, and every 12 months thereafter
- Imaging with contrast CT chest/PETCT with follow-ups

ANNOTATED BIBLIOGRAPHY

NON–SMALL-CELL LUNG CANCER

Stages IA/IB and IIA/IIB

Ref 1. Butts et al. (2010). Randomized phase III trial of vinorel-EEbine plus cisplatin compared with observation in completely resected stage IB and II non–small-cell lung cancer: updated survival analysis of JBR-10. *J Clin Oncol*;28(1):29–34.

In this study, 482 patients with stage IB, II NSCLC, after complete resection, were randomized to observation versus postoperative four cycles of cisplatin/vinorelbine chemotherapy. Results at 9.3 years showed that the following:

	Stage IB	Stage II	5-year
	Median Survival (Years)	Median Survival (Years)	Overall Survival (%)
Surg	11	3.6	56
Surg + post-op Chemo	9.8 ns	6.8 ns	67 ss

Adjuvant cisplatin-based chemotherapy improves overall survival among patients with completely resected early-stage NSCLC. The benefit, however, was limited to only N1 patients.

Ref 2. Strauss et al. (2011). Adjuvant chemotherapy (AC) in stage IB non-small cell lung cancer (NSCLC): long-term follow-up of cancer and leukemia group B (CALGB) 9633. *J Clin Oncol*;29(15 Suppl.):7015. CALGB 9633 Trial.

In this study, 344 patients with pathologically confirmed T2N0 NSCLC and who had undergone lobectomy or pneumonectomy were randomly assigned to adjuvant chemotherapy or observation within 4–8 weeks of resection. Chemotherapy consisted of paclitaxel 200 mg/m² intravenously over 3 h and carboplatin at an area under the curve dose of 6 mg/mL per minute intravenously over 45–60 min every 3 weeks for four cycles. Result at a median follow-up of 9 years showed the following:

	Median Survival (Years)		Median OS (%)	
	>4 cm	All	>4 cm	All
Surgery	6.6	6.6	43	44
Surgery + chemo	8.9	8.2	53	51
P value	—	—	.059	.087

Adjuvant chemotherapy should not be considered standard care for stage IB NSCLC patients, as this study showed no significant survival benefit. However, a statistically significant trend for survival advantage for patients who had tumors >4 cm supports consideration of adjuvant paclitaxel/carboplatin for stage IB patients who have large tumors.

Ref 3. Weteel V et al. (2013). A randomized trial comparing preoperative to perioperative chemotherapy in early-stage non-small-cell lung cancer (IFCT 0002 trial). *Eur J Cancer*;49(12):2654–64. IFCT 0002 Trial.

In this trial, 528 patients with resectable stage I–II non–small-cell lung cancer were randomized with a 2 × 2 factorial design compared with two chemotherapy strategies (PRE vs. PERI), and then two chemotherapy regimens (gemcitabine–cisplatin vs. paclitaxel–carboplatin). The PRE group received two preoperative cycles followed by two additional preoperative cycles, whereas the PERI group underwent two preoperative cycles followed by two postoperative cycles (given only to responders in both cases). The results were as below:

	3-Year DFS (%)	**3-Year OS (%)**
PRE group	No	67.4
PERI group	Difference	67.7
P value	—	.92

This study failed to demonstrate any difference in survival between patients receiving preoperative and perioperative chemotherapy in early-stage NSCLC.

Stage III—Resected

Ref 4. Douillard et al. (2008). Impact of postoperative radiation therapy on survival in patients with complete resection and stage I, II, or IIIA non-small-cell lung cancer treated with adjuvant chemotherapy: the adjuvant Navelbine International Trialist Association (ANITA) randomized trial. *Int J Radiat Biol Phys*;72(3):695–701. ANITA Trial.

In this study, 840 patients with stage IB–IIIA NSCLC were randomly assigned to observation or to 30 mg/m^2 vinorelbine plus 100 mg/m^2 cisplatin. Postoperative radiotherapy was not mandatory and was undertaken according to every center's policy. Results after a median follow-up of 76 months were as below:

	Median Survival (months)	**Overall Survival (%)**
Observation	43.7	42.6
Post-op chemotherapy	65.7 ss	51.2
FOR PN2 PATIENTS		
Observation and RT	22.7	
Chemo and RT	47.4 ss	

*Subgroup analysis suggested that patients with stage IB disease did not benefit from adju-
vant chemotherapy. However, patients with resected stage IIIA disease derived significant
benefit from postoperative radiotherapy. Adjuvant vinorelbine and cisplatin should be considered the standard of care for patients with resected stage II and IIIA NSCLC. Results also
showed a positive effect of PORT in pN2 disease.*

Ref 5. Arrigada et al. (2010). Long-term results of the international adjuvant lung
cancer trial evaluating cisplatin-based chemotherapy in resected lung cancer. *J Clin
Oncol*;28(1):35–42.

*In this study, 1867 patients with stage I, II, and III NSCLC, after complete resection, were
randomized to observation or postoperative cisplatin-based chemotherapy. Before randomization, however, patients were pathologically staged to incorporate chemotherapy and postoperative radiation therapy. Results at a median follow-up of 7.5 years were as below:*

	Median Survival (months)	Disease-free Survival (%)	Overall Survival (%)
Surgery	45	34	40 ss
Surgery + post-op chemo	54	40	45 ss

*Cisplatin-based adjuvant chemotherapy given to NSCLC patients after complete resection
improves DFS and OS at 5 years.*

Stage III—Resectable

Ref 6. van Meerbeeck et al. (2007). Randomized controlled trial of resection versus
radiotherapy after induction chemotherapy in stage IIIA-N2 non-small-cell lung cancer.
J Natl Cancer Inst;99(6):442–50. EORTC 08941.

*In this study, 332 patients with stage IIIA—N2 NSCLC, after receiving platinum-based in-
duction chemotherapy × 3 cycles, achieving minor response were randomized to receive either
radical surgery or thoracic radiation therapy. Patients with incomplete resection also received
postoperative RT (60 Gy). The results at a median follow-up of 6 years were as follows:*

	5-year Overall Survival (months)	Median Survival (%)
Induction chemoRT	17.5	14
Induction chemo + surgery	16.4	5.7
P-value	.61	ns

The study revealed that there was no significant difference between the two arms in terms of survival. Therefore, chemoradiotherapy is now the standard treatment for future trials for stage IIIA–N2 NSCLC patients.

Ref 7. Albain et al. (2009). Radiotherapy plus chemotherapy with or without surgical resection for stage III non-small-cell lung cancer: a phase III randomized controlled trial. *Lancet*;374(9687):379–86.

This study followed 429 patients with NSCLC, pathologically + IIIA (N2) and IIIB treated with induction chemoRT followed by resection. Induction was chemotherapy PE × 2 cycles concurrent RT 4500 cGy. Resection was attempted if response or stable disease occurred. A chemoRT boost was given if either unresectable disease, positive margin, or positive lymph node(s) were found. Results at 5 years were as follows:

5-Year	Median PFS (months)	5-year PFS (months)	Overall Survival (%)
CT/RT	11	11	20
CT/RT + surgery	13	22	27
P-value	.17		.10

The study did not show improved survival in the surgical arm.

Ref 8. Pless M et al. (2015). Induction chemoradiation in stage IIIA/N2 non-small-cell lung cancer: a phase 3 randomized trial. *Lancet*;386(9998):1049–56.

In this trial, 232 patients with stage IIIA/N2 NSCLC were randomly assigned to neoadjuvant chemotherapy alone versus neoadjuvant chemoradiotherapy. Chemotherapy was given 100 mg/m^2 CDDP and 85 mg/m^2 docetaxel × 3 cycles followed by RT with 44 Gy in 22 fractions over 3 weeks. The data showed the following:

	Median EFS (m)	Median OS (m)
Chemo + surg	11.6	26.2
chemoRT + surg	12.8	37.1
P value	.67	—

This study analysis showed that RT did not add a significant benefit to induction chemotherapy followed by surgery.

Ref 9. Eberhardt WE et al. (2015). Phase III study of surgery versus definitive concurrent chemoradiotherapy boost in patients with resectable stage IIIA(N2) and selected IIIB non-small-cell lung cancer after induction chemotherapy and concurrent chemoradiotherapy (ESPATUE). *J Clin Oncol*;33(35):4194–201. ESPATUE Trial.

In this trial, 246 patients with pathologically proven IIA (N2) and selected patients with IIIB received induction chemotherapy, which consisted of three cycles of CDDP 50 mg/m^2 on *days 1 and 8 and paclitaxel 175 mg/m^2 on day 1 every 21 days, as well as concurrent chemo-radiotherapy to 45 Gy given as 1.5 Gy BID, concurrent CDDP 50 mg/m^2 on days 2 and 9, and concurrent vinorelbine 20 mg/m^2 on days 2 and 9. Those patients whose tumors were reevaluated and deemed resectable in the last week of radiotherapy were randomly assigned to receive a chemoradiotherapy boost between 65 and 71 Gy in arm A or to undergo surgery arm B. At a median follow-up of 78 months, the results showed the following:*

	5-Year PFS (%)	5-Year OS (%)
Arm A	35	40
Arm B	32	44
P value	.75	.34

This study revealed that for patients with resectable stage III NSCLC, receiving both definitive concurrent chemoRT and surgical resection after pre-op chemoRT is acceptable.

Stage III—Unresectable

Ref 10. Curran et al. (2011). Sequential vs concurrent chemoradiation for stage III non-small cell lung cancer: randomized phase III trial RTOG 9410. *J Nat Cancer Ins*;103(19):1452–60. RTOG 9410.

In this study, 611 patients with unresected NSCLC stage II, III, KPS 70, weight loss 5% or less were randomized to sequential chemoRT, versus concurrent chemoRT QD, versus concurrent chemoRT b.i.d. In the sequential arm, chemotherapy was given CDDP 100 mg/m^2 days 1, 29 and vinblastine 5 mg/m^2 weekly × 5 cycles; RT was given 60 Gy beginning day 50. In the concurrent QD arm, the same chemotherapy and RT was given beginning day 1. In the concurrent b.i.d. arm, CDDP 50 mg/m^2 was given on days 1, 8, 29, and 36 and VP16 50 mg b.i.d. × 10 on weeks 1, 2, 5, and 6. RT was given 120 cGy b.i.d. beginning day 1. Results at a median follow-up time of 11 years were as follows:

	Median Survival (m)	5-Year Overall Survival (%)	Esophageal Toxicity Gr 3–4 (%)
Sequential	14.6	10	4
Concurrent QD	17 ss	16	25
Concurrent b.i.d.	15.6	13	—

ss, statistical significant.

Results showed concurrent CDDP-based chemotherapy and QD RT both improve median survival and OS without increasing late toxicity.

Ref 11. Jalal SI et al. (2012). Updated survival and outcomes for older adults with inoperable stage III non-small-cell lung cancer treated with cisplatin, etoposide, and concurrent chest radiation with or without consolidation docetaxel: analysis of a phase III trial from Hoosier Oncology Group (HOG) and US Oncology. *Ann Oncol*;23(7):1730–38. HOG Trial.

In this study, 203 patients with inoperable, stage IIIA/B NSCLC, PS 0–1, FEV 1 L, and <5% weight loss received cisplatin 50 mg/m² IV days 1, 8, 29, 36 and etoposide 50 mg/ m² IV days 1–5, 29–33 concurrently with chest XRT to 5940 cGy and without progressing, patients were randomized to docetaxel 75 mg/m² IV every 21 days for three cycles versus observation.

	Median Survival (months)	*Overall Survival at 5 years (%)*	*Toxicity*	
			Grade 3/4 (%)	*Grade 5 (%)*
Observation	*26.1*	*23.8*	—	—
Docetaxel	*24.2 ns*	*16.4*	*19*	*5.5*

The data showed that consolidation docetaxel does not improve survival following concurrent cisplatin/etoposide, and is associated with significant toxicities and can no longer be considered as standard treatment for patients with inoperable stage III NSCLC.

Ref 12. Bradley et al. (2017). Long-term results of RTOG 0617: A randomized phase 3 comparison of standard dose versus high dose conformal chemoradiation therapy +/− cetuximab for stage III NSCLC. *Int J Radiat Oncol Biol*;99(2 Suppl.):S105. RTOG 0617.

In this two-by-two factorial study, 544 patients with Stage III unresectable NSCLC treated with concurrent chemoradiation with platinum based chemotherapy [concurrent carboplatin (AUC 2)/paclitaxel (45 mg/m²), two cycles of consolidation (AUC 6/200 mg/m²)] were accrued. Randomization was applied to those receiving 60 Gy versus 74 Gy and receiving cetuximab versus not. At a median follow-up of 5.1 years, the data were as given below:

	Median Survival (months)	*5-Year PFS (%)*	*5-Year OS (%)*
60 Gy	*28.7*	*18.3*	*32.1*
74 Gy	*20.3*	*13*	*23*
P *value*	*.0072*	*.055*	*.004*

This study showed that 60 Gy with concurrent chemotherapy should remain the standard of care with an OS rate. Cetuximab had no effect on OS.

Ref 13. Liang J et al. (2017). Etoposide and cisplatin versus paclitaxel and carboplatin with concurrent thoracic radiotherapy in unresectable stage III non-small cell lung cancer: a multicenter randomized phase III trial. *Ann Oncol;*28(4):777−83.

In this trial, 200 patients with stage III NSCLC randomly received 60−66 Gy of thoracic radiation therapy concurrent with either etoposide 50 mg/m^2 on days 1−5 and cisplatin 50 mg/m^2 on days 1 and 8 every 4 weeks for two cycles (EP arm), or paclitaxel 45 mg/m^2 and carboplatin (AUC 2) on day 1 weekly (PC arm). The data from a median follow-up of 73 months were as follows:

	3-Year (%)	Median (m)	
	OS	*OS*	*Pneumonitis*
EP arm	41.1	23.3	18.9
PC arm	26	20	33
P value	.024	.095	.036

This study concluded that EP might be superior to weekly PC in terms of OS in the setting of concurrent chemoradiation for unresectable stage III NSCLC.

Ref 14. Antonia SJ et al. (2018). Overall survival with durvalumab versus placebo after chemoradiotherapy in stage III NSCLC: Updated results from PACIFIC. 2018 World Conference on Lung Cancer. Abstract PL02.01. Presented September 25, 2018. PACIFIC Trial.

In this trial, 713 patients with stage III NSCLC without disease progression after two or more cycles of platinum-based chemoRT, compared with the anti-PDL 1 antibody durvalumab as consolidation therapy with placebo. Durvalumab was given at a dose of 10 mg/kg of body weight IV or placebo every 2 weeks for up to 12 months. At median follow up of 25.2 months the data showed

	PFS (m)	*OS (%)*	*Toxicity (%)*
Placebo	5.6	55.6	26.1
Durvalumab	17	66.3	30.5
p *value*	<0.001	0.005	-

The study showed that Durvalumab therapy resulted in significantly longer overall survival than placebo. No new safety signals were identified.

Stage IV

Ref 15. Gomez et al. (2018). Local Consolidative Therapy (LCT) Improves Overall Survival (OS) Compared to Maintenance Therapy/Observation in Oligometastatic Non-Small Cell Lung Cancer (NSCLC): Final Results of a Multicenter, Randomized, Controlled Phase 2 Trial. Presented at ASTRO 60th Annual Meeting, San Antonio, TX, October 21, 2018.

In this study, 49 patients were randomized following completion of first-line chemotherapy for stage IV NSCLC to receive local consolidative therapy (ablative radiotherapy or surgery) or maintenance chemotherapy alone. The highest number of nonregional mets considered for enrollment was 3. The data at 38.8 months shows

	Progression Free Survival (m)	Overall Survival (m)
Maintenance TX	4.4	17
Local consolidation	14.2	41.2
P-value	0.014	0.017

The study concluded that with long-term follow-up, compared to maintenance therapy, local consolidation therapy in patients with oligometastatic disease (<3 mets) who do not progress after front-line systemic therapy improves PFS and is associated with an improvement in OS.

SUPERIOR SULCUS TUMORS

Ref 16. Rusch et al. (2007). Induction chemoradiation and surgical resection for non–small-cell lung carcinomas: Long term results of Southwest Oncology Group Trial 9416 (Intergroup Trial 0160). *J Clin Oncol*;25(3):313–18. Int 9416 Trial.

In this study, 110 patients with superior sulcus tumor T3-T4 N0-N1 are treated by induction chemoRT followed by surgical resection. RT was given 4500 cGy concurrently with Eto/CDDP chemotherapy. Results showed the following:

pCR	56%
5-year OS	44% for all patients
5-year OS	54% for patients after complete resection

T3 or T4 did not make any difference. Primary site of relapse is in brain.

This study revealed that adding chemotherapy to RT for superior sulcus tumor provides high rates of pathologic CR; local control and overall survival was improved relative to previous studies of radiation plus resection.

MEDICALLY INOPERABLE TUMORS

Ref 17. Timmerman et al. (2013). RTOG 0618: stereotactic body radiation therapy (SBRT) to treat operable early-stage lung cancer patients. *J Clin Oncol*;31 (15 Suppl.):7523. RTOG 0618 Trial.

In this study, 33 patients were accrued with a median FEV1 and DLCO of 72% and 68% predicted in attempt to better appreciate survival in patients who were otherwise qualified to undergo an operation. Median follow-up was 25 months.

	2-Year (%)
Local failure (including lobe)	19.2
Regional failure	11.7
Distant failure	15.4
PFS	65.4
OS	84.4

This trial revealed that SBRT has high rate of primary tumor control, inadequate need for surgical salvage in operable early-stage lung cancer patients with peripheral lesions.

Ref 18. Nyman J et al. (2016). SPACE — a randomized study of SBRT vs conventional fractionated radiotherapy in medically inoperable stage I NSCLC. *Radiother Oncol*;121(1):1–8. SPACE Trial.

In this trial, 102 patients with stage I medically inoperable NSCLC were randomized to receive SBRT to 66 Gy in three fractions (1 week) or 3DCRT to 70 Gy (7 weeks). At a median follow-up of 37 months, the data showed the following:

	3-Year PFS	OS	Pneumonitis
3DCRT	42	59	34
SBRT	42	54	19
P value	ns	ns	.26

This trial showed that there was no difference in PFS and OS between SBRT and conventionally treated patients. SBRT should be considered standard treatment for patients with inoperable stage I NSCLC.

Ref 19. Videtic et al. (2017). Long-term follow-up on NRG Oncology RTOG 0915 (NCCTG N0927): a randomized phase 2 study comparing 2 stereotactic body radiation therapy schedules for medically Inoperable patients with stage I peripheral non-small cell lung cancer. *Int J Radiat Oncol Biol*;99(2 Suppl.):S15–16. RTOG 0915 Trial.

In this trial, 94 patients with medically inoperable NSCLC with biopsy-proven peripheral (≥2 cm from the central bronchial tree) T1 or T2, N0 (PET negative), M0 were randomized.

SBRT of 34 Gy in one fraction (arm 1) versus 48 Gy in four fractions (arm 2). Median follow-up data after 3.8 years were as given below:

	5 median OS (year)	5-Year OS (%)	Grade ≥3 Toxicity
34 Gy	*4.1*	*28.8*	*no*
48 Gy	*4*	*40.2*	*diff*

This study showed absence of late-appearing toxicity in either arm; primary tumor control rates at 5 years were similar by arm.

Ref 20. Ball DL et al. (2017). A randomized trial of SABR vs conventional radiotherapy for inoperable stage I non-small cell lung cancer: TROG 09.02 (CHISEL). Presented at: international association for the study of lung cancer 18th world conference on lung cancer; Yokohama, Japan. Abstract OA 01.01. CHISEL Trial.

In this study, 101 patients with stage I (T1-T2a N0M0) NSCLC based on PET that was medically inoperable or who refused surgery, had ECOG 0 or 1, and the tumor had to be at least 2 cm or more from the bifurcation of the lobar bronchus, were randomized 2:1 to SABR (54 Gy in three fractions, or 48 Gy in four fractions, depending on proximity to the chest wall, to the isodose covering the PTV) or to CRT (66 Gy in 33 fractions or 50 Gy in 20 fractions). The data at 2 years are given below.

Patients randomized to SABR had superior freedom from local failure (HR = 0.29, 95% CI 0.130, 0.662, P = 0.002) and longer overall survival (HR = 0.51, 95% CI 0.51, 0.911, P = 0.020).

The study concluded that patients with inoperable stage I NSCLC, receiving SABR compared to CRT experienced superior freedom from local failure and had improved overall survival.

LIMITED-STAGE SMALL-CELL LUNG CANCER

Ref 21. Yang CF et al. (2016). Role of adjuvant therapy in a population-based cohort of patients with early-stage small-cell lung cancer. *J Clin Oncol*;34(10):1057.

In this study, 1574 patients with pathologic T1-2N0M0 SCLC who underwent complete resection in the NCDB are stratified by adjuvant therapy regimen of chemotherapy with or without PCI. At a median follow-up of 43 months, the data were as follows:

	5 Years	
	MS (m)	OS (%)
No adjuvant chemotherapy	*42.1*	*40.4*
Adjuvant chemotherapy/PCI	*66*	*52.7*
P value	*<.01*	*<.01*

This analysis showed that patients with pT1-2N0M0 SCLC treated with surgical resection alone have worse outcomes than those who undergo resection with adjuvant chemotherapy or chemotherapy with PCI.

Ref 22. Turrisi et al. (1999). Twice-daily compared with once-daily thoracic radiotherapy in limited small-cell lung cancer treated concur-rently with cisplatin and etoposide. *N Engl J Med*;340(4):265–71.

In this study, 417 patients with limited-stage disease, FEV1 > 1 L, were randomized to receive RT 180 cGy every day to 45 Gy over 5 weeks versus 150 cGy b.i.d. to 45 Gy over 3 weeks. Those patients who achieved complete response also received PCI 250 cGy to 25 Gy. All patients received concurrent chemotherapy with CDDP 60 mg/m² on day 1, etoposide 120 mg/m² on days 1–3 every 3 weeks × 4 cycles. Cord dose was kept at 36 Gy in b.i.d. arm. Results at 5 years were as follows:

5-Year	Median Survival (m)	Local Failure (%)	Overall Survival (%)	Esophagitis/ Grade 3 (%)
CT + QD RT	19	52	16	11
CT + BID RT	23	36	26	27

Four cycles of CDDP + etoposide and a course of b.i.d. RT 45 Gy beginning with cycle 1 of chemotherapy resulted in improved survival rates in patients with limited-stage SCLC.

Ref 23. Takada et al. (2002). Phase III study of concurrent versus sequential thoracic radiotherapy in combination with cisplatin and etoposide for limited-stage small-cell lung cancer: results of the Japan Clinical Oncology Group Study 9104. *J Clin Oncol*;20(14):3054–60.

In this study, 231 patients with limited-stage SCLC were randomized between sequential chemoRT versus concurrent chemoRT. RT consisted of 45 Gy over 3 weeks (1.5 Gy twice daily), and the patients were randomly assigned to receive either sequential or concurrent RT. All patients received four cycles of cisplatin plus etoposide every 3 weeks (sequential arm) or 4 weeks (concurrent arm). RT was initiated following the fourth cycle in the sequential arm and on day 2 of the first cycle of chemotherapy in the concurrent arm. The results showed the following

	Median Survival (months)	5-year Survival (%)
Sequential chemoRT	19.7	18.3
Concurrent chemoRT	27.2	23.7
P-value	.097	

This study strongly suggests that cisplatin plus etoposide and concurrent radiotherapy is more effective for the treatment of limited stage SCLC than cisplatin plus etoposide and sequential radiotherapy.

Ref 24. Faivre-Finn et al. (2017). Concurrent once-daily versus twice-daily chemoradiotherpy in patients with limited-stage small-cell lung cancer (CONVERT): an open label, phase 3, randomized, superiority trial. *Lancet Oncol*;18(8):1116−25. CONVERT Trial.

In this study, 547 patients with LS-SCLC were randomized to receive BID concurrent chemoradiotherapy (45 Gy/30) or once daily concurrent chemoradiotherapy (66 Gy/33). Chemotherapy given cisplatin/etoposide (four to six cycles). Patients started RT on day 22 of cisplatin−etoposide. Median follow-up was 45 months.

	Median Survival	2-Year OS (%)	5-Year OS (%)	Grade 3−4 Esophagitis (%)
BID ChemoRT	30 months	56	34	18
OD ChemoRT	25 months	51	31	19
P-value	.14			.85

The authors concluded that the survival outcomes did not differ significantly with a similar toxicity profile. Because the trial was designed to show superiority of OD RT and not equivalence, BID RT should continue to be the standard of care.

EXTENSIVE-STAGE SMALL-CELL LUNG CANCER

Ref 25. Slotman et al. (2007). Prophylactic cranial irradiation in extensive small-cell lung cancer. *N Engl J Med*;357:664−72.

In this study, 286 patients with ES-SCLC who completed platinum-based chemotherapy with at least a partial response were randomized to receive or not receive PCI. Patients were randomized following chemotherapy and OS; DFS is calculated from the time of randomization.

	Median Survival (months)	1-Year OS (%)	1-Year Risk of Brain Mets (%)
PCI	6.7	27.1	14.6
No PCI	5.4	13.3	40.4
P-value	.003		<.001

The study concluded that PCI improved survival.

Ref 26. Slotman et al. (2014). Use of thoracic radiotherapy for extensive stage small-cell lung cancer: a phase 3 randomised controlled trial. *Lancet Oncol;*385:36–42.

In this study, 495 patients with ES-SCLC who completed and had a response to chemotherapy were randomized to receive either thoracic RT (30 Gy/10) or not. All patients were given PCI. The primary endpoint was 1-year OS and results were as given below:

	1-Year OS (%)	2-Year OS (%)	6-Month PFS (%)
Thoracic RT	33	13	24
No thoracic RT	28	3	7
P-value	.07	.004	.001

Despite the lack of difference at the primary endpoint (1-year OS), there was a significant OS benefit at 2 years and the authors concluded that thoracic RT in addition to PCI should be considered in ES-SCLC.

Ref 27. Takahashi et al. (2017). Prophylactic cranial irradiation versus observation in patients with extensive-disease small-cell lung cancer: a multicentre, randomised, open-label, phase 3 trial. *Lancet Oncol;*18(5):663–71.

In this trial, 224 patients with extensive-disease small-cell lung cancer who had any response to platinum-based doublet chemotherapy and no brain metastases by MRI were randomly assigned (1:1) to receive prophylactic cranial irradiation (25 Gy in 10 daily fractions of 2.5 Gy) or observation. All patients were required to have brain MRI at 3-month intervals up to 12, 18, and 24 months after enrolment. Results were as below:

	Brain Met (%)	Median OS (m)
PCI	48	11.6
Observation	69	13.7
P value	<.0001	.094

This study showed that prophylactic cranial irradiation did not improve overall survival compared with observation in patients with extensive-disease small-cell lung cancer. Prophylactic cranial irradiation is therefore not essential for patients with extensive-disease small-cell lung cancer with any response to initial chemotherapy and a confirmed absence of brain metastases when patients receive periodic MRI examination during follow-up.

Gastrointestinal Cancers

ESOPHAGEAL CANCER

The estimated incidence in the United States is 17,290 with estimated 15,850 deaths in 2018.

The most common type of esophageal cancer worldwide is squamous cell carcinoma (SCCa), although the incidence of adenocarcinoma is increasing, especially in white males. In the United States, the most common type of esophageal cancer is adenocarcinoma (75% of all esophageal cancers) with the most common location of esophageal cancer being the lower third of the esophagus involving the gastroesophageal (GE) junction.

The length of the **esophagus** is 25–30 cm. It begins at the cricoid C6 level, which is 15 cm from the incisors. It has four parts.

- Cervical, from C7 to thoracic inlet, approximately 20 cm from the incisors
- Upper thoracic, starting at 20 cm from the incisors to 25 cm
- Midthoracic, starting at 25 cm and ending 30 cm from the incisors
- Lower thoracic, ending 40 cm from the incisors to the GE junction

Lymphatic channels drain to the cervical, mediastinal, and celiac lymph nodes. Lymph node (LN) risks are as follows:

Location of the Tumor	Subclavian Int. Jugular Lymph Node (%)	Superior/Middle Mediast/Mid Lower/ Mediastinal Lymph Node (%)	Celiac Lymph Node
Cervical tumor	6	70	10
Upper thoracic tumor	—	70	30
Midthoracic tumor	—	60	40
Lower thoracic tumor	—	30	70

Data from Akiyama H, Tsurumaru M, Kawamura T, Ono Y. Principles of surgical treatment for carcinoma of the esophagus: analysis of lymph node involvement. Ann Surg 1981;194(4):438–46.

Fundamentals of Radiation Oncology
https://doi.org/10.1016/B978-0-12-814128-1.00018-0

Workup

Risk Factors
- Diet (e.g., high irritants, fermented foods), obesity, high body mass index (BMI), alcohol, and tobacco
- Achalasia
- Plummer–Vinson syndrome
- Caustic injury to the esophagus, GERD
- Barrett esophagus, atrophic gastritis

Symptoms and Signs
- Weight loss, dysphasia initially to bulky solid food progressing to soft foods and liquids, odynophagia, or hoarseness. Chronic cough suggesting tracheal irritation by LNs or extension of tumor
- Cervical adenopathy, SVC syndrome, Horner syndrome (physical exam including HEENT), organomegaly, and bone pain

Investigations
- CBC, chemistry (liver and renal function), HER 2 and PDL1 testing
- Double contrast esophagogram can show ragged mucosal pattern and luminal narrowing of the esophageal lumen
- Upper endoscopy with brushings and biopsy, endoscopic ultrasound (EUS) is better for depth of invasion and nodal assessment
- Tracheobronchoscopy to exclude tracheal invasion in tumors at or above carina (also helpful to exclude synchronous head and neck cancer in patients with history of tobacco and alcohol use)
- Mediastinoscopy to evaluate suspicious paratracheal and subcarinal nodes on CT. Laparoscopic staging performed to rule out LN or vascular involvement that may prevent curative surgery
- CT chest/upper abdomen with oral and IV contrast, bone scan if symptomatic or if alkaline phosphatase is elevated, PET/CT is useful in the detection of metastatic disease

TNM Staging (Esophageal Cancer)

TX	Primary tumor cannot be assessed
T0	No evidence of primary tumor
Tis	High-grade dysplasia[a]
T1	Tumor invades lamina propria, muscularis mucosae, or submucosa
T1a	Tumor invades lamina propria or muscularis mucosae
T1b	Tumor invades submucosa
T2	Tumor invades muscularis propria
T3	Tumor invades adventitia

T4   Tumor invades adjacent structures

T4a   Resectable tumor invading pleura, pericardium or diaphragm

T4b   Unresectable tumor invading other adjacent structures, such as aorta, vertebral body, trachea, etc.

^aHigh-grade dysplasia includes all noninvasive neoplastic epithelia that were formerly called carcinoma in situ, a diagnosis no longer used for columnar mucosae anywhere in the gastrointestinal tract.

NX	Regional lymph node(s) cannot be assessed
N0	No regional lymph node metastasis
N1	Regional lymph node metastases involving one to two nodes
N2	Regional lymph node metastases involving three to six nodes
N3	Regional lymph node metastases involving seven or more nodes
M0	No distant metastasis
M1	Distant metastasis

Stage Grouping

Squamous Cell Carcinoma

Stage	T	N	M	Grade	Tumor Location
Stage 0	Tis	N0	M0	n/a	Any
Stage IA	T1a	N0	M0	1, X	Any
Stage IB	T1a	N0	M0	2–3	Any
	T1b	N0	M0	1–3, X	Any
	T2	N0	M0	1	Any
Stage IIA	T2	N0	M0	2,3, X	Any
	T3	N0	M0	Any	Low
	T3	N0	M0	1	Upper/Middle
Stage IIB	T3	N0	M0	2–3	Upper/middle
	T3	N0	M0	X, Any	Any, X
	T1	N1	M0	Any	Any

(Continued)

Stage	T	N	M	Grade	Tumor Location
Stage IIIA	T1	N2	M0	Any	Any
	T2	N1	M0	Any	Any
Stage IIIB	T2	N2	M0	Any	Any
	T3	N1, 2	M0	Any	Any
	T4a	N0, 1	M0	Any	Any
Stage IVA	T4a	N2	M0	Any	Any
	T4b	N0, 2	M0	Any	Any
	Any	N3	M0	Any	Any
Stage IVB	Any	Any	M1	Any	Any

Stage Grouping

Adenocarcinoma

Stage	T	N	M	Grade
Stage 0	Tis	N0	M0	n/a
Stage IA	T1a	N0	M0	1, X
Stage IB	T1a	N0	M0	2
	T1b	N0	M0	1–2, X
Stage IC	T1	N0	M0	3
	T2	N0	M0	1, 2
Stage IIA	T2	N0	M0	3, X
Stage IIB	T1	N1	M0	Any
	T3	N0	M0	Any
Stage IIIA	T1	N2	M0	Any
	T2	N1	M0	Any
Stage IIIB	T2	N2	M0	Any
	T3	N1, 2	M0	Any
	T4a	N0, 1	M0	Any
Stage IVA	T4a	N2	M0	Any

Stage	T	N	M	Grade
	T4b	N0, 1, 2	M0	Any
	Any	N3	M0	Any
Stage IVB	Any	Any	M1	Any

Histologic Grade (G)

GX	Grade cannot be assessed—stage grouping as G1
G1	Well differentiated
G2	Moderately differentiated
G3	Poorly differentiated, undifferentiated

M, (distant metastasis); N, (regional lymph nodes); TNM, T (tumor).*Used with permission of the American Joint Committee on Cancer (AJCC), Chicago, Illinois. The original source for this material is the AJCC Cancer Staging Manual, Eight Edition (2017) published by Springer Science Business Media LLC, www.springer.co*m.

Treatment

- **Stage Tis and T1a**—endoscopic mucosal resection and endoscopic submucosal dissection with or without ablation.
- **Stage T1bN0M0**—esophagectomy should be considered for all medically fit patients. Several operative techniques are acceptable for patients with resectable esophageal cancer. Transthoracic (Ivor Lewis esophagogastrectomy and McKeown esophagogastrectomy) and transhiatal esophagogastrectomy are common surgical approaches. Gastric conduit is the preferred approach for esophageal reconstruction.
- **Stage T1b-4aN0-N+**—neoadjuvant chemoRT followed by surgery or definitive concurrent chemoRT [1, 2, 3, 3a].
  - Neoadjuvant chemo carboplatin AUA of 2, paclitaxel 50 mg/m^2 weekly for ×5 cycles.
  - Concurrent chemoRT is CDDP 75 mg/m^2, 5FU 1000 mg/m^2/day CIV every 4 weeks ×4 cycles.
- Patients with SCCa receiving neoadjuvant chemoRT with complete clinical response may be observed. All others are considered for surgical resection. For adenocarcinoma, patients with complete clinical response to preoperative chemoRT proceed to surgery.
- **Stage T4b, inoperable**—concurrent chemoRT.
- **Stage pT3-T4, pN+, or positive margin**—postoperative adjuvant chemotherapy or chemoRT.

RT Technique

3D Technique

Patient is CT simulated in the supine position, arms above head with oral and IV contrast. Patient avoids heavy meal 3 h before simulation. Use a VacLok device. **Borders:** superior thyroid groove/includes bilateral supraclavicular nodes if tumor is above carina or 5 cm above tumor; inferior 5 cm below tumor. Include celiac nodes if lower thoracic/GE junction tumor, laterals 2 cm margin. Boost with 3-cm longitudinal margin. Treat AP/PA to 39.6–45 Gy, then off cord to AP/RAO/LAO obliques versus laterals to 50.4 Gy; the supraclavicular nodes are treated with electrons to 50.4 Gy; cord dose is kept below 42.5–45 Gy (Fig. 18.1).

IMRT Technique

Patient setup is similar as 3D technique. Patient is CT simulated. CT scan of the entire thorax and upper abdomen is done, including the liver and kidneys. Fuse PETCT with planning CT. For 6 MV photons, use equally spaced nine-field coplanar IMRT beams or two-arc VMAT. Respiratory motion may be significant for distal esophagus cancer and GE junction tumors. When 4D planning or other motion management techniques are used, PTV margins may be modified to account for observed motion and may also be reduced (Figs. 18.2–18.5).

Volumes

GTV = gross disease + enlarged LNs identified on CT or PET scan.
CTV1 = GTV (or postop tumor bed) + 3–4 cm superior and inferior margins, 1 cm radial margin for primary tumor and 0.5–1.5 cm for enlarged LNs (respecting anatomic tissue boundaries) + elective LNs depending on primary tumor location.

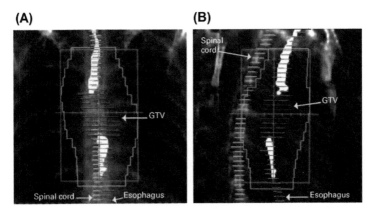

(A)   **(B)**

FIGURE 18.1 (A) A 3D-CRT DRR of a midesophageal cancer, AP field, showing superior border 5 cm above and inferior border 5 cm below the tumor; lateral borders have a 2 cm margin from the tumor. (B) Oblique field, showing sparing of the spinal cord from the radiation field.

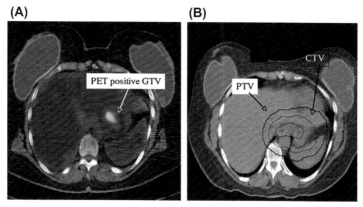

FIGURE 18.2 PET-CT scan showing GE junction tumor (A), which is fused to the planning CT scan to delineate the GVT, CTV, and PTV (b).

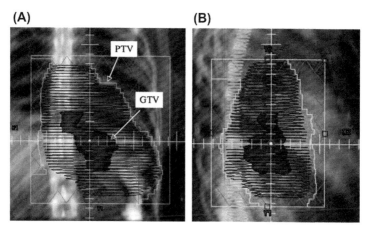

FIGURE 18.3 GE junction tumor patient DRR showing AP view (A) and oblique view (B) of the seven-field IMRT plan.

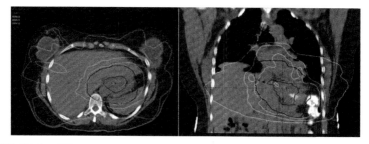

FIGURE 18.4 GE junction tumor patient seven-field IMRT treatment plan isodose lines conforming to PTV shown in axial (A) and coronal (B) views.

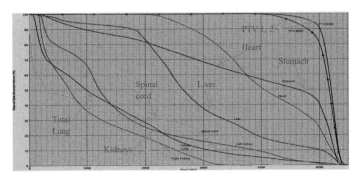

FIGURE 18.5 GE junction tumor patient IMRT plan DVH showing PTV receiving 95% of the prescription dose. All critical normal structures are within dose constraints. A dose of 45 Gy to PTV1 and of 50.4 Gy to PTV2 is prescribed.

CTV2 = GTV (or postop tumor bed) + 2 cm superior and inferior margin and 1 cm radial margin and 0.5−1.5 cm for enlarged LNs (respecting anatomic tissue boundaries).
PTV = CTV + 0.5−1 cm margin.

Elective Nodal Regions for Primary Tumor Location

Cervical esophagus: supraclavicular lymph nodes and higher echelon cervical lymph nodes (when ≥ N1 disease)
Proximal 1/3 esophagus: supraclavicular lymph nodes, mediastinal and paraesophageal lymph nodes
Middle 1/3 esophagus: paraesophageal lymph nodes
Distal 1/3 esophagus: paraesophageal, lesser curvature, splenic nodes, and celiac axis nodes

Doses

Preoperative chemoRT = 180 cGy/fx to 41.4−50.4 Gy
Definitive chemoRT = 180 cGy/fx 50.4−54 Gy
Postoperative chemoRT = 180 cGy/fx to 45−50.4 Gy
Cervical: chemoRT = 180 cGy/fx to 59.4−66.6 Gy

Constraints

Lung	RT alone V20 ≤ 40%; concurrent chemoRT V20 ≤ 30%; post-op chemoRT V20 ≤ 20%; V40 ≤ 10%; V30 ≤ 15%; V10 ≤ 40%; V5 ≤ 50%; mean lung dose 13−20 Gy
Heart	V25 < 10%; V30 ≤ 30%; mean dose <30 Gy
Liver	Mean dose <25 Gy; V20 ≤ 30%; V30 ≤ 20%
Kidney	V18 < 33 Gy; mean dose <15−18 Gy

Spinal cord	45–50 Gy
Bowel	Max bowel dose < Max PTV dose; D05 ≤ 45 Gy
Stomach	Mean < 30 Gy (if not within PTV); max dose <54 Gy

Outcome

The 5-year survival rate for esophageal carcinoma is 43% for localized disease (T1–3, N0), 23% for regional disease (T4, N+), and 5% for metastatic disease (M1).

Complications

- Skin reactions: erythema, hair loss and pigmentation, dry desquamation, blistering
- Dysphagia and odynophagia
- Weight loss and fatigue, dehydration
- Radiation pneumonitis (cough, low-grade fever, and shortness of breath)
- Radiation fibrosis of the lung, esophageal stricture requiring dilatation
- Pericarditis

Follow-Up

- Every 3–6 months for 1–2 years, every 6–12 months for 3–5 years, then every 12 months thereafter
- Posttreatment PETCT
- EGD and imaging with follow-up visits
- Nutritional assessment and counseling

GASTRIC CANCER

The estimated incidence in the United States is 26,240 with estimated 10,800 deaths in 2018.

GE junction is at T10 level through the left dome of the diaphragm and from there the stomach descends to the midlumbar level.

Lymphatic drainage is from the left side of the stomach and the upper two-thirds of the stomach to the suprapancreatic nodes, from the right lower one-third of the stomach to the subpyloric nodes and eventually to the submesenteric nodes.

Regional first echelon lymph nodes involve the suprapancreatic and subpyloric, lesser curvature and greater (gastroepiploic) curvature, right and left pericardial nodes. Second echelon lymph nodes involve the common hepatic, left gastric, splenic hilum and splenic artery nodes, celiac axis, and lower esophageal nodes.

Workup

Risk Factors

- Low fiber diet, high salt intake, N-nitroso compounds, smoking
- Atrophic gastritis, obesity
- *H. pylori* (*Helicobacter pylori*)

Symptoms and Signs
- Weight loss, weakness, vague epigastric discomfort, indigestion, occasional vomiting, and early satiety
- Anemia, hepatomegaly, and abdominal mass (metastatic ovarian tumor—Krukenberg tumor)
- Remote lymph node metastasis involving left supraclavicular (Virchow node), periumbilical (Sister Mary Joseph nodule), or left axillary lymph nodes (Irish node)
- Ascites, positive fecal occult blood

Investigations
- CBC and liver function tests
- Esophagogastroduodenoscopy or endoscopy with cytology/biopsy
- CT chest/abdomen/pelvis with oral and IV contrast. Double contrast upper GI PET scan may be useful
- *H. pylori* test

TNM Staging (Gastric Cancer)

TX	Primary tumor cannot be assessed
T0	No evidence of primary tumor
Tis	Carcinoma in situ: intraepithelial tumor without invasion of the lamina propria, high-grade dysplasia
T1	Tumor invades lamina propria, muscularis mucosae, or submucosa
T1a	Tumor invades lamina propria or muscularis mucosae
T1b	Tumor invades submucosa
T2	Tumor invades muscularis propria[a]
T3	Tumor penetrates subserosal connective tissue without invasion of visceral peritoneum or adjacent structures[b,c]
T4	Tumor invades serosa (visceral peritoneum) or adjacent structures[b,c]
T4a	Tumor invades serosa (visceral peritoneum)
T4b	Tumor invades adjacent structures

[a]*A tumor may penetrate the muscularis propria with extension into the gastrocolic or gastrohepatic ligaments, or into the greater or lesser omentum, without perforating the visceral peritoneum covering these structures. In this case, the tumor is classified T3. If there is perforation of the visceral peritoneum covering the gastric ligaments or the omentum, the tumor is classified T4.*
[b]*The adjacent structures of the stomach include the spleen, transverse colon, liver, diaphragm, pancreas, abdominal wall, adrenal gland, kidney, small intestine, and retroperitoneum. Intramural extension to the duodenum or esophagus is classified by the greatest depth invasion in any of these sites, including the stomach.*
[c]*A designation of pN0 should indicate that all examined lymph nodes are negative, regardless of the total number removed and/or examined.*

NX	Regional lymph node(s) cannot be assessed
N0	No regional lymph node metastasis[a]
N1	Metastasis in 1–2 regional lymph nodes
N2	Metastasis in 3–6 regional lymph nodes
N3	Metastasis in 7 or more regional lymph nodes
N3a	Metastasis in 7–15 regional lymph nodes
N3b	Metastasis in 16 or more regional lymph nodes

[a]pN0 designation used if all examined lymph nodes are negative, regardless of the total number removed and examined.

M0	No distant metastasis
M1	Distant metastasis

Histologic Grade (G)

GX	Grade cannot be assessed
G1	Well differentiated
G2	Moderately differentiated
G3	Poorly differentiated

PATHOLOGICAL (PTNM) STAGING

Stage	T	N	M
Stage 0	Tis	N0	M0
Stage IA	T1	N0	M0
Stage IB	T1	N1	M0
	T2	N0	M0
Stage IIA	T1	N2	M0
	T2	N1	M0
	T3	N0	M0
Stage IIB	T1	N3a	M0

(Continued)

Stage	T	N	M
	T2	N2	M0
	T3	N1	M0
	T4a	N0	M0
Stage IIIA	T2	N3a	M0
	T3	N2	M0
	T4a	N1, 2	M0
	T4b	N0	M0
Stage IIIB	T1, 2	N3b	M0
	T3	N3a	M0
	T4b	N1, 2	M0
Stage IIIC	T3, 4a	N3b	M0
	T4b	N3a, 3b	M0
Stage IV	Any T	Any N	M1

M, (distant metastasis); *N*, (regional lymph nodes); *TNM*, T (tumor).
Used with permission of the American Joint Committee on Cancer (AJCC), Chicago, Illinois. The original source for this material is the AJCC Cancer Staging Manual, Eighth Edition (2017) published by Springer Science Business Media LLC, www.springer.com.

Treatment

- **Stage Tis and Tia**—endoscopic resection or surgery. Surgery involves total gastrectomy. For distal lesions, subtotal gastrectomy is recommended. Either procedure is followed by reconstruction such as esophagojejunostomy, Roux-en-Y, or gastrojejunostomy Billroth II. Prophylactic splenectomy is not indicated.
- **Stage T1b-4N0−N+**—perioperative chemotherapy or preoperative chemoRT followed by surgery [4, 5].
- Perioperative chemotherapy consisting of three preoperative and three postoperative cycles of ECF (epirubicin, cisplatin, 5FU) 50/60/200 mg/m^2/day CIV.
- **Stage pT2N0**—observation or post-op chemoRT.
- Stage pT3-4N0−N+, positive margin/gross disease—post-op chemoRT [6, 7, 8]. Post-op concurrent chemotherapy is 5FU/leucovorin 425/20 mg/m^2 ×1 followed by concurrent 5FU/leucovorin and RT (400/20 mg/m^2 every 4 weeks ×2 cycles) followed by further 5FU/leucovorin 425/20 mg/m^2 ×2 cycles.
- **Inoperable/unresectable**—concurrent chemoRT.
- **Stage IV** - systemic chemotherapy with or without palliative RT is indicated. Chemotherapy consist of FOLFOX, cisplatin with 5FU, capecitabine and oxaliplatin, and taxane-containing regimens. Her 2 Neu positive patients should receive trastuzumab in addition to the above regimens in the first line setting.

RT Technique

3D Technique

CT simulation and conformal treatment planning should be used. The patient should not intake heavy meal 3 h before simulation and treatments. 4D-CT planning or other motion management is recommended, when necessary. Patient is supine, arms above head, oral/IV contrast, and CT simulated. Use of an immobilization device is recommended. **Borders:** Superior T9/T10 or 2 cm above stomach; inferior L3/L4 (cover celiac axis); laterals 3 cm margin around tumor or tumor bed, 3–4 cm to the right lateral of vertebral body (cover porta hepatis), 3/4 of the left hemidiaphragm (cover splenic hilum). For lesions through gastric wall, include entire left hemidiaphragm. For cardiac lesion, include 3–5 cm of esophagus. For near gastroduodenal junction lesion, include 3–5 cm of duodenum. Four-field approach is appropriate if pre-op volume is available for more conformal 3D treatment planning. A 2 cm margin is added for the boost treatment.

IMRT Technique

Setup and CT simulation are similar as 3D. Fuse PETCT with planning CT. For 6 MV photons, use nine-field beam IMRT or two-arc VMAT. Motion management and daily IGRT are recommended.

Volumes

GTV = gross disease based on EGD and imaging
CTV = GTV (or post-op tumor bed) + remaining stomach +
elective LNs depending on the location of the primary
PTV=CTV + 0.5 cm

Elective Nodal Regions for Primary Tumor Location

Proximal 1/3 gastric: 3–5 cm distal esophagus and nodal areas including perigastric, celiac, splenic hilar, hepatic artery, and porta hepatis
Middle 1/3 body gastric: perigastric, celiac, splenic hilar, porta hepatis, and pancreaticoduodenal lymph nodes
Distal 1/3 gastric: 3–5 cm of duodenum and nodal areas perigastric, suprapancreatic, celiac, porta hepatis, and pancreaticoduodenal lymph nodes

Dose

Preoperative chemoRT=180 cGy/fx to 45–50.4 Gy
Definitive chemoRT=180 cGy/fx to 50.4–54 Gy
Postoperative chemoRT=180 cGy/fx to 45 Gy

Constraints

Lungs	V20 ≤ 30%; mean dose ≤20 Gy
Spinal cord	45–50 Gy
Bowel	V45 < 195 cc

(Continued)

Heart	V30 $\leq$ 30%; mean dose <30 Gy
Kidney	V20 $\leq$ 33%; mean dose <18 Gy
Liver	V30 $\leq$ 33%; mean dose <25 Gy

Outcome

Median survival is 27 months. Five-year overall survival for surgery is only 20%, whereas surgery with chemoRT is 39%–52%. According to stages, 5-year overall survival rates for stages I, II, III, and IV were approximately 57%–71%, 33%–46%, 9%–20%, and 4%, respectively.

Complications

- Fatigue, weakness, nausea/vomiting, weight loss, heartburn, gastric indigestion, diarrhea, gastric ulcer
- Bowel damage causing obstruction, ulceration, and bleeding
- Kidney and liver damage causing high blood pressure or abnormal liver function

Follow-Up

- Every 3–6 months for 1–2 year, every 6–12 months for 3–5 year, and every 12 months thereafter
- CBC, liver and renal function tests, endoscopic examination (for patients who had partial or subtotal gastrectomy) and imaging as clinically indicated
- For resected patients, monitor vitamin B12 and iron
- For early lesions imaging should be considered when clinically indicated. For locally advanced gastric cancer CT chest/abdomen/pelvis with oral and IV contrast every 6-12 months for first 2 years, then annually up to 5 years and/or can consider PET/CT as clinically indicated.

PANCREATIC CANCER

The estimated incidence in the United States is 55,440 with estimated 44,330 deaths in 2018.

The pancreatic gland lies transversely across the abdomen, the head within the concavity of the duodenum at about the L2 level with the body in front of L1, and the tail obliquely in direct contact with the spleen. The celiac trunk lies at the upper border of the pancreas and the superior mesenteric vessels travel from just inferior to the celiac vessels down to the L3 level. Blood supply is from the splenic artery and the inferior pancreatic artery, while the lymphatic drainage is diffuse.

Workup

Risk Factors

- Smoking, high-fat diet, alcohol, diabetes mellitus (DM)
- Chemists and metal workers (benzidine)
- Nonhereditary chronic pancreatitis

Symptoms and Signs

- Anorexia, asthenia, early satiety, weight loss, nausea and vomiting, abdominal pain radiating to mid/low back, lessened by assuming fetal position, constipation due to decreased gut motility, or diarrhea due to malabsorption
- Jaundice may be associated with pruritus
- Trousseau sign involves migratory thrombophlebitis

Investigations

- CBC, chemistry including amylase, lipase, liver function test (LFT), and alkaline phosphatase
- Tumor marker is CA 19—9
- Transabdominal ultrasound or EUS with FNA if available, endoscopic retrograde cholangiopancreatography (ERCP)
- Chest X-ray, dynamic phase spiral CT to assess operability. If vascular invasion [celiac, SMA (superior mesenteric artery), portal] or extensive nodal disease is present, then it is considered unresectable, and usually fine needle aspiration (FNA) is performed for confirmation. PET/CT may be helpful and its role is evolving.
- Laparoscopic procedure can be done—to rule out peritoneal seeding and to get biopsy

TNM Staging (Pancreatic Cancer)

TX	Primary tumor cannot be assessed
T0	No evidence of primary tumor
Tis	Carcinoma in situ This includes high-grade pancreatic intraepithelial neoplasia (PanIn-3), intraductal papillary mucinous neoplasm with high-grade dysplasia, intraductal tubulopapillary neoplasm with high-grade dysplasia, and mucinous cystic neoplasm with high-grade dysplasia
T1	Tumor $\leq$2 cm in greatest dimension
T1a	Tumor $\leq$0.5 cm in greatest dimension
T1b	Tumor >0.5 cm and <1 cm in greatest dimension
T1c	Tumor 1—2 cm in greatest dimension
T2	Tumor >2 cm and $\leq$4 cm in greatest dimension
T3	Tumor >4 cm in greatest dimension
T4	Tumor involves celiac axis, superior mesenteric artery, and/or common hepatic artery, regardless of size
NX	Regional lymph nodes cannot be assessed
N0	No regional lymph node metastases
N1	Metastasis in one to three regional lymph nodes

(Continued)

N2	Metastasis in four or more regional lymph nodes	
M0	No distant metastasis	
M1	Distant metastasis	

Stage Grouping

Stage	T	N	M
Stage 0	Tis	N0	M0
Stage IA	T1	N0	M0
Stage IB	T2	N0	M0
Stage IIA	T3	N0	M0
Stage IIB	T1,2,3	N1	M0
Stage III	T1,2,3	N2	M0
	T4	Any N	M0
Stage IV	Any T	Any N	M1

AJCC, American Joint Committee on Cancer; *TNM*, tumor, node, metastasis; *UICC*, Union for International Cancer Control.
Used with permission of the American Joint Committee on Cancer (AJCC), Chicago, Illinois. The original and primary source for this information is the AJCC Cancer Staging Manual, Eighth Edition (2017) published by Springer Science+Business Media, LLC, www.springer.com.

Treatment

- **Resectable**—surgery followed by chemotherapy or concurrent chemoRT [9, 10]. Surgical procedure is Whipple partial pancreaticoduodenectomy, which removes distal stomach, gall bladder and cystic duct, head of pancreas, and duodenum. This is followed by reconstruction with choledochojejunostomy, pancreaticojejunostomy, and gastrojejunostomy.
  - Postoperative chemotherapy is with gemcitabine, or gemcitabine/capecitabine or 5FU/leucovorin.
  - Postoperative chemoRT consists of one course of gemcitabine 1000 mg/m^2 IV days 8 and 15, followed by 5FU CIV at 250 mg/m^2/day, followed by additional course of gemcitabine on the same schedule repeated every 20 days. RT is given with concurrent 5FU chemotherapy.
- **Borderline Resectable** - Preoperative chemo alone or preoperative chemoRT may provide a better chance for margin-negative resection. Preop chemotherapy consider FOLFIRINOX, nab-paclitaxel and gemcitabine. If induction chemotherapy results in stable but still unresectable disease, the patient should be considered for combined chemoRT with concurrent 5FU or capecitabine (11).

- **Unresectable** pancreatic cancer—definitive concurrent chemoRT [12, 13, 14]. Concurrent chemo is 5FU 220 mg/m^2 CVI. Additional chemotherapy with gemcitabine 1000 mg/m^2/days 1, 8 ×2 cycles with or without oral erlotinib 100 mg/day may be given before chemoRT followed by further gemcitabine/erlotinib using the same schedule for ×2−4 cycles.

RT Technique

3D Technique

Patient is immobilized with a vaclock (R), CT simulated, supine, arms above head, with IV and oral contrast. The scan extends from approximately T4/5 to L5/S1. For body and tail lesions it may be ideal to simulate with an empty stomach to increase the separation from the tumor. Respiratory motion of target should be accounted for using ITV method—breath hold [with or without active breathing control (ABC)], abdominal compression, or respiratory gating.

Borders: AP/PA fields; superiorly T10/T11 to encompass celiac axis node; inferiorly L3/L4 to encompass paraaortic nodes; laterally 2 cm margin around the tumor or tumor bed, 3 cm to the right lateral vertebral body (cover porta hepatis), 2 cm from the left edge of the vertebral bodies (cover splenic hilum). Lateral fields: anteriorly 2 cm anterior to the tumor or 3−4 cm from the anterior edge of the vertebral body to cover paraaortic node and porta hepatis; posteriorly split vertebral body in half to avoid kidneys. Boost pre-op primary tumor with 2 cm margin.

IMRT Technique

Setup and CT simulation are the same as 3DCRT. Fuse PETCT. For 6 MV photons, use nine-field IMRT or two-arc VMAT. Use motion management and daily IGRT.

Volumes

GTV = gross disease
CTV1 = GTV (or post-op tumor bed, anastomotic sites) + 1.5 cm + elective LNs
CTV2 = GTV (or post-op tumor bed, anastomotic sites) + 1.5 cm
PTV=CTV+0.5 cm[1]

Elective Nodal Regions for Primary Tumor Locations

Pancreatic head tumor: peri/suprapancreatic, celiac, porta hepatis, and paraaortic lymph nodes
Body/tail tumor: peri/suprapancreatic, celiac, splenic hilum
Postop tumor bed area: tumor bed based on pre-op imaging, surgical clips, anastomotic sites (pancreatojejunostomy, hepatojejunostomy)

---

[1]If motion management is not used, then PTV margin is expanded to 1−2 cm.

Doses

Preoperative chemoRT—180 cGy/fx to 50.4—54 Gy
Definitive chemoRT:
PTV1 = 180 cGy/fx to 45 Gy
PTV2 = 180 cGy/fx 54—59.4 Gy
Postoperative chemoRT:
PTV1 = 180 cGy/fx to 45 Gy
PTV2 = 180 cGy/fx to 50.4 Gy

Constraints

Kidney: combined mean ≤ 18
Liver: mean ≤ 25 Gy for post-op RT, and mean ≤ 30 Gy for
definitive or pre-op RT
Small bowel/stomach: maximum dose ≤55 Gy, V45 < 150 cc, V30 < 300 cc;
V50 < 10%, V45 < 15%, and V20 < 50%
Spinal cord: maximum ≤45 Gy

Outcome

Survival if untreated is 4 months and with bypass surgery is 7 months. Resectable patients have median survival of 20 months, and unresectable patients have median survival of 10 months, when treated with chemoRT. Five-year survival rates for stages I, II, III, and IV pancreatic cancer are 12%—14%, 5%—7%, 3%, and 1%.

Complications

- Fatigue, weakness, nausea/vomiting, anorexia, weight loss, heartburn, indigestion, stomach ulcer, diarrhea, and change in bowel habits
- Small bowel obstruction (SBO) due to radiation fibrosis
- Hepatotoxicity and nephrotoxicity
- Spinal cord injury

Follow-Up

- Every 3—6 months for 1—2 year and every 6—12 months thereafter
- CA 19—9 and imaging as clinically indicated

COLON AND RECTAL CANCER

The estimated incidence of colon cancer in the United States is 97,220—and for rectal cancer, 43,030—with estimated combined deaths of 50,630 in 2018.

The rectum is 12—15 cm in length. The rectum begins from the third sacral vertebrae and ends at the anorectal ring, which is the upper border of the anal columns and can be felt by palpating the upper border of the anal sphincter.

Lymphatic drainage of the upper rectum follows the superior rectal vessels and drains to the inferior mesenteric lymph node and eventually to the portal system. The middle and lower rectum follow the middle and inferior rectal vessels, eventually draining to the internal iliac nodes, then to the inferior vena cava. The most common lymph nodes involved with rectal cancer are the perirectal lymph nodes, located laterally and posteriorly to the rectum.

Workup

Risk Factors
- High-fat, low-fiber, high red-meat diet, obesity, and smoking
- Inflammatory bowel disease (more risk with ulcerative colitis than Crohn disease)
- Familial adenomatosis polyposis (includes Gardner and Turcot syndrome)
- Hereditary nonpolyposis syndrome (HNPCC)—Lynch syndrome

Symptoms and Signs
- Tumors located in the right colon are usually exophytic and possibly associated with iron deficiency anemia. Tumors located in the left colon are invasive and can be associated with obstruction and rectal bleeding
- Anorexia, weight loss and change in bowel habit
- Blood in the stool or rectal bleeding and abdominal deep-pelvic or rectal pain
- Pencil-thin stool
- Enlarged lymph nodes (organomegaly)
- Mass palpated during rectal exam

Investigations
- CBC and chemistry with carcinoembryonic antigen (CEA) and liver function test (LFT)
- Proctosigmoidoscopy or colonoscopy with biopsy (5% synchronous disease)
- Transrectal ultrasound or pelvic MRI with contrast
- Chest X-ray, air-contrasted barium enema [barium enema (BE) misses low lesions], CT of the chest, abdomen, and pelvis with IV and oral contrast, PET scan is not routine

TNM Staging (Colon Cancer)

TX	Primary tumor cannot be assessed
T0	No evidence of primary tumor
Tis	Carcinoma in situ: intramucosal or invasion of lamina propria
T1	Tumor invades submucosa, muscularis mucosa
T2	Tumor invades muscularis propria
T3	Tumor invades through the muscularis propria into pericolorectal tissues
T4a	Tumor penetrates to the surface of the visceral peritoneum (including gross perforation of the bowel through tumor and continuous invasion of tumor to the surface of the visceral peritoneum)
T4b	Tumor directly invades or adheres to other organs or structures
NX	Regional lymph nodes cannot be assessed
N0	No regional lymph node metastasis
N1a	Metastasis in one regional lymph node
N1b	Metastasis in two to three regional lymph nodes

(Continued)

N1c   Tumor deposit(s) in the subserosa, mesentery, or nonperitonealized pericolic or perirectal tissues without regional nodal metastasis

N2a   Metastasis in four to six regional lymph nodes

N2b   Metastasis in seven or more regional lymph nodes

M0   No distant metastasis

M1   Distant metastasis

M1a   Metastasis confined to one organ (liver, lung, ovary, or nonregional lymph node) without peritoneal metastases

M1b   Metastases in more than one organ without peritoneal metastases

M1c   Metastasis to the peritoneum with or without other organ involvement

Stage Grouping

Stage 0	Tis	N0	M0
Stage I	T1, 2	N0	M0 (Dukes A)
Stage IIA	T3	N0	M0 (Dukes B[a])
Stage IIB	T4a	N0	M0 (Dukes B)
Stage IIC	T4b	N0	M0 (Dukes B)
Stage IIIA	T1, 2	N1,1c	M0 (Dukes C)
	T1	N2a	M0 (Dukes C)
Stage IIIB	T3, 4a	N1, 1c	M0 (Dukes C)
	T2, 3	N2a	M0 (Dukes C)
	T1, 2	N2b	M0 (Dukes C)
Stage IIIC	T4a	N2a	M0 (Dukes C)
	T3, 4a	N2b	M0 (Dukes C)
	T4b	N1, 2	M0 (Dukes C)
Stage IVA	Any T	Any N	M1a
Stage IVB	Any T	Any N	M1b
Stage IVC	Any T	Any N	M1c

M, (distant metastasis); *N*, (regional lymph nodes); *TNM*, T (tumor).
[a]*Dukes B is a composite of better (T3 N0 M0) and worse (T4 N0 M0) prognostic groups, as is Dukes C (any T N1 M0 and any T N2 M0).*
Used with permission of the American Joint Committee on Cancer (AJCC), Chicago, Illinois. The original source for this material is the AJCC Cancer Staging Manual, Eighth Edition (2017) published by Springer Science Business Media LLC, www.springer.com.

Treatment

Colon Cancer

- **Resectable**—surgery with colectomy and en bloc dissection of the regional lymph nodes for patients with colonic tumors to remove at least 12 lymph nodes. Postop RT is not needed.
- **Stage pT3-T4N0**—postoperative chemotherapy is individualized. Chemotherapy may involve CAPEOX or FOLFOX [15].
- **Stage N+** − should receive adjuvant oxaliplatin/5FU chemotherapy for 3−6 months. Six months is recommended for T4, N2 patients.
- **Stage T4** disease with contained perforation, fistula or abdominal wall invasion, or patients with residual gross disease—consider post-op RT concurrent with 5FU-based chemotherapy.
- **Unresectable** − neoadjuvant chemoRT followed by surgical assessment.

Rectal Cancer

- **Stage T1-2**—surgery is transanal or transabdominal.
  - Criteria for transanal excision are tumor within 8 cm of anal verge, <3 cm, <30% circumferential involvement, not fixed, well differentiated, and no LVI/PNI.
  - Postop chemoRT is recommended for T2, positive margin, poorly differentiated, positive LVI.
- **Stage T3-4N0-anyN+** − pre-op concurrent chemoRT followed by transabdominal resection 6−8 weeks later, and then followed by further chemotherapy [16, 17, 18, 19, 20, 21]. The surgical procedure is total mesorectal excision (TME), Low anterior resection (LAR), or abdominal perineal resection (APR), depending on tumor location from anal sphincter.
- Preop concurrent chemotherapy 5FU 225 mg/m^2 continuous intravenous infusion (CVI) followed by further 5FU 450 mg/m^2 ×2 cycles; maintenance chemo is for 4 months. Alternatively, capecitabine or FOLFOX can be used.
- **Stage pT3-4, pN+ or positive margin**—adjuvant chemotherapy with 5FU/leucovorin ×1−2 cycles followed by post-op concurrent chemoRT is recommended. Chemotherapy is as above every 4 weeks; maintenance chemotherapy is for 4 months. Alternatively, FOLFOX, XELOX (Xeloda plus oxaliplatin) ×2 cycles followed by 5FU/RT CIV and maintenance chemotherapy.
- **Synchronous metastasis:**
  - Nonobstructing—systemic chemotherapy (+/-preoperative pelvic RT), then resection of the synchronous metastasis and rectal lesion, followed by maintenance chemotherapy as above.
  - Obstructing—resection of the rectal cancer followed by systemic therapy.
- **Metachronous metastasis, resectable**—treat with neoadjuvant chemotherapy ×2−3 months followed by resection, followed by further maintenance chemotherapy as above.

RT Technique

3D Technique

Patient is CT simulated prone, on a belly board, IV contrast, bladder full, empty rectum, mark anus, wire over perineal scar. Initial pelvic field: three or four fields (opposed lateral and PA ± AP) to 45 Gy. **Borders:** superior L5/S1, inferior (pre-op/LAR) 5 cm below tumor or at anal verge, if APR, flash APR scar; lateral: 2 cm on bony pelvis; anterior: behind pubic symphysis (for T4 tumors, 1 cm front of pubic symphysis); posterior: 1 cm posterior to sacrum (flash, if APR). Boost with 2–3 cm margin proximally and distally. Include perirectal lymphatics located laterally and posteriorly in sacral hollow; treat with opposed laterals. RT fields should cover the tumor or tumor bed (2–5 cm margin), presacral nodes, and internal iliac nodes. Include external iliac lymph nodes for T4 tumors.

IMRT Technique

Patient is CT-simulated supine for IMRT technique. Fuse PETCT with planning CT. For 6 MV photons, use equally spaced seven- to nine-field coplanar IMRT beams or two-arc VMAT (Figs. 18.6–18.8).

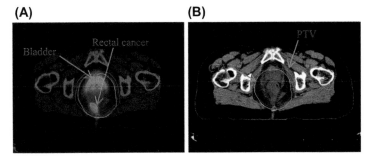

FIGURE 18.6   (A) PET CT showing primary rectal cancer. (B) Planning CT images fused with PET scan delineating target volumes GTV, CTV, PTV.

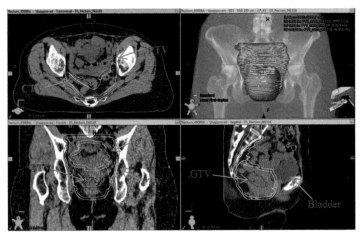

FIGURE 18.7   CT images of target volumes for a rectal cancer GTV, CTV, and PTV.

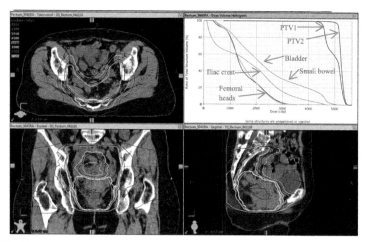

FIGURE 18.8   Rectal cancer patient CT images of two-arc VMAT treatment plan isodose lines showing conforming to PTV and DVH showing meeting all constraints. The prescription dose is PTV1 to 45 Gy and PTV2 to 50.4 Gy.

Volumes

GTV = gross disease + enlarged LNs as seen on CT or PET scan

CTV1 = GTV (or post-op tumor bed) + 2–3 cm margin superior inferior including the presacral space and 1–2 cm margin radial + elective LNs

CTV2 = GTV (or postop tumor bed)+2–3 cm margin superior inferior including the presacral space and 1 cm margin radial

PTV = CTV+0.5 cm margin, modified to exclude 0.5 cm near the skin

Elective Nodal Regions for Primary Tumor Locations

Internal iliac (include external iliac for T4 disease), perirectal fat, and presacral space (presacral space extends 1 cm tissue anterior to the anterior sacrum border from mid S1 to S5).

Tumors invading the anal canal: include inguinal and external iliac lymph nodes.

Post-op APR: include the APR wound.

Doses

Preoperative chemoRT

PTV1 = 180 cGy/fx to 45 Gy

PTV2 = 180 cGy/fx to 50.4 Gy

Postoperative chemoRT

PTV1 = 180 cGy/fx to 50 Gy

PTV2 = 180 cGy/fx to 50.4 cGy for negative margin (54–59.4 Gy considered for positive margin/gross residual disease)

Constraints

Small bowel (peritoneal cavity): V35 < 180 cc, V40 < 100 cc, V45 < 65 cc, Dmax < 50 Gy.
Femoral heads: V45 ≤ 25%, V40 ≤ 40%, Dmax <50 Gy.
Bladder: V45 ≤ 15%, V40 ≤ 40%, Dmax <50 Gy.
Iliac crest: V30 ≤ 50%, V50 ≤%
External genitalia: V20 ≤ 50%, V40 ≤ 5%

Outcome

- Local control with combined modality treatment is 80%−90%. For stage I, II, III, and IV patients, the 5-year overall survival rates are 87%, 49%−80%, 58%−84%, and 12%, respectively.

Complications

- Early: Skin reaction (erythema, irritation, soreness, and/or blistering), fatigue, nausea, anorexia, change in bowel habit, diarrhea, cramps, rectal discomfort or soreness, rectal bleeding, and urinary frequency or dysuria.

  Late: Change in bowel habits, rectal stenosis, mucosal telangiectasia or ulceration, and bleeding from rectal mucosa. Bladder telangiectasia or ulcer of bladder wall leads to hematuria.

Follow-Up

- Every 3−6 months for the first 2 years, every 6 months for 3−5 years, and every 12 months thereafter
- CEA is monitored every 3−6 months for the first 1−2 years, then every 6 months for 5 years
- Colonoscopy in 12 months. If negative, then repeat in 3 years followed by repeat in 5 years
- CT of the chest, abdomen, and pelvis every 12 months for 5 years
- Proctoscopy (with EUS or MRI with contrast) every 3−6 months in the first 2 years and every 6 months thereafter for 5 years

ANAL CANCER

The estimated incidence in the United States is 8580 with estimated 1160 deaths in 2018.
The anal canal is 3−4 cm in length. The superior margin of the anal canal is the upper border of the anal columns, the anorectal ring, and the inferior margin of the anal canal is the anal verge. Below the anal verge is the anal margin, extending to a 5−6 cm radius around the anal verge. The anus is divided into upper and lower parts by the Dentate Line, which is formed by the anal valves located at the inferior aspect of the anal columns. Above the dentate line, the lymphatic drainage in sequence is to the internal pudendal, then hypogastric, then obturator, and, finally, to the internal iliac

vessels. Below the dentate line, lymphatic drainage is in sequence to the anal verge, then perianal skin, then superficial inguinal nodes, then femoral nodes, and, finally, to the external iliac system.

Workup

Risk Factors
- Smoking, genital warts
- Anal intercourse
- Infection with HPV 16, 18, HSV 2 and HIV

Symptoms and Signs
- Alteration in bowel habits, sensation of mass in the anus and anal pain, discharge, and bleeding
- Enlarged lymph nodes and anal mass
- Anal or perianal ulcers

Investigations
- CBC, chemistry with liver and renal function
- HIV test is suggested if positive, then CD4 count is performed
- Digital rectal examination (DRE)
- Gynecologic exam for women, including cervical cancer screen
- Endoscopic exam with biopsy, and fine needle aspiration (FNA) for palpable inguinal lymph nodes, cystoscopic exam, and transanorectal ultrasound
- Chest X-ray or chest/abdomen CT with IV and oral contrast + pelvic CT or MRI, PET scan

TNM Staging (Anal Cancer)

TX	Primary tumor cannot be assessed
T0	No evidence of primary tumor
Tis	High-grade squamous intraepithelial lesion (previously termed carcinoma in situ, Bowen disease, anal intraepithelial neoplasia II–III, high-grade anal intraepithelial neoplasia)
T1	Tumor <2 cm in greatest dimension
T2	Tumor >2 cm but <5 cm in greatest dimension
T3	Tumor >5 cm in greatest dimension
T4	Tumor of any size invades adjacent organ(s), e.g., vagina, urethra, and bladder[a]

[a]*Direct invasion of the rectal wall, perirectal skin, subcutaneous tissue, or the sphincter muscle(s) is not classified as T4.*

NX	Regional lymph nodes cannot be assessed
N0	No regional lymph node metastasis
N1	Metastasis in inguinal, mesorectal, internal iliac, or external iliac nodes
N1a	Metastasis in inguinal, mesorectal, or internal iliac lymph nodes
N1b	Metastasis in external iliac lymph nodes
N1c	Metastasis in external iliac with any N1a nodes
M0	No distant metastasis
M1	Distant metastasis

Stage Grouping

Stage	T	N	M
0	Tis	N0	M0
I	T1	N0	M0
IIA	T2	N0	M0
IIB	T3	N0	M0
IIIA	T1,2	N1	M0
IIIB	T4	N0	M0
IIIC	T3,4	N1	M0
IV	Any T	Any N	M1

AJCC, American Joint Committee on Cancer; *TNM*, tumor, node, metastasis; *UICC*, Union for International Cancer Control.
Used with permission of the American Joint Committee on Cancer (AJCC), Chicago, Illinois. The original and primary source for this information is the AJCC Cancer Staging Manual, Eighth Edition (2017) published by Springer Science+Business Media, LLC, www.springer.com.

Treatment

- **Stage T1N0, well-differentiated, anal margin**—wide local excision and primary closure. Postoperative chemoRT is recommended for close or positive surgical margin.
- **Stage T1, poorly differentiated, T2-4, N+**—definitive concurrent chemoRT [22, 23, 24, 25].
- Concurrent chemotherapy is given with 5FU 1000 mg/m^2 CVI, MMC 10 mg/m^2 every 4 weeks ×2 cycles. Using MMC with capecitabine as concurrent chemotherapy is also an acceptable option.

- **HIV-positive patients with CD4 count <200 cells/µL**, treatment-related toxicity may be worse. Patients with a history of HIV-related complications may require dosage adjustment or treatment without mitomycin. Patients unable to tolerate chemotherapy because of HIV should receive RT alone.
- **Local recurrence after chemoRT**—treatment response should be clinically assessed 8−12 weeks after completion of chemoRT. Patients with persistent disease can be observed to rule out local progression. Large lesion may require several months to regress. Lesions that persist beyond 6 months should undergo biopsy for histologic confirmation. Patients with persistent or progressive disease are offered APR, and in patients with distant metastases, 5FU/CDDP or docetaxel containing regimen (DCF) chemotherapy is recommended.
- **Metastatic disease**—docetaxel containing regimen (DCF) has shown excellent front line therapy in metastatic patients. Patients who responds well to systemic chemotherapy can be considered for concurrent chemoRT to the primary site.

RT Technique

3D Technique

Patient is supine, anus marked, arms above chest, frog leg in a VacLock and CT simulated. For 3D conformal RT, the inguinal nodes and the pelvis, anus, and perineum should be included in the initial radiation field. **Borders:** superiorly to L5/S1 (to include the common iliac, upper presacral and rectosigmoid nodes); inferiorly flash with 3 cm margin on primary tumor, laterally AP field to ASIS, PA to 1.5−2 cm on pelvic brim. PA fields do not cover the inguinal LNs; therefore, anterior inguinal electron fields are needed to treat the inguinal nodes. The electron field borders are superiorly at the bottom of sacroiliac joint, inferiorly at the bottom of greater trochanter, medially matched with the exit PA field, and laterally at the ASIS. Electron field treatment should be at least 3 cm depth, or planning CT can be used for depth assessment. The electron field lateral border should be 1 cm more than the photon field. Note to use bolus on palpable groin lymph nodes. Treat up to 30.6 Gy, then decrease superior border to bottom of SI joint; if N0, treat to 36 Gy, then block inguinal fields and treat primary tumor to 50.4 Gy; if N+, treat involved lymph nodes to 50.4 Gy. If T2 with residual after 45 Gy, T3, T4, N+, then boost with 2 cm margin to both primary and lymph nodes to 54−59.4 Gy (Figs. 18.9 through 18.13).

IMRT Technique

Patient is CT simulated (with ≤3 mm slice thickness), supine, and immobilized with arms above chest, frog leg. Fuse PETCT with planning CT. In IMRT cases where the CTV does not involve the skin, but comes within 1 cm of the skin surface, bolus is not recommended. The distal point of macroscopic disease or anal verge is wired before imaging. A vaginal marker may be considered. All patients must be scanned with a comfortably full bladder (>250 ml). Use of IV contrast is strongly recommended to aid delineation of pelvic vessels. For 6 MV photons, use seven- to nine-field IMRT or two-arc VMAT. Daily IGRT is recommended (Figs. 18.14 and 18.15).

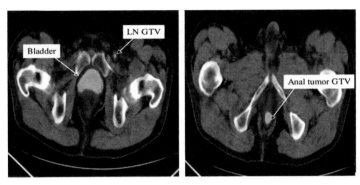

FIGURE 18.9   PETCT scan shows anal cancer and left inguinal positive LN.

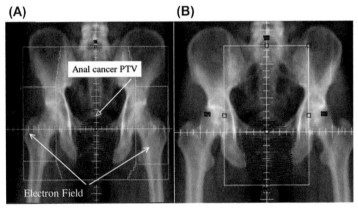

FIGURE 18.10   (A) Anal cancer patient DRR showing 3D-CRT AP field and (b) 3D PA field for the initial 30.6 Gy of prescription dose. The superior border is at L5/S1; inferiorly flash the perineum with 3 cm margin on primary tumor, laterally extend AP field to ASIS and PA field at the pelvic brim. The supplementary electron field from the AP is also shown in (A).

IMRT Dose Painting Plan per RTOG 0529

Volumes

GTVA = gross primary anal tumor volume
GTVN50 = nodal regions containing macroscopic disease <3 cm (50.4 Gy)
GTVN54 = nodal regions containing macroscopic disease >3 cm (54 Gy)
CTV = GTV + areas considered to contain potential microscopic disease
CTVA = GTVA +2.5 cm (except into bone or air)
CTV42/CTV45 = elective nodal regions (described below) + 1 cm
CTV50 = GTV50 + 1 cm
CTV54 = GTV54 + 1 cm

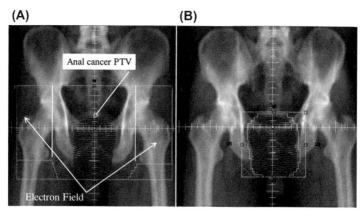

FIGURE 18.11 (A) Anal cancer patient DRR showing 3D-CRT reduced AP field after 30.6 Gy, with the superior border at the bottom of SI joint. (B) IMRT boost PA field is shown with 0.5 cm margin around the PTV.

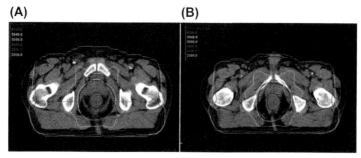

FIGURE 18.12 (A) Anal cancer patient showing isodose distribution LN coverage in superior axial, and (B) anal tumor coverage in inferior axial. Treatment plan performed by combining initial 3D-CRT and IMRT boost plan for the anal tumor PTV.

PTV = CTV + 0.5–1 cm

CTV expansion for 8 mm around the iliac vessels, respecting muscles and bony margins. Gross LN add 1 cm margin. Inguinal LNs may need greater margins. Organ movement for the bladder and/or uterus can also be in the order of 1 cm. It is recommended that the CTV extends ~1–2 cm into the bladder or uterus.

CTVA: internal iliac, presacral, perirectal LNs

In the upper pelvis, coverage of the presacral region mandates that the nodal CTV include at least 1 cm anterior to the sacrum up to the level of the sacral promontory.

In the midpelvis, the nodal target volume should be somewhat round in the posterior pelvis, with extensions anteriorly along each pelvic sidewall to cover the iliac nodal regions.

(A)   **(B)**

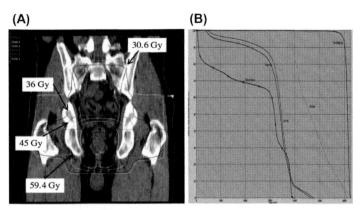

FIGURE 18.13   (A) Anal cancer treatment plan showing isodose distribution in the coronal plane. The doses of 30.6, 36, 45, and 59.4 Gy are prescribed for the treatment fields and the planning target volume. (B) DVH showing 95% coverage of the PTV and all organs at risk within dose constraints.

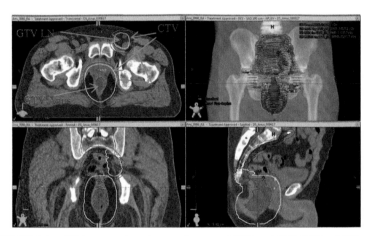

FIGURE 18.14   CT images showing anal cancer GTV and LN GTVs, CTV and PTV.

In the lower pelvis, to adequately cover the perirectal nodal region, the nodal CTV should extend posteriorly and laterally to the bones of the pelvic sidewall, the levators at the floor of the pelvis, and the posterior–lateral pelvic fascia cephalad to the levators.

CTVB: external iliac LNs

Extends from external iliac LNs to inguinal LNs at the level of the inferior level of the internal obturator vessels at the upper edge of the superior pubic rami.

CTVC: inguinal LNs

The caudate extent of the inguinal region should be 2 cm caudate to the saphenous/femoral junction.

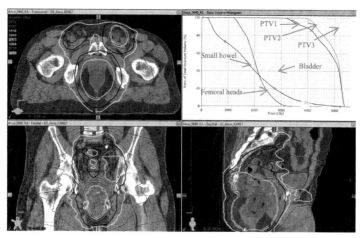

FIGURE 18.15 Anal cancer patient CT images of two-arc VMAT plan isodose lines conforming to targets and DVH meeting all constraints. The prescription dose is PTV1 to 39.6 Gy, PTV2 to 45 Gy, and PTV3 to 50.4 Gy to the gross disease. The treatments were to be delivered sequentially.

Doses for Dose Painting plan per RTOG

T2N0 disease:

   PTVA = 50.4 Gy in 28 fractions at 1.8 Gy per fraction
   PTVN = 42 Gy in 28 fractions at 1.5 Gy per fraction

T3-T4N0 disease:

   PTVA = 54 Gy in 30 fractions at 1.8 Gy per fraction
   PTVN = 45 Gy in 30 fractions at 1.5 Gy per fraction

For N+ disease:

   PTVA = 54 Gy in 30 fractions at 1.8 Gy per fraction
   PTVN = 45 Gy in 30 fractions at 1.5 Gy per fraction (elective nodal)
   PTV50 = 50.4 Gy in 30 fractions at 1.68 Gy per fraction (all nodal regions containing involved nodes < 3 cm in greatest dimension)
   PTV54 = 54 Gy in 30 fractions at 1.8 Gy per fraction (all nodal regions containing involved nodes > 3 cm in greatest dimension)
   T2 neg LN 42 Gy, gross disease 50.4
   T3−4 neg LN 45 Gy, <3 cm LN 50.4 Gy, >3 cm LN 54 Gy, gross disease 54 Gy

IMRT Sequential Plan

Volumes

GTV − primary tumor + enlarged LNs as seen on CT or PET scan
GTVM = GTV +2.5 cm
T2 disease
CTV1 = GTVM + CTVA + CTVB + CTVC
CTV2 = GTVM
T3−4 disease
CTV1 = GTVM + CTVA + CTVB + CTVC
CTV2 = GTVM (LN < 3 cm)
CTV3 = GTVM (LN > 3 cm)
PTV = CTV + 0.5−1 cm margin, exclude 0.5 cm near the skin

Doses for Sequential Plan

T2 disease
PTV1 = 180 cGy/fx to 39.6 Gy
PTV2 = 180 cGy/fx to 50.4 Gy

T3-4 disease
PTV1 = 180 cGy/fx to 43.2 Gy
PTV2 = 180 cGy/fx to 50.4 Gy (LN < 3 cm)
PTV3 = 180 cGy/fx to 54 Gy (LN > 3 cm)

Constraints

Small bowel: V45 < 20 cc, V35 < 150 cc, V30 < 200 cc
Large bowel: V45 < 20 cc, V35 < 150 cc, V30 < 200 cc
Femoral heads: V44 ≤ 5%, V40 ≤ 35%, V30 ≤ 50%
Bladder: V50 ≤ 5%; V40 ≤ 35%, V35 ≤ 50%
Genitalia: V40 ≤ 5%, V30 ≤ 35%, V20 ≤ 50%
Bone marrow: V50 ≤ 5%, V40 ≤ 35%, V30 ≤ 50%.

Outcome

- Local control is 85% in all.
- Colostomy-free survival is 70%.
- Five-year overall survivals for stages I, II, IIIA, IIIB, and IV are 77%, 67%, 58%, 51%, and 15%, respectively.

Complications

- Fatigue and weight loss, nausea and anorexia, skin irritations, including redness, soreness, and ulceration, change in bowel habits, including diarrhea
- Bowel/rectal damage causing narrowing, ulceration, and bleeding requiring surgical intervention and anal incontinence
- Bladder damage and increased urinary frequency

Follow-Up

- Digital rectal examination (DRE) and inguinal examination every 3—6 months for 5 years
- Anoscopy every 6—12 months for 3 years
- Chest/abdomen/pelvic CT with contrast imaging annually for 3 years in patients with inguinal lymph node positivity or T3—4 tumor

ANNOTATED BIBLIOGRAPHY

ESOPHAGEAL CANCER

Ref 1. Shapiro et al. (2015). Neoadjuvant chemoradiotherapy plus surgery versus surgery alone for oesophageal or junctional cancer (CROSS): long-term results of a randomised controlled trial. *Lancet Oncol;16(9):1090.* CROSS Trial.

In this study, 368 patients with clinically resectable cancer of the esophagus or esophagogastric junction (clinical stage T1N1M0 or T2-3N0-1M0, according to the TNM cancer staging system, sixth edition) were randomly assigned to neoadjuvant chemoRT [intravenous carboplatin (AUC 2 mg/mL per min) and intravenous paclitaxel (50 mg/mL of body surface area) for 23 days] with concurrent radiotherapy (41.4 Gy, given in 23 fractions of 1.8 Gy on 5 days per week) followed by surgery, or surgery alone. Median follow-up data after of 32 months were as given below:

	Median Survival (m)	Median Survival (m)	
	SCCa	*Adenocarcinoma*	*5-Year OS (%)*
Surgery only	*21.1*	*27.1*	*34*
ChemoRT + surg	*81.6*	*43.2*	*47*
P *value*	*0.008*	*0.0038*	*0.003*

The trial confirms the OS benefit for neoadjuvant chemoRT when added to surgery in patients with resectable esophageal EGJ cancer, for both SCCa and adenocarcinoma.

Ref 2. Klevebro F et al. (2016). A randomized clinical trial of neoadjuvant chemotherapy versus neoadjuvant chemoradiotherapy for cancer of oesophagus or gastro-oesophageal junction. *Ann Oncol;27(4):660—7.*

In this trial, 181 patients with carcinoma of esophageal or gastroesophageal junction who were candidates for curative intended treatment were randomized to neoadjuvant chemo or neoadjuvant chemoRT, followed by surgery. Three cycles of platin/50FU were administered in both arms, whereas 40 Gy of concomitant RT were added in the neoadjuvant CRT arm. The data showed the following:

	pCR (%)	LN Mets (%)	R0 resection (%)	OS (%)
chemo + surg	9	62	74	No
chemoRT + surg	28	35	87	Difference
P value	0.002	0.001	0.04	No

The study showed that addition of RT to neoadjuvant chemotherapy results in higher pathologic CR, lower frequency of LN metastases, and higher R0 resection rate, without affecting survival.

Ref 3. Stahl M et al. (2017). Preoperative chemotherapy versus chemoradiotherapy in locally advanced adenocarcinoma of the oesophageal junction (POET): long-term results of a controlled randomized trial. *Eur J Cancer*;81:183—90. POET Trial.

In this trial, 119 patients with locally advanced adenocarcinoma of GE junction were randomized to chemotherapy (group A) or induction chemotherapy and chemoRT (group B) followed by surgery. Induction chemotherapy was given cisplatin, fluorouracil, leucovorin, and concurrent chemo was given cisplatin, etoposide with RT 30 Gy. The results were as follows:

pCR (%)	5-Year	Local PFS (pts)	5-Year OS (%)
Chemo + surg	15.6	12 pts (10%)	24.4
ChemoRT + surg	2	20 pts (15%)	39.5
P value	0.03	0.055	

Long-term follow-up data suggest a benefit in local PFS when RT was added to preoperative chemotherapy in patients with advanced adenocarcinoma of esophageal junction.

Ref 3a. Xu et al. (2018). Phase III Randomize study of Preoperative versus Postoperative Chemoradiaotherapy in Resectable Locally Advanced Esophageal Squamous cell Carcinoma. *Int J Rad Onc Bio Phys* Vol 102, Num 35, Nov 1, 2018, Abstract 58.

In this trial, 149 patients with clinically resectable, locally advanced (cT1-2N1M0 or T3-4N0-1M0) SCCa of the esophagus were randomly assigned to receive either preoperative CRT (weekly administration of carboplatin/paclitaxel for 6 weeks and concurrent radiation therapy 50.4 Gy) followed by surgery or surgery followed by concurrent postoperative CRT (initially the same regimens as preoperative CRT). However, concurrent postoperative CRT was modified to sequential chemoradiation (carboplatin/paclitaxel per 3 weeks for two cycles followed by radiation therapy 50.4 Gy). After a median follow-up of 42 months, the data show the following:

	DFS (%)	OS (%)	Gr 3-4 toxicity (%)
Preop chemoRT	56.2	63.8	Not
Postop chemoRT	34.5	49	Different
P value	0.008	0.044	

This study concluded that preoperative CRT, as compared with postoperative CRT, prolongs DFS and OS with acceptable toxicities in resectable locally advanced esophageal SCCa.

GASTRIC CANCER

Ref 4. Cunningham et al. (2006). Perioperative chemotherapy versus surgery alone for resectable gastroesophageal cancer. *N Engl J Med*;355(1):11–20. MAGIC trial.

In this study, 503 patients with resectable adenocarcinoma of the stomach, esophagogastric junction, or lower esophagus were randomized to either perioperative chemotherapy and surgery or surgery alone. Chemotherapy consisted of three preoperative and three postoperative cycles of intravenous epirubicin (50 mg/m^2 of body surface area) and cisplatin (60 mg/m^2) on day 1, and a continuous intravenous infusion of fluorouracil (200 mg/m^2) for 21 days. The results were as given below:

	5-Year Overall Survival (%)
Surg + chemo	23
Pre-op chemo + surg + chemo	36
P-value	0.009

This study showed that in patients with operable gastric or lower esophageal adenocarcinomas, a perioperative regimen of ECF significantly improved progression-free and overall survival.

Ref 5. Ychou et al. (2011). Perioperative chemotherapy compared with surgery alone for resectable gastroesophageal adenocarcinoma: an FNCLCC and FFCD multicenter phase III trial. *J Clin Oncol*;29(13):1715. French FNCLCC/FFCD trial.

In this study, 224 patients with potentially resectable stage II or greater adenocarcinoma of the stomach, EGJ, or distal esophagus were randomly assigned to two to three cycles of preoperative chemotherapy (infusional FU 800 mg/m^2 daily for 5 days plus cisplatin 100 mg/m^2 on *day 1 or 2, every 4 weeks) or to surgery alone. Patients in the chemotherapy arm were to receive three to four cycles of postoperative chemotherapy as well. Median 5.7-year follow-up data are given below:*

Tx Group	5-Year DFS (%)	5-Year OS (%)
Surgery	*19*	*24*
Chemo + surgery + chemo	*34*	*38*
P-value	*0.003*	*0.02*

This trial showed that in patients with resectable adenocarcinoma of the lower esophagus, GEJ, or stomach, perioperative chemotherapy using FU/CDDP significantly increased the curative resection rate, DFS, and OS.

Ref 6. Smalley et al. (2012). Updated analysis of SWOG-directed intergroup study 0116: a phase III trial of adjuvant radio-chemotherapy versus observation after curative gastric cancer resection. *J Clin Oncol*;30(19):2327. Int 0016 Trial.

In this study, 559 patients with primaries $\geq$ T3 and/or node-positive gastric cancer were randomly assigned to observation versus chemoRT after R0 resection. Chemotherapy was given ×1 cycle 5FU/leucovorin (425 mg/m^2 and 20 mg/m^2 days 1–5), then 5FU/leucovorin (400 mg/m^2 and 20 mg/m^2 days 1–4 of weeks 1 and 5) concurrent with RT 180 cGy to 45 Gy; 1 month after completion of RT, patient received two more cycles of 5FU 425 mg/m^2 and leucovorin 20 mg/m^2 at monthly interval. Results at more than 10 years of median follow-up were as follows:

Tx Group	5-Year Overall Survival (%)	Disease-Free Survival (%)	Median Survival (Months)
Surgery	*28*	*19*	*27*
Surgery + chemoRT	*43*	*27*	*36*
P-value	*0.0046*	*<0.001*	

Post-op chemoRT may now be considered a standard of care for high-risk R0 resected locally advanced adenocarcinoma of the stomach and GE junctions.

Ref 7. Park et al. (2015). Phase III trial to compare adjuvant chemotherapy with capecitabine and cisplatin versus concurrent chemoradiotherapy in gastric cancer: final report of the adjuvant chemoradiotherapy in stomach tumors trial, including survival and subset analyses. *J Clin Oncol*;33(28):3130 ARTIST Trial.

In this study, 458 patients with completely resected gastric cancer and a D2 lymph node dissection were randomly assigned to six courses of postoperative XP or to two courses of postoperative XP followed by chemoRT [45 Gy RT with concurrent daily capecitabine (825 mg/m^2

twice daily)] and two additional courses of XP. Median follow-up results after 84 months were as follows:

Tx Group	3-year Disease-Free Survival (%) in LN(+) Patients	3-Year Disease-Free Survival (All Patients)	5-Year Overall Survival (All Patients)
Surgery + chemotherapy	72	74	73
Surgery + chemoRT	77.5	78	75
P-value	0.0365	0.862	0.0484

The results showed that chemoRT significantly improved DFS in patients with node-positive disease and with intestinal-type gastric cancer.

Ref 8. Verheij M et al. (2016). A multicenter randomized phase III trial of neo-adjuvant chemotherapy followed by surgery and chemotherapy or by surgery and chemoradiotherapy in resectable gastric cancer: first results from the CRITICS study. *J Clinical Oncol*;34.15_suppl.4000. CRITICS Trial.

In this trial, 788 patients with stage Ib-Iva resectable gastric cancer were randomized after diagnosis to neoadjuvant CT in both arms and consisted of three courses of ECC/EOC. After gastric cancer resection, patients received another three courses of ECC/EOC or CRT (45 Gy combined with weekly CDDP and daily capecitabine). Median follow-up data after 50 months were as given below:

	5 Year Survival (%)	Toxicity (%)	
		Hemato gr > 3	gastric > 3
CT arm	41.3	44	37
CRT arm	40.9	34	42
P value	0.99	0.01	0.14

The trial revealed no significant difference in OS between postoperative chemotherapy and chemoRT.

PANCREATIC CANCER

Resectable Pancreatic Cancer

Ref 9. Regine et al. (2011). Fluorouracil-based chemoradiation with either gemcitabine or fluorouracil chemotherapy after resection of pancreatic adenocarcinoma: 5-year analysis of the U.S Intergroup/RTOG 9704 phase III trial. *Ann Surg Oncol*;18(5):1319–26. RTOG 9704 Trial.

In this study, 451 patients with locally advanced pancreatic adenocarcinoma after gross total resection were randomized to chemotherapy with either fluorouracil (continuous infusion of 250 mg/m² per day) or gemcitabine (30-minute infusion of 1000 mg/m² once per week) for 3 weeks before chemoRT therapy and for 12 weeks after chemoRT. ChemoRT with a continuous infusion of fluorouracil (250 mg/m² per day) was the same for all patients (50.4 Gy). The results for the patients with pancreatic head tumor were as follows:

	5-Year Median Survival (Months)	Overall Survival (%)
Surg + 5FU + ChemoRT + 5FU	No	18
Surg + Gem + ChemoRT + Gem	Difference	22
P-value		0.08

This study showed that the addition of gemcitabine to pre- and postfluorouracil-based chemoRT did not result in a significant survival benefit for patients with resected pancreatic cancer.

Ref 10. Oettle et al. (2013). Adjuvant chemotherapy with gemcitabine and long-term outcomes among patients with resected pancreatic cancer: the CONKO-001 randomized trial. *JAMA*;310(14):1473. CONKO 001 Trial.

In this study, 354 patients with grossly complete (R0 or R1) surgical resection and a preoperative carbohydrate antigen 19−9 (CA 19−9) level <2.5 times the upper limit of normal were randomly assigned to gemcitabine (1000 mg/m², days 1, 8, and 15 every 4 weeks for 6 months) or no treatment after surgery. Patients were stratified by resection margins (which were positive in approximately 17% of patients) and tumor (T) and nodal (N) status; the primary endpoint was disease-free survival (DFS). After 136 months of median follow-up period, the results showed the following:

Tx Group	Median Disease-Free Survival (m)	5-Year Overall Survival (%)	10-Year Overall Survival (%)
Surg + gemcitabine	13.4.	20.7	12.2
Surgery control group	6.7	10.4	7.7
P-value	<0.001		

Among patients with macroscopic complete removal of pancreatic cancer, the use of adjuvant gemcitabine for 6 months compared with observation alone resulted in increased overall survival as well as disease-free survival. These findings provide strong support for the use of gemcitabine in this setting.

Ref 11. Van Tienhoven et al (2018). Preoperative chemoradiotherapy versus immediate surgery for resectable and borderline resectable pancreatic cancer (PREOPANC-1): A randomized, controlled, multicenter phase III trial. *Journal of Clinical Oncology* 36, no. 18_suppl.

In this study 246 patients with (borderline) resectable pancreatic cancer, were randomized between immediate surgery (arm A) and preoperative chemoradiotherapy (arm B), both followed by adjuvant chemotherapy. The preoperative chemoradiotherapy consisted of 15 times of 2.4 Gray (Gy) combined with gemcitabine, 1,000 mg/m2 on days 1, 8 and 15, preceded and followed by a cycle of gemcitabine. The data showed that

	R0 resection (%)	LRFI (%)	DFS (m)	OS (m)
Surgery	31	30	7.9	13.5
chemoRT+surgery	65	50	9.9	17.1
p value	0.0001	0.002	0.023	0.047

This study preliminary data show that preoperative chemoradiotherapy significantly improves outcome in (borderline) resectable pancreatic cancer compared to immediate surgery.

Unresectable Pancreatic Cancer

Ref 12. Loehrer et al. (2011). Gemcitabine alone versus gemcitabine plus radiotherapy in patients with locally advanced pancreatic cancer: an Eastern Cooperative Oncology Group trial. *J Clin Oncol*;29(31):4105—12. ECOG 4201 Trial.

In this study, patients with localized unresectable adenocarcinoma of the pancreas were randomly assigned to receive gemcitabine alone (at 1,000 mg/m^2/wk for weeks 1—6, followed by 1 week rest, then for 3 of 4 weeks) or gemcitabine (600 mg/m(^{2})/wk for weeks 1—5, then 4 weeks later 1000 mg/m^2 for 3 of 4 weeks) plus radiotherapy (starting on day 1, 1.8 Gy/fx for total of 50.4 Gy). The results were as follows:

Tx Group	Overall Survival (m)	Toxicity (Gr 4-5) (%)
Chemotherapy alone (gemcitabine)	9.2	9
ChemoRT (gemcitabine + RT)	11.1	41
P-value	0.017	

This trial demonstrates improved overall survival with chemoRT. Additionally, no statistical differences were seen in quality of life measurements at 6, 15—16, and 36 weeks.

Ref 13. Hammel P et al. (2016). Effect of chemoradiotherapy vs chemotherapy on survival in patients with locally advanced pancreatic cancer controlled after 4 months of gemcitabine with or without Erlotinib: The LAP07 randomized clinical trial. *JAMA*;315(17):1844–53. LAP07 Trial.

In this trial, 223 patients with locally advanced pancreatic cancer in the first randomization received 1000 mg/m² weekly of gemcitabine alone versus 219 patients who received 1000 gemcitabine mg/m² plus 100 mg/d of erlotinib. In the second randomization involving patients with progression-free disease after 4 months, 136 patients received 2 months of the same chemotherapy and 133 underwent chemoRT (54 Gy plus capecitabine). At a median follow-up of 36.7 months, the results were as follows:

	Local Progression (%)	OS (m)
Chemo	46	16.5
Chemo + RT	32 ss	15.2 ns
Gemcitabine		13.6
Gemcitabine + erlotinib		11.9 ns

There was no significant difference in OS with chemoRT compared with chemo alone, and there was no significant difference in OS with gemcitabine compared with gemcitabine plus erlotinib used as maintenance therapy.

Ref 14. Hurt et al. (2017). *Long-term results and recurrence patterns from SCALOP: a phase II randomized trial of gemcitabine or capecitabine-based chemoradiation for locally advanced pancreatic cancer. Br J Cancer;116(10):1264–70. SCALOP Trial.*

In this trial, 114 patients with locally advanced pancreatic cancer (with a tumor diameter of <7 cm) were given 12 weeks of gemcitabine (1000 mg/m² on days 1, 8, and 15 of a 28-day cycle) and capecitabine (830 mg/m² twice daily on days 1–21 of a 28-day cycle); patients with stable or responding disease, tumor diameter of <6 cm and WHO PS 0–1 were randomly assigned to receive a further cycle of gemcitabine and capecitabine chemotherapy followed by either gemcitabine (300 mg/m² once per week) or capecitabine (830 mg/m² twice daily, Monday through Friday), both in combination with RT (50.4 Gy in 28 fractions). Results from a median follow up of 10.9 months were as below:

	Median PFS (m)	Median OS (m)	12 Months OS (%)
Gemcitabine CRT	10.4	14.6	64.2
Capecitabine CRT	12	17.6	79.2
P value	0.12	0.18	ns

The results suggest that a capecitabine-based regimen might be preferable to a gemcitabine regimen in the context of consolidation chemotherapy after a course of induction chemotherapy for locally advanced pancreatic cancer.

COLON CANCER

Ref 15. André et al. (2015). Adjuvant fluorouracil, leucovorin, and oxaliplatin in stage II to III colon cancer: updated 10-year survival and outcomes according to BRAF mutation and mismatch repair status of the MOSAIC study. *J Clin Oncol*;33(35):4176–87. MOSAIC Trial.

In this study, 2246 patients with stage II–III colon cancer after curative resection were randomized to adjuvant fluorouracil/leucovorin versus fluorouracil/leucovorin plus oxaliplatin for 6 months. At a median follow-up of 9. 5 years, the results were as follows:

		Overall Survival (%)	
		All	
	Disease-Free Survival (%)	Patients	Stage III
Fluorouracil/leucovorin	67.4	67.11	59.0
Fluorouracil/leucovorin + oxaliplatin	73.3	71.7	67.1
P-value	0.003	0.043	0.016

This study showed that adding oxaliplatin to a regimen of fluorouracil/leucovorin significantly improved disease-free survival for all patients and overall survival for stage III colon cancer patients.

RECTAL CANCER

Pre-op RT

Ref 16. van Gjin et al. (2011). Preoperative radiotherapy combined with total mesorectal excision for resectable rectal cancer: 12-year follow-up of the multicentre, randomised controlled TME trial. *Lancet Oncol*;12(6):575–88. Dutch Trial.

In this study, 1861 patients with mostly resectable stage I, II, or III were randomized to total mesorectal excision (TME) versus pre-op RT + TME. RT was given 5 Gy/fraction to a total dose of 25 Gy. Tumors had to be within 15 cm of anal verge. Median follow-up results at 12 years were as follows:

	Local Recurrence (%)	Distant Metastases (%)	Overall Survival (%)
TME	11.1	28.1	48.8
Pre op RT + TME	5.1	24.9	47.6
P-value	<0.001	NS	NS

This study showed that preoperative short-term RT reduced 10-year local recurrence by more than 50% relative to surgery alone without an overall survival benefit. For patients with TNM stage III cancer with a negative circumferential resection margin, 10-year survival was 50% in the preoperative RT group versus 40% in the surgery-alone group (P = 0.032).

Ref 17. Sauer et al. (2012). Preoperative versus postoperative chemoradiotherapy for locally advanced rectal cancer: results of the German CAO/ARO/AIO-94 randomized phase III trial after a median follow-up of 11 years. *J Clin Oncol*;30(16):1926−33. German Trial.

In this study, 823 patients with stage II and III rectal cancer were randomly assigned to preoperative chemoRT with fluorouracil (FU), total mesorectal excision surgery, and adjuvant FU chemotherapy, or the same schedule of chemoRT used postoperatively. The preoperative treatment consisted of 5040 cGy delivered in fractions of 180 cGy per day, 5 days per week, and fluorouracil, given in a 120-h continuous intravenous infusion at a dose of 1000 mg/m^2 of body surface area per day during the first and fifth weeks of radiotherapy. Surgery was performed 4−6 weeks after the completion of chemoRT. One month after surgery, four 5-day cycles of fluorouracil (500 mg/m^2/day) were given. ChemoRT was identical in the postoperative treatment group, except for the delivery of a boost of 540 cGy. The results at 10 years were as follows:

Tx Group	10-year Overall Survival (%)	10-year Local Relapse (%)	10-year Distant Metastases
Pre-op ChemoRT	59.6	7.1	29.8
Post-op ChemoRT	59.9	10.1	29.6
P-value	0.85	0.048	0.9

This study showed that preoperative chemoRT, as compared with postoperative chemoRT, improved local control; however, there was no effect on overall survival.

Ref 18. Allegra CJ et al. (2015). Neoadjuvant 5-FU or capecitabine plus radiation with or without oxaliplatin in rectal cancer patients: a phase III randomize clinical trial. *J Natl Cancer Inst*;107(11):djv248. R04 Trial.

In this trial, 1608 patients with stage II, III rectal cancer receiving preoperative radiation were randomly assigned to one of four chemotherapy regimens in a 2 × 2 design: CVI 5FU or oral capecitabine with or without oxaliplatin. CVI 5FU dose is 225 mg/m^2/d, capecitabine dose is 825 mg/m^2/d, oxaliplatin dose is 50 mg/m^2/qwk, and RT dose is 50.4 Gy. The data were as given below:

	5-Year DFS (%)	5-Year OS (%)	Toxicity diarrhea (%)
5FU	66.4	79.9	
Capecitabine	67.7	80.8	

	5-Year DFS (%)	5-Year OS (%)	Toxicity diarrhea (%)
No oxaliplatin	64.2	79	7
Oxaliplatin	69.2	81.3	16
P value	—	—	<0.0001

This study showed that CVI 5FU produced outcomes for DFS and OS similar to those obtained with oral capecitabine combined with RT. Oxaliplatin did not improve DFS or OS.

Ref 19. Deng et al. (2016). Modified FOLFOX6 with or without radiation versus fluorouracil and Leucovorin with Radiation in neoadjuvant treatment of locally advanced rectal cancer: initial results of the Chinese FOWARC multicenter, open-label, randomized three-arm phase III trial. *J Clin Oncol*;34(27):3300—7. Chinese Trial.

In this phase III trial, 495 patients with stage II/III rectal cancer were randomly assigned to receive neoadjuvant therapy with fluorouracil plus RT (fluorouracil—RT group: five 2-week cycles of infusional fluorouracil (leucovorin 400 mg/m², fluorouracil 400 mg/m², and fluorouracil 2.4 g/m² over 48 h) plus RT (46—50.4 Gy delivered in 23—25 fractions during cycles 2 through 4) followed by surgery and seven cycles of infusional fluorouracil), mFOLFOX6 plus RT (mFOLFOX6-RT group: the same treatment plus intravenous oxaliplatin 85 mg/m² on day 1 of each cycle), or mFOLFOX6 without RT (mFOLFOX6 group: four to six cycles of mFOLFOX6 followed by surgery and six to eight cycles of mFOLFOX6) followed by TME resection and postoperative adjuvant chemotherapy. The results were as given below:

Tx Group	pCR (%)	Downstaging (%)
FU + RT	14	37.1
FOLFOX + RT	27.5	56.4
FOLFOX	6.6	35.5

This study showed that FOLFOX + RT resulted in higher pCR and downstaging than FU + RT. Neoadjuvant chemotherapy with FOLFOX alone had inferior results and a lower pCR rate than chemoRT; however, results were similar regarding downstaging rates with FU + RT, with less toxicity, and post-op complications.

Ref 20. Erlandsson et al. (2017). Optimal fractionation of preoperative radiotherapy and timing to surgery for rectal cancer (Stockholm III): a multicentre, randomised, non-blinded, phase 3, non-inferiority trial. *Lancet Oncol*;18(3):336—46. Stockholm Trial.

In this study, 840 patients with all stages of resectable rectal cancer were randomly assigned with permuted blocks, stratified to receive either 5 × 5 Gy radiation dose with surgery within 1 week (short-course radiotherapy) or after 4—8 weeks (short-course radiotherapy with delay) or 25 × 2 Gy radiation dose with surgery after 4—8 weeks (long-course radiotherapy with delay). Results were as follows:

Tx Group	Post-op Complication (%)	Surgical Complication (%)
Short-course RT	50	31
Short-course RT with delay	38	26
Long-course RT with delay	39	23
P-value	0.075	0.038

This study showed that RT with delayed surgery is also a useful alternative offering similar oncological outcomes and lower postoperative complications.

Ref 21. Azria D et al. (2017). Late toxicities and clinical outcome at 5 years of the ACCORD 12/0405-PRODIGE 02 trial comparing two neoadjuvant chemoradiotherapy regimens for intermediate-risk rectal cancer. *Ann Oncol*;28(10):2436—42. ACCORD Trial.

In this trial, 598 patients with rectal adenocarcinoma T3-T4 NxM0 (or T2Nx distal anterior rectum) were randomized to RT45 + capecitabine and RT50 + capecitabine and oxaliplatin. Median follow-up results of 60.2 months were as follows:

	Local	DFS Control	OS
Cap45	8.8	60.4	76.4
Capox50	7.8	64.7	81.9
P value	0.78	0.25	0.06

The study showed that CAPOX50 regimen did not improve local control, DFS, or OS in ACCORD12 trial.

ANAL CANCER

Ref 22. Northover et al. (2010). Chemoradiation for the treatment of epidermoid anal cancer: 13-year follow-up of the first randomised UKCCCR Anal Cancer Trial (ACT I). *Br J Cancer*;102(7):1123. ACT I Trial.

In this study, 577 patients with T1—4 epidermoid anal cancer were randomized to receive RT alone (45 Gy) or combined modality therapy using 5-fluorouracil (1,000 mg/m² for 4 days or 750 mg/m² for 5 days) by continuous infusion during the first and the final weeks of RT and mitomycin (12 mg/m²) on day 1 of the first course. All patients were scheduled to receive 45 Gy by external beam irradiation. Patients who responded to treatment were recommended to have boost RT, with either an iridium implant or external beam irradiation (15 Gy external beam or 25 Gy brachytherapy boost). Twelve-year posttreatment results were as follows:

Tx Groups	Event (Number of Patient)		Anal Cancer-Related
	LRR	*DM*	*Death*
RT alone	155	21	125
RT + chemo	94	29	93

The clear benefit of chemoradiation outweighs an early excess risk of nonanal cancer deaths and can still be seen 12 years after treatment.

Ref 23. Gunderson et al. (2012). Long-term update of US GI intergroup RTOG 98-11 phase III trial for anal carcinoma: survival, relapse, and colostomy failure with concurrent chemoradiation involving fluorouracil/mitomycin versus fluorouracil/cisplatin; 30(35):4344−51. RTOG 9811 Trial.

In this study, 649 patients with stage T2−4, any N, SCCa of the anus were randomized between 5FU (1,000 mg/m^2/day by continuous infusion on days 1−4, 29−32)/mitomycin (10 mg/m^2 IV bolus on days 1 and 29)+ RT versus induction 5FU (1,000 mg/m^2/day by continuous infusion on days 1−4, 29−32, 57−60 and 85−88)/CDDP (75 mg/m^2 IV over 60 min on days 1, 29, 57, 88). RT dose was given 180 cGy/fx to 45−59 Gy to both arms; RT was started on day 57 of chemotherapy. The results of long-term follow-up periods were as given below:

Tx Groups	5 Year Rates			
	DFS (%)	*OS (%)*	*Local Relapse (%)*	*Distant Metastasis (%)*
RT + MMC/5FU	67.8	78.3	20	13.1
CDDP/5FU-RT/CDDP/5FU	57.8	70.7	26.4	18.1
P-value	0.006	0.026	0.087	0.12

This study revealed that concurrent RT with FU/MMC has a statistically significant, clinically meaningful impact on DFS and OS versus induction plus concurrent FU/CDDP. Therefore, concurrent RT + FU/MMC remains the preferred standard of care.

Ref 24. Peiffert D et al. (2012). Induction chemotherapy and dose intensification of the radiation boost in locally advanced anal canal carcinoma: final analysis of the randomized UNICANCER ACCORD 03 trial. *J Clin Oncol*;30(16):1941−48. ACCORD 03 Trial.

In this trial, 307 patients with locally advanced anal canal carcinoma (tumors >4 cm or <4 cm and N1-3M0) were randomly assigned to one of four treatment arms. Group A: two ICT (induction) cycles (fluorouracil 800 g/m²/d IV infusion, days 1 through 4 and 29 to 32; and CDDP 80 mg/m² IV on days 1 and 29, RTC (concomitant chemoRT) (45 Gy in 25 fractions over 5 weeks, fluorouracil and CDDP during weeks 1 and 5), and standard dose boost (SD 15 Gy). Group B: two ICT cycles, RCT, and high-dose boost (HD 20—25 Gy); group C: RCT and SD boost (reference arm) and group D: RTC and HD boost. Median follow-up results of 50 months were as follows:

	5-Year CFS (%)
Group A ICT, RCT, 45 + 15	69.6
Group B ICT, RTC, 45 + 20—25	82.4
Group C RCT, 45 + 15	77.1
Group D RCT, 45 + 20—25	72.7
P value	0.37

This study showed that there is no advantage for either ICT or HD radiation boost for CFS for locally advanced anal canal cancer.

Ref 25. James RD et al. (2013). Mitomycin or cisplatin chemoradiation with or without maintenance chemotherapy for treatment of squamous-cell carcinoma of the anus (ACT II): a randomized, phase 3, open-label, 2 × 2 factorial trial. *Lancet Oncol*;14(6):516—24. ACT II Trial.

In this trial, 940 patients with SCCa of the anus without metastatic disease were randomly assigned to one of four groups, to receive mitomycin (12 mg/m² on day 1), cisplatin (60 mg/m² on days 1 and 29), fluorouracil (1,000 mg/m² per day on days 1—4 and 29—32), or radiotherapy (50.5 Gy in 28 daily fractions) with or without two courses of maintenance chemotherapy (fluorouracil and cisplatin at weeks 11 and 14). Median follow-up of 5.1 years results were as given below:

	pCR (%)	3-year PFS (%)	OS (%)
RT + PF	89.6	74	no
RT + MMC/F	90.5	73	diff
P value	0.64	0.70	ns

The results of this trial show that fluorouracil and mitomycin with 50.4 Gy RT should remain standard practice.

Ref 26. Kachnic LA et al. (2017). NRG Oncology/RTOG 0529: Long-term outcomes of dose-painted intensity modulated radiation therapy, 5-fluorouracil, and mitomycin-c in anal canal cancer. *Int J Radio Biol*;99(2 supplement):S64—5. RTOG 0529 Trial.

In this trial, 63 patients with T2-4N0-3M0 anal cancer received 5FU/MMC days 1 and 29 of DP-IMRT, prescribed per stage-T2N0: 42 Gy elective nodal and 50.4 Gy anal canal tumor planning target volumes in 28 fractions, T3-4N0-3: 45 Gy elective nodal, 50.4 Gy < 3 cm or 54 Gy > 3 cm metastatic nodal and 54 Gy anal canal tumor PTVs in 30 fractions. Median follow-up results of 7.9 years were as follows:

	LRF (%)	DFS (%)	CFS (%)	OS (%)	Toxicity (%)				
					gr1	gr2	gr3	gr4	gr5
RTOG 9811	22	57	63	69					
RTOG 0529	16	60	66	68	18	55	16	0	2

The study showed that chemoRT using DP-IMRT for anal cancer provided reduced acute mortality with comparable long-term efficacy and late effects as compared with nonconformal radiation therapy.

Genitourinary Cancers

RENAL CELL CANCER

The estimated incidence in the United States is 65,340 with an estimated 14,970 deaths in 2018.

The right and left kidneys are located between the eleventh ribs and the third lumbar vertebrae in the retroperitoneal fatty tissue. The left kidney resides slightly higher than the right kidney in the posterior abdominal wall. The kidneys and renal pelvis lymphatics drain to the renal hilar, paraaortic (PA), and paracaval lymph nodes (LNs).

Workup

Risk Factors
- Smoking, analgesic abuse (containing phenacetin)
- Hypertension
- Von Hippel—Lindau disease

Symptoms and Signs
- Occasionally constitutional symptoms such as malaise, fever, night sweats, weight loss,"classic triad" of abdominal pain/flank pain, flank mass, and hematuria.
- Paraneoplastic syndromes such as erythrocytosis and hypercalcemia.
- Physical exam should note flank mass, any supraclavicular LN, organomegaly, and lower extremity edema.

Investigations
- CBC, with hepatic and renal function, urinalysis, and cytology.
- Ureteroscopy.
- Consider needle biopsy if indicated.
- Chest X-ray, CT abdomen/pelvis (or MRI), bone scan (if elevated alkaline phosphatase or bone pain are present), brain MRI, if indicated.

Fundamentals of Radiation Oncology
https://doi.org/10.1016/B978-0-12-814128-1.00019-2

TNM STAGING (RENAL CANCER)

T1	Tumor 7 cm or less in greatest dimension, limited to the kidney
T2	Tumor more than 7 cm in greatest dimension, limited to the kidney
T3	Tumor extends into major veins or perinephric tissues but not into the ipsilateral adrenal gland and not beyond Gerota's fascia
T4	Tumor invades beyond Gerota's fascia (including contiguous extension into the ipsilateral adrenal gland)
N0	No regional lymph node metastasis
N1	Regional lymph node metastasis
M0	No distant metastasis (no pathologic M0; use clinical M to complete stage group)
M1	Distant metastasis

Stage Grouping

Stage I	T1	N0	M0
Stage II	T2	N0	M0
Stage III	T1, 2	N1	M0
	T3	N0, 1	M0
Stage IV	T4	Any N	M0
	Any T	Any N	M1

M, (distant metastasis); N, (regional lymph nodes); TNM, T (tumor).
Used with permission of the American Joint Committee on Cancer (AJCC), Chicago, Illinois. The original source for this material is the AJCC Cancer Staging Manual, Eighth Edition (2017) published by Springer Science Business Media LLC, www.springer.com.

Treatment

- **Stage I, II, III**: Partial or radical nephrectomy is the standard treatment. Radical nephrectomy involves complete removal of Gerota's fascia and its contents (kidney, adrenal gland). Patients with renal vein involvement may require aggressive surgical approach and may consider regional lymphadenectomy.
  - Stage I: Select patients can undergo active surveillance or ablative techniques.
  - T1a, select patients: Not surgical candidates or failed ablative techniques can consider SBRT [1, 2].

- **Stage IV**: Cytoreductive nephrectomy and metastectomy recommended for solitary metastasis. Post-op if margin positive or residual disease, then tyrosin kinase inhibitors may be indicated.

- Resected high risk clear cell RCC (Stage 3, positive regional nodal disease, or both) can consider adjuvant sunitab ×1 year.
- Consider SBRT to the primary and to the solitary metastasis (depending on the site) for up to three to five metastatic sites [1, 2].

- **Medically unresectable**: Consider tyrosine kinase inhibitors such as sunitinib, sorafenib, pazopanib, and temsirolimus. A novel TKI Cabozantinib has greater activity in the front line setting and, if available, is an appropriate first line agent.
  - Asymptomatic patients with low tumor burden and favorable risk stratification may be followed with active surveillance.
  - Intermediate and high risk group consider combined immunotherapy with nivolumab and ipillimumab.
  - Chemotherapy had limited success; however, interleukin 2 and interferon A have shown 10%–20% objective responses.

- **Postoperative radiation**: It can be considered in high-risk patients with features such as large tumors (>=7 cm), positive margins, invasion of Gerota's fascia, positive LNs, renal vein and/or inferior vena cava involvement, and sarcomatoid features.

Radiation Therapy Technique

3D Technique

Simulation: Supine, arms-up, immobilization with Vac-Lok bag or knee/ankle fix, wire scar, CT planning scan fuse with pre-op imaging. **Borders**: Superior, top of T12; inferior, bottom of L4; contralateral transverse processes; ipsilateral renal bed with clips. If possible, scar should be included in the target.

IMRT Technique

Patient set up as 3D-CRT, fuse MRI with planning CT. 6-MV photons, seven to nine fixed-beam IMRT or two-arc VMAT.

Volumes

GTV = none in post-op (or primary gross tumor)
CTV1 = post-op nephrectomy bed, surgical clips, scar (or GTV) + at risk
LNs + 0.5–1.5 cm (respecting anatomical borders)
CTV2 = post-op nephrectomy bed, surgical clips, scar (or GTV) + 0.5–1.5 cm (respecting anatomical borders)
PTV = CTV + 0.5 cm

At risk LN: PA nodes

Doses

PTV1 = 180 cGy/fx to 45 Gy
PTV2 = 180 cGy/fx to 50.4–59.4 Gy (positive margins or gross residual disease)

SBRT/SRS Doses
Intact disease, SBRT: Single fraction 14–26 Gy (median dose 25 Gy);
Multiple fractions 24–70 Gy (median dose 40 Gy) delivered in 2–10 fractions.

Extracranial metastases, SBRT: 16—60 Gy delivered in 1—10 fractions. Dose and fractionation is greatly dependent on size, location, and proximity to other organs at risk.

Intracranial metastases, SRS: tumor size <2 cm is 24 Gy, <2—3 cm is 18 Gy, >3—4 cm is 15 Gy.

Constraints

Consider organs at risk in the treatment area, and make sure to follow standard constraints; liver, bowel, contralateral kidney, spinal cord, and stomach.

Contralateral kidney: maximum dose <20 Gy. If both kidneys are irradiated, one must not receive more than 15 Gy.

Liver: V36 < 30%

Spinal cord: maximum dose <45 Gy

Small bowel: V45 < 195 cc

SBRT: Dose constraints vary because of fractionation and treatment site.

Outcome

Five-year overall survival rates for stage I is 80%; stage II is 74%; stage III is 50%—55%; stage IV is 10%—30%.

Complications

- Fatigue, nausea, vomiting, increased bowel frequency, and loose stool
- Damage to the kidney and small bowel

Follow-Up

- Every 3 months for the first year, every 6 months for the second year, then every 12 months thereafter
- Imaging with chest X-ray and abdominal CT as indicated

BLADDER CANCER

The estimated incidence in the United States is 81,190 with 17,240 estimated deaths in 2018.

The anterosuperior portion of the bladder (apex) lies behind the symphysis pubis and peritoneum. The base is the posteroinferior part, which lies adjacent to the vagina or rectum. The portion adjacent to the prostate or urethra (in females) is the neck of the bladder. The triangle formed by the ureteral and urethral orifices is the trigone and the base of the bladder. Lymphatic drainage is from the bladder to the external and internal iliac and presacral nodes.

Workup

Risk Factors

- Aniline dye, tobacco, chronic bladder infection, and bladder stones
- Schistosoma hematobium (squamous cell cancer)

Symptoms and Signs

- Microscopic or gross hematuria, increase urination frequency, bladder irritability, and dysuria
- Bimanual exam and examination under anesthesia (EUA)

Investigations

- CBC, chemistry with renal function, urine cytology
- Evaluation of entire genitourinary (GU) tract with IVP
- Cystoscopy with biopsy, EUA, transurethral resection of bladder tumor (TURBT), biopsy of prostatic urethra, and mapping biopsies if diffuse in situ disease
- Chest X-ray, CT of the abdomen and pelvis, bone scan if symptomatic or for increase in alkaline phosphatase

TNM STAGING (BLADDER CANCER)

Ta	Noninvasive papillary tumor
Tis	Urothelial carcinoma in situ: flat tumor
T1	Tumor invades subepithelial connective tissue
T2	Tumor invades muscularis propria
T2a	Tumor invades superficial muscularis propria (inner half)
T2b	Tumor invades deep muscularis propria (outer half)
T3	Tumor invades perivesical tissue
pT3a	Microscopically
pT3b	Macroscopically (extravesical mass)
T4	Tumor invades any of the following: prostatic stroma, seminal vesicles, uterus, vagina, pelvic wall, abdominal wall
T4a	Tumor invades prostatic stroma, uterus, vagina
T4b	Tumor invades pelvic wall, abdominal wall
N0	No regional lymph node metastasis
N1	Single regional lymph node metastasis in the true pelvis (perivesical, obturator, internal and external iliac or sacral lymph node)
N2	Multiple regional lymph node metastasis in the true pelvis (perivesical, obturator, internal and external iliac or sacral lymph node)
N3	Lymph node metastasis to the common iliac lymph nodes
M0	No distant metastasis (no pathologic M0; use clinical M to complete stage group)
M1a	Distant metastasis limited to lymph nodes beyond the common iliac
M1b	Non–lymph node distant metastases

Stage Grouping

Stage 0a	Ta	N0	M0
Stage 0is	Tis	N0	M0
Stage I	T1	N0	M0
Stage II	T2a, 2b	N0	M0
Stage IIIA	T3a, 3b,4a	N0	M0
	T1, 2, 3, 4a	N1	M0
Stage IIIB	T1, 2, 3, 4a	N2, 3	M0
Stage IVA	T4b	N0	M0
Stage IVA	Any T	Any N	M1a
Stage IVB	Any T	Any N	M1b

M, (distant metastasis); *N*, (regional lymph nodes); *TNM*, T (tumor).
Used with permission of the American Joint Committee on Cancer (AJCC), Chicago, Illinois. The original source for this material is the AJCC Cancer Staging Manual, Eighth Edition (2017) published by Springer Science Business Media LLC, www.springer.com.

Treatment

Superficial Disease (Ta, Tis, T1)
- Low-grade Ta—TURBT only.
- High-grade Ta/Tis, T1—TURBT followed by intravesical BCG (Bacillus Calmette–Guerin vaccine). BCG is given, 50 mg intravesical every week ×6 cycles. Consider a single dose of intravesicular mitomycin C within 24 h of TURBT, before BCG is given.
- Radical cystectomy is considered in patients who have no response to one to two courses of BCG, tumors >5 cm in size, involvement of the ureters, bladder neck, and multiple recurrences.
- ChemoRT therapy can be considered for patients who are medically inoperable or refuse cystectomy for the abovementioned indications.

Invasive Disease, N0
- Pre-op chemotherapy followed by partial or radical cystoprostatectomy or anterior exenteration in women.
  - Pre-op chemotherapy is with gemcitabine 1000 mg/m^2 days 1, 8, 15 and cisplatin 70 mg/m^2 on day 2 [3, 4].
  - Post-op pT3–T4 tumor or node positive can also be considered for chemotherapy provided they have not received any pre-op chemotherapy [5].
  - Post-op RT benefit is unclear; however, it can be considered for gross residual disease, positive margins, pathological nodal involvement, pT3-T4, LVI, and high-grade disease.

- Bladder preservation management: maximum TURBT followed by concurrent chemoRT [6, 7]. Chemotherapy CDDP 100 mg/m^2 every 3 weeks × 2 cycles. The patients then have UA cytology and a biopsy done after 4–6 weeks of treatment. The patient with pathologic complete response (pCR) continues with chemoRT, while the patient with pathologic partial response/no response (pPR/NR) undergoes cystectomy.
- Patients refusing surgery or medically unable to have a cystectomy should undergo maximum TURBT followed by concurrent chemoRT. Chemotherapy CDDP 15 mg/m^2 and 5-FU 400 mg/m^2 × 3 cycles (preferred) or CDDP 100 mg/m^2 every 3 weeks × 2 cycles.
- In elderly, medically unfit patients, bladder preservation therapy can be expedited with hypofractionated chemoRT. After maximum TURBT, followed by concurrent chemoRT. Chemotherapy is weekly gemcitabine 100 mg/m^2 or CDDP 40 mg/m^2. In elderly, medically unfit patients, bladder preservation therapy can be expedited with hypofractionated chemoRT. After maximum TURBT, followed by concurrent chemoRT. Chemotherapy is weekly gemcitabine 100 mg/m^2 or CDDP 40 mg/m^2.

Invasive Disease, N+, and Metastatic
- Chemotherapy or concurrent chemoRT. Combination chemotherapy with gemcitabine and cisplatin (GC) is preferred over M-VAC (methotrexate, vinblastine, adriamycin, cisplatin).
- Multiple PD-1 and PD-L1 monoclonal antibodies such as pembrolizumab, nivolumab, durvalumab can be considered for metastatic urothelial cancer progressing on chemotherapy.

Radiation Therapy Technique

3D Technique
Patient is supine, arms above chest, CT simulated for four-field box. CT scan is done twice, once with empty bladder for initial whole bladder treatment then with full bladder for the boost treatment. **Borders** are superior S2/S3, inferior bottom of obturator foramen, lateral 2 cm on bony pelvis, anterior 2 cm anterior to bladder wall, posterior 2 cm posterior to bladder wall/tumor. Treat to 39.6 Gy (45 Gy for patients refused/medically unfit) then cone down with 2-cm margin around the tumor to final dose of 64.8 Gy. Patient always voids before each treatment.

IMRT Technique
Patient supine, CT simulate as 3D technique. Bladder mapping from biopsies and placement of fiducial markers to define tumor bed. Initial treatment is with empty bladder and boost treatment is with full bladder. 6-MV photons, with seven to nine IMRT beams or two-arc VMATS for treatment. Daily CBCT is recommended. Fig. 19.1.

Volumes
GTV = gross disease defined by cystoscope and/or CT/MRI imaging
CTVtumor = GTV + tumor bed (defined by bladder mapping)
CTVbladder = entire bladder
CTVother = elective LN + radical cystectomy structures

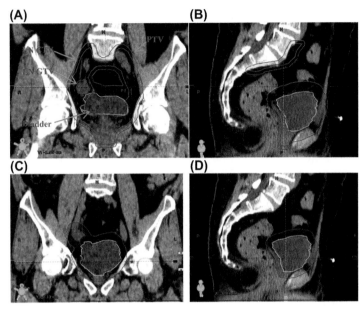

FIGURE 19.1   Coronal CT (A) and sagittal CT (B) of bladder cancer treated with definitive chemoRT with PTV1 (outer red line) delivering 45 Gy. Sagittal (C) and coronal CT (D) of the boost field PTV2 (red) delivering 64.8 Gy to the whole bladder and an involved lymph node. Superior border at L4/L5 and inferior border below the prostate at the genitourinary diaphragm. PTV1 includes the prostate, seminal vesicles, bladder, internal and external iliac nodes, and common iliac nodes (due to involved node). PTV2 includes the gross tumor, whole bladder, and involved node with margin.

> PTVtumor = CTVtumor + 2 cm
> PTVbladder = CTVbladder +2 cm
> PTVother = CTVother + 0.5 cm
> PTV1 = PTVtumor + PTVbladder + PTVother
> PTV2 = PTVtumor + PTVbladder
> PTV3 = PTVtumor

Elective Lymph Nodes/Radical Cystectomy Structures

Internal, obturator, and external iliac LNs up to S2/S3 structures included in radical prostatectomy: prostate/urethra/SVs in men; uterus/Fallopian tube/upper vagina in women.

Doses

> PTV1 = 180 cGy/fx to 45 Gy
> PTV2 = 180 cGy/fx to 54 Gy
> PTV3 = 180 cGy/fx to 64.8–66.6 Gy
> Hypofractionated RT = 250 cGy/fx to 50 Gy

Constraints

Small bowel: V45 < 195 cc
Femoral heads: V45 < 25%, V50 < 5%
Urethra: maximum dose<70 Gy

Outcome

- Overall survival for Ta is 95%; HG T1 is 50%; T2, T3 is 50%; LN + 20%.
- Bladder conservation is 40%, and overall survival is 50%.

Complications

- Urinary frequency with burning sensation, hematuria, bladder damage with shrinkage, loss of capacity, urethral stricture (<5%), and recurrent bladder infection; change in bowel habit, diarrhea, cramps, rectal inflammation, soreness, rectal bleeding, bowel or rectal damage requiring surgical correction (5%–15%), bone damage with softening or fracture.
- Impotence with loss of erection.

Follow-Up

- Every 3 months for the first year, every 6 months for the second year, then every 12 months thereafter
- Cystoscopy and urine cytology every 3 months for 2 years, then every 12 months
- CT scan of the abdomen and pelvis every 12 months and as indicated

PROSTATE CANCER

The estimated incidence in the United States is 164,690 with 29,430 estimated deaths in 2018.

The prostate gland is located deep in the pelvis and is surrounded anteriorly by the dorsal vein complex, posteriorly by the rectum, and superiorly by the bladder. The subcapsular lymphatic system drains to a periprostatic lymphatic network, which drains into the internal iliac, obturator, external iliac, and less frequently presacral LNs. Nonregional (distant) nodes = aortic, common iliac, inguinal, and superficial femoral.

Pelvic LN involvement can be predicted by the following equations and nomograms:

Percent LN risk = 2/3 PSA + (GS-6) × 10 (Roach formula)

Percent LN risk = (GS-5) × (PSA/3 + 1.5 × T) (Yale formula)

Where GS is gleason score, T = 0, 1, two for cT1c, cT2a, and cT2b/c.

Percent LN risk = Memorial Sloan-Kettering nomogram: http://www.mskcc.org/mskcc/html/10088.cfm.

Workup

Risk Factors

- Advanced age
- Family history
- Race—African-American

Symptoms and Signs
- Many patients are asymptomatic, hesitancy, frequency, nocturia, weak urinary stream, urinary tract infection, impotence (secondary to invasion to neuromuscular bundle).
- DRE: palpate for gland dimension, consistency, sensitivity, mobility presence/size of nodules, involvement of any lateral rectal sulci.
- Bone pain (secondary to bony metastasis).

Investigations
- CBC, CMP, LFTs, testosterone (baseline)
- Prostate-specific antigen (PSA):
  - Screening discuss at the age of 45
  - African-American patients offer screening at the age of 40
  - High-risk patients with positive family history offer annual screening at the age of 45–50
- Biomarkers such as 4K (estimates probability of high-risk prostate cancer) or PCA3 >35 (may be indicative of prostate cancer) are not recommended as first-line screening tests.
  - TRUS-guided biopsy (12 cores)
  - CT or MRI of the pelvis for T3/4 or T1/2 with LN nomogram risk of >10%
  - Bone scan for T1 with PSA over 20, T2 with PSA >10, T3/4, gleason score >8, for symptoms or if elevated alkaline phosphatase
- Calculation of life expectancy: https://www.ssa.gov/OACT/STATS/table4c6.htm

International Society of Urological Pathology Grade Groups[a]

ISUP Grade Group	Gleason Score
1	< = 6
2	3 + 4 = 7
3	4 + 3 = 7
4	8
5	9 or 10

[a]Epstein JI, et al. The 2014 international society of urological pathology (ISUP) consensus conference on gleason grading of prostatic Carcinoma: definition of grading patterns and proposal for a new grading system. Am J Surg Pathol February 2016;40(2):244–52.

TNM Staging (Prostate Cancer)

T1	Clinically inapparent tumor not palpable
T1a	Tumor incidental histologic finding in 5% or less of tissue resected
T1b	Tumor incidental histologic finding in more than 5% of tissue resected
T1c	Tumor identified by needle biopsy (because of elevated PSA)[a]

T2	Tumor confined within prostate			
T2a	Tumor involves one-half of one side or less			
T2b	Tumor involves more than one-half of one side but not both sides			
T2c	Tumor involves both sides			
T3	Tumor extends through the prostate capsule[b]			
T3a	Extracapsular extension (unilateral or bilateral)			
T3b	Tumor invades seminal vesicle(s)			
T4	Tumor is fixed or invades adjacent structures other than seminal vesicles: such as external sphincter, rectum, bladder, levator muscles, and/or pelvic wall			

Note: There is no pathological T1 classification.
[a]*Tumor found in one or both lobes by needle biopsy, but not palpable or reliably visible by imaging, is classified as T1c.*
[b]*Invasion into the prostatic apex or into (but not beyond) the prostatic capsule is classified as T2 not as T3.*

N0	No regional lymph node metastasis
N1	Metastasis in regional lymph node(s)
M0	No distant metastasis (no pathologic M0; use clinical M to complete stage group)
M1	Distant metastasis

Stage Grouping

Stage	T	N	M	PSA	GG
Stage I	T1a–c	N0	M0	PSA < 10	GG1
	T2a, T2	N0	M0	PSA < 10	GG1
Stage IIA	T1a–c, T2a, T2	N0	M0	PSA > 10 < 20	GG1
	T2b–c	N0	M0	PSA < 20	GG1
Stage IIB	T1, 2	N0	M0	PSA < 20	GG2
Stage IIC	T1, 2	N0	M0	PSA < 20	GG3
	T1, 2	N0	M0	PSA <20	GG4
Stage IIIA	T1, 2	N0	M0	PSA > 20	GG1-4
Stage IIIB	T3, 4	N0	M0	Any PSA	GG1-4
Stage IIIC	Any T	N0	M0	Any PSA	GG5
Stage IVA	Any T	N1	M0	Any PSA	Any
Stage IVB	Any T	N0	M1	Any PSA	Any

M, (distant metastasis); *N*, (regional lymph nodes); *TNM*, T (tumor).
Used with permission of the American Joint Committee on Cancer (AJCC), Chicago, Illinois. The original source for this material is the AJCC Cancer Staging Manual, Eighth Edition (2017) published by Springer Science Business Media LLC, www.springer.com.

Treatment

Very Low-Risk

(T1c and gl < 6/GG1 and PSA <10 and < 3 cores with <50% cancer in each core and PSA density <0.15 ng/ml/g)

- Life expectancy <10 years: observation
- Life expectancy 10–20 years: active surveillance with DRE and PSA every 6–12 months; repeat biopsy at 12 months
- Life expectancy >20 years:
  - Active surveillance [8, 9, 10]
  - Radical prostatectomy, which involves complete removal of prostate and surrounding capsule, SVs, ampulla, the vas deference, with the option of the bilateral pelvic LN dissection [8, 9, 10].
  - External beam radiation therapy (no nodal treatment) [17–19]. Hypofractionated RT is recommended to prostate only [20, 21].
  - Brachytherapy radiation alone [11, 12]. For prostate gland volume more than 60 cc, recommend neoadjuvant hormonal therapy for 3–6 months.

Low-Risk

(T1–T2a and gl < 6/GG1 and PSA <10)

- Life expectancy <10 years: observation
- Life expectancy >10 years:
  - Active surveillance [8, 9, 10].
  - Radical prostatectomy, with the option of the bilateral pelvic LN dissection [8, 9, 10],
  - Radiation therapy options involve EBRT (no nodal treatment) [17–19]. Hypofractionated RT is recommended to prostate only [20, 21].
  - Brachytherapy radiation alone [11, 12]. For prostate gland volume more than 60 cc, recommend neoadjuvant hormonal therapy for 3–6 months.

Favorable Intermediate-Risk

(T2b-c or gl 3 + 4/GG2 or PSA 10–20* and percent positive cores <50%)
  cannot have >1 intermediate risk factor

- Life expectancy <10 years: observation or EBRT or brachytherapy
- Life expectancy >10 years:
  - Radical prostatectomy with a pelvic node dissection option [8, 9, 10].
  - EBRT initially to prostate and proximal seminal vesicle, followed by a boost dose to prostate only (no nodal treatment) [17–19]. Hypofractionated RT is recommended to prostate ± SV [21–23].
  - Brachytherapy alone [11–13].

Unfavorable Intermediate-Risk

(T2b-c or gl 3 + 4/GG2 or gl 4 + 3/GG3 or PSA 10–20)

- Life expectancy <10 years: observation or EBRT or brachytherapy
- Life expectancy >10 years:
  - Radical prostatectomy with a pelvic node dissection option.

- EBRT initially to prostate and proximal seminal vesicle, followed by a boost dose to prostate [17–19]. Consider pelvic node RT for gl score 4 + 3 (15, 16).
- Brachytherapy alone or EBRT combination with brachytherapy boost can be considered for these patients [11–13].

- Recommend short-term ADT (4–6 months). Hormonal therapy is given with bicalutamide 50 mg orally every day × 4 months, goserelin 3.6 mg every month × 4–6 months [24, 26, 27].

High-risk

(T3a or gl 8/GG > 4 or gl 4 + 5/GG5 or PSA >20)

Very high-risk

(T3b–T4, or primary gl five or >4 cores gl 8–10/GG 4–5)

Regional (N+)

- EBRT to pelvic nodes, seminal vesicle, and prostate, followed by boost dose to prostate and seminal vesicle, followed by boost dose to prostate [17–19]. Treat pelvic node [15, 16].
- EBRT combination with brachytherapy boost can be considered for this group of patient (13, 14). Treat pelvic node.
- Long-term ADT (28 months) with 2 months before and 2 months during the RT with bicalutamide and goserelin as above, followed by adjuvant hormonal therapy with goserelin 10.8 mg every 3 months × 2 years is recommended [25, 26, 28].
- Consider chemotherapy with docetaxel in addition to ADT [29, 30]. Docetaxel dose is 75 mg/m^2 × 6 cycles with or without prednisone.
- Consider abiraterone combined with ADT [31]. Abiraterone dose is 1000 mg/day for ×2 years.

Postprostatectomy Radiation Therapy

The definition of a failure after radical prostatectomy: PSA >=0.2 ng/mL followed by a second PSA also >=0.2 ng/mL (AUA definition)

- Adjuvant RT is recommended for ECE, positive SV, and positive margin. RT is given after urinary incontinence resolves, may take up to 1 year [32, 33].
- Salvage RT is recommended for persistent PSA, rising PSA after initial undetectable PSA from RP, gross disease by imaging or biopsy. Salvage RT is recommended while PSA is still low <1 ng/mL [34, 35, 37].
- Androgen deprivation is indicated for patients with a rising PSA after RP and specifically for patients with pT3 disease, high PSA (>0.7), positive margins, high Gleason score (8–10), positive nodes [35, 36]. ADT duration is 6–24 months with bicalutamide or goserelin.

Post–Radiation Rising PSA

The definition of failure after RT: a rise of the PSA >=2 ng/mL above PSA nadir (Phoenix definition).

- Patients who meet the phoenix definition of biochemical failure after RT should have repeat staging workup. If patient has no distant metastasis, then consider prostatectomy or salvage brachytherapy, cryotherapy, or HIFU.
- Alternatively, androgen ablation therapy can be considered.

Metastatic Disease
- ADT and docetaxel 75 mg/m2 × 6 cycles with or without prednisone [23, 24].
- ADT and abiraterone is recommended [25].
- LHRH agonist and antiandrogen with Casodex 50 mg orally every day × 1 month and Zoladex 10.8 mg subcutaneously every 3 months until PSA failure.
- LHRH antagonist with degarelix initial dose 120 mg SC for two doses (i.e., two separate injections totaling 240 mg), then, after 28 days, begin maintenance dose of 80 mg SC q28 days.
  - Patients with bony metastasis should be considered for bisphosphonate treatment.

Hormonal Refractory Prostate Cancer
- Abireterone with prednisone
  - Systemic chemotherapy with docetaxel and prednisone every3 weeks for × 6 cycles; alternatively, estramustine, etoposide, paclitaxel × 4 cycles is the recommended treatment.
- Enzalutamide 160 mg/d can be considered.
- Ketoconazole 400 mg t.i.d. with or without glucocorticoids can be considered.
- Provenge, a cancer vaccine for metastatic hormone refractory prostate cancer patients. Treatment involves three courses in a month with weeks in between courses.
- Patients with bony metastasis should be considered for bisphosphonate treatment.

Radiation Therapy Technique

3D Technique
- Patient is supine, arms on chest, on Vac-Lok, IV contrast, mark anus, perform urethrogram, bladder full, rectum empty, patient CT simulated. Borders are: superior at bottom of SI joint; inferior border is 1 cm below urethrogram beak, lateral at 2 cm on bony pelvis; anterior to symphysis pubis, posterior at S3/S4. Boost prostate with a margin of 1 cm (rectal margin 0.5 cm) to a total final dose, depending on the risk stratification of the prostate cancer. If treating more than 72 Gy, patients must have image-guided radiation therapy (IGRT). Treat small pelvis with four-field box and prostate boost with six-field conformal radiation therapy. Figs. 19.2 and 19.3.
- For post-op patients, it is necessary for the incontinence to resolve, which takes about 3 months. Patient position is same as above, small bowel contrast in place. Borders are superior, 10 cm above inferior border; inferior, 1 cm below urethrogram beak, lateral 10 cm across; anterior, 1 cm behind symphysis; posterior, cm posterior to most anterior portion of anterior rectal wall. Boost with small bowel block and 10 × 10 field to a total final dose.
- Brachytherapy is done in selected patients with small prostate glands of <60 cc. In patients receiving brachytherapy alone, the implant is done with ultrasound guidance. Postimplant dosimetry should be performed within 1 month.

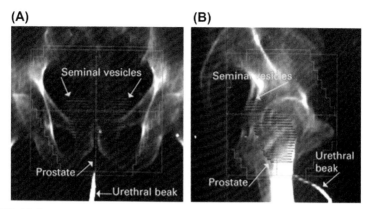

FIGURE 19.2 (A) DRR for prostate cancer, 3D AP field, showing superior border at the bottom of SI joint and inferior border 1 cm below the urethral beak. Lateral borders have a 2-cm margin on the bony pelvis. (B) DRR for prostate cancer, 3D right lateral field, showing the anterior border is anterior to the symphysis pubis and the posterior border is at S3/S4.

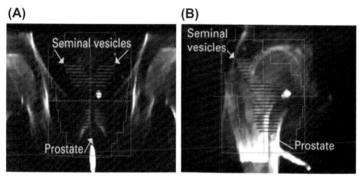

FIGURE 19.3 (A) DRR for prostate cancer, cone down 3D AP field, showing treating seminal vesicles and the prostate with a 1-cm margin. (B) DRR for prostate cancer, cone down 3D right lateral field, showing treating seminal vesicles and the prostate with a 1-cm margin.

IMRT Technique
- Simulation: Patient is supine, bladder full; rectum empty (a 3 cm diameter or less). Consider fiducials (placed before SIM). Knee and ankle fix for immobilization. MRI prostate with CT simulation for contouring (typically use T2 sequence).
  - Planning technique: 6-MV photons, use equally spaced 7–9 coplanar IMRT beams or two arcs with VMAT (6 MV or 15 MV). Daily IGRT is recommended.

- Contouring:
  - Prostate is contoured using the MRI for more precise delineation. Attention should be given to contouring the prostatic apex.
  - Rectum is drawn from ischial tuberosity to the top of the seminal vesicles. Sigmoid colon is drawn to the top of the pelvic inlet (11−15 cm from ischial tuberosity).
  - Nodal volume is contoured using a 7 mm around vessels from L5/S1 interspace to top of pubis (include the obturator nodes)
- To reduce the rectal toxicity, rapid dose fall-off posteriorly is important; the 50% isodose line should not cover the entire circumference of the rectum. See Figs. 19.4 and 19.5.

Volumes

Intact prostate volume

    GTV = prostate + extracapsular extension
    Low/favorable intermediate risk
    CTV1 = GTV + proximal 1 cm SV
    CTV2 = GTV
    Select unfavorable intermediate risk/high risk
    CTV1 = GTV + entire SV + pelvic elective LNs
    CTV2 = GTV + entire SV
    CTV3 = GTV
    PTV = CTV +0.8 cm margin with rectal margin 0.5 cm

    SBRT

    PTV = Prostate ± proximal 1 cm SVs with 5 mm superior and lateral, 3 mm anterior and posterior

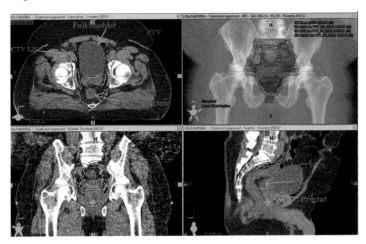

FIGURE 19.4 Prostate cancer CT images showing target volumes SV, prostate, LNs, CTV, PTV and critical structures bladder, and rectum.

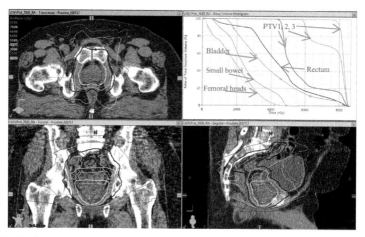

FIGURE 19.5   Prostate cancer CT images showing two-arc VMAT planning isodose lines conforming to PTVs and DVH meeting all constraints. The prescription dose is PTV1 45 Gy, PTV2 55.8 Gy, PTV3 79.2 Gy.

Postprostatectomy Prostate Bed Volume*

GTV = none
CTV = prostate bed (as below) + pelvic LN (for salvage RT)

Superior level of cut end of vas deferens or 3–4 cm above top of symphysis (vas may retract postoperatively; include seminal vesicle remnants if pathologically involved)

Inferior 8–12 mm below vesicourethral anastomosis (may include more if concern for apical margin, can extend to slice above penile bulb if vesicourethral anastomosis not well visualized)

Anterioposterior edge of pubic bone, posterior 1–2 cm of bladder wall.

Posterioanterior rectal wall (may need to be concave around lateral aspects), mesorectal fascia.

Lateral levator ani muscles, obturator internus, sacrorectogenitopubic fascia (if concern about extraprostatic disease at base may extend to obturator internus)

PTV = CTV + 0.8 cm margin with rectal margin 0.5 cm.

(Michalski JM, Lawton C, El Naqa I, Ritter M, O'Meara E, Seider MJ, et al. Development of RTOG consensus guidelines for the definition of the clinical target volume for postoperative conformal radiation therapy for prostate cancer. Int J Radiat Oncol Biol Phys (2010) 76(2):361–8)

Pelvic Elective LNs:

External iliac, internal iliac, presacral and periprostatic LNs (superior border for the LNs at L5/S1, inferior border of external iliac is at the superior border of femoral head, inferior border of internal iliac LN at the top of SV, inferior border of obturator LN is at the top of the pubis presacral LN anterior border is 1 cm anterior to the sacrum, superior and inferior border is at S1–S3)

Brachytherapy Technique

Brachytherapy is performed in select patients.

- Ideal criteria include patients with prostate glands of 30−60 cc, with AUA score of <=15, no pubic arch interference.
  - Monotherapy: patients with very low risk, low risk, and favorable intermediate risk
  - Boost therapy: patients with unfavorable intermediate risk and high risk
- Implants can be done with low-dose rate (LDR) or HDR, and CT or US guidance is used.
- Large prostate gland of >60 cc recommend short course of ADT of 4−6 months.

Low-Dose Rate Brachytherapy

This is a permanent brachytherapy technique. Pre-op bowel preparation is needed, appropriate anesthesia is required. TRUS images are used for preplanning. PTV is 3−5 mm margin around the prostate. In the OR intra-op TRUS-guided images are matched with the pre-op images. Preloaded needles are inserted through the template until the correct location is established. Seeds are then deposited, and needles are withdrawn. The patient is discharged from the hospital the same day or the next day after he is able to urinate. When treating with LDR, postimplant dosimetry should be done within 1 month (Figs. 19.4 and 19.5).

High-Dose Rate Brachytherapy

This is a temporary brachytherapy technique. Afterloading catheters are inserted using template under TRUS guidance. CT simulation is done with the catheters in place. Treatment planning is done via computer optimization of the dwell times. HDR Ir 192 sources are used for treatment using a computer-driven afterloading machine. The catheters and the template are removed after each treatment. After appropriate radiation safety monitoring, the patient is discharged home the same day.

Doses for External Beam Radiation Therapy and Brachytherapy

Definitive RT
Low/intermediate risk
PTV1 = 180−200 cGy/fx to 54−55.8 Gy
PTV2 = 180−200 cGy/fx 75.6−80 Gy

High risk
PTV1 = 180−200 cGy/fx to 45−46 Gy
PTV2 = 180−200 cGy/fx to 54−55.8 Gy
PTV3 = 180−200 cGy/fx to 79.2−80 Gy

Hypofractionated RT
PTV1 = 250 cGy/fx to 78 Gy or 270 cGy/fx to 70.2 Gy

SBRT
6.5 Gy/fx in five fxs to 32.5 Gy or 7.25 cGy/fx to 36.25 Gy (NRG Gu005)

Post-op RT
180 cGy/fx to 66.6–72 Gy
Gross disease: 180 cGy/fx to 73.8–75.6 Gy

Brachytherapy mono dose
I-125: mono dose 145 Gy
Pd-103: mono dose 125 Gy
Goals: V100 > 95%–99%, V150 < 70%, V200 <20%, D90 >90–100%
HDR Ir-192: 9.5 Gy in four fxs to 38 Gy or 13. 5 Gy/fx in two fxs to 27 Gy
Goals: V100 > 90–9%, V150 <40%, D90 > 90%

Brachytherapy boost dose (EBRT40–50 Gy)
I-125: 110 Gy
Pd-103: 90–100 Gy
HDR Ir-192: 4 Gy/fx in four fxs to 16 Gy or 10.5 Gy/fx to 21 Gy

Constraints

Standard Fractionation (180–200 cGy/fx)

Rectum: V72 Gy<10cc, V65 Gy<17%, V40Gy<35%
Anus: V60 Gy<1cc, V35Gy<40%
Bladder: V65 Gy<25%, V40 Gy<50%
Femoral heads: V50 Gy<10%
Bowel: V50 Gy<5%, V40 Gy<20%
Penile bulb: V15 Gy < 10%
Corporal bodies: V7 Gy<10%

Moderate Hypofractionation (270 cGy/fx)

Rectum: V65 Gy<10cc, V50 Gy<17%, V31 Gy<35%
Anus: V48 Gy<1cc, V32 Gy<40%
Bladder: V50 Gy<25%, V31 Gy<50%
Femoral heads: V40 Gy< 10%
Bowel: V40 Gy<5%, V30 Gy<20%
Penile bulb: V12 Gy<10%
Corporal bodies: V 5.5 Gy < 10%

Combination EBRT + Brachytherapy (HDR) Boost

Rectum: V41 Gy<10cc, V40 Gy<17%, V30 Gy<35%
Anus: V35Gy<1cc, V20Gy<40%
Bladder: V40Gy<25%, V30 Gy<50%
Femoral heads: V31 GY <10%
Bowel: V50 Gy<5%, V40 Gy<20%
Penile bulb: V10 Gy<10%
Corporal bodies: V4.5Gy<10%

Brachytherapy

LDR: Rectum D0.1 cc <200 Gy, D2 cc <100%, RV <1 cc; urethra V100 <60%, D30 <130%, Dmax <150%

    HDR: Rectum V75 <1 cc; urethra V120 <0.8 cc

Outcome

- After radiation, PSA is halved in 2—3 months. PSA remains detectable in majority of patients after RT with no clinical evidence of failure. It can take years for patients to reach nadir.
- Biochemical disease-free survival (bDFS) for low-risk patients is 80—90+%, intermediate risk 75%—85%, high risk 60%
- For post-op patients treated with adjuvant or salvage radiation, the 5-year freedom from biochemical failure overall is 56%, 71% for PSA 0.01—2 ng/mL, 63% for PSA 0.21—0.5, 54% for PSA 0.51—1, 43% for PSA 1.01—2, and 37% for PSA>2.

Complications

EBRT

- Likely: Fatigue, urinary frequency/urgency, dysuria, diarrhea/loose stools, gas, occasionally rectal irritation/inflammation or exacerbation of hemorrhoids
- Less likely: Permanent changes in bowel habits, rectal bleeding, proctitis, bowel or rectal damage requiring surgical correction, hematuria, cystitis
- Erectile dysfunction in long term
- Second malignancy (bladder 0.1%—3.8%, rectal 0.3%—1.2%)*

Wallis CJD, et al. Second malignancies after radiotherapy for prostate cancer: systematic review and meta-analysis. BMJ 2016;352. https://doi.org/10.1136/bmj.i851 (Published 02 March 2016).

Brachytherapy

- Urinary frequency, dysuria, hematuria
- Urinary retention—resolves within 3 days
- Obstructive symptoms—resolve within 12 months

Hormone Therapy Toxicity

- Fatigue, hot flashes, energy changes, decreased energy, increased appetite, weight gain, risk of metabolic syndrome, risk of DM/CAD, risk of bone density loss
- Bicalutamide also carries the risk of gynecomastia
- Treated with tamoxifen or prophylactic breast RT

Follow-Up

- Every 3 months for the first year, every 6 months for the second year, and every 12 months thereafter.
- DRE and PSA measurement with each visit.
  - PSA failure after EBRT: PSA rise by > 2 ng/mL above the nadir. Nadir after EBRT may take up to 3 years (after brachytherapy up to 5 years). Transient rise of PSA may happen after EBRT/brachytherapy.
- Patients receiving androgen ablation treatment should be considered for a baseline bone density study.

TESTICULAR CANCER

The estimated incidence in the United States is 9310 with 400 estimated deaths in 2018.

Testicular cancer is most common between the ages of 20 and 34. Lymph drainage is to the PA nodes between the T11-L4 vertebrae. The left testicle drains to the left renal vein, and the right testicle drains to the inferior vena cava below the renal vein level.

Workup

Risk Factors
- Prior testicular cancer
- Cryptorchidism
- Klinefelter's syndrome

Symptoms and Signs
- Painless heavy feeling of the testicles, low back pain
- Testicular mass in almost all patients
- Check for adenopathy in supraclavicular fossa, axilla, inguinal region, with attention to cryptorchidism
- Gynecomastia (associated with high HCG and choriocarcinoma)

Investigations
- CBC and routine chemistries
  - LDH: the serum level of LDH has prognostic value in patients with metastatic disease and is included for staging.
- Serum markers
  - HCG (half-life = 1 day); HCG is secreted by syncytiotrophoblast. It is elevated in SGCT-pure seminoma and NSGCT-embryonal and choriocarcinoma.
  - AFP (half-life = 5 days); AFP is elevated in nonseminomatous embryonal, teratoma, teratocarcinoma, yolk sac tumor; AFP is not elevated in pure seminoma, choriocarcinoma, or germinoma.
  - Serum tumor markers are obtained immediately after orchiectomy and if elevated should be performed serially after orchiectomy according to the normal decay for HCG and AFP to assess for persistent serum tumor marker elevation.
- Testicular ultrasound differentiates tumor from cyst, spermatocele, varicocele.
- Evaluate contralateral testis for subclinical tumor.
- Chest X-ray with or without CT chest, CT of the abdomen and pelvis, brain MRI, if clinically indicated.
- Semen analysis and banking of sperm, if adequate quality, for patient's fertility desires.

TNM Staging (Testicular Cancer)

pTX	Primary tumor cannot be assessed
pTis	Germ cell neoplasia (carcinoma in situ)
pT1	Tumor limited to the testis and epididymis without vascular/lymphatic invasion; tumor may invade into the tunica albuginea but not the tunica vaginalis

(Continued)

pT2　Tumor limited to the testis and epididymis with vascular/lymphatic invasion, or tumor invading hilar soft tissue or epididymis or penetrating visceral mesothelial layer covering the external surface of tunica albuginea with or without lymphovascular invasion

pT3　Tumor invades the spermatic cord with or without vascular/lymphatic invasion

pT4　Tumor invades the scrotum with or without vascular/lymphatic invasion

---

Except for pTis and pT4, extent of primary tumor is classified by radical orchiectomy.

N0　No regional lymph node metastasis

N1　Metastasis with a lymph node mass 2 cm or less in greatest dimension; or multiple lymph nodes, none more than 2 cm in greatest dimension

N2　Metastasis with a lymph node mass more than 2 cm but not more than 5 cm in greatest dimension; or multiple lymph nodes, any one mass greater than 2 cm but not more than 5 cm in greatest dimension

N3　Metastasis with a lymph node mass more than 5 cm in greatest dimension

M0　No distant metastasis

M1　Distant metastasis

M1a　No retroperitoneal nodal or pulmonary metastasis

M1b　Nonpulmonary visceral metastases

Stage Grouping

Stage I	**pT1–4**	**N0**	**M0**	**SX**
Stage IA	pT1	N0	M0	S0
Stage IB	pT2	N0	M0	S0
	pT3	N0	M0	S0
	pT4	N0	M0	S0
Stage IS	Any pT/Tx	N0	M0	S1–3 (postorchiectomy)
Stage II	Any pT/Tx	N1–3	M0	SX
Stage IIA	Any pT/Tx	N1	M0	S0
	Any pT/Tx	N1	M0	S1
Stage IIB	Any pT/Tx	N2	M0	S0
	Any pT/Tx	N2	M0	S1

Stage I	pT1–4	N0	M0	SX
Stage IIC	Any pT/Tx	N3	M0	S0
	Any pT/Tx	N3	M0	S1
Stage III	Any pT/Tx	Any N	M1	SX
Stage IIIA	Any pT/Tx	Any N	M1a	S0
	Any pT/Tx	Any N	M1a	S1
Stage IIIB	Any pT/Tx	N1–3	M0	S2
	Any pT/Tx	Any N	M1a	S2
Stage IIIC	Any pT/Tx	N1–3	M0	S3
	Any pT/Tx	Any N	M1a	S3
	Any pT/Tx	Any N	M1b	Any S

Required for staging: Serum tumor markers (S)

S0	Marker study levels within normal limits
S1	LDH $< 1.5 \times N^a$ **AND** hCG (mIu/ml) < 5000 **AND** AFP (ng/mL) < 1000.
S2	LDH $1.5–10 \times N$ **OR** hCG (mIu/ml) 5000–50,000 **OR** AFP (ng/mL) 1000–10,000
S3	LDH $> 10 \times N$ **OR** hCG (mIu/ml) $> 50,000$ **OR** AFP (ng/mL) $> 10,000$

M, (distant metastasis); *N*, (regional lymph nodes); *TNM*, T (tumor).
ᵃN indicates the upper limit of normal for the LDH assay.
Used with permission of the American Joint Committee on Cancer (AJCC), Chicago, Illinois. The original source for this material is the AJCC Cancer Staging Manual, Eighth Edition (2017) published by Springer Science Business Media LLC, www.springer.com.

Treatment

Seminoma

Initial surgical management is radical orchiectomy with high spermatic cord ligation, followed by RT if indicated. Sperm banking should be discussed with the patient before any RT is initiated.

- **Stage I treatment options:**
  - Observation for compliant patient (preferred).
  - Post-op chemotherapy carboplatin $\times$ 1–2 cycles with AUC of 7 [39]
  - Post-op RT to PA LNs (38). Note: Contraindication for RT, such as horseshoe kidney or inflammatory bowel disease, these patients should undergo observation after orchiectomy.

- **Stage IIA:** Post-op RT to PA and ipsilateral pelvis followed by boost to gross LNs.
- **Stage IIB treatment options:**
  - Postop chemotherapy PEB × 3 cycles or EP × 4 cycles
  - Post-op RT to PA and ipsilateral pelvis followed by boost to gross LN (s)

Stage IIC/III: Chemotherapy PEB (cisplatin, etoposide, bleomycin) $20/100$ mg/m^2/ 30 units per week every 4 weeks × 3–4 cycles. After chemotherapy, residual tumors of 3 cm or more or progressive disease may require surgery or RT.

- **Unresectable:** In patients with a massive primary tumor that cannot be resected, the treatment is with RT alone to a field that includes the hemiscrotum, the PA nodes, ipsilateral pelvis, and groin (especially if the scrotum is involved).

Nonseminoma

Initial surgical management is radical inguinal orchiectomy with high spermatic cord ligation.

- **Stage I:**
  IA: Surveillance.
  IB: Retroperitoneal lymph node dissection (RPLND) or chemotherapy PEB × 1 cycle.
- **Stage IIA:** RPLND is performed. If patients have persistently elevated markers after RPLND, then PEB × 3 cycles are given.
- **Stage IIB, IIC, III:** No RPLND, chemo PEB every 4 weeks × 4 cycles.
- **Residual mass after chemotherapy:** Resections are recommended for these patients. If the patient has a residual mass and negative markers but the mass is unresectable, then the patient can either be observed or have radiation therapy. If, after initial complete response or partial response to chemotherapy, the mass grows, then the recommendation is to resect the mass.
- **Mixed tumor:** Postorchiectomy-elevated AFP indicates mixed tumor, which should be treated as nonseminoma.

Radiation Therapy Technique

3D Technique

Patient is supine, arms by side, testicles in clam shell, IV contrast, CT simulated. **Borders**: Superior T10/T11; inferior for PA field L5/S1; if treating dogleg, then top of symphysis pubis; laterals for PA field 2 cm from vertebral edge (cover left renal hilum for left-sided tumor); if treating dogleg, then ipsilateral border 2 cm on pelvic bone; contralateral at transverse process up to L5/S1, then diagonally parallel with ipsilateral border then vertically to medial border of obturator and block humeral head. See Figs. 19.6 and 19.7. With coffee table and extended tray block 5 cm beyond field, there is about 0.5% dose to the testis (fractionated tolerance dose for sterility is 1–2 Gy). Recovery of sperm count is dependent on dose and can take up to a year or more.

Volumes

GTV = gross disease (none after surgery) or nodal mass

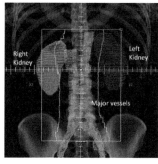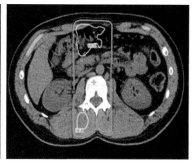

FIGURE 19.6   The **left panel** shows a stage I testicular cancer treated adjuvant RT, paraaortic field 3D AP view with the superior border at T11/T12, and the inferior border at L5/S1. The **right panel** shows axial CT with isodose distribution for a 3D-CRT treatment plan.

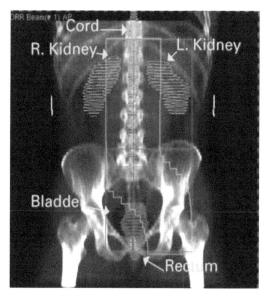

FIGURE 19.7   DRR for stage IIA testicular cancer, 3-D AP field, showing a dogleg field. The superior border is at T10/T11 and the inferior border is at the symphysis pubis.

CTV1 = GTV (none after surgery) + grossly involved LNs with 2–3 cm margin - + elective retroperitoneal LNs with 1.2–1.9 cm expansion on the inferior vena cava and aorta
CTV2 = cone down to nodal mass with 2–3 cm margin
PTV = CTV + 0.5 cm

Elective LNs

Stage I: paracaval, precaval, and interaortocaval LNs for right sided tumors and at least the preaortic and lateral aortic nodes for left-side tumors. Contour the inferior vena cava and aorta from bottom of T11 to L5/S1 where the blood vessels end +1.2−1.9 cm expansion on vessels.

Stage II: stage I elective LNs and ipsilateral common iliac, external and proximal internal iliac veins and arteries down to the upper border of the acetabulum +1.2−1.9 cm expansion on vessels.

Doses

PTV1 = 150−200 cGy/fx to 20−25.5 Gy
PTV 2:
Stage IIA = 150−200 cGy/fx to 30 Gy
Stage IIB = 150−200 cGy/fx to 36 Gy

Constraints

Kidney: V20 < 30%, if horseshoe kidney then RT is contraindicated.

Outcome

Seminoma local relapse of tumor <3 cm is 6%; 3−6 cm is 18%; >6 cm is 36%. Stage I disease-free survival is 97%, OS is 100%, stage IIA,B disease-free survival is 90%, stage IIC is 85%.

Complications

- Nausea/vomiting and diarrhea
- Transient azoospermia
- Decrease in fertility
- RT dose 15−20 cGy: temporary reduction in sperm count
- RT dose 20−200 cGy: transient azoospermia
- RT dose >200 cGy: permanent azoospermia
- Second malignancy: 5% at 15 years

Follow-Up

- Every 3 months for the first year, every 4 months for the second and third years, every 6 months for the fourth and fifth years, and every 12 months thereafter
- AFP and bHCG with every visit
- Chest X-ray, CT of the abdomen and pelvis with every visit

ANNOTATED BIBLIOGRAPHY

RENAL CELL CANCER

Ref 1. Siva et al. (2017). Stereotactic ablative body radiotherapy for inoperable primary kidney cancer: a prospective clinical trial. *BJU Int* 2017;120:623−30.

This was a prospective interventional clinical trial with 37 patients with T1−T2 primary renal cell carcinoma underwent SABR. Dose was 26 Gy in one fx if primary tumor <5 cm *in maximal dimension, or 14 Gy/fx to 42 Gy in three fxs if primary tumor =>5 cm. At median follow-up of 24 months, the data showed that*

Two-year outcomes:

Freedom from local progression: 100%

Distant progression: 89%

Overall survival: 92%

No grade 4, 5 toxicity, grade 3 toxicity 3%, grade 1–2 toxicity 78%

The study results show that SABR for primary RCC was feasible and well tolerated. The data showed encouraging cancer control, functional preservation, and early survival outcomes in an inoperable cohort.

Ref 2. Siva et al. (2018). Pooled analysis of stereotactic ablative radiotherapy for primary renal cell carcinoma: a report from the international radiosurgery oncology consortium for kidney (IROCK). *Cancer* March 1, 2018;124(5):934–42.

Data from 233 patients treated with SABR from nine international data sets from a consortium were pooled. Median dose was 25 Gy in one fx, of those treated with >1 fx median dose was 40 Gy in four fx.

Four year outcomes:

Local control: 97.8%

Cancer-specific survival: 91.9%

Progression-free survival: 65.4%

Grade 3, 4 toxicity 1.3%, grade 1, 2 toxicity 35.6%

The authors concluded that SABR is well tolerated and locally effective for primary RCC. In addition, they found that patients treated with single fraction SABR had less distant progression/death from RCC.

BLADDER CANCER

Neoadjuvant/Adjuvant Chemotherapy

Ref 3. International Collaboration of Trialists (2011). International phase III trial assessing neoadjuvant cisplatin, methotrexate, and vinblastine chemotherapy for muscle-invasive bladder cancer: long-term results of the BA06 30,894 trial. *J Clin Oncol* 1;29(16)2171–7. BA06 Trial.

In this trial, 976 patients with muscle-invasive bladder cancer (T2 gr 3, T3, T4, N0/Nx, M0) were randomized no neoadjuvant chemo versus CMV chemo × 3 cycles followed by cystectomy and/or radiotherapy. Each institution selected its preferred local treatment option (radiotherapy/cystectomy) to reduce individual bias in selection of treatments for specific patients. At median follow-up of 8 years, the data showed the following:

	10-Year Overall Survival
No neoadjuvant chemo	30
Neo adjuvant chemo	36
P value	0.037

The trial showed that CMV chemotherapy improves OS outcome as first-line adjunctive treatment for invasive bladder cancer and should be viewed as state of the art compared with cystectomy or radiotherapy alone for deeply invasive bladder cancer.

Ref 4. Kitamura H et al. (2014). Randomised phase III study of neoadjuvant chemotherapy with methotrexate, doxorubicin, vinblastine and cisplatin followed by radical cystectomy compared with radical cystectomy alone for muscle-invasive bladder cancer: Japan clinical oncology group study JCOG0209. *Ann Oncol*;25(6):1192–8. JCOG0209 Trial.

In this trial, 130 patients with muscle-invasive bladder cancer (T24aN0M0) patients were randomized to receive two cycles of neoadjuvant MVAC followed by radical cystectomy or radical cystectomy alone. At median follow-up of 55 months, the data showed the following:

	pT0 (%)	5-Year Progression-Free Survival (%)	5-Year Overall Survival (%)
No neoadjuvant chemo	9	56.4.	62.4
Neoadjuvant chemo	34	67.9	72.3
P value	<0.01	0.04	0.07

This trial showed that a significantly increased pT0 proportion and favorable OS of patients who received neoadjuvant MVAC chemotherapy.

Ref 5. Sternberg CN et al. (2015). Immediate versus deferred chemotherapy after radical cystectomy in patients with pT3-pT4 or N+M0 urothelial carcinoma of the bladder (EORTC 30,994): an intergroup, open label, randomized phase 3 trial. *Lancet Oncol*;16(1):76–86. EORTC 30994.

In this trial, 284 patients with muscle-invasive bladder cancer were randomized to immediate versus deferred combination chemotherapy MVAC ×6 cycles after radical cystectomy. After a median follow-up of 7 years, the data showed the following:

	5-Year Progression-Free Survival (%)	Overall Survival (%)
Deferred chemo	31.8	no
Immediate chemo	47.6	diff
P value	<0.0001	ns

The data did not show a significant improvement in OS with immediate versus deferred chemotherapy after radical cystectomy.

ChemoRT Bladder Conservation

Ref 6. Mitin T et al. (2016). Long-term outcomes among patients who achieve complete or near-complete responses after the induction phase of bladder preserving combined modality therapy for muscle-invasive bladder cancer: a pooled analysis of NRG Oncology/RTOG 9906 and 0233. *Int J Radiat Biol Phys*;94(1):67–74. RTOG 9906 Trial.

A pooled analysis was performed on 119 patients with muscle-invasive bladder cancer enrolled on NRG 9906 and RTOG 0233, who were classified as having a complete (T0) or near complete (Ta or Tis) response after induction chemoRT and completed consolidation with a total RT dose or at least 60 Gy. At median follow-up of 5.9 years, the data showed the following:

	Bladder Recurrence-Free Survival (%)	5-Year Disease-Free Survival (%)	5-Year Overall Survival (%)
Near complete response	72	67	61
Complete response	68	85	72
P value	0.70	0.11	0.12

The analysis shows that the outcomes are similar between patients who achieve a complete response (T0) or near-complete response (Ta or Tis) after the induction phase of bladder-preservation trimodality therapy and suggests that it is reasonable to continue with bladder-preservation therapy in patients who achieve near-complete response to the induction phase.

Ref 7. Emma H et al. (2017). BC2001 long-term outcomes: a phase III randomized trial of chemoradiotherapy versus radiotherapy (RT) alone and standard RT versus reduced high-dose volume RT in muscle-invasive bladder cancer. *J Clin Oncol* February 2017;35(6_suppl):280. BC 2001 Trial.

In this study, 458 patients with MIBC (pT2-T4a N0 M0) were randomized in a 2×2 factorial design (stratified by center and use of neoadjuvant chemotherapy [neoCT]) to CRT versus RT alone and/or to standard RT (sRT) (to tumor and whole bladder with 1.5 cm margin) versus reduced high-dose volume RT (rvRT) (tumor +1.5 cm margin treated to 100 (+/−5)% target dose and remaining bladder to 80% target dose). RT was 64 Gy/32 fx in 6.5 weeks (wks) or 55 Gy/20 fx in 4 wks (as per center policy). CRT was mitomycin C (12 mg/m^2 iv bolus, MMC) day one of RT and 5-fluorouracil (5-FU) continuous infusion at 500 mg/m^2/24 h for 10 days in total corresponding to fx 1–5 (wk 1) and fx 16–20 (wk 4) of RT. At median follow-up of 118 months, the results showed the following:

	5-Year LRC (%)	2-Year Salvage Cystectome (%)	Overall Survival (%)
RT	49	17	no
cRT	63 ss	11	diff

(Continued)

	5-Year LRC (%)	2-Year Salvage Cystectome (%)	Overall Survival (%)
P value		0.03	
sRT	no		no
rvRT	diff		diff

This study showed that in medically inoperable bladder cancer, (1) CRT using MMC-5FU is well tolerated and significantly improves local recurrence DFS compared with RT alone with good bladder function and no increase in late toxicity and (2) reducing dose to uninvolved bladder has minimal effect on either local control or toxicity.

PROSTATE CANCER

Conservative Treatment

Ref 8. Bill-Axelson et al. (2014). Radical prostatectomy or watchful waiting in early prostate cancer. *N Eng J Med*;370:932−942.

In this study, 695 patients with localized prostate cancer were randomly assigned to watchful waiting versus radical prostatectomy. The results at median follow-up of 23.2 years showed the following:

	Death from (%)	All cumulative (%)
	Prostate Cancer (%)	Death (%)
Watchful waiting	28.7	68.9
Prostatectomy	17.7	56.1
P value 0.006	0.001	<0.001

This study showed that extended follow-up confirmed a substantial reduction in mortality after radical prostatectomy.

Ref 9. Hamdy et al. (2016). 10-year outcomes after monitoring, surgery, or radiotherapy for localized prostate cancer. *N Eng J Med*;375(15):1415−24. PROTECT Trial.

In this trial, 643 men between 50 and 69 years of age were randomized active monitoring, radical prostatectomy, and external beam radiotherapy for treatment of clinically localized prostate cancer. RT given 200 cGy/fx to 74 Gy. RT patients also received 3−6 months of neoadjuvant and concurrent ADT. At median follow-up of 10 years, the data showed the following:

	Incidence of Metastasis (%)	Prostate Cancer−Specific Survival (%)
Observation	6.3	98.8
RP	2.4	99
RT + ADT	3 ss	99.6 ss

This trial revealed that at 10 years, prostate cancer—specific mortality was low irrespective of the treatment assigned, with no significant difference among treatments. Surgery and RT were associated with lower incidences of disease progression and metastases than active monitoring.

Ref 10. Wilt TJ et al. (2017). Follow-up of prostatectomy versus observation for early stage prostate cancer. *N Eng J Med*;377(2):132—42. PIVOT trial.

In this trial, 731 patients with localized prostate cancer were randomized to observation or radical prostatectomy. At median follow-up of 12.7 years, the data showed the following:

	Death Due to Prostate Cancer (%)	*Total Death*
Observation	11.4	66.8
Surgery	7.4	61.3
P *value*	0.06	0.06

The trial showed after nearly 20 years of follow-up among men with localized prostate cancer, surgery was not associated with significantly lower all-cause or prostate-cancer mortality than observation.

Brachytherapy

Ref 11. Kittel et al. (2015). Long-term efficacy and toxicity of low-dose-rate 125I prostate brachytherapy as monotherapy in low-, intermediate-, and high-risk prostate cancer. *IJROBP*;92(4):884—93.

In this study, 1989 patients with low, intermediate, or high-risk prostate cancer were treated with prostate seed implant with 125I and followed on a prospective registry at a single institution. PSI dose was 144 Gy. Median follow-up was 5.8 years.

	10-Year Outcomes (All Groups) (%)
bRFS	81.5
DMFS	91.5
OS	76.1
PCSM	2.5

LDR monotherapy is an effective treatment even for select high or unfavorable intermediate-risk patients. Long-term toxicity rates were low.

Ref 12. Hauswald et al. (2016). High-dose-rate monotherapy for localized prostate cancer: 10 year results. *IJROBP*;94(4):667—75.

In this study, 448 men with low, intermediate-risk prostate cancer treated with HDR mono-
therapy and a median dose of 43.5 Gy in six fractions. Median follow-up was 6.5 years.
10-year PSA PFS (progression-free survival) = 97.8%
10-year OS = 76.7%
LC 99.7%
DMFS 98.9%
CSS 99.1%
HDR monotherapy for low- and intermediate-risk prostate cancer is safe and effective.

Ref 13. Morris WJ et al. (2017). Androgen suppression combined with elective nodal and dose escalated radiation therapy (the ASCENDE-RT trial): an analysis of survival endpoints for a randomized trial comparing a low-dose-rate brachytherapy boost to a dose-escalated external beam boost for high- and- intermediate-risk prostate cancer. *Int J Radiat Oncol Biol*;98(2):275–85. ASCENDE Trial.

In this trial, 398 men had high-tier intermediate and high-risk prostate cancer were random-
ized to a standard arm with 12 months of androgen deprivation therapy (ADT), pelvic RT to
46 Gy, followed by a dose-escalated external beam RT (DE-EBRT) boost of 32 Gy, or an exper-
imental arm of a low-dose brachytherapy (LDR-PB) boost of I-125 dose of 115 Gy. At median
follow-up of 6.5 years the data showed the following:

	9-Year bPFS (%)	*9-Year Intermediate-Risk bPFS (%)*	*9-Year High-Risk bPFS (%)*
DE-EBRT	62	70	58
LDR-PB	83	94	78
P *value*	<0.001	<0.001	0.05

This study showed that compared with 78 Gy EBRT, men randomized to LDR-PB were
twice as likely to be free of biochemical failure at a median follow-up of 6.5 years.

Ref 14. Ennis et al. (2018). Brachytherapy-based radiotherapy and radical prostatectomy are associated with similar survival in high-risk localized prostate cancer. *JCO*;36(12):1192–6.

In this study, 42,765 prostate cancer patients with high risk, localized disease from National
Cancer Data Base treated with radical prostatectomy, EBRT + ADT or EBRT + BT ± ADT.
At median follow-up of 36 months, the data showed the following:

	HR Compared With RP Unweighted
EBRT + ADT	1.95
EBRT + BT ± ADT	1.45

This study showed that high-risk prostate cancer patients treated with EBRT + BT ± ADT
have similar survival to those treated with radical prostatectomy.

Lymph Node Treatment

Ref 15. Roach et al. (2013). Radiation therapy oncology group (RTOG) 9413: a randomized trial comparing whole pelvic radiation therapy (WPRT) to prostate only (PORT) and neoadjuvant hormonal therapy (NHT) to adjuvant hormonal therapy (AHT). *Int J Radiat Oncol Biol* October 1, 2013;87(2 supplement):S106–7. RTOG 9413 Trial.

This is a phase III trial comparing whole pelvis RT followed by a cone-down boost to boost RT only and comparing neoadjuvant to adjuvant TAB. 1300 patients with any T stage, LN risk >15%, PSA <100, ineligible for 9408 randomized to four arms as NHT + RT: small field RT dose 70.2 Gy versus NHT + RT: large field, RT dose 50.4 + 19.8 = 70.2 Gy versus RT + AHT: small field, 70.2 Gy versus RT + AHT: large field, 50.4 + 19.8 = 70.2 Gy. PSA failure was defined as two consecutive rises or a PSA >4 at last follow-up after a nadir. At a median follow-up of 10 years, the results showed the following:

	BF (%)	*Progression-Free Survival (%)*	*Overall Survival (%)*
NHT + PORT	—	—	*No*
NHT + WPRT	*Improved*	*Improved*	*Diff*
P *value*	*0.01*	*0.03*	*Ns*

The RTOG 9413 continues to demonstrate that NHT + WPRT improve biochemical failure compared with NHT + PORT.

Ref 16. Pommier P et al. (2016). Is there a role for pelvic irradiation in localized prostate adenocarcinoma? Update of the long-term survival results of the GETUG -01 randomized study. *Int Radiat Oncol Biol*;96(4):759–69. GETUG 01 Trial.

In this trial, 446 patients with T1b-T3, N0pNx, M0 patients were randomized to prostate-only versus pelvic nodes + prostate. Short-term 6-month neoadjuvant and concomitant hormonal therapy was allowed only for high-risk (T3 or gleason score <6, or PSAx3 upper normal limit of laboratory) patients. The total RT dose increased from 66 to 70 Gy during the course of the study. At median follow-up of 11.4 years, the data showed the following:

		Overall survival	
	LR	*HR*	*All*
NHT + PORT	*84*	*71.2*	*73.6*
NHT + WPRT	*87.7*	*71*	*74.9*
P *value*	*0.79*	*0.56*	*0.53*

The trial showed that pelvic nodes irradiation did not statistically improve event-free survival or OS in the whole population.

Dose Escalation With Higher Radiation Dose Treatment

Ref 17. Pasalic et al. (2018). A Twenty-Y Update on the Outcome of a Randomized Dose-Escalation Trial for Prostate Cancer. *IJROBP*; vol 102. num 35. supp 2018, abs 61, S31.

In this study, 301 patients with T1b-T3 prostate cancer randomized to EBRT with 70 Gy versus 78 Gy. RT given initially four fields to 46 Gy, then six fields conformal to boost dose, specified to isocenter. PSA failure defined as nadir +2. At median follow-up was 14.3 years, the data showed the following:

	Freedom From Biochemical/ Clinical Failure (%)	DSF (%)	Overall Survival (%)	Grade >2 toxicity (%)	
				GI	GU
70 Gy	53.8	68.4	No	13	8
78 Gy	74.3	82.3	diff	26	13
P value	0.0018	0.074	n/a	ns	ns

This study confirmed that dose escalation improved freedom from biochemical failure and clinical progression, however, had no impact on OS. Although GI toxicity was higher in the high-dose arm, GU toxicity was less and no significant.

Ref 18. Heemsbergen WD et al. (2014). Long-term results of the Dutch randomized prostate cancer trial: impact of dose-escalation on local, biochemical, clinical failure and survival. *Radiother Oncol*;110(1):104–9. Dutch Trial.

In this study, 664 patients with T1b-T4N0 prostate cancer were randomized between 68 and 78 Gy. RT used was 3D-CRT. Hormonal treatment was permitted and was at the discretion of the treating physician. At median follow-up of 110 months, the data showed the following:

	Biochemical Failure(%)	LF (%)	Prostate Cancer death	Overall Survival (%)
68 Gy	—	—	No	No
78 Gy	20% less	50% less	diff	diff
P value	<0.05	<0.05	ns	ns

The study observed significantly less biochemical failure and LF in the high-dose arm; however, similar rates of prostate cancer death and OS were observed in both arms.

Ref 19. Dearnalaley DP et al. (2014). Escalated-dose versus control-dose conformal radiotherapy for prostate cancer:long-term results from MRC RT01 randomized controlled trail. *Lancet Oncol*;15(4):464–73. MRC Trial.

In this trial, 843 patients with T1b–T3a prostate cancer with PSA of less than 50 ng/mL were randomly assigned to 200 cGy/fx to 64 Gy versus 74 Gy. All patients received neoadjuvant ADT for 3–6 month before the start of conformal radiotherapy, which continued until the end of conformal radiotherapy. At median follow-up of 10 years, the data showed the following:

	Biochemical Progression-Free Survival (%)	Overall Survival (%)
64 Gy	43	71
74 Gy	55	71
P value	0.0003	0.96

This study showed that escalated dose conformal RT with neoadjuvant ADT showed an advantage in biochemical PFS, but this advantage did not translate into an improvement on OS.

Hypofractionated Radiation Treatment

Ref 20. Lee WR et al. (2014). Randomized phase III noninferiority study comparing two radiotherapy fractionated schedules in patients with low risk prostate cancer. *J Clin Oncol*;34(20):2325–32. RTOG 0415 Trial.

In this trial, 1115 men with low-risk (T1b-2c, gleason score two to six, PSA <10) prostate cancer were randomized to C-RT (180 cGy/fx to 73.8 Gy) versus H-RT (250 cGy/fx to 70 Gy). At median follow-up of 5.8 years the data showed the following:

	Biochemical Recurrence (%)	5-Year Disease-Free Survival (%)	5-Year Overall Survival (%)	Late GI Grade 2 −3 (%)
C-RT	8.1	85.3	93.2	13.8
H-RT	6.3	86.3	92.5	22.4
P value	<0.001	<0.001	0.008	0.0021

This study showed that men with low-risk prostate cancer, the efficacy of 70 Gy in 28 fractions over 5.6 weeks is not inferior to 73.8 Gy in 41 fractions in 8.2 weeks, although an increase in late GI adverse events was observed in patients treated with H-RT.

Ref 21. Dearnaley D et al. (2016). Conventional versus hypofractionated high-dose intensity-modulated radiotherapy for prostate cancer: 5-year outcomes of the randomised, non-inferiority, phase 3 CHHip trial. *Lancet Oncol*;17(8):1047–60. CHHip Trial.

In this trial, 3216 men with localized prostate cancer (pT1b-T3aN0M0) were randomized to conventional (74 Gy given in 37 fractions) or one of two hypofractionated schedules (60 Gy in 20 fractions or 57 Gy in 19 fractions), all given with IMRT. Patients were given RT with 3—6 months of neoadjuvant and concurrent androgen suppression. At median follow-up of 62.4 months the data showed the following:

| | 5-Year (%) bFS/cFS | Overall Survival (%) | Toxicity Grade >2 | |
			GI	GU
74 Gy	88.3	no	13.7	9.1
60 Gy	90.6 (0.0018)	diff	11.9	11.7
57 Gy	85.9 (0.48)	no diff	11.3	6.6

This study showed that hypofractionated RT using 60 Gy in 20 fractions in noninferior to conventional fractionations using 74 Gy for localized prostate cancer.

Ref 22. Catton C et al. (2017). Randomized trial of hypofractionated radiation regimen for the treatment of localized prostate cancer. *J Clin Oncol* June 2017; 35(17):1884—90. PROFIT Trial.

In this trial, 1206 men with intermediate-risk prostate cancer (T1-2a, gleason score <6, and PSA 10.1—20 ng/mL, or T1-2, gleason score 7, and PSA <20 ng/mL), were randomized to 200 cGy/fx to 78 Gy versus 300 cGy/fx to 60 Gy. ADT was not permitted with therapy. At median follow-up of 6 years, the data showed the following:

| | Biochemical Disease-Free Survival (%) | Prostate Death | All (pt) Death | Late Toxicity (%) | |
				GI > gr3	GU > gr3
78 Gy	85	12	78	1.5	2.8
60 Gy	85ns	10ns	76	2.7ns	2

This trial showed that the hypofractionated RT regimen used in this trial was not inferior to conventional RT and was not associated with increased late toxicity.

Ref 23. Widmark et al. (2018). Ultrahypofractionation for prostate cancer: outcome from the Scandinavian phase 3 HYPO-RT-PC trial. *Radiother Oncol* April 2018;127(1):S-314; Abstract OC-0599 at ESTRO 37.

In this study, 1200 men with intermediate-risk prostate cancer patients with tumor stages of T1c-T3a, prostate-specific antigen (PSA) levels of 20 or below, and one or two of three risk factors: stage T3a, a Gleason tumor score of seven or higher, or a PSA level greater than 10.

Patients were randomized to one of two treatment arms: 200 cGy/fx to 78 Gy in 8 weeks versus 6.1 Gy/fx to 42.7 Gy in 2.5 weeks. ADT was not allowed among study participants. At median follow-up of 60 months the data showed the following:

	5-Year FFS (%) Biochemical/Clinical	Late Grade 2 (%)	
		Urinary	Bowel
CF 78 Gy	83.8	3.5	2.3
U−HF42.7 Gy	83.7	2.5	1.2
P value	ns	0.75	0.69

The authors deemed that the U−HF regimen is noninferior to conventional fractionation.

Neoadjuvant and Adjuvant Hormonal Treatment

Ref 24. Pisansky TM et al. (2015). Duration of androgen suppression before radiotherapy for localized prostate cancer: radiation therapy oncology group randomized clinical trail 9910. *J Clin Oncol*;33(4):332−9. RTOG 9910 Trial.
In this trial, 1579 men with intermediate-risk prostate cancer were randomly assigned 8 weeks of AS followed by RT with an additional 8 weeks of concurrent AS (16 weeks total) or to 28 weeks of AS followed by radiotherapy with an additional 8 weeks of AS (36 weeks total). At median follow-up of 10 years, the data showed the following:

	10-Year PSA Failure (%)	10-Year Disease-Free Survival (%)	10-Year Overall Survival (%)
8 weeks + RT	27	95	66
28 weeks + RT	27	96	67
P value	0.77	0.45	0.62

This study showed that extending AS from 8 to 28 weeks before RT did not improve outcomes in intermediate-risk group prostate cancer patients.

Ref 25. Mason MD et al. (2015). Final report of the Intergroup randomized study of combined androgen-deprived therapy radiotherapy versus androgen-deprivation therapy alone in locally advanced prostate cancer. *J Clin Oncol*;33(19):2143−50. Intergroup Trial.
In this trial, 1205 patients with locally advanced prostate cancer (T3-4,N0/Nx, M0 or T1-2 with either PSA more than 40 ug/L or PSA of 20−40 ug/L plus gleason score of 8−10, were randomly assigned to lifelong ADT alone or to ADT + RT. The RT dose was 64−69 Gy in

35−39 fractions to the prostate and pelvis or prostate alone. At a median follow-up of 8 years, the data showed the following:

	PSA (%) Progression-Free	Disease (%) Progression-Free	10-Year Overall Survival (%)
ADT	27	46	49
ADT + RT	63	74	55
P value	ss	ss	0.001

The analysis of this study showed that benefit of survival is maintained at a median follow-up of 8 years and firmly establishes the role of RT in the treatment of locally advanced prostate cancer.

Ref 26. Fossa SD et al. (2016). Ten and 15-year prostate cancer-specific mortality in patients with nonmetastatic locally advanced or aggressive intermediate prostate cancer, randomized to lifelong endocrine treatment alone or combined with radiotherapy: final results of Scandinavian Prostate Cancer Group-7. *Eur Urol;*70(4): 684−91. Scandinavian Trial.

In this trial, 875 patients with high-risk or intermediate PCa were randomized to ET (endocrine treatment) or ET + RAD. After 3 mo with total androgen blockade in all patients, all individuals continued lifelong antiandrogen monotherapy. Those randomized to ET + RAD started prostate radiotherapy (70 Gy) at 3 mo. At median survival of 12 years, the data showed the following:

	15-Year PCa-Specific Mortality Rate (%)
ET	34
ET + RAD	17
P value	<0.001

The study analysis showed that adding radiation therapy to lifelong antiandrogen therapy halves the absolute risk of death from prostate cancer.

Ref 27. Dubray et al. (2016). Does short-term androgen depletion add to high dose radiotherapy (80 Gy) in localized intermediate risk prostate cancer? Final analysis of GETUG 14 randomized trial (EU-20503/NCT00104741). *J Clin Oncol* May 2016;34(15_suppl):5021.

In this study, 377 patients with intermediate-risk localized prostate adenocarcinoma patients randomly assigned to high-dose conformal radiotherapy (prostate 80 Gy/40 fractions; seminal vesicles 46 Gy/23 fractions) either alone (group RT) or in combination with 4-month androgen deprivation (flutamide + triptorelin starting 2 months before radiotherapy, group AD-RT). At median follow-up of 84 months, the data showed the following:

	Biochemical-Free Survival (%)	*Overall Survival (%)*
RT	*76*	*94*
ADT + RT	*84*	*93*
P *value*	*0.02*	*0.54*

This study revealed that 4 months of androgen blockade improves event-free survival at 5 years in pts with intermediate-risk prostate adenocarcinoma when treated with high dose radiotherapy.

Ref 28. Lawton AF et al. (2017). Duration of androgen deprivation in locally advanced prostate cancer: Long-term update of NRG Oncology RTOG 9202. *Int J Radiat Oncol Biol* 98(2):296–303. RTOG 9202 Trial.

In this study, 1500 patients with LAPC T2c-T4 with PSA <150 ng/mL were randomized. All patients received flutamide and Zoladex ×2 months before and ×2 months during RT and were randomized to no further therapy (STAD) or 2 years of additional Zoladex (LTAD). A radiation dose of 65–70 Gy was given to the prostate and a dose of 44–50 Gy to the pelvic LNs. At median follow-up of 19.6 years the results showed the following:

	Local (RR%) Progression	*Distant (RR%) Metastases*	*Disease-Free Survival (%)*	*Overall Survival (%)*
STAD	–	–	–	–
LTAD	*46 reduced*	*36 reduced*	*29 improved, 12 improved*	
P *value*	*0.02*	*<0.0001*	*<0.0001*	*0.03*

This study showed that LTAD and RT are superior to STAD and RT for the treatment of locally advanced nonmetastatic adenocarcinoma of the prostate and should be considered the standard of care.

RR—relative reduction.

Hormonal Treatment and Chemotherapy

Ref 29. Sandler HM et al. (2015). A phase III protocol of androgen suppression (AS) and 3DCRT/IMRT versus AS and AS and 3DCRT/IMRT followed by chemotherapy (CT) with docetaxel and prednisone for localized, high-risk prostate cancer (RTOG 0521). *J Clin Oncol*;33(18), suppl-published online. RTOG 0521 Trial.

In this trial, 612 patients with high risk prostate cancer (1) gl seven to eight, any T stage, PSA >20 or (2) gl 8, >2 T, any PSA, or (3) gl 9–10, any T stage, any PSA (all had PSA <150). RT dose 75.6 Gy. CT consisted of 6, 21-day cycle of docetaxel + prednisone starting 28 days after RT. At median follow-up of 5.5 years, the data showed the following:

	5-Year Disease-Free Survival (%)	4-Year Overall Survival (%)
AS + RT	66	89
AS + RT + CT	73	93
P value	0.05	0.03

This study analysis showed that for high risk, localized PCa, adjuvant CT improved OS at 4 years. Toxicity was acceptable.

Ref 30. James ND et al. (2016). Addition of docetaxel, zoledronic acid, or both to first-line long-term hormone therapy in prostate cancer (STAMPEDE): survival results from an adaptive, multiarm, multistage, platform randomized controlled trial. *Lancet*;387(10024):1163–77. STAMPEDE Trial.

In this trial 2962 patients with high risk, locally advanced, metastatic or recurrent prostate cancer were randomized hormone therapy for at least 2 years + RT (SOC) versus SOC + ZA versus SOC + Doc versus SOC + ZA + Doc. Zoledronic acid (4 mg) was given for six 3-weekly cycles, then 4-weekly until 2 years, and docetaxel (75 mg/m2) for six 3-weekly cycles with prednisone 10 mg daily. At median follow-up of 43 months, the data showed the following:

	Median Overall Survival (Months)
SOC	71
SOC + ZA	Not reached
SOC + Doc	81ss
SOC + ZA + Doc	76ss

The analysis of this trial showed that adding Zoledronic acid no evidence of survival improvement and should not be part of standard care for this population. Docetaxel chemotherapy, given at the time of long-term hormone therapy initiation, showed evidence of improved survival. Docetaxel should be part of standard of care for adequately fit men commencing long-term hormone therapy.

Ref 31. James ND et al. (2017). Abiraterone for prostate cancer not previously treated with hormone therapy. *N Eng J Med* 2017;377:338–51. STAMPEDE Trial.

In this trial, 1917 patients with high risk locally advanced or metastatic prostate cancer patients, hormone naïve, were randomized to ADT alone or ADT + abiraterone acetate (1000 mg daily) and prednisone (5 mg daily). Local RT was mandatory for node negative, non-metastatic disease and encouraged for those with positive nodes. Treatment continued for 2 years or until any type of progression. At median follow-up of 40 months, the data showed the following:

	3-Year Overall Survival (%)	Toxicity Grade 3, 4
ADT	76	33
ADT + Abiraterone	83	47

This study concluded that among men with locally advanced or metastatic prostate cancer, ADT plus abiraterone and prednisone was associated with higher rates of OS than ADT alone.

Postoperative Radiation Treatment

Postoperative Radiation Treatment and Hormone Therapy

Ref 32 Bolla M et al. (2012). Postoperative radiotherapy after radical prostatectomy for high-risk prostate cancer: long-term results of a randomized controlled trial (EORTC trial 22911). *Lancet*;380(9858):2018−27. EORTC 22911 Trial.

In this study, 1005 patients with prostate cancer, s/p prostatectomy with pN0 M0 tumors and one or more pathological risk factors—capsule perforation, positive surgical margins, invasion of seminal vesicles—were randomized to wait-and-see policy versus immediate postoperative radiotherapy (60 Gy conventional irradiation delivered over 6 weeks). At median follow-up of 10.6 years, the results showed the following:

	Biochemical Progression-Free Survival (%)	Late Adverse Effects (%)
Surgery alone	39.4	59.7
Surgery + post-op RT	61.8	70.8
P value	<0.000	0.001

The study analysis shows that conventional postoperative irradiation significantly improves biochemical PFS and local control compared with a wait and see policy.

Ref 33. Wiegel T et al. (2014). Adjuvant radiotherapy versus wait-and-see after radical prostatectomy: 10-year follow-up of the ARO 96-02/AUO AP 09/95 trial. *Eur Urol*;66(2):243−50. ARO/AUO Trial.

In this trial, 388 patients after RP, with pT3pN0 prostate cancer were randomized to WS (wait and see) or three-dimensional conformal ART with 60 Gy. At median follow-up of 113 months the data showed the following:

	10-Year Progression-Free Survival (%)	Mets-Free (%) Survival	Overall Survival (%)
WS	35	No	No
ART	56	Diff	Diff
P value	<0.0001		

The analysis showed that compared with WS, ART reduced the risk of PFS in pT3 PCa.

Ref 34. Tendulkar et al. (2016). Contemporary update of a multi-institutional predictive nomogram for salvage radiotherapy after radical prostatectomy. *JCO*; 34(30):3648−54.

In this study, 2460 patients node-negative patients with a detectable post-RP prostate-specific antigen (PSA) treated with Salvage RT with or without concurrent ADT were obtained from 10 academic institutions. At median follow-up of 5 years, the data showed the following:

PreRT PSA	5-Year FFBF (%)
All patients	56
0.01−0.2	71
0.21−0.5	63
0.51−1	54
1.01−2	43
>2	37

The authors conclude that early salvage radiation with a low preradiation PSA was associated with improved FFBF, DM. On MVA, pre-RT PSA, Gleason score, ECE, SVI, margin status, ADT, and dose were associated with FFBF.

Ref 35. Carrie C et al. (2016). Salvage radiotherapy with or without short-term hormone therapy for rising prostate-specific antigen concentration after radical prostatectomy (GETUG-AFU 16): a randomized, multicenter, open-label phase 3 trial. *Lancet Oncol*;17(6):747−56. GETUG Trial.

In this trial, 743 patients who underwent radical prostatectomy, who has stage pT2, pT3, or pT4a (bladder neck involvement only) in patients who had rising PSA of 0.2 to less than two ug/ L after prostatectomy were randomly assigned RT of 200 cGy/fx to 66 Gy or RT + short-term androgen suppression using 10.8 mg goserelin by SC injection on the first day of irradiation and 3 months later. The data showed the following:

	5-Year Progression-Free Survival
RT	62
RT + ADT	80
P *value*	<0.0001

The study showed that adding short-term androgen suppression to salvage radiotherapy benefits men who have had radical prostatectomy and whose PSA rises after a postsurgical period when it is undetectable.

Ref 36. Shipley WU et al. (2017). Radiation with or without antiandrogen therapy in recurrent prostate cancer. *N Engl J Med*;376(5):417. RTOG 9601 Trial.

In this trial, 760 patients who has undergone prostatectomy with a lymphadenectomy, with a tumor stage of T2 (confined to prostate but with a positive surgical margin) or T3 (histologic extension beyond the prostatic capsule), no nodal involvement, and a detectable PSA level of 0.2−4 ng/mL to undergo radiation therapy and receive either antiandrogen therapy (24 months of bicalutamide at a dose of 150 mg daily) or daily placebo tablets during and after RT. At median follow-up of 13 years the data showed the following:

	Metastatic (%) Prostate Cancer	Overall Survival (%)
Post-op RT	23	71.3
Post-op RT + antiandrogen	14.5	76.3
P *value*	0.005	0.04

The study showed that addition of 24 months of antiandrogen therapy with daily bicalutimide to salvage RT resulted in significantly higher rates of long-term OS and lower incidences of metastatic prostate cancer and death from prostate cancer than radiation therapy plus placebo.

Ref 37. Pollak et al (2018). Short Term Androgen Deprivation Therapy Without or With Pelvic Lymph Node Treatment Added to Prostate Bed Only Salvage Radiotherapy: The NRG Oncology/RTOG 0534 SPPORT Trial. Presented at ASTRO 60th Annual Meeting, San Antonio, TX, October 2018. RTOG 0534 Trial.

In this study 1,792 men who had persistently detectable or rising PSA levels were randomly placed into three treatment groups: prostate bed radiation therapy (PBRT) alone, PBRT plus short-term androgen deprivation (hormone) therapy (STAD), and PBRT plus pelvic lymph node radiotherapy (PLNRT) plus STAD. Hormone therapy consisted of four-to-six months of

androgen deprivation. The RT dose was 45 Gy to the PLNRT and 64.8−70.2 Gy to the PBRT.
The data at 5 years showed that

	FFP (%)	Distant mets (pts)	OS (%)
PBRT	71	45	no
PBRT+STAD	81	38	statistical
PBRT+STAD+PLNRT	87	25	difference
p value	<0.0001	0.014	-

This study reveled that PLNRT+ PBRT+STAD superior to PBRT alone; PBRT+STAD superior to PBRT alone; PLNRT+PBRT+STAD superior to PBRT+STAD for prostate cancer patients in salvage RT.

TESTICULAR CANCER

Ref 38. Jones et al. (2005). Randomized trial of 30 versus 20 Gy in the adjuvant treatment of stage I testicular seminoma: a report on Medical Research Council Trial TE18, European Organisation for the Research and Treatment of Cancer Trial 30942 (ISRCTN18525328). *J Clin Oncol*;23(6):1200−8.

In this study 625 patients with stage I seminoma were randomly assigned 20 Gy/10 fx over 2 weeks or 30 Gy/15 fx during 3 weeks after orchidectomy. RT given was PA field with dogleg field for prior inguinal surgery. The results at 5 years showed the following:

	Relapse-Free Survival (%)	Moderate/Severe Lethargy (%)
30 Gy	97	20
20 Gy	96.4 ns	5

The study showed that treatment with 20 Gy in 10 fractions is unlikely to produce relapse rates more than 3% higher than for standard 30-Gy radiation therapy, and reductions in morbidity enable patients to return to work more rapidly.

Ref 39. Oliver RT et al. (2011). Randomized trial of carboplatin versus radiotherapy for stage I seminoma: mature results on relapse and contralateral testis cancer rates in MRC TE19/EORTC 30,982 study (ISRCTN27163214). *J clin Oncol*; 29(8):957−62. EORTC 30,981.

In this trial, 1447 patients with stage I seminoma postsurgery randomly assigned between RT and one infusion of carboplatin dosed at seven × (glomerular filtration rate+25) on the basis of EDTA and 90% of this dose if determined on the basis of creatinine clearance. RT was given to PA field to a dose between 20 and 30 Gy. At a median follow-up of 6.5 years, the data showed the following:

	RFR (%)	Contralat (%) GCT-Free
RT	96	99.8
Carboplatin	94.7	98.8
P value	0.36	0.03

This trial confirmed the noninferiority of single-dose carboplatin (at 7xAUC dose) versus RT in terms of RFR and establishes a statistically significant reduction in the medium-term risk of second GCT produced by treatment.

20

Gynecological Cancers

ENDOMETRIAL CANCER

The estimated incidence in the United States is 63,230 with an estimated 11,350 deaths in 2018.

The bladder and the rectum lie in front of and behind the uterus, respectively. The upper two-thirds of the uterus, the corpus, are separated by an isthmus from the lower one-third of the uterus, the cervix. The cervix itself is again divided into subvaginal and vaginal parts.

Lymphatics of the uterus are as follows:

- Superior part: drains through broad ligament to external iliac lymph node (LN) near the ovary, then to the paraaortic (PA) LN
- Inferior part: drains through broad ligament to LN at bifurcation of the common iliac

Pelvic/Paraaortic Node Risk

Involvement of the pelvic and PA LN is a function of the depth of invasion and grade of the carcinoma. In stage I patients, the depth of invasion is most important.

Invasive	Pelvic Lymph Node (%)			Paraaortic Lymph Node (%)		
	G1	G2	G3	G1	G2	G3
None	0	0	3	0	0	2
<50%	1	3	5	0	1	2
>50%	15	15	25	3	5	10

Data from Creasman WT, Morrow CP, Bundy BN, Homesley HD, Graham JE, Heller PB. Surgical pathologic spread patterns of endometrial cancer: a gynecologic oncology study group. Cancer 1987;60(8 Suppl):2035–41.

Fundamentals of Radiation Oncology
https://doi.org/10.1016/B978-0-12-814128-1.00020-9

Workup

Risk Factors
- Obesity, diabetes mellitus, hypertension, and tamoxifen use
- Early menarche, late menopause, prolonged estrogen exposure, and unopposed estrogens in postmenopausal patient
- Nulliparity
- Family history of uterine cancer
- Gonadal dysgenesis (Turner's syndrome)
- Sclerocystic ovaries (Stein-Leventhal syndrome)

Symptoms and Signs
- Abnormal vaginal bleeding, foul smelling vaginal discharge
- Bladder/bowel symptoms for advanced tumors
- Low back pain radiating to abdominal wall
- Physical exam should note organomegaly, palpation for uterine size, bimanual pelvic examination

Investigations
- CBC, chemistry (CA125 marker for extrauterine disease), Pap smear
- Pregnancy test, when indicated
- Outpatient aspiration curettage, endometrial biopsy
- Perform D&C if endometrial biopsy is nondiagnostic
- Surgical staging of simple hysterectomy with LN sampling (pelvic/PA) or sentinel LN biopsy
- Chest X-ray, CT abdomen/pelvis (in the suspicion of extrauterine disease), myometrial, and cervical invasion can be evaluated with MRI in preoperative staging. PETCT can be considered but not routinely performed.

TNM Staging (Endometrial Cancer)

TNM FIGO

Tis	*	Carcinoma in situ (preinvasive carcinoma)
T1	I	Tumor confined to corpus uteri
T1a	IA	Tumor limited to endometrium or invades less than one-half of the myometrium
T1b	IB	Tumor invades one-half or more of the myometrium
T2	II	Tumor invades stromal connective tissue of the cervix but does not extend beyond uterus**
T3a	IIIA	Tumor involves serosa and/or adnexa (direct extension or metastasis)
T3b	IIIB	Vaginal involvement (direct extension or metastasis) or parametrial involvement
T4	IVA	Tumor invades bladder mucosa and/or bowel mucosa (bullous edema is not sufficient to classify a tumor as T4) *FIGO staging no longer includes Stage 0 (Tis). **Endocervical glandular involvement only should be considered as Stage I and not Stage II

N0   No regional lymph node metastasis

N1   IIIC1   Regional lymph node metastasis to pelvic lymph nodes

N2   IIIC2   Regional lymph node metastasis to paraaortic lymph nodes, with or without positive pelvic lymph nodes

M0   No distant metastasis (no pathologic M0; use clinical M to complete stage group)

M1   IVB   Distant metastasis (includes metastasis to inguinal lymph nodes, intraperitoneal disease, lung, liver or bone. Excludes metastasis to paraaortic lymph nodes, vagina, pelvic serosa or adnexa)

Stage Grouping

Stage I	T1	N0	M0
Stage IA	T1a	N0	M0
Stage IB	T1b	N0	M0
Stage II	T2	N0	M0
Stage III	T3	N0	M0
Stage IIIA	T3a	N0	M0
Stage IIIB	T3b	N0	M0
Stage IIIC1	T1,2,3	N1	M0
Stage IIIC2	T1,2,3	N2	M0
Stage IVA	T4	Any N	M0
Stage IVB	Any T	Any N	M1

FIGO, International Federation of Gynecology and Obstetrics; M, (distant metastasis); *N*, (regional lymph nodes); *TNM*, T (tumor).
Used with permission of the American Joint Committee on Cancer (AJCC), Chicago, Illinois. The original source for this material is the AJCC Cancer Staging Manual, Eighth Edition (2017) published by Springer Science Business Media LLC, www.springer.com.

Treatment

Stage IA (Gr 1, 2)

Surgery TAH-BSO involving peritoneal washing. The uterus is bisected and checked for myometrial invasion and endocervical involvement, pelvic/PA LN sample, and gross LN excision followed by observation. Consider vaginal brachytherapy if multiple intermediate risk factors (age, positive lymphovascular invasion, tumor size, and lower uterine (cervical/glandular) involvement).

Stage IA (Gr 3)

TAH-BSO and surgical nodal staging followed by postop intracavitary vaginal brachytherapy [1, 2]. High risk (serous, clear cell [CC], carcinosarcoma) may consider platinum-based chemotherapy.

Stage IB (Gr 1, 2)

Surgery TAH-BSO, post-op intracavitary vaginal brachytherapy is indicated.

Stage IB (Gr 3), II, III

- TAH-BSO and surgical nodal staging. Postoperatively, stage II disease may receive brachytherapy alone in lower risk patients (microscopic cervical invasion, Grade 1/2 and adequately staged); for stage III disease postoperatively whole pelvic RT (WPRT) [2]. Consider brachytherapy boost after WPRT to the upper one-third of vagina for high risk patients [3, 4].
  - Stage IIIB (vaginal metastasis), recommended treatment is post-op RT to whole pelvis, then boost the vagina and parametrium followed by additional low dose rate (LDR) brachytherapy or alternatively, HDR brachytherapy.
  - IIIC patients at risk of positive margin after surgery, may consider preoperative whole pelvic ± paraaortic LNs radiation followed by ML block, then boost lateral pelvic wall to be followed by low-dose rate tandem and ovoid (LDR T&O) applicators or HDR; or, if treated postoperatively, then treat as above.
- Platinum-based concurrent or sequential chemotherapy is recommended for stage III [5, 6, 7].

Stage IV

- Surgical debulking followed in select patients by post-op WPRT and vaginal brachytherapy is recommended as noted above.
- Platinum-based concurrent or sequential chemotherapy [5, 6, 7].

Medically Inoperable

- Stage I, FIGO Gr 1/2 no pelvic LN by MRI and superficial muscle invasion—brachytherapy alone.
- All other stages—whole pelvis RT followed by brachytherapy boost.
- Stage III—consider platinum-based concurrent chemotherapy.

Papillary Serous or Clear Cell Carcinoma

- Stage I, select II—TAH-BSO and surgical nodal staging followed by chemotherapy (commonly, carboplatin and paclitaxel) and vaginal brachytherapy or pelvic radiation
- Stage II–IV—TAH-BSO and surgical nodal staging followed by chemotherapy and external beam radiation therapy (EBRT) with or without vaginal brachytherapy.

Uterine Sarcoma

- Recommended treatment is TAH/BSO. Lymphadenectomy is not required for leiomyosarcoma; however, for endometrial stromal sarcoma and carcinosarcoma (mixed müllerian tumors), lymphadenectomy is performed.

- Low-grade endometrial stromal sarcoma—hormonal treatment with progestational agents, tamoxifen or aromatase inhibitor is recommended.
- High-grade undifferentiated sarcoma and leiomyosarcoma—consider chemotherapy. Single-agent doxorubicin or combination regimen such as gemcitabine and docetaxel can be considered.
- Stage II, III high grade—consider post-op RT to increase local control.
- Medically inoperable sarcomas—treatment options are pelvic RT, chemotherapy, and hormonal therapy.

Radiation Therapy Technique

3D Technique

Patient is supine, arms above chest, on Vac-Lok system, CT simulated with vaginal/rectal marker in place. Use a four-field technique for whole pelvis to spare bowel. **Borders** are superior, L4/L5 (if PA+, then T12/L1); inferior, bottom of obturator foramen; and at least 4 cm below vaginal cuff; laterals, 2 cm on bony pelvis; anterior, anterior to symphysis pubis, posterior S2/S3. Custom blocks used to shield small bowel and femoral heads medially. Constraint for small bowel dose is 45–55 Gy; bladder dose is 70 Gy; rectum is 65 Gy; and vaginal surface is 100 Gy.

IMRT Technique

Preferred for post-op patients (RTOG 1203). The patient setup is similar to the 3D technique. 6-MV photons, use five to seven coplanar IMRT beams or two-arc VMAT for planning. Place radiopaque markers at the end of a long Q-tip into the vaginal apex to identify the vaginal apex on CT or can use intravaginal barium. The patient should have two CT scans: one with full bladder followed by empty bladder for simulation. The two CT scans then should be fused to account for vaginal cuff motion. The IMRT plan and daily treatments need to be done with full bladder. Figs. 20.1 and 20.2.

Volume

GTV = Postoperatively, there will be no GTV (or for medically inoperable T2 MRI gross disease, LNs)

CTV vagina full = vaginal target from full bladder CT scan (or for medically inoperable CTV Gyn target)

CTV vagina empty = vaginal target from empty bladder CT scan (or for medically inoperable CTV Gyn target)

ITV vagina = CTV vagina full + CTV vagina empty + additional margin 0.5–1 cm if rectal distension (or ITV Gyn = CTV Gyn full + CTV Gyn empty + additional margin 0.5–1 cm if rectal distension)

CTV LN = the iliac LNs and vessels +0.7 cm margin

PTV = ITV vagina (or ITV Gyn) + CTV LN + 0.5–1 m margin

Vaginal Target and Lymph Nodes

Gyn target: entire uterus, cervix, and upper 1–2 cm of vagina.

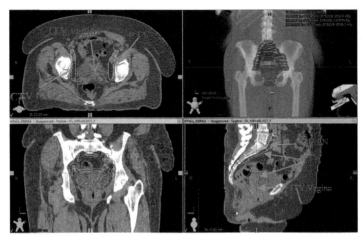

FIGURE 20.1   A uterine cancer patient with postoperative IIIC1 endometrial cancer with cervical stromal invasion (S1–S3 contoured). CT images showing target volumes CTV lymph node, ITV vagina, and PTV, for a patient with postoperative IIIC1 endometrial cancer with cervical stromal invasion (S1–S3 contoured).

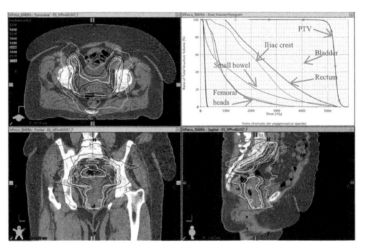

FIGURE 20.2   A uterine cancer patient with postoperative IIIC1 endometrial cancer with cervical stromal invasion. CT images showing a two-arc VMAT treatment plan isodose lines conforming to PTV and DVH meeting all constraints. A prescription dose to PTV is 50.4 Gy.

Vaginal target: vaginal cuff and paravaginal tissue, the upper border is delineated by the vaginal marker on Q-tip or via intravaginal barium, the inferior border is 1 cm below the obturator foramen.

LNs: common, external, obturator, internal iliac LNs. Nodal CTV should starts at 0.5–1 cm below the L4/L5 interspace, inferior border of external iliac is at the superior border of femoral head, inferior border of internal iliac and obturator LN is at the top of the pubic bone, presacral LN anterior border is 1 cm anterior to the sacrum and inferior border is at S3 (if cervix is involved with uterine cancer)

Dose for External Beam Radiation Therapy and Brachytherapy

Definitive RT: WPRT 180 cGy/fx to 45 Gy, boost gross pelvic LNs to 54–61.2 Gy. Followed by brachytherapy boost.

Post-op WPRT RT: 180 cGy/fx to 45–50.4 Gy

Stage IA (Gr 3): Post-op LDR vaginal brachytherapy surface dose to 50–70 Gy over 72 h. Alternatively, High-dose rate (HDR) brachytherapy RT to 6 Gy/fx to 30 Gy to the vaginal surface (or 7 Gy/fx to 21 Gy or 5 Gy/fx to 25 Gy to 0.5 cm) to the vaginal cuff and upper one-third of vagina.

Stage IB (Gr 3), II, III: Post-op WPRT to 45–50.4 Gy. Consider additional brachytherapy boost with intracavitary LDR dose to 30–35 Gy. Alternatively, HDR intracavitary RT to 6 Gy/fx to 12–18 Gy to vaginal surface (or 5 Gy/fx to 10–15 Gy to 0.5 cm) to the upper one-third of vagina.

Stage IIIB: Post-op RT to whole pelvis to 45 Gy, then boost the vagina and parametrium to 7.2 Gy to a total dose of 52.2 Gy, followed by additional LDR brachytherapy to 30–35 Gy. Alternatively, HDR brachytherapy RT to 6 Gy ×2 fx = 12 Gy to vaginal surface.

Stage IV: Post-op RT to whole pelvis to 45 Gy, then boost the vagina and parametrium to 7.2 Gy to a total dose of 52.2 Gy, followed by additional LDR brachytherapy to 30–35 Gy. Alternatively HDR brachytherapy RT to 6 Gy ×2 fx = 12 Gy to vaginal surface.

Medically inoperable:

Stage I, FIGO Gr 1/2, no pelvic LN by MRI and superficial muscle invasion: brachytherapy alone HDR RT to 8.5 Gy/fx to 34 Gy or 5 Gy/fx to 45 Gy to 2 cm from midpoint of the intrauterine source or to CTV (per Schwartz et al., 2015)*

All other stage: WPRT to 45 Gy followed by brachytherapy boost. LDR T&O in two 48-hour insertions to 30–35 Gy (load one tandem 10-15-10 mg and the other with 10 mg in the tip. If there is cervical stromal involvement, add ovoids for 60 Gy surface dose). Alternatively, HDR RT to 8.5 Gy/fx to 17 Gy or 5 Gy/fx to 25 Gy at 2 cm lateral from midpoint of intrauterine source or to CTV (per Schwartz et al.)*. Use two tandems (#1 and #2 curvature) curving away from each other (Y applicator).

Schwarz et al., 2015. Consensus statement for brachytherapy for the treatment of medically inoperable endometrial cancer. Brachytherapy September–October 2015;14(5):587–99.

Vaginal cuff recurrence: WPRT to 45 Gy followed by; if thickness <0.5 cm then HDR RT to 7 Gy/fx to 21 Gy to vaginal surface (or 5.5–22 Gy to 0.5 cm; if thickness >0.5 cm then interstitial brachytherapy.

Constraints

Upper vagina mucosa = 150 Gy, midvagina mucosa = 90 Gy, lower vagina mucosa = 60 Gy.

Small bowel (peritoneal cavity) V45 < 195 cc; V40 < 30%
Rectum V30 < 60%; V50 < 50%
Bladder V45 < 35%
Femoral head V30 < 15%; V50 < 5%
Iliac crest V40 < 37%

Outcome

- Stage I local control, 99%; overall survival (OS), 90%
- Stage II local control, 90%; OS 80%
- Stage IIIA disease-free survival, 70%
- Stage IIIB disease-free survival, 45%
- Stage IIIC disease-free survival, 45%
- Stage IV OS, 10%
- Medically inoperable early-stage disease-free survival, 80%.

Complications

- Skin reactions, pubic hair loss, diarrhea, cramps, rectal soreness and bleeding, anal discomfort, bowel or rectal damage, scarring or narrowing of bowel causing obstruction requiring surgical correction
- Urinary frequency/dysuria/nocturia, bladder damage with shrinkage, loss of capacity, and recurrent bladder infection
- Ovarian damage, such as cessation of menstrual periods, sterility
- Vaginal damage, such as soreness, irritation, dryness, or shrinkage with resulting difficulty during intercourse. **Note:** Post radiation, maintain sexual activity or prescribe vaginal dilator.

Follow-Up

- Every 3 months for the first year, every 6 months for the second year, and every 12 months thereafter
- CT chest, abdomen, and pelvis every 12 months for high-risk patients/histologies

CERVICAL CANCER

The estimated incidence in the United States is 13,240 with an estimated 4170 deaths in 2018.

Invasive cervical cancer is the third most common female cancer in the United States. However, it is the most common gynecologic cancer worldwide. It arises at the squamo-columnar junction of the endocervical canal and is associated with chronic inflammation of the cervix and carcinoma in situ (CIS). CIS precedes invasive carcinoma.

Lymph Node Risk

Stage	Pelvic Lymph Node (%)	Paraaortic Lymph Node (%)
IA	<5	—
IB	15	7
IIA	25	12
IIB	35	18
IIIA	45	25
IIIB/IV	>60	>30

Data from: 1. Morton DG, Lagasse LD, Moore JG, Jacob M, Amromin GD. Pelvic lymphnodectomy following radiation in cervical carcinoma. Obstet Gynecol Surv 1964;88:932. 2. Tanaka Y, Sawada S, Murata T. Relationship between lymph node metastases and prognosis in patients irradiated postoperatively for carcinoma of the uterine cervix. Acta Radiol Oncol 1984;23(6):455–59. 3. Sudarsanam A, Charyulu K, Belinson J, Averette H, Goldberg M, Hintz B, Thirumala M, Ford J. Influence of exploratory celiotomy on the management of carcinoma of the cervix: A preliminary report. Cancer 1978;41(3):1049–53. 4. Nelson JH Jr, Boyce J, Macasaet M, Lu T, Bohorquez JF, Nicastri AD, Fruchter R. Incidence, significance, and follow-up of paraaortic lymph node metastases in late invasive carcinoma of the cervix. Am J Obstet Gynecol 1977;128(3):336–40. 5. Berman ML, Keys H, Creasman W, DiSala P, Bundy B, Blessing J. Survival and patterns of recurrence in cervical cancer metastatic to periaortic lymph nodes (a Gynecologic Oncology Group study). Gynecol Oncol 1984;19(1):8–16.

Workup

Risk Factors
- Human papillomavirus 16, 18, 31, 33 (HPV 16: SCCa; HPV 18: adenocarcinoma)
- Poor access to routine health care, smoking, early sexual activity and multiple sexual partners, history of sexually transmitted disease, large number of pregnancies
- Oral contraceptive use
- Immune suppression
- Exposure to DES (diethylstilbestrol)—CC cancer

Symptoms and Signs
- Fatigue and anemia, postcoital spotting, and intermenstrual bleeding, foul-smelling vaginal discharge, hematuria/rectal bleeding in advanced stage, pelvic pain.
- Physical exam note for enlarged LNs (tumors involving lower vagina can metastasize to inguinal LNs), organomegaly, bony tenderness, and bilateral lower extremity edema. Pelvic exam should include bimanual examination.

Investigations
- CBC, liver/renal function tests, and Pap smear
- Pregnancy test, when indicated

- Colposcopy with biopsy of any suspicious areas and four quadrants
- LEEP (loop electrosurgical excision procedure)
- Conization if no apparent gross lesion(s) visible by colposcope but tumor suspected
- EUA to determine parametrial or pelvic sidewall tumor extension
- Cystoscopy, proctosigmoidoscopy as indicated (for stage IIB and above)
- Chest X-ray, IVP, barium enema as indicated for FIGO staging, CT chest/ abdomen/pelvis with contrast, MRI pelvis if suspicious of vaginal, bladder, or rectal involvement (for stage IIB and above). PET/CT to evaluate supraclavicular and PA LN involvement (for stage IIB and above)

Note: CT, MRI, and PET/CT imaging are used for accurate definition of the extent of disease and RT volumes but do not change the FIGO clinical stage.

TNM Staging (Cervical Cancer)

TNM FIGO

Tis	*	Carcinoma in situ (preinvasive carcinoma)
T1	I	Cervical carcinoma confined to uterus (disregard extension to corpus)
T1a**	IA	Invasive carcinoma diagnosed only by microscopy. Stromal invasion with a maximum depth of 5.0 mm measured from the base of the epithelium and a horizontal spread of 7.0 mm or less. Vascular space involvement, venous or lymphatic, does not affect classification
T1a1	IA1	Measured stromal invasion 3.0 mm or less in depth and 7.0 mm or less in horizontal spread
T1a2	IA2	Measured stromal invasion more than 3.0 mm and not more than 5.0 mm with a horizontal spread 7.0 mm or less
T1b	1B	Clinically visible lesion confined to the cervix or microscopic lesion > T1a/IA2
T1b1	IB1	Clinically visible lesion 4.0 cm or less in greatest dimension
T1b2	IB2	Clinically visible lesion >4.0 cm in greatest dimension
T2	II	Cervical carcinoma invades beyond uterus but not to pelvic wall or lower third of vagina
T2a	IIA	Tumor without parametrial invasion
T2a1	IIA1	Clinically visible lesion <4.0 cm in greatest dimension
T2a2	IIA2	Clinically visible lesion >4.0 cm in greatest dimension
T2b	IIB	Tumor with parametrial invasion
T3	III	Tumor extends to pelvic wall and/or involves lower third of vagina, and/or causes hydronephrosis or non functioning kidney
T3a	IIIA	Tumor involves lower third of vagina, no extension to pelvic wall

T3b	IIIB	Tumor extends to pelvic wall and/or causes hydronephrosis or nonfunctioning kidney
T4	IVA	Tumor invades mucosa of bladder or rectum, and/or extends beyond true pelvis (bullous edema is not sufficient to classify a tumor as T4) *FIGO staging no longer includes Stage 0 (Tis). **All macroscopically visible lesions—even with superficial invasion—are T1b/IB.
N0		No regional lymph node metastasis
N1		Regional lymph node metastasis
M0		No distant metastasis (no pathologic M0; use clinical M to complete stage group)
M1	IVB	Distant metastasis (including peritoneal spread, involvement of supraclavicular or mediastinal lymph nodes, lung, liver, or bone)

Stage Grouping

Stage I	T1	Any N	M0
Stage IA	T1a	Any N	M0
Stage IA1	T1a1	Any N	M0
Stage IA2	T1a2	Any N	M0
Stage IB	T1b	Any N	M0
Stage IB1	T1b1	Any N	M0
Stage IB2	T1b2	Any N	M0
Stage II	T2	Any N	M0
Stage IIA	T2a	Any N	M0
Stage IIA1	T2a1	Any N	M0
Stage IIA2	T2a2	Any N	M0
Stage IIB	T2b	Any N	M0
Stage III	T3	Any N	M0
Stage IIIA	T3a	Any N	M0
Stage IIIB	T3b	Any N	M0
Stage IVA	T4	Any N	M0
Stage IVB	Any T	Any N	M1

FIGO, International Federation of Gynecology and Obstetrics; M, (distant metastasis); *N*, (regional lymph nodes); *TNM*, T (tumor).
Used with permission of the American Joint Committee on Cancer (AJCC), Chicago, Illinois. The original source for this material is the AJCC Cancer Staging Manual, Eighth Edition (2017) published by Springer Science Business Media LLC, www.springer.com.

Treatment

Cervical Intraepithelial Neoplasia

If PAP shows dysplasia or cancer, then examine by colposcopy and biopsy. If atypia is seen, then treat as infection and repeat the process.

Carcinoma in situ

Recommended treatments are cryosurgery, laser surgery, and LEEP. Consider simple hysterectomy if there is recurrence. Consider conization to retain fertility.

Stage IA1, IA2
- Cervical conization or patients with stage IA1 disease without LVSI can be managed with trachelectomy or extrafascial hysterectomy.
- Modified radical hysterectomy for patients with IA1 with positive LVSI and IA2.
- For fertility sparing vaginal radical trachelectomy.

Stage IB1, IIA1
- Treatment is modified radical hysterectomy and pelvic LN dissection with optional PA LN sampling.
- Intermediate-risk patients (Sedlis criteria: tumor size >4 cm, deep stromal invasion, presence of LVI) will receive post-op RT.
- High-risk patients (positive parametrium, positive LN, positive margin) will receive post-op concurrent chemoRT.
- Chemotherapy is CDDP 40 mg/m^2 every week X6 weeks, given concurrently with RT.

Stage IB2–IVA
- Treatment is definitive concurrent chemoRT involving pelvic RT and brachytherapy [8, 9, 10, 12, 13] to define RT fields accurately, radiological, or surgical determination of PA involvement is recommended.
  - If imaging or surgery is negative for PA LN metastasis, RT dose to whole pelvis is followed by brachytherapy.
  - If imaging or surgery is positive for PA LN metastasis, RT dose to PA and pelvis with PA LN boost dose is followed by brachytherapy.
  - Consider parametrial boost after midline block, if indicated.
- Chemotherapy 40 mg/m^2 cisplatin every week X6 weeks given concurrently during weeks of external beam radiation.
- Adding gemcitabine or paclitaxel to weekly cisplatin may improve treatment results and is investigational [11].

Stage IVB
- Chemotherapy with platinum-based regimen.
- Bevacizumab can be considered [14].
- Palliative RT as indicated.

Medically Inoperable
- Pelvic RT and brachytherapy for medically inoperable patients or those who refuse surgery.
- For high-risk patients, consider adding chemotherapy.

Radiation Therapy Technique

3D Technique
- Patient is supine, arms above chest, on Vac-Lok, IV contrast, and CT simulated for EBRT. Place radiopaque markers are at the end of a long Q-tip into the vaginal apex to identify the vaginal apex on CT. The patient should have two CT scans: one with full bladder followed by empty bladder for simulation. The two CT scans then should be fused to account for organ motion. The 3D plan and daily treatments need to be performed with full bladder.
- AP pelvic RT **borders** are superior, L4/L5 (if PA+, then to renal vessels or T12/L1); inferior, bottom of ischial tuberosity (for IIIA marker at distal tumor, include all of vagina, bilateral inguinal if lower one-third vagina involved); lateral, 2 cm on contoured vessels or bony pelvis (Fig. 20.3).
- Midline block should block midline structures with 4–5 cm blocks. Typically, superior border is at bottom of SI joints (Fig. 20.5). You can use 50% isodose lines from brachytherapy to construct the midline block. For LDR brachytherapy, deliver 40–60 cGy/h to point A.
- GTV, CTV, PTV, and OARs should be defined for 3D-CRT.

IMRT Technique
- Consider IMRT to reduce GI toxicity in the intact setting and for dose-painting and PA node positive disease. In the post-op setting, IMRT is recommended as per RTOG 0418. IMRT for intact cervix is under investigation.
- Routine image guidance is necessary for proper delivery of IMRT.
- The IMRT planning and daily treatments need to be performed with full bladder (Figs. 20.4–20.6).

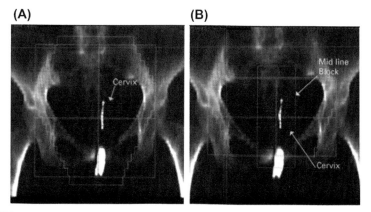

(A) **(B)**

FIGURE 20.3 (A). DRR for cervical cancer, 3D AP field, showing superior border at L4/L5, inferior border at ischial tuberosity, and lateral border 2 cm on bony pelvis. (B) DRR of cervical cancer, bilateral pelvic boost after midline block, 3D AP field showing superior border lowered to SI joint.

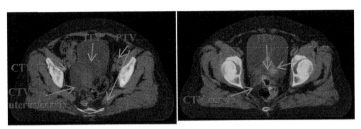

FIGURE 20.4 PET scan showing mildly PET-positive cervical cancer. PET scan is fused with planning CT scan to delineate GTV, CTV Gyn (uterus/cervix), CTV LN, ITV, and PTV.

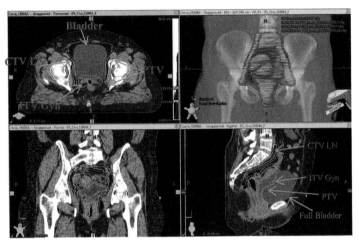

FIGURE 20.5 CT images of a cervical cancer patient showing intact cervix GTV, CTV Gyn (uterus/cervix), CTV LN, ITV, PTV, and full bladder for treatment plan.

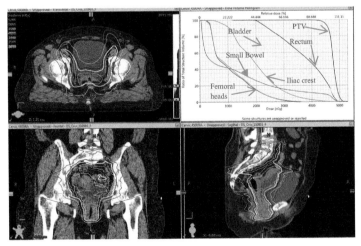

FIGURE 20.6 CT images of a cervical cancer patient showing two-arc VMAT planning isodose lines conforming to target volumes and DVH meeting all constraints. The prescription dose is PTV 50.4 Gy.

Volumes

GTV = gross disease + enlarged LNs seen on CT scan.
CTV Gyn target Full = volume of Gyn targets from full bladder CT scan.
CTV Gyn target Empty = volume of Gyn targets from empty bladder CT scan.
ITV Gyn target = CTV Gyn target full + CTV Gyn target empty +1 cm.
CTV LN = the iliac LNs (+PALNs, +inguinal LNs) + 0.7 cm margin.
PTV = ITV Gyn target + CTV LN + 0.5–1 cm.

Gyn Targets and Lymph Nodes

Gyn targets: Clinical or radiological gross disease, uterus, cervix, parametrium, upper 1/2 vagina (upper 2/3 vagina if upper vagina involved, entire vagina if extensive vaginal involvement, upper 3 cm of vagina if post-op). If parametrial extension, include entire parametrium and mesorectum in the target.

LNs: common iliac, external iliac, obturator, internal iliac, presacral, PA (if PA at high risk or positive), inguinal (if lower 1/3 vagina involved)

Nodal volume should start from 0.5 to 1 cm below the L4/L5 interspace and stop at the level of the femoral heads for external iliac, inferior border of internal iliac and obturator LN is at the top of the pubic bone and inferior border of presacral at the level of S3.

Brachytherapy Technique

- BRT is recommended for all patients with intact cervix usually initiated near the end or after EBRT.
- Performed using intracavitary approach, combined with CT- or MRI-compatible intrauterine tandem and ovoids or ring (Fig. 20.7). Interstitial implant for large or lateral targets.

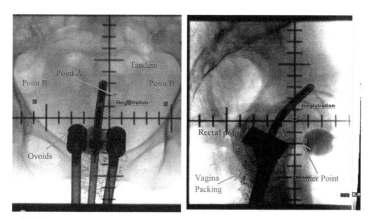

FIGURE 20.7 A pair of low dose rate Fletcher applicators in patient acquired by a conventional simulator. The left panel shows an AP view, and the right panel shows an RL view of the implant, showing tandem, ovoids, points A and B, bladder point and rectal point.

- Typically, the total dose is prescribed to point A, which represents the paracervical tissues. Point A is 2 cm above and 2 cm lateral to where the tandem intersects the line connecting the top of the ovoids and point B is 5 cm lateral to the tandem. Bladder point is posterior point on mid-Foley balloon filled with 7 cc of fluid, rectal point is 5 mm posterior to vaginal wall at the lower intrauterine source level.
- However, the point A dosing system does not take into account the tumor stage, size, and response to EBRT or tumor to OAR correlations.
- Image-guided BRT for definitive treatment of cervical cancer allows for individualization of treatment with dose escalation to the high-risk clinical target volume (HR-CTV) while sparing OARs. Thus, this technique can improve outcomes and decrease toxicity (Fig. 20.8).
- MRI is recommended to assess residual tumor size and geometry immediately before BRT, ideally with MRI with applicators in place, or alternatively, CT can be used.
- Accurate target definition is vitally important. For this purpose, Gynaecological GEC-ESTRO Working Group published their recommendations for image-guided BRT (MRI-based) (ref Radiother Oncol March 2005;74(3):235—45).
  - GTV: Macroscopic tumor at brachytherapy, high signal intensity mass(es) (FSE, T2) in cervix/corpus, parametria, vagina, bladder, and rectum.
  - High-risk CTV: includes GTV, whole cervix, presumed extracervical tumor extension, gray zones in parametria, uterine corpus, vagina or rectum, and bladder
  - Intermediate-risk CTV: encompasses HRCTV with margins added according to tumor size and regression; minimum margins of 5—15 mm, extensive disease: with good remission HR-CTV and initial tumor extension
- If adequate dose coverage cannot be achieved with intracavitary BRT, supplemental dose with interstitial needles should be considered using hybrid applicators or interstitial approach.

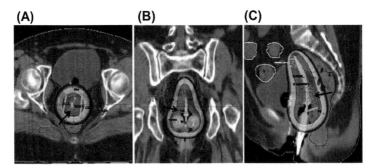

(A)   **(B)**   **(C)**

FIGURE 20.8   Dose distribution of CT-based brachytherapy application in (A) axial, (B) coronal and (C) sagittal images. The dose is prescribed to target volume (CTV) (arrow). The prescribed dose is demonstrated in red area. *From Onal and Oymak (2011). CT-Guided Brachytherapy Planning, chapter 6, Computed Tomography - Special Applications. InTech:113, Chapters published November 21, 2011 under CC BY 3.0 license.*

- Most commonly used HDR BRT regimens: 5.5 Gy/fx to 27.5 Gy, 6 Gy/fx to 30 Gy, or 7 Gy/fx to 28 Gy.
- Prescribed the equivalent dose at 2 Gy (EQD2) to the HR-CTV of ≥80−90 Gy.
- Postoperatively close or positive vaginal margins may be treated with vaginal cylinder BRT. The HDR is prescribed to vaginal surface (6−18 Gy) or 5 mm depth from the mucosal surface (5.5−11 Gy).
- Overall treatment time of EBRT and BRT should be less than 8 weeks to improve OS.

External Beam Radiation Therapy and Brachytherapy Doses

Stage IB2−IIA2: RT dose to whole pelvis to 45 Gy followed by LDR implant is 15−20 Gy/fx ×2 to point A dose to 85 Gy total, after ML block boost PM point B for IIB to 55 Gy, and for III−IVA to 60 Gy. If using HDR implant, then the dose is 5.5−6 Gy/fx for ×5 fractions to a total dose of 27.5−30 Gy or 7 Gy/fx ×4 to 28 Gy to point A.

Stage IIB−IVA

Negative PA: RT dose to whole pelvis to 45 Gy followed by LDR implant is 15−20 Gy/fx ×2 to point A dose to 85 Gy total, after ML block boost PM point B for IIB to 55 Gy, and for III−IVA to 60 Gy. If using HDR implant, then the dose is 5.5−6 Gy/fx for ×5 fractions to a total dose of 27.5 Gy−30 or 7 Gy/fx ×4 to 28 Gy to point A.

Positive PA: RT dose to PA and pelvis to 45 Gy, then dose paint or boost PA LN to 54−61.2 Gy, followed by implant LDR 15−20 Gy/fx ×2 to point A 85 Gy. Point B 55−60 Gy. If using HDR implant, then the dose is 5.5−6 Gy/fx for ×5 fractions to a total dose of 27.5−30 Gy or 7 Gy/fx ×4 to 28 Gy to point A.

Medically inoperable: Recommended treatment is EBRT to whole pelvis to 45 Gy followed by LDR implant is 15−20 Gy/fx ×2 to point A to a dose total dose of 75 Gy; point B dose to 55 Gy. If using HDR implant, then the dose is 5.5−6 Gy/fx for ×5 fractions to a total dose of 27.5−30 Gy or 7 Gy/fx ×4 to 28 Gy.

GEC ESTRO Planning Target Goals
D98 GTV EQD2: >95 Gy
D90 HRCTV EQD2: >90 Gy, <95 Gy
D98 HRCTV EQD2: >75 Gy
D98 IRCTV EQD2: >60 Gy
Point A EQD2: >65 Gy

Constraints

OAR doses should be limited with D2cc rectum ≤65−75 Gy, D2cc sigmoid ≤65−75 Gy, and D2cc bladder ≤80−90 Gy.

Small bowel (peritoneal cavity) V45 < 195 cc; V40 < 30% rectum V30 < 60%; V50 < 50%
Bladder V45 < 35%
Femoral head V30 < 15%; V50 < 5%

Note: Use ABS worksheet to calculate cumulative target and OAR doses.

Outcome

OS for stage IA is 100%; IB is 85%; IIA is 75%; IIB is 65%; IIIA is 55%; IIIB/IV is 15%.

Complications of Radiation Therapy

- Skin reactions, including hair loss, diarrhea, cramps, rectal soreness and bleeding, anal discomfort, scarring or narrowing of bowel causing obstruction requiring surgical correction.
- Urinary frequency/dysuria/nocturia, bladder damage, loss of capacity, and recurrent bladder infection.
- Ovarian damage, early menopause, and sterility.
- Vaginal damage, such as soreness, irritation, dryness or shrinkage with resulting difficulty during intercourse, vaginal vault necrosis, and leg edema.
- When RT is combined with surgery, the rate of complications is higher because of injury to the ureter of the bladder.

Follow-Up

- Every 3 months for the first year, every 6 months for the second and third years, and every 12 months thereafter
- Pelvic exam during each visit
- Pap smear annually Chest X-ray every 12 months, other imaging techniques only as clinically indicated
- Consider posttreatment PETCT

OVARIAN CANCER

The estimated incidence in the United States is 22,240 with estimated 14,070 deaths in 2018.

Ovarian cancer deaths are the highest among the gynecological cancers in the United States. The ovary is histologically a very complex structure and gives rise to a variety of tumors. The most common is epithelial (serous, mucinous, endometrioid, and CC), germ cell, and stromal cell tumors. Lymphatic drainage is to the external iliac, internal iliac, and PA LNs.

Workup

Risk Factors
- Obesity, low parity or infertility, unopposed estrogen, and exposure to asbestos and talc
- Family history of breast cancer (genetic mutations in the BRCA 1 or BRCA 2)

Symptoms and Signs
- Nausea and abdominal pain, mass/pressure in the pelvis, urinary frequency and feeling of rectal pressure.
- Note any abdominal swelling, ascites, and LNs or bimanual pelvic exam.

Investigations

- CBC, routine chemistry.
- Pregnancy test, when indicated.
- HCG is useful for embryonal, choriocarcinoma, and sometimes germinoma tumors; AFP useful to follow endodermal sinus tumors; CEA most likely elevated with mucinous tumor and CA-125 levels >35μ/ml are compared with most nonmucinous epithelial tumors.
- Tissue diagnosis via exploratory/staging laparotomy, which is mandatory with debulking.
- Ultrasound of the abdomen, Chest X-ray, CT abdomen/pelvis.

TNM Staging (Ovarian Cancer)
TNM FIGO

TNM	FIGO	
T1	I	Tumor limited to ovaries (one or both)
T1a	IA	Tumor limited to one ovary; capsule intact, no tumor on ovarian surface on ovarian surface. No malignant cells in ascites or peritoneal washings
T1b	IB	Tumor limited to both ovaries; capsules intact, no tumor on ovarian surface. No malignant cells in ascites or peritoneal washings
T1c	IC	Tumor limited to one or both ovaries with any of the following: capsule ruptured tumor on ovarian surface, malignant cells in ascites or peritoneal washings
T2	II	Tumor involves one or both ovaries with pelvic extension and/or implants
T2a	IIA	Extension and/or implants on uterus and/or tube(s). No malignant cells in ascites or peritoneal washings
T2b	IIB	Extension to and/or implants on other pelvic tissues. No malignant cells in ascites or peritoneal washings
T3	III	Tumor involves one or both ovaries with microscopically confirmed peritoneal metastasis outside the pelvis
T3a	IIIA2	Microscopic peritoneal metastasis beyond pelvis (no macroscopic tumor)
T3b	IIIB	Macroscopic peritoneal metastasis beyond pelvis 2 cm or less in greatest dimension
T3c	IIIC	Peritoneal metastasis beyond pelvis more than 2 cm in greatest dimension and/or regional lymph node metastasis Note: Liver capsule metastasis T3/Stage III; liver parenchymal metastasis M1/Stage IV. Pleural effusion must have positive cytology for M1/Stage IV
N0		No regional lymph node metastasis
N1	IIIA1	Regional lymph node metastasis
M0		No distant metastasis (no pathologic M0; use clinical M to complete stage group)
M1	IV	Distant metastasis (excludes peritoneal metastasis)

Stage Grouping

Stage I	T1	N0	M0
Stage IA	T1a	N0	M0
Stage IB	T1b	N0	M0
Stage I C	T1c	N0	M0
Stage II	T2	N0	M0
Stage IIA	T2a	N0	M0
Stage IIB	T2b	N0	M0
Stage IIIA1	T1, 2	N1	M0
Stage IIIA2	T3a	N0, 1	M0
Stage IIIB	T3b	N0, 1	M0
Stage III C	T3c	N0, 1	M0
Stage IV	Any T	Any N	M1

FIGO, International Federation of Gynecology and Obstetrics; M, (distant metastasis); *N*, (regional lymph nodes); *TNM*, T (tumor).
Used with permission of the American Joint Committee on Cancer (AJCC), Chicago, Illinois. The original source for this material is the AJCC Cancer Staging Manual, Eighth Edition (2017) published by Springer Science Business Media LLC, www.springer.com.

Treatment
Stage IA, IB (G1, 2)
• Surgery TAH/USO. Unilateral salpingo-oophorectomy in IA disease; bilateral salpingo-oophorectomy in IB disease for fertility maintenance. Grade 2 patients may be considered for post-op chemotherapy with carboplatin/Taxol X3-6 cycles.

All Other Stages
• TAH-BSO and optimally debulked (<1−2 cm residual disease) surgery followed by IV chemotherapy. The combination of carboplatin (5−6 AUC) and paclitaxel (175 mg/m^2) every 3 weeks X6 cycles is the most commonly used regimen.
• For appropriately selected patients intraperitoneal (IP) chemotherapy. The most commonly used IV/IP regimen consists of six cycles of IV paclitaxel (135 mg/m^2 over 24 h) on day 1, IP cisplatin (100 mg/m^2 in a liter of normal saline) on day 2, IP paclitaxel (60 mg/m^2) on day 8. Repeat every 3 weeks × six cycles. After a suboptimal resection, dose-dense IV therapy (carboplatin every 3 weeks with paclitaxel administered every week for a total of 15 weeks of treatment over conventional dosing) can be used in patients with tumors are not of CC or mucinous type.

- Whole abdominopelvic RT (WART) is rarely used, but can be considered as curative if not a chemotherapy candidate in select stage III patients [15, 16]. With IMRT technique, side effects may be more tolerable.
- Consider fractionated or stereotactic radiation for palliation or for metastases
- For nonsurgical patients, consider neoadjuvant chemotherapy X3 cycles with carboplatin and paclitaxel as above followed by surgical debulking with chemotherapy postoperatively.

Radiation Therapy Technique

3D Technique

Patient is supine, arms by side, on Vac-Lok, and CT simulated. The CTV includes the entire peritoneal cavity. Conventionally, **borders** are superior, 1 cm above right dome of diaphragm; inferior, bottom of ischial tuberosity; laterals, 1 cm on peritoneal reflection. Treat up to 30 Gy/150 cGy, then close superior border for pelvic boost to 51.6 Gy, superior L5/S1. An additional boost may be delivered to PA LNs to 45–50 Gy. Kidney and liver blocks should be applied at 15 and 25 Gy, respectively. Recently, IMRT has been investigated versus 3D-CRT in the treatment of ovarian cancer. It may improve the tolerability of WART.

Outcome

Disease-free survival: low risk 95%, intermediate risk 70%, high risk 35%; all OS 45%.

Complications

- WART is morbid treatment.
- Nausea, vomiting, diarrhea, acute weight loss, malabsorption.
- Bowel obstruction.
- Serious complications can occur when given after chemotherapy, but when limited to three cycles, tolerance is purportedly much better.

Follow-Up

- Every 3 months for first year, every 6 months for the second and third years, and every 12 months thereafter
- Pelvic exam and CA 125 for epithelial tumors during each visit
- CT of the chest, abdomen, and pelvis as indicated

VAGINAL CANCER

The estimated incidence in the United States is 5170 with an estimated 1330 deaths in 2018.

Vaginal cancer is most commonly located at the posterior wall and in the upper one-third of the vaginal vault. Lymphatics drain from upper two-thirds of the vagina to the pelvic LNs, then to the PA nodes. The lower one-third drains to the inguinal–femoral LNs, then to the pelvic LNs. Lesions can also spread along the vaginal wall to involve the cervix and/or vulva.

Workup

Risk Factors
- Smoking, multiple partners, DES used by their mothers can cause CC vaginal cancer in patients.
- HPV infection.
- Prior SCCa of the genital tract.

Symptoms and Signs
- Vaginal bleeding/discharge, urinary symptoms such as dysuria or rectal symptoms, pelvic pain
- Physical exam should note any enlarged LNs and organomegaly, pelvic examination should include bimanual exam.

Investigations
- CBC, routine chemistry with liver and renal functions, exfoliative cytology, HPV and HIV status
- Colposcopy with directed biopsies
- EUA with multiple cervical biopsies to rule out cervical cancer
- Cystoscopy, proctoscopy/barium enema for advanced stage
- Chest X-ray, intravenous pyelogram (IVP), CT abdomen/pelvis, MRI to assess primary tumor extent and for brachytherapy planning. PET/CT to evaluate LN and distant metastases.

Note: If vaginal tumor is extended to another tissue/organ which may be the source of the disease, the tumor is treated as if the nonvaginal origin.

TNM Staging (Vaginal Cancer)

TNM FIGO

Tis	*	Carcinoma in situ (preinvasive carcinoma)
T1	I	Tumor confined to vagina
T1a	I	Tumor confined to vagina <2 cm
T1b	I	Tumor confined to vagina >2 cm
T2	II	Tumor invades paravaginal tissues but not to pelvic wall
T2a	II	Tumor invades paravaginal tissues but not to pelvic side wall, <2 cm
T2b	II	Tumor invades paravaginal tissues but not to pelvic side wall, >2 cm
T3	III	Tumor extends to pelvic wall**
T4	IVA	Tumor invades mucosa of the bladder or rectum and/or extends beyond the true pelvis (bullous edema is insufficient evidence to classify a tumor as T4) *FIGO staging no longer includes Stage 0 (Tis). **Pelvic wall is defined as muscle, fascia, neurovascular structures, or skeletal portions of the bony pelvis.

N0		No regional lymph node metastasis
N1	III	Pelvic or inguinal lymph node metastasis
M0		No distant metastasis (no pathologic M0; use clinical M to complete stage group)
M1	IVB	Distant metastasis

Stage Grouping

Stage IA	T1a	N0	M0
Stage IB	T1b	N0	M0
Stage IIA	T2a	N0	M0
Stage IIB	T2b	N0	M0
Stage III	T1,3	N1	M0
	T3	N0	M0
Stage IVA	T4	Any N	M0
Stage IVB	Any T	Any N	M1

FIGO, International Federation of Gynecology and Obstetrics; M, (distant metastasis); *N*, (regional lymph nodes); *TNM*, T (tumor).
Used with permission of the American Joint Committee on Cancer (AJCC), Chicago, Illinois. The original source of this material is the AJCC Cancer Staging Manual, Eighth Edition (2017) published by Springer Science Business Media LLC, www.springer.com.

Treatment

Vaginal Intraepithelial Neoplasia
- Surgical excision, CO_2 laser or topical 5FU.

Carcinoma in situ
- Surgery is wide local excision (WLE).
- Intracavitary RT for organ preservation.

Stage I
- Surgery is WLE or partial vaginectomy and pelvic or inguinal LN dissection, depending on the depth and the location of the tumor. Indications for postop RT include close or positive surgical margins and/or LN metastases.
- Alternatively can treat with RT. Tumor thickness <0.5 cm use intracavitary brachytherapy; tumor >0.5 cm treat whole pelvis RT followed by interstitial or intracavitary brachytherapy boost.

Stage II
- Subvaginal infiltration: WPRT followed by interstitial or intracavitary brachytherapy boost.

Stage II (Paravaginal/Parametrial Invasion), III and IV
- WPRT followed by interstitial and intracavitary brachytherapy boost
- Cisplatin-based chemotherapy given concurrently with RT for vaginal cancer treatments. Dosage extrapolated from cervical cancer data.

External Beam Radiation Therapy Technique

Patient is supine with frog leg (if distal vaginal involvement), arms by side and CT simulated Place a BB marker in the vagina/rectum to mark the distal extent of the tumor. RT can be given with 3DCRT or IMRT. 3D AP/PA fields. **Borders:** Superior L5/S1, inferior flash vagina, lateral 2 cm on bony pelvis (for lower one-third lesions, anterior superior iliac spine). Then brachytherapy followed with EBRT to complete adequate treatment to the nodes and parametrial tissue. No bolus unless LNs ulcerate through skin because it can increase chances of moist desquamation and skin toxicity. The dose to the parametria is 60−65 Gy if gross invasion or extension to the pelvic sidewall occurs.

Volumes
GTV = primary tumor.
CTV = primary tumor with a margin, entire vagina, paravaginal tissues and pelvic LNs (iliac, obturator, presacral) and inguinal LNs if the tumor involves the distal third of the vagina + 1−2 cm
PTV = CTV + 0.5 cm.

Intracavitary Technique

An acrylic dome cylinder is used for the vaginal intracavitary radiotherapy (ICRT). The cylinder can be loaded with 137Cs sources in configuration of 20-10-20 mgs or similar distribution with HDR 192Ir source. The dose is prescribed t o 0.5 cm depth if > 0.5 cm residual thickness, 60 Gy t o the entire vaginal mucosa with additional boost doses of 10−15 Gy to the gross disease site.

The superiority of MRI-guided adaptive brachytherapy over conventional brachytherapy has been recently demonstrated for treating cervical cancer is also applicable to vaginal cancer.

Interstitial Technique

An Syed/Neblett template is most commonly used for interstitial brachytherapy, although variety of templates are available. The template has a central opening for a vaginal obturator and an opening for a tandem through the obturator. Multiple openings for plastic, steel, or titanium needles in a circumferential pattern around the central opening are also present. In addition, needles can also be loaded on vaginal obturator.

The template is positioned with the patient in lithotomy position and under general anesthesia. The vaginal obturator is then placed, with its needles around it. The deepest part of the tumor is usually implanted with the needles first. Additional needles are placed anteriorly to posteriorly, insuring that they are 1 cm beyond the tumor. After the screws are tightened to secure the needles or needles glued to template, the template is sutured to the perineum.

Orthogonal films with dummy sources are taken for dosimetry (or MRI and CT-based planning is recommended). A treatment plan is established with low dose 192Ir sources for a dose rate of 30–55 Gy/h, making sure that the periphery of the entire tumor volume is enclosed within the prescription isodose line. If treated after EBRT, then the implant boost dose is 30–35 Gy.

Doses

CIS: Intracavitary brachytherapy giving 60 Gy to the entire vagina, then boost the involved vaginal mucosa to 70 Gy.

Stage I: Superficial lesions of less than 0.5 cm: intracavitary brachytherapy to 60 Gy mucosa dose followed by an additional boost dose of 15 Gy to the involved site.

Lesions thicker than 0.5 cm: the whole pelvis is treated to 45 Gy with EBRT; this is then followed by interstitial brachytherapy with implant to treat the gross tumor to a boost dose of 30 Gy prescribed 0.5 cm beyond the implant.

Stage II (Subvaginal Infiltration): Whole pelvis to 45 Gy, then midline block to treat the parametria to 50 Gy. Then boost lesion with implant to 35 Gy, prescribed to 0.5 cm beyond the implant.

Stage II (Paravaginal/Parametrial Invasion), III and IV: Whole pelvis with 45–50 Gy, then midline block and treat parametrium to 60 Gy, then boost lesion with implant to 35 Gy, prescribed to 0.5 cm beyond the implant.

Note: For tumors involving the lower third of the vagina: inguinal LNs should be electively treated to 50.4 Gy. For patients with clinically positive LNs, an additional boost dose of 25 Gy is given.

Note: HDR boost dose is 4.5–5.5 Gy ×5 fractions to 22.5–27.5 Gy.

Outcome

OS rates for stages I, IIA, IIB/III, and IV are 90%, 50%, 40%, and 0%, respectively.

Complications

- Vaginal damage, such as soreness, irritation, dryness, or shrinkage with resulting difficulty during intercourse, vaginal vault necrosis
- Rectovaginal or vesicovaginal fistulas
- Radiation cystitis or proctitis.

Follow-Up

- Every 3 months for the first year, every 6 months for the second and third years and every 12 months thereafter
- Pelvic exam during each visit
- Chest X-ray every 12 months
- Cervical or vaginal cytology annually.

VULVAR CANCER

The estimated incidence in US is 6190 with an estimated 1200 deaths in 2018.

The vulva comprises the mons pubis, the labia majora, the labia minora, the perineal body, the clitoris and the vaginal vestibule. Lymphatics drain from labia to superficial inguinal and femoral LNs, then to the deep femoral nodes and from the vestibule to deep inguinal and femoral LNs and finally to the pelvic LNs. Clitoral lymphatics drain directly into the pelvic LNs. Vulvar lymphatics generally do not cross the midline.

Workup

Risk Factors
- Increasing age, human papillomavirus (HPV) infection, smoking, chronic irritant vaginitis and immunosuppression.
- Vulvar intraepithelial neoplasia.
- Vulvar dystrophy, including lichen sclerosus and squamous hyperplasia.
- Prior SCCa of vaginal tract.

Symptoms and Signs
- Can be asymptomatic at presentation, long history of pruritus, pain, and bleeding.
- Frequently present with exophytic mass.
- Physical exam should note any enlarged inguinal LNs and organomegaly, bimanual pelvic exam.

Investigations
- CBC, routine chemistry with liver and renal functions, PAP smear, exfoliative cytology.
- Biopsy-wedge or punch of the lesion, FNA for any suspicious LNs.
- Colposcopy with multiple cervical biopsies (insure it is not a cervix metastasis).
- Consider cystoscopy, proctoscopy/BE/IVP in advanced stages or when symptomatic.
- Chest X-ray, chest/abdomen/pelvic CT or PET/CT for larger tumors or when metastasis is apparent; Pelvic MRI for treatment planning (surgery or RT).

TNM Staging (Vulvar Cancer)
TNM FIGO

Tis	*	Carcinoma in situ (preinvasive carcinoma)
T1a	IA	Lesions <2 cm in size, confined to the vulva or perineum and with stromal invasion <1 mm**
T1b	IB	Lesions >2 cm in size **or** any size with stromal invasion >1 mm, confined to the vulva or perineum
T2***	II	Tumor of any size with extension to adjacent perineal structures (Lower/distal 1/3 urethra, lower/distal 1/3 vagina, anal involvement)
T3****	IVA	Tumor of any size with extension to any of the following: upper/proximal 2/3 of urethra, upper/proximal 2/3 vagina, bladder mucosa, rectal mucosa, or fixed to pelvic bone.

*FIGO staging no longer includes Stage 0 (Tis).
**The depth of invasion is defined as the measurement of the tumor from the epithelial-stromal junction of the adjacent most superficial dermal papilla to deepest point of invasion.
***FIGO uses the classification T2/T3. This is defined as T2 in TNM.
****FIGO uses the classification T4 (defined as T3 in TNM).

N0		No regional lymph node metastasis
N1		One or two regional lymph nodes with the following features:
N1a	IIIA	One or two lymph node metastasis each 5 mm or less
N1b	IIIA	One lymph node metastasis 5 mm or greater
N2		Regional lymph node metastasis with the following features:
N2a	IIIB	Three or more lymph node metastases each <5 mm
N2b	IIIB	Two or more lymph node metastases >5 mm
N2c	IIIC	Lymph node metastasis with extracapsular spread
N3	IVA	Fixed or ulcerated regional lymph node metastasis. An effort should be made to describe the site and laterality of lymph node metastases.
M0		No distant metastasis (no pathologic M0; use clinical M to complete stage group)
M1	IVB	Distant metastasis (including pelvic lymph node metastasis)

Stage Grouping

Stage I	T1	N0	M0
Stage IA	T1a	N0	M0
Stage IB	T1b	N0	M0
Stage II	T2	N0	M0
Stage IIIA	T1,2	N1	M0
Stage IIIB	T1,2	N2a,b	M0
Stage IIIC	T1,2	N2c	M0
Stage IVA	T1,2	N3	M0
	T3	Any N	M0
Stage IVB	Any T	Any N	M1

FIGO, International Federation of Gynecology and Obstetrics; M, (distant metastasis); *N*, (regional lymph nodes); *TNM*, T (tumor).
Used with permission of the American Joint Committee on Cancer (AJCC), Chicago, Illinois. The original source for this material is the AJCC Cancer Staging Manual, Eighth Edition (2017) published by Springer Science Business Media LLC, www.springer.com.

Treatment

Carcinoma In Situ: The recommended treatment is surgery with WLE for localized lesion and skinning vulvectomy for multifocal lesion.

Stage IA: The recommended treatment is WLE with a more than 8 mm margin. If the margin is < 8 mm, then options are either reexcision or post-op RT to vulva only.

Stage IB, II:
- Recommended treatment is surgery with radical local resection/modified radical vulvectomy. For lateralized vulvar tumor (>2 cm from midline), then perform ipsilateral groin node evaluation with SLNs or ipsilateral groin LN dissection. If the vulvar lesion is midline, then perform contralateral groin node evaluation with SLNs or bilateral inguinofemoral LN dissection.
- If the margin is < 8 mm, then the options are either reexcision or post-op RT. Consider post-op RT for risk factors positive LVI, tumor T2-3, depth of invasion >5 mm, pattern of invasion (spray or diffuse), and positive LN [17].
- If SLNs positive—post-op RT and consider concurrent chemotherapy or completion inguinofemoral LN dissection. If any groin is positive with two or more LNs and with one LN with extracapsular extension or with >2-mm metastasis, after inguinofemoral LN dissection, then post-op RT and consider concurrent chemotherapy. RT is given to the bilateral groins and the pelvis.

Stage III–IVA:
- Unresectable disease may be treated with definitive RT and concurrent weekly cisplatin to primary tumor and lymphatics [18, 19].
- May also consider pre-op RT and weekly cisplatin (40 mg/m^2) to improve operability rates. No benefits of surgery in patients with clinical complete response. If a complete response is not achieved, surgical resection of residual disease is recommended. Consider additional RT for patients with unresectable disease.
- If unable to tolerate chemotherapy, then RT alone for organ preservation.

Radiation Therapy Technique

Patient is supine, arms on chest, IV contrast with CT simulated. Patient in frog-leg position with bolus on vulva. Radioopaque markers are placed on the vulvar skin and scars during simulation to define the primary target volume.

RT field **borders** for vulva alone, superior 1 cm above pubic symphysis, inferior flash, laterals 3 cm on lesion. For regional LNs, superior L4/L5, inferior 4 cm below the lowest extent of disease; laterals ASIS, ±midline block (6 cm wide), extends from 2 cm above pubis to the bottom of the field. For organ preservation, superior L4/L5, inferior 4 cm below the lowest extent of disease/flash vulva, laterals from AP ASIS, from PA 2 cm on pelvis, exit gets wired on skin.

RT can be given with 3D-CRT or IMRT. The vulvar and nodal targets should be contoured on the planning CT. More conformal techniques may reduce pelvic bone marrow, femoral head and neck, small bowel, rectum, and bladder doses, depending on tumor extent and patient anatomy.

Note: IMRT contouring guidelines are reported by Gaffney et al. Red Journal 2016.

Volumes

GTV = gross disease on physical exam and imaging
CTV = Definitive or preoperatively treating: gross disease +
entire vulva + 1–3 cm margin + elective LNs
PTV = CTV +0.5 cm

Gross Disease and Elective Lymph Nodes

Primary: CTV = entire vulva + 1 cm (if GTV extends beyond vulva).
   Invasion of vagina: gross disease + 3 cm (if LVSI include entire vagina).
   Invasion of anal canal, bladder or rectum: gross disease + 2 cm.
   Invasion of periurethra: gross disease + 2 cm of urethra.
   Invasion of periclitora: gross disease + 2 cm.
   LNs: for patients with LN positive, CTV should include the inguinal, external iliac, internal iliac, and obturator regions bilaterally. If LN negative after lymphadenectomy, RT applied only to vulva. Recommend local RT to vulva, if treating regional LNs.
   Note: A thermoluminescent dosimeter should be placed externally over the vulvar skin to confirm doses to the target areas at first treatment for IMRT. Image-guided IMRT is an essential component of treatment.

Doses

Stage IA: RT dose is 180 cGy/fx to 45–50.4 Gy for negative margins, 50–55 Gy for close margins and 54–59.9 Gy for positive margins.

Stage IB, II: post-op RT dose is 180 cGy/fx to 45–50.4 Gy for negative margins, 50–55 Gy for close margins and 54–59.9 Gy for positive margins. If SLNs positive, post-op RT is given to the bilateral groins and the pelvis. The RT dose is 45–50.4 Gy to the pelvis and to the groins.

Stage III, IVA: Pre-op RT: 180 cGy/fx to 45–60 Gy to the gross primary and depending on LN risk treat inguinal LNs and pelvic LNs.
   Definitive RT: 180 cGy/fx to 45 to the gross disease, inguinal LNs, and pelvic LNs, followed by boost dose of 60–65 Gy to the gross disease.
   Post-op RT: 180 cGy/fx to 45–50.4 Gy, if positive margin or gross residual disease treat boost dose to 60–65 Gy.

Constraints

Lower vagina 60–80 Gy
Small bowel (peritoneal cavity) V45 < 195 cc; V40 < 30%
Rectum V30 < 60%; V50 < 50%
Bladder V45 < 35%
Femoral head V30 < 15%; V50 < 5%

Outcome

OS rates for stages I, II, III and IV are 85%, 60%, 25%, 0%, respectively.

Complications

- As noted for cervical and vaginal cancer
- Lower extremity lymphedema

Follow-Up

- Every 3–6 months for 2 years, every 6–12 months for years three to five, and every 12 months thereafter
- Pelvic exam during each visit
- Chest X-ray every 12 months or as clinically indicated

ANNOTATED BIBLIOGRAPHY

ENDOMETRIAL CANCER

Ref 1. Nout et al. (2010). Vaginal brachytherapy versus pelvic external beam radiotherapy for patients with endometrial cancer of high-intermediate risk (PORTEC-2): an open-label, non-inferiority, randomised trial. *Lancet*;375:816–23. PORTEC 2 Trial.

In this study, 427 patients with high-intermediate risk (HIR) endometrial cancer (age >60 and stage 1C grade 1–2 or stage 1B grade 3; any age and stage 2A grade 1–2 or grade 3 with <50% invasion) after surgery were randomized to pelvic EBRT (46 Gy in 23 fractions) or vaginal brachytherapy (21 Gy HDR in three fractions, or 30 Gy LDR). The results at 5 years were as follows:

	Vaginal Relapse (%)	*Pelvic Relapse (%)*	*Disease-Free Survival (%)*	*Overall Survival (%)*
Surgery + Pelvic RT	*1.6*	*0.5*	*78.1*	*79.6*
Surgery + Vaginal RT	*1.8*	*3.8*	*82.7*	*84.8*
P-value	*0.74*	*0.02*	*0.74*	*0.57*

This study showed that vaginal brachytherapy is effective in preventing vaginal recurrence in patients with HIR endometrial carcinoma. Despite the slightly but significantly increased pelvic failure rate in the vaginal RT arm, rates of distant metastases, recurrence-free survival and OS were similar.

Ref 2. Creutzberg et al. (2011). Fifteen-year radiotherapy outcomes of the randomized PORTEC-1 trial for endometrial carcinoma. *Int J Radiat Oncol Biol Phys*;81(4):e631–38. PORTEC one Trial.

In this study, 715 patients with endometrial cancer stage FIGO I, invasion <50% and Gr 3, invasion ≥50% and Gr 1, any invasion and Gr 2,3 after TAH/BSO, no lymphadenectomy, were randomized to observation versus post-op RT. RT was given at 46 Gy to whole pelvis. HIR *definition: Age >60 years, Gr 3, invasion >50%; two of those three factors present (except for Gr 3 with deep invasion). Results at median follow-up of 13.3 years were as follows:*

	15-Year Locoregional Recurrence (%)	15-Year Vaginal Recurrence	15-Year Overall Survival (%)
Surgery	15.5	15.5	60
Surgery + RT	6	11	52
P-value	<0.0001		0.14

74% of the locoregional recurrences were isolated vaginal recurrences.

Post-op RT in stage I endometrial cancer reduced locoregional recurrences but had no impact on OS. The 15-year outcomes of PORTEC-1 trial confirm the relevance of HIR criteria for adjuvant treatment selection.

Ref 3. Sorbe et al. (2012). External pelvic and vaginal irradiation versus vaginal irradiation alone as postoperative therapy in medium-risk endometrial carcinoma: a prospective randomized study. *Int J Radiat Oncol Biol Phys*;82(3):1249–55. Swedish Trial.

In this study, 527 patients with medium-risk (stage IA–IC) endometrial cancer were randomized to vaginal BRT or adjuvant external beam pelvic RT (1.8–2 Gy/46 Gy) and vaginal BRT. BRT doses were (EQD2) 19.5–23.5 Gy at a depth of 5 mm and 29.3–35.3 Gy at the surface of the vaginal applicator. The results at 5 years were as follows:

	Locoregional Relaps (%)	Overall Survival (%)	Endometrial Ca-Related Death (%)
BRT	5	90	6.8
BRT + EBRT	1.5	89	3.8
P value	0.013	0.548	0.118

Although BRT and EBRT showed significant locoregional control benefit, there was no survival advantage and increased late toxicity with combined modality. This treatment modality should be preferred in high-risk patients with two or more high-risk factors. BRT alone should be the adjuvant treatment option for purely medium-risk patients.

Ref 4. Onsrud et al. (2013). Long-term outcomes after pelvic radiation for early-stage endometrial Cancer. *J Clin Oncol*;31:3951–56. Norwegian Trial.

In this study, 540 patients with stage I endometrial cancer after surgery (TAH + BSO, no LN dissection) were randomized to intravaginal BRT or intravaginal BRT followed by postoperative external pelvic RT. Vaginal Brachytherapy was given LDR 60 Gy at vaginal surface. After median 20.5 years of follow-up,

	Median Overall Survival (%)	2nd Cancer <60 Years
VBRT	20.48	25.6
EBRT	20.50	39.7
P value	0.186	0.014

There was no statistically significant difference in OS between the two groups. However, external pelvic RT significantly decreased survival and increased the risk of secondary cancer in patients with low-risk endometrial cancer who were <60 years old.

Ref 5. Matei et al. (2017). A randomized phase III trial of cisplatin and tumor volume directed irradiation followed by carboplatin and paclitaxel versus carboplatin and paclitaxel for optimally debulked, advanced endometrial carcinoma. *J Clin Oncol*:35S, (abstract #5505). GOG 258 Trial.

In this study, 813 patients with stage III to IVA (<2 cm residual disease) endometrioid or stage I/II serous or CC endometrial cancer were randomized to adjuvant chemoRT (concurrent cisplatin and EBRT followed by carboplatin and paclitaxel X four cycles) or chemotherapy alone (carboplatin and paclitaxel X 6 cycles). Median follow-up was 47 months.

	Vaginal (%) Recurrence	Pelvic/PA LN (%) Recurrence	Distant (%) Recurrence
Chemo	7	21	21
ChemoRT	3	10	28

Preliminary results showed no differences in relapse-free survival for those receiving chemoRT versus chemotherapy alone. Addition of RT decreased vaginal recurrences, pelvic, and PA relapses. This study showed that adjuvant chemoRT can be recommended to patients with high risk of local relapse to increase locoregional control.

Ref 6. Randall et al. (2017). A phase III trial of pelvic radiation therapy versus vaginal cuff brachytherapy followed by paclitaxel/carboplatin chemotherapy in patients with high-risk, early-stage endometrial cancer: a gynecology oncology group study. *Int J Radiat Oncol Biol Phys* (abstract #LBA-1). GOG 249 Trial.

In this study, 601 patients with stage I endometrioid histology with GOG 99-based HIR criteria (based on age, tumor Gr, depth of invasion, and presence of LVI), stage II, or stage I–II serous (S) or CC tumors were randomized to pelvic RT (45 Gy over 5 weeks) or vaginal cuff BRT (LDR or HDR) and chemotherapy (paclitaxel 175 mg/m^2 and carboplatin AUC 6 q 21 days × 3 cycles). Median follow-up data of 53 months are given below.

	5-year PA/Pel LN Recurrence (%)	3-Year Overall Survival (5)	Toxicity Grade 3
VCB/Chemo	9.2	88	62
PXRT	4.4	91	10
P value	—	0.57	—

No significant differences in OS; however, pelvic or PA nodal recurrences were significantly more common in the chemotherapy arm. Acute toxicity was more common and more severe with chemotherapy. This study showed that adjuvant pelvic RT should remain the standard of care for high-risk, early-stage endometrial cancer.

Ref 7. Boer SM de et al. (2018). Adjuvant chemoradiotherapy versus radiotherapy alone for Women with high-risk endometrial Cancer (PORTEC-3): final results of an international, open-label, multicentre, randomised, phase 3 trial. *Lancet Oncol*; 19(3):295−309. PORTEC three.

In this trial, 686 women with HREC (FIGO stage 1 grade 3 with deep myometrial invasion and/or LVSI; stage II or III; serous/CC histology) were randomized to RT (48.6 Gy in 1.8 Gy fractions) or CTRT (two cycles of carboplatin AUC5 and paclitaxel 175 mg/m^2 at 3 week intervals). Median follow-up results of 60.2 months were:

	5-Year FFS (%)		5-Year Overall Survival (%)	
	All	Stage III	All	Stage III
RT	68.9	58	76.7	69.8
ChemoRT	75.5	69.3	81.8	78.7
P value	0.078	0.032	0.183	0.114

This study showed that adjuvant chemotherapy given during and after pelvic RT for treatment of HREC did not significantly improve 5-year FFS and OS compared with RT alone but for women with stage III EC FFS, FFS and OS were significantly improved with CTRT.

CERVICAL CANCER

Ref 8. Duenas-Gonzalez et al. (2011). Phase III, open-label, randomized study comparing concurrent gemcitabine plus cisplatin and radiation followed by adjuvant Gemcitabine and Cisplatin versus concurrent Cisplatin and radiation in patients with stage IIB to IVA Carcinoma of the Cervix. *J Clin Oncol*;29:1678−16685.

In this study, 515 patients with stage IIB to IVA disease and Karnofsky performance score ≥70 were randomly assigned to arm A (cisplatin 40 mg/m^2 and gemcitabine 125 mg/m^2

weekly for 6 weeks with concurrent EBRT (50.4 Gy), followed by BRT (30–35 Gy in 96 h), and then two adjuvant 21-day cycles of cisplatin, 50 mg/m² on day 1, plus gemcitabine, 1000 mg/m² on days 1 and 8) or to arm B (cisplatin and concurrent EBRT followed by BRT). Efficacy results at 3 years were as follows:

	Progression-Free Survival	Overall Progression-Free Survival	Overall Survival	Time to Progressive Disease
Arm A	74.4%	log-rank P = 0.0227; HR, 0.68; 95% CI, 0.49–0.95	log-rank P = 0.0224; HR, 0.68; 95% CI, 0.49–0.95	log-rank P = 0.0012; HR, 0.54; 95% CI, 0.37–0.79
Arm B	65.0% ss			

Incorporation of gemcitabine in addition to cisplatin improved progression-free survival and OS but was associated with significantly increased but clinically manageable grade 3–4 toxicities.

Ref 9. Wang et al. (2015). A randomized trial comparing concurrent chemoradiotherapy with single-agent cisplatin versus cisplatin plus gemcitabine in patients with advanced cervical cancer: an Asian Gynecologic Oncology Group study. *Gynecol Oncol*;137:462–7. AGOG Trial.

In this study, 74 patients with FIGO stage III/IVA or stage I/II with PET positive pelvic/PA nodal metastasis were randomized to arm C (weekly cisplatin 40 mg/m²) or arm CG (weekly cisplatin 40 mg/m² and gemcitabine 125 mg/m²), for six cycles. After an interim analysis, accrual was closed early. Results at 3 years were as follows:

	Progression-Free Survival (%)	Overall Survival (%)
Arm C	65.1	74.1
Arm CG	71.0 ns	85.9 ns

The OS and progression-free survival rates were similar in both arms. Despite limitation in power, it suggests that only adding gemcitabine at the chemoRT duration does not improve treatment results, but treatment toxicities could increase.

Ref 10. Chopra S et al. (2016). Phase III RCT of postoperative adjuvant Conventional radiation (3DCRT) versus IGIMRT for reducing late bowel toxicity in cervical cancer (PARCER) (NCT01279135/CTRI2012): results of interim analyses. *Int J Radiat Oncol Biol*;93(3 Supplement):54. PARCER Trial.

In this trial, 120 patients with cervical cancer after hysterectomy randomized to 3D-CRT versus IMRT. RT dose given 200 cGy/fx to 50 Gy +/1 and weekly cisplatin (40 mg/m²), which was followed by two brachytherapy of 6 Gy each. IMRT arm ensured that no more than 200 and 100 cc of small bowel received 15 and 40 Gy, respectively. Median follow-up results of 20 follow.

	Acute Grade 2 (%) Bowel Toxicity	*Late Grade 2 (%) Bowel Toxicity*
3D-CRT	58.9	25
IMRT	54	11.4
P value	0.59	0.02

This study showed that there is no acute bowel toxicity with the use of IGIMRT; however, significant reduction is observed in incidence of late bowel toxicity.

Ref 11. Thakur et al. (2016). Prospective randomized study comparing concomitant chemoradiotherapy using weekly cisplatin & paclitaxel versus weekly cisplatin in locally advanced carcinoma cervix. *Ann Transl Med;*4(3):48.

In this prospective study, 81 patients with FIGO stage IIA to IIIB cervical cancer were randomized to RT and concurrent weekly cisplatin (control arm, 40 mg/m²) versus weekly cisplatin and paclitaxel (study arm, cisplatin 30 mg/m², and paclitaxel 50 mg/m²). EBRT was delivered to a total dose of 50 Gy in 25 fractions followed by intracavitary BRT or supplement EBRT at 20 Gy in 10 fractions with two cycles of respective chemotherapy. Results at median follow-up of 29 months follow.

	Disease-Free Survival (%)	*Overall Survival (%)*
RT + CDDP	64.3	78.6
RT + CDDP + paclitaxel	79.5 ns	87.2 ns

Despite the increased risk of toxicities, these early results favor the addition of paclitaxel into the standard cisplatin-based chemoRT protocol.

Ref 12. Kloop AH et al. (2016). A phase III randomized trial comparing patient-reported toxicity and quality of life (QOL) during pelvic intensity modulated radiation therapy as compared to conventional radiation therapy. *Int J Radiat Oncol Biol;*96(2 Supplement):S3. RTOG 0213.

In this trial 278 patients with cervical and endometrial cancer receiving post-operative RT were randomized to standard four field radiation or IMRT. RT dose was 45—50.4 Gy. Acute GI and GU toxicities and QOL were measured via multiple patient questionnaires such as EPIC, PRO-CTCAE and FACT-Cx. The data showed.

	Bowel Domain Score	Diarrhea (%) Frequency	Urinary Score
3D-CRT	−23.6	51.9	−10.4
IMRT	−18.6	33.7	−5.6
P value	0.048	0.01	0.03

This study showed that IMRT reduces acute patient reported GI and GU toxicity compared with standard RT.

Ref 13. Gupta et al. (2017). Neoadjuvant chemotherapy followed by surgery (NACT-surgery) versus concurrent cisplatin and radiation therapy (CTRT) in patients with stage IB2 to IIB squamous carcinoma of cervix: a randomized controlled trial (RCT). *Ann Oncol*;28(Suppl 5) (abstract 9280_PR).

In this study, 635 patients with clinical stages IB2, IIA, or IIB squamous cervical cancer were randomized to NACT-surgery (paclitaxel and carboplatin X3 cycles) or CTRT (pelvic radiation with cisplatin X5 cycles). Post-op RT was given as per protocol criteria. After a median 58.5 months follow-up, treatment results were as follows:

	5-Year Disease-Free Survival (%)	5-Year Overall Survival (%)
NACT-Surgery	67.5	74.8
CTRT	72.2 ns	74.7 ns

This is the first randomized trial to test NACT followed by surgery with chemoRT. Neoadjuvant chemotherapy followed by radical surgery is not superior to cisplatin-based concurrent chemoRT. ChemoRT should remain the standard treatment for patients with locally advanced SCCa of cervix.

Ref 14. Tewari K et al. (2017). Bevacizumab for advanced cervical cancer: final overall survival and adverse event analysis of a randomized controlled, open-label, phase 3 trial (Gynecologic Oncology Group 240). *Lancet*;390(10103):1654−63. GOG 240 Trial.

In this trial, 452 patients with metastatic, persistent, or recurrent cervical carcinoma randomized to CDDP (50 mg/m^2 on day 1 or 2) plus paclitaxel (135 mg/m^2 or 175 mg/m^2 on day 1) or topotecan (0.75 mg/m^2 on days 1—3 plus paclitaxel (135 mg/m^2 on day 1) with or without bevacizumab (15 mg/kg on day 1) in 21-day cycle. The data are given below.

	Overall Survival (Months)	Fistula (%) Grade >3
Chemo alone	13.3	<1
Chemo + bevacizumab	16.8	6
P value	0.007	—

This study showed that incorporation of bevacizumab into the chemotherapy regimen significantly improved OS in metastatic, persistent or recurrent cervical cancer patients.

OVARIAN CANCER

Ref 15. Rochet et al. (2014). Intensity-modulated whole abdomen irradiation following adjuvant carboplatin/taxane chemotherapy for FIGO stage III ovarian cancer: 4-year outcomes. *Strahlenther Onkol*;191(7):582—9.

In this prospective study, 16 patients with optimally resected FIGO stage III ovarian cancer, who had received six cycles of adjuvant carboplatin/taxane chemotherapy, were treated with consolidation intensity-modulated WART. RT was given, 30 Gy in 1.5 Gy fractions to entire peritoneal cavity, the diaphragm, the liver capsule, and the pelvic and PA node regions. Median follow-up was 44 months.

Median recurrence-free survival is 27.6 months.
Median OS is 42.1 months.
Gr 3 toxicities were diarrhea (25%), leucopenia (19%), nausea/vomiting (6%), and thrombocytopenia (6%). No Gr 4 toxicities occurred.
Small bowel obstruction occurred in a total of six patients due to postsurgical adhesions (19%) or local tumor recurrence (19%).
The peritoneal cavity was the most frequent site of initial failure.

This study showed that consolidation intensity modulated WART after surgery and adjuvant chemotherapy is feasible and can be performed with manageable acute and late toxicity.

Ref 16. Arians et al. (2017). Adjuvant intensity modulated whole-abdominal radiation therapy for high-risk patients with ovarian cancer (international federation of gynecology and obstetrics stage III): first results of a prospective phase 2 study. *Int J Radiat Oncol Biol Phys*;99(4):912—20.

In this phase II study, 20 patients with optimally debulked FIGO stage III ovarian carcinoma with complete remission after carboplatin/paclitaxel chemotherapy were treated with consolidative intensity-modulated WART. WART dose was 30 Gy at 1.5 Gy per fraction. All patients completed WART.

No gastrointestinal acute toxicities higher than Gr 2.
Only one patient experienced acute Gr 4 hematologic toxicity (thrombocytopenia).
The use of IMRT for WART resulted in excellent treatment tolerability rate (>70).

During WART, mean global health status decreased by 18.1 points. Six weeks after WART, global health status had already increased, with a mean score difference of 4.6 relative to baseline.

This study showed that intensity-modulated WART resulted in excellent coverage of the whole peritoneal cavity, with an effective sparing of OARs. Intensity-modulated WART offers a new therapeutic option for consolidation treatment of patients with advanced ovarian cancer.

VULVAR CANCER

Ref 17. Kunos et al. (2009). Radiation therapy compared with pelvic node resection for node-positive vulvar cancer: a randomized controlled trial. *Obstet Gynecol*;114:537−46 GOG 37.

Long-term results of GOG 37 study. In this study, 114 patients with SCCa of the vulva and positive inguinal/femoral LNs after radical vulvectomy and groin dissection were randomized to pelvic lymphadenectomy versus groin/pelvic RT.

Results at 6 years were as follows:

	Overall Survival (%)	Recurrence-Free Survival (%)	Cancer-Related Deaths (%)
Surg + pelvic dissection	*41*	*48*	*51*
Surg + RT	*51 ns*	*59 ss*	*29 ss*

The addition of adjunctive groin and pelvic RT after radical vulvectomy and inguinal lymphadenectomy proved superior to pelvic node resection but was limited to those patients with clinically positive groin nodes and two or more positive groin nodes.

Ref 18. Moore et al. (2012). A phase II trial of radiation therapy and weekly cisplatin chemotherapy for the treatment of locally-advanced squamous cell carcinoma of the vulva: A gynecologic oncology group study. *Gynecol Oncol*;124:529−33 GOG 205.

In this study, 58 patients with unresectable (T3−T4) vulvar SCCa were treated with RT (1.8 Gy/57.6 Gy) plus weekly cisplatin (40 mg/m^2) followed by surgical resection of residual tumor (or biopsy to confirm complete clinical response). Surgery was performed 6−8 weeks after chemoRT with a median follow-up time of 24.8 months.

Clinical complete response 64% of patients (37/58)

Pathological complete response 78% (29/34)

This study showed that RT and concurrent weekly cisplatin chemotherapy achieved a high complete clinical and pathologic response with acceptable toxicity.

Ref 19. Chapman et al. (2017). Adjuvant radiation therapy for margin-positive vulvar squamous cell Carcinoma: defining the ideal dose-response using the National Cancer data base. *Int J Radiat Oncol Biol Phys*;97(1):107−17.

In this study, the impact of adjuvant RT on OS in the case of positive surgical margins after radical vulvectomy was analyzed using the National Cancer Data Base. In total, 3075 patients with vulvar SCCa who underwent initial extirpative surgery with positive margins from 1998 to 2012 were included. The 3-year OS significantly improved with adjuvant RT. Dose of RT was positively associated with OS, the greatest mortality reduction occurred in cumulative doses ≥54 Gy. No survival benefit was seen with ≥60 Gy compared with 54.0–59.9 Gy.

Results at 3 years were as follows:

Dose Range	Overall Survival (%)
30–45 Gy	54.3
45.1–53.9 Gy	55.7
54.0–59.9 Gy	70.1
>60 Gy	65.3

In patients with vulvar SCCa and positive surgical margins, adjuvant RT improves OS with the optimal dose in the range of 54.0–59.9 Gy.

21

Lymphoma and Hematologic Cancers

HODGKIN LYMPHOMA

The estimated incidence in the United States is 8500 with estimated 1050 deaths in 2018.

Hodgkin lymphoma is most prevalent in early life (age 15–30) and after the fifth decade (after 55 years). Reed–Sternberg cells are mononuclear variants (large binucleate cells with central nucleoli and perinuclear clearing) and are a pathognomonic of classical Hodgkin lymphoma, whereas nodular lymphocyte-predominant Hodgkin lymphoma lacks Reed–Sternberg cells. Majority of patients present with supradiaphragmatic disease.

Workup

Risk Factors
- Epstein–Barr virus
- HIV-associated with advanced stage disease
  - Immunosuppression, solid organ transplantation
  - Autoimmune disorders such as rheumatoid arthritis, SLE, sarcoidosis*

Symptoms and Signs
- Fatigue, alcohol-induced pain and pruritus, respiratory symptoms due to mediastinal mass
- Systemic B symptoms:
  - Unexplained weight loss of more than 10% body weight over 6 months before staging
  - Unexplained, persistent, or recurrent fever (Pel-Ebstein pattern waxing and waning) with temperatures above 38 °C during the previous month
  - Recurrent drenching night sweats
- Palpable lymph nodes (number, size, shape, consistency, mobility, and location), palpable abdominal organs—liver, spleen, and bony tenderness

---

*(Ref: Landgren O, et al. J Natl Cancer Inst 2006;98:1321–30.)

Fundamentals of Radiation Oncology
https://doi.org/10.1016/B978-0-12-814128-1.00021-0

Investigations

- CBC with differential, comprehensive metabolic panel, LFTs, T3, T4, TSH, ESR, LDH, pregnancy test (if child-bearing age)
- Excisional biopsy of the lymph node with immunohistochemistry evaluation. Basic IHC panels on FFPET (formalin fixed paraffin-embedded tissue) are CD3, CD15, CD30, CD45, CD20
- Bone marrow biopsy recommended if cytopenias and for negative PET scan; staging laparotomy is not recommended
- Contrast CT chest/abdomen/pelvis
- PET scan is recommended before treatment and is needed for posttreatment assessment
- PFTs if bleomycin is considered
- Echocardiogram if anthracycline-based chemotherapy is considered

Classifications

Rye Classification	WHO Classification

• Nodular sclerosis
• Mixed cellularity
• Lymphocyte predominant
• Lymphocyte depleted
	• Nodular lymphocyte predominant (CD20/CD45+)
	• Classical (CD15/CD30+):
	  Nodular sclerosis
	  Mixed cellularity
	  Lymphocyte rich
	  Lymphocyte depleted

STAGING

Ann Arbor Staging System Updated by Lugano Classification (2012) (see Fig. 21.1)

Limited Stage

Stage I: Involvement of a single lymphatic site (i.e., nodal region, Waldeyer ring, thymus, or spleen)

    Stage IE: Single extralymphatic site in the absence of nodal involvement (rare in Hodgkin lymphoma)

    Stage II: Involvement of two or more lymph node regions on the same side of the diaphragm

    Stage IIE: Contiguous extralymphatic extension from a nodal site with or without involvement of other lymph node regions on the same side of the diaphragm

    Stage II bulky: Bulk in Hodgkin lymphoma is defined as a mass greater than one-third of the thoracic diameter on CT of the chest or a mass >10 cm

Advanced Stage

Stage III: Involvement of lymph node regions on both sides of the diaphragm; nodes above the diaphragm with spleen involvement

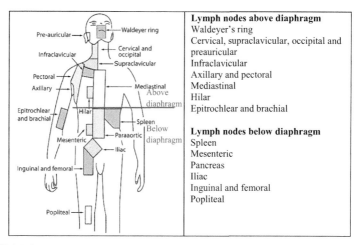

Lymph nodes above diaphragm
Waldeyer's ring
Cervical, supraclavicular, occipital and
preauricular
Infraclavicular
Axillary and pectoral
Mediastinal
Hilar
Epitrochlear and brachial

Lymph nodes below diaphragm
Spleen
Mesenteric
Pancreas
Iliac
Inguinal and femoral
Popliteal

FIGURE 21.1 The lymph node regions as defined in the Ann Arbor staging system.
Reproduced from Wikibooks, Radiation Oncology/Hodgkin/Staging, page 1. Wikimedia Foundation, Inc, 2017.

Stage IV: Diffuse or disseminated involvement of one or more extralymphatic organs, with or without associated lymph node involvement; or noncontiguous extralymphatic organ involvement in conjunction with nodal stage II disease.

OR

Any extralymphatic organ involvement in nodal stage III disease includes any involvement of the CSF, bone marrow, liver, or multiple lung lesions (not direct extension in stage IIE disease)

Note: For HL, each stage should be classified as A or B according to the absence or presence of B symptoms, respectively (as above).

Used with permission of the American Joint Committee on Cancer (AJCC), Chicago, Illinois. The original source for this material is the AJCC Cancer Staging Manual, Eighth Edition (2017) published by Springer Science Business Media LLC, www.springer.com.

Note: *Per AJCC Cancer Staging Manual, Eighth Edition (2017), involvement of pleura, liver, bone marrow and CSF is stage IV.*

Note: *All ipsilateral neck nodes on one side are considered one site. Waldeyer's ring (tonsils, base of tongue, nasopharynx) is a separate site; supraclavicular is a separate site from infraclavicular; axilla is a separate site from epitrochlear/brachial; hilar is separate from mediastinal; spleen, periaortic, iliac, and mesenteric are all separate sites. Inguinal and femoral are combined in one site.*

Patients with Hodgkin Lymphoma are Classified into Groups

1. Early stage favorable (stage I–II with no risk factors)
2. Early stage unfavorable (stage I–II with a risk factor)
3. Stage IIB bulky
4. Advanced stage (stage III–IV)

Risk factors according to the GHSG, EORTC, and NCCN:

Risk Factor	GHSG	EORTC	NCCN
Age		≥50	
ESR and B symptoms	ESR > 50 (A) or > 30 (B)	ESR > 50 (A) or > 30 (B)	ESR ≥ 50 or any B symptoms
Mediastinal mass	MMR>0.33	MTR>0.35	MMR>0.33
Nodal sites	≥3[a] (>2)	>3[a]	>3
Extranodal lesion	any		
Bulky			>10 cm

GHSG = German Hodgkin Study Group; EORTC = European Organization for the Research and Treatment of Cancer; MMR = mediastinal mass ratio, maximum width of mass/maximum intrathoracic diameter; MTR = mediastinal thoracic ratio, maximum width of mediastinal mass/intrathoracic diameter at T5-6.
[a]EORTC combines the Ann Arbor sites infraclavicular/axilla and mediastinum/hilum as one region.

PETCT Response Assessment

Deauville Score*
    Score 1: No uptake
    Score 2: Uptake ≤ mediastinum
    Score 3: Uptake > mediastinum but ≤ liver
    Score 4: Uptake moderately higher than liver
    Score 5: Uptake markedly higher than liver and/or new lesions
    Score 4–5: Considered positive
    *(Ref: Barrington SF, et al. J Clin Oncol 2014;32(27):3048–58)

Treatment

Early Stage Favorable (Stage I, II No Risk Factors)*
- Chemotherapy ABVD ×2, restage with PET, followed by ISRT 20 Gy [1, 3, 4, 5, 7].

Early Stage Unfavorable (Stage I, II with Risk Factors)*
- Chemotherapy ABVD ×4, restage with PET, followed by ISRT 30 Gy [2, 3, 4, 5, 7].

Stage II B Bulky*
- Chemotherapy ABVD ×4–6, restage with PET, followed by ISRT 30 Gy [2, 3, 4, 5, 7].

Advanced Stage (Stage III, IV)*

- Chemotherapy ABVD ×6, restage with PET, followed by consideration for consolidation RT to initial bulky sites or residual disease to 30 Gy for CR; 36—45 Gy for PR [8, 9, 10, 11].

Note: All patients with positive PETCT (FPS 4 or 5) after planned initial chemotherapy should have additional evaluations and/or chemotherapy before initiating radiation, which could include biopsy, additional ABVD, or escalated chemotherapy treatment and/or HD/ASCR [2, 6, 12]. Following HD/ASCR, patients should receive maintenance Brentuximab vedotin; this has been shown to improve PFS.

Nodular Lymphocyte Predominant Hodgkin Lymphoma (NLPHL)**

Early-Stage disease

STAGE 1A, IIA (NONBULKY)
- Observation in a completely excised lymph node or ISRT to 30 Gy.

STAGE IB, IIB (NONBULKY)
- ABVD x2—4 cycles and rituximab, followed by ISRT to 30 Gy.

STAGE I, II (BULKY)
- Chemotherapy ABVD ×4, followed by ISRT 30 Gy.

Advanced-Stage Disease
- **Stage III/IV**: ABVD ×6, followed by ISRT to 30 Gy to bulky disease and to PR sites.

**NCCN guidelines 3.2018.*

Outcome

Stage	Therapy	Progression Free Survival at 5 Years (%)	Overall Survival at 5 Years (%)
Early stage favourable	CMT	92	96
Early stage unfavorable	CMT	87	94
Advanced-stage disease (III/IV)	Chemotherapy ± RT (RT to initial bulky disease or PR after two to four cycles of chemotherapy_	70	85

Ref: GHSG HD10 study, NEJM 2010;363:640—52; Eich HT, et al. GHSG HD11; J Clin Oncol 2010;28(27):4199—206; Merli F, et al. HD2000 study (Fondazione Italiana Linfomi). J Clin Oncol 2016;34(11):1175—81.

International Prognostic Score for Advanced Disease: 1 Point Per Factor

(ref Hasenclever D, Diehl V. A prognostic score for advanced Hodgkin's disease. International Prognostic Factors Project on Advanced Hodgkin's Disease. N Engl J Med. 1998 Nov 19;339(21):1506-14)

- Age above 45 years
- Albumin less than 4 g/dL
- Stage IV disease
- Hemoglobin less than 10.5 g/dL
- Lymphocyte count < 600/μL and/or < 8% of WBC count
- White blood cell count ≥15,000/μL
- Male gender

5-year PFS for IPS: 0 factors—84%, 1 factor—77%, 2 factors—67%, 3 factors—60%, 4 factors—51%, 5 or more factors—42%.

0 Points: 84% Freedom from progression and 89% overall survival

1 Point: 77% Freedom from progression and 90% overall survival

2 Points: 67% Freedom from progression and 81% overall survival

3 Points: 60% Freedom from progression and 78% overall survival

4 Points: 51% Freedom from progression and 61% overall survival

5 to 7 Points: 42% Freedom from progression and 56% overall survival

NON-HODGKIN LYMPHOMA

The estimated incidence in the United States is 74,680 with estimated 19,910 deaths in 2018.

Patients with non-Hodgkin lymphoma (NHL) present quite differently from the Hodgkin patients. Fewer patients present with B symptoms compared with Hodgkin disease. In addition, the common Ann Arbor staging system does not quite predict the clinical presentation of non-Hodgkin disease. As such, non-Hodgkin lymphomas are divided into indolent, aggressive, and highly aggressive lymphomas that more appropriately reflect the clinical behaviors of the disease. Each kind has more subtypes with distinctly different behaviors.

Workup

Risk Factors

- Immunodeficiency (HIV) virus infection or immunosuppression secondary to organ transplant, Epstein—Barr virus infection
- *Helicobacter pylori* bacterial infection
- Alkylating agents and prior radiation exposure

Symptoms and Signs
- Palpable lymph node (number, size, location, shape, texture, mobility), pleural effusion, and pericardial rub
- Examination of pharynx and oral cavity to evaluate Waldeyer ring, palpable abdominal organs—liver, spleen
- Site-specific findings, such as thyroid mass for thyroid lymphoma or bony tenderness for bone lymphoma
- Symptoms A and B are no longer used in NHL

Investigations
- CBC with differential, comprehensive metabolic panel, ESR, LFTs, LDH, HIV, hepatitis B, pregnancy test (if child-bearing age).
- Biopsy of peripheral lymph node/excisional biopsy, basic IHC panel on FFPET are CD3, CD5, CD10, CD45, CD20, CD23, MIB labeling Index (KI 67)
- Cytogenetics t(11; 14), 17p-, t(11q; v), del(13q)
- Bilateral bone marrow biopsy/aspiration
- Echocardiogram if anthracycline-based chemotherapy is considered
- Contrast CT neck/chest/abdomen/pelvis
- PET scan

In select cases, consider:

- Discussion of fertility issues/sperm banking if applicable
- Hepatitis C, beta-2-microglobulin
- Esophagogastroduodenoscopy (EGD) and/or colonoscopy for GI involvement
- CSF cytology with flow cytometry in patients with high-grade lymphoma, primary CNS lymphoma or DLBCL (CNS risk score 4–6*, HIV infection, Testicular involvement, $> = 2$ extranodal sites, Double hit lymphoma)
- Plain bone radiographs and/or MR imaging in patients with bone disease
- MRI brain for patients with CN palsy or suspicion of brain disease/LMD, MRI spine for spine disease/LMD

CNS risk score (1 point per factor): IPI risk factors and adrenal/renal site.

STAGING/GRADING

Note: The standard staging system is the Ann Arbor system same as per Hodgkin disease.

The following is the NCCN classification and WHO classification for non-Hodgkin disease.

NCCN Classification	WHO Classification
B-cell lymphomas:	**B-cell neoplasms:**
Indolent lymphomas	Precursor B-lymphoblastic leukemia
Chronic lymphocytic	CLL/B-cell SLL
leukemia/small lymphocytic	B-cell promyelocytic lymphoma
lymphoma (CLL/SLL)	Lymphoplasmacytic lymphoma
Follicular lymphoma	Hairy cell Leukemia
Marginal zone lymphoma	Plasma cell myeloma/plasmacytoma
(MZL)	MALT lymphoma
• MALT lymphoma	Nodal marginal zone B-cell lymphoma
• Splenic MZL	Follicular lymphoma
• Nodal MZL	Mantle cell lymphoma
	Diffuse large B-cell lymphoma
Aggressive lymphomas	Burkitt lymphoma/leukemia
Diffuse large B-cell	
lymphoma	**T- & NK-cell neoplasms:**
Mantle cell lymphoma	Precursor T-cell ALL
Highly aggressive lymphomas	T-cell promyelocytic lymphoma
Burkitt lymphoma	T-cell large granular lymphocytic
Lymphoblastic lymphoma	lymphoma
AIDS-related B-cell lymphoma	Aggressive T-cell lymphoma
	Adult T-cell lymphoma
	Extranodal NK/T cell
T-cell lymphomas:	lymphoma
Peripheral T-cell lymphoma	Enteropathy-type T-cell lymphoma
Mycosis fungoides	Hepatosplenic T-cell lymphoma
	Subcutaneous panniculitis-like T-cell lymphoma
	Mycosis fungoides
	Primary cutaneous anaplastic large cell lymphoma
	Peripheral T-cell lymphoma, NOS
	Angioimmunoblastic T-cell lymphoma
	Anaplastic large cell lymphoma

MALT, mucosa-associated lymphoid tissue; *WHO*, World Health Organization.

Follicular Lymphoma International Prognostic Index

- Age >60 years
- Serum lactate dehydrogenase concentration above normal
- Hemoglobin level <12.0 g/dL
- Ann Arbor stage III or IV
- Number of involved nodal areas >4

One point is given for each of the above characteristics.
Risk group: low 0–1, intermediate 2, high >3.

Revised International Prognostic Index for Non-Hodgkin Lymphoma

- Age >60 years
- Serum lactate dehydrogenase concentration above normal
- ECOG performance status ≥2
- Ann Arbor stage III or IV
- Number of extranodal disease sites >1

One point is given for each of the above.
Risk group: low 0–1, low intermediate 2, high intermediate 3, high 4–5.

Treatment

Indolent, Stage I/II

NONBULKY
- Treatment is ISRT 24 Gy. Slowly regressing or bulky disease requires higher dose of RT of 30 Gy [13, 14, 15].
- Patient with no response to RT treated with chemotherapy such as cyclophosphamide, bendamustine, and rituximab.

NONCONTIGUOUS, BULKY
- Rituximab with or without chemotherapy. Most common chemotherapy is bendamustine followed by ISRT 30 Gy [16, 17].

Indolent, Stage III/IV

- Treatment is watch and waits.
- However, for symptomatic patients with bulky disease, cytopenia due to lymphoma, progression of disease, or end-organ threat, consider rituximab-based chemotherapy. There are a variety of regimens, including bendamustine*, CHOP[1], CVP[2], FCR[3], FND[4]. In older patients or those with multiple comorbidities and poor performance status, consider single agent Rituxan.
- RT is reserved for palliative control of local symptoms [15].

*(Ref: Mondello P. Oncologist April 2018;23(4):454–60)
[1]CHOP: [cyclophosphamide/adriamycin (doxorubicin/hydroxydoxorubicin)/vincristine (Oncovin)/prednisone].
[2]CVP: [cyclophosphamide, vincristine, prednisone]
[3]FCR: [fludarabine, cytoxan, Rituxan]
[4]FND: [fludarabine, Novantrone, dexamethasone]

Follicular Grade 3B

- Consider treating as DLBCL
- Stage I/II: R-CHOP ×3–4 cycles followed by ISRT 30–36 Gy
- Stage III/IV: R-CHOP ×6 cycles, restage with PET, followed by ISRT 30–45 Gy to bulky sites or PR

Aggressive, Stage I/II

NONBULKY, IPI 0-1

- Treatment is R-CHOP ×3 followed by ISRT 30 Gy. RT for partial responders requires higher RT dose of 36 Gy [18, 19, 20, 21, 22, 23].

BULKY, IPI >1

- Treatment is R-CHOP ×6 followed by ISRT 30–36 Gy.

Aggressive, Stage III/IV

- Treatment is combination chemotherapy with R-CHOP ×6–8 cycles.
- RT may be used to improve local control in partial responders, and for those patients with initial bulky disease, ISRT dose is 30–45 Gy.

Highly Aggressive

High-grade non-Hodgkin lymphomas are treated with a variety of non-CHOP combination chemotherapy with stem cell rescue, such as Hyper CVAD[5] alternating with methotrexate–cytarabine, CODOX-M/IVAC[6], or regimens such as those employed for acute lymphoblastic leukemia can be used.

[5]*Hyper CVAD: [cyclophosphamide, vincristine, doxorubicin (adriamycin), dexamethasone]*

[6]*CODOX-M/IVAC: [cyclophosphamide, vincristine (Oncovin), doxorubicin–high-dose methotrexate alternating with Ifosfamide, etoposide (VP-16), high-dose cytarabine (Ara-c)]*

Gastric MALT Lymphoma

Symptoms include dyspepsia, abdominal pain; B symptoms are rare. Most patients have localized stage I/II disease. Endoscopic biopsy is required with IHC analysis. *H. pylori* status must be performed on histopathology; if negative, perform confirmatory noninvasive testing (stool antigen, urea breath, blood antibody). Translocation t(11.18) is associated with disseminated disease and resistance to antibiotic treatment.

- Early-stage patients with *H. pylori* positive are recommended to receive antibiotic therapy with a proton pump inhibitor. Stable or regression disease can be monitored for up to 18 months before treatment with RT. Patients positive for lymphoma after antibiotic treatment are recommended for ISRT 24–30 Gy. Treat entire stomach and any perigastric LNs. *H. pylori*-negative patients are treated with ISRT 24–30 Gy.
- For advanced-stage patients, treatment is chemotherapy involving rituximab-based chemotherapy. Alternatively, local RT can also be considered.

Extranodal Marginal Zone B Cell Lymphoma (Nongastric MALT Lymphoma)

Most common sites include salivary glands (18%–26%), skin (12%–26%), orbit (7%–14%), head and neck (11%), lung (8%–9%), thyroid (6%), and breast (2%–3%). Following are the treatments:

- Consider empiric doxycycline for cutaneous or ocular disease
- For early stage—ISRT 24 Gy or surgical resection followed by postoperative RT for positive margin

- Advanced stage—the recommended treatment is watch and waits; however, for symptomatic patients with bulky disease, cytopenia due to lymphoma, or progression of disease, consider rituximab-based chemotherapy

Mantle Cell Lymphoma

Propensity for extranodal sites includes head and neck and GI tract. Immunohistochemical profile: CD5+, CD20+, cyclin D1+. Characterized by t(11; 14) resulting in overexpression of cyclin D1. Ki67 proliferation rates <30% associated with more favorable prognosis. Following are the treatments:

- Early-stage limited disease in patients with favorable subtypes can be treated with ISRT 30—36 Gy. Alternatively, combination chemotherapy with rituximab can also be considered.
- For advanced stage disease, the recommended treatment is watch and wait; however, for symptomatic patients due to bulky disease, or cytopenia due to lymphoma, or progression of disease, consider rituximab-based chemotherapy.
- RT is reserved for palliative control of local symptoms; RT dose is 30—36 Gy.

Primary CNS Lymphoma

Treatment of primary CNS lymphoma is R-MPV (rituximab, high-dose methotrexate, procarbazine, vincristine, ± intrathecal chemotherapy) and WBRT.

- Patient CR after chemo WBRT dose is 23.4 Gy, PR patient WBRT to 30—36 Gy followed by a residual disease boost dose to 45 Gy.
- Patients who are not candidates for chemotherapy may receive WBRT to 24—36 Gy followed by residual disease boost dose to 45 Gy.

Chemo and WBRT improve tumor response rates and survival compared with WBRT alone but are also associated with significant neurotoxicity, especially when radiation is followed by methotrexate.

Primary Testicular Lymphoma

Male >60 years old is common presentation. Workup includes lumbar puncture.
Treatment per IELSG trial 10* is
- Radical inguinal orchiectomy
- R-CHOP x 3 cycles every 21 days along with CNS prophylaxis IT-MTX x 4. Followed by additional R-CHOP x 3—5 depending on stage I versus II and response CR versus PR.
- After completion of chemoimmunotherapy, patients receive prophylactic RT to the contralateral testis to 25—30 Gy. In addition, stage II patients receive IFRT to 35 Gy.

*Vitolo U et el (2011). 'First-line treatment for primary testicular diffuse large B-cell lymphoma with rituximab-CHOP, CNS prophylaxis, and contralateral testis irradiation: final results of an international phase II trial.' J Clin Oncol. 2011 Jul 10;29(20):2766-72.

RT performed using lead skin collimation and electrons. Toxicity of RT includes low testosterone.

Primary Mediastinal B-Cell Lymphoma

Young female with bulky mediastinal mass is the most common presentation. B symptoms are common presentation and can present with SVC syndrome.
Treatment is:

- DA-R-EPOCH x 6–8 followed by sequential PETCT to assess response and to determine total chemoimmunotherapy cycles.*
- If R-CHOP is given or low burden residual disease after DA-R-EPOCH, consolidate with RT to 30–36 Gy.

*Dunleavy et al (2015). 'Dose-Adjusted EPOCH-Rituximab Therapy in Primary Mediastinal B-Cell Lymphoma'. N Engl J Med. 2013 Apr 11; 368(15): 1408–1416.

NK-T Cell Lymphoma

Stage I/II: Low risk ISRT to 50–54 Gy alone; High risk ISRT to 45–54 Gy with concurrent/sequential chemotherapy
Stage III/IV: SMILE* followed by ISRT to 45–54 Gy (residual disease)
*SMILE: dexamethasone, methotrexate, ifosfamide, L-asparaginase, etoposide

Outcome

Based on revised FLIPI score

FLIPI score	10-year survival
Low risk 0–1	71%
Intermediate risk 2	51%
High risk >3	36%

(Ref: Smith SM. Hematology 2013:561–7).

Based on revised IPI score

Risk Group	No. of IPI Factors	4-year PFS (%)	4-year OS (%)
Very good	0	94	94
Good	1, 2	80	79
Poor	3, 4, 5	53	55

(ref Hasenclever D, Diehl V. A prognostic score for advanced Hodgkin's disease. International Prognostic Factors Project on Advanced Hodgkin's Disease. N Engl J Med. 1998 Nov 19;339(21):1506-14)

Low-grade follicular lymphomas:
Stage I, II: 10-year PFS is 44%; 10-year OS is 64%
(Ref: Mac Manus MP. J Clin Oncol 1996;14(4):1282—90)
Stage III, IV: 5-year PFS is 58%; 5-year OS is 89%
(Ref: Cheah CY, Ann Oncol 2016;27:895—901)

High-grade lymphomas:
Stage I, II DFS is 75%, OS is 85%
Stage III, IV OS is 55%.

Marginal-zone lymphomas:
Stage I/II: 10-year DFS is 68%; 10-year OS is 87%
(Ref: Goda JS. Cancer 2010;116(16):3815—24)
Stage III/IV: 5-year DFS is 23%; 5-year OS is 69%
(Ref: Arciani L. Oncologist 2006;11:285—91)

Primary CNS lymphoma:
3-year PFS is 51%; 3-year OS is77%
(Ref: Morris PG. J Clin Oncol 2013;31:3971—79)

NK-T cell lymphoma:
Stage I/II(low risk): 5-year PFS is 65%; 5-year OS is 70%
Stage I/II (high risk): 5-year PFS is 64%; 5-year OS is 72%
(Ref: Yang Y. Blood 2015;126:1424—32)
Stage III/IV: 4-year DFS is 60%; 5-year OS is 47%
(Ref: Kwong YM. Blood 2012;120(15):2973—80)

RT Technique

Note: modern RT volume and doses have evolved to improve therapeutic ratio, and uses mostly involved site (ISRT) and involved node (INRT) radiation therapy, utilizing either 3DCRT or IMRT technique. In addition modern imaging is also used to limit RT doses to the critical structure to minimize long term complications.

3D Technique

PREAURICULAR FIELD

Borders: Superiorly at the top of the zygomatic arch, inferiorly below the mandible. Preauricular field is matched on the skin with the mantle field. Anteriorly posterior to third molar and posteriorly to the external auditory canal.

WALDEYER FIELD

Borders: Superiorly at the top of the zygomatic arch, inferiorly below the mandible, anteriorly at the mandibular symphysis, and posteriorly beyond spinous process.

MANTLE FIELD

Patient is supine, arms akimbo, neck extended. Patient is generally treated at 100 cm SSD. BBs are placed at neck, spinal cord, supraclavicular fossa, axilla, superior/middle/lower mediastinum point, and any palpable lymph nodes are wired. **Borders:** Superiorly at the mandible/mastoid, inferiorly at T10 or T11 (one vertebral body above maximal diaphragm excursion to avoid matching through spleen if spleen and paraaortic lymph nodes

(A)   **(B)**

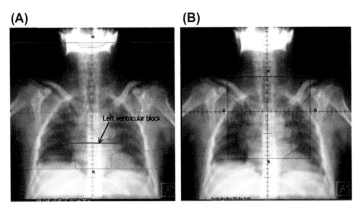

FIGURE 21.2   AP DRR showing 3-D mantle RT field and mediastinal involved field (IF). (A) The mantle field showing a mouth, humeral heads, lung, and left ventricular blocks. The superior border of the mantle field is at mandible/mastoid; inferior border is at T10/T11. (B) The superior border of the IF is C5/C6, inferior border at 5 cm below carina or 2 cm below prechemotherapy inferior extent of the disease; lateral border at postchemotherapy volume with a 1—1.5 cm margin to block edge. *Reproduced from A comparison of mantle vs. involved-field radiotherapy for Hodgkin's lymphoma: reduction in normal tissue dose and second cancer risk. Koh ES, Tran TH, Heydarian M, Sachs RK, Tsang RW, Brenner DJ, Pintilie M, Xu T, Chung J, Paul N, Hodgson DC, Figures 1 and 2, Radiat Oncol;2:13, © 2007 in accordance with BioMed Central Open Access Charter.*

are to be treated); laterally the fields are set clinically to include the axillae inferiorly to the fourth rib. The following blocks are used for the mantel field (see Fig. 21.2).

- **PA C-spine** block placed for PA field after 30 Gy. If bulky cervical nodes approach the midline, then no PA C-spine block.
- **Mouth** block placed for AP/PA fields.
- **Humeral head** block for AP/PA fields. If arms are above head, then no humeral block.
- **Larynx** block for AP field after 19.8 Gy.
- **Lung** blocks for AP/PA fields laterally following the inner rib margins. (Do not block hilar.)
- **Left ventricle** block for AP field. If no pericardial or subcarinal disease is noted, then block the left ventricle from start of the treatment; if pericardium is being treated electively, then block after 14.4 Gy; if subcarina is being treated, then block at 30.6 Gy.

PA FIELD

Patient is supine; generally treated at 100 cm SSD with AP/PA fields. **Borders:** Superior is at T10 or T11; inferior border is at L4/L5, laterals 2 cm from vertebral body edge. PA field is matched at midplane with a 3-mm safety margin extra to the skin gap. The field is extended laterally to encompass the entire spleen, if present.

   Note: PA field is often treated 1 month after the mantle field treatment is completed to limit toxicity.

PELVIC FIELD/INVERTED FIELD

Patient is supine, and AP/PA fields are used. **Borders:** Superior is at L4/L5; inferiorly at 2.5 cm below ischial tuberosity; laterally to encompass inguinal lymph nodes; need a midline block to avoid unnecessary radiation to bladder/bowel and to encompass iliac nodes. Pelvic field is matched at midplane to PA field.

INVOLVED SITE AND INVOLVED NODE FIELD

The involved site field (ISRT) encompasses the originally involved lymph node with a margin to account for uncertainties in pre- and postchemotherapy imaging. Involved-node field (INRT) encompasses the original extent of disease (Fig. 21.3).

INVOLVED FIELD

The involved field encompasses the entire nodal area in which the involved nodes are observed. In general, all ipsilateral neck nodes on one side are considered one involved field (IF) site, such as ipsilateral cervical and supraclavicular region. However, supraclavicular is a separate site from infraclavicular. Axilla includes the ipsilateral supraclavicular and infraclavicular region; however, axilla is a separate site from epitrochlear/brachial. Hilar is separate from mediastinal; spleen, periaortic, iliac, and mesenteric are all separate sites. Inguinal IF includes external iliac and femoral region.

EXTENDED FIELD

The extended field encompasses multiple involved nodal areas and clinically uninvolved contiguous nodal areas at high risk of subclinical disease. When multiple nodal areas are located to the upper side of the diaphragm the extended field is mantle field, and below the diaphragm the extended field if inverted Y field.

IMRT Technique

Patient supine, CT simulation with IV contrast, PETCT fusion. Use 6 MV photons, nine-field IMRT, or two-arc VMAT. Use daily IGRT (Figs. 21.4–21.6).

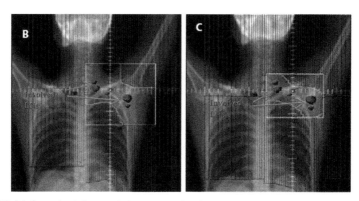

FIGURE 21.3   The left panel shows involved site field (ISRT). The right panel shows the involved node field (INRT). *Reproduced from Kelsey CR, et al. 2012. Combined-modality therapy for early-stage Hodgkin lymphoma: maintaining high cure rates while minimizing risks. Oncology (Williston Park). December 2012;26(12):1182–9, 1193.*

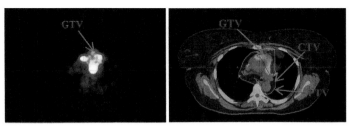

FIGURE 21.4 An HL patient's PET scan shows postchemo gross residual disease, PET fusion with planning CT image shows target volumes GTV, CTV, and PTV based on PET fusion.

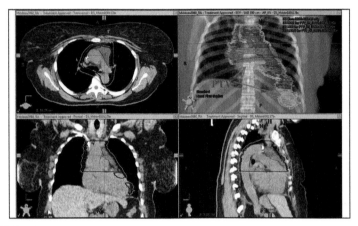

FIGURE 21.5 An HL patient's planning CT images showing target volumes GTV, CTV, ITV, and PTV.

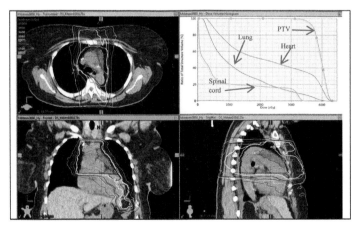

FIGURE 21.6 An HL patient's postchemotherapy CT images showing two-partial arc VMAT treatment plan isodose lines conforming to PTV and DVH meeting all the constraints. The prescription dose is 36 Gy.

Volumes

GTV = prechemotherapy PETCT + postchemotherapy CT (PET) gross disease and lymph nodes

CTV = GTV + 1.5 cm margin superior and inferior + residual disease and involved LNs and suspected clinical involvement (margin can be up to 5 cm superior inferiorly), respecting anatomic boundaries

(ITV = CTV inspiration + CTV expiration for thoracic and abdominal sites)

PTV = CTV/ITV + 0.5–1 cm

Volumes for site-specific extranodal lymphoma

(Ref: ILROG guidelines, Yahalom J et al, Int J radiat Oncol Biol Phys 2015, Vol 92, (1),11–31)

GASTRIC MALT LYMPHOMA

GTV = gross dz + enlarged lymph nodes.

CTV = GTV + stomach from GE junction to beyond the duodenal bulb; whole stomach wall and visible perigastric nodes are included.

ITV = CTV + 1–2 cm.

PTV = ITV + 0.5–1 cm.

CONJUNCTIVAL AND EYELID MALT LYMPHOMA

CTV = Entire conjunctival reflection to the fornices

RETROBULBAR, LACRIMAL GLAND, AND DEEP CONJUCTIVAL LYMPHOMAS MALT LYMPHOMA

CTV: Entire orbit

NASAL NK T-CELL LYMPHOMA

Unilateral, anterior (stage IE) or middle nasal cavity without extension into adjacent organs or bilateral nasal cavity involvement.

CTV = bilateral nasal cavity, ipsilateral maxillary sinus (bilateral maxillary sinus if bilateral nasal cavity involvement), bilateral anterior ethmoid sinuses, and hard palate.

Nasal tumor extending into the nasopharynx: CTV + nasopharynx.

Disease extending into anterior ethmoid sinuses: CTV + posterior ethmoid sinuses.

Disease extending into adjacent structures (extended stage I) or with cervical lymph node involvement (stage IIE): CTV + involved paranasal organs/tissues or cervical lymph nodes.

WALDEYER'S RING NK T-CELL LYMPHOMA

CTV = Waldeyer's ring + adjacent organs/structures with disease extension + cervical LN

Doses

HODGKIN LYMPHOMA

Combined modality

Stage I, II, favorable

PTV1, ISRT = 200 cGy/fx to 20 Gy

Stage I, II (unfavorable), III, IV
PTV1, ISRT = 200 cGy/fx 30 Gy (bulky 36 Gy)
LPHL
Combined modality, PTV, ISRT = 200 cG/fx 20 Gy
RT alone, PTV, IFRT = involved LN 200 cGy/fx to 30−36 Gy, uninvolved LN 24−30 Gy

NON-HODGKIN LYMPHOMA

Indolent (follicular, gastric MALT, nongastric MALT)
PTV = 200 cGy/fx to 24−30 Gy (mantle 30−36 Gy)
Aggressive (DLBCL)
PTV, CR after chemo = 200 cGy/fx to 30−36 Gy
PTV, PR after chemo = 200 cGy/fx to 40−50 Gy
PTV, no chemo = 180 cGy/fx to 45−54 Gy

Constraints

As per the primary disease site planning and treatment—brain, H&N, lung, breast, abdomen. RT dose to critical organs as low as possible to minimize early side effects and long term complications.

Complications

- Fatigue, nausea, vomiting, sore throat, and skin reaction
- Hypothyroidism, pulmonary pneumonitis, and chronic fibrosis
- Acute and chronic pericarditis, cardiomyopathy, myocardial infarction, early coronary artery disease, change in bowel habits with diarrhea and bowel, or rectal damage
- Infertility for males and females with pelvic radiation
- Radiation-induced malignancies
- Herpes zoster
- Neurocognitive decline in elderly PCNSL patients receiving radiotherapy

Follow-Up

- Every 3 months for the first year, every 6 months for the second to fifth year, then every 12 months thereafter
- TSH and CT chest, abdomen, pelvis every 12 months
- Influenza vaccination for patients treated with chest RT or bleomycin every 12 months
- Baseline stress test and echocardiogram 10 years posttreatment
- Breast screening with mammogram and breast MRI 10 years posttreatment, then every 12 months

ANNOTATED BIBLIOGRAPHY

EARLY-STAGE HODGKIN DISEASE

Ref 1. Engert et al. (2010). Reduced treatment intensity in patients with early-stage Hodgkin's lymphoma. *N Engl J Med*;363(7):640. HD 10 Trial.

In this study, 1370 patients with favorable stage I—II HD were randomized to chemotherapy ABVD ×4 cycles versus ABVD ×2 cycles followed by IFRT t o 2 0 Gy versus IFRT to 30 Gy. At 5 years, the data showed the following:

	PFS (%)	OS (%)
ABVD ×2+IFRT 20 Gy	93.2	97.3
ABVD ×4+IFRT 20 Gy	91.6	96.6
ABVD ×2+IFRT 30 Gy	93.9	96.9
ABVD ×4+IFRT 30 Gy	90.8	96.9

This study showed that in patients with early-stage Hodgkin lymphoma and a favorable prognosis, treatment with two cycles of ABVD followed by 20 Gy of involved-field radiation therapy is as effective as, and less toxic than, four cycles of ABVD followed by 30 Gy of involved-field radiation therapy.

Ref 2. Eich et al. (2010). Intensified chemotherapy and dose-reduced involved-field radiotherapy in patients with early unfavorable Hodgkin's lymphoma: final analysis of the German Hodgkin Study Group HD11 trial. *J Clin Oncol*;28(27):4199. HD 11 Trial.

In this study, 1395 patients with newly diagnosed early unfavorable HL were randomly assigned in a 2 × 2 factorial design to

1. *four cycles of ABVD + 30 Gy IFRT*
2. *four cycles of ABVD + 20 Gy IFRT*
3. *four cycles of BEACOPP + 30 Gy IFRT*
4. *four cycles of BEACOPP + 20 Gy IFRT*

At 5 years, OS was 94.5%, and PFS was 86%.

BEACOPP+ 20 Gy was more effective than ABVD+ 20 Gy; however, there was no difference between the results when the chemotherapy was followed by 30 Gy RT. Moderate dose escalation using BEACOPP (baseline) did not significantly improve outcome in early unfavorable HL. Four cycles of ABVD should be followed by 30 Gy of IFRT.

Ref 3. von Tresckow et al. (2012). Dose-intensification in early unfavorable Hodgkin's lymphoma: final analysis of the German Hodgkin Study Group HD14 trial. *J Clin Oncol*;30(9):907. HD 14 Trial.

In this trail, 1528 patients with stage IA, IB, or IIA histologically proven HL with at least one of the following risk factors: bulky mediastinal mass (≥one-third maximum transverse thorax diameter); extranodal involvement; erythrocyte sedimentation rate (ESR) ≥ 50 mm/h (without B symptoms) or ESR ≥ 30 mm/h (with B symptoms); or three or more lymph node areas involved were randomized to either four cycles of ABVD or two cycles of BEACOPP+ 2 cycles ABVD. Both arms received 30 Gy IFRT. At a median follow-up of 43 months, the data showed the following.

	5-Year (%) FFTF	5-Year (%) OS
Arm A	87.7	96.8
Arm B	94.8	97.2
P value	—	—

This study showed that two cycles of BEACOPP+ 2 cycles ABVD arm resulted in a superior FFTF with a difference of 7.2% at 5 years. The difference in 5-year PFS was 6.2%. Intensification of chemotherapy resulted in an improved control in patients with early unfavorable HL.

Ref 4. Radford J et al. (2015). Results of a trial of PET-directed therapy for early-stage Hodgkin's Lymphoma. *N Eng J Med* 2015;372:1598−607. RAPID Trial.

In this trial, patients with newly diagnosed stage IA or stage IIA Hodgkin lymphoma received three cycles of ABVD and then underwent PET scanning. Patients with negative PET findings were randomly assigned to receive IFRT or no further treatment. Patients with positive PET findings received a fourth cycle of ABVD and IFRT. At a median follow-up of 60 months, the data showed the following.

	3-year (%) PFS	3-year (%) OS
PET NEGATIVE		
ABVD ×3+IFRT 30 Gy	94.6	97.1
ABVD ×3	90.8	99
PET POSITIVE		
ABVD ×4+IFRT 30 Gy	87.6 (5 year)	94.5
P values	0.016	

The results of this study did not show the noninferiority of no further treatment after chemotherapy with regard to PFS; nevertheless, patients in this study with early-stage HL and negative PET findings after three cycles of ABVD had a good prognosis either with or without consideration of RT.

Ref 5. Andre M P F et al. (2017). Early positron emission tomograpy response-adapted treatment in stage I and II Hodgkin Lymphoma: final results of the randomized EORTC/LYSA/FL H 10 trial. *J Clin Oncol* June 2017;35(16):1786−94. HD 10 Trial.

In this trial, 1925 patients were randomized on the basis of early PET after two cycles of ABVD—according to EORTC criteria favorable and unfavorable—stage I and II HL The standard arm consisted of ABVD followed by INRT regardless of ePET results. In the experimental arm, ePET-negative patients received ABVD only, whereas ePET-positive patients switched to BEACOPPesc ×2 cycles and INRT. RT dose was 30 Gy. At a median follow-up of 4.5 years, the data showed the following:

	PET Negative 5-Year PFS (%)	
	F	*U*
AVBD alone	*87.1*	*89.6*
ABVD + INRT	*99*	*92.1*
P *value*	*0.017*	*0.026*
	PET Positive 5-Year PFS (%)	
ABVD + INRT	*77.4*	
BEACOPPesc + INRT	*90.6*	
P *value*	*0.002*	

This study concluded that in stage I and II, PET response after two cycles of ABVD allows for early treatment adaptation. In the PET-negative group, risk of relapse increased when INRT is omitted, and in the PET-positive group, switching to BEACOPPesc + INRT improved 5-year PFS.

Ref 6. Fermé et al. (2017). ABVD or BEACOPP baseline along with involved-field radiotherapy in early-stage Hodgkin Lymphoma with risk factors: results of the European Organisation for Research and Treatment of Cancer (EORTC)-Groupe d'Étude des Lymphomes de l'Adulte (GELA) H9-U intergroup randomised trial. *Eur J Cancer* 81:45. H9 U Trial.

From 1998 to 2002, 808 patients with untreated supradiaphragmatic HL with at least one risk factor (age $\geq$ 50, involvement of four to five nodal areas, mediastinum/thoracic ratio $\geq$ 0.35, erythrocyte sedimentation rate (ESR) $\geq$ 50 without B-symptoms or ESR $\geq$ 30 and B-symptoms) were randomized to

- *6-ABVD-IFRT (n = 276)*
- *4-ABVD-IFRT (n = 277)*
- *4-BEACOPP baseline-IFRT (n = 255).*

Five-year EFS rates in the 4-ABVD-IFRT (85.9%) and the 4-BEACOPP baseline-IFRT (88.8%) were not inferior to 6-ABVD-IFRT (89.9%), and the 5-year overall survival estimates were 94%, 93%, and 93%, respectively. However, patients treated with BEACOPP developed serious adverse more often.

Ref 7. Sasse S et al. (2017). Long-term follow-up of contemporary treatment in early-stage Hodgkin Lymphoma: updated analyses of the German Hodgkin Study Group HD7, HB8, HD10, and HD11 trials. *J Clin Oncol June* 2017;35(18):1999−2007. HD 11 Trial.

In this study, 4276 patients with early-stage favorable and unfavorable HL treated within HD 7, 8, 10, and 11 were analyzed for long-term efficacy and safety. At a median follow-up of 120 months, the data showed the following:

	10/15-Year (%) PFS	OS (%)
HD7		
EFRT	52	No
Chemo + RT	73	Difference
HD10		
ABVD ×4+IFRT 30 Gy	87	94
ABVD ×2+IFRT 20 Gy	87	94
HD8		
COPP/ABVD ×2+EFRT 30 + 10 Gy	No	No
COPP/ABVD ×2+IFRT 30 + 10 Gy	Difference	Difference
HD11		
ABVD	No	No
BEACOPP	Difference	Difference
ABVD+30 Gy	84	No
ABVD+20 Gy	76	Difference
BEACOP+30 Gy	84	No
BEACOPP+20 Gy	84	Difference
P value	<0.001	

This analyses shows that long-term follow-up data of the four randomized trials support the current risk-adapted therapeutic strategies in early-stage HL.

ADVANCED-STAGE HODGKIN DISEASE

Ref 8. Borchmann P et al. (2011). Eight cycles OS escalated-dose BEACOPP compared with four cycles OS escalated-dose BEACOPP followed by four cycles of baseline-dose BEACOPP with or without radiotherapy in patients with advanced-stage Hodgkin's lymphoma: final analysis of the HD12 trial of the German Hodgkin Study Group. *J Clin Oncol*;29(32):4234–42. HD 12 Trial.

In this trial, 1670 patients with advanced stage HL two chemotherapies (escalated BEACOPP ×8 vs. escalated BEACOPP ×4 + 4 baseline BEACOPP) plus either no RT *or 30 Gy on bulk+ 30 Gy on residual tumor were compared with each other. At 5 years, the data showed the following:*

	FFTF (%)	OS (%)
BEACOPP escalated	86.4	92
BEACOPP 4 + 4	84.8	90.3
RT arm	90.4	—
No RT	87	—

The analysis showed that the reduction in BEACOPP to the 4 + 4 regimen might decrease efficacy, and the results do not support the omission of consolidation RT for patients with residual disease.

Ref 9. Advani RH et al. (2015). Randomized phase III Trail comparing ABVD plus radiotherapy with the stanford V regimen in patients with stages I or locally extensive, bulky mediastinal Hodgkin Lymphoma: A subset analysis of the North American Intergroup E2496 trial. *J Clin Oncol*;33(17):1936−42. Intergroup E2496 Trial.

In this trial, 794 patients with stage I or II bulky mediastinal HL were randomly assigned to six to eight cycles of ABVD every 28 days or Stanford V once per week for 12 weeks. Two to three weeks after completion of chemotherapy, all patients received 36 Gy of IFRT to the mediastinum, hila, and supraclavicular regions. Patients on Stanford V arm received IFRT to the additional sites >5 cm at diagnosis. At a median follow-up of 6.5 years, the data showed the following:

	5-Year FFS (%)	5-Year OS (%)
Stanford V	79	92
ABVD	85	96
P value	0.22	0.19

The analysis showed that for patients with stage I and II bulky mediastinal HL, no substantial statistically difference was detected between the two regimens.

Ref 10. Carde P et al. (2016). Eight cycles of ABVD versus four cycles of BEACOPP escalated plus four cycles of BEACOPP baseline in stage III to IV, International Prognostic scores >3, high-risk Hodgkin Lymphoma: first results of the phase III EORTC 20012 intergroup trial. *J Clin Oncol*;34(17):2028−36. EORTC 20012 Trial.

In this trial, 549 patients with clinical stage III or IV HL, IPS of 3 or higher, and age 60 years or younger received ABVD ×8 or escalated-dose BEACOPP ×4 followed by baseline BEACOPP ×4 without RT. At a median follow-up of 3.6 years, the data showed the following:

	4-Year EFS (%)	DFS (%)	OS (%)
ABVD8	63.7	85.8	86.7
BEACOPP4+4	69.3	91	90.3
P value	0.312	0.076	0.208

The analysis showed that ABVD8 and BEACOPP4+4 resulted in similar EFS and OS in patients with high-risk advanced-stage HL.

Ref 11. Borchmann P et al. (2017). PET-guided treatment in patients with advanced-stage Hodgkin's Lymphoma (HD18): final results of an open-label, international, randomized phase 3 trial by the German Hodgkin Study Group. *Lancet* December 2017;390(10114):2790−802. HD 18 Trial.

In this trial, 2101 patients with advanced-stage HL (IIB, III, IV) were enrolled to investigate metabolic response determined by PET after two cycles of standard regimen of eBEACOPP (PET2) results. Patients with positive PET2 were randomized to receive six additional cycles of either standard eBEACOPP (8 × eBEACOPP total) or eBEACOPP with rituximab (8 × R-eBEACOPP). Those with negative PET2 were randomized between standard treatment with six additional cycles of eBEACOPP (8 × eBEACOPP) or experimental treatment with two additional cycles (4 × eBEACOPP). After 2011, an amendment to reduce standard therapy to a 6 × eBEACOPP and patients with positive PET2 were not randomized anymore. The data showed the following:

	5-Year PFS (%)
PET2 positive	
eBEACOPP	89.7
R eBEACOPP	88.1ns
PET2 negative	
eBEACOPP ×6−8	90.8
eBEACOPP ×4	92.2ns

The analysis showed that the favorable outcome of patients treated with eBEACOPP could not be improved by adding rituximab after positive PET2. However, PET2 negative allows reduction to only four cycles of eBEACOPP without loss of tumor control.

Ref 12. Engert A et al. (2017). Reduced-intensity chemotherapy in patients with advanced-stage Hodgkins Lymphoma: updated results of the open-label, international, randomized phase 3 HD15 trial by the German Hodgkin Study Group. *HemaSphere* December 2017;1(1):e5. HD 15 Trial.

In this trial, 2182 patients with clinical stage III—IV or stage II with B symptoms and one or both risk factors of large mediastinal mass [$\geq$1/3 of the maximal thoracic diameter] or extranodal lesions were to receive eight cycles of eBEACOPP, six cycles of eBEACOPP, or eight cycles of the more dose-dense BEACOPP-14 in a 1:1:1 ratio. In all three groups, radiotherapy was recommended in case of lesions of at least 2.5 cm in the largest diameter with residual FDG uptake after chemotherapy. At a median follow up of 102 months, the data showed the following:

	10-Year (%) PFS	10-Year (%) OS	10-Year (%) Second Cancer
8×eBEACOPP	*81*	*88*	*10*
6×eBEACOPP	*84*	*90*	*7*
8×BEACOPP-14	*84*	*92*	*7*

This updated analysis of the HD15 trial thus confirms the efficacy and long-term safety of the shortened first-line chemotherapy consisting of 6× eBEACOPP followed by PET-guided RT in advanced-stage HL.

NON-HODGKIN LYMPHOMA

Indolent Non-Hodgkin Lymphoma

Ref 13. Pugh et al. (2010). Improved survival in patients with early stage low-grade follicular lymphoma treated with radiation: a surveillance, epidemiology, and end results database analysis. *Cancer*;116(16):3843.

The Surveillance, Epidemiology, and End Results database for stage I—II, grade 1—2 follicular lymphoma were analyzed. A total of 6568 patients were identified.

DSS	5 Years	10 Years	15 Years	20 Years
RT	*90%*	*79%*	*68%*	*63%*
No RT	*81%*	*66%*	*57%*	*51%*
OS	*5 Years*	*10 Years*	*15 Years*	*20 Years*
RT	*81%*	*62%*	*45%*	*35%*
No RT	*71%*	*48%*	*34%*	*23%*

P < 0.0001 both for DSS and OS.
On multivariate analysis, upfront RT remained independently associated with improved DSS and OS. This SEER analysis showed that upfront RT was associated with improved DSS and OS compared with alternate management approaches.

Ref 14. Lowry et al. (2011). Reduced dose radiotherapy for local control in non-Hodgkin lymphoma: a randomised phase III trial. *Radiother Oncol*;100(1):86.

In this study, 361 sites of indolent NHL (predominantly follicular NHL and marginal zone lymphoma) were randomized to receive 40–45 Gy in 20–23 fractions or 24 Gy in 12 fractions. Also 640 sites of aggressive NHL (predominantly diffuse large B cell lymphoma as part of combined-modality therapy) were randomized to receive 40–45 Gy in 20–23 fractions or 30 Gy in 15 fractions. At a median follow-up of 5.6 years, the data showed the following:

	Indolent NHL		**Aggressive NHL**	
	40–45 Gy	*24 Gy*	*40–45 Gy*	*30 Gy*
Overall response rate	93%	92%	91%	91%

The analysis of this study showed that in a large, randomized trial, there was no loss of efficacy associated with RT doses of 24 Gy in indolent NHL and 30 Gy in aggressive NHL, compared with previous doses of 40–45 Gy.

Ref 15. Hoskin et al. (2014). 4 Gy versus 24 Gy radiotherapy for patients with indolent lymphoma (FORT): a randomised phase 3 non-inferiority trial. *Lancet Oncol*;15(4):457–63. FORT Trial.

This trial explored the dose response for follicular lymphoma and compared 4 Gy in two fractions with 24 Gy in 12 fractions. 299 sites were randomly assigned to 24 Gy and 315 sites to 4 Gy. After a median follow-up of 26 months:

21 local progressions had been recorded in the 24 Gy group.
70 local progressions had been recorded in the 4 Gy group.
Time to local progression with 4 Gy was not noninferior to 24 Gy.

The authors concluded that 24 Gy in 12 fractions was more effective than 4 Gy for indolent lymphoma and should be regarded as the standard of care. However, 4 Gy remains a useful alternative for palliative treatment.

Ref 16. Ardeshna KM et al. (2014). Rituximab versus watch-and-wait approach in patients with advanced-stage, asymptomatic, non-bulky follicular lymphoma: an open-label randomised phase 3 trial. *Lancet Oncol*;15(4)424–35.

In this trial, 379 patients with low-tumor-burden follicular lymphoma (grades 1, 2, and 3a) stage II, III, or IV were asymptomatic (no B symptoms or severe pruritus) and were randomized to watchful waiting versus induction rituximab (375 mg/m^2 weekly for 4 weeks followed by *a maintenance schedule of 12 further infusions given at 2-monthly intervals for 2 years. The data showed the following:*

	At 3 Years (%) Not Needing therapy	PFS (%)	OS (%)
Watch and wait	46	36	94
Rituximab	88	82	97
P *value*	<0.0001	<0.0001	0.40

The analysis of the study concluded that rituximab monotherapy should be considered as a treatment option in patients with asymptomatic, advanced-stage, low-tumor burden follicular lymphoma.

Ref 17. MacManus MP et al. (2016). Treatment with 6 cycles of CVP or R-CVP after involved field radiation therapy (IFRT) significantly improves progression-free survival compared to IFRT alone in stages I-II low grade follicular lymphoma: results of an international randomized trial. *Int J Radia Oncol Biol* December 1, 2016;96(5):938.

In this trial, 150 patients with stage I—II low-grade FL (grade 1—3a) were randomized to IFRT alone or IFRT followed by six cycles of R-CVP (cyclophosphamide 1000 mg/m^2, vincristine1.4 mg/m^2, prednisone 50 g/m^2) D1—5, rituximab 375 mg/m^2 D1. RT dose to bulky sites was 36 Gy. At a median follow-up of 9.6 years, the data showed the following:

	10-Year (%) PFS	10-Year (%) OS
IFRT	41	86
IFRT + R-CVP	59	95
P *value*	0.033	0.40

This study revealed that systemic therapy with R-CVP after IFRT significantly improved PFS.

Aggressive Non-Hodgkin Lymphoma

Ref 18. Coiffier et al. (2010). Long-term outcome of patients in the LNH-98.5 trial, the first randomized study comparing rituximab-CHOP to standard CHOP chemotherapy in DLBCL patients: a study by the Groupe s'Etudes des Lymphomes de I'Adulte. *Blood*;116(12):2040—45.

In this study, 399 patients between 60 and 80 years with stage II–IV DLBC lymphoma were randomized to receive CHOP ×8 every 3 weeks versus CHOP ×8 plus rituximab on day 1 of each cycle. The results at a median follow-up of 10 years showed the following:

	PF Survival (%)	Overall Survival (%)
CHOP ×8	20	27
CHOP ×8 + rituximab	36 ss	43 ss

This study showed that the results from the 10-year analysis confirm the benefits and tolerability of the addition of rituximab to CHOP.

Ref 19. Pfreundschuh et al. (2011). CHOP-like chemotherapy with or without rituximab in young patients with good-prognosis diffuse large-B-cell lymphoma: 6-year results of an open-label randomized study of the MabThera International Trail (MInT) Group. *MINT Trial.*

In this study, 824 patients aged 18–60 years with IPI 0–1, stage II–IV, or bulky stage I DLBC lymphoma were randomized to CHOP ×6 versus CHOP ×6 plus rituximab. In addition, bulky and extranodal sites were given radiation therapy. The results at 72 months showed the following:

	Event-Free Survival (%)
CHOP ×6	55
CHOP ×6 + rituximab	74
P-value	<0.0001

This study showed that rituximab added to CHOP ×6 improved long-term outcomes for young patients with good-prognosis diffuse large-B-cell lymphoma.

Ref 20. Held G et al. (2014). Role of radiotherapy to bulky disease in elderly patients with aggressive B-cell Lymphoma. *J Clin Oncol* April 2014;32(11):1112–8. RICOVER-60 trial.

In this trial, 472 patients with Aggressive CD20+ B-cell lymphomas any stage or IPI were randomly assigned to four arms: CHOP-14 ×6 versus R-CHOP-14 ×6 versus CHOP-14 ×8 versus R-CHOP-14 ×8. The trial stopped at planned interim analysis because R-CHOP-14 ×6 showed improved PFS/OS. Amendment of RICOVER-north—R-CHOP-14 ×6 + 2 plus IFRT and no IFRT. RT was given to those with either bulky disease >7.5 cm or ENI. RT dose was 36 Gy. At median observation of 39 months, the data showed the following:

	PFS (%)	OS (%)
R-CHOP	62	65
R-CHOP + RT	88	90
P value	<0.001	<0.001

The study concluded that additive RT to bulky sites abrogates bulky disease as a risk factor and improves outcome of elderly patients with aggressive B-cell lymphoma.

Ref 21. Stephens DM et al. (2016). Continued risk of relapse independent modality in limited-stage diffuse large B-Cell Lymphoma: final and long-term analysis of Southwest oncology group study S8736. *J Clin Oncol* 1;34(25):2997–3004. SWOG 8736.

In this study, 401 patients with intermediate-/high-grade stage I, II nonbulky non-Hodgkin lymphoma were randomized between CHOP ×8 versus CHOP ×3+IF (involved-field) RT. RT was given 40 Gy with boost to 50 Gy for residual disease. Results at a median follow up of 17.7 years showed the following:

	PFS (Years)	OS (Years)
CHOP ×8	12	13
CHOP ×3+RT	11.1	13.7
P value	0.73	0.38

The study showed that although, at 5 years, CHOP (3) + IFRT showed improved DFS and OS, extended survival data showed similar PFS and OS, with continuous treatment failure.

Ref 22. Pfreundschub M et al. (2017). Radiotherapy to bulky disease PET-negative after immunochemotherapy in elderly DLBCL patients: results of planned interim analysis of the first 187 patients with bulky disease treated in the OPTIMAL>60 study of DSHNHL. *J Clin Oncol* May 2017;35(15_suppl):7506. OPTIMAL Trial.

In this study, 61- to 80-year-old patients were randomized in a 2 × 2 factorial design to 6× CHOP-14 or 6× CHLIP-14 plus 8× rituximab or 12× rituximab. Patients with bulk (>7.5 cm) PET positive after six cycles of chemotherapy were assigned to RT (39.6 Gy), while PET-negative bulks were observed. The data showed the following:

	2-Year (%) PFS	2-Year (%) OS
OPTIMAL trial	79	88
RICOVER trial	75	78
P value	0.345	0.154

This study concluded that RT can be spared in bulky disease PET negative after chemotherapy.

Ref 23. Lamy T et al. (2017). R–CHOP 14 with or without radiotherapy in no-bulky limited-stage diffuse large B-cell lymphoma (DLBCL). *Blood* October 23, 2017. Blood-2017-07-793,984. Lysa/Goelams Group Trial.

In this trial, 334 patients with nonbulky (tumor size <7 cm) limited-stage DLBC received four or six consecutive cycles of R-CHOP delivered every 2 weeks, followed or not by RT at 40 Gy delivered 4 weeks after the last R-CHOP cycle. At a median follow-up of 64 months, the results showed the following:

	5-Year EFS (%)	OS (%)
R-CHOP	89	92
R-CHOP + RT	92	96
P value	0.18	ns

The study concluded that R-CHOP alone is not inferior to R-CHOP followed by RT in patients with nonbulky limited-stage DLBCL.

Sarcomas

SOFT-TISSUE SARCOMAS

The estimated incidence in the United States is 13,040 with estimated 5150 deaths in 2018.

These tumors are mesenchymally derived and can occur in any part of the body but most commonly in the extremities (60%) and predominantly in muscle groups, although patients can present with head and neck, chest, and retroperitoneal tumors.

Sarcomas most commonly metastasize to the lungs and rarely to the lymph nodes (~5%). Angiosarcoma and rhabdomyasarcoma are the most common subtypes associated with lymph node metastases (14%) followed by synovial cell, malignant peripheral nerve sheath tumor, and clear cell sarcoma.

Workup

Risk Factors
- Inherited disorders:
  - Hereditary retinoblastoma—osteosarcoma, soft-tissue sarcoma, and melanoma
  - Li Fraumeni syndrome—breast cancer, brain tumors, acute leukemia, soft-tissue sarcomas, bone sarcomas, and adrenal cortical carcinoma
  - Neurofibromatosis type I—benign and malignant nerve sheath tumors and gastrointestinal stromal tumors (GIST)
- Radiation (therapeutic, diagnostic, or accidental)—angiosarcoma, osteosarcoma
- Environmental toxins—polyvinyl chloride, thorium dioxide (*Thorotrast*)—angiosarcoma, fibrosarcoma, neurofibrosarcomas, spindle cell sarcomas, extraskeletal chondrosarcoma
- Human herpesvirus 8—etiologic agent responsible for all types of Kaposi sarcoma in immunocompromised patients

Symptoms and Signs
- Symptoms secondary to effects of pressure or direct invasion by the tumor, such as numbness, edema, and pain and are site specific
- Painless lump, growing over time

Fundamentals of Radiation Oncology
https://doi.org/10.1016/B978-0-12-814128-1.00022-2

Investigations

All suspected soft-tissue sarcomas should be referred to a specialist sarcoma unit.

- CBC, chemistry panel, BUN/CR, ESR, LDH
- Carefully planned biopsy to reduce risk of seeding at time of surgery—FNA may be adequate for histopathological subtyping or grade assessment, but core needle biopsy, or incisional biopsy, is preferred
- Imaging should be performed before biopsy or surgery
  - CT thorax, CT abdomen for myxoid liposarcomas and retroperitoneal sarcomas
  - MRI should be performed to locally stage the tumor. Consider angiography if concerned about the vessels
  - PET-CT if distant metastatic disease has not already been discovered, or where the decision for amputation or mastectomy would be altered by discovery of metastatic disease

TNM STAGING (SOFT-TISSUE SARCOMAS) TRUNK AND EXTREMITIES

Tx	Primary tumor cannot be assessed
T0	No evidence of primary tumor
T1	Tumor $\leq$5 cm in greatest dimension
T2	Tumor >5 cm in greatest dimension, $\leq$10 cm
T3	Tumor >10 cm in greatest dimension, $\leq$15 cm
T4	Tumor >15 cm in greatest dimension
N0	No regional lymph node metastasis
N1	Regional lymph node metastasis
M0	No distant metastasis
M1	Distant metastasis

FNCLCC HISTOLOGIC GRADE

GX	Grade cannot be assessed
G1	Total differentiation, mitotic count, and necrosis score of 2 or 3
G2	Total differentiation, mitotic count, and necrosis score of 4 or 5
G3	Total differentiation, mitotic count, and necrosis score of 6, 7, or 8

Stage Grouping

Stage IA	T1	N0	M0	G1, GX
Stage IB	T2,3,4	N0	M0	G1, GX
Stage II	T1	N0	M0	G2, G3
Stage IIIA	T2	N0	M0	G2, G3
Stage IIIB	T3,4	N0	M0	G2, G3
Stage IV	Any T	N1	M0	Any G
	Any T	Any N	M1	Any G

TNM, T (tumor), N (regional lymph nodes), and M (distant metastasis).
Used with permission of the American Joint Committee on Cancer (AJCC), Chicago, Illinois.
The original source for this material is the AJCC Cancer Staging Manual, Eighth Edition (2017)
published by Springer Science Business Media LLC, www.springer.com.

Treatment

Stage 1a/b, Extremity, Superficial Trunk, and H&N Lesions
- Surgical wide local excision with oncologically acceptable margins
- Patients with positive margins—recommendation reresection to obtain negative margins
- Stage 1a with clear margins—observe
- Stage 1b with clear margins—consider post-op radiotherapy
- Positive margins, or gross residual disease—perform post-op radiotherapy

Stage II, III, Extremity, Superficial Trunk, and H&N Lesions
- Preoperative radiotherapy should be considered for all patients, especially for large tumor, or where surgery will provide less than a wide negative resection margin [1—3].
- For positive margins or residual disease, postoperative RT is recommended with EBRT or brachytherapy [4—6].
- The use of adjuvant chemotherapy to treat adults with localized resectable soft-tissue sarcoma remains controversial. Benefits are further improved with the addition of ifosfamide to doxorubicin-based regimens but must be weighed against associated toxicities [7,8].

Unresectable, Node-Positive, Distant Metastasis
- Unresectable disease—definitive RT with consideration for concurrent chemotherapy
- Consider regional node dissection and metastasectomy for limited disease followed by localized radiotherapy and chemotherapy

- Disseminated disease—treatment is driven by histology.
  - For doxorubicin sensitive tumors, treatment with olaratumab and doxorubicin has replaced ifosfamide-doxorubicin. Second line agents in this setting include pegylated liposomal doxorubicin, gemcitabine in combination with other agents or gemcitabine alone.
  - For patients with dematofibrosarcima protuberant(DMFP) or giant cell tenosynovial tumor, imatinib is recommeded.
  - For advanced liposarcoma and leiomyosarcoma, trabectin is recommended after doxorubicin-based treatment.

Retroperitoneal/Intraabdominal Sarcomas
- Preoperative radiation followed by surgery. Potential benefits of using pre-op RT are lower doses; the tumor displaces radiosensitive viscera outside the field of radiation.
- Surgery if margin negative observation, margin positive consider reresection or post-op RT.
- Adjuvant chemotherapy regimens following surgical resection have demonstrated decreased local recurrence rates, but the effect on overall survival is less clear.
- Patients with unresectable or progressive disease, the recommendation is best supportive care.

GIST
- Resectable disease surgery followed by possible post-op imatinib
- Lesions determined not to be resectable, treat with imatinib, then reassess response before evaluating whether suitable for surgery
- Metastatic disease—treat with imatinib and consider changing to sunitinib depending on response/progression
- Disease progresses—consider regorafenib, or clinical trial or best supportive care

Kaposi sarcoma
- Optimal control of HIV infection using highly active antiretroviral therapy.
- HAART may be tried as the sole modality in nonvisceral disease; for visceral disease, chemotherapy may be added.
- For palliation of local symptoms, radiotherapy can be used but caution should be used with regard to local toxicities such as mucositis. RT dose is 200 cGy/fx to 20–40 Gy.

RT Technique

CT simulated with extremity in a cast and wire on scar if treating postoperatively. Pre-op CT or MRI can be fused for target delineation. Multifield 3DCRT or IMRT can be used for planning. Use 6 MV photons, nine noncoplanar beams, or two-arc VMAT. A strip of healthy skin/limb circumference is spared, and treatment of whole circumference of bone is avoided. Block growth plates and joint, if possible. Put bolus on the scar. Daily IGRT is recommended (Figs. 22.1 and 22.2).

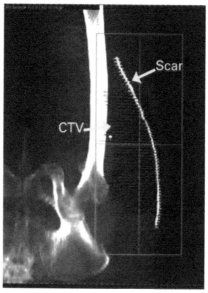

FIGURE 22.1 A right upper thigh STS patient DRR of extremity, sarcoma, oblique field, showing 4–5 cm margin on the post-op tumor site and including the entire scar.

(A)   **(B)**

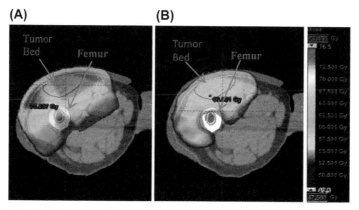

FIGURE 22.2 Example of transaxial isodose distribution for a patient with soft-tissue sarcoma of the thigh treated with (A) 3D-CRT and (B) IMRT techniques showing minimizing dose to the femur and surrounding normal tissue. *From Sladoska A, et al. Application of IMRT in adjuvant treatment of soft tissue sarcomas of the thigh—Preliminary results. Reports of Practical Oncology & Radiotherapy May–June 2011;16(3):110–4.*

Volumes

Preoperative

GTV = gross disease based on imaging (MRI TI postcontrast)

   CTV1 = GTV + 4–5 cm craniocaudally and 1.5 cm radially, respecting anatomical barrier, include peritumoral edema (MRI T2)

   PTV = CTV + 0.5 cm

Postoperative

GTV = none

   CTV1 = tumor bed, surgical clips + 4–5 cm craniocaudally and 1.5 cm radially, respecting anatomical barrier

   CTV2 = tumor bed, surgical clips + 1.5–2 cm craniocaudally and 1.5 cm radially respecting anatomical barrier

   PTV = CTV + 0.5 cm

Doses

Preoperative: 200 cGy/fx to 50 Gy

   Postoperative:

   Negative margin: 180–200 cGy/fx to 50–50.4 Gy, followed by boost dose to 63 Gy (60–66 Gy is acceptable)

   Microscopic positive margin: 200 cGy/fx to 50 Gy, followed by boost dose to 66–68 Gy

   Residual gross disease: 200 cGy/fx to 50 Gy, followed by boost dose to 70–76 Gy

   Brachytherapy boost: Postoperative boost can also be given via low-dose interstitial implant to the tumor bed. Based on the margin status, the radiation dose is 16–18 Gy. The catheters are loaded on or after the sixth post-op day after the wound healing is complete. For boost, use dose rate of 40–60 cGy/h. Start with 1 mCi seeds with 1 cm spacing. For implant >10 cm, use 1 cm spacing; for 10–20 cm, use 1.2 cm spacing; for >20 cm, use 1.5 cm spacing; consider increasing the end seeds by 25%.

Constraints

Depends on location of treatment site such as retroperitoneal or extremity.

   Spared healthy strip of limb circumference <20 Gy.

   Bone V40 < 64%, mean dose <37 Gy, hot spots<59 Gy*

   Joint space <45 Gy

   (*Ref: Dickie et al. Bone fractures following external beam radiotherapy and limb-preservation surgery for lower extremity soft tissue sarcoma: relationship to irradiated bone length, volume, tumor location and dose. Int J Radiat Oncol Biol Phys. 2009 Nov 15; 75(4):1119–24)

Complications

- Delays wound healing (particularly preoperative radiotherapy, but long-term functional outcomes are better in patients who receive pre-op RT, likely due to higher radiotherapy doses and larger treatment sizes needed in postoperative radiotherapy)
- Traumatic fractures, fibrosis with limitation of motion, nerve and vascular injuries, and lymphedema

- Risk of second malignancy
- Reduced fertility, depending on area treated
- Site-specific toxicities, depending on site treated such as renal impairment, enteritis, mucositis, etc.

Outcome

- The 5-year overall survival rates for localized sarcomas, regional stage sarcomas, and sarcomas with distant metastases are 83%, 54%, and 16%, respectively
- For patients with retroperitoneal sarcoma who underwent complete resection, the 5-year survival rate was 58.3%, whereas it was 0% in cases of incomplete or no resection

Follow-up

- Consider baseline postoperative and periodic imaging of site unless site is easily followed by physical examination
- Follow patients every 3 months for the first 2–3 years and every 6–12 months thereafter
- Chest X-ray or CT at each visit

ANNOTATED BIBLIOGRAPHY

PREOPERATIVE RT

Ref 1. Sampath S et al. (2011). Preoperative versus postoperative radiotherapy in soft-tissue sarcoma: multi-institutional analysis of 821 patients. *Int J Radiat Oncol Biol* 81(2):498–505.

In this retrospective analysis, 821 patients with STS of all major anatomic sites who received definitive surgery and either pre-op or post-op RT were included. The median follow-up time was 63 months and the results were as given below:

	5-year (%) CSS
Pre-op RT	79
Post-op RT	74
P values	<0.05

The analysis showed preoperative RT is associated with a reduced cancer-specific mortality compared with postoperative RT in STS.

Ref 2. O'Sullivan B et al. (2013). Phase 2 study of preoperative image-guided intensity-modulated radiation therapy to reduce wound and combined modalities in lower extremity soft tissue sarcoma. *Cancer* 15:119(10):1878–84.

In this trial, 70 patients with histologically proven LE-STS appropriate for preoperative RT and surgery received 50 Gy in 25 daily fractions. Patients received IMRT using daily

CBCT. GTV was delineated per CT or MRI, CTV extended 4 cm superiorly and inferiorly and 1.5 cm radially, restricted at the anatomic barriers, included peritumoral edema. CTV was expanded 0.5 cm to delineate PTV. Data from a median follow-up of 49 months were as follows:

	Wound (%) Complications	Primary (%) Closure	Local (%) Recurrence
This study	30.5	93.2	6.8
NCIC SR2 trial	No difference	71.4	
P value	0.2	0.002	

This study revealed that preoperative IG-IMRT significantly diminished the need for tissue transfer RT chronic morbidities and the need for subsequent secondary operations for wound complications was lowered although not significantly.

Ref 3. Wang D et al. (2015). Significant reduction of late toxicities in patients with extremity Sarcoma treated with Image-Guided Radiation Therapy to a reduced target volume: Results of Radiation Therapy Oncology Group RTOG-0630 Trial. *J Clin Oncol* July 2015;33(20):2231–2238. RTOG 0630 Trial.

In this trial, 98 patients with extremity STS received IGRT with (cohort A) or without (cohort B) chemotherapy followed by limb-sparing resection. Cohort A was closed for poor accrual. All patients in cohort B received IG-RT to 50 Gy in 25 fractions. For G2/3 tumor <8 cm: CTV sup/inf margins 2 cm, radial 1 cm, also cover edema on T2 MR; for G2/3, tumor > 8 cm: CTV sup/inf margins 3 cm, radial 1.5 cm, also cover edema on T2 MR. RT dose prescribed to reduced targeted volume plus 0.5 cm margin for PTV. IMRT or 3DCRT was used for RT. At a median follow-up of 3.6 years, results were as follows:

	Toxicity (%) Grade >2	2 year (%) LC
Cohort B	10.5	94
CAN–NCIC–SR2 trial	37	—
P value	<0.001	

The significant reduction of late toxicities in patient with extremity STS who were treated with preoperative IGRT and absence marginal-field recurrences suggests that the target volumes used in the RTOG 0630 study are appropriate for preoperative IGRT for extremity STS.

POSTOPERATIVE RT

Ref 4. Beane JD et al. (2014). Efficacy of adjuvant radiation therapy in the treatment of soft tissue sarcoma of the extremity: 20-year follow-up of a randomized prospective trial. *Ann Surg Oncol* 21(8):2484–9. NCI Trial.

In this trial, 141 patients with extremity STS were randomized to limb-sparing surgery (LSS) alone or receiving adjuvant EBRT. The study results at a median follow-up of 17.9 years were as follows:

	Local (%) Recurrence	20 year (%) OS	Wound (%) Complication	Edema (%)
LSS	4	64	12.5	12
LSS + RT	0	71	17	25
P value	0.44	0.22	0.72	0.31

The study results show that adjuvant EBRT following surgery for STS of the extremity provides excellent local control with acceptable treatment-related morbidity and no significant improvement in OS.

Ref 5. Folkert MR et al. (2014). Comparison of local recurrence with conventional and intensity-modulated radiation therapy for primary soft-tissue sarcomas of the extremity. *J Clin Oncol* 32(29):3236–41.

In this trial 319, consecutive adult patients with primary nonmetastatic extremity STS were treated with limb-sparing surgery and adjuvant RT. RT dose was generally 50 Gy in 2 Gy fractions for preoperative treatment and was prescribed to the planning target volume (PTV). In the postoperative setting, the PTV is treated to 45 Gy in 1.8 Gy fractions, and then the PTV volume is reduced and treated to an additional 18–21.6 Gy in 1.8 Gy fractions to a total dose of 63–66.6 Gy. Median follow-up data from 90 months were as follows:

	LC	5-year (%) Joint Stiffness	Toxicity Gr > 2 Edema
3DCRT	15.1		
IMRT (80% post-op)	7.6 ss	14.5	7.9
CAN–NCIC–SR2 trial	–	17.8	15.1

The study results showed that IMRT was associated with significantly reduced local recurrence compared with 3DCRT for primary STS of the extremity and late toxicity appear to be less with IMRT.

Ref 6. Robinson MH et al. (2016). Vortex Trial: A randomized controlled multicenter phase 3 trial of volume of postoperative radiation therapy given to adult patients with extremity soft tissue sarcoma (STS). *Int J Radiat Oncol Biol* October 1, 2016; 96(2 Suppl.):S1. VORTEX Trial.

In this trial, 216 patients with extremity STS after tumor resection were treated either in the control arm (C): 50 Gy in 25 fractions to CTV1 (GTV + 5 cm craniocaudally and 2 cm axially) followed by 16 Gy in eight fractions to CTV2 (GTV + 2 cm c-c and axially) or the research arm (R): 66 Gy in 33 fractions to CTV2 alone. No adjuvant chemotherapy was permitted. At a median follow-up of 4.8 years, the results were as follows:

	5-year (%) LRFS	5-year (%) OS	Toxicity Gr > 1	bone joint
Arm C	86	72	11	18
Arm R	84	67	15	18

The study results indicated there was no significant difference in limb function at 2 years between the control and research arms. Because of the small number of events, it was not possible to state whether or not the research arm was inferior for LRFS.

NEOADJUVANT AND ADJUVANT CHEMOTHERAPY

Ref 7. Cesne Le et al. (2014). Doxorubicin-based adjuvant chemotherapy in soft tissue sarcoma: pooled analysis of two STBSG-EORTC phase III trials. *Ann Oncol* 25(12): 2425–32. EORTC 627711/62931 Trial.

In this study, 819 individual patient's data from two EORTC trials (EORTC 62771 and EORTC 62931) were pooled. Adjuvant RT was given to both study arms. At a median follow-up of 8.2 years, results were as follows:

1. Adjuvant chemotherapy CYVADIC reduced the local recurrence rate without any impact on survival (EORTC 62771).
2. Adjuvant chemotherapy AI (EORTC 62931) failed to demonstrate any advantage for both RFS and OS.

This current study showed that adjuvant CT is not associated with a better OS in young patients or any subgroup and therefore is not recommended for routine standard of care.

Ref 8. Pallasini E et al. (2016). Short, full-dose adjuvant chemotherapy (CT) in high-risk adult soft tissue sarcomas (STS): Long-term follow-up of a randomized clinical trial from the Italian Sarcoma Group and the Spanish Sarcoma Group. *J Clin Oncol* May 2016;34(15 Suppl.):1045–11045.

In this trial, 328 patients with high-risk extremity/trunk STS were randomized to receive three preoperative cycles of epirubicin 120 mg/m^2 and ifosfamide 9 g/m^2 (arm A) or to receive the same three preoperative cycles plus two postoperative cycles (arm B). Radiotherapy (RT) could be either delivered in the preoperative or in the postoperative setting. A total dose of 44–50.4 Gy was given in the preoperative setting and 60–66 Gy in the postoperative setting. Patients treated with preoperative RT could also receive an intraoperative (10–12 Gy) or *postoperative boost (16–20 Gy) at the discretion of the treating physician. At a median follow-up of 116 months, results were as follows:*

	10-year DM (%)	10-year OS (%)
Arm A	34.1	64
Arm B	34.8	59

The study results show that at a longer FU, three cycles of a full-dose conventional CT in comparison with five resulted in about 60% patients alive and disease-free at 10 years.

Pediatric Cancers

HODGKIN'S LYMPHOMA

Childhood Hodgkin's lymphoma affects more male than female children. In general, one-third of all patients may present with B symptoms of weight loss, unexplained fever, and night sweats.

On pathology, Reed–Sternberg cells are seen which are positive for CD15 and CD30, while negative for CD20 and CD45. There are four subtypes of Hodgkin's lymphoma. In order of highest to lowest incidence they are as follows: nodular sclerosing, mixed, lymphocyte rich, and lymphocyte depleted. Lymphocyte-depleted Hodgkin's lymphoma is associated with the poorest prognosis.

Radiologically, Hodgkin's lymphoma classically has contiguous spread between lymph node regions (as opposed to non-Hodgkin's lymphomas, which often involve noncontiguous regions).

Workup

Symptoms and Signs
- Systemic B symptoms:
    1. Unexplained weight loss of >10% body weight over 6 months prior to staging.
    2. Unexplained, persistent, or recurrent fever (Pel–Ebstein pattern waxing and waning) with temperatures above 38°C during the previous month.
    3. Recurrent drenching night sweats.
- Loss of energy, pruritus, cough, or dyspnea
- Palpable lymph nodes (number, size, location, shape, consistency, and mobility) and splenomegaly

Investigations
- CBC, ESR, LFTs, creatinine, alkaline phosphatase.
- Excisional biopsy of the lymph node with immunohistochemistry evaluation. Basic IHC panel on FFPET (formalin-fixed paraffin-embedded tissue) are CD3, CD15, CD30, CD45, and CD20.
- Bone marrow biopsy recommended if cytopenias and negative PET scan; staging laparotomy is not recommended.
- Contrast CT chest/abdomen/pelvis.

Fundamentals of Radiation Oncology
https://doi.org/10.1016/B978-0-12-814128-1.00023-4

- PET scan is recommended before treatment and is needed for posttreatment assessment.
- Fertility consultation.

Staging

Ann Arbor Staging System updated by Lugano classification (2012).

LIMITED STAGE[1]

Stage I
Involvement of a single lymphatic site (i.e., nodal region, Waldeyer's ring, thymus, or spleen)

Stage IE
Single extralymphatic site in the absence of nodal involvement (rare in Hodgkin's lymphoma)

Stage II
Involvement of two or more lymph node regions on the same side of the diaphragm

Stage IIE
Contiguous extralymphatic extension from a nodal site with or without involvement of other lymph node regions on the same side of the diaphragm

Stage II bulky
Bulk in Hodgkin's lymphoma is defined as a mass greater than one-third of the thoracic diameter on CT of the chest or a mass >10 cm

ADVANCED STAGE

Stage III
Involvement of lymph node regions on both sides of the diaphragm; nodes above the diaphragm with spleen involvement

Stage IV
Diffuse or disseminated involvement of one or more extralymphatic organs, with or without associated lymph node involvement; or noncontiguous extralymphatic organ involvement in conjunction with nodal Stage II disease; OR Any extralymphatic organ involvement in nodal stage III disease
(Includes any involvement of the CSF, bone marrow, liver, or multiple lung lesions [not direct extension in Stage IIE disease]).

Note: For HL, each stage should be classified as A or B according to the absence or presence of B symptoms, respectively (as above).
Used with permission of the American Joint Committee on Cancer (AJCC), Chicago, Illinois. The original source for this material is the AJCC Cancer Staging Manual, Eighth Edition (2017) published by Springer Science Business Media LLC, www.springer.com.
Note: Per AJCC Cancer Staging Manual, Eighth Edition (2017), involvement of pleura, liver, bone marrow, and CSF is stage IV.
Note: All ipsilateral neck nodes on one side are considered one site. Waldeyer's ring (tonsils, base of tongue, nasopharynx) is a separate site; supraclavicular is a separate site from infraclavicular; axilla is a separate site from epitrochlear/brachial; hilar is separate from mediastinal; spleen, periaortic, iliac, and mesenteric are all separate sites. Inguinal and femoral are combined in one site, not separate.

Children's Oncology Group Risk Classification and Response Definitions

The Children's Oncology Group categorizes patients into low-, intermediate-, or high-risk disease depending on stage, B symptoms, bulk, and degree of response.

Low-risk: stage IA/IIA without bulk (sometimes IIIA is included as well)
Intermediate-risk: all other categories
High-risk: stage IIIB/IVB (sometimes includes IIB)

The definitions of radiologic response are as follows:

Rapid early response (RER): ≥60% reduction in the product of perpendicular diameters of all nodal abnormalities and PET negative.
- RER is evaluated after two cycles of chemotherapy (ABVE-PC). Those not meeting RER criteria are designated slow early responders (SER).

Complete response (CR): ≥80% reduction in the product of perpendicular diameters of all nodal abnormalities and PET negative.

Treatment

Low-Risk Hodgkin's Lymphoma (Favorable Stages I and IIA)
- The recommended treatment is ABVE X2 (doxorubicin, bleomycin, vinblastine, etoposide), then restage. If there is CR, 150 cGy to 15–25.5 Gy involved-field radiation therapy (IFRT); if there is partial response, then ABVE X2; restage then 25.5 Gy/150 cGy IFRT [1, 2, 3].
- Lower radiation doses (15 Gy) are considered for patients with CR after two cycles of chemotherapy and no bulky disease. If bulky disease exists at diagnosis or persistent mass after maintenance chemotherapy, consider higher radiation dose to optimize local control.
- Current low-risk protocol AHOD 0431 schema: AV-PC X3, restage, and determine radiation therapy upon response.

Intermediate-Risk Hodgkin's Lymphoma (Unfavorable Stage I, II, and IIIA)
- Treatment is adapted to response [4, 5]. ABVE-PC (doxorubicin, bleomycin, vinblastine, etoposide, prednisone, cyclophosphamide) is given for two cycles.
  - Individuals who achieve RER, two more cycles of ABVE-PC are given. For those in CR, no further treatment is given.
  - Consider radiotherapy (RT) for those with negative prognostic factors with anemia or bulky disease [4].
  - For those with less than CR, RT is given (150 cGy/fx to 21 Gy).
  - For individuals who are SER with PET-positive disease at the time of response assessment, consider giving augmented therapy with DECA (dexamethasone, etoposide, cisplatin, and cytarabine) for two cycles followed by 150 cGy/fx to 21 Gy.

High-Risk Hodgkin's Lymphoma (Stages IIIB/IVB, ± Unfavorable IIB)

- The recommended treatment is ABVE-PC X3; if CR, then 150 cGy to 21 Gy IFRT [6, 7, 8]; if partial response, then additional ABVE-PC X2 cycles followed by IFRT; if progressive disease, consider alternative chemotherapy regimen and stem cell transplant.
- Alternatively, non–cross-resistant, alternate X8 cycles of chemotherapy with ABVD and MOPP can be considered [6, 7].
- Current clinical trial AHOD 0831: ABVE-PC x 2C; if CR, then two additional cycles of ABVE-PC followed by risk-adapted radiation therapy; if PR or stable disease (SD), then additional ABVE-PC x2cycles with IFOS/VINO x two cycles followed by risk-adapted radiation therapy.

Radiotherapy Technique

The patient is supine in a vacuum immobilization bag (VakLok). CT simulation obtained with 4DCT to assess organ movement. Individuals with treatment targets in the neck should have a thermoplastic frame. For older patients, deep inspiratory breath hold may be considered to move the heart inferiorly reducing cardiac toxicity. Prechemotherapy CT and imaging at response assessment should be fused with the CT simulation dataset.

ISRT is recommended (adapted from AHOD1331 protocol):

GTV = all imaging abnormalities persisting after chemotherapy.
CTV = lymph nodes and tissues originally involved with lymphoma (i.e., the prechemotherapy GTV), but must consider the reduction in axial diameter that occurred with chemotherapy. Typically, on a given axial cut, the whole nodal level that contained the initially abnormal lymph node will be contoured as the CTV. A margin 1.5 cm above and below involved lymph nodes is recommended. For mediastinal targets, an ITV should be created to account for respiratory motion.
PTV= CTV/ITV +0.5 cm

Note: alternatively consider IFRT (per AHOD 0031)—treatment limited to areas of disease involved at presentation.

GTV = lymph nodes >1.5 cm on CT
CTV = Anatomic compartment as defined per protocol
PTV = CTV +1 cm margin

Organs at risk that should be avoided include the following: salivary glands, thyroid, breasts, lungs, heart, liver, kidneys, and gonads. Consider use of a clamshell device for young men receiving RT to the abdomen or pelvis.

Photon

Most patients should be treated with opposed AP/PA beams. In selected cases, 3D-CRT or IMRT may be used (with use of primarily anterior and posterior beam angles to minimize lung doses).

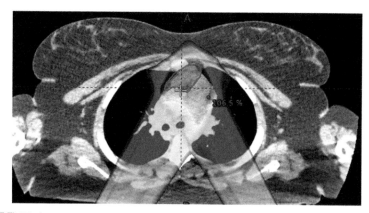

FIGURE 23.1 In this pediatric patient with mediastinal Hodgkin's lymphoma, the target is shown in red and the color wash represent >10% isodoses. Intensity-modulated proton therapy was planned using robust planning, to account for the presence of breathing motion and heterogeneous tissues. The posterior oblique beams can spare breast tissue.

Proton

In selected cases where movement of mediastinal structures is minimal (<5 mm), proton therapy can be considered. Various gantry arrangements are possible, depending on the geometry of target volumes. Posterior beams will spare breast tissue (Fig. 23.1), while anterior beam(s) will spare cardiac structures. 4D CT imaging is essential to measure organ motion, and plans should be created with increased robustness or smearing to account for range uncertainty.

Outcome

For early stage Hodgkin's lymphoma, disease-free survival is 90%; overall survival is 100%. For advanced-stage Hodgkin's lymphoma, disease-free survival is 80%; overall survival is 95%.

Complications

- Thyroid dysfunction
- Heart problems (from anthracycline chemotherapy and RT exposure)
- Impairment of growth such as decreased mandibular growth, infraclavicular narrowing, shortened sitting height, and decreased muscle development
- Radiation-induced second cancer risk ∼0.5—1% per year, most common acute myeloid leukemia and breast cancer.

NEUROBLASTOMA

Neuroblastoma arises from neural crest cells and is typically located in the adrenal glands or paraspinal sympathetic ganglia. It is the most common malignancy of infants, with half of the infants presenting with metastatic disease.

On diagnostic imaging, neuroblastoma typically displaces, rather than arises from the kidney. It frequently crosses midline and contains calcifications on CT.

Workup

Symptoms and Signs
- Fever, weight loss, anorexia, malaise, and lethargy
- Proptosis and orbital ecchymosis
- Spinal cord compression
- Failure to thrive
- Abdominal mass
- Other syndromes
  - Blueberry muffin sign: skin metastases, as observed in neonatal neuroblastoma
  - Horner's syndrome: due to sympathetic dysfunction, seen in the neck or thorax primaries
  - Hutchinson's syndrome: patients have widespread bone pain
  - Kerner-Morrison syndrome: patient have intractable watery diarrhea caused by vasoactive intestinal peptide secretion
  - Opsoclonus–polymyoclonus syndrome: patients with acute cerebellar, truncal ataxia, and dancing eyes
  - Pepper syndrome: infants with massive liver involvement, that compromises respiration

Investigations
- CBC, chemistry, potassium, coagulation panels, urine catecholamines (VMA, HVA), ferritin levels, LDH
- Bilateral bone marrow biopsies and aspirates
- X-ray of the abdomen, CT chest/abdomen/pelvis, and bone scan and PET-CT for tumors that are not MIBG-avid
- MIBG (^{131}I-metaiodobenzylguanidine) scan is specific for tumors of neural crest origin
- Cytogenetics for N-MYC amplification and 11q or 1p loss of heterozygosity

Staging

International Neuroblastoma Staging System (INSS)

Stage 1	Localized tumor with gross total resection with negative regional lymph node (attached lymph node may be positive) and margins negative
Stage 2A	Localized tumor with incomplete gross excision; regional lymph nodes negative
Stage 2B	Localized tumor ± complete resection with involved ipsilateral regional lymph node
Stage 3	Unresectable unilateral tumor infiltrating across the midline involved regional lymph nodes; midline tumor with bilateral extension by infiltration (unresectable) or by lymph node involvement, localized unilateral tumor with contralateral lymph node involvement
Stage 4	Dissemination to distant lymph node(s), liver, bone marrow, and/or skin
Stage 4S	Limited to infants < 1 year AND localized primary tumor with dissemination limited to skin, liver, and/or bone marrow (<10%)

Note: Only 20%–40% of patients present with localized disease.

International Neuroblastoma Risk Group (INRGSS)

Because INSS staging is a surgical staging system, the INRG developed a clinical staging system in 2009 based on radiological features.

Stage L1	Localized tumor not involving vital structures, as defined by a list of image-defined risk factors (IDRFs), and confined to one body compartment
Stage L2	Locoregional tumor with presence of $\geq$1 IDRF
Stage M	Distant metastatic disease
Stage MS	Limited to infants <18 months of age with dissemination limited to skin, liver, and/or bone marrow

Treatment

Low Risk (Stage 1, 2A/B N-MYC Nonamplified)

Recommended treatment is surgery alone [9]. Chemotherapy is used for recurrent or progressive disease, consisting of VAdrC or OPEC (Oncovin [vincristine], prednisone, etoposide, chlorambucil). Radiation therapy is reserved for local failure following treatment with surgery and chemotherapy.

In selected cases of low-risk disease in infants, observation without surgery is a feasible option [9, 11].

Intermediate Risk (Stage 3, 4N-MYC Nonamplified)

Recommended treatment is surgery followed by chemotherapy and second-look surgery to remove any residual disease. Radiation therapy is given if residual disease is present (21.6 Gy) or in the setting of local failure after treatment with surgery and chemotherapy [10].

High Risk (Stage 3N-MYC Nonamplified Unfavorable Histology, Stage 2A/B, 3, 4N-MYC Amplified)

The recommended treatment is induction chemotherapy followed by surgery. Patients then receive further high-dose chemotherapy and tandem autologous stem cell transplant [12, 14]. All patients receive consolidative RT to the primary site (21.6–23.4 Gy) and up to five metastatic sites (21.6 Gy). Patients with gross residual disease after chemotherapy receive boost RT to a total dose of 36 Gy. Following RT, patients receive oral cis-retinoic acid [12] and immunotherapy anti-GD2 antibody, ch14.18 [13].

Stage 4S

The recommended treatment is RT to the primary tumor site and enlarging liver causing the respiratory distress. Localized treatment to massive hepatic metastases (Pepper syndrome) is 150 cGy X3, using a field-based technique or clinical markup (from the nipple line to the pubis). Reevaluation and additional radiation may be delivered as needed.

Treatment Technique

A CT-based treatment planning is performed. 4DCT is helpful to measure organ motion. Vacuum bag immobilization devices are used to reduce torso movement. A one-phase treatment plan is for patients with no residual disease, whereas two-phase treatment plan is used to treat residual disease. IMRT should be used for most cases. In select cases with low magnitude of organ motion and retroperitoneal primaries, proton therapy with one or two posterior beams can be considered (Fig. 23.2).

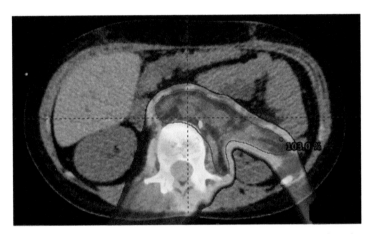

FIGURE 23.2   A patient with retroperitoneal neuroblastoma treated with intensity-modulated proton therapy (IMPT). In this patient, two posterior oblique beams were used to avoid the left kidney. The red line represents the CTV, while the color wash represents the 50% isodose line. Note the relatively homogeneous dose over the corpus of the vertebral body.

Volumes

GTV1 = postchemotherapy preoperative treatment volume
CTV1 = GTV1 + 1.0−1.5 cm (ANBL1531 will use 1 cm)
GTV2 = postoperative, pretransplant disease
CTV2 = GTV2 + 1.0 cm
ITV/PTV = CTV + 0.5 cm, use 4DCT information to create a patient-specific volume

Dose

PTV1: 180 cGy/fx to 21.6−23.4 Gy
PTV2: 180 cGy/fx to 36 Gy
Depending on the treatment protocol, vertebral bodies may require treatment to 18−20 Gy to prevent scoliosis in skeletally immature patients.

Constraints

For organs at risk, the following dose constraints should be used (adapted from ANBL1531):

LIVER	
V30	<15%
Mean	<15 Gy
KIDNEY (FOR LATERALIZED PRIMARY)	
Ipsilateral kidney V18	<75%
Ipsilateral kidney mean	≤18 Gy
Contralateral kidney V18	<25%
LUNG	
Total Lung V20	<30%
Ipsilateral Lung V20	<30%
Contralateral Lung V20	<10%
VERTEBRA	
If adjacent to treatment field, the vertebrae should have a mean dose	≥18 Gy

Outcome

For early stage disease (stage 1−2), disease-free survival is 90%. For advanced disease (stage 3−4), disease-free survival is 30%−60%.

Complications

- Decreased creatinine clearance and lower renal tolerance
- Sinusoidal obstruction syndrome (veno-occlusive disease) of the liver, a posttransplantation complication that can be exacerbated by RT
- Spinal deformity in long-term survivors
- Soft tissue and muscular hypoplasia
- Secondary malignancy

WILMS' TUMOR (NEPHROBLASTOMA)

Wilms' tumor is composed of immature renal cells and is the most common abdominal tumor in children. Anaplastic Wilms' tumors with hyperdiploid mitotic figures and enlarged nuclei have poor prognosis. In addition to anaplastic Wilms' tumor, other unfavorable histologies are clear cell sarcoma and rhabdoid tumor. Wilms' tumor has a tendency to metastasize to lung and liver. On the other hand, clear cell sarcomas typically metastasize to the brain and bone, while rhabdoid tumors primarily metastasize to the brain.

Workup

Symptoms and Signs
- Abdominal pain, hematuria, fever, hypertension
- Unilateral flank mass
- Associated genetic syndromes:
  - WAGR: Wilms' tumor, aniridia, genitourinary malformation, mental retardation; deletion at 11p13/WT1
  - Beckwith–Wiedemann syndrome: microcephaly, ear lobe grooves, macroglossia, umbilical hernia, organomegaly, postnatal gigantism, hemihypertrophy; results from alterations at WT2
  - Denys–Drash syndrome: pseudohermaphroditism, renal disease; mutation at 11p13/WT1.

Investigations[1]
- CBC, chemistry with liver and renal function tests, urine catecholamines (to rule out neuroblastoma)
- Biopsy only for unresectable or bilateral disease
- Chest X-ray, CT chest/abdomen/pelvis, bone scan, bone marrow and skeletal survey in clear cell only, and brain MRI in rhabdoid tumors. Doppler ultrasound to assess renal mass and look for vascular thrombus
- Cytogenetics including WT1 (11p13) and evaluation for 1p16q loss of heterozygosity

Histology

Favorable
- Triphasic
- 90% nephrogenic rests
- Focal anaplasia

Unfavorable
- Diffuse anaplasia
- Hyperdiploid

Note: Clear cell sarcoma of the kidney or rhabdoid tumors are no longer considered Wilms' tumors.

Staging

Children's Oncology Group Staging System

Stage I	Tumor limited to kidney and completely excised, no rupture, no capsular penetration, margins negative
Stage II	Tumor extends beyond the kidney but is completely excised, extra renal vessels infiltrated or contain tumor thrombus, margins negative

[1]**Note:** In all pediatric tumors, except Wilms', obtain bone marrow biopsy.

Stage III	Residual nonhematogenous tumor confined to the abdomen, or (a) positive lymph nodes, (b) diffuse peritoneal contamination, (c) peritoneal implants, (d) margins positive, (d) tumor spillage or rupture A tumor that is biopsied before surgery is stage III.
Stage IV	Hematogenous metastases, e.g., lung, liver, or brain
Stage V	Bilateral renal involvement at diagnosis; each side should be staged separately

Treatment

Stage I Favorable Histology

Recommended treatment is nephrectomy. During nephrectomy, the contralateral kidney and liver are palpated and para-aortic and renal hilar lymph nodes are biopsied. No post-op RT is indicated. Consider chemotherapy VA (vincristine, actinomycin D) is recommended for 10 weeks for ≥ 2 years, tumor ≥ 550 gm [15].

Stage I Unfavorable Histology, Stage II Favorable Histology

The recommended treatment is nephrectomy and VA chemotherapy for 1 year.
For stage II favorable histology (FH), no post-op RT is indicated [15, 16].
For stage I with focal or diffuse anaplasia, flank RT to 1080 cGy.

Stage II Unfavorable Histology, Stage III, IV Favorable Histology/Unfavorable Histology

The recommended treatment is nephrectomy followed by post-op RT given concurrently with VAA chemotherapy (vincristine, actinomycin D, adriamycin) for 1 year. RT must start within 9 days postoperatively [15, 16, 17].

Stage III, IV FH: RT dose is 1080 cGy to the flank
Stage II-IV with focal anaplasia: RT dose is 1080 cGy to the flank
Stage II with diffuse anaplasia: RT dose is 1080 cGy to the flank
Stage III, IV with diffuse anaplasia: The RT dose is 1980 cGy to the flank [18, 19]

For any residual disease of 3 cm or more, a focal boost dose of 1080 cGy is also given.

Stage III with positive ascites, preoperative tumor rupture, diffuse surgical spillage, and peritoneal seeding: The RT dose is 1050 cGy whole abdomen RT (150 cGy/day). Patients with gross residual tumor will receive a focal boost dose of 1050 cGy.
Stage III with diffuse, unresectable peritoneal implants: RT dose is 2100 cGy whole abdomen RT.

Stage IV Lung Metastases

The dose for pulmonary metastases is 150 cGy/fx to 12 Gy (whole lung) +/− 7.5 Gy boost for residual disease.

Stage V

Each site is biopsied separately. A tumor biopsy might not reveal anaplasia due to tumor heterogeneity and sampling error.

Nephron-sparing surgery is recommended, with partial nephrectomy(ies) +/− biopsy of the contralateral side if possible, and biopsy of the lymph nodes during the initial exploration. Partial nephrectomy(ies) may be done after 5 weeks of chemotherapy as a second-look surgery. RT dose is adapted to clinicopathologic findings on each side. RT is also recommended if persistent disease is noted during reassessment at 12 weeks.

Unresectable

The recommended treatment is to give 5 weeks of pre-op VAA chemotherapy (vincristine, dactinomycin, adriamycin), then re-evaluate at week 6. If still unresectable, then give pre-op RT; many will not get to surgery, so RT doses may be > 1200 cGy with vincristine chemotherapy. If resectable, treat with RT 1080 cGy postoperatively.

Clear Cell Sarcoma

The recommended treatment for all stages is to post-op RT and chemotherapy with etoposide, cyclophosphamide, doxorubicin, and vincristine. The RT dose is 1080 cGy. If residual disease is present, boost with 1080 cGy.

Patients with stage III disease due to preoperative tumor rupture, peritoneal metastases, or spillage outside the tumor bed receive whole abdomen RT to 1050 cGy. Patients with diffuse, unresectable peritoneal implants receive whole abdomen RT to 2100 cGy.

Rhabdoid

Recommended treatment for all stages is to give post-op RT for any stage of tumor, followed with chemotherapy (carboplatin, etoposide, and cyclophosphamide).

RT dose is 1080 cGy in children aged ≤12 months, and 1980 cGy for those aged >12 months. If residual disease is present, a boost of 1080 cGy may be given.

For those with stage III disease due to rupture, peritoneal metastases, or tumor spill outside the tumor bed, whole abdomen RT is given. The dose is 1050 cGy in children aged ≤12 months and 1050 cGy plus a 900 cGy flank boost in those aged >12 months.

For those with stage III disease due to diffuse unresectable peritoneal implants, whole abdomen RT is given. The dose is 1050 cGy in children aged ≤12 months and 2100 cGy in those aged >12 months.

Radiotherapy Technique

Patients should undergo CT simulation. The radiation therapy should start within 9 days of surgery. Initial RT is given concurrently with chemotherapy (vincristine and actinomycin D), with anthracycline (doxorubicin) added at week 4 after chemotherapy initiation.

Tumor Bed Field (Flank)

The tumor on the preoperative CT should be outlined on the CT simulation scan. The superior, inferior, and lateral field borders should be placed 1 cm from the preoperative kidney volume (including any vascular tumor thrombus). The medial border should extend across midline to include 1 cm beyond the vertebral body but exclude the contralateral kidney.

If lymph nodes were positive, the entire para-aortic lymph node chain should be included. This includes a superior border at the diaphragmatic crura and an inferior border at the bottom of L5.

For residual tumors, a boost dose is given with a 1 cm margin.

The treatment should be delivered using opposed AP/PA fields.

Whole Abdomen Field

Whole abdomen RT is indicated for patients with preoperative tumor rupture, diffuse abdominal spill (but not localized flank spill), or peritoneal metastases. The field should include the entire peritoneal cavity, which extends from the dome of the diaphragm to the bottom of the obturator foramen. Whole abdomen dose is 150 cGy per fraction to 1050 cGy. Blocks are placed 1 cm beyond the dome of the diaphragm. The femoral heads, acetabuli, and 1 cm beyond the lateral abdominal wall and heart are shielded. The kidney dose must be <1440 cGy. The liver dose is <1980 cGy.

Whole abdomen RT should be delivered using opposed AP/PA fields (Fig. 23.3).

Whole Lung Field

For metastatic disease to the lungs, the whole lung dose is 1200 cGy (150 cGy per day). For children aged <12 months, the dose is 1050 cGy.

The target volume includes the entire lung, pleural surfaces, and diaphragmatic recesses. The superior, lateral, and inferior field edges should extend 1 cm beyond this volume. The inferior border is often located at the L1 level. Whole lung RT should be delivered using opposed AP/PA fields (Fig. 23.3).

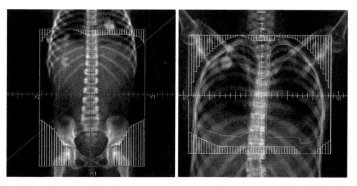

FIGURE 23.3   (Left) AP whole abdominal radiotherapy (RT) field. Shielding to block pelvic soft tissues should be placed with care to ensure that the peritoneal cavity is still included in the field with ≥1 cm margin. (Right) AP whole lung RT field. Note thyroid shielding superiorly.

Note: In AREN0533, for patients who have whole lung RT delayed until 6 weeks after chemo, those who have rapid CR of lung metastasis can avoid whole lung radiation [20].

Outcome

For early stage disease (stage I/II), disease-free survival is 80%–90% and overall survival is 95%. For advanced-stage disease (stage III/IV), disease-free survival is 50%–80% and overall survival is 60%–90%.

Complications

- Cardiomyopathy or coronary artery disease
- Hypothyroidism
- Skeletal growth disturbances (short sitting height)
- Radiation-induced nephropathy
- Radiation-induced malignancies including lung cancer and soft tissue sarcoma

RHABDOMYOSARCOMA

Rhabdomyosarcomas (RMS) are composed of immature mesenchymal cells of the striated muscles. Histologically, they are small round blue cell tumors.

The risk of lymph node involvement is higher for patients with RMS in the bladder/prostate, head and neck, extremity, and paratesticular (age >10 years) locations. Common distant sites of metastasis for RMS are the brain, bone, and lungs.

Workup

Symptoms and Signs
- Tumor causing volume and pressure effects on the respective organs of origin
- Examination of HEENT for H&N and bimanual examination for GU sites
- A genitourinary mass causes
  - urinary frequency
  - hematuria
  - urinary or rectal obstruction
- Cranial nerve palsies for base of skull/parameningeal lesions

Investigations
- Laboratory tests with CBC, chemistry with liver and renal function tests
- CSF cytology for parameningeal sites
- Biopsy of tumor, bilateral bone marrow aspiration, and core needle biopsy
- Chest X-ray, CT/MRI of primary, CT chest/abdomen/pelvis, PET-CT

Histology

Favorable
- Embryonal
- Botryoid (GU in infants)

Unfavorable
- Alveolar (older children)
- Pleomorphic (adults)
- Undifferentiated

Note: In the Children's Oncology Group study ARST1431, treatment for Group I tumors is adapted based on FOXO1 fusion status (presence of a FOXO1-PAX3 or FOXO1-PAX7 fusion is a negative prognostic factor).

Staging

Favorable sites: Orbit, nonparameningeal H&N, nonbladder/-prostate GU, biliary tract

Unfavorable sites: Parameningeal (nasopharynx, nasal cavity, middle ear, paranasal sinuses, mastoid, infratemporal fossa, pterygopalatine fossa, parapharyngeal space), bladder/prostate, extremity/trunk

Note: The orbit is *not* a parameningeal site.

TNM Pretreatment Staging System

Stage	Site	Size	Node	Mets
1	Favorable	Any	Any	M0
2	Unfavorable	5 cm	N0	M0
3	Unfavorable	>5 cm	N0	M0
		Any	N1	M0
4	Any site	Any	Any	M1

Clinical Group Staging

Group IA	Localized disease, completely resected, confined to the organ/muscle of origin
Group IB	Localized disease, completely resected, contiguous infiltration outside organ/ muscle, lymph node negative
Group IIA	Microscopic residual, lymph node negative
Group IIB	No microscopic residual, lymph node positive
Group IIC	Microscopic residual, lymph node positive
Group III	Incomplete resection or biopsy with gross residual
Group IV	Distant metastases at diagnosis

Note: Stage determines chemotherapy; Group determines RT.

Risk Grouping
Low Risk
>Embryonal, stages 1, groups I–III
>Embryonal, stage 1, group III orbit
>Embryonal, stage 2–3, group I–II

Intermediate Risk
>Embryonal, stages 2–3, group III
>Alveolar, stages 1–3, groups I–III

High Risk
>Any histology, stage 4, group IV

Treatment

Local Control
Resectable tumors should receive an upfront maximum safe resection.

Unresectable tumors should receive a biopsy followed by neoadjuvant chemotherapy. The patient should undergo reevaluation for local control at 13 weeks, which may consist of surgery and/or chemoRT.

Patients with head and neck tumors with visual compromise, cranial nerve palsy, or intracranial extension may receive RT for local control upfront to prevent acute worsening of symptoms.

Tumors that are generally treated nonsurgically include orbit, parameningeal, bladder/prostate, and special pelvic sites (vagina, cervix, uterus), which by definition are Group III (since biopsy used to establish diagnosis).

For orbit and bladder/prostate primaries, biopsies of the primary and regional lymph nodes are followed by chemotherapy and radiation therapy.

For special pelvic sites (vagina, cervix, uterus), chemotherapy is given. For patients with a pathologic complete response (pCR), the traditional approach has been to omit radiation. However, this approach may lead to a higher local failure rate; thus, meticulous examination under anesthesia, biopsies, and/or local excision are essential to ensure that a true pCR is achieved before omitting RT.

Chemotherapy
The recommended treatment is to use combination chemotherapy of VAC (vincristine, actinomycin D, cyclophosphamide) for patients with localized disease. Patients with metastatic disease may also be treated with additional IE (ifosfamide/etoposide). Alternatively, chemotherapy (VAC) with an escalating dose of cyclophosphamide followed by recombinant human G-CSF can also be considered for localized disease. In some protocols, topotecan is also given. The latter approach has been used for high-risk patients with alveolar and undifferentiated histology.

Chemotherapy (VAC) is for 12 weeks after initial biopsy/surgery, followed by concurrent radiation with chemotherapy at week 12–13 [21–27].

Radiotherapy	Site	Radiotherapy Dose/Volume
Group I	Unfavorable histology	36 Gy
Group II	N0	36 Gy
Group I or II	N+	41.4 Gy
Group III	Orbit	45 Gy
	Other sites (with gross residual disease)	50.4 Gy (<5 cm) 59.4 Gy (≥5 cm)[a]

[a]*Tumors ≥5 cm treated with 50.4 Gy have a higher local failure rate [26]. Thus, ARST1431 is evaluating the role of dose-escalation in patients with large tumors (≥5 cm).*

Radiation in Stage IV

In patients with stage IV disease, local control is delivered at 20 weeks. Following all chemotherapy, consolidation RT or surgery are given to **all** metastatic sites, including whole lung RT for any lung metastases seen at diagnosis 150 cGy/fx to 15 Gy.

Metastatic sites may be treated with conventionally fractionated RT or stereotactic body RT (SBRT). Sites in CR may receive 40 Gy in 20 fractions; sites with a partial response or less should receive 50 Gy in 25 fractions.

Radiotherapy Technique

Radiation simulation is dependent on the site to be treated, but generally requires CT and MRI simulation with fusion of imaging at diagnosis. IMRT or proton therapy is appropriate.

Radiotherapy Volume
GTV1 = prechemotherapy tumor volume
CTV1 = GTV1 + 1–1.5 cm
GTV2 = postchemotherapy tumor volume
CTV2 = GTV2 + 1 cm

For patients with N1 nodes, the entire lymph node chain is included in the clinical target volume.

PTV = CTV+0.5 cm

Keep critical structure dose limits as follows:

Liver	V50 < 30%
Whole liver	<23.4 Gy

(*Continued*)

Kidney	V50 < 24%
Whole kidney	V10 < 14.4 Gy
Lung	V20 < 20%
Bilateral lungs	V10 < 15 Gy
Optic nerve/chasm	<54 Gy
Spinal cord	<45 Gy
Small bowel	<45 Gy
Whole abdomen	<24 Gy
Whole heart	<30 Gy
Lacrimal gland/cornea	<41.4 Gy
Lens	<14.4 Gy

Outcome

Disease-free survival rate for group I is 80%—90% and for group II is 75%—85%. Overall survival rate for group I is 90%—95%; group II is 80%—85%; group III is 70%—75%; and group IV is 30%.

Complications

Complications are treatment site specific and include the following:

- Brain: neurocognitive dysfunction
- Hypothalamus—pituitary axis: neuroendocrine dysfunction, especially growth hormone deficiency
- Head and neck: facial deformity, cataracts, hearing loss, trismus
- Pelvis: hypogonadism, soft tissue hypoplasia, and infertility

EWING'S SARCOMA

Ewing's sarcoma originates from either mesenchymal or neuroectodermal cells. The most common site is distal femur. It frequently involves the diaphysis of long bones and commonly metastasizes to the lungs and bone marrow. Occult metastases are frequent; thus, chemotherapy is essential for successful treatment. **Askin tumor** is a variant of Ewing's sarcoma with small, round cells involving the chest wall with a large soft tissue component. It is similar to extracranial peripheral neuroectodermal tumor (PNET).

Ewing's sarcoma is a small round blue cell tumor. Negative prognostic factors include male sex, older age (>15 years), pelvic primary site, large size (>8 cm), and metastatic dissemination.

Workup

Symptoms and Signs
- Pain (common presenting symptom)
- Fever (negative prognostic factor)
- Neurologic symptoms from nerve compression
- Pelvic tumors can present with bladder voiding difficulty
- X-ray can show a bony lytic lesion along with a soft tissue mass
- Classic appearances on X-ray include an onion-skin lesion or Codman's triangle

Investigations
- CBC, chemistry with renal and liver function tests, ESR, LDH
- Biopsy of the soft tissue tumor component
- Bone marrow biopsy
- Chest X-ray and CT thorax, CT/MRI of primary, PET-CT
- Cytogenetics for t(11; 22) fusion (EWS-FLI1 fusion)

Treatment

Chemotherapy

Recommended treatment is induction chemotherapy regimen VDC alternating with IE (vincristine, doxorubicin, cyclophosphamide with ifosfamide, etoposide) [28–32].

Surgery
- Fewer than 20% of the tumors are resectable at the time of diagnosis. Local therapy is given at week 12 of chemotherapy. If the tumor can be resected with negative margins and functionality, surgery is recommended.
- If margins are negative, then post-op RT is not recommended. For individuals with positive margins, adjuvant RT should follow surgery.

Radiotherapy

PRIMARY SITE
- For a positive margin, post-op RT is recommended within 2 weeks of surgery.
- For microscopic positive margin, treat the prechemotherapy volume to 50.4 Gy.
- For gross residual disease, treat the prechemotherapy volume to 45 Gy, followed by a boost to 55.8 Gy.
- For unresected disease, treat the entire prechemotherapy bony and soft tissue mass with a 1 cm margin to 45 Gy; this is followed by treatment of the prechemo bony tumor volume and postchemo soft tissue volume with a 1 cm margin to a final dose of 55.8 Gy.
- Patients with resectable disease in select sites (such as pelvis, and chest wall) can be considered for pre-op radiation to 36 Gy followed by surgery within 2 weeks to minimize risk of positive margin.

LYMPH NODES
For individuals with positive lymph nodes, the first phase of treatment should include the entire lymph node drainage chain. Gross, unresected disease should be followed by a boost.

Resected lymph nodes: 50.4 Gy (phase 1 plan)
Unresected patients with resectable disease in select lymph nodes: 45 Gy (phase 1),
55.8 Gy (total dose, phase 2)

ASKIN TUMOR

Recommended treatment is biopsy of the tumor, followed by chemotherapy, then
resection if possible; otherwise, RT. For patients with positive pleural cavity
cytology, treating the entire pleura is recommended.

METASTATIC DISEASE

All sites of metastases (except bone marrow) are treated at the conclusion of
chemotherapy. RT doses are as follows:
Lung metastases: Age <6 years receive 12 Gy, >6 years receive 15 Gy at 150 cGy/
day. For unresected lung metastases, give a 34.2−36 Gy boost.
Bone metastases: 45−56 Gy or treat with SBRT 30−40 Gy in five fractions.
Malignant ascites/diffuse peritoneal involvement: Whole abdomen RT to 24 Gy in
1.5 Gy/fx.

Radiotherapy Technique

Simulation parameters are adapted to the site being treated. IMRT or proton therapy
may be used for most treatment sites. Ensure that no beams are passing or exiting
through a contralateral extremity.

For extremity lesions, use a small vacuum bag and a small thermoplastic frame to
immobilize the limb distal to the treatment site. For extremity targets, spare a small
strip of soft tissue, avoid treating both epiphyses of a joint and do not treat the whole
bone. Fig. 23.4.

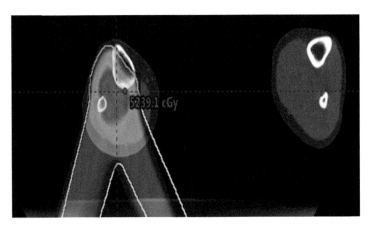

FIGURE 23.4   Proton treatment of a patient with a right leg Ewing sarcoma and
prominent soft tissue component. Red color wash represents prescription dose, while
green and blue color wash represent low isodoses. Two posterior oblique beams are
used. Note the ability of the proton beams to spare a large strip of tissue from receiving
any radiation.

Volumes

PRE-OP VOLUMES

GTV1 = prechemotherapy extent of the bone and soft tissue disease
CTV1 = GTV1+1−2 cm
GTV2 = prechemotherapy extension of the bone disease and postchemotherapy soft tissue disease
CTV2 = GTV2+1−2 cm
PTV = CTV+0.5 cm

POST-OP VOLUMES

GTV1 = none
CTV1 = GTV1
GTV2 = residual bone, microscopic margin soft tissue abnormality
CTV2 = GTV2 + 1 cm
PTV= CTV+0.5 cm

Doses, No Chemo

PTV1 = 180 cGy/fx to 45 Gy
PTV2 = 180 cGy/fx to 55.8−61.2 Gy (vertebral body lesion max dose 50.4 Gy)

Doses, Post-op

PTV1 = 50.4 Gy, <90% necrosis (+/− microscopically positive margin)
PTV2 = 50.4 Gy, microscopic+ and >90% necrosis, 55.8 Gy gross disease

Outcome

Nonmetastatic, nonpelvic disease-free survival is 70% and overall survival is 80%. Nonmetastatic, pelvic disease-free survival is 50%−60% and overall survival is 60%−70%.

5-year overall survival is 60%−80% for all patients localized disease and 5%−30% for all individuals with metastatic disease. Bone marrow metastases are associated with poorer prognoses than bone or lung metastases.

Complications

- Posttreatment fracture and soft tissue fibrosis
- Hip dysfunction and pelvic growth disturbance, joint contracture
- Radiation cystitis
- Lymphedema
- Secondary tumors
- Loss of fertility (for pelvic primaries)

Follow-Up

- Every 3 months for the first year
- Every 6 months for the second year and every 12 months thereafter
- CT chest and imaging of the primary site every 3 months
- Bone scan or PET-CT as clinically indicated

RETINOBLASTOME

Retinoblastoma is the most common childhood ocular malignancy. Retinoblastoma is usually unilateral (75%) but also can be bilateral (25%), particularly in patients with germline RB1 mutations. The retinoblastoma (RB1) gene is located on the long arm of 13q. It is an autosomal recessive gene, but acts in a dominant fashion in the hereditary disease due to spontaneous loss of heterozygosity. Of those with unilateral disease, 10% are familial in etiology; of those with bilateral disease, 25% are familial.

Bilateral disease is typically hereditary and multifocal and presents at a younger age. Trilateral retinoblastoma is bilateral retinoblastoma associated with a pineal tumor. Retinoblastomas can metastasize to the neuraxis (including leptomeningeal spread), lymph nodes, bone, liver, spleen, and bone marrow; however, lung metastases are rare.

Note: The diameter of the eye globe is ~22 mm. The bony canthus is at the equator, ~5 mm behind the lens; the posterior aspect of the lens is ~3 mm from the limbus.

Workup

Symptoms and Signs
- The majority of patients present with leukocoria, strabismus, poor vision, vitreous seeding, or retinal detachment.
- Cat's eye reflex.
- Patients with retinoblastoma in developing countries may have extensive disease within or beyond the eye at diagnosis with massive tumors involving over half of the retina, multiple tumors diffusely involving the retina, obvious seeding of the vitreous, or extraocular involvement.
- Possible examination of parents and siblings.

Investigations
- Slit-lamp examination and indirect ophthalmoscopy
- Orbital ultrasound
- EUA of both eyes with mapping of the tumors
- Orbital/head CT/MRI (vitreous calcification, also assess degree of ocular/orbital involvement)
- Biopsy is contraindicated due to possible choroidal seeding
- For disease beyond the retina, a lumbar puncture, biopsy, bone marrow biopsy, and bone scan are recommended
- Genetic counseling and testing

Staging

Reese–Ellsworth Classification
This system is commonly used but does not predict survival well. It was developed in the 1960s when most patients were treated with external beam RT and predicts the chance of eye preservation.

Note: Disk diameter = 1.5 mm.

Group I	Very favorable for maintenance of sight
	a. Solitary tumor, less than 4 disc diameters in size, at or behind the equator
	b. Multiple tumors, none over 4 disc diameters in size; all at or behind the equator
Group II	Favorable for maintenance of sight
	a. Solitary tumor, 4 to 10 disc diameters in size, at or behind the equator
	b. Multiple tumors, 4 to 10 disc diameters in size behind the equator
Group III	Possible for maintenance of sight
	a. Any lesion anterior to the equator
	b. Solitary tumors larger than 10 disc diameters behind the equator
Group IV	Unfavorable for maintenance of sight
	a. Multiple tumors, some larger than 10 disc diameters
	b. Any lesion extending anteriorly to the ora serrata
Group V	Very unfavorable for maintenance of sight
	a. Massive tumors involving over half the retina
	b. Vitreous seeding

Note: Approximately 85% of patients present with one or both eyes categorized as group V.

International Classification for Intraocular Retinoblastoma

This local staging system is useful for describing the extent of disease within the eye.

Group A	Tumor ≤3 mm in the retina; 1.5 mm away from optic disc and 3 mm away from fovea
Group B	Any tumor >3 mm, confined to the retina; ≤3 mm subretinal fluid at base of tumor without subretinal seeding
Group C	Tumor with subretinal and/or vitreous seeding ≤3 mm, or local subretinal fluid >3 but ≤6 mm
Group D	Diffuse vitreous or subretinal seeding >3 mm, or subretinal fluid >6 mm
Group E	Presence of any of the following:

- >2/3 of globe filled with tumor
- Tumor in anterior segment or on ciliary body
- Iris neovascularization or neovascular glaucoma
- Opaque media from hemorrhage
- Tumor necrosis with aseptic orbital cellulitis
- Phthisis bulbi

Treatment

Limited Disease <4 Disc Diameters

Limited local treatment should only be considered when the risk for multifocal disease is low (older child and nonhereditary). However, with the use of chemotherapy, local treatments may also be reasonable for multifocal disease.

- **Photocoagulation** is best used for lesions posterior to the equator with little elevation. Laser beam treatment is not directed at the retinoblastoma lesion but aims to obliterate the feeding vessels.
- **Cryotherapy** is used for lesions anterior to the equator without vitreous seeding. A freeze—thaw cycle is repeated at least 3 times. It is contraindicated in posterior lesions and with vitreous seeding.
- **Radioactive brachytherapy plaques** are used for 4—12 mm solitary lesions, >3 mm from the disc of fovea with a thickness <10 mm. Lesion plus 2 mm margins are treated. I-125 radioactive seeds are used for treatment. RT dose is 1000—1500 cGy/d to 40—45 Gy, prescribed to the apex of the lesion.

Advanced Unilateral Disease

- The recommended treatment is multiagent chemotherapy with carboplatin, vincristine, and etoposide followed by local treatment.
- Enucleation is performed only on a blind eye or eye which does not have a reasonable expectation of sight after treatment. In enucleation, at least 10 mm of optic nerve should be resected. If the optic nerve has a positive margin, then post-op RT should be given.

Indications for adjuvant external beam RT include residual disease, invasion of the cut end of the optic nerve, prior intraocular operative procedure, and/or extrascleral extension. Patients with these adverse factors require external beam treatment of the orbit and optic nerve to a dose of 45—54 Gy. If patients have dural or brain extension, then whole brain RT or CSI is indicated.

Bilateral Disease

- One eye usually has more advanced disease, with less involvement of the other eye. Enucleation of the eye with more advanced diseased is indicated only if the eye is blind.
- If both eyes are blind, then give a trial of RT before enucleation.
- If both eyes have sight, then make an effort to preserve both eyes with chemotherapy and focal treatment [33]. Close follow-up is necessary to determine the need for further focal treatment.

External Beam Technique

The patient is supine and has face mask on and arms by side, CT simulation. Proton therapy or photon IMRT may be used; use of proton therapy may reduce the risk of secondary cancers, particularly for patients with germline RB1 mutation.

Per ARET 0321, patients with stage 2 and 3 disease will undergo RT within 42 days after ×4 cycles of consolidation chemo. Stage 4a and 4b patients will start after stem cell infusion.

The target volume for external EBRT is the entire orbit, as well as the orbital nerve to the optic chiasm. RT dose is 180–200 cGy/fx to 40–45 Gy.

Note: When using anesthesia, avoid ketamine, as it can give a lateral nystagmus.

Outcome

Intraocular involvement: 5-year disease-free survival >90%
Extraocular extension: 5-year disease-free survival <10%

Complications

- Alopecia, including loss of eyelashes
- Radiation dermatitis
- Cataract formation
- Severe soft tissue and orbital hypoplasia (may require reconstructive surgery)
- Retinopathy and vision loss
- Secondary cancers (extremely high risk for RB1 germline mutants)
  - Propensity to develop soft tissue sarcomas, osteosarcoma, and melanoma

ANNOTATED BIBLIOGRAPHY

LOW-RISK HODGKIN'S LYMPHOMA

Ref 1. Kung et al. (2006). POG 8625: a randomized trial comparing chemotherapy with chemoradiotherapy for children and adolescents with Stages I, IIA, IIIA1 Hodgkin disease: a report from the Children's Oncology Group. *J Pediatr Hematol Oncol*;28(6):362–8. POG 8625 Trial.

In this study, children <21 years of age with biopsy-proven, pathologically staged I, IIA, or IIIA1 Hodgkin disease were randomized between six courses of chemotherapy of alternating nitrogen mustard, oncovin, prednisone, and procarbazine/doxorubicin, bleomycin, vinblastine, and dacarbazine versus four courses of chemotherapy of alternating nitrogen mustard, oncovin, prednisone, and procarbazine/doxorubicin, bleomycin, vinblastine, and dacarbazine + IFRT to 2550 cGy. At 3 years the results showed the following:

	Event-Free Survival (%)	Overall Survival (%)
Chemo alone	90	No
Chemo + IFRT	90	difference

This study showed that for pediatric patients with asymptomatic early stage and intermediate-stage Hodgkin disease, chemotherapy and chemoradiotherapy both resulted in statistically indistinguishable EFS and overall survival.

Ref 2. Wolden et al. (2012). Long-term results of DDG 5942: a randomized comparisons of chemotherapy with and without radiotherapy for children with Hodgkins' lymphoma — a report from the Children's Oncology Group. *J Clin Oncol*;30(26):3174—80. CCSG 5942.

In this study, 498 patients who achieved an initial CR after receiving COPP/ABVD X4—6 cycles chemotherapy were randomized to receive low-dose involved-field radiation (21 Gy LD-IFRT) versus observation. At median follow-up of 7.7 years the result showed the following:

	Event-Free Survival (%)	Overall Survival (%)
COPP/ABVD + IFRT	91.2	97
COPP/ABVD	82.9	95.9
P-value	0.057	0.50

This study showed that IFRT improved statistically significant event-free survival (EFS) but did not lead to an overall survival advantage.

Ref 3. Castellino S et al. (2014). Outcomes and patterns of failure in children/adolescents with low risk Hodgkin lymphoma (HL) who are FDG-PET (PET3) positive after AVPC therapy. *Klin Padiatr*; 226(O_06). AHOD0431 Trial.

In this trial, 287 patients with low-risk HL stage I/II, without bulk, received three cycles of AVPC chemotherapy. FDG-PET was captured after cycles 1 (PET1) and 3 (PET3). CR was defined as > 80% reduction in the size of nodal masses, or return to normal size on CT, and negative findings on PET3. Patients who achieved a CR received no further therapy. Those with a partial response (PR) received 21 Gy IFRT. The data show the following:

Four year EFS was 79.8%, and overall survival (OS) was 99.6%.
Four year EFS for PET1 positive 68.4% versus negative 88.1% (P = 0.0008).
Four year EFS for CR patients 78% versus PR patients 83%
Four year EFS for PET3 positive 72% versus negative 80% (P = 0.38).
EFS for patients received RT, PET3 positive 72% versus negative 85% in (P = 0.18).

This study demonstrates that PET1 is a highly significant prognostic indicator in low-risk HL among children/adolescents treated with three cycles of AVPC, PET-3 appears less predictive. AVPC ×3 cycles alone not standard of care.

INTERMEDIATE-RISK HODGKIN'S LYMPHOMA

Ref 4. Friedman et al. (2014). Dose-intensive response-based chemotherapy and radiation therapy for children and adolescents with newly diagnosed intermediate-risk Hodgkin lymphoma: a report from the Children's Oncology Group Study AHOD0031. *J Clin Oncol*;32(32):3651—8. AHOD0031 Trial.

In this randomized controlled trial, 1712 patients with intermediate-risk Hodgkin lymphoma were enrolled. Patients were initially treated with two cycles of ABVE-PC chemotherapy, followed by interim response assessment. Those with a rapid early response (RER) received an additional two cycles of ABVE-PC, followed by CR evaluation. Those with RER and CR were randomly assigned to involved-field RT (IFRT) or no further treatment. Patients with slow early response were randomized to receive augmented therapy with DECA for two cycles and IFRT versus IFRT alone. The results were as follows:

	4-Year Event-Free Survival (%)	P-Value
ALL PATIENTS WITH RER AND CR		
RT	87.9	0.11
No RT	84.3	
PATIENTS WITH RER, PET-NEGATIVE AFTER 2 CYCLES, AND CR		
RT	86.7	0.87
No RT	87.3	
ALL PATIENTS WITH SER		
DECA	79.3	0.11
No DECA	75.2	
PATIENTS WITH SER, PET-POSITIVE AFTER 2 CYCLES		
DECA	70.7	0.05
No DECA	54.6	

This study supported early response assessment in selecting patients suitable for omission of RT. It also suggested that the addition of DECA for patients with slow early response and PET-positive disease at interim assessment may improve event-free survival.

Ref 5. Charpentier et al. (2016). Predictive factor analysis of response-adapted radiation therapy for chemotherapy-sensitive pediatric Hodgkin lymphoma: analysis of the Children's Oncology Group AHOD 0031 Trial. *Int J Rad Oncol Biol Phys*;96(5):943–50. AHOD 0031 Trial.

In this secondary analysis of AHOD0031, which evaluated the role of IFRT in patients with RER, various clinicopathologic factors and their association with outcome were analyzed. In the subgroup of 190 patients with anemia and bulky disease who achieved RER and CR after chemotherapy, 4-year results were as follows:

	4-Year Event-Free Survival (%)	P-Value
PATIENTS WITH ANEMIA AND BULK WITH RER AND CR		
IFRT	89.3	0.19
No IFRT	77.9	

Thus, individuals with bulky stage I/II disease and anemia may benefit from RT, despite achieving RER and CR after chemotherapy.

HIGH-RISK HODGKIN'S LYMPHOMA

Ref 6. Hunger et al. (1994). ABVD/MOPP and low-dose involved-field radiotherapy in pediatric Hodgkin's disease: The Stanford experience. *J Clin Oncol*;12(10):2160–6.

In this study, 57 children with HL stage I–IV were treated using six cycles of MOPP/ABVD and low-dose IFRT. They received one cycle of ABVD and one cycle of MOPP. Patients were fully reevaluated after the two cycles of chemotherapy. RT was then given to 150–180 cGy to 15 Gy to involved fields. If the patient had massive mediastinal disease, nodal masses >6 cm, or sites that had not responded completely to the two initial cycles of chemo, then boost RT dose was given to a total dose of 25 Gy. The boost doses (10 Gy) were administered after the fourth and sixth cycles of chemotherapy. For patients with disease above and below the diaphragm, RT was STNI or TNI. Oophoropexy was done in females prior to pelvic RT. Results at 10 years showed the following:

	Disease-Free Survival (%)	Overall Survival (%)
All patients	93	96
Stage IV patients	69	85

All patients had normal growth and development. No patient developed a second malignancy, symptomatic cardiac, pulmonary, or thyroid disease. This older study showed that this treatment was effective, but the sample size was insufficient to accurately describe late radiation-induced toxicities.

Ref 7. Weiner et al. (1997). Randomized study of intensive MOPP- ABVD with or without low-dose total-nodal radiation therapy in the treatment of stages IIB, IIIA2, IIIB, and IV Hodgkin's disease in pediatric patients: a Pediatric Oncology Group study. *J Clin Oncol*;15(8):2769–79. POG 8725.

In this study, 183 children with HD stages IIB, IIIA2, IIIB, and IV were randomized to receive alternating MOPP-ABVD X 8 cycles with or without low dose TNI. RT was given at the completion of eight cycles of chemo to patients in CR. Patients with no disease below aortic bifurcation received STNI, with pelvic disease received TNI; fields were treated sequentially with a 2-week rest period between each port. All lymphoid tissue including spleen received 150 cGy to 21 Gy; nonlymphoid tissue lung, pericardium, liver, and kidney received 10.5 Gy. Chemo was given for four 1-month cycles of MOPP alternating with four 1-month cycles of ABVD. Results at 5 years showed as follows:

	Elapse-Free Survival	Overall Survival
MOPP-ABVD X8	79	96
MOPP-ABVD X8+RT	80	87

This study showed that after the delivery of eight cycles of MOPP—ABVD, the addition of low-dose RT does not improve the estimated EFS or OS in pediatric patients with advanced-stage Hodgkin's disease.

Ref 8. Kelly KM et al. (2015). Phase III study of response adapted therapy for the treatment of children with newly diagnosed very high risk Hodgkin lymphoma (stages IIIB/IVB) (AHOD0831): a report from the Children's Oncology Group. Abstract 3927, session 623. Lymphoma: Chemotherapy, excluding pre-clincial models: poster III. AHS 57th Annual Meeting, Orlando. AHOD0831 Trial.

In this trial 165 patients aged ≤21 years with stage IIIB or IVB HL were nonrandomly assigned to receive two 21-day courses of ABVE-PC (doxorubicin, bleomycin, vincristine, etoposide, prednisone, cyclophosphamide). RER was defined by FDG-PET negativity (i.e., no activity above background), irrespective of size of residual masses. Patients with RER were consolidated with two additional cycles of ABVE-PC. SER received two cycles of ifosfamide/vinorelbine (IFOS/VINO) followed by two more cycles of ABVE-PC. RT, 21 Gy in 14 fractions, was administered to sites of initial bulky involvement (large mediastinal mass, nodal aggregate >6 cm, splenic macronodular involvement) and regions of SER. At median follow-up of 42 months the data showed as follows:

Four year second EFS 89.9%; RER 91.9%, SER 87.8%, Stave 89.6%
Four year OS 95.9%

This study revealed that among pediatric patients with very high-risk HL (IIIB, IVB), a response directed approach utilizing limited chemotherapy (4 cycles for RER; six cycles for SER) and risk directed RT did not reach the ambitiously high pre-specified target for second EFS. Similar outcomes to POG 9425 despite reduction in RT volumes. Persistent PET at end of chemotherapy identifies a cohort at an especially high risk for relapse/early progression.

NEUROBLASTOMA

Ref 9. Nitschke et al. (1988). Localized neuroblastoma treated by surgery: a pediatric oncology group study. *J Clin Oncol*;6(8):1271—9. POG 8104.

In this study, 101 patients with localized resectable neuroblastoma without regional lymph node involvement received no therapy beyond surgical resection. The result showed as follows:

	2-Year Disease-Free Survival (%)
Surgery only	*89*

This study showed that complete gross removal of the localized tumors is adequate therapy to ensure the survival of the majority of these lower risk patients.

Ref 10. Castleberry et al. (1991). Radiotherapy improves the outlook for patients older than 1 year with pediatric oncology group stage C neuroblastoma. *J Clin Oncol*;9(5):789—95.

In this study, 62 stage C neuroblastoma patients of older than 1 year of age received cyclo-phosphamide 150 mg/m² orally days 1−7 and doxorubicin 35 mg/m² intravenously (IV) on day 8, every 3 weeks for five courses. These patients were randomized to RT to primary tumor and regional lymph nodes (24−30 Gy/16 to 20 fractions) versus observation. All patients were advised to undergo a second-look surgery to remove residual disease followed by further chemo-therapy. The results showed the following:

	Complete Response (%)	Disease-Free Survival (%)
Chemo alone	45	31
ChemoRT	67	58
P-value	0.013	0.009

The study revealed that POG stage C neuroblastoma in children older than 1 year of age is a higher risk group and that chemoradiation provides superior initial and long-term disease con-trol compared with chemotherapy alone in this patient subset.

Ref 11. Hero et al. (2008). Localized infant neuroblastomas often show spontaneous regression: results of the prospective trials NB95−S and NB97. *J Clin Oncol*;26(9):1504−10. NB95−S, NB97 Trials.

In this study of infants with localized neuroblastoma without N-MYC amplification, patients were treated in a nonrandomized fashion with resection alone (if the risk of surgery was low) or observation. Among 93 patients with observed tumors, 44 developed spontaneous regression, 28 developed local progression, 7 progressed to stage 4S, and 4 progressed to stage 4. Among the entire group of patients with unresected tumors the following result was observed:

	3-Year Overall Survival (%)	3-Year Metastasis-Free Survival (%)
Observation	99	94

The authors concluded that infants with localized neuroblastoma can be managed with close observation.

Ref 12. Matthay et al. (2009). Long-term results for children with high-risk neuro-blastoma treated on a randomized trial of myeloablative therapy followed by 13-cis-ret-inoic acid: A Children's Oncology Group study. *J Clin Oncol*;27(7):1007−13.

In this study, 539 patients with high-risk, stage IV, or stage III with MYCN amplification, elevated ferritin, or unfavorable histology received initial chemotherapy with five cycles of cisplatin, doxorubicin, etoposide, and cyclophosphamide, followed by surgery and RT (given be-tween cycles 4 + 5 for gross residual disease). Patients were then randomized between myeloa-blative therapy and ABMT with TBI versus intensive nonmyeloablative chemo (cisplatin, etoposide, doxorubicin, ifosfamide X 3 cycles). A second randomization was done with six cycles of 13-cis-retinoic acid (isotretinoin) versus observation. The results at five years showed the following:

	EFS (%)		OS (%)
FIRST RANDOMIZATION			
ABMT	30	ABMT/cis-RA	59
Chemotherapy alone	19 ss	ABMT/no cis-RA	41 ss
SECOND RANDOMIZATION			
13-cis-retinoic acid	42	Chemo/cis-RA	38
Observation	31 ns	Chemo/no cis-RA	36 ns

This study showed that myeloablative therapy and autologous hematopoietic cell rescue resulted in significantly better 5-year EFS and OS than nonmyeloablative chemotherapy; cis-retinoic acid given after consolidation independently results in significantly improved OS.

Ref 13. Yu et al. (2010). Anti-GD2 antibody with GM-CSF, interleukin-2, and isotretinoin for neuroblastoma. N Eng J Med;363(14):1324–34. ANBL0032 Trial.

This study (ANBL0032) was a phase III randomized controlled trial evaluating the role of ch14.18, a monoclonal antibody against tumor-associated disialoganglioside GD2. 226 eligible patients with high-risk neuroblastoma were randomized and assigned to receive ch14.18 with isotretinoin along with GM-CSF and interleukin-2, versus isotretinoin alone. Study treatments were given after autologous stem cell transplant. The study was stopped early due to efficacy. Median follow-up was 2.1 years. Results are shown below:

	2-Year Event-Free Survival (%)	P-Value	2-Year Overall Survival	P-Value
ch14.18	66	0.01	86	0.02
No ch14.18	46		75	

Grade 3 or higher toxicity was higher in the treatment arm receiving immunotherapy, with 52% reporting neuropathic pain (vs. 6%, due to presence of GD2 antigen on pain fibers) and 39% developing fever (vs. 6%). Nonetheless, because of improved survival found in this study, immunotherapy is a standard of care for high-risk neuroblastoma.

Ref 14. Park J R et al. (2016). A phase III randomized clinical trial (RCT) of tandem myeloablative autologous stem cell transplant (ASCT) using peripheral blood stem cell (PBSC) as consolidation therapy for high-risk neuroblastoma (HR-NB): a Children's Oncology Group (COG) study. J Clin Oncol;34(18). https://doi.org/10.1200/JCO.2016.34.18_suppl.LBA3.

This study (ANBL0532), published only in abstract form, was a phase III randomized controlled trial of two treatments: single autologous stem cell transplant with carboplatin, etoposide, and melphalan versus tandem transplant (two back-to-back transplants, thiotepa–cyclophosphamide transplant then modified carboplatin, etoposide, melphalan transplant). 355 patients were randomized. 3-year results are shown as follows:

	3-Year Event-Free Survival (%)	P-Value	3-Year Overall Survival (%)	P-Value
ALL PATIENTS				
Single	48.8	0.008	69.0	0.26
Tandem	61.8		73.8	
PATIENTS WHO RECEIVED MAINTENANCE IMMUNOTHERAPY				
Single	55.4	0.0009	75.7	0.016
Tandem	73.7		86.3	

The authors concluded that tandem consolidation and stem cell transplant improves survival for patients with high-risk neuroblastoma receiving immunotherapy. It should be noted that immunotherapy is now part of the standard of care for high-risk neuroblastoma (see ref 8a).

WILMS' TUMOR

Ref 15. D'Angio et al. (1976). The treatment of Wilms' tumor: results of the national Wilms' tumor study. *Cancer*;38(2):633–46 (NWTS-1).

In this study, 359 Wilms' tumor patients with stage I–IV were randomized between surgery, post-op RT, and chemotherapy. The results showed the following:

Stage I	RT not beneficial for patients less than 1 year
Stage II, III	Chemo VA better than V or A
Stage IV	Preoperative VCR showed no benefit

This study also revealed that the radiation should be started within 9 days of surgery. Whole abdomen RT was not necessary for local tumor spills confined to the flank or for prior tumor biopsy.

Ref 16. D'Angio et al. (1981). The treatment of Wilms' tumor: results of the Second National Wilms' Tumor Study. *Cancer*;47(9):2302–11 (NWTS-2).

In this study, 188 patients with stage I and 268 patients with stage II–III were randomized between surgery, post-op RT, and chemotherapy. The results showed the following:

Stage I	RT is not needed for any patient
Stage II–IV	Adriamycin benefited favorable histology

RT delay beyond postoperative day 10 increased flank relapse rate.

Ref 17. D'Angio et al. (1989). Treatment of Wilms' tumor. Results of the Third National Wilms' Tumor Study. *Cancer*;64(2):349—60 (NWTS-3).

In this study, 1439 patients with Wilms' tumor stage I—IV were randomized between surgery, post-op RT, and chemotherapy. The results showed the following:

Stage II	No RT = RT 20 Gy; thus, RT is not needed
Stage III	RT 10 Gy = RT 20 Gy, VAA better than VA
Stage IV	Cyclophosphamide had no benefit

This study revealed that less intensive therapy does not produce inferior outcome for low-risk patients and cyclophosphamide did not benefit the high-risk patients.

Ref 18. Green et al. (1998). Effect of duration of treatment on treatment outcome and cost of treatment for Wilms' tumor: A report from the National Wilms' Tumor Study Group. *J Clin Oncol*;16(12):3744—51 (NWTS-4).

In this study, 905 patients with stage I—IV Wilms' tumor were randomized after the completion of 6 months of chemotherapy to discontinue (short) or to continue for nine additional months (long) of treatment with chemotherapy regimens that included vincristine and either divided-dose (standard [STD]) courses (5 days) or single-dose (pulse-intensive [PI]) treatment with dactinomycin. High-risk patients also received either divided-dose (STD) courses (3 days) or single-dose (PI) treatment with doxorubicin. The results of the study showed the following:

Stage I/II	No RT, only VA chemotherapy
Stage III	10 Gy WART plus 10 Gy boost if > 3 cm residual (VAA)
Stage IV	If lung metastases on chest X-ray persistent after 4 weeks of chemo (VAA), then WLI 150 cGy to 12 Gy, wait 2 weeks and if still visible on chest X-ray, either resect or 150—750 cGy boost
Stage I/UF/ anaplasia	Age-adjusted flank RT

The study also showed that the short chemotherapy schedule for the treatment of children with stage I—IV Wilms' is no less effective than the long chemotherapy schedule and can be administered at a substantially lower total treatment cost.

Ref 19. Dome et al. (2006). Treatment of anaplastic histology Wilms' tumor: results from the fifth National Wilms' Tumor Study. *J Clin Oncol*;24(15):2352—8 (NWTS-5).

In this study, a total of 2596 patients with Wilms' tumor were enrolled onto NWTS-5, of whom 281 had anaplastic histology (AH). Patients with stage I AH were treated with vincristine and dactinomycin for 18 weeks. Patients with stages II to IV diffuse AH were treated with vincristine, doxorubicin, cyclophosphamide, and etoposide for 24 weeks plus flank/abdominal radiation. The results at 4 years showed the following:

	Event-Free Survival (%)	Overall Survival (%)
Stage I	69.5	82.6
Stage II	82.6	82.6
Stage III	64.7	64.7
Stage IV diffuse	33.3	33.3
Bilateral	43.8	55.2

The study showed that the stage I AH patients had poor outcome with only two drugs and no radiation. Poor outcomes were seen overall for those with anaplasia. Novel treatment strategies are needed to improve outcomes for patients with AH, especially those with stage III to V disease.

Ref 20. Dix DB et al. (2018). Treatment of stage IV favorable histology Wilms tumor with lung metastases: a report from the Children's Oncology Group AREN0533 Study. *J Clin Oncol.*

In this trial, 292 patients with FH Wilms' tumor and isolated lung metastases showing complete lung nodule response (CR) after 6 weeks of DD4A continued receiving chemotherapy without lung RT. Patients with incomplete response (IR) or loss of heterozygosity at chromosomes 1p/16q received lung RT and four cycles of cyclophosphamide/etoposide in addition to DD4A drugs (Regimen M). The results showed the following:

1. *Among patients with complete lung nodule response, 4-year event-free survival and 4-year overall survival were 79.5% and 96.1%, respectively.*
2. *Among patients with incomplete lung nodule response, 4-year event-free survival and 4-year overall survival were 88.5% and 95.4%, respectively.*

The study concluded that excellent OS was achieved after omission of primary lung RT in patients with lung nodule CR. EFS was significantly improved, with excellent OS, in patients with lung nodule IR using four cycles of cyclophosphamide/etoposide in addition to DD4A drugs. The overall AREN0533 treatment strategy yielded EFS and OS estimates that were superior to previous studies.

RHABDOMYOSARCOMA

Ref 21. Maurer et al. (1988). The intergroup Rhabdomyosarcoma Study-I. A final report. *Cancer;61(2):209−20.*

In this study, 686 patients younger than 21 years of age with RMS or undifferentiated sarcoma were randomized after surgery by the groups as below. RT doses were given as follows:

<3 years	40 Gy
<6 years and <5 cm tumor	50 Gy
≥6 years or ≥5 cm tumor	55 Gy
≥6 years and ≥5 cm tumor	60 Gy

The results at 5 years showed the following:

	Disease-Free Survival (%)	Overall Survival (%)
Group I		
VAC	80	93
VAC + RT	80	81 ns
Group II		
VA + RT	72	72
VAC + RT	65 ns	72
Group III		
"pulse" VAC + RT	—	53
"pulse" VAC + adriamycin + RT	—	51
Group IV		
"pulse" VAC + RT	—	14
"pulse" VAC + adriamycin + RT	—	26

The study revealed that there was no benefit for radiation in the treatment of Clinical Group I disease, or cyclophosphamide given as a daily low-dose oral regimen in the treatment of Clinical Group II disease, or adriamycin in the treatment of Clinical Groups III and IV diseases.

Ref 22. Maurer et al. (1993). The intergroup Rhabdomyosarcoma study-II. *Cancer;*71(5):1904–22.

In this study, 999 patients with rhabdomyosarcoma were randomized after surgery by the groups as below. RT doses were given as follows:

Group I	no RT
Group II	40–45 Gy
Group III <6 years and <5 cm	40–45 Gy
Group III ≥6 years or >5 cm	50–55 Gy

The results at 5 years were as follows:

	Disease-Free Survival (%)	Overall Survival (%)
Group I		
VA	70 ns	84
VAC	80	85
Group II		
VA + RT	69	88
VAC + RT	74 ns	79 ns
Group III		
VAC + RT	—	66
Vadrac-VAC + RT	—	65
Group IV		
VAC + RT	—	26
Vadrac-VAC + RT	—	27

In comparison to the IRS-I study, OS was improved among nonmetastatic patients. Within IRS-II, VAC did not improve DFS or OS for group I/II, and Vadria-VAC did not improve outcomes in group III/IV patients.

Ref 23. Crist et al. (1995). The third intergroup Rhabdomyosarcoma study. *J Clin Oncol*;13(3):610–30 (IRS-III).

In this study, 1062 patients after surgery were randomized to treatment by clinical group (I through IV), histology (unfavorable or favorable), and site of the primary tumor. RT was given to group I unfavorable/group II to 41.4 Gy, group III if <6 years and <5 cm tumor to 41.4 Gy, if ≥6 years and ≥5 cm tumor to 50.4 Gy. RT was given at day 0 for those with CNS palsy, base of skull invasion, and intracranial extension, at week 2 for group II favorable/group III orbit and head and neck, all other at week 6. The results at 5 years showed the following:

	Overall Survival (%)
Group I	93
Group II	81
Group III	73
Group IV	30

The study revealed that the overall outcome of patients in IRS-III was significantly better than in IRS-II. For group I/favorable patients chemotherapy with VA is adequate; cyclophosphamide is not needed. For group II/FH tumors, excluding orbit, head, and paratesticular sites, results were inconclusive regarding the benefit from addition of doxorubicin (ADR) to VA. For group III tumors, excluding those in special pelvic, orbit, and other selected nonparameningeal head and neck sites, patients fared much better on the more intensive regimens of IRS-III than on pulsed VAC or VAC-VAdrC in IRS-II. Clinical group IV did not benefit significantly from the more complex therapies evaluated in IRS-III, however.

Ref 24. Crist et al. (2001). Intergroup rhabdomyosarcoma study-IV: results for patients with nonmetastatic disease. *J Clin Oncol*;19(12):3091−102 (IRS-IV).

In this study, 883 patients with nonmetastatic rhabdomyosarcoma after surgery were randomized to treatment by primary tumor site, group (1−3), and stage (I to III) as follows:

Stage	Chemo	Group I	Group II	Group III
I	VAC versus VAI	No RT	Conv/4140	HF RT of 1.1 Gy
II	VAC versus VAI versus VIE	No RT	Conv/4140	BID to 59.4 Gy
III	VAC versus VAI versus VIE	Conv/4140	Conv/4140	versus conv RT to 50.4 Gy
IV	VM versus IE versus IA	Conv/5040	Conv/5040	Conv/5040 (all with VAC)

The results at 3 years showed the following:

	Failure-Free Survival (%)		Local Control (%)
VAC	75	conv RT	87
VAI	77	HF RT	87
VIE	77		

The study revealed that VAC and VAI or VIE with surgery (with or without RT) are equally effective for patients with local or regional RMS. Hyperfractionated (HF) twice-daily RT did not result in any local control benefit; 50.4 Gy daily RT became the standard treatment.

Ref 25. Arndt et al. (2009). Vincristine, actinomycin, and cyclophosphamide compared with vincristine, actinomycin, and cyclophosphamide alternating with vincristine, topotecan, and cyclophosphamide for intermediate-risk rhabdomyosarcoma: Children's Oncology Group study D9803. *J Clin Oncol*;27(31):5182−8.

In this study, 617 patients with intermediate-risk RMS, defined as stages 2 and 3, clinical group III embryonal (including botryoid and spindle cell) RMS, and all nonmetastatic alveolar (defined as any part of the tumor having an alveolar component) RMS, undifferentiated sarcoma, or ectomesenchymoma were randomly assigned to 39 weeks of VAC versus VAC/VTC; local therapy began after week 12. Patients with parameningeal primary tumors with intracranial extension were assigned to treatment with VAC and immediate RT (nonrandomized VAC). At median follow-up of 4.3 years, the results showed the following:

	Local Failure (%)	Failure-Free Survival (%)	Overall Survival (%)
VAC	16.5	73	79
VAC/VTC	18.5	68	79
P-value	0.5	0.3	0.9

This study revealed that for intermediate-risk RMS, VAC/VTC does not significantly improve FFS compared with VAC.

Ref 26. Walterhouse DO et al. (2014). Shorter-duration therapy using vincristine, dactinomycin, and lower-dose cyclophosphamide with or without radiotherapy for patients with newly diagnosed low-risk Rhabdomyosarcoma: a report from the soft tissue Sarcoma Committee of the Children's Oncology Group. *J Clin Oncol*;32(31):3547−52. ARST0331 Trial.

In this trial, 271 patients enrolled newly diagnosed patients with subset-one low-risk embryonal RMS (ERMS; stage 1/2 group I/II ERMS or stage 1 group III orbit ERMS). Therapy included four cycles of VAC followed by four cycles of VA over 22 weeks. Patients with microscopic or gross residual disease at study entry received RT. Total RT doses were based on the extent of residual disease; no RT for group I tumors, 36 Gy for group IIA tumors, 41.4 Gy for group IIB/C tumors, and 45 Gy for group III orbit tumors in 1.8-Gy fractions. At median follow-up of 4.3 years, the data showed the following:

Three year FFS 89%
Three year OS 98%

This study showed that shorter duration therapy that included lower dose cyclophosphamide and RT did not compromise FFS for patients with subset-one low-risk ERMS.

Ref 27. Wolden et al. (2015). Local control for intermediate-risk Rhabdomyosarcoma: results from D9803 according to histology, goup, site, and size: a report from the Children's Oncology Group. *Int J Rad Oncol Biol Phys*;93(5):1071−76.

In this secondary analysis of D9803, 423 patients with group III embryonal or group I−III alveolar RMS were included. Patients received 42 weeks of VAC or VAC/VTC (as described above) with local therapy at week 12. Those with group I/II alveolar RMS received

36–41.4 Gy, while others received 50.4 Gy. With a median follow-up of 6.6 years, the following results were observed:

	5-Year Event-Free Survival	Local Failure	P-Value
Group I/II alveolar RMS	69%	10%	
Group III RMS	70%	19%	
Tumor size			
≥5 cm		25%	0.0004
<5 cm		10%	

Because tumors ≥5 cm were more likely to fail locally, the current COG study (ARST1431) is evaluating dose-escalation for these tumors.

EWING'S SARCOMA

Ref 28. Nesbit et al. (1990). Multimodal therapy for the management of primary, nonmetastatic Ewing's sarcoma of bone: A long-term follow-up of the First Intergroup study. *J Clin Oncol*;8(10):1664–74 (IESS-I).

In this study, 342 patients were randomized between treatment 1 (VAC plus Adr) or treatment 2 (same as treatment 1 without Adr) or treatment 3 (same as treatment 2 plus whole lung RT, VAC plus BPR). The results at 5 years showed the following:

Treatment	Relapse-Free Survival (%)	Overall Survival (%)	Metastases (%)	Comments
VACAdr	60	65	30	1 versus 2, P = 0.001
VAC	20	28	72	Arm 2 closed early
VAC + lung RT	44	53	42	

This study revealed that the addition of either doxorubicin or bilateral lung RT (150–200 cGy to 15–18 Gy) to VAC significantly improved DFS and OS.

Note: *No dose response in the primary tumor if an adequate volume was treated to between 40 and 68 Gy.*

Ref 29. Burgert et al. (1990). Multimodal therapy for the management of nonpelvic, localized Ewing's sarcoma of bone: Intergroup study IESS-II. *J Clin Oncol*;8(9):1514–24 (IESS-II).

In this study, 214 patients with Ewing's sarcoma were randomized as below. Surgical resection was encouraged, but not mandatory. Post-op RT was given 45 Gy to the whole bone ±10 Gy boost. The results at 5 years showed the following:

Treatment	Relapse-Free Survival (%)	Overall Survival (%)	Local Failure (%)
NONMETASTATIC, NONPELVIC TUMORS			
High-dose VACA	73	77	8
Standard VACA	66	63	11
NONMETASTATIC, PELVIC TUMORS			
High-dose VACA	55	63	12 (vs. 28% in IESS-I)

This study revealed that better results with high-dose intermittent VACA as compared to moderate-dose standard VACA.

Ref 30. Donaldson et al. (1998). A multidisciplinary study investigating radiotherapy in Ewing's sarcoma: End results of POG #8346. Pediatric Oncology Group. *Int J Radiat Oncol Biol Phys*;42(1):125−35 (POG 8346).

In this study, 178 patients with Ewing's sarcoma were treated with induction chemotherapy of cyclophosphamide/doxorubicin (C/A) × 12 weeks, followed by local treatment (either surgery or radiation therapy) and C/A, dactinomycin, and vincristine for 50 weeks. Resection was advised for patients with small primary tumors if accomplished without functional loss. 40 patients were randomized to whole bone radiation to 39.6 Gy plus a 16.2 Gy boost (total 55.8 Gy) or involved-field (IF) radiation to 55.8 Gy, and the remainder of the patients were assigned to IF radiation only. The results at 5 years showed the following:

	Local Control (%)	Event-Free Survival (%)
Whole bone RT	No	No
IFRT	difference	difference

With adequate IF radiotherapy treatment to appropriate volumes as defined by MR imaging, there was no difference in LC/EFS between those randomized to whole bone versus IF for Ewing's sarcoma patients. This study established a standard of care for RT field size in Ewing's sarcoma.

Ref 31. Grier et al. (2003). Addition of ifosfamide and etoposide to standard chemotherapy for Ewing's sarcoma and primitive neuroectodermal tumor of bone. *N Engl J Med*;348(8):694−701 (IESS-III).

In this study, 398 patients 30 years of age or younger with nonmetastatic Ewing's sarcoma, primitive neuroectodermal tumor of bone, or primitive sarcoma of bone were randomized to receive 49 weeks of standard chemotherapy with doxorubicin, vincristine, cyclophosphamide, *and dactinomycin or experimental therapy with these four drugs alternating with courses of ifosfamide and etoposide. The results at 3 years showed the following:*

Treatment	Relapse-Free Survival (%)	Overall Survival (%)
High-dose VACA	54	61
VACA + IE	69	72
P-value	0.005	0.01

This IESS-III study showed that VACA/IE was better than high-dose intermittent VACA.

Ref 32. Whelan J et al. (2016). Efficacy of busulfan-melphalan high dose chemotherapy consolidation (BuMel) in localized high-risk Ewing sarcoma (ES): Results of EURO-EWING 99-R2 randomized trial (EE99R2Loc). *J Clin Oncol*;34(suppl; abstr 11,000).
In this trial, 477 patients with high-risk localized disease received six VIDE courses (vincristine, ifosfamide, doxorubicin, etoposide) and one VAI (vincristine, actinomycin D, ifosfamide) before randomization to BuMel with stem cell rescue or VAI x seven courses. At median follow-up of 8 years the data show the following:

	3-Year EFS(%)	3-Year OS(%)
VAI	53.1	69.9
BuMel/stem	66.9	77.8
P value	—	0.19

This study showed that BuMel conferred improvement in EFS and OS with acceptable toxicity for patients with localized ES and poor histological response to chemotherapy or large tumor volume unresected or initially resected. It should be considered as a standard of care for this group of patients with localized high-risk ES and no contraindication to BuMel.

RETINOBLASTOMA

Ref 33. Brennan et al. (2017). Ocular salvage and vision preservation using a topotecan-based Regimen for advanced intraocular retinoblastoma. *J Clin Oncol*;35(1):72—7.
In this study of 27 patients with bilateral retinoblastoma, participants were treated with topotecan and vincristine, alternating with carboplatin and vincristine. In some patients, periocular carboplatin was injected. Focal treatment was given after the second course of chemotherapy; options included cryotherapy, laser photocoagulation, thermotherapy, or plaque brachytherapy.

Event-free survival was defined as avoidance of external beam RT and/or enucleation. Results were as follows:

10-year cumulative incidence of external beam RT	5.9%
10-year event-free survival	77.5%

The authors concluded that a topotecan-based regimen was effective for bilateral retinoblastoma.

Benign Diseases

Benign tumors are nonmalignant and involve several organs and systems of the body, including skin, brain, head, neck, connective tissue, and bone. Benign tumors are masses of well-differentiated cells that grow locally and do not invade or metastasize to distant locations. The cause of benign tumors can be local trauma or injury, inflammation, hyper-proliferation, or functional in nature. Local growth of these tumors can be symptomatic, causing mass effects, nerve damage, and overproduction of certain hormones causing further symptoms and signs in patients. Most benign diseases can be treated with sur-gery. Some benign tumors may respond to radiation treatments. This chapter is a brief review of the clinical indications and treatments for common benign diseases in radiation oncology.

SKIN AND CONNECTIVE TISSUE DISORDERS

Keloid

Keloid is excessive fibrous tissue formed at the site of a surgical scar or injury from heat or chemical burns to the skin. It can be symptomatic, causing pain, pruritus, ulceration, and disfigurement. Treatment includes intralesion steroid injections and surgery. Recurrent keloids that present major cosmetic problems or cause significant morbidity symptoms are candidates for low-dose RT treatment.

RT Technique: RT is given immediately postoperatively within 1–2 days [1]. Use enface electron 6–12 MeV to 90% IDL, appropriate thickness bolus is required qd.

Dose: 300–400 cGy/fx to 12–18 Gy.

Desmoid Tumor/Aggressive Fibromatosis

A desmoid tumor is an abnormal growth of connective tissue arising from the muscles, tendons, and scars. These can be intra-abdominal or extra-abdominal from head and neck, shoulder, and thigh area. Desmoid tumors that are locally aggressive are known as aggressive fibromatosis and can be life-threatening by compressing blood vessels, nerves, intestines, and kidneys. Surgical resection with wide margins is the recommen-ded treatment. Recurrent desmoid tumors can be inoperable or may require mutilating surgery. Post-op RT can reduce the risk of recurrences.

Fundamentals of Radiation Oncology
https://doi.org/10.1016/B978-0-12-814128-1.00024-6

RT Technique: CT simulation, 6–18 MV photon, 3DCRT, or IMRT.
Dose: 200 cGy/fx to 50 Gy, gross disease to 60 Gy.

Peyronie Disease

This is a chronic inflammatory connective tissue disorder involving tunica albuginea of the penis, causing pain and abnormal curvature of the penis. Treatment results with medications such as pentoxifylline are mixed. Corrective surgical procedure and penile prosthesis may benefit. RT may improve symptoms including pain.

RT Technique: Patient is supine, shield testicles; enface electrons 6–12 Mev with appropriate bolus qd; or 6 MV photon, 3DCRT.
Dose: 200 cGy/fx to 20–30 Gy.

Dupuytren's Contracture

Hand deformity involving one or more fingers becoming permanently flexed. It is a connective tissue disorder with unknown cause. Clostridial collagenase injections can soften and weaken the contracture. The surgical procedure fasciectomy and dermofasciectomy removes the affected tissue from the hand and may provide relief; however, relapse is common. RT may prevent or improve the contracture.

RT Technique: Enface electrons 6–9 Mev, 90% IDL, appropriate thickness bolus qd, shield uninvolved areas of the palm.
Dose: 300 cG/fx to 30 Gy.

Gynecomastia

Gynecomastia is enlargement of male breasts, due to hormonal imbalance. An increase in the ratio of estrogen to androgen may be responsible for the male breast enlargement. Prostate cancer patients receiving antitestosterone hormone can develop gynecomastia. Patients present with breast pain and unilateral or bilateral breast enlargement. Medical management with tamoxifen may improve breast pain. Patients with chronic gynecomastia can undergo subcutaneous mastectomy. Radiation therapy is also an effective treatment for gynecomastia.

RT Technique: Enface electron 9–12 Mev, 90% IDL, 1–1.5 cm bolus qd.
Dose: 300 cGy/fx to 12–15 Gy.

BENIGN NEOPLASMS OF THE BRAIN, HEAD, AND NECK

Meningioma

Meningioma is an extraaxial tumor that originates from the meninges. Common locations are in the convexity of the brain, the sphenoid wing, and cerebellopontine angle. Most meningiomas are benign (WHO grade I), atypical (WHO grade II), or malignant (WHO grade III). Patients most commonly present with headache or localizing symptoms [2]. Small, incidentally detected meningioma may be observed with serial MR imaging. Patients with progression or symptoms are treated with maximal safe resection. Post-op RT is recommended for subtotal resection or recurrence, and definitive RT is recommended for poor surgical candidates with skull base meningioma or involving intracerebral vasculature.

RT Technique: Patients are CT simulated in a thermoplastic mask, fuse MRI with planning CT scan, 3D or IMRT, 6 MV photons, multiple noncoplanar beams or two-arc VMAT, GTV = enhancing tumor and tumor bed ± dural tail (controversial: T2-weighted sequence can help distinguish vasculature from dural tail with nodular enhancements).

Grade I CTV = GTV
Grade II CTV = GTV + 1−2 cm respecting natural barrier
Grade III CTV = GTV + 2−3 cm, respecting natural barrier
PTV = CTV + 0.3−0.5 cm

Dose: Grade I: PTV = 180 cGy/fx to 45−54 Gy; Grade II: PTV = 180 cGy/fx to 54−59.4 Gy; Grade III: PTV = 200 cGy/fx to 60 Gy.

Pituitary Adenoma

Pituitary adenomas are benign tumors, classified as either microadenomas (<10 mm in size) or macroadenomas (>10 mm in size). In addition, they can be chromophobic—inactive or secreting prolactin; acidophilic-secreting GH; basophilic-secreting ACTH (adrenocorticotropic hormone), or TSH-secreting. Patients present with headache, hypopituitarism, infertility, acromegaly, Cushing disease, and/or hyperthyroidism.
    Treatment [3]:

- Trans-sphenoidal surgery is the primary treatment for GH- and ACTH-secreting tumors. In addition, nonfunctional tumors are symptomatic and progressive, or in younger patients, they are often treated with TSS.
- Medical management with bromocriptine and cabergoline for prolactinomas with prolactin 500 mg/mL is recommended. If there is no response by 4−6 weeks, then transsphenoidal surgery (TSS), followed by further medical management, is recommended.
- Radiation therapy is indicated for all pituitary macroadenomas with persistently elevated hormonal levels. Radiation therapy is also recommended for nonsurgical patients or for patients with recurrent tumors.

RT Technique: 3DCRT—patient is set up in the supine position with the chin tucked and head immobilized with a face mask. Two lateral opposed fields are used. The vertex field is placed with the couch rotated 90 degrees. IMRT/SRS—patient is supine, with face mask on for immobilization, CT, and MRI simulation. For 6 MV photon IMRT, multiple coplanar and/or nonplanar beams may be used. IGRT is needed. SRS is not recommended for tumors near optic nerves or with cavernous sinus involvement or tumor volume size <3−4 cm.

Volumes

GTV = tumor bed and residual disease
CTV = GTV+ and at-risk regions
PTV = CTV+0.5 cm (0−1 mm if treating with SRS)

Dose

3D or IMRT
Nonfunctioning tumor 180 cGy/fx to 45—50.4 Gy
Functioning tumors 180 cGy/fx 50.4—54 Gy
SRS
Nonfunctioning tumor 12—20 Gy to 50% isodose line.
Functioning tumor 15—30 Gy to 50% isodose line

Craniopharyngioma

Craniopharyngiomas are benign neoplasms arising from Rathke's pouch in the sellar or suprasellar region. Although classified as benign, they can be locally recurrent and cause substantial morbidity. The peak age is 5—14 years. Patients may present with headache, nausea/vomiting, endocrine dysfunction, and/or bitemporal hemianopsia. On CT, calcifications are common and are useful for target delineation. On MR imaging, these tumors contain cystic and solid components. Recommended treatment is maximal safe resection while avoiding neurological deficits. Cystic fenestration may help reduce the possibility of cystic regrowth. Adjuvant radiation therapy is indicated for subtotal resection or recurrent disease after initial surgery.

RT Technique: IMRT—patient is supine, with face mask on for immobilization and with CT and MRI simulation. All MR imaging preceding simulation date should be fused and used to guide target delineation. For 6 MV photon IMRT, multiple coplanar and/or nonplanar beams may be used.

Volumes

GTV = tumor bed and residual solid or cystic components on MRI, as well as tumor-related calcifications on CT.

CTV = GTV + 0.5—1 cm and at-risk regions, confined to anatomic barriers. At-risk regions are defined with the assistance of imaging (including preoperative images) before RT.

PTV = CTV + 0.3—0.5 cm.

Dose: 180 cGy/fx to 54 Gy.

Acoustic Neuroma

Acoustic neuroma is a benign intracranial growth that develops from the Schwann cells of the eighth cranial nerve. It arises from the vestibular portion of the vestibulocochlear nerve. Patients present with sensorineural hearing loss, tinnitus, vertigo, and facial nerve symptoms. Active surveillance with serial MRI and audiometry for asymptomatic patients with small tumor is appropriate. Treatment options include microsurgery, fractionated radiation, or stereotactic radiosurgery.

RT Technique: Patient supine, in face mask, and CT simulated 6 MV, IMRT with multiple coplanar beams or two-arc VMAT.

Dose

3D or IMRT 200 cGy to 50—54 Gy
SRS 12—13 Gy to 50% IDL

Chordoma

This is a slow-growing benign tumor of the neuroaxis. The most common locations of chordoma are clivus/skull base, vertebrae, and sacrum. Local growth of the tumor can cause pain in the back and weakness or numbness of arms or legs. Treatment is surgical resection followed by post-op RT [4].

Technique: Patient supine, in immobilization device, and CT simulated. Fuse MRI with planning CT scan, proton radiation is an option for treatment. GTV = none or residual gross disease, CTV = GTV + 1–2 cm, PTV = 0.5 cm.

Dose

Photon 200 cGy/fx to 50–60 Gy.
Proton 180–200 GyE to 63–79.2 GyE.

PARAGANGLIOMA/PHEOCHROMOCYTOMA (GLOMUS TUMOR)

This is a benign neuroendocrine tumor of neural crest origin, which can develop in the carotid bodies in head and neck, aortic bodies in the thorax, and adrenal gland in the abdomen. Depending on the tumor's location, the patient may present with headache, vertigo, or high blood pressure. Embolization and surgery is the treatment of choice. Radiation treatment can be considered after subtotal resection, for recurrence or skull base tumors.

RT Technique: Patient supine, in immobilization device, and CT simulated. Fuse MRI with planning CT scan, GTV = none or residual gross disease, CTV = GTV + 1–2 cm, PTV = 0.5 cm.

Dose: 180 cGy/fx to 45–54 Gy.

EYE/ORBIT DISEASES

Pterygium

This is fibrovascular proliferation arising from the conjunctival and corneal border. Patients may present with foreign body sensation, excessive tearing, and/or persistent redness of the conjunctiva and in advanced stages, difficulty with vision and may require surgical excision. Post-op RT with ^{90}Sr decreases recurrence.

RT Technique: The surgical resection bed is the target volume. An appropriately sized epibulbar plaque applicator with central radioactive disc (^{90}Sr sources) is selected during the surgical procedure. The first treatment is at the time of the surgery or within 24–48 h thereafter. Treatment requires only a few minutes, as the dose rate from ^{90}Sr is 5–20 Gy/min.

Dose: 8–10 Gy/fx to 24–60 Gy once a week.

Graves Opthalmopathy

Autoimmune disease of the orbit and periorbital tissue reacting to activated T lymphocytes with the TSH-R located in the orbital and periorbital tissue. Patients complain of irritation, blurred vision, and may present with upper eye lid retraction, proptosis, or periorbital swelling. Treatment involves normalization of thyroid function, steroids, and decompressive surgery. Orbital radiation therapy can be considered as an alternative treatment [5].

RT Technique: Patient is supine, in a face mask, and CT simulated; 6 MV photon, 3DCRT with opposed lateral fields, include both orbits/extraocular muscles in the fields, using a half beam block to place isocenter a few millimeters behind the lens to minimize dose to the lens.

Dose: 200 cGy/fx to 20 Gy.

VASCULAR DISORDERS

Arteriovenous Malformation/Cavernous Hemangioma

This is a congenital disorder of the vascular system in which abnormally thin-walled blood vessels form between arteries and veins in the brain. The cavernous hemangioma is a vascular malformation where dilated thin-walled blood vessels form benign tumors. Surgery is the treatment of choice; however, if the locations of the lesions within the brain are high risk for surgery, then stereotactic radiosurgery is recommended.

RT Technique: Patient is supine, and CT and MRI imaging are performed with the positional frame attached to the patient. Slice thickness of <2 mm images are recommended for SRS planning. Fusion of MRI with CT is recommended for target delineation.

Volume

GTV includes only tumor volume on MRI. For the fixed frame—based SRS technique, CTV and PTV are the same as GTV without any additional margin. For the frameless SRS technique, CTV is the same as GTV, and a 1—2 mm margin is added to the CTV.

Dose: Tumor size <4 cm is 20—25 Gy to 50% IDL.

FUNCTIONAL DISORDERS

Trigeminal Neuralgia

This is a chronic pain syndrome of the trigeminal nerve (fifth cranial), possibly due to loss of the myelin sheath of the trigeminal nerve. Treatment options are medical management with carbamazepine, balloon compression, microvascular decompression, and stereotactic radiosurgery.

RT Technique: SRS technique as above AV malformation. The target volume is trigeminal root entry zone at the pons to the semilunar ganglion.

Dose: 70—90 Gy to the 50% IDL.

Parkinson Disease

This is a chronic degenerative disorder of the central nervous system. The motor symptoms of Parkinson disease are due to the lack of dopamine due to cell death from the midbrain area of substantia nigra. Treatment options are medical managements with levodopa, MAO-B inhibitors, thalamotomy/pallidotomy, and stereotactic radiosurgery.

RT Technique: SRS technique as above AV malformation. The target volume is ventralis medialis nucleus for treating tremor; globus pallidus internus for treating rigidity.

Dose: 120–140 Gy.

DISEASES OF THE BONE

Heterotopic Ossification

This is abnormal growth of bone around the hip. The mesenchymal cells around the periarticular soft tissue form osteoblastic stem cells due to trauma, such as total hip replacement. Patient may complain of pain and decreased range of motion in the hip joint. Plain film X-rays and bone scans can confirm heterotopic ossification of the hip joint. Surgical excision of the heterotopic ossification followed by prophylactic radiation treatment is recommended.

RT Technique: Patient supine, in an immobilization device and CT simulated. 6–18 MV photons, 3DCRT, RT is given within 24–48 h of surgery either pre- or postoperatively.

Dose: 7–8 Gy in a single fraction.

Radiation treatment is an effective modality for benign diseases, most of which require low doses of radiation treatment. Nevertheless, one must carefully consider any long-term side effects of radiation from these treatments. Radiation treatments for pituitary adenoma can cause vision deterioration or can cause meningioma many years after the treatments. The risk of radiation-induced malignancy is a real concern as well, especially for young children receiving radiation therapy [6]. As such, whenever possible, other forms of treatment for benign disease may be preferred.

References

Ref 1. *Berman B, Bieley HC. Adjunct therapies to surgical management of keloids. Dermatol Surg 1996;22(2):126–30.*

Ref 2. *Rogers, et al. Low-risk meningioma: initial outcomes from NRG oncology/RTOG. ASTRO abstract 2016 Int J Rad Oncol Biol Phys 2016;96(5):939–40. RTOG 0539 Trial.*
(a) Rogers L, et al. Intermediate-risk meningioma: initial outcomes from NRG Oncology RTOG 0539. J Neurosurg October 2017;6:1–13. https://doi.org/10.3171/2016.11.JNS161170 [Epub ahead of print].
(b) Rogers L, et al. High-risk meningioma: initial outcomes from NRG oncology/RTOG- 0539. Neuro Oncol November 6, 2017;19(6):vi133.

Ref 3. *Laws ER, Sheehan JP, Sheehan JM, Jagnathan J, Jane Jr JA, Oskouian R. Stereotactic radiosurgery for pituitary adenomas: a review of the literature. J Neuro Oncol 2004;69(1—3):257—72.*

Ref 4. *Carpentier A, Polivka M, Blanquet A, Lot G, George B. Suboccipital and cervical chordomas: the value of aggressive treatment at first presentation of the disease. J Neurosurg 2002;97(5):1070—7.*

Ref 5. *Bahn RS. Graves' ophthalmopathy. N Engl J Med 2010;362(8):726—38.*

Ref 6. *McKeown SR, et al. Radiotherapy for benign disease; assessing the risk of radiation-induced cancer following exposure to intermediate dose radiation. Br J Radiol December 2015;88(1056). 20150405.*

PALLIATIVE CARE AND RADIATION TREATMENT TOXICITY

Metastatic Cancers

METASTATIC BRAIN CANCER

The estimated incidence in the United States is between 200,000 and 500,000 cases in 2018.

The most common brain tumors are intracranial metastatic tumors. They are primarily located in the cerebral hemisphere, less commonly in the cerebellum, or brainstem. Frequent sites of primary malignancy are lung, breast, melanoma, and colorectal.

Workup

Symptoms and Signs
- Generalized headache, often present throughout the day, which may worsen with positional changes
- Vomiting, secondary to increased intracranial pressure (ICP)
- Difficulty with vision, hearing, speech, and memory
- Changes in personality
- Focal or generalized seizures, motor function difficulty with loss of balance during ambulation

Investigations
- CT/MRI brain with contrast
- Biopsy of primary and/or metastatic lesion for tissue diagnosis

Treatment

- Asymptomatic: close observation with initiation of steroids as needed
- If symptomatic then dexamethasone 10 mg IV loading, 2—4 mg orally every 6 h. Zantac/Prilosec as directed.
- If impending cerebral herniation, use mannitol or glycerol IV.
- If seizure is a presenting symptom, then for generalized seizures, use Dilantin, Tegretol or phenobarbitol, and for partial seizures, use valproic acid and Tegretol. The phenytoin dose is 300—400 mg/day. Serum anticonvulsant level should be monitored. Do not use anticonvulsive prophylaxis.

Fundamentals of Radiation Oncology
https://doi.org/10.1016/B978-0-12-814128-1.00025-8

Limited brain disease:

- Surgery is indicated for patients with metastatic lesions 1–3, and aggregate tumor volume is <4 cm3, no visceral metastases, and >3 months expected survival.
- Postop SRS is preferred; fractionated RT or WBRT can be considered if SRS is not available [1, 4].
- If unresectable or uncontrolled systemic disease, then SRS followed by WBRT [2, 3].

Disseminated disease (not meeting criteria for limited disease): WBRT and SRS can be considered for patients with good performance status and low total tumor volume.

Multiple brain metastases (>4) causing mass effect: surgery of the dominant lesion followed by WBRT.

RT Technique

Patient is supine, fiducial markers on bony canthus, face mask on. For SRS, use appropriate immobilization devices (fixed-type invasive frames or noninvasive masks). If frameless, then image guidance is used for treatment. Otherwise, frame-based techniques are preferred.

For patients with CNS lymphoma, include posterior $^1/_2$ $-^2/_3$ of orbit in the field.

Volume/Borders

3DCRT: superior, anterior, posterior borders to flash 2 cm; inferior border is at bottom of C2. Angle gantry to superimpose BBs. Block 1 cm margin on cribiform plate and temporal fossa (Fig. 25.1).

SRS: contrast-enhanced tumor or tumor bed + 1–2 mm margin (Fig. 25.2).

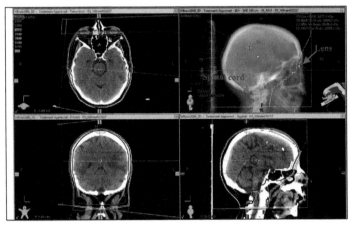

FIGURE 25.1   CT images showing 3D RT lateral field DRR and isodose lines for whole-brain RT. The lateral fields are blocking the lens.

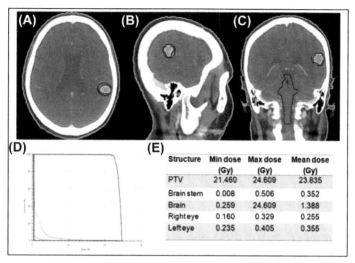

Structure	Min dose (Gy)	Max dose (Gy)	Mean dose (Gy)
PTV	21.460	24.609	23.835
Brain stem	0.008	0.506	0.352
Brain	0.259	24.609	1.388
Right eye	0.160	0.329	0.255
Left eye	0.235	0.405	0.355

FIGURE 25.2 LINAC-based SRS plan for a left brain lesion: (A) axial; (B) sagittal; (C) coronal view; (D) dose–volume histogram; (E) evaluation metrics (courtesy of Ugur Selek, M.D. Koc University, Istanbul, Turkey).

Doses

WBRT

Standard fractionation is 300 cGy/fx to 30 Gy.

For patients with very good prognosis, consider protracted course of treatment 200 cGy/fx to 40–46 Gy.

For patients with very poor performance, consider supportive care only and accelerated WBRT 400 cGy/fx to 2000 cGy.

SRS

Tumor <2 cm dose is 20–24 Gy.
Tumor 2 cm to <3 cm dose is 18 Gy.
Tumor 3 cm to <4 cm dose is 15 Gy.
LINAC-based SRS prescription is to 80% isodose line.
Gamma Knife–based SRS is to 50% isodose line.

Constraints

WBRT: lens <10 Gy.
SRS: brain stem Dmax 15 Gy, optic chiasm Dmax 15 Gy, cochlea Dmax 12 Gy, brain volume limit 20 Gy, lens Dmax 3 Gy.

Outcome

- The median survival for a single metastatic lesion treated with radiation therapy alone is 6 months. Surgery plus RT is 12 months.

- Surgery plus post-op radiation improves overall survival to 25% at 1 year.
- Whole-brain RT followed by stereotactic radiosurgery results in improved local control, but not survival.

Complications

- Headache, nausea, vomiting, seizures, transient neurologic symptom deterioration, vertigo, regional alopecia, and fatigue.
- Radiation necrosis.

Follow-Up

- Clinical judgment/patient symptoms and MRI every 3 months for patients who have and have not received WBRT, respectively.
- Then as clinically indicated.

SPINAL CORD COMPRESSION

Spinal cord compression is one of the few radiation oncology emergencies. Most spinal cord compressions are extramedullary, resulting from extension of the tumor into the spinal cord epidural space, leading to paralysis if not treated quickly.

Workup

Symptoms and Signs
- Back pain (most prevalent symptom). Pain is worse when lying down and with ambulation.
- Loss of sensation, urinary frequency, incontinence, and constipation
- Extremity weakness, causing difficulty walking and climbing stairs.
- Vertebral bony involvement.

Investigations
- Plain film X-ray, CT/MRI with contrast of the entire spinal axis.
- Biopsy if patient has no cancer diagnosis.

Treatment

- Dexamethasone 10 mg IV bolus, 2–4 mg orally every 4 h.
- Zantac/Prilosec as directed.
- Surgery is indicated for:
  - unknown diagnosis
  - rapidly deteriorating neurologic symptoms
  - unifocal vertebral body disease
  - no visceral systemic disease
  - previous radiation therapy
  - stabilization if vertebrae fracture/retropulsion of bone fragments
  - relative radioresistant tumors such as melanoma, renal cell cancer
- Surgery followed by post-op RT improves patient's ability to walk [4, 5, 6].
- Radiation therapy alone is often the treatment of choice because many patients present with multiple or pending sites of cord compression and/or disseminated disease.

- Chemotherapy should be used for very young patients and for chemosensitive tumors such as lymphoma, germ cell, neuroblastoma, Ewing sarcoma, or small-cell lung cancer. Chemotherapy is used in pediatric cases, because of the risk of secondary malignancies following spinal radiation therapy.

RT Technique

Volume/Borders

3D technique: Radiation therapy portals should center on the site of epidural compression and included two vertebrae above and below the site. However, with CT- or MRI-based planning, one vertebra above and below the site of compression is adequate. It is important to include the entire soft tissue extent of tumor.

SRS: GTV = gross disease, CTV = GTV + body of the vertebrae, pedicles and dorsal elements of the vertebra, PTV = CTV + 1–3 mm with appropriate image guidance.

Dose

3D technique

Treat cervical spine with opposed laterals (to avoid the pharynx), thoracic spine with PA or AP/PA, and lumbar spine with AP/PA.

- Very poor prognosis and small volume: 400 cGy/fx to 2000 cGy
- Standard prognosis/volume: 300 cGy/fx to 3000 cGy
- Very large field with documented dose to bowel above tolerance: consider 250 cGy/fx to 3750 cGy

SBRT

16–18 Gy; spinal cord should be at least 3 mm away from the bony metastatic lesion. Maximum spinal cord point dose is 14 Gy, and 10% of the spinal cord volume is constrained to <10 Gy.

Outcome

- Back pain improves in most patients.
- More than 50% of patients will be able to walk. Ambulation recovery has been shown to correlate strongly with duration of nonambulatory status before treatment: 24 h, <72 h, and 1 week, 90, 70, and 20% regain ambulation.

Complications

Depends on the location of the spinal cord compression and the treatment site (e.g., a lower lumbar vertebrae site may cause fatigue, nausea, and bowel frequency).

Follow-Up

As clinically indicated.

SUPERIOR VENA CAVA SYNDROME

Superior vena cava (SVC) syndrome is a medical emergency due to the risk of airway obstruction and cerebral edema. The majority of SVC involvement is caused by bronchogenic cancers, followed by malignant lymphoma and benign tumors.

Workup

Symptoms and Signs
- Shortness of breath, cough, facial edema, and ipsilateral upper extremity edema.
- Venous distention of the neck and anterior chest wall with visible development of dermal collateral vessels.

Investigations
Same as for lung cancer.

Treatment

- Steroids were shown not to be beneficial, but not harmful if given to lymphoma or small cell cancer patients; dexamethasone 10 mg IV bolus, 2—4 mg orally every 4 h.
- Zantac/Prilosec as directed.
- Furosemide 20—80 mg QD for 3—5 days.
- If a thrombus is identified, consider anticoagulant treatment with urokinase, streptokinase, or a plasminogen activator.
- Prompt evaluation by pulmonologist for stent placement, particularly for distressed patients.
- Following stent placement, oncologic therapy is required due to risk of progressive and/or recurrent SVC syndrome. If SVC is caused by small-cell lung cancer, it may be effectively managed with chemotherapy.
- RT is the treatment standard for many patients, either after stent placement, or alone. RT dose is 250—300 cGy to 30—37.5 Gy.

Outcome

More than 90% of patients obtain relief from stenting. More than 60% of patients experience symptoms relief within 1—2 weeks of treatment.

Complications

Same as for lung cancer.

Follow-Up

As clinically indicated.

METASTATIC BONE CANCERS

Pain from metastatic bone lesions results from stimulation of nerve endings in endostium as a result of release of prostaglandin, bradykynin, substance P, and histamine from destroyed bone. Also stretching of the periostium by increasing tumor size can cause pain.

Workup

Symptoms and Signs
- Bone pain, neurologic symptoms related to compression of any nerves due to bony lesions
- Pathologic fracture

Investigations
- Whole-body bone scan provides the best overview of the extent of disease.
- For patients with a negative bone scan and/or neurologic findings, CT/MRI of the bone is recommended.
- Skeletal survey in multiple myeloma may show radiographic bone destruction in locations that may not show increased uptake in bone scans.
- Biopsy of primary and/or metastatic lesion for tissue diagnosis can be considered if radiologic studies are nondiagnostic.

Treatment

- Adequate pain management with nonnarcotic and narcotic medications.
- Surgery is indicated for patients with lesions in weight-bearing bones (femur/humerus) with more than 50% destruction of the cortex. Intramedullary rod placement is performed to decrease the risk of pathologic fracture until palliative radiation has taken effect.
- Bisphosphonate pamidronate treats hypercalcemia, relieving bone pain as well as preventing additional fractures.
- Radiation therapy is the mainstay of treatment either alone or with pain medication. There are three forms of radiation that should be considered for patients:
  1. Radionuclides (all have palliative benefit, but ^{223}Ra has been shown to improve survival) [8]
  2. SBRT: The eligibility for SBRT includes all of the following factors:
     a. Limited disease
     b. Excellent performance status
     c. Bony lesion is >3 mm away from spinal cord
     d. Retreatment
     e. Radioresistant tumors

Dose for spinal SBRT: 16–18 Gy
Constraints for spinal SBRT: Maximum spinal cord point dose is 14 Gy, and 10% of the spinal cord volume is constrained to <10 Gy

  3. External beam radiation:
     Patient is CT-simulated supine or prone, depending on treatment site. Often placing a BB at the location of the painful lesion helps to identify the treatment site on CT scan. Treat with involved field radiation therapy technique by outlining the bony lesion and adding 2 cm margin to treat the volume. For metastatic bony lesions involving vertebrae, treatment should include one vertebrae superiorly and inferiorly in the treatment field. Protect bone joints from radiation when possible.

EBRT dose [7]:
Fractionation schemes that have proven effective include the following:

1. 800 cGy/fx to 800 cGy
2. 400 cGy/fx to 2000 cGy
3. 300 cGy/fx to 3000 cGy

The larger dose per fraction schedules are used with limited fields and/or poor systemic control of disease.

Outcome

Overall 60%–90% of the patients experience pain relief.

Complications

- No significant side effects from external beam RT treatment.
- Radionuclide treatments can cause myelosuppression.

Follow-Up

As clinically indicated.

ANNOTATED BIBLIOGRAPHY

METASTATIC BRAIN CANCERS

Ref 1. Kocher M et al. (2011). Adjuvant whole-brain radiotherapy versus observation after radiosurgery or surgical resection of one to three cerebral metastases: results of the EORTC 22952–26001 study. *J Clin Oncol*;29(2):134–41. EORTC 22952 Trial.

In this trial, 359 patients with 1–3 brain metastases of solid tumors (small-cell lung cancer excluded) with stable systemic disease or asymptomatic primary tumors and WHO performance status of 0–2 were treated with complete surgery or radiosurgery and randomly assigned to adjuvant WBRT (30 Gy in 10 fractions) or observation (OBS). The results were as below:

	Intracranial (%) *Progression Causing Death*	*OS (Months)*
Surg or SRS	*44*	*10.7*
Surg or SRS + WBRT	*28*	*10.9*
P *value*		*0.89*

The study showed that following radiosurgery or surgery of a limited number of brain metastases, adjuvant WBRT reduces intracranial relapses and neurologic deaths but fails to improve OS.

Ref 2. Brown PD et al. (2015). NCCTG N0574 (Alliance): A phase III randomized trial of whole brain radiation therapy (WBRT) in addition to radiosurgery (SRS) in patients with 1 to 3 brain metastases. *J clin Oncol*;33(18_suppl). Alliance Trial.

In this trial, 213 patients with 1−3 brain metastases, each <3 cm, were randomized to SRS alone or SRS + WBRT. The WBRT dose schedule was 30 Gy in 12 fractions; the SRS dose was 18−22 Gy in the SRS plus WBRT group and 20−24 Gy for SRS alone. Results were as given below:

	Cognitive Progression	1-Year (%) Brain Control	Median OS (%)
SRS	62	51	10.7
SRS + WBRT	88	85	7.5
P value	0.002	0.001	0.93

This study showed that decline in cognitive function was more frequent with the addition of WBRT to SRS. Adjuvant WBRT did not improve OS, despite better brain control.

Ref 3. Yamamoto M et al. (2017). A multi-institutional prospective observational study of stereotactic radiosurgery for patients with multiple brain metastases (JLGK0901 study update): Irradiation-related complications and long-term maintenance of mini-mental state examination scores. *Int J Radiat Biol Phys*;99(1):31−40. JLGK0901 Trial.

In this study, 1194 patients with 1−10 newly diagnosed brain metastases (largest tumor <10 mL in volume and <3 cm in longest diameter; total cumulative volume <15 mL) and KPS of 70 or higher were prospectively enrolled for observational study. SRS dose at the tumor periphery was 22 Gy for tumor volumes <4 mL, and 20 Gy for tumor volumes of 4−10 mL. Data from a median follow-up of 12 months were as given below:

	Median OS (Months)	Gr 3−4 Toxicity (%)	
		12 Months	48 Months
1 tumor	13.9	7	12
2−4 tumors	10.8	8	12
5−10 tumors	10.8	6	13
P value	0.78	0.89	0.38

The study concluded that SRS without WBRT in patients with 5−10 brain metastases does not differ from that in patients with 2−4 brain metastases. Neither MMSE score maintenance nor post-SRS complication incidence differed among groups further supporting noninferiority hypothesis of SRS alone for patients with 5−10 BMs versus 2−4 BMs.

Ref 4. Brown PD et al. (2017). Postoperative stereotactic radiosurgery compared with whole brain radiotherapy for resected metastatic brain disease (NCCTG N107C/CEC 3): a multicenter, randomized, controlled, phase 3 trial. *Lancet Oncol*;18(8):1049−60. NCCTG N107C Trial.

In this trial, 194 patients with one resected brain metastasis and a resection cavity less than 5 cm were randomly assigned to either postoperative SRS (12−20 Gy single fraction with dose determined by surgical cavity volume) or WBRT (30 Gy in 10 daily fractions or 37.5 Gy in 15 fractions of 2.5 Gy). Data from a median follow up of 11.1 months were as follows:

	Cognitive Progression Free Survival (Months)	1-Year LC (%)	Median OS (Months)
Surg + SRS	3.7	56	12.2
Surg + WBRT	3	78	11.6
P value	<0.0001	0.04	0.70

This study clearly showed that decline in cognitive function was more frequent with WBRT than with SRS, but there was no different in OS between the treatment groups.

SPINAL CORD COMPRESSION

Ref 5. Patchell et al. (2005). Direct decompressive surgical resection in the treatment of spinal cord compression caused by metastatic cancer: a randomised trial. *Lancet*;366(9486):643−8.

In this study, 101 patients with spinal cord compression caused by metastatic cancer were randomized to either surgery followed by radiotherapy or radiotherapy alone. Radiotherapy for both treatment groups was given in 300 cGy/fx to 30 Gy. The results were as follows:

	Able to Walk (%)	Duration of Walk (Days)	Steroid Requirement
RT alone	57	13	
Surgery + RT	84	122	Significantly less
P value	0.001	0.003	

This study revealed that surgery + RT provides better outcome than RT alone for patients with spinal cord compression caused by metastatic cancer.

Ref 6. Hoskin P et al. (2017). SCORAD III: randomized noninferiority phase III trial of single-dose radiotherapy (RT) compared to multifraction RT in patients (pts) with metastatic spinal canal compression (SCC). *J Clin Oncol*;35(18_Suppl).

In this trial, 688 patients with spinal cord or cauda equine compression (C1−S2) were randomized to receive external beam RT as a single dose of 8 Gy or 20 Gy in five fractions. The results were as follows:

	Ambulatory Status 1−2	OS (%)	Toxicity (%)	
			Gr 1−2	Gr 3−4
Multifraction RT	73.3	13.7	56.9	20.4
Single-dose RT	69.5	12.4	51	20.6
P value		0.81		

The study showed that using a single dose of 8 Gy was equivalent to multifraction RT in patients with metastatic SCC.

METASTATIC BONE CANCERS

Ref 7. Meeuse JJ (2010). Efficacy of radiotherapy for painful bone metastases during the last 12 weeks of life: results from the Dutch bone metastasis study. Cancer;116(11):2716−25.

In this trial, 1157 patients with painful bone metastases were randomized to single fraction (1 × 8 Gy or multiple fraction 6 × 4 Gy) radiotherapy. A total of 274 patients who died within 12 weeks following randomization were included in this analysis. The study concluded that pain responded in about half of the patients who survived <12 weeks after randomization. When considering RT, single fraction is preferred.

Ref 8. Parker C et al. (2016). Efficacy and Safety of Radium-223 Dichloride in Symptomatic Castration-resistant Prostate Cancer Patients With or Without Baseline Opioid Use From the Phase 3 ALSYMPCA Trial. European Urology Volume 70, Issue 5, November 2016, Pages 875−883.

In this trial, 921 patients with castration-resistant prostate cancer and bone metastases were randomly assigned six injections of ^{223}Ra (at a dose of 50 kBq per kg of body weight, IV) or matching placebo. Six injections were given every 4 weeks. At the interim analysis, the data showed the following:

	Non opiod MS (m)	Opiod MS (m)
Placebo	12.8	10.4
Ra-223	16.4	13.9
p value	0.013	0.001

The study concluded that Radium-223 versus placebo significantly prolonged OS and reduced symptomatic skeletal event risk with a favorable safety profile in castration-resistant prostate cancer patients with symptomatic bone metastases, regardless of baseline opioid use.

Radiation Treatment, Toxicity, and Their Management*

Radiation treatment side effects generally fall into two categories: early and late side effects. Early side effects occur during and immediately after completion of radiation treatment, whereas late radiation side effects occur many months or years after completion of radiation treatment. It is the early radiation side effects that can cause significant difficulty for the patient to continue radiation treatment and may require a break from the treatment, compromising the treatment outcome. It is imperative that radiation oncologists learn how to treat the side effects of radiation to prevent such breaks in the treatment. It is also noteworthy that the concurrent treatment of chemotherapy with radiation worsens both early and late radiation side effects. This chapter will discuss the common radiation side effects and their management during the radiation therapy.

NORMAL TISSUE TOLERANCE TO THERAPEUTIC IRRADIATION

Radiation therapy side effects and complications are dose and volume dependent. It is important for radiation oncologists to know the normal tissue tolerances to radiation therapy. Table 26.1 contains information on tolerance of normal tissues/organs, including the partial volume effects [1]. In the modern era of 3D-CRT and IMRT, the following tolerance doses to full and partial volumes can be used as a guideline when designing normal tissue/organ constraints for the radiation treatment planning. Table 26.2 presents recent quantitative analyses of normal tissue effects in the clinic [2, 3, 4].

---

*The unreferenced contents are primarily an organized compilation of the author's (T.W. Dziuk, M.D.) personal prescribing notes and practices; no warranty, expressed or implied, is made as to accuracy. Although every attempt has been made, both in writing and in editing, to ensure accuracy, the reader is urged to carefully review information.

Fundamentals of Radiation Oncology
https://doi.org/10.1016/B978-0-12-814128-1.00026-X

TABLE 26.1 Normal Tissue Late Toxicity as a Function of Volume and Dose

TD 5/5 and T/D 50/5 = Tumor Dose (cGy) Causing 5% and 50% Complication Rate in 5 Years

Organ Volume Irradiated (3/3, 2/3, 1/3) (Selected End Point)	TD 5/5			TD 50/5		
	3/3	2/3	1/3	3/3	2/3	1/3
Bladder (contracture and volume loss)	6500	8000	—	8000	8500	—
Bone (child) (growth arrest)	(10 cm³) 2000			(10 cm³) 2000		
Brachial plexus (clinically apparent nerve damage)	6000	6100	6200	7500	7600	7700
Brain (necrosis/infraction)	4500	5000	6000	6000	6500	7500
Brainstem (necrosis/infraction)	5000	5300	6000	6500	—	—
Cauda equina (clinically apparent nerve damage)	6000	—	—	7500	—	—
Colon (obstruction, perforation, ulceration)	4500	—	5500	5500	—	6500
Ear (acute serous otitis)	3000	3000	3000	4000	4000	4000
Ear (chronic serous otitis)	5500	5500	5500	6500	6500	6500
Esophagus (stricture, perforation)	5500	5800	6000	6800	7000	7200
Femoral head (necrosis)	5200	—	—	6500	—	—
Heart (pericarditis)	4000	4500	6000	5000	5500	7000
Kidney (clinically apparent nephritis)	2300	3000	5000	2800	4000	—

Larynx (necrosis)	7000	7000	7900	8000	8000	9000
Larynx (edema)	4500	4500	—	8000	—	—
Lens (cataract)	1000	—	—	1800	—	—
Liver (liver failure)	3000	3500	5000	4000	4500	5500
Lung (pneumonitis)	1750	3000	4500	2450	4000	6500
Muscle (clinical myositis)	5000	—	—	—	—	—
Optic chiasm (blindness)	5000	—	—	6500	—	—
Optic nerve (blindness)	5000	—	—	6500	—	—
Oral mucosa (ulcer, fibrosis)	(50 cm²) 6000	—	—	(50 cm²) 7500	—	—
Ovary (sterility)	300	—	—	1200	—	—
Parotid gland (xerostomia)	3200	3200	—	4600	4600	—
Pituitary (hypopituitarism)	4500	—	—	—	—	—
Rectum (severe proctitis, necrosis, fistula, stenosis)	6000	—	—	8000	—	—
Retina (blindness)	4500	—	—	6500	—	—
Rib cage (pathologic fracture)	—	—	5000	—	—	6500
Skin (necrosis, ulceration)	(100 cm²) 5000	(30 cm²) 6000	(10 cm²) 7000	(100 cm²) 6500	—	—
Spinal cord (myelitis, necrosis)	(20 cm) 4700	(10 cm) 5000	(5 cm) 5000	—	(10 cm) 7000	(5 cm) 7000
Small intestine (obstruction, perforation)	4000	—	5000	5500	—	6000

(Continued)

TABLE 26.1 Normal Tissue Late Toxicity as a Function of Volume and Dose—cont'd

Organ Volume Irradiated (3/3, 2/3, 1/3) (Selected End Point)	TD 5/5 and T/D 50/5 = Tumor Dose (cGy) Causing 5% and 50% Complication Rate in 5 Years					
	TD 5/5			TD 50/5		
	3/3	2/3	1/3	3/3	2/3	1/3
Stomach (ulceration, perforation)	5000	5500	6000	6500	6700	7000
Testes (sterility)	500	–	–	–	2000	–
TMJ mandible (limitation of joint function, fracture)	6000	6000	6500	7200	7200	7700
Thyroid (hypothyroidism)	4500	–	–	7000	–	–
Vagina (ulcer, fistula)	9000 (5 cm³)	–	–	10,000	–	–

Adapted from ref 1 Emami B, Lyman J, Goitein M, Munzenrider JE, Shank B, Solin LJ, Wesson M. Tolerance of normal tissue to therapeutic irradiation. Int J Radiat Oncol Biol Phys;21(1):109–22, © 1991, with permission from Elsevier.

TABLE 26.2 Quantitative Analyses of Normal Tissue Effects in the Clinic (QUANTEC)

Critical Structure		Conventional Fractionated 3D-CRT				
	Volume	Dose/Volume	Maximum Dose (Gy)	Toxicity Rate (%)	Toxicity Endpoint	
Brain	—	—	<60	<3	Symptomatic necrosis	
Brain	—	—	72	5	Symptomatic necrosis	
Brain	—	—	90	10	Symptomatic necrosis	
Brain stem	—	—	<54	<5	Neuropathy or necrosis	
Brain stem	D1–10 cc	≤59 Gy	—	<5	Neuropathy or necrosis	
Brain stem	—	—	<64	<5	Neuropathy or necrosis	
Optic nerve/chiasm	—	—	<55	<3	Optic neuropathy	
Optic nerve/chiasm	—	—	55–60	3–7	Optic neuropathy	
Optic nerve/chiasm	—	—	60	7–20	Optic neuropathy	
Spinal cord	—	—	50	0.2	Myelopathy	
Spinal cord	—	—	60	6	Myelopathy	
Spinal cord	—	—	69	50	Myelopathy	
Cochlea	Mean	≤45 Gy	—	<30	Sensory–neural hearing loss	
Parotid, bilateral	Mean	≤25 Gy	—	<20	Long-term salivary function <25%	
Parotid, bilateral	Mean	≤39 Gy	—	<50	Long-term salivary function <25%	
Parotid, unilateral	Mean	≤20 Gy	—	<20	Long-term salivary function <25%	
Pharyngeal constrictors	Mean	≤50 Gy	—	<20	Symptomatic dysphagia and aspiration	

(*Continued*)

TABLE 26.2 Quantitative Analyses of Normal Tissue Effects in the Clinic (QUANTEC)—cont'd

| Critical Structure | Volume | Conventional Fractionated 3D-CRT | | | Toxicity Endpoint |
		Dose/Volume	Maximum Dose (Gy)	Toxicity Rate (%)	
Larynx	—	—	<66	<20	Vocal dysfunction
Larynx	Mean	<50 Gy	—	<30	Aspiration
Larynx	Mean	<44 Gy	—	<20	Edema
Larynx	V50	<27%	—	<20	Edema
Lung	V20	≤30%	—	<20	Symptomatic pneumonitis
Lung	Mean	7 Gy	—	5	Symptomatic pneumonitis
Lung	Mean	13 Gy	—	10	Symptomatic pneumonitis
Lung	Mean	20 Gy	—	20	Symptomatic pneumonitis
Lung	Mean	24 Gy	—	30	Symptomatic pneumonitis
Lung	Mean	27 Gy	—	40	Symptomatic pneumonitis
Esophagus	Mean	<34 Gy	—	5–20	Grade 3 + esophagitis
Esophagus	V35	<50%	—	<30	Grade 2 + esophagitis
Esophagus	V50	<40%	—	<30	Grade 2 + esophagitis
Esophagus	V70	<20%	—	<30	Grade 2 + esophagitis
Heart (pericardium)	Mean	<26 Gy	—	<15	Pericarditis
Heart (pericardium)	V30	<46%	—	<15	Pericarditis

Organ	Metric	Value		Rate	Endpoint
Heart	V25	<10%	—	<1	Long-term cardiac mortality
Liver	Mean	<30–32 Gy	—	<5	RILD (in normal liver function)
Liver	Mean	<42 Gy	—	<50	RILD (in normal liver function)
Liver	Mean	<28 Gy	—	<5	RILD (in Child–Pugh A or HCC)
Liver	Mean	<36 Gy	—	<50	RILD (in Child–Pugh A or HCC)
Kidney, bilateral	Mean	<15–18 Gy	—	<5	Clinical dysfunction
Kidney, bilateral	Mean	<28 Gy	—	<50	Clinical dysfunction
Kidney, bilateral	V12	<55%	—	<5	Clinical dysfunction
Kidney, bilateral	V20	<32%	—	<5	Clinical dysfunction
Kidney, bilateral	V23	<30%	—	<5	Clinical dysfunction
Kidney, bilateral	V28	<20%	—	<5	Clinical dysfunction
Stomach	D100	<45 Gy	—	<7	Ulceration
Small bowel (individual loops)	V15	<120 cc	—	<10	Grade 3 + toxicity
Small bowel (peritoneal cavity)	V45	<195 cc	—	<10	Grade 3 + toxicity
Rectum	V50	<50%	—	<10	Grade 3 + toxicity
Rectum	V60	<35%	—	<10	Grade 3 + toxicity
Rectum	V65	<25%	—	<10	Grade 3 + toxicity
Rectum	V70	<20%	—	<10	Grade 3 + toxicity
Rectum	V75	<15%	—	<10	Grade 3 + toxicity

(Continued)

IV. PALLIATIVE CARE AND RADIATION TREATMENT TOXICITY

TABLE 26.2 Quantitative Analyses of Normal Tissue Effects in the Clinic (QUANTEC)—cont'd

| Critical Structure | Volume | Conventional Fractionated 3D-CRT | | | Toxicity Endpoint |
		Dose/Volume	Maximum Dose (Gy)	Toxicity Rate (%)	
Bladder (bladder cancer)	—	—	<65	<6	Grade 3 + toxicity
Bladder (prostate cancer)	V65	<50%	—	—	Grade 3 + toxicity
Bladder (prostate cancer)	V70	<35%	—	—	Grade 3 + toxicity
Bladder (prostate cancer)	V75	<25%	—	—	Grade 3 + toxicity
Bladder (prostate cancer)	V80	<15%	—	—	Grade 3 + toxicity
Penile bulb	Mean dose to 95% gland	<50 Gy	—	<35%	Severe erectile dysfunction
Penile bulb	D90	<50 Gy	—	<35	Severe erectile dysfunction
Penile bulb	D60–70	<70 Gy	—	<55	Severe erectile dysfunction

Note: The "pericardium volume" was defined as a "rind" within the previously contoured heart volumes. The manually contoured heart volumes served as the outer border, and the inner border was automatically contoured 1 cm within these same contours using the planning. The heart pericardium contours on successive axial CT slices were meshed into a 3-D structure [3].

Stereotactic Radiosurgery (Single Fraction)					
Critical Structure	Volume	Dose/Volume	Maximum Dose (Gy)	Toxicity Rate (%)	Toxicity Endpoint
Brain	V12	<5 –10 cc	–	<20	Symptomatic necrosis
Brain stem (acoustic tumors)	–	–	<12.5	<5	Neuropathy or necrosis
Optic nerve/chiasm	–	–	<12	<10	Optic neuropathy
Spinal cord (single-fx)	–	–	13	1	Myelopathy
Spinal cord (hypo-fx)	–	–	20	1	Myelopathy
Cochlea	Prescription dose	≤14 Gy	–	<25	Sensory-neural hearing loss
Liver/HCC (three fractions)	Mean	<13 Gy	–	<5	RILD
Liver/Mets (three fractions)	Mean	<15 Gy	–	<5	RILD
Liver (three fractions)	700 cc	<15 Gy	–	<5%	RILD

Reprinted from ref 2, Marks LB, Yorke ED, Jackson A, 10 Haken RK, Constine LS, Eisbruch A, Bentzen SM, Nam J, Deasy JO. Use of normal tissue complication probability models in the clinic. Int J Radiat Oncol Biol Phys;76(3 Supplement):S10—9, © 2010, with permission from Elsevier; reproduced from ref 4 Wikipedia, the free Encyclopedia. Radiation Oncology/Toxicity/QUANTEC, page 1. Wikimedia Foundation, Inc., http://www.en.wikibooks.org/wiki/Radiation_Oncology/Toxicity/QUANTEC.

SKIN

Early Radiation Dermatitis and Focal Pruritus

Early radiation dermatitis manifests as pruritus, erythema, and/or scaly, flaky dry desquamation. *RadiaPlexRX Gel* and *Miaderm* are used to prevent and treat radiation dermatitis. *Aquaphor* or other moisturizers provide relief for early dry desquamation and minor irritation. As symptoms progress, *Domeboro* compresses provide relief to intact skin and appears to delay further reaction; add *Miaderm L* or *Sarna Sensitive* to further reduce irritation. Eventually **aquaphor/xylocaine,** topical **lidocaine**, and *EMLA* may be needed. Limit application of prescription topical anesthetics to intact skin.

Miliaria rubra (inflammation of sweat glands) may develop early or late and is a pruritic, erythematous punctate rash, which can extend outside the treatment field; use **hydrocortisone 1%** initially; if refractory, advance to *Topicort.*

Aquaphor Healing Ointment (OTC)—apply tid
Dermoplast (OTC topical anesthetic)—apply to the affected area tid
Domeboro compresses (OTC)—dissolve 1 tablet or packet in 1 pint water, apply moist (not wet) soak 20 min tid to qid
EMLA Cream (lidocaine 2.5%, prilocaine 2.5%)—apply prn
Eucerin (OTC moisturizer)—apply prn
Hydrocortisone 1% (OTC, e.g., Cortaid, Cortizone-10)—apply qid prn
Lidocaine—apply to the affected area prn for topical anesthesia
• L.M.X.4 & L.M.X.5 (OTC 4% and 5% lidocaine cream)
Lidoderm 5% patch—apply for 12 h q 24 h
• apply up to three patches at a time for wound coverage
Miaderm (OTC)—apply tid at initiation of XRT; or for symptoms
• Miaderm L—also contains 4% lidocaine
RadiaPlex Rx Gel (with hyaluronic acid)—apply tid
Sarna Sensitive (OTC, 1% hydrocortisone; 1% pramoxine (a topical anesthetic)—apply tid
Topicort (desoximetasone)—apply bid

Dry and Moist Desquamation

Areas preparing to desquamate develop a dusky erythematous appearance. Once that develops, begin *Domeboro* soaks, followed by *Regenecare HA* (gel or spray) or **Aquaphor/Xylocaine** when dry. Cover with *Telfa* if needed to protect clothing and to minimize abrading. **Hydrogel Wound Dressings** are preferred for persistent dry desquamation; for moist desquamation coverage, consider **Hydrocolloids** dressings (also, see **Ulceration—Slow Healing**).

If deep moist desquamation develops with greater than 500 to 1000 cGy XRT remaining, continue as above, with radiation held until new skin islets appear (about 7–10 days). If more than 2000 cGy remain, allow additional time for skin recovery. If malodorous or discolored exudate, consider *Silvadene* or *SilverMed* (if allergic to sulfa drugs) or systemic therapy.

Domeboro soaks (OTC)—dissolve 1 tablet or packet in 1 pint water
- apply moist (not wet) soak 20 min tid to qid
- packets or tablets of 12 and 100

Hydrocolloids (e.g., *Dyoderm, Tegasorb, Comfeel*)

Hydrogel Wound Dressings (e.g., *Vigilon, Geliperm, Cool Magic*)
- apply prn

Regenecare (hydrogel with 2% **lidocaine**)—bid to tid
- Regenecare Wound Gel—3 oz
- Regenecare HA (my preference)—3 oz
- Regenecare HA Spray—4 oz

Silvadene cream 1%—apply to the affected area tid

SilverMed—apply tid to bid

Telfa (OTC nonstick adhesive pads)—cover wound prn

Ulceration—Slow Healing

To promote healing, wounds need to be free of infection, bacteria debris, and moist. For debridement, use **normal saline** or *MPM Wound and Skin Cleanser*, then apply **Aquaphor** or *Regenecare HA*; *Silvadene* or *SilverMed* as an overcoat to prevent infection. Vascularization is important—consider *Xenaderm*, a capillary bed stimulant, or *Trental* with *Vitamin E.* To maintain a moist environment, cover with a **Hydrocolloid,** or **Hydrogel** if dry.

For more aggressive therapy, consider a physical therapy or home health. Vacuum-assisted wound closure systems (VACS) facilitate rapid wound healing of smaller sites. Hyperbaric oxygen and/or surgical intervention may also be necessary.

Domeboro soaks (OTC)—dissolve 1 tablet or packet in 1 pint water, apply moist (not wet) soak 20 min qid

Hydrocolloids (e.g., Dyoderm, Tegasorb, Comfeel)

Hydrogel Wound Dressings (e.g., **Vigilon, Geliperm, Cool Magic**)

MPM Wound and Skin Cleanser (OTC)—spray, allow time to soften, adjust nozzle to "STREAM" to loosen debris

Pentoxifylline (Trental, generic)—400 mg po tid

Regenecare (hydrogel with 2% **lidocaine**)—bid to tid
- Regenecare Wound Gel—3 oz
- Regenecare HA (my preference)—3 oz
- Regenecare HA Spray—4 0z

Silvadene cream 1%—apply to the affected area tid

SilverMed—apply tid to bid

Vitamin E (OTC)—1000 IU po qd

Xenaderm (Balsam Peru, trypsin, and castor oil)—apply bid to tid

Antibiotics/Wound Infection Treatment

Polysporin, Bactroban, or *Bacitracin* is effective for superficial skin/open wound infections (caution regarding *Neosporin,* as approximately 10% of patients are allergic to **neomycin**). *Silvadene* or *Silvermed* are used for mild wound sepsis.

Keflex, Bactrim, and *Augmentin* are effective for subcutaneous infection/involvement as systemic treatment; if considerable erythema and warmth, use *Levaquin, Cipro,* or a *Z-pak.* For skin infections/cellulitis in diabetic patients or for groin and perineum infections, add *Cleocin.* If pseudomonas is suspected (foul smelling, greenish exudate), *Cipro* or *Levaquin* are systemic choices.

> *Acetic acid* 0.05% (OTC)—apply qd or qod to open wound
> * for superficial pseudomonas infection
> **Amoxicillin/clavulanate** (*Augmentin,* generic)—500 mg tid, 875 mg bid
> **Azithromycin** (*Z-Pak*)—as directed
> **Bacitracin** (OTC)—apply bid to tid
> *Bactrim DS* (**sulfamethoxazole/trimethropim,** generic)—1 po bid
> *Bactroban* (**mupirocin**)—apply to the affected area tid
> **Cephalexin** (*Keflex,* generic)—250–500 mg po q 6 h
> **Ciprofloxacin** (*Cipro,* **Cipro XR,** generic)—250–750 mg po bid
> **Clindamycin** (*Cleocin,* generic)—150–450 mg po q 6 h
> * MRSA and nonaerobic coverage
> **Levofloxacin** (*Levaquin*)—500–750 mg qd
> *Neosporin* (OTC, **neomycin/polymyxinB/bacitracin**)—apply bid to tid
> *Neosporin + Pain Relief* (OTC, with pramoxine)—apply bid to tid
> *Polysporin* (OTC, **polymyxinB/bacitracin**)—apply bid to tid
> *Silvadene cream 1%*—apply to the affected area tid
> *SilverMed*—apply tid to bid

Antifungals/Antivirals

For yeast or fungal infections, use topical OTC medications initially. If dry, scaly, annular, or suspect fungus, use *Lamisel.* If moist and popular or suspect yeast, use *Lotrimin.* If refractory to OTC medications, prescribe topical *Naftin* or oral **fluconazole.** In regions of chronic drainage, use *Aquaphor* as a barrier/protectant. For herpetic infections, prescribe *Zovirax, Valtrex,* or *Famvir,* with different dosing for h. simplex versus h. zoster.

> **Fluconazole** (*Diflucan,* generic)—200 mg day 1, then 100 mg qd
> *Famvir* (**famciclovir**) (h. simplex)—1000 mg bid × 1 day
> * h. simplex suppressive therapy 250 mg qd
> * h. zoster—500 mg tid × 7 days
> * tablets 125, 250, and 500 mg
> *Lamisel* (**terbinafine**—OTC antifungal)—apply bid
> *Lotrimin Antifungal* (OTC antifungal)—apply bid
> * AF (clotrimazole) Ultra (butenafine)
> *Naftin* (**naftifine** 1%)—apply qd
> *Valtrex* (**valacyclovir**) (h. simplex)—1 gm bid × 7 days
> *Zovirax* (**acyclovir**) (h. simplex)— 200 mg po 5 times daily × 10 d
> * h. zoster—800 mg po 5 times daily × 7–10 d

Generalized Pruritus

Most generalized (or focal) pruritus responds to the treatments below. Additional etiologies include renal pruritus, cholestatic pruritus, hematologic pruritus, lymphoma, etc.

Aveeno Bath Treatments (OTC)—soak in bath prn
Diphenhydramine (OTC, e.g., *Benadryl*)—25–50 mg po qid
Dexamethasone (*DexPax*, 1.5 mg **dexamethasone**)—as directed—.6-day, 10-day, 13-day tapering dose packs.
Doxepin (*Sinequan*, generic)—10–75 mg po qd

Note: antidepressant/anxiolytic effect; low dose initially with gradual escalation.

Hydroxyzine (*Vistaril*, generic)—10–25 mg po tid

Note: nonbenzodiazepam anxiolytic.

Medol Dosepak (**methylprednisolone**)—as directed—6-day dose pack (4 mg)

HEAD AND NECK

Radiotherapy of the head and neck impacts many structures. Acute effects include radiation dermatitis (see skin section), loss of taste, mucositis, odynophagia/dysphagia, and xerostomia. With head and neck cancer, local control rates decrease with radiotherapy breaks—the patient should be well informed of the need for continued treatment regardless of the severity of side effects. Minimizing alcohol and (especially) tobacco use decreases the probability and duration of side effects ($\sim$20%); eliminating tobacco use increases the local control rate ($\sim$20%).

Weight loss usually begins in week 3 or 4 and continues for 3–4 weeks post-XRT. Despite aggressive pain management, a feeding tube is required in one-third of patients. Consider initial placement of a peg tube for severe dysphagia, or for poor performance status with planned combined modality therapy.

Skin reactions and odynophagia begin to resolve at 3–6 weeks (possibly longer with chemotherapy or hyperfractionated radiotherapy). Decreased taste, decreased hearing, dysphagia, laryngeal edema, and xerostomia persist longer.

Xerostomia increases dental caries risk, which can rapidly progress despite fluoride prophylaxis. The potential for tooth extraction causing bone necrosis increases with doses above 5000 cGy; prophylactic pre- and postextraction hyperbaric oxygen is usually advised. If minor osteonecrosis develops, manage conservatively, evaluating periodically for possible infection. For refractory or large radionecrotic lesions, **pentoxifylline** and **vitamin E** may be beneficial; often, hyperbaric oxygen ($+/-$ subsequent flap reconstruction) is necessary. Radiation to the lower neck can cause thyroid failure. A rare, but debilitating, side effect is carotid stenosis.

Eye

A common combination used during pterygium irradiation is *Proparacaine* as a topical analgesic and **tobramycin** post-XRT. If ocular inflammation from XRT, prescribe *Cortisporin Ophthalmic.*

> *Cortisporin Ophthalmic* (combination of steroid and antimicrobial)—apply ointment or 1—2 gtts q 3—4 h
> Note: Do not use more than 5—10 days.
> *Proparacaine hydrochloride 0.5%*—2 gtts before procedure
> **Tobradex** (*tobramycin 0.3% + dexamethasone*)—3 gtts after procedure

Dry Eye

Most preparations are mild antiinflammatory or tear replacement agents. For dry eye irritation, use OTC tear lubricants, and advance to *Lacrisert* if minimal relief. *Restasis* increases tear production and is suppressed by ocular inflammation (as in keratoconjunctivitis sicca). For refractory dry eye, plugging the lacrimal duct (**silicone plugs,** surgery) or trapping devices (**corneal shields**) is advised.

> Cyclosporin emulsion (*Restasis*)—1 gtt q 12 h
> *Lacrisert*—insert as directed qd
>
> Note: consider for severe dryness.
>
> *Refresh* (OTC)—usually 1—2 gtts to the affected eye qid
> * *Tears* (mild to moderate dry eye)
> * *Celluvisc* (moderate to severe dry eye)
> * *Endura* (severe dry eye)
> * *Liquigel* (moderate to severe dry eye)
> *Tears Naturale* (OTC)—1—2 gtts prn
> * *Tears Naturale Forte*—15 and 30 cc bottles
> * *Tears Naturale Free*—small, multiuse vials
> Visine (OTC)—usually 1—2 gtts to the affected eye qid
> * *Visine Original*—for minor redness
> * *Visine-A*—contains antihistamine; for redness due to allergens
> * *Visine Advanced Relief*—addition of a lubricant
> * *Visine Tears*—lubricant only; use prn

Ear

For allergy-induced eustachian tube dysfunction, use an antihistamine (see Sinuses section). For XRT-induced eustachian tube edema, prescribe **pseudoephedrine,** an OTC decongestant. If refractory, prescribe *Mucinex*, and if needed, a short course of tapering steroids (e.g., **Medrol Dosepak** or **DexPax**); eventually, TM tube placement may be required. For external otitis, use **Otitis Externa Mix** (OTC), *Cipro HC Otic*, or *Cortisporin Otic*. For uncomplicated otitis media, **amoxicillin** is commonly prescribed and advanced to *Augmentin* or *Levaquin* if no improvement after 3 days. For XRT-induced external otitis, *Tympagesic Otic Solution* has analgesic and anesthetic properties.

Amoxicillin (*Amoxil,* generic)—250 mg q 8 h (500 mg q 8 h if severe); 875 mg bid, or 775 mg ER qd

Amoxicillin/clavulanate (*Augmentin,* generic)—500 mg tid, **Dexamethasone** (*DexPax,* 1.5 mg **dexamethasone**)—as directed—6-day, 10-day, 13-day tapering dose packs.

Diphenhydramine (OTC, e.g., *Benadryl*)—25 mg po q 6–8 h

Ciprodex (**Ciprofloxacin** and **dexamethasone**)—four gtts bid × 7 days—7.5 cc Drop-Tainer system

CiproHC Otic (**Ciprofloxacin** and **prednisone**)—3 gtts bid × 7 days

Cortisporin Otic—4 gtts to the affected ear q 6 h

Levofloxacin (*Levaquin*)—500–750 mg qd

Methylprednisolone (*Medrol Dosepak*)—po as directed—.4 mg tablets, given over a 6-day taper

Otitis Externa Mix (OTC)—2–4 gtts to the affected ear, bid to qid— mix 1:1 water:white vinegar

Pseudoephedrine (OTC decongestant)—as directed

Tympagesic Otic Solution—fill canal q 4 h, place stopper

Mucositis

Mucositis (mouth to anus) or stomatitis (mouth alone) is variable in time to onset, extent of involvement, and impact to the patient. A clinical trial demonstrated decreased oral pain using *MuGard* prophylactically. To minimize the impact of mucositis impact, good oral hygiene including baking soda gargle, soft toothbrush, mild toothpaste (e.g., *Biotene*), minimal flossing, fluoride carriers or toothpaste, use of a humidifier, and minimizing spicy foods, alcohol, caffeine, and tobacco are encouraged.

Candida can present in an atypical, patchy fashion. If in doubt, treat gastric reflux exacerbates mucositis, and it can be improved with a proton pump inhibitor (e.g., *Prevacid, Prilosec*). For very early or unusually severe mucositis (especially with associated early skin reaction), rule out HIV infection or collagen vascular disease. Treat focal aphthous ulcers (an excessive immune response to minor trauma) with topical medications such as OTC *Ulcerease* or *Orabase,* or **Triple Mix** (Rx).

Severe mucositis can cause rapid weight loss necessitating a feeding tube. Initially, consider topical medications (**Triple Mix)** and anesthetics (**phenol, benzocaine lidocaine** preparations and *UlcerEase* with ice chips). *RadiCare Oral Wound Rinse, Gelclair, OraMagic RX* or *Plus* are also used, but typically, systemic pain medication is eventually required. A normal progression is **NSAID,** *Tramadol* or **hydrocodone,** then **fentanyl** (or other long-acting pain medication). *Carafate slurry* may also help the healing process.

Baking Soda mouthwash—1–3 tsp gargle and spit, >4–6 qd
* mix 1 tbs baking soda, 1 tbs salt, 1 quart water

Carafate suspension (**sucralfate**)—2 tsp swish and swallow qid

Gelclair—swish in oral cavity 1 minute, spit; avoid eating or drinking for 1 h—use up to tid
* provides relief for 1–6 h

Lidocaine—topical absorption, 5 min to onset, 40 min duration
- *Xylocaine Oral Spray* 10%—po prn (10 mg per dose)
- *Xylocaine Viscous 2%*—2 tsp po swish and swallow/swish and spit prn

Miracle Mouthwash—2 tsp po swish and swallow/spit qid
- mix 60 mL tetracycline oral suspension (125 mg/5 mL), 30 mL **mycostatin oral suspension** (100,000 u/mL), 30 mL

Hydrocortisone oral suspension (10 mg/5 mL) and 240 mL
Benadryl syrup (12.5 mg/5 mL)
MuGuard—5 mL four to six times per day
Omeprazole (*Prilosec*, generic, OTC)—20 mg po qd
Orabase Paste (20% **benzocaine**)—apply prn
OraMagic (OTC)—swish and spit qid
OraMagic Rx—regular formulation
OraMagic Plus—with benzocaine
RadiCare Oral Wound Rinse—15 cc swish/gargle qid
Triple mix—1:1:1 Benadryl elixir:Maalox:viscous xylocaine 2%
Ulcerease (OTC topical anesthetic)—2 tsp swish and swallow or spit prn—mix with ice chips for posterior pharyngitis

Oral Infection and Candidiasis

For oral infections, consider **clindamycin** or *Augmentin*. **Mycelex troche** and **nystatin** oral suspension can be used initially for candidiasis, with **fluconazole** for severe or refractory cases. Xerostomia may make troches difficult to tolerate. If candidiasis develops within severe mucositis, the infection may require a longer (4–8 weeks) course of systemic antifungal therapy.

Amoxicillin/clavulanate (*Augmentin*, generic)—250–500 mg po tid—875 mg po bid
- *Augmentin extended release*—2 tablets bid

Chlorhexidine (*Peridex*)—1/2 oz swish 30 s and spit bid
- Note: used as a prophylactic oral antibiotic

Clindamycin (*Cleocin*, generic)—150–450 mg po q 6 h
- MRSA and nonaerobic coverage

Fluconazole (*Diflucan*)—200 mg po day 1, then 100 mg po qd × 7 days (if candida recurs, repeat for 21 days)
Mycelex troche—dissolve lozenge in mouth, five per day, × 14 days
Nystatin suspension (*Nystatin*, generic)—5 cc swish well for 2 min and swallow qid; or dissolve 2 lozenges orally bid; through 2 days postclinical resolution

Sialdenitis

Acute sialdenitis is a mild to severe swelling of the parotid or submandibular glands, occurring within 24–48 h of radiotherapy. The patient is often alarmed and describes swelling, dry mouth, and/or pain. Usually self-limiting to 24–48 h. Reassure patient and prescribe NSAID and heating pad. If associated with temperature >101° and parotid is hot, treat with **oxacillin** or **vancomycin**.

Sinuses

Allegra, Claritin, and *Zyrtec* are used for allergy-induced nasal congestion and/or Eustachian tube dysfunction and can be used in hypertensive patients. To promote sinus drainage, use decongestants and/or high-dose expectorants (e.g., 1200 mg) that help thin nasal secretions. For infection, *Augmentin* or *Levaquin* are initial choices. If pseudomonas is suspected (foul-smelling green purulent discharge), use *Cipro* or *Levaquin.*

> *Actifed* (OTC antihistamine and decongestant)—1 po q 6 h
> **Amoxicillin/clavulanate** (**Augmentin**)—250–500 mg po tid; –875 mg po bid
> • Augmentin extended release—2 tablets bid
> *Benadryl* 25 mg (OTC antihistamine)—25–50 mg po q 4–6 h
> **Cetirizine** (*Zyrtec*, OTC)—10 mg po qd
> • *Zyrtec-D*—po bid
> **Ciprofloxacin** (*Cipro, Cipro XR,* generic)—250–750 mg q 12 h
> **Fexofenadine** (*Allegra*)—60 mg po bid or 180 mg po qd
> *Allegra D 12 Hr*—po bid (60 mg + 120 mg pseudoephedrine)
> *Allegra D 24 Hr*—po qd (180 mg + 240 mg pseudoephedrine)
> **Loratadine** (*Claritin*, OTC)—po qd
> • *Claritin-D* 12 h (with 120 mg pseudoephedrine)—bid
> • *Claritin-D* 24 h (with 240 mg pseudoephedrine)—qd
> **Levofloxacin** (*Levaquin*)—500–750 mg qd
> *Mucinex* (**guaifenesin**, OTC)—600–1200 mg po bid
> • *Mucinex DM*—with cough suppressant
> • *Mucinex D*—with pseudoephedrine
> **Pseudoephedrine** (OTC decongestant)—1 po q 6 h

Teeth and Osteoradionecrosis

Whenever possible before XRT, restorable teeth should be repaired, and nonrestorable and questionably restorable teeth extracted. Full mouth extraction is recommended when there is extensive decay, poor or undependable oral hygiene, moderate peridontal problems (pockets greater than 3 mm deep), and less than 50% of remaining alveolar bone support. XRT can begin as soon as 1 week after simple extraction and 3–4 weeks after more complex extractions.

Osteoradionecrosis occurs in 3%–10% of patients postradiotherapy, through damage of intraosseous small blood vessels. The primary treatment is hyperbaric oxygen, which is also used prophylactically for teeth extraction postradiotherapy (especially when the mandible has received high dose) or the extracted teeth are within the irradiated field.

For posttreatment, start antibiotics 1 day before extraction, if required. For multiple extractions, removal of one at a time with alveoplasty (if indicated) reduces risk of osteoradionecrosis.

Xerostomia

Xerostomia may begin in the third week of XRT. Initially, serous cells produce thickened saliva; at higher doses, the mucous cells fail and saliva diminishes. Posttreatment, salivation may worsen up to 6 months and then improve up to 3 years. Symptomatic relief can be obtained with saliva substitutes, or stimulation.

Artificial salivas (e.g., *Numosyn, Aquoral, Salivart, Moi-Stir*), glycerin, or baking soda gargles can provide symptomatic relief. In nonedentulous patients, fluoride protection must be provided, either with a fluoride toothpaste (*GelKam, Biotene*, or *Prevident*) or with a fluoride carrier. Avoid OTC mouthwashes since the alcohol can dry oral tissues. Moisture stimulants include **Biotene Products,** chewing gum, and sugar-free candy.

XRT-induced xerostomia is worsened by, or confused with, dehydration. For symptomatic thickened saliva, **baking soda gargle** is an initial approach; an expectorant (e.g., **guaifenesin**) and/or hydration may provide significant relief.

Occasionally a patient develops a severe gag response to the thickened saliva, refractory to baking soda gargle, or normal antiemetics—*Ativan* may benefit this situation. Xerostomia can be caused or worsened by candidiasis, anticholinergic drugs (e.g., tricyclic antidepressants), opioids, antihistamines, decongestants, antidepressants, anxiolytics, and antidiarrheals.

For prophylaxis, *Amifostine* during XRT has a statistically significant benefit (20% absolute improvement in late xerostomia, 35% versus 57%). A small study has shown prophylactic benefit with *NeutraSal*. *Salagen* has no significant prophylactic benefit but does benefit post-XRT as primary treatment. *Evoxac*, approved for Sjogren Syndrome, has statistically significant benefit for XRT-associated xerostomia.

Aquoral—2 sprays po tid to qid prn
Amifostine (**Ethyol**)—200 mg/m^2 IV over 3 min, daily 15—30 min before XRT
Artificial saliva (OTC)—apply to oral mucosa prn
- *Salivart*—25 and 75 g containers
- *Saliva Substitute*—120 mL squirt bottle
Baking Soda Mouthwash (OTC)—1—3 tsp swish and spit prn
- mix 1 tbs baking soda, 1 tbs salt, 1 quart water
Biotene Antibacterial Mouthwash (OTC)—15 cc swish and spit prn
Biotene Dry Mouth Toothpaste (OTC)—bid to tid brushing
Biotene Dental Gum (OTC)—chew one to two pieces prn
Cevimeline (*Evoxac*)—30 mg po tid
Fluoride carriers—arranged via dental consultation
GelKam (**fluoride toothpaste**)—brush 10 min bid
Glycerin (OTC)—mix 1/4 tsp in 8 oz water, use prn
Moi-Stir (OTC)—spray prn
Mouth Kote 1% (OTC)—5 cc po gargle, swish, hold for 1 min, and then spit
Mucinex (**guaifenesin**, OTC)—600—1200 mg po bid
- tablets 600 mg
- *Mucinex DM*—with cough suppressant
- *Mucinex D*—with pseudoephedrine

NeutraSal—swish and spit qid
Numosyn—2 cc swish and swallow prn
Pilocarpine (*Salagen*)—5 mg po tid initially; consider 10 mg po tid prn (12 weeks required to assess efficacy)
SalvaSure (OTC)—dissolve po prn

THORAX

Air Hunger

Narcotics
    Codeine—30 mg po q 4–6 h
    Morphine sulfate—7.5–30 mg po q 4 h
Anxiolytics
    Alprazolam (*Xanax*)—start at 0.25–0.5 mg tid
    • *Xanax XR* (extended release)—start at 0.5–1.0 mg/d
    Diazepam (*Valium*)—2–10 mg po bid to qid
    Lorazepam (*Ativan*)—0.5–2 mg po bid to qid

Obstructive Airways Disease (Asthma, COPD)

Asthma produces intermittent dyspnea, whereas COPD (chronic bronchitis and/or emphysema) produces nonfluctuating, progressive dyspnea. First-line therapy for COPD exacerbation is short-acting beta-agonists (SABA) inhalation, adding anticholinergics or combination and eventually steroids (the classes have different mechanisms, so can be used simultaneously).

    SABA
    Albuterol sulfate (e.g., *Proventil, Ventolin*, generic)
    • Inhalation aerosol—2 puffs q 4 h prn
    Levalbuterol (*Xopenex*, generic)—2 puffs q 4–6 h
    Anticholinergics
    Ipratropium bromide (*Atrovent*)—2 puffs q 4–6 h
    Combinations
    Advair (**Fluticasone + Salmeterol**)—1 puff bid
    Oral Steroids
    Prednisone—30–40 mg po qd × 7–10 days, then taper
    Dexamethasone (*Decadron*)—8–16 mg po qd × 7 d, then taper
    • *exPax*, (1.5 mg **dexamethasone**)—as directed

Cough

A sudden increase in cough and/or dyspnea should be evaluated, and antibiotics started if purulent sputum, increased temperature (>101°), or marked increase in sputum production with worsening of dyspnea, or a pneumonia is identified. Often, antibiotics are administered empirically. If no infectious etiology is suspected, and the main complaint is dyspnea, initiate COPD airway management. Supplemental oxygen is indicated for resting O_2 saturation <88%.

For chronic cough, initially rule out postnasal drip etiology—inhaled glucocorticoid (e.g., *Flonase, Nasonex*), advancing to an oral first-generation antihistamine OTC medication containing **bromopherinamine** (e.g., *Dimetapp Cold and Allergy Elixir*) or **chlorpheniramine** (e.g., *Chlor-Trimeton*), **diphenhydramine**, or combination (e.g., *Bromofed-DM*). If too sedating, use a less anticholinergic second-generation antihistamine (**cetirizine, fexofenadine, loratadine**). For GERD, use H2 blockers or promotility agents (*Reglan*). Antibiotics may be required for bronchitis, or pneumonia with increased or purulent secretions and worsening dyspnea.

Initial acute cough management is OTC cough suppressants with **dextromethorphan** (centrally acting antitussive); if thickened secretions, include an expectorant such as **guaifenesin** (liquefies and reduces the viscosity of thickened secretions). If persistent, add *Tessalon Perles* (especially for dry cough with inspiration). If this combination does not provide adequate relief, advance to narcotic-containing cough suppressants (**codeine, hydrocodone, morphine**). If refractory, consider **gabapentin.**

Bromopheniramine (e.g., *Dimetapp*, OTC)—4—8 mg tid
Chlorpheniramine (e.g., *Chlor-Trimeton*, OTC)—4 mg q 4—6 h
• hydrocodone/chlorpheniramine (Tussionex)—5 mL bid
Fexofenadine (*Allegra*, OTC)—60 mg po bid, or 180 mg po qd
Allegra D 12 Hr—po bid
Allegra D 24 Hr—po qd
Benadryl (**diphenhydramine**—OTC)—25—50 mg q 4—6 h
Cetirizine (*Zyrtec*, OTC)—10 mg po qd
Zyrtec-D12 Hr—bid
Dextromethorphan + guaifenesin (OTC expectorant & antitussive, e.g., *Robitussin DM*)—2 tsp q 4 h
Guaifenesin (OTC expectorant, e.g., *Robitussin*)— 2—4 tsp q 4 h
Guaifenesin with codeine—2 tsp po q 4 h; maximum 8 tsp per day
• codeine 10 mg/5 mL, guaifenesin 100 mg/5 mL
Fluticasone (*Flonase*, OTC)—1 spray bid or 2 sprays qd
Loratadine (*Claritin*, OTC)—po bid or qd
• *Claritin* 24 h—qd
• *Clairitn-D 12* h (with 120 mg pseudoephedrine)—bid
• *Claritin-D 24* h (with 240 mg pseudoephedrine)—qd
Gabapentin (*Neurontin*, generic)—300 mg qd to 600 mg tid
Hydrocodone—*Hydromet* (with homatropine antitussive)
• 5 mg q 4 h
• 5 mg tablets—alcohol-free syrup 5 mg/5 mL
• *Tussionex* (with chlorpheniramine)—5 mL q 12h
• 10—8 mg/5 mL extend release syrup
• *HYCOTUSS* (with **guaifenesin**)—5—15 mL q 4 h
• 5—100 mg per 5 mL
• **Guaifenesin with hydrocodone, pseudoephedrine** (generic)—5 mL q 4 h
• 30 mg per day maximum
Mucinex (**guaifenesin**, OTC)—600—1200 mg po bid
• *Mucinex DM*—with cough suppressant
• *Mucinex D*—with pseudoephedrine

Mometasone (*Nasonex*, generic, OTC)—two sprays each nostril qd
* 120 sprays per container

Pseudoephedrine (OTC decongestant, e.g., **Sudafed**)—1 po q 6 h

Tessalon (**benzonatate**)—100–200 po q 8 h

Infectious Processes

Determining the etiologic agent helps, but empiric therapy is often required. If influenza is suspected, antivirals (*Relenza, Tamiflu*) may be used early in the infection or prophylactically.

For outpatient pneumoniae, with immune compromise or comorbidities, category 1 recommendations are **Moxifloxacin**, or a combination of macrolide (*Biaxin* or *Zithromax*) and *Augmentin* or **Clindamycin**. If no immune compromise or comorbidities, **azithromycin** or **doxycycline** are appropriate.

If aspiration or an anaerobic infection are suspected, consider **Clindamycin**. For purulent bronchitis or sinusitis, many of the above drugs are effective as well as **trimethaphan/sulfamethoxazole** and cephalosporins (*Keflex, Ceftin*).

Amoxicillin/clavulanate (*Augmentin*, generic)—250–500 mg po tid; 875 mg po bid
* Augmentin Extended Release—2 tablets bid

Azithromycin (*Zithromax*, Z-Pak, generic)—500 mg po qd day 1, then 250 mg po qd × 4d

Bactrim and *Bactrim DS* (generic)—2 regular or 1 DS tablet po bid

Cefuroxime (*Ceftin*, generic)—250–500 mg po bid

Cefpodoxime (*Vantin*, generic)—200 mg po bid

Cephalexin (*Keflex*, generic)—250–500 mg po qid

Ciprofloxacin (*Cipro, Cipro XR*, generic)—250–750 mg q 12 h
* XR 500–1000 mg qd

Clarithromycin (*Biaxin*, generic—250–500 mg po bid; *Biaxin XL* 500 mg qd)

Clindamycin (*Cleocin*, generic)—150–450 mg po tid to qid
* MRSA and nonaerobic coverage

Doxycycline (e.g., *Vibramycin*, generic)—100 mg po bid

Levofloxacin (*Levaquin*, generic)—500–750 mg qd

Moxifloxacin (*Avelox*)—400 mg po qd

Oseltamivir (*Tamiflu*, antiviral)—75 mg bid × 5 days
* prophylaxis 75 mg po qd × 10 days

Zanamivir Inhalation (*Relenza*)—Inhale bid × 5 days
* Use Diskhaler and five Rotadisks

Radiation Pneumonitis and Pulmonary Fibrosis

Radiation pneumonitis is an inflammatory response in the lung to radiation, occurring at 2 weeks to 6 months following radiotherapy. There are multiple variables, but V20 is the most important: V20 < 22%—no pneumonitis; V20 22%–31%—8% grade 2+ pneumonitis; V20 > 35%–15%, with ~5% grade 5 pneumonitis.

It presents with dyspnea, tachycardia, cough, pleuritic chest pain, and/or hypoxia. CT scan is more sensitive than CXR, demonstrating an infiltrate within parts of the radiation treatment field. Mild symptoms can be treated with **NSAID**, advancing to systemic steroids as needed. Rule out infectious process before starting steroids.

Pulmonary fibrosis can appear months to years after radiation, seen as a sharply demarcated fibrous lesion, versus some haziness with radiation pneumonitis (see Radiation Fibrosis section).

NSAID

- **Ibuprofen**—200–800 mg po q 6 h
- **Naproxen** (*Naprosyn*, generic)—500–750 mg po initially, then 250–500 mg po q 6–12 h
- **Indomethacin** (*Indocin*, generic)—25 mg bid to tid initially; **Oral Steroids**— **Prednisone**—20 mg po q 8 h (or 60 mg po qd) is a reasonable starting dose; published recommendations include 1 mg/kg at diagnosis maintained for several weeks followed by slow taper

Smoking Cessation

More effective with a behavior modification program, in addition to medical management. The US Public Health Service recognizes five first-line medications: **bupropion, nicotine gum, nicotine inhaler, nicotine nasal spray**, and the **nicotine patch**.

> **Bupropion** (*Zyban*, generic)—150 mg po qd before quitting, then 150 mg po bid × 7–12 weeks
> *Nicorette Lozanges* (**nicotine lozenge**, OTC)—2–4 mg q 1–8 h
> *Nicoderm CQ* (transdermal, OTC)—variable dosing, 7–21 mg/day—worn 16–24 h/day
> - >10 cigarettes per day: 6 weeks at 21 mg/d; 2–4 weeks at 14 mg/d; then 4–8 weeks at 7 mg/d
> - <10 cigarettes or weight < 45 kg: 6 weeks at 14 mg/d; 8 weeks at 7 mg/d
> *Nicorette Gum* (OTC)—chew gum several minutes, then store in cheek 30 min
> - weeks 1–6 at q 1–2 h; weeks 7–8 at q 2–4 h; weeks 9–10 at q 4–8 h
> - 2 mg (<25 cigarettes/day), 4 mg > 25 cigarettes/day)
> **Nicotine Inhaler** (*Nicotrol Inhaler*, OTC)—6–16 cartridges per day, up to 12 weeks; then gradual reduction over 12 weeks
> **Varenicline** (*Chantix*)—0.5 mg/d × 3 d; bid × 4 days, then
> - 1 mg qd × 12–24 weeks

BREAST

Skin erythema is expected during breast irradiation, and desquamation is not uncommon. Avoidance of deodorants (especially aluminum containing) during breast irradiation is no longer practiced. Also, no studies demonstrate worse outcome with lotions applied before breast irradiation.

A pruritic, erythematous, punctate rash that originates in the upper inner quadrant breast is likely miliaria rubra (inflamed sweat glands). Treat with topical steroids (see page 1).

Fungal infections are prevalent in the inframammary.

Breast edema may develop during radiation, producing swelling, increased warmth, and erythema (from internal body heat transmission). This warmth/erythema is usually mild, with gradual onset. Local or diffuse infectious processes present suddenly, with marked warmth and erythema, and often tenderness of the breast. If refractory to antibiotic therapy, rule out abscess, and then consider collagen vascular disease associated vasculitis (steroids) or progression to an inflammatory breast cancer (biopsy).

There are two types of cords that can develop in the arm, postlymph node dissection. With Axillary Web Syndrome, a tight cord of tissue extends from the midaxilla to the antecubital fossa. Treatment involves physical therapy, including myofascial release and home program for arm stretching.

Occasionally, patients develop one or more superficial blood clots (vs. a DVT). The usual presentation is a palpable, linear, tender cord traceable beyond the antecubital fossa, with no distal edema. These commonly resolve within 3–4 weeks. Reassure the patient, and prescribe a heating pad 30 min tid and aspirin (unless contraindicated). Mondor disease is a variant, where the patient initially presents with a red, tender superficial thrombophlebitis that scleroses to form a tough fibrous band, causing pain and skin retraction. Manage conservatively. Note: Although Mondor disease usually occurs in the axilla, it can also present in the breast, and as one or more linear bands extending caudally to the abdomen.

Irradiation of prosthetically augmented breasts can result in capsule contracture (the probability of contracture increases with increased prosthesis to breast tissue volume, smoking, and diabetes). Some surgeons recommend *Singular* 10 mg qd for 3 months, followed by *Trental* 400 mg tid with **Vitamin E** 1000 mg qd for 6 months.

Abscess/Infection

For generalized erythema, swelling, and warmth (greater than ~2 vs. the opposite breast), treat for mastitis with **dicloxacillin**, **cephalexin**, *Bactrim DS*, or **clindamycin**.

For nonsubareolar abscesses and localized warmth/erythema, drain abscess and prescribe **dicloxacillin, cephalexin,** and **clindamycin.** If subareolar and odoriferous, add **metronidazole** (preferably) or **clindamycin** for anaerobic coverage. If there is an obvious localized abscess with marked erythema/warmth of the breast, drainage and IV antibiotics (**Vancomycin**) are recommended.

> *Bactrim DS* (sulfamethoxazole/trimethoprim, generic)—1 po bid
> Cephalexin (*Keflex*, generic)—250–500 mg po qid
> Clindamycin (*Cleocin*, generic)—150–450 mg po tid to qid
> • MRSA and nonaerobic coverage
> Dicloxacillin (generic)—500 mg qid
> Metronidazole (*Flagyl*, generic)—500 mg po tid

Note: IV metronidazole for serious anaerobic infections.

Costochondritis

Costochondritis presents as a highly localized point tenderness along the anterior costochondral junctions and may involve one or multiple joints. Costochondritis usually responds to a short course of **NSAIDs** (600 mg tid, × 3 d) or *Celebrex* 100 mg bid to 200 mg qd.

Lymphedema

Lymphedema can involve the upper extremity and/or the treated breast. Arm and breast edema is most prominent after axillary node dissection. Following sentinel node biopsy, a supraclavicular field will slightly increase the risk for upper extremity lymphedema. A moderate risk of edema of the irradiated breast still exists.

Lymphedema consult should be initiated early for the upper extremity. For the breast, refer early if there is moderate pain or pore prominence with pitting edema. Otherwise, allow 6 months for resolution and improvement.

The National Lymphedema Network (lymphnet.org) has an excellent website.

Hot Flashes

Hot flashes from decreased estrogen availability impact the thermoregulatory functions of the hypothalamus. Randomized clinical trials show a placebo effect >20% (the reason for the large number of anecdotal remedies).

Relieving "triggers" may reduce the severity or length of hot flashes. Avoid or minimize (admittedly, some easier said than done):

- stress, alcohol, hot foods, hot beds
- caffeine, diet pills, hot tubs, hot rooms
- saunas, smoking

Increase activity level.
Initiate relaxation techniques.
Begin a low-fat diet.
Neurontin, newer antidepressants (*Effexor, Paxil*), and antihypertensives (*CatapresTTS, Aldomet*) have shown significant benefit in randomized clinical trials.

A recommended algorithm: for mild, nondisruptive hot flashes, prescribe **Vitamin E** (800—1000 IU qd). For severe symptoms, prescribe *Effexor* or *Paxil*. Advance to *Catapress* or *Aldomet*, and finally *Neurontin* if symptoms continue. If symptoms persist, consider, after discussion with patient, advancing to progestational agents (*Megace* or *Depo-Provera*).

Gabapentin (*Neurontin*, generic)—300 mg qd × 3 days, then 300 mg tid or titrate down to effective level
Clonidine patch (*CatapressTTS*)—0.1 mg patch q week
Medroxyprogesterone (*Depo-Provera*)—150 mg I.M. q 3 month
Megestrol (e.g., *Megace*)—20 mg po bid initially; 10 mg qd or qid once responsive
Methyldopa (*Aldomet*)—250 mg po bid
Paroxetine (*Paxil CR*)—12.5 + mg po qd
Venlafaxine (*Effexor XR*)—75 mg po qhs (titrate upward from −37.5 mg)

GASTROINTESTINAL TRACT

Esophagitis can begin as early as 2 weeks into radiotherapy, with healing 2—8+ weeks following treatment. A prominent long-term effect is stricture from submucosal fibrosis, usually remedied with single or multiple dilatations. For stricture refractory to dilatation, consider an XRT fibrosis protocol and redilatation.

Irradiation of the stomach often results in anorexia, nausea, and vomiting. Abdominal irradiation can cause hypomotility, hypermotility, flatus/gas cramping, and diarrhea (both chronic and postprandial). Irradiation of the colon and rectum can produce tenesmus, proctitis, urgency, hemorrhoidal inflammation, and rectal bleeding. Extending the field inferiorly can produce severe perianal irritation.

Long-term effects may include chronic diarrhea, bowel adhesions, bleeding from ulceration and neovasculaturity, and protein losing enteropathy.

Antacids/Hypersecretion Medications

For short-term antacid relief, consider OTC extrastrength liquid antacids. For chronic antacid/GERD treatment, consider H-2 blockers (H2B), either OTC or Rx, or proton pump inhibitors (PPI). Stomach ulcers may develop 1—2 months following doses >5000 cGy. **Carafate** protects the stomach with a coating action and may have some prophylactic benefit. For erosive gastritis or esophagitis, consider doubling the recommended doses for H2B and PPI.

> **Aluminum**, **Magnesium,** and **Simethicone** (OTC combination), e.g.,:
> * Maalox Max Antacid/Anti-gas—2—4 tsp qid
> *Mylanta Double Strength*—2—4 tsp prn; maximum 12 per day
> **Cimetidine** (*Tagamet*, OTC, generic, H2B)—300 mg po q ac and qhs or 800 mg po qhs
> * For steroid prophylaxis, 400 mg po qhs × tablets 300, 400, 800 mg
> **Dexlansoprazole** (*Kapidex*, PPI)—60 mg po qd × 8 weeks, then 30 mg po qd maintenance
> **Esomeprazole** (*Nexium*, PPI)—20—40 mg po qd
> **Famotidine** (*Pepcid*, OTC, generic, H2B)—10—20 mg po bid
> * *Pepcid Complete*, 10 mg with antacid
> **Lansoprazole** (*Prevacid*, generic PPI)—esophagitis 30 mg qd
> **Omeprazole** (*Prilosec*, PPI, OTC, generic)—20 mg po qd
> **Pantoprazole** (*Protonix*, generic, PPI)—40 mg po qd
> **Rabeprazole** (*Aciphex*, PPI)—20 mg po qd
> **Ranitidine** (*Zantac*, OTC, generic, H2B)—150 mg po bid or 300 mg po qhs

Diarrhea

History is important for proper management of diarrhea. Assess watery diarrhea (po antidiarrheals) versus loose/soft stool (dietary modification alone), frequency, flatus/gas cramping (antiflatulent ± antidiarrheal), urgency or rectal/hemorrhoidal pain (rectal suppository), and whether urination triggers bowel movement (GU antispasmodic). The goal should be normalization of bowel movements using dietary modifications and prophylactic medications. Monitor weight loss, fluid loss (tenting and dry mucous membranes), and electrolyte imbalance (especially potassium).

For XRT-induced diarrhea, begin with post—bowel movement mild OTC antidiarrheals (e.g., *Pepto-Bismol, Kaopectate*). For more aggressive therapy, *Imodium* (OTC) is more accessible, whereas *Lomotil* is cheaper but with more side effects. *Lomotil* or *Imodium* are usually prescribed after each loose bowel movement. However, once multiple daily antidiarrheals are required, attempt a prophylactic regimen: $^1/_2$ —2 tablets po q AM (pre–bowel movement) to bid, titrating up to 8 per day to normalize bowel movements. If refractory, include a low residue diet, and increase foods high in pectin (e.g., oatmeal, ripe bananas, and applesauce, which help bind stool).

Lomotil and *Imodium* may be combined to a total of 16 tablets per day. Before pursuing this combination, consider **tincture of opium** or antimotility agents (increasing order of preference—see antimotility section): **Bentyl, Donnatal, Levsin,** or **Librax.** This may benefit the patient by controlling diarrhea, associated bloating, cramping, and urgency. Postprandial diarrhea may be controlled with antimotility agents given q AC and qHS.

For severe, refractory diarrhea, obtain stool cultures to rule out C. difficile (which can be caused by high doses of antibiotics). If negative, consider possible infection (e.g., perforation, diverticulitis). If there has been 5FU administration, administer subcutaneous *Sandostatin* (expensive).

Bismuth subsalicylate (*Kaopectate, Pepto-Bismol,* OTC, generic)
- suspension—2 tbs after each loose BM; 16 tbs qd maximum
- Extrastrength *Kaopectate*—2 tbs prn; 8 tbs qd maximum

Diphenoxylate/atropine (*Lomotil,* generic is *Lonox*)—1/2–2 tablets or 10 mL po initially or qam, then 1 after each loose stool as needed
- diphenoxylate 2.5 mg/atropine 0.025 mg per tablet or per 5 mL

Note: maximum 8 tablets or 40 mL per day.

Loperamide (*Imodium A-D,*OTC, generic)—1–4 mg po qam, then 2 mg po prn; 1–4 mg qd to bid as prophylaxis prn
- *Imodium Advanced* (2 mg), with simethicone 125 mg/chewable tablet

Note: maximum 16 mg loperamide per day.

Octreotide (*Sandostatin*)—50–200 mcg SQ bid to tid
- 50, 100, 500 mcg/mL
- *Sandostatin LAR Depot*—20 mg IM q 4 weeks; 30 mg IM maximum

Tincture of Opium
- *Optium tincture*, deodorized—0.6 cc po qid
- 10 mg anhydrous morphine per ml
- *Paregoric*—5–10 cc po qd to qid
- 2 mg anhydrous morphine per 5 mL

Antiflatulents

Increased gas production, especially when associated with hypermotility, can produce severe abdominal cramping. Initially, use **simethicone,** antiflatulents, and antidiarrheal medications as needed. *Bean-O* may enable a normal diet, and in some cases, reduce postprandial diarrhea. If cramping symptoms persist, consider a low residue diet, followed by antimotility agents.

Bean-O (OTC, **alpha-galactosidase** enzyme)—5 drops or 3 tablets q 3 servings
Simethicone (OTC antiflatulent + generics)—variable dosing, see individual products

- **Gas-X** Regular, Extra Strength, Maximum Strength
- **Maalox**, Maximum Strength, Regular Strength
- **Phazyme** 125 mg, 180 mg

Imodium Advanced (OTC, generic)—2–4 mg po qam, then 2 mg po prn; 1–4 mg po qd

- bid as prophylaxis if needed
- **loperamide** (2 mg), with **simethicone** 125 mg/chewable tablet

Note: maximum 16 mg loperamide per day.

Anorexia/Appetite Stimulant

Anorexia/weight loss may be multifactorial, beyond simple appetite loss.

Underlying issues and potential treatments include *Reglan* for early satiety, antiemetics for nausea, antacids for gastric hyperacidity, antiflatulents for gas cramping, motility agents for postprandial diarrhea, laxatives for constipation, zinc for altered taste, analeptics for fatigue, and antidepressants.

The strongest weight-based clinical support is for **corticosteroids** and **megestrol**; there is also support for **dronabinol**.

Oxandrin is an anabolic steroid which promotes appetite and weight gain, especially muscle mass. It is generally safe and, when effective, provides the patient a sense of physical well-being. Observe women for signs of virilization.

Dronabinol (*Marinol*)—2.5 po qhs to bid initially; maximum 10 mg bid
Megesterol (*Megace ES, Megace* & generic)
- *Megace* & generic oral suspension—800 mg qd
- *Megace ES*—625 mg/5 mL po qd
Prednisone—10–40 mg q day
Oxandrolone (*Oxandrin*)—2.5–20 mg qd, in 2–4 divided doses
Zinc—may improve taste

Chronic Radiation Enteritis, Proctitis, or Rectal Bleeding

Following abdominal or pelvic irradiation, chronic diarrhea/malabsorption, with associated weight loss, can persist or develop after one to several years. Malabsorption (e.g., short bowel syndrome, radiation enteritis, pancreatic insufficiency, HIV) should be suspected if there is continued weight loss despite normal thyroid function and adequate caloric intake. Fecal fat assays may be helpful to determine if malabsorption or maldigestion are present. Endoscopic and radiographic evaluations are typically performed.

The first attempt to control chronic diarrhea beyond dietary modifications is with prophylactic antidiarrheals, *Imodium*, or *Lomotil* (*Lomotil* is preferred for "short bowel syndrome"). For refractory classic radiation enteritis, a combination of *Imodium* and *Lactulose* should be considered. If still no improvement, consider 2-week trial courses of **Pancrelipase**, **Questran**, and finally **prednisone**. In some patients, elemental formulas as sole source of nutrition provide the only remedy.

For chronic proctitis or rectal bleeding, begin with **steroid suppositories** or a "*Rectal Rocket*." If minimal improvement, change to a 2-week trial *Colocort* (**hydrocortisone retention enema**); if improvement, continue four additional weeks. If symptoms persist, oral *Asulfidine* or *Colazal* may be helpful. One study showed a significant decrease in proctitis with prophylactic *Colazal*.

Obtain a GI consult if symptoms persist. Sigmoidoscopy is indicated when refractory to the above, as evidenced in one study that showed a 6% incidence of malignancy. For refractory bleeding, studies have shown benefit from direct application (by the gastroenterologist) of dilute **formalin** (usually 4%) by a gastroenterologist. Nd:YAG laser therapy or Argon plasma coagulation have also been shown to be beneficial. Finally (or before formalin/coagulation), begin a 3-month course of **Trental** and **Vitamin E** (extend to 6 months if improvement) or proceed to hyperbaric oxygen.

Balsalazide (*Colazal*)—2250 mg po tid
Cholestyramine (*Questran*, generic)—1 packet or 1 scoopful mixed per directions po qd initially; may increase to 1—2 packets or scoopfuls po bid
Colocort (**hydrocortisone retention enema**)—1 pr qhs, retain for 1 h to all night
• single dose units, 100 mg hydrocortisone/60 mL
Diphenoxylate/atropine (*Lomotil*, generic is *Lonox*)—2 tablets or 10 mL po qam or initially; 1 after each loose stool as needed
• **diphenoxylate** 2.5 mg/**atropine** 0.025 mg per tablet or 5 mL

Note: maximum 8 tablets or 40 mL per day.

Formalin—apply directly to the involved area; most use a 4% solution.
Hydrocortisone Rectal Suppository (*Anusol-HC*, generic)—1 pr bid to tid
Lactulose (*Cephulac*, generic)—adjust from 30—45 cc po qd to qid
Kristalose (less sweet)—10—20 mg po qd, up to 40
Loperamide (*Imodium AD*, generic)—2—4 mg po qam, then 2 mg po prn
• 1—4 mg po qd to bid as prophylaxis if needed
Pancrelipase (*Pancrease*)—400—2500 units/kg/meal
Creon 10 & *Creon* 20—1 po with meals
Pentoxifylline (*Trental*, generic)—400 mg po tid with meals

Note: do not use if history or cerebral or retinal bleeding.

Prednisone—10—40 mg po q day
Rectal Rocket—1 per rectum qhs × 5 days
• custom formulation or **hydrocortisone** 5%, **lidocaine** 2.5% (or 5%), **nifedipine** 0.3% (to 0.4%)
Sulfasalazine (*Azulfidine*, generic) 500 mg po bid to qid; up to 1000 mg qid
• *Azulfidine-EN*—enteric coated tablet
Vitamin E (**tocopherol**)—1000 IU po qd

Esophagitis

For early esophagitis without CTX (especially with steroid therapy), suspect candida and treat with aggressive systemic medication (**fluconazole**). For XRT esophagitis, initially prescribe topical anesthetics (*Triple mix, miracle mouthwash*), adding prn systemic pain medications (e.g., **hydrocodone elixir**) and scheduled pain medications (e.g., **transdermal patches**). If exacerbated by reflux, prescribe antacids, PPI, or H2B initially (consider doubling PPI or H2B). Follow with *Carafate*. *Advera*, a peptide-based semi-elemental nutrition supplement, enhances the body's ability to heal the alimentary tract (see nutrition section).

Erosive pill esophagitis presents as a sudden onset, very localized, severe odynophagia (**hydrocodone** is one pill commonly involved). Healing can take up to 3 weeks, and pain management often requires class II narcotics. For prevention (especially in patients with dysphagia), coat pills with cooking or olive oil before ingesting.

Carafate suspension (**sucralfate**)—2 tsp swish and swallow qid
Fluconazole (*Diflucan*, generic)—200 mg po day 1, then 100 mg po qd, × 7 days (if candida recurs, repeat for 21 days)
Hydrocodone/acetaminophen elixir (generic)—15 mL po q 4 h
- *Lortab elixir*—7.5/500 mg per 15 mL
- *Hycet*—7.5 mg/325 mg per 15 mL

Miracle Mouthwash—2 tsp po swish and swallow qid
- mix 60 cc tetracycline oral suspension (125 mg/5 mL), 30 cc mycostatin oral suspension (100,000 µ/mL), 30 cc hydrocortisone oral suspension (10 mg/5 mL), and 240 cc Benadryl syrup (12.5 mg/5 mL)

Triple mix—2 tsp qac and qhs
- mix 1:1:1 Benadryl elixir:Maalox:viscous Xylocaine 2%

Enteral/Oral Nutritional Supplements
Maintaining adequate nutrient, fluid, and electrolyte intake/balance with the myriad of potential radiation side effects can be challenging. Other sections address issues of intake and diarrhea management.

Maintaining oral intake may require management of anorexia, loss of taste, xerostomia, nausea, or odynophagia/dysphagia. If available, a registered dietitian can provide support. Tube feeding may be indicated once the patient begins weight loss. Parenteral feeding (TPN) is a last resort in some circumstances (e.g., vomiting, severe diarrhea, etc). It is important to monitor weight closely in late radiation treatment and subsequently until the patient "turns the corner," which varies considerably from patient to patient.

General Guidelines for Calculating Basic Nutritional Needs

Minimal daily caloric needs:
Normal weight: weight (kg) × 25 cal/kg
Decreased weight: weight (kg) × 35 cal/kg
Stressed weight loss: weight (kg) × 45 cal/kg
Minimum daily protein needs:
Normal weight: weight (kg) × 0.8 gm protein/kg
Decreased weight: weight (kg) × 1.0 gm protein/kg
Stressed weight loss: weight (kg) × 1.5 g protein/kg
Fluid needs: 1 mL per calorie

When using a tube feeding formula, fluid needs are unchanged and fluid in the supplement plus tube flushing fluid are included in the total amount.

Oral Intake/Supplements

Patients should be maintained on regular diets as long as possible. Eventually, they may require addition of liquid supplements, and eventually liquid supplements alone.

The reality of caloric intake can be quite different versus the patients' perspective—daily calorie counting can be invaluable to demonstrate inadequate intake to the patient, and as a guide to adequate diet.

A common issue—the desire to start or resume a healthy diet can exacerbate weight loss due to low calorie to volume ratio (early satiety reduces total caloric intake) and a healthy high fiber diet (painful to swallow, and again with decreased caloric volumes).

Examples of Oral Supplements—per 8 oz can
Retail:

Boost—240 cals and 10 gm protein
Boost Plus—360 cals and 13 gm protein
Boost High Protein—240 cals and 15 gm protein
Boost with Fiber—240 cals and 10 gm protein and 3 gm fiber
Boost Glucose Control—190 cals and 3 gm fiber
Ensure—250 cals and 9 gm protein
Ensure Plus—355 cals and 13 gm protein
Ensure High Protein—230 cals and 12 gm protein
Ensure with Fiber—250 cals and 9 gm protein and 3 gm fiber
Enlive Juice Drink—300 cals and 10 gm protein
Glucerna—220 cals (for diabetics; contains sugar alcohols)
Nutritional Support (Walgreen's, lower cost)—335 cals and 13 gm protein
Prosure (introduce in small amounts and increase to a maximum of two cans daily)—300 cals and 16 gm protein; high ratio of omega fatty acids

Also:

Carnation Instant Breakfast, with 1 cup whole milk—315 cals and 12 gm protein
Scandi-Shake, 3 oz with 1 cup whole milk—600 cals and 12 gm protein

Impact products by Nestle—Prescription lactose-free and gluten-free products that taste well and are to improve immune response: *Impact, Impact Advanced Recovery, Impact Glutamine, Impact Peptide 1.5.*

Oral supplements are available retail at the local drugstore or supermarket. Tube feeding supplements are available through a medical supply company (doctor's order required for insurance reimbursement, which is typically only when it is the patient's sole source of nutrition).

Tube feeding supplements (medical supply only)—per 8 oz can

Jevity 1—250 cals and 10.5 gm protein
Jevity 1.2—285 cals and 13 gm protein
Jevity 1.5—355 cals and 15 gm protein
Osmolite—250 cals and 9 gm protein
Osmolite—1—250 cals and 10.5 gm protein
Osmolite—1.2—285 cals and 13.2 gm protein

General Guidelines for Tube Feedings

- Transition patient to feeding tube when they are unable to consume 75% of dietary needs orally
- Be aware of fluid and electrolyte needs (increased with vomiting, diarrhea, and ostomy drainage)
- Most patients tolerate a standard formula. Others may require specialized formulas (e.g., organ dysfunction, diabetes, etc).
- For cancer patients, tubes are typically gastrostomy or jejunostomy

Feedings May Be

Bolus (via syringe). ~ 250 mL over 10–20 min. Best for ambulatory patients. May cause cramping, pain, nausea, or vomiting.

Intermittent (gravity or feeding pump). 250–500 mL over 60 min.

Cyclic (feeding pump). Specific volume for 8–20 h per day. Used when transitioning back to normal diet.

Continuous (feeding pump). For jejunal feeding, and those unable to tolerate bolus feedings (reflux, aspiration, medically unstable).

Potential Problems

Metabolic issues—fluid, electrolyte, and glucose imbalances
- prevented by appropriate monitoring and using appropriate formula

Gastric—nausea/vomiting, aspiration, diarrhea, bloating, and pain
- minimized by using appropriate formula and feeding type

Mechanical—tube clogging or migration, skin irritation
- keep head of bed elevated 30–45° during and 30 min postfeeding
- flush every 4 h during continuous feeding and before and after bolus feedings
- G-tubes with skin disks anchors; J-tube with skin anchor
- do not use dressings
- clean around site daily

Hiccups

Hiccups may be remedied by a number of physical maneuvers:

- breath holding, Valsalva maneuver
- pharyngeal stimulation—sipping cold water, swallowing a teaspoon of dry sugar
- pressing on eyeballs
- pulling knees hard into chest

Hiccups can be secondary to reflux—consider a proton pump inhibitor.

Baclofen is a good initial choice followed by **Reglan**. **Thorazine** is used for refractory hiccups, as well as **scopolamine, amphetamine, prochlorperazine, phenobarbital**, and narcotics. Phrenic nerve block has been used in severe cases.

Baclofen (*Gablofen*, generic)—5–20 mg po tid; titrating up at 2 day intervals.

Metoclopramide (*Reglan*, generic)—10–20 mg po q 4 h.

Chlorpromazine (*Thorazine*)—25 mg IV or IM, or 50 mg po tid (range 25 mg po tid –50 mg po qid); maintenance 10–50 mg po tid.

Motility Agents

Antimotility agents serve as a second-line therapy for refractory diarrhea and bowel/gas cramping (see Diarrhea section).

Levsin is a good first choice for spastic colon. *Librax* is another antispasmodic, with the added benefit of sedation.

For early satiety, ***Reglan*** is used to increase motility. It can also be used following esophagectomy with stomach pull-through, to improve food passage through the thorax.

Dicyclomine (*Bentyl*, generic)—20 mg po qid, to 40 mg po qid if tolerated.
Hyoscyamine (*Levsin*, generic)—0.125–0.25 mg po/sl tid to qid

- Levsinex TIMECAPS—0.375–0.75 mg po bid to tid

Chlordiazepoxide/clidinium (Librax)—1–2 po qac and qhs.
Metoclopramide (*Reglan*, generic)—10–20 mg po q 4 h

Nausea/Vomiting

Nausea can result from chemotherapy, opioid-induced constipation or direct nausea, anxiety, delayed gastric emptying, excess flatus, diarrhea, vertigo, brain mets, etc. For XRT-induced nausea, the chronology is important. If anticipatory, initially use **ondansetron** 45 min before XRT, advancing to *Ativan* if needed. For nausea occurring 30 min to 4 h post XRT, po/IM/IV *Compazine* or *Phenergan* 15–30 min before XRT is good initial option, then advance to **ondansetron**.

For chronic XRT-induced nausea, consider a longer-acting, prophylactic antiemetic, such as *Zofran* or *Kytril*. If nausea persists, consider addition of **metoclopramide**, anxiolytic, or steroid. If the patient can tolerate the side effects, *Marinol* (Class III) can be effective.

Educate the patient as to whether the antiemetic is to be taken prn or scheduled, and ensure the patient is following prescription instructions. The patient may benefit by decreasing fat or being on a clear liquid diet during the time the nausea is worst. Clear liquid supplements, such as ***Resource Juices***, are a consideration.

Ativan (**lorazepam**, generic)—anticipatory—1–2 mg po 45 min before XRT
- adjunct to antinausea medications 0.5–1 mg po tid
Compazine (prochlorperazine, generic)
- oral—5–10 mg po q 6–8 h
- oral spansules—10–15 mg q 12 h, or 15–30 mg qam
- suppositories—25 mg bid
Dexamethasone (*Decadron*, generic)—2–4 mg po q 8 h
Kytril (**granisetron**)—2 mg tablet po 1 h within XRT
Marinol (**dronabinol**)—2.5–10 mg po q 6–8 h
Metoclopramide (*Reglan*, generic)—10–20 mg po q 4 h
Phenergan (**promethazine**)—12.5–25 mg po/pr q 4–6 h
- suppositories 12.5 mg, 25 mg, 50 mg

Note: sedating may potentiate CNS depressants.
Note: reduction: 6.75–12.5 mg IV/IM q 4–6 h

Zofran (**ondansetron**, generic)—8 mg po q 8 h
- also *Zofran ODT* (orally disintegrating tablet, generic) and
- *Zuplenz*—orally dissolving film

Constipation

Chronic constipation occurs in 20%–40% of patients receiving narcotic pain medications; tolerance does not develop. Patients may manage using their personal historic approaches: high fiber diet, prunes or prune juice, *MOM*, stool softeners, etc.

For chronic constipation, bulking agents alone may be successful (high-fiber diets and bulking agents can cause obstipation if fluid intake is inadequate). Daily **docusate** or *Miralax* may be required, advancing to stimulant laxatives as needed.

If more aggressive therapy is required (especially recent onset and/or narcotic induced), rule out fecal impaction. Daily **senna** with or without **docusate** is a good first choice. Advance to **magnesium citrate** to initiate bowel movement, then **senna**. If refractory, begin **lactulose**. If still no benefit in the setting of opioid-induced constipation, advance to *Amitiza* or *Movantik*. A new drug for opioid-induced constipation is Class II subcutaneous *Relistar*.

If fecal impaction has occurred, arrange for admission or home health consult, and manual disimpaction and/or soap suds or tap water enema.

Rectal suppositories should be placed against the rectal wall and not in stool. **Senna**, **lactulose**, and *MiraLax* can cause bloating and abdominal cramping. Add an antiflatulent (**simethicone**) if needed. Electrolyte levels should be monitored, except for patients solely on stool softeners or bulking agents.

Amitiza (lubiprostone)—24 µg bid
Bulking agents
- calcium polycarbophil (e.g., *FiberCon*)—1 gm po qid
- methylcellulose (e.g., *Citrucel*)—2 gm po qd to tid
- psyllium (e.g., *Metamucil*)—1–2 tsp po qd to tid
- wheat dextrin (*Benefiber*)—2 tsp tid (dissolves in beverages and soft foods; used in cooking)
Lactulose (*Cephulac*, generic)—adjust from 30 to 45 cc po qd to qid
- *Kristalose* (less sweet)—10–20 mg po qd, up to 40
Bisacodyl (e.g., *Dulcolax*, OTC laxative)—10–30 mg po prn
- 5–10 mg per rectum prn po effective in 6–1 h; pr effective in ~15 min
Fleets enema (generics available, OTC)—1–2 as directed pr prn
- *Fleets* Biscadoyl Enema—if phosphate or sodium enema contraindicated
- *Fleets* Mineral Oil Enema—for passage of hard stools
- *Fleets* Enema—regular formula
Magnesium citrate (OTC)—1/2–1 bottle po prn (may titrate to lower dose)
Magnesium hydroxide (*Milk of Magnesia*, OTC)—2–4 tbs po qd
Miralax (polyethylene glycol)—17 gm in 8 oz fluid qd
Movantik (naloxegol, schedule II)—25 mg qam (reduce to 12.5 mg prn)

Relistar (methylnaltrexone, schedule II)—8—12 mg subcutaneous qod
- weight 84 to 134 #, 8 mg subcutaneous qod
- weight 135 to 250#, 12 mg subcutaneous qod
- weight 251#, 0.15 mg/kg subcutaneous qod

Senna (e.g., *Senokot*, generic, OTC)—1—4 tablets qd to tid
- some preparations have stool softener (e.g., *Senokot-S*)
- *SenokotXTRA*—double strength

Texas cocktail (OTC)—30 mL mineral oil in 8 oz juice; follow at 1 h with 10 oz magnesium citrate

Acute Proctitis/Tenesmus

OTC *Preparation* H suppositories are a good initial choice for hemorrhoid inflammation. Prescribe *Anusol HC* or **Proctocort** suppositories for internal hemorrhoids and *Proctofoam HC* or *Cortifoam* for external hemorrhoids. If persistent pain or bleeding, use a *Rectal Rocket*.

For XRT-induced proctitis or tenesmus/urgency, determine whether the irritation is external or internal to the anal verge. If internal, use stool softeners and OTC medications initially, then *Anusol HC* or **Proctocort** suppositories, *Proctofoam HC*, or *Cortifoam*. Advance to a *Rectal Rocket*. If unresponsive, use *Colocort* enema, and eventually *mesalamine*.

For perianal irritation, use OTC *Tuck's Ointment* (previously Anusol HC), *Nupercainal Ointment* or *ELA-Max* for relief. If refractory, prescribe *Proctofoam HC* or *Cortifoam*, advancing to *Pramosone* or *Analpram* if needed. For extensive perianal skin breakdown, a combination of *Domeboro* soaks and **Aquaphor/Xylocaine** are usually beneficial.

For sudden onset, severe pain with bowel movement and tenesmus, rule out rectal fissure (managed differently). *Analpram* and high-fiber diet are the mainstay with a longer perirecovery period.

Analpram-HC—apply tid to qid cream
- *Analpram* cream 1%, 2.5%—*Analpram* lotion 2.5%

Aquaphor-**Original Formula/Xylocaine 5% Ointment**—apply tid

Colocort (**hydrocortisone retention enema**)—1 pr qhs, retain for 1 h to all night
- single dose units, 100 mg hydrocortisone/60 mL

Cortifoam (**hydrocortisone 10%**)—1 pr qd to bid

ELA-Max 5 Anorectal Cream (5% lidocaine—OTC)—apply to intact skin

Hydrocortisone Rectal Suppository (*Anusol-HC*, generic)

LMX.5 (5% lidocaine cream OTC) 15, 30 gm tubes Mesalamine
- *Rowasa*—rectal suspension enema—1 per rectum qhs
- *Canasa*—rectal suppository—1 per rectum bid to tid

Nupercainal Hemorrhoidal and Anesthetic Ointment (OTC)
- apply per rectum bid and after each bowel movement

Pramosone (**hydrocortisone + pramoxine**)—apply to intact skin qid
- *Pramosone* Cream 1%—1 oz, 2 oz
- *Pramosone* Lotion 1%—2 oz, 4 oz, 8 oz

- *Pramosone* Ointment—1%, 2.5% —1 oz (combination topical steroid and anesthetic)

Preparation H
- Preparation H Hydrocortisone 1% (OTC)—apply qid
- Preparation H Suppositories (OTC)—1 pr 3–5 daily
- Preparation H Cooling Gel (OTC, with aloe)
- Preparation H Maximum Strength (OTC, with topical anesthetic)

Proctocort (**hydrocortisone**)—30 mg suppository—1–2 prn bid
- 1% cream—apply bid to qid prn

Proctofoam HC—apply prn as directed tid to qid
- 10 gm (14 unit dose) aerosol container

Note: contains hydrocortisone 1% and pramoxine 1%.

Rectal Rocket—1 per rectum qhs × 5 days
- custom formulation or **hydrocortisone** 5%, **lidocaine** 2.5% (or 5%), **nifedipine** 0.3% (to 0.4%)

Tuck's Ointment (1% hydrocortisone, OTC)—apply tid to id

GENITOURINARY

Radiation of the bladder can cause cystitis, urgency, frequency, dysuria, and nocturia. Bladder infections may occur during the first week if bacteria are introduced with contrast at simulation, or during the third to fifth week (bladder wall integrity compromised by XRT). Noninfectious cystitis is mild and intermittent initially, beginning in the third to fifth week. Patients with enlarged prostates are at risk for increased urinary obstructive symptoms (often with dysuria) secondary to XRT-induced prostate edema, as early as the second treatment.

Increased frequency and volume without increased fluid intake suggests diabetes; urinalysis will establish infection versus glucosuria. Urgency, frequency, and/or dysuria, with a good stream and no hesitation, suggests bladder spasms and/or cystitis—treat with analgesics or antispasmodics if UA is negative; antibiotics if positive. Urgency, frequency, and/or dysuria, with hesitancy and intermittent or decreased stream, suggests obstruction—treat with a urinary obstruction modifier, adding analgesics if needed.

Note: **Finasteride** compounds, *Propecia* (used for hair growth), *Avodart*, and *Proscar* can dramatically reduce (50% up to 90%) prostate-specific antigen (PSA) levels.

Note: To rule out UTI after hours or on weekends, consider home urine tests, such as **UTI Tests** or **AZO Test Strips**.

Analgesics/Antispasmodics/Incontinence

Infectious or XRT-cystitis and bladder spasms can cause dysuria from the tip of the penis to the suprapubic region. Once UTI has been ruled out then for painless increased frequency with good force of stream, or for pain through the course of urination, treat topically with **phenazopyridine**. If dysuria remains severe, advance to *Urised* or *Prosed DS*, and then *Elmiron* or systemic pain medications. Caution the patient regarding urine discoloration with some of these medications.

If flow is good, and without urgency, pain at initiation or completion of urination, or urge incontinence, then treat for bladder spasms with antispasmodics (*Enablex, VESIcare, Detrol LA, Ditropan XL,* or *Urispas*). If symptoms persist, one study showed benefit with the drug combination *Ditropal XL* and *Detrol LA.* If severe symptoms persist, consider **Hyoscyamine, Donnatal Extentabs,** or **B&O Suprettes.**

The most common types of urinary incontinence in XRT patients are [1] urge incontinence [2], mechanical incontinence (postprostatectomy, or TURP), and [3] overflow incontinence. For urge and mechanical incontinence, antispasmodics are the initial treatment of choice. For refractory mechanical incontinence, placement of a "urethral blocking device" may provide significant benefit. See the **Urinary Obstruction Modifiers** section for recommendations regarding overflow incontinence.

B & O Supprettes (belladonna/opium, Class II)
- 1 supprette PR qd to qid
- 15A: 30 mg opium, 16.2 mg belladonna
- 16A: 60 mg opium, 16.2 mg belladonna

Detrol LA (tolterodine)—4 mg po qd
Ditropan XL (oxybutynin, generic)—5–10 mg qd; increase 5 mg qd weekly to 30 qd maximum
Elmiron (pentosan)—100 mg po tid
Enablex (darifenacin)—7.5 mg, advancing to 15 mg po qd
Hyoscyamine (Levsin, generic)—0.125–0.25 mg po/sl tid to qid
- Levsinex TIMECAPS—0.375–0.75 mg po bid to tid
- Donnatal Extentabs—1 po bid (to tid)
- hyoscyamine + phenobarbital, atropine, scopolamine

Oxytrol (Oxybutynin Transdermal System)—1 patch q 3–4 days
Prosed DS (combination of local analgesic, antiseptic, and parasympatholytic)

Note: contraindicated in glaucoma, urinary bladder neck obstruction, pyloric or duodenal obstruction, or cardiospasm; do not use with sulfonamides.

Formulation includes atropine.
Phenazopyridine (Pyridium, or OTC Azo-Standard)—200 mg po tid
Urispas (flavoxate)—100–200 mg po tid to qid
VESIcare (solifenacin)—5 mg, advancing to 10 mg po qd

Antibiotics

For acute cystitis/UTI, consider *Bactrim/Septra* initially, with *Cipro* or *Levaquin* as second-line therapy for 7–14 days. Additional options include *Keflex* and *Augmentin.* Prostatitis (boggy, tender prostate on exam) requires longer therapy—28 days of *Levaquin* or 3 months of *Bactrim.*

For uncomplicated implant procedures, *Ancef* 1 gm IV or *Levaquin* 500 mg IV is recommended. If bacterial endocarditis prophylaxis is indicated, *Ampicillin* 2 g and *Gentamicin* 1.5 mg/kg (120 mg maximum) 30 min preprocedure and *Ampicillin* 1 g at 6 h are recommended. Alternately, *Vancomycin* 1 gm and *Gentamicin* 1.5 mg/kg (120 mg maximum), 30 min preprocedure can be used.

Amoxicilin/clavulanate (*Augmentin*, generic)—500/125 mg tid
Cephalexin (*Keflex*, generic)—500 mg qid
Ciprofloxacin (*Cipro, Cipro XR*, generic)—250–750 mg po bid
* *Cipro XR*—500–1000 mg qd
Levofloxacin (*Levaquin*)—500–750 mg qd
Nitrofurantoin (*Macrobid*, generic)
* treatment—50–100 mg qid
* long-term suppression—50–100 mg po qhs
Trimethoprim/sulfamethoxazole (Bactrim, *Bactrim DS*, generic)
* treatment—2 regular or 1 DS tablet po q 12 h
* long-term suppression—1 regular po qd

Erectile Dysfunction Therapy

Erectile dysfunction can have many causes. The onset following XRT is typically 8–16 months. The primary etiology in XRT-induced ED is arteriogenic. Studies indicated that limiting dose to the penile bulb and corporal bodies decreases risk. Prostatectomy more commonly involves a neurogenic compromise.

Other etiologies include antiandrogen therapy, pharmaceuticals (e.g., blood pressure medications, antidepressants), and psychological issues.

Viagra, Levitra, Cialis, or *Stendra* (PDE5 inhibitors) are effective approximately half the time for XRT-induced erectile dysfunction. They are prescribed as one dose per day maximum, except low-dose *Cialis* that may be taken on a daily basis. *Viagra* or *Levitra* are taken approximately 1 h before intercourse; *Stendra* can be taken 30 min before activity. Duration of benefit is 4–5 h, except *Cialis* may provide benefit up to 36 h (single dose regimen). Contraindications include organic nitrates in heart patients, and alpha blockers (except *Flomax*).

Erectile dysfunction refractory to medication is managed by the urologist. Options include "the pump," Caverject injections to the penile shaft, and *MUSE* urethral suppositories.

Cialis (**tadalafil**)—10 mg qd prn (range 5–20 mg) as single dose
* 2.5 mg qd (up to 5 mg qd) for continuous dosing
Levitra (**vardenafil**)—10 mg po prn (range 5–20 mg)
Stendra (*avanafil*)—100 mg qd prn (range 50–200 mg)
Viagra (**sildenafil**)—50 mg qd prn (range 25–100 mg)
Male hot flashes
Progestational agents (e.g., *Megace, Depo-Provera*) and certain antidepressants (e.g., *Effexor XR*) provide the most consistent relief.
Depo-Provera (**Medroxyprogesterone**)—150 mg I.M. q 3 months
Effexor XR (**Venlafaxine**)—75 mg po qhs
Megestrol (*Megace*, generic)—20 mg po bid, 10 mg qd or qod once responsive.

Hematuria and Chronic Radiation Cystitis

Sudden onset hematuria can be caused by UTI, radiation cystitis, tumor retraction, or bleeding diathesis. If during XRT, rule out UTI, and then provide supportive care, unless bleeding is severe or has not improved 4 weeks postradiation. For acute bleeding following an implant procedure, manage initially with bladder irrigation (saline or distilled water). If this fails after 24 h, or there is severe clot formation disrupting the irrigation process (and platelets are normal and coagulation is not an issue), *Amicar* may be of benefit.

For late or persistent bleeding, rule out UTI, assess and adjust (if possible) anticoagulation therapies (e.g., decrease **aspirin** from 325 mg/d to 81 mg/d). Several studies have shown benefit from direct application of dilute **formalin** (usually 4%), or argon plasma coagulation. Finally, try a 3-month course of *Trental* and **Vitamin E** (extend to 6 months if improvement). Proceed to hyperbaric oxygen if needed.

Managing late radiation cystitis symptoms can be complex and frustrating for everyone involved. Occasionally, chronic prostatitis or a UTI deep in the bladder walls will produce symptoms and may require long-term antibiotics. An antispasmodic may be required, and some patients will require urinary obstruction modifiers (UOBs) and antispasmodics. If symptoms persist, bladder analgesics are the next choice—consider *Elmiron* before using systemic narcotics. Eventually, long-term pain management may be the only option.

If decreased flow does not respond to urinary obstruction modifier (UOB) medications, cystoscopy is indicated to reduce any urethral strictures and assess for bladder outlet obstruction. If TURP is indicated, it should be staged in multiple procedures, removing as little tissue as possible for relief of symptoms.

> *Amicar* (**aminocaproic acid**)—5 g in 250 mL IV, or 5 mg PO first hour; then 1 g po or IV q h—maximum 8 g qd
> *Elmiron* (**pentosan**)—100 mg po qd
> **Formalin**—apply a 4% solution directly to the involved area
> **Pentoxifylline** (*Trental*, generic)—400 mg po tid with meals
> • 3 months trial, extend additional 3 months if effective
>
> Note: do not use if history or cerebral or retinal bleeding.
>
> **Vitamin E** (**tocopherol**)—1000 IU po qd

Urinary Obstruction Modifiers

Radiation can cause edema of the prostate very early in the course of treatment, further obstructing a compromised stream. With normal urination, the onset will be slower. Obstruction can also occur in the acute and chronic postimplant phase. Ensure that the patient is not on antihistamines, decongestants, antispasmodics, or anticholinergics, which increase urinary obstruction symptoms.

For acute and chronic urinary obstructive symptoms secondary to BPH and/or XRT oedema, alpha-1 blockers are the treatment of choice (decreasing smooth muscle tone in the prostate, prostate capsule, and proximal urethral sphincter). *Flomax, Rapaflo*, and *Uroxatral* often provide excellent relief. *Proscar* and *Avodart* provide antiandrogen therapy (5a reductase inhibitors; also lower PSA) and require months for effectiveness but may be especially useful in treatment of chronic obstruction. For severe symptoms, use a combination of alpha-1 blocker and 5a reductase inhibitor such as the new drug *Jalyn.*

Occasionally, an indwelling or suprapubic catheter is required throughout the course of therapy or in the postimplant phase versus intermittent self-catherization (patient's preference). External XRT-induced edema usually subsides 2—4 weeks post-treatment. In patients presenting with severe obstructive symptoms before XRT, obstruction may require surgical intervention or permanent catheter.

Avodart (dutasteride)—0.5 mg qd
Flomax (tamsulosin, generic)—0.4—0.8 mg qd
Jalyn (*dutasteride/tamsulosin*)—1 tablet after same meal qd
Proscar (finasteride, generic)—5 mg qd
Rapaflo (sildosin)—8 mg po with same meal
Uroxatral (alfuzosin)—10 mg po following same meal qd

GYNECOLOGICAL

Perineal Reaction

Radiation to the labia, perineum, and inguinal folds often results in severe skin reaction, necessitating a break in treatment. Use steroid creams cautiously, as fungal infections can develop in moist skin. Distal dysuria from desquamation around the meatus can be reduced using **aquaphor** as a barrier. *Domeboro* soaks should be started early, with *Silvadene* or *SilvaMed* applied after drying. Add oral pain medications or topical anesthetics as needed.

Acute Vaginitis

Vaginal irritation may be secondary to radiation or to superinfection. Normal vaginal discharge (nonirritating, milky white or mucoid, odorless) often increases during radiotherapy and does not indicate infection.

The most common etiology for vaginitis is candida; clinicians should have a low threshold for suspicion, and treat early. Candidal vaginitis risk increases with diabetes, steroid use, and immune compromise. Use OTC topical Rx initially (e.g., *Monistat*, *Femstat*, or *Mycelex*), and *Diflucan* if refractory.

Bacterial vaginosis produces a profuse, gray, thin discharge, often with a fishy smell. Topical **metronidazole** or **clindamycin** are the drugs of choice (oral **metronidazole** also works, but with increased side effects).

Trichomoniasis (8%—13% in older populations) produces a greenish-yellow purulent discharge. Confirm with laboratory testing, and then treat with **metronidazole**.

Betadine douche and suppositories or *Replens* moisturizer may soothe noninfected vaginitis. If symptoms persist, topical **lidocaine** usually provides relief. For postmenopausal atrophic vaginitis, consider topical hormonal therapy (e.g., *estradiol vaginal cream*, vaginal tablets, or *estradiol rings*).

Betadine medicated douche (povidine—iodine 10%; OTC mixtures)
• 2 tbsp concentrate to quart warm water qd
Betadine medicated gel (povidine—iodine 10%, OTC)

- one applicator full qhs; may apply externally as well

Betadine-medicated vaginal suppositories (povidine–iodine 10%, OTC)—insert intravaginally qhs

Butoconazole—(*Femstat-3*, generic, OTC)—q d to q 3 d

Cleocin Vaginal Ovules (clindamycin)—one ovule intravaginally qhs × 3 d

Clotrimazole (*Mycelex*, generic, OTC)—qd × 1, 3, or 7 d
- e.g., Mycelex-3, Mycelex-7

Diflucan (fluconazole, generic)—150 mg po × 1 d; if refractory, 100 mg qd × 14 d

Lidocaine—apply to the affected area prn for topical anesthesia
- *LMX 4* and *LMX 5* (OTC 4% and 5% cream)

EMLA Cream (lidocaine 2.5%, prilocaine 2.5%)
- apply topically prn

Metronidazole (*Flagyl*, generic)—375–500 mg po bid
- *Flagyl ER*—750 mg po qd × 7 d
- *Metrogel-Vaginal* (0.75%)—1 applicator qd to bid × 5 days

Miconazole (*Monistat*, generic, OTC)—100 mg intravaginally qd × 7 d or 200 mg qd × 3 d

Replens Vaginal Moisturizer (OTC)—one applicator full q 2–3 d prn

Vaginal Late Toxicity

Severe acute vaginal radiation toxicity predicts for late vaginal necrosis or fistula formation. Conservative management of vaginal necrosis includes local debridement, hydrogen peroxide douches, antibiotics, antifungals, and topical estrogen. Hyperbaric oxygen has also demonstrated benefit. Alternately, consider **Trental** and **Vitamin E.**

Stenosis of the vaginal apex is common postbrachytherapy. Initially, there may be stricture formation that must be manually lysed by the clinician, through vaginal dilator use or by sexual intercourse. Long-term prevention of vaginal stenosis requires routine use of a **vaginal dilator** or regular sexual intercourse. Sexual intercourse also helps decrease vaginal shortening. Topical medications, such as **estrogen** creams, may alleviate discomfort.

Estrogen creams (e.g., Premarin Vaginal Cream, generic)
- three times weekly for 6–9 months

Vaginal Dilators—use three to five times weekly, essentially forever
- lubricate and advance into vagina for 10 min

NERVOUS SYSTEM

Edema Management

Primary or metastatic cancer of the brain and the spinal cord are often associated with symptomatic edema, which can worsen during radiotherapy (especially during the first several fractions). Steroids decrease existing or developing edema and help prevent increased edema from radiotherapy. Onset is rapid, with peak plasma levels at 1 h for IV and 1–2 h for oral administration.

Steroids should never be abruptly discontinued. Depending on the potential morbidity of progressive edema, a steroid taper can be initiated during the radiotherapy, reversing the taper if symptoms develop. A taper is begun or continued at treatment completion, with one approach involving a 50% reduction every 2 weeks. Oral decadron has a $2^1/_2$ day duration, so equal spacing is not required.

Studies show up to 60% steroid myopathy with steroid use. This is a distinctive proximal lower extremity weakness (similar to Eaton–Lambert Syndrome). Resolution (or at least improvement) of symptoms may occur during steroid taper but usually begins at 1–3 months poststeroid discontinuation. The weakness should be differentiated from progressive disease and the patient reassured.

Steroids can dramatically elevate blood glucose levels, especially in diabetics, causing fatigue and altered mental status, easily confused with disease progression or XRT-induced edema. Other common side effects include hypertension, candidiasis, gastritis, and Cushingoid appearance.

Steroids often cause insomnia, managed initially by alternating the schedule with no dosing after 2 pm. Sleep medications are often indicated. Mood disorders (from hypermania to hypomania) may require psychotropic medication. Occasionally, steroid psychosis may develop.

Dexamethasone (*Decadron*, generic)
- XRT-induced symptomatic edema or prophylaxis
- 2–6 mg po q6–8h; + 8 mg load initially
- tumor-induced symptomatic edema
- 10–25 mg IV initially, then 4–10 mg IV/po q 6 h
- severe sudden symptoms/impending herniation or compression

Vertigo

Benign positional vertigo (<60 s episodes with certain head positions) can be controlled with repositioning manuevers (e.g., **Epley manuever**). For other causes, symptomatic relief requires vestibular nerve suppressants, such as **diazepam** or **meclizine**. **Scopolamine patches** are used for prophylaxis.

Diazepam (*Valium*, generic)—2–5 mg qid to tid
Meclizine (*Antivert*, generic)—25–50 mg po tid
- tablets 12.5, 25, 50 mg
Scopolamine patches (*Transderm Scop*)—apply to skin behind ear; effective for several days per patch

Seizure

Seizures associated with primary or metastatic brain tumors are usually focal but may generalize. Incidence is 30%–40%. Many are managed with **phenytoin** or **divalproex** and newer agents, such as **levetiracetam**, **pregabalin**, or **topiramate**, which are preferred for their lower side effect profile. Begin with a single-drug regimen.

Depakote ER (**divalproex**)—initial 10–15 mg/kg/day. Titrate upward 5–10 mg/kg/day in weekly intervals for optimal response; maximum 60 mg/kg/day

Keppra (**levetiracetam**)—500–750 mg bid; maximum 3000 mg qd
Lyrica (**pregabalin**)—50 mg tid; increase to 200 mg tid maximum
Phenytoin (*Dilantin*, generic)—100 mg tid initially, increase 100 mg every 2 weeks
to desired response (usually 300–600 mg)
Once stabilized, change to extended release daily ER capsules
Tegretol (**carbamazepine**)—200–600 mg bid
Topamax (**topiramate**)—200 mg bid; weekly increase 50 to 800 mg bid maximum

PAIN MANAGEMENT

Effective pain management is tailored to the type and intensity of pain. Initial management should target the cause of the pain, and if ineffective, then central acting medications are initiated. Some common examples are as follows:

Bone pain/costochondritis—steroid or **NSAID**
Mucositis/esophagitis—topical medications
Breast (tumor bed) pain—**NSAID**
Neuropathic pain—**neurontin**
Brain metastases/edema—steroids
Gas cramping—*Gas-X*

Chronic pain management usually involves a two-drug approach. Long-acting narcotics are administered q 12–24 h, with short-acting, prn medication for breakthrough
pain. The long-acting narcotic dose is adjusted, so that 2–3 prn doses are required
daily. Coanalgesics are added as needed.

If concerned about drug seeking or addictive behavior, attempt to control pain with
long-acting medications alone.

Equianalgesic effects are usually related to oral morphine.

Oral **morphine**	Oral dose of **opioid**
2 mg	30 mg **codeine** 5 g **hydrocodone**
5 mg	5 mg **oxycodone**
15 mg	4 mg **hydromorphone**

For opioid-naive patients, following initial doses are recommended:

Morphine	2.5–5 mg q 6 h
Long-acting morphine	15 mg bid
Hydromorphone	0.5–1 mg q 4 h
Fentanyl	12.5 µg/h

For all opioids, caution is recommended in patients with impaired respiratory function, bronchial asthma, increased intracranial pressure, and liver failure.

Constipation is most common and tolerance is uncommon. After acute impaction is resolved, chronic management can be initiated. Begin with a cathartic (e.g., **senna** 1 qd to 2 tid, with **simethicon** if gas cramps develop) as needed. If ineffective, advance to an osmotic agent (e.g., **lactulose** 30 cc bid to tid). *Amitiza* or *Movantik* are also medical alternatives.

Nausea may develop, but tolerance develops over several days to weeks. Management may be local (e.g., **ranitidine** or **NSAID**) or central (e.g., **prochlorperazine** 10 mg q 6 h, **promethazine** 25 mg q 4 h). If persistent, advance to **ondansetron**.

If sedation and altered mental state occur, symptoms usually resolve after several days:

- for persistent sedation, consider *Ritalin* (5–10 mg bid) or *Provigil* (100–200 mg qam)
- for persistent confusion, consider *Haldol* (0.5–1.0 mg tid)

Sudden onset of nausea or confusion without a change in medications warrants evaluation for brain metastases, liver failure, hypercalcemia, hyponatremia, hypoxemia, or hyperglycemia.

Nonopioid Analgesics

Acetaminophen (*Tylenol*, generic, OTC)—325–650 mg q 4–6 h

Note: 4000 mg/d maximum; not antiinflammatory

Aspirin (OTC)—325–1000 mg po q 4–6 h

Note: 4000 mg/d maximum; antiinflammatory.

Celecoxib (*Celebrex*)—100–200 mg po bid
Ibuprofen (Rx, OTC)—200–800 mg po q 4–6 h
Indomethacin (*Indocin*, generic)—25–50 mg bid to tid
- begin at 25 mg bid, advance q week.
- extended release capsules 75 mg; Rx 75 mg qd to bid
Naproxen (*Naprosyn*, generic)—250–500 mg bid
- OTC (*Aleve*, generic)—caplets, gelcaps, tablets 220 mg
- *Anaprox DS* (rapid onset)—550 mg bid
  Note: 1500 mg/d maximum
Tramadol (*Ultram*, generic)—50–100 mg q 4–6 h—300 mg/d
- *Ultram ER*—100–300 mg qd
- *Ultracet*—37.5 mg tramadol/325 mg acetaminophen 2 po q 4–6 h
- 8 tablets per day maximum; limit therapy to 5 days
Opioid Analgesics for Mild to Moderate Pain
Codeine—15–60 mg po q 4 h
- **Codeine** (CII)—tablets 15, 30, 60 mg
- syrup—15 mg/mL

- **Codeine/acetaminophen** (e.g., *Tylenol #3*)—30 mg, *Tylenol #4*—60 mg; acetaminophen 300 mg maximum: **codeine** 360 mg/d maximum, **acetaminophen** 4000 mg/d

Hydrocodone—5–10 mg po q 4–6 h
- maximum 5/300 8 per day; 7.5 and 10/300 6 per day
- *hydrocodone/acetaminophen* (most combinations generic)
- *Lortab* tablets 2.5/500, 5/500, 7.5/500, 10/500 mg
- *Lorcet* tablets 5/500, 7.5/650, 10/650 mg
- *Lortab Elixir* 7.5/500 mg per 15 mL
- *Vicodin* 5/500 mg
- *Vicodin ES* 7.5/750 mg, *Vicodin HP* 10/660 mg
- *Norco* (generic) 5/325, 7.5/325, 10/325 mg
- **hydrocodone/guaifenesin** (generic)—5 and 15 mg per 5 mL
- *HYCOTUSS* (5/100 mg per 5 mL)—5–15 mL q 4 h
- 30 mg per day maximum
- **hydrocodone/chlorpheniramine** (*Tussionex*)
- 5 mL bid
- 10 mg hydrocodone, 8 mg chlorpheniramine per 5 mL
- **hydrocodone/ibuprofen**—7.5/200 mg
- *Vicoprofen*—1 po q 4–6 h maximum 5/day

Opioid Analgesics for Severe Pain (Class II Narcotics)

Morphine and **oxycodone** are available in immediate release, standard release, and delayed/extended release forms.

Fentanyl
- transdermal system (*Duragesic*, generic)—12 μg/h + q 3 days—patch 12, 25, 50, 75, 100 μg/h
- oral transmucosal (*Actiq*)—200 + μg q 30 min prn breakthrough pain
- 100, 200, 400, 600, 800, 1200, 1600 μg
- buccal transmucosal films (*Onsolis*)—200 μg
- dosing separated by minimum 2 h
- once correct dose established, 4 doses per day maximum
- films 200, 400, 600, 800, 1200 μg
- sublingual spray (*Subsys*)—100+ μg, 1–2 doses, q 4 h
- first dose, then can deliver second dose at 30 min
- begin at 100 μg—no more than four episodes per day
- 100, 200, 400, 600, 800, 1200, 1600 μg per spray

Hydromorphone (*Dilaudid*, generic)—2 mg–8+ mg po q 4–6 h
- extended release (*Dilaudid-HP*)

Morphine
- immediate release—5 mg + po q 4 h
- generic: tablets 10, 15, 30 mg
- solution 10, 20, 20 mg/cc
- suppositories—5, 10, 20, 30 mg
- delayed release—30 mg + po q 8–12 h

- *M.S. Contin*—tablets 15, 30, 60, 100, 200 mg
- generic CR: tablets 15, 30, 60, 100, 200 mg
- sustained release—20 mg + po q 24 h
- *Avinza*—capsules 30, 45, 60, 75, 90, 120 mg
- *KADIAN*—capsules 20–200 mg
- both can be sprinkled into applesauce
- injectable—5–20 mg IM/SQ q 4 h
- 5–15 mg IV q 4 h
- IV/IM to po conversion factor ~1:4

Oxycodone—4.5–10 mg po q 4–6 h
Oxycodone (generic)—tablets 5 mg; solution 5 mg/5 mL
- *OxyIR*—immediate release 5 mg oral capsules
- *OxyFast*—oral concentrate 20 mg/1 mL
- oxycodone/aspirin (*Percodan*, generic)—tablet 4.5/325
- oxycodone/acetaminophen
- *Percocet*—7.5/325, 10/325 mg
- generic—5/325, 7.5/325, 10/325, 5/500, 7.5/500, 10/650 mg
- delayed release—10–40 mg + po bid
- *Oxycontin*—10, 20, 40, 80, 160 mg
- generic, CR—10, 20, 40, 80 mg

Oxymorphone (*Opana*)—5–20 mg q 4–6 h
- tablets 5, 10 mg
- *Opana ER*—5–20 + mg q 12 h

Coanalgesics

Nonsteroidal antiinflammatory drugs are effective for treating prostaglandin-associated pain, such as bone mets, arthritis, and acute surgical pain (see drugs in preceeding section). **Steroids** can reduce edema and are useful for tumor-induced nerve compression, increased intracranial pressure, and soft tissue infiltration. Neuropathic pain can be rapidly relieved with **gabapentin**. Other coanalgesics include analeptics, anxiolytics, antispasmodics, topical anesthetics, and muscle relaxants (see subsequent sections). **Amitriptyline** is an antidepressant that has shown most benefit as an adjunct, especially in neuropathic pain. See *uptodate.com* for more complete information.

Amitriptyline (*Elavil*, generic)—as an adjunct, begin at 25 mg tid; titrate to 50 mg tid
Neurontin (**gabapentin**)—300 mg tid, increase to 600 mg tid prn

Narcotic Antagonist

Narcan (**naloxone**)—0.4–2.0 mg IV, IM, or SQ; repeated q 2–3 min
- prefilled syringes and ampules—0.4 mg/mL 1 mg/mL

PSYCHOTROPIC MEDICATIONS

Anxiety, depression, and altered sleep patterns are common in cancer patients. Antianxiety medication is a good first intervention, but many patients also benefit from antidepressants. Depression is generally undertreated in this group of patients.

Somnolence and Fatigue

Before attempting to remedy somnolence and fatigue, rule out comorbid factors such as anemia, electrolyte imbalances, nutritional issues, endocrine, pain, and depression. *Ritalin* and *Provigil* are the drugs most commonly prescribed for cancer-related fatigue.

> *Navigil* (**armondafinil**, Class IV)—50–150 mg (elderly), (nonelderly) 250 mg qam
> *Provigil* (**Modafinil**, Class IV)—100 mg (elderly), 200 mg po qam
> *Ritalin* (**Methylphenidate**, generic, Class II)
> * 10–20 mg po bid to tid
> * *Ritalin* SR—20 mg tab—20 mg po tid
> * *Ritalin* LA—20 mg po qam; increase 10 mg q week to 60 mg qd maximum

Antianxiety

Ativan is useful for anticipatory anxiety and nausea and may have a slight amnestic effect. *Librium* and *Valium* are useful for managing withdrawal symptoms. *Valium* has additional benefit as a muscle relaxant. *Xanax* is a good choice for associated panic disorder. Try to avoid long-term daily use (longer than 2 months) and use with caution in patients with a history of addiction. For patients unable to take benzodiazepines, **hydroxyzine**, **gabapentin**, or **propranolol** can be considered.

> **Lorazepam** (*Ativan*, generic)—0.5–2 mg po tid for anxiety
> 1–4 mg po qhs prn insomnia
> **Chlordiazepoxide** (*Librium*, generic)
> * mild anxiety: 5–10 mg tid to qid
> * severe anxiety: 20–25 mg po tid to qid
> **Diazepam** (*Valium*, generic)—2–10 mg po bid to qid
> **Alprazolam** (*Xanax*, generic)—0.25–1 mg po tid (maximum 4 mg/d)
> * *Xanax XR* (extended release)—2–6 mg po qd
> **Clonazepam** (*Klonopin*)—0.25–2 mg bid to qid

Antidepressants

Clinical depression, depressed mood, and anhedonia (marked loss of interest or pleasure in all activities) occur in up to 20% of cancer patients. Newer classes of antidepressants (see listed drugs), with increased patient tolerance, include selective serotonin-reuptake inhibitors (SSRIs), serotonin norepinephrine-reuptake inhibitors

(SNRIs), and serotonin antagonist-reuptake inhibitors (SARIs). Tricyclic antidepressants also have anticholinergic side effects.

Antidepressants, such as *Trazadone* and *Mitazapine*, enhance the serotonergic system and can be helpful when insomnia and anxiety are the major symptoms. *Wellbutrin* enhances dopamine and is useful when the primary symptoms are lack of energy, concentration, and motivation.

Monamine oxidase inhibitors should be avoided (unless previously successful for the patient). Dose escalation should be performed on a weekly basis.

Celexa (**citalopram**, SSRI)—20 mg po qd; to 40 mg qd maximum
Cymbalta (**duloxetine**, SNRI)—20–120 mo qd
Effexor (venlafaxine, generic, SNRIs)—25 mg tid; 75 mg tid maximum
Effexor XR (extended release)—75–225 mg/day maximum
Lexapro (**escitalopram**, SSRI)—10 mg po qd; 20 mg po qd maximum
• tablets 5, 10, 20 mg—solution 5 mg/5 mL
Paxil (**paroxetine**, generic—SSRI)—20 mg po qam (50 mg/d maximum)
• debilitated patients: 10 mg po qam (40 mg/d maximum)
• *Paxil CR* (continuous release)—25–62.5 mg/day maximum
Pristiq (**desvenlafaxine**, SNRI)—25–200 mg qd
Prozac (**fluoxetine**, generic SSRI)—20 mg qd to 40 mg bid
• *Prozac Weekly*—delayed release capsule, 90 mg q week
Remeron (**mirtazapine**)—15–45 mg qhs
Wellbutrin (**bupropion,** generic)—100 mg po bid; 300 mg tid maximum
• *Wellbutrin XL* (extended release)—150–300 mg qd
Zoloft (**sertraline**, SSRI)—50 mg po qd; 200 mg/d maximum

Antipsychotics

Antipsychotics are occasionally used during XRT for patients with moderate to severe agitation, combativeness, or who have altered mental status and are noncooperative. For milder cases, anxiolytic medication such as *Ativan* may be appropriate. Choice is usually based on the patient's history and physician's clinical experience. *Haldol* can cause severe extrapyramidal syndromes but is appropriate for severe psychoses. The newer antipsychotics have fewer side effects and may be more appropriate for less severe psychoses.

Haloperidol (*Haldol*, generic)—moderate: 0.5–2.0 mg po tid
• severe: 3.0–5.0 mg po tid
• acute: 2–5 mg IM q 4 h; maximum 100 mg/day
Abilify (**aripiprazole**)—10–15 mg po qd
Risperdal (**risperidone**)—1 mg po bid; 3 mg po bid maximum
Zyprexa (**olanzapine**)—5 mg po qd; 20 mg po qd maximum

Hypnotics/Sleep Aids

Benadryl and/or **Melatonin** can be effective sleep aids and are a good initial choice as they do not cause tolerance or dependence problems. *Roserem* (which works through the melatonin system), **trazadone** (an antidepressant, with antianxiety benefit), and **neurontin** (an antiepileptic) are good initial treatment options.

For patients not previously treated with **benzodiazepines**, *Ambien* is a good first Rx choice. The three listed **benzodiazepines** are approximately equal in efficacy of sleep induction and maintenance—*Dalmane, ProSom,* and *Restori.* If patients are awakening after 2–4 h of sleep, consider a longer-acting anxiolytic such as *Xanax, Ativan,* or *Ambien CR;* however, there can be problems with dependence, amnesia, falls, and depression with long-term use, especially in the elderly.

Ambien (**zolpidem**, generic)—10 mg po qhs; elderly patients 5 mg
- *Ambien CR*—6.25–12.5 mg po qhs
- caution of sleepwalking

Benadryl (**diphenhydramine**, OTC)—50 mg po qhs

ProSom (**estazolam**, generic)—1.0–2.0 mg po qhs

Dalmane (**flurazepam**, generic)—30 mg po qhs
- elderly patients 15 mg po qhs

Lunesta (**eszopiclone**)—2–3 mg po qhs

Neurontin (**gabapentin**)—300 mg qhs, increase to 600 mg prn

Sonata (**zalepon**)—5–20 mg po qhs

Restoril (**temazepam**, generic)—15–30 mg po qhs

Rozerem (**ramelteon**)—8 mg po qhs

Trazadone (generic)—50–100 mg qhs

Sedatives

Sedatives are used with agitated patients to facilitate treatment, either XRT or with other office procedures. *Ativan* is a good initial choice for XRT anxiety or claustrophobia.

Lorazepam (*Ativan*, generic)
- injectable: IM 0.05 mg/kg, 4 mg maximum
- IV smallest of 2 mg or 0.044 mg/kg
- TUBEX Units and vials—2, 4 mg/cc
- oral: 0.5–3 mg po

Diazepam (*Valium*, generic)—2–10 mg IV or IM q 3 h
- 2–10 mg po

Versed (midazolam)
- age < 60 IV 1–2.5 mg, then small boosts q 2 min to maximum 8–10 mg
- debilitated/age > 60: IV 0.5–1.5 mg, then small boosts q 2 min to maximum 3.5 mg
- injectable 1, 5 mg/cc

Note: use cardiorespiratory monitoring and slow IV administration.

Benzodiazepine Receptor Antagonist
Romazicon (flumazenil)—0.2 mg IV over 30 s, then 0.3 mg IV over 30 s, then 0.5 mg over 30 s q min up to 3.0 mg maximum until benzodiazepine overdose reversed

RADIATION FIBROSIS AND MUSCLE RELAXANTS

Muscle spasms may be a secondary response to anxiety over treatment, positioning for therapy, splinting, or nerve stimulation. **Flexeril** or **Zanaflex** are good initial choices, but the patient may have previous success with other relaxants. **Valium** serves as an anxiolytic as well as a muscle relaxant.

Radiation fibrosis is relatively common and can be debilitating.

Statistically significant regression has been demonstrated using a combination of **Vitamin E** and **Trental** for a 6-month period. Another potentially useful drug is **Potaba**, which increases oxygen uptake at the tissue level. **Potaba** has shown clinical efficacy for Peyronie's, scleroderma, dermatomyositis, and morphea patients.

Aminobenzoate (*Potaba*)—3 g po qid
Carisoprodol (*Soma*, generic)—1 tablet po qid
Carisoprodol/aspirin (*Soma Compound*, generic)—1–2 po qid
Cyclobenzaprine (*Flexeril*, generic)—5–20 mg po tid
Diazepam (*Valium*, generic)—2–10 mg po tid to qid
Pentoxifylline (*Trental*)—400 mg tid
Tocopherol (Vitamin E, OTC)—1000iu qd

COMMON TOXICITY (SIDE EFFECT) CRITERIA

Although it is common practice to describe the adverse events associated with radiation treatment as side effects of the treatment, cooperative groups like Radiation Therapy Oncology Group (RTOG) recommend not to call such events side effects to minimize confusion. Instead, it is better to define the side effects of radiation treatment. The RTOG has provided descriptive terminology for any adverse acute and/or late event (the toxicity) that is associated with the radiation treatment. This is called the RTOG acute toxicity criteria and was developed as part of the common toxicity criteria by the National Cancer Institute (NCI). For each adverse event, a grading scale from 0 (no radiation adverse effect) to 5 (radiation adverse effect causing patient death) is provided for documentation and reporting. The acute toxicity criteria can be used to monitor the treatment effects during treatment, justifying any necessary supportive measures for any adverse event. Following are the RTOG acute toxicity criteria for different sites of treatment (Table 26.3).

TABLE 26.3 RTOG Acute Toxicity Criteria for Different Treatment Sites

Toxicity	Grade 0 (Absent or None)	Grade 1 (Mild)	Grade 2 (Moderate)	Grade 3 (Severe and Undesirable)	Grade 4 (Life Threatening and Disabling)
Skin	No change over baseline	Follicular, faint, or dull erythema/epilation/dry desquamation decreased sweating	Tender or bright erythema, patchy moist desquamation/ moderate edema	Confluent moist desquamation other than skin folds, pitting edema	Ulceration, hemorrhage, necrosis
Mucous Membrane	No change over baseline	Injection/may experience mild pain not requiring analgesic	Patchy mucositis, which many produce an inflammatory serosanguineous discharge/ may experience moderate pain requiring analgesia	Confluent fibrinous mucositis/may include severe pain requiring narcotic	Ulceration, hemorrhage, or necrosis
Eye	No change	Mild conjunctivitis with or without scleral injection/ increased tearing	Moderate conjunctivitis with or without keratitis requiring steroids and/or antibiotics/dry eye requiring artificial tears/iritis with photophobia	Severe keratitis with corneal ulceration/objective decrease in visual acuity or in visual fields/acute glaucoma/panophthalmitis	Loss of vision (unilateral or bilateral)
Ear	No change over baseline	Mild external otitis with erythema, pruritis, 2* to dry desquamation not requiring medication. Audiogram unchanged from baseline	Moderate external otitis requiring topical medication/serous otitis medius/hypoacusis on testing only	Severe external otitis with discharge or moist desquamation, symptomatic hypoacusis/tinnitus not drug related	Deafness
Salivary Gland	No change over baseline	Mild mouth dryness/slightly thickened saliva/may have slightly altered taste such as metallic taste/these changes not reflected in alteration in baseline feeding behavior, such as increased use of liquids with meals	Moderate to complete dryness/thick, sticky saliva/ markedly altered taste	—	Acute salivary gland necrosis

Pharynx and Esophagus	No change over baseline	Mild dysphagia or odynophagia/may require topical anesthetic or nonnarcotic analgesics/may require soft diet	Moderate dysphagia or odynophagia/may require narcotic analgesics/may require puree or liquid diet	Severe dysphagia or odynophagia with dehydration or weight loss 15% from pretreatment baseline, requiring NG feeding tube, IV fluids, or hyperalimentation	Complete obstruction, ulceration, perforation fistula
Larynx	No change over baseline	Mild or intermittent hoarseness/cough not requiring antitussive erythema of mucosa	Persistent hoarseness but able to vocalize/referred ear pain, sore throat, patchy fibrinous exudates, or mild arytenoid edema not requiring narcotic cough requiring antitussive	Whispered speech, throat pain, or referred ear pain requiring narcotic/confluent fibrinous exudate, marked arytenoid edema	Marked dyspnea, stridor, or hemoptysis with tracheostomy or intubation necessary
Upper GI	No change	Anorexia with $\leq$5% weight loss from pretreatment baseline/nausea not requiring antiemetics abdominal discomfort not requiring parasympatholytic drugs or analgesics	Anorexia with $\leq$15% weight loss from pretreatment baseline/nausea and/or vomiting requiring antiemetics abdominal pain requiring analgesics	Anorexia with 15% weight loss from pretreatment baseline or requiring NG tube or parenteral support. Nausea and/or vomiting requiring tube or parenteral support/abdominal pain, severe despite meds/hematemesis, or melena/abdominal distension (flat plate radiograph shows distended bowel loops)	Ileus subacute or acute obstruction, perforation, GI bleeding requiring transfusion/abdominal pain requiring tube decompression or bowel diversion

(Continued)

TABLE 26.3   RTOG Acute Toxicity Criteria for Different Treatment Sites—cont'd

Toxicity	Grade 0 (Absent or None)	Grade 1 (Mild)	Grade 2 (Moderate)	Grade 3 (Severe and Undesirable)	Grade 4 (Life Threatening and Disabling)
Lower GI including pelvis	No change	Increased frequency or change in quality of bowel habits not requiring medication/rectal discomfort not requiring analgesics	Diarrhea requiring parasympatholytic drugs (e.g., Lomotil)/mucous discharge not necessitating sanitary pads/rectal or abdominal pain requiring analgesics	Diarrhea requiring parenteral support/severe mucous or blood discharge necessitating sanitary padsabdominal distension (flat plate radiograph demonstrated distended bowel loops)	Acute or subacute obstruction, fistula, or perforation; GI bleeding requiring transfusion; abdominal pain or tenesmus requiring tube decompression or bowel diversion
Lung	No change	Mild symptoms of dry cough or dyspnea on exertion	Persistent cough requiring narcotic, antitussive agents/dyspnea with minimal effort but not at rest	Severe cough unresponsive to narcotic antitussive agent or dyspnea at rest/clinical or radiologic evidence of acute pneumonitis/intermittent oxygen or steroids may be required	Severe respiratory insufficiency/continuous oxygen or assisted ventilation
Genitourinary	No change	Frequency of urination or nocturia twice pretreatment habit/dysuria, urgency not requiring medication	Frequency of urination of nocturia, which is less frequent than every hour. Dysuria urgency, bladder spasm requiring local anesthetic (e.g., Pyridium)	Frequency with urgency and nocturia hourly or more frequently/dysuria, pelvis pain or bladder spasm requiring regular, frequent narcotical gross hematuria with/without clot passage	Hematuria requiring transfusion/acute bladder obstruction not secondary to clot passage, ulceration, or necrosis
Heart	No change over baseline	Asymptomatic but objective evidence of ECG changes or pericardial abnormalities without evidence of other heart disease	Symptomatic with ECG changes and radiologic findings of congestive heart failure or pericardial disease/no specific treatment required	Congestive heart failure, angina pectoris, pericardial disease responding to therapy	Congestive heart failure, angina pectoris, pericardial disease, arrhythmias not responsive to nonsurgical measurement

	No change	Fully functional status (i.e., able to work) with minor neurologic findings, no medication needed	Neurologic findings present sufficient to require home care/nursing assistance may be required/medications including steroids/antiseizure agents may be required	Neurologic findings/requiring hospitalization for initial management	Serious neurologic impairment which includes paralysis, coma, or seizures 3 per week despite medication/hospitalization required
Central nervous system	No change	Fully functional status (i.e., able to work) with minor neurologic findings, no medication needed	Neurologic findings present sufficient to require home care/nursing assistance may be required/medications including steroids/antiseizure agents may be required	Neurologic findings/requiring hospitalization for initial management	Serious neurologic impairment which includes paralysis, coma, or seizures 3 per week despite medication/hospitalization required
Hematologic WBC ($\times 1000$)	4.0	3.0:S4.0	2.0–4*.0	1.0 < 2.0	<1.0
Platelets ($\times 10\ 3/mm^3$)	100	75:S100	50:S73	25:S50	<25 or spontaneous bleeding
Neutrophils ($\times 1000$)	≥ 1.9	1.3:S1.9	1.0:S1.5	0.5:S1.0	<0.5 or sepsis
Hemoglobin (gm%)	11	11–9.5	<9.5–7.5	<7.5–5.0	—
Hematocrit (%)	≥ 32	28:S32	<28	Packed cell transfusion required	—

Adapted from ref 5, Cox JD, Stetz J, Pajak TF. Toxicity criteria of the Radiation Therapy Oncology Group (RTOG) and the European Organization for Research and Treatment of Cancer (EORTC). Int J Radiat Oncol Biol Phys;31(5):1341–6, © 1995 with permission from Elsevier; and from ref 6 Arbuck SG, Ivy SP, Setser A, et al. The Revised Common Toxicity Criteria: Version 2.0. Cancer Therapy Evaluation Program (CTEP). http://ctep.info.nih.gov.

References

Ref 1. *Emami B, Lyman J, Goitein M, Munzenrider JE, Shank B, Solin LJ, Wesson M. Tolerance of normal tissue to therapeutic irradiation. Int J Radiat Oncol Biol Phys 1991;21(1):109—22.*

Ref 2. *Marks LB, Yorke ED, Jackson A, Ten Haken RK, Constine LS, Eisbruch A, Bentzen SM, Nam J, Deasy JO. Use of normal tissue complication probability models in the clinic. Int J Radiat Oncol Biol Phys 2010;76(3 Suppl):S10—9.*

Ref 3. *Martel MK, Sahijdak WM, Ten Haken RK, Kessler ML, Turrisi AT. Fraction size and dose parameters related to the incidence of pericardial effusions. Int J Radiat Oncol Biol Phys 1998;40(1):155—61.*

Ref 4. *Wikipedia, the Free Encyclopedia. Radiation Oncology/Toxixity/QUANTAC, page 1. Wikimedia Foundation, Inc. http://www.en.wikibooks.org/wiki/Radiation_Oncology/Toxicity/ QUANTEC.*

Ref 5. *Cox JD, Stetz J, Pajak TF. Toxicity criteria of the radiation therapy Oncology group (RTOG) and the European Organization for Research and treatment of cancer (EORTC). Int J Radiat Oncol Biol Phys 1995;31(5):1341—6.*

Ref 6. *Arbuck SG, Ivy SP, Setser A, et al. The Revised common toxicity criteria: version 2.0. Cancer therapy evaluation program (CTEP). http://ctep.info.nih.gov.*

Acronyms and Abbreviations

AA	Anaplastic astrocytoma
ABMT	Autologous bone marrow transplant
ABTR	All breast recurrences
ABV	Adriamycin, bleomycin, and vinblastine
ABVD	Adriamycin, bleomycin, vinblastine, and dacarbazine
ABVE	Adriamycin, bleomycin, vinblastine, and etoposide
AC	Adriamycin, cytoxan
ACBE	Air-contrasted barium enema
ACTH	Adrenocorticotropic hormone
ADCL	Accredited Dosimetry Calibration Laboratory
ADH	Antidiuretic hormone
ADR	Adriamycin
ADT	Androgen deprivation therapy
AE	Ary-epiglottic
AFP	Alpha fetoprotein
AFx	Accelerated fractionation
AH	Anaplastic histology
AH	Atypical hyperplasia
AJCC	American Joint Committee on Cancer
ALARA	As low as reasonably achievable
ALL	Acute lymphoblastic leukemia
ALND	Axillary lymph node dissection
AML	Acute myelogenous leukemia
ANITA	Adjunct Navelbine International Trialist Association
AP	Anterior-posterior
AP/PA	Anterior-posterior/posterior-anterior
AP/Rt/Lt	Anterior-posterior/right/left
APC	Adenomatous polyposis of the colon)
APC	Anaphase promoting complex
APE	AP endonuclease
APR	Abdomino perineal resection
ARR	Absolute risk reduction
ASCO	American Society of Clinical Oncology
ASIS	Anterior superior iliac spine
ASTRO	American Society for Radiation Oncology
ATAC	Arimidex, Tamoxifen, Alone, or in Combination
AUC	Area under curve
BCC	Basal cell carcinoma
BCG	Bacillus Calmette-Guerin (vaccine)
BCNU	Carmustine

BCT	Breast conservation therapy
bDFS	Biochemical disease-free survival
BE	Barium enema
BEACOPP	Bleomycin, etoposide, adriamycin, cyclophosphamide, Oncovin, prednisone, procarbazine
BED	Biologically effective dose
BEIR	Biological Effects of Ionizing Radiation (committee)
BEP	Bleomycin, etoposide, cisplatin (regime)
BER	Base excision repair
BEV	Beam's-eye view
bFGF	Basic fibroblast growth factor
bFS	Biochemical-free survival
bHCG	Beta human chorionic gonadotropin
b.i.d.	Twice a day
BMRC	British Medical Research Council
BOS	Base of skull
BOT	Base of tongue
BPH	Benign prostatic hyperplasia
Bq	Becquerel
BRCA	Breast cancer gene
bRFS	Biochemical relapse-free survival
BS	Bone scan
BSA	Body surface area
BSF	Backscatter factor
BSO	Bilateral salpingo-oophorectomy
BUDR	5-bromodeoxyuridine
BUN	Blood urea nitrogen
BUN−CR	Blood urea nitrogen−creatine ratio
C	Coulomb
CA 125	Cancer antigen 125
CAF	Cyclophosphamide, adriamycin, and 5-fluorouracil
CALGB	Cancer and Leukemia Group B (trial)
CAM	Cell adhesive matrix
CAMF	Cyclophosphamide, adriamycin, methrotrexate, and 5-Fluorouracil
CAMFPT	Cyclophosphamide, adriamycin, methrotrexate, and 5-Fluorouracil and prednisone/tamoxifen
CAP	Cancer of the prostate
CAP	Cyclophosphamide, doxorubicin, cisplatin
CAT	Choramphenicol acetyl transferase
CAV	Cytoxan, adriamycin, vincristine
CAX	Central axis
CBC	Complete blood count
CBT	Contralateral breast tumor
CBTR	Contralateral breast tumor recurrence
CCG	Children's Cancer Group
CCNU	1-(2-chloroethyl)-3-cyclohexyl-1-nitrosourea

cCR	Clinical complete response
CDDP	Cisplatin
CDT	Complete Decongestive Therapy
CEA	Carcinoembryonic antigen
CFR	Code of Federal Regulations
cGy	Centigray
CHOP	Cyclophosphamide, hydroxydaunomycin (doxorubicin), Oncovin (vincristine), and prednisone
Ci	Curie
CIN	Cervical intraepithelial neoplasia
CIS	Carcinoma in situ
CIV	Continuous intravenous infusion
CLF	Cell loss factor
CLL	Chronic lymphocytic leukemia
cm	Centimeter
CM	Cisplatin plus methotrexate
CME	Cervical mediastinal exam
CMF	Cyclophosphamide, methotrexate, and 5-fluorouracil
CMFPT	Cyclophosphamide, methotrexate, 5-fluorouracil and prednisone/tamoxifen
CML	Chronic myelogenous leukemia
CMT	Combined modality therapy
CMV	Cisplatin, methotrexate, and vinblastine
CN	Cranial nerve
CNS	Central nervous system
CODOX-M/IVAC	Cyclophosphamide, vincristine (Oncovin), doxorubicin—high-dose methotrexate alternating with ifipfomide, etoposide, high-dose Cytarabine
colstFS	Colostomy-free survival
CON	Continuous
COPD	Chronic obstructive pulmonary disease
COT	Completion of treatment
CPA	Cerebellopontine angle
CR	Complete response
CR	Creatine ratio
CREST	Calcinosis, Raynaud's phenomenon, esophageal motility dysfunction, sclerodactyly, telangiectasia (syndrome)
CRI	Cranial irradiation
CRT	Chemo-radiotherapy
CRT	Conformal radiation therapy
CRu	Complete response − unconfirmed
CS	Clinical stage
CSF	Cerebrospinal fluid
CSS	Cancer-specific survival
CSS	Cause-specific survival
cSv	Centisievert
CT	Chemotherapy

CT	Computed tomography
CTCL	Cutaneous T cell lymphoma
CTEP	Cancer Therapy Evaluation Program
CTX	Chemotherapy
CTV	Clinical target volume
CVAD	Cyclophosphamide, vincristine, adriamycin, dexamethasone
CVD	Collagen vascular disease
CVI	Continuous intravenous infusion
CVP	Cyclophosphamide, vincristine, prednisone
CW	Chest wall
CXR	Chest x-ray
CYC/ADR	Cyclophosphamide/adriamycin
D&C	Dilation and curettage
DATECA	Danish Testicular Carcinoma database
DBCG	Danish Breast Cancer Group
DCIS	Ductal carcinoma in situ
DDGS	Daumas-Duport Grading System
DES	Diethylstilbestrol
DF	Distant failure
DFP	Dermatofibrosarcoma protuberans
DFS	Disease-free survival
DHBI	Double hemi-body irradiation
DL	Direct laryngoscope
DLBC	Diffuse large-B-cell (lymphoma)
DLCO	Diffusing capacity of the lung for carbon monoxide
DM	Diabetes mellitus
DM	Distant metastasis
dMLC	Dynamic multileaf collimation
DNA	Deoxyribonucleic acid
DOT	U.S. Department of Transportation
dps	Disintegrations per second
DRE	Digital rectal examination
DRF	Dose reduction factor
DRR	Digitally reconstructed radiograph
DSB	Double-strand break
DSS	Disease-specific survival
DVH	Dose-volume histogram
DVT	Deep venous thrombosis
EBCTG	Early Breast Cancer Trialists' Group
EBRT	External beam radiation therapy
EBV	Epstein-Barr Virus
EBVP	Epirubicin, bleomycin, vinblastine, and prednisone
EC	Extracapsular
ECE	Extracapsular extension
ECF	Epirubicin, cisplatin, and 5FU
ECOG	Eastern Cooperative Oncology Group

EDP	End damage processors
EFS	Event-free survival
EGF-R	Epidermal growth factor-receptor
EIC	Extensive intraductal cancer
ELCG	Early Lung Cancer Group
ENE	Extranodal extension
EORTC	European Organization for Research and Treatment of Cancer
EORTC-GPMC	European Organization for Research and Treatment of Cancer–Groupe Pierre-et-Marie-Curie
EP	Etoponite, platinum
EPID	Electronic portal imaging device
ER	Enhancement ratio
ER	Estrogen receptor
ERCP	Endoscopic retrograde cholangopancreatography
ESPAC	European Study Group for Pancreatic Cancer
ESR	Erythrocyte sedimentation rate
ET	Endotracheal
EUA	Examination under anesthesia
EUS	Endoscopic ultrasound
eV	Electron volt
exlap	Exploratory laparotomy
5FU/FA	5-Fluorouracil/folinic acid
FEV	Forced expiratory volume
FAM	5-Fluorouracil, doxorubicin, and mitomycin
FAP	Familial adenomatous polyposis (of the colon)
FCR	Fludarabine, cytoxan, Rituxan
FDA	U.S. Food and Drug Administration
FFF	Freedom from failure
FFP	Freedom from (disease) progression
FFS	Failure-free survival
FFTF	Freedom from treatment failure
FH	Favorable histology
FIGO	International Federation of Gynecology and Obstetrics
FISH	Fluorescent in situ hybridization
FNA	Fine needle aspiration
FND	Fludarabine, Novantrone, dexamethasone
FOLFOX	Folinic acid (leucovorin) Fluorouracil Oxaliplatin
FOM	Floor of mouth
FSU	Functional subunit
FU	Fluorouracil
FVC	False vocal cords
FVC	Forced vital capacity
Fx	Fractions
GBM	Glioblastoma multiforme
GC	Gemcitabine and cisplatin

GCT	Germ cell tumor
GE	Gastroesophageal
GELA	Groupe d'Etude des Lymphomes de l'Adulte
GF	Growth fraction
GGR	Global genome repair
GH	Growth hormone
GI	Gastrointestinal
GIST	Gastrointestinal stromal tumor
GITSG	Gastrointestinal Tumor Study Group
GK	Gamma Knife
GM	Geiger-Mueller (counter)
GND	Groin node dissection
GOG	Gynecologic Oncology Group
GORTEC	Groupe Oncologie & Radiotherapie de la Tete et du Cou (Oncology and Radiotherapy Group for Head and Neck Cancer)
GSD	Genetically significant dose
GSHG	German Hodgkin Study Group
GTV	Gross tumor volume
GU	Genitourinary
GVHD	Growth versus host disease
Gy	Gray
GyE	Gray equivalent
Hb	Hemoglobin
HBI	Hemi-body irradiation
hCG	Human chorionic gonadotropin
HCT	Hematopoietic stem cell transplant
HD	Hodgkin's disease
HDR	High dose rate
HEENT	Head, ears, eye, nose, throat
HFx	Hyperfractionated
HG	High grade
HIV	Human immunodeficiency virus
HN2	Topical mechlorethamine
HNPCC	Hereditary non-polyposis colorectal cancer
HOB	Head of bed
HP	Hypopharynx
HPOA	Hypertropic pulmonary osteoarthropathy
HPV	Human papillomavirus
HR	Homologous recombination (also called HRR)
HTN	Hypertension
HU	Hydroxyurea
HVA	Homovanillic acid
HVL	Half-value layer
HVS	Herpes simplex virus

IBC	Inflammatory breast cancer
IBD	Inflammatory bowel disease
IBT	Ipsilateral breast tumor
IBTR	Ipsilateral breast tumor recurrence
ICP	Intracranial pressure
ICRP	International Commission on Radiological Protection
ICRT	Inracavitary radiotherapy
ICRU	International Commission on Radiation Units and Measurements
IDC	Infiltrating ductal carcinoma
IDL	Intermediate-density lipoprotein
IESS	Intergroup Ewing's Sarcoma Study
IF	Involved field
IFN	Interferon
IFRT	Involved-field radiation therapy
IGRT	Image-guided radiation therapy
IJ	Intrajugular
IL-2	(Proleukin® IL-2)
ILC	Infiltrating lobular carcinoma
IM	Intramuscularly
IMC	Internal mammary chain
IMLN	Internal mammary lymph node
IMRT	Intensity-modulated radiation therapy
INSS	International Neuroblastoma Staging System
IP	Interstitial pneumonitis
IP	Intraperitoneal
IPI	International Prognostic Index
IT MTX	Intrathecal methotrexate
ITV	Internal target volume
IU	International unit
IV	Intravenous
IVP	Intravenous pyelogram
J	Joule
JAMA	Journal of the American Medical Association
JD	Jugulodigastric
KPS	Karnofsky performance status
kerma	Kinetic energy released in matter
keV	Kiloelectron volt
kg	Kilogram
LABC	Locally advanced breast cancer
LABT	Locally advanced breast tumor
LAG	Lymphangiogram
LAN	Low anterior neck

LAO	Left anterior oblique
LAP	Laparotomy
LAR	Low anterior resection
LC	Local control
LCIS	Lobular carcinoma in situ
LCSG	Lung Cancer Study Group
LD	Lymphocyte depleted
LD IFRT	Low-dose involved-field radiation therapy
LDH	L-lactate dehydrogenase
LDR	Low dose rate
LE	Local excision
LE	Lower extremity
LEEP	Loop electrosurgical excision procedure
LET	Linear energy transfer
LF	Local failure
LFT	Liver function test
LHRH	Luteinizing hormone−releasing hormone
linac	Linear accelerator
LMDS	Locally multiply damaged sites
LIQ	Lower inner quadrant
LN	Lymph node
LND	Lymph node dissection
LOQ	Lower outer quadrant
LP	Lymphocyte predominate
LPHD	Lymphocyte predominate Hodgkin's disease
LPO	Left posterior oblique
LQ	Linear quadratic
LRC	Locoregional control/local regional control
LRF	Local-regional failure
LUL	Left upper lobe
LUS	Lower uterine segment
LV	Left ventricle
LV	Leukovorin
LVEF	Left ventricular ejection function
LVI	Lymphovascular invasion
m/s	Meters per second
m	Month
MAGIC	Medical Research Council Adjuvant Gastric Infusional Chemotherapy (trial)
MALT	Mucosa-associated lymphoid tissue
MAO	Monamine oxidase inhibitor
MAPK	Mitogen activated protein kinase
mCCNU	Methyl-CCNU (lomustine)
MC/LD	Mixed cellularity/lymphocyte depleted
MCV	Methotrexate, cisplatin, and vinblastine
MDA/MDACC	M.D. Anderson Cancer Center (Houston, TX)

MDAH	M.D. Anderson Hospital (Houston, TX)
MDFS	Median disease-free survival
MDR	Medium dose rate
MEN	Multiple endocrine neoplasia
mets	Metastatic (metastases)
MeV	Megaelectron volt
MF	Mycosis fungoides
MFH	Malignant fibrous histiocytoma
MFL	Methotrexate, 5-Fluorouracil, leukovorin
MG	Myasthenia gravis
MGH	Massachusetts General Hospital (Boston, MA)
MGUS	Monoclonal of undetermined significance
MIBC	Muscle invasive bladder cancer
MIBG	Meta-iodobenzyl guanidine
ML	Mid line
MLC	Multileaf collimator
MLD	Mean lung dose
mm	Micrometer
MM	Multiple myeloma
MMC	Mitomycin
mmHg	Milligrams of mercury
MMM	Massive mediastinal mass
MMP	Matrix metalloproteinases
MMR	Mismatch repair (gene)
MMT	Mixed müllerian tumor
MOF	MethylCCNU/oncovin/fluorouracil
MOPP	Mechlorethamine, vincristine, procarbazine, and prednisone
MOSAIC	Multicenter International Study of Oxaliplatin/ 5-Fluorouracil/Leucovorin in the Adjuvant Treatment of Colon Cancer
MPD	Maximum peripheral dose
MPD	Maximum permissible dose
MPV	Methotrexate, procarbazine, and vincristine
MRA	Magnetic resonance angiography
MRC	Medical Research Council
MRC TTWG	Medical Research Council Testicular Tumor Working Group
MRI	Magnetic resonance imaging
MS	Median survival
MSKCC	Memorial Sloan-Kettering Cancer Center
MST	Median survival time
mSv	Millisievert
MTC	Medullary thyroid cancer
MU	Monitor unit
MV	Megavoltage
M-VAC	Methotrexate, vinblastine, doxorubicin, cisplatin
M-VEC	Methotrexate, vinblastine, epirubicin, cisplatin
MZL	Marginal zone lymphoma

nat hx	Natural history
NCBI	National Center for Biotechnology Information
NCCN	National Comprehensive Cancer Network
NCCTG	North Central Cancer Treatment Group
NCI	National Cancer Institute
NCOG	Northern California Oncology Group
NCRP	National Council on Radiation Protection and Measurements
NE	Norepinephrine
NED	No evidence of disease
NER	Nucleotide excision repair
NES	Nuclear export system
NF	Neurofibromatosis
NF1	Neurofibromatosis 1
NHD	Non-Hodgkin's disease
NHL	Non-Hodgkin's lymphoma
NHR	Nonhomologous recombination (also called NHEJ)
NORM	Naturally occurring radioactive material
NP	Nasopharynx
NR	No response
NRC	Nuclear Regulatory Commission
ns	Not statistically significant
NSABP	National Surgical Adjuvant Breast and Bowel Project
NSAID	Nonsteroidal anti-inflammatory drug
NSCLC	Non-small-cell lung cancer
NS/LP	Nodular sclerosis/lymphocyte predominant
OA	Oligoastrocytoma
OAR	Organ-at-risk
OC	Oral cavity
ODT	Orally disintegrating tablet
OER	Oxygen enhancement ratio
OOB	Out of bed
OP	Oropharynx
OPEC	Oncovin (vincristine), prednisone, etoposide, chlorambucil
OR	Operating room
OR	Overall risk
OS	Overall survival
OSL	Optically stimulated luminescence
OTC	Over the counter
PA	Para-aortic
PA	Posterior-anterior
PAB	Posterior axillary boost
PALN	Para-aortic lymph node
PC	Prednisone/cytoxan
PCA	Patient-controlled analgesia (pump)
PCI	Prophylactic cranial irradiation

pCR	Pathologic complete response
PCR	Polymerase chain reaction
PCV	Procarbazine, CCNU, vincristine
PDD	Percentage depth dose
PE	Physical exam
PE	Platinum etoposide
PE	Pulmonary embolism
PEB	Cisplatin, etoposide, bleomycin
PEG	Percutaneous endoscopic gastrostomy
PET	Positron emission tomography
PF	Cisplatin and fluorouracil
PFS	Progression-free survival
PFT	Pulmonary function test
PLGF	Platelet derived growth factor
PLM	Percent labeled mitoses
PI	Pulse-intensive
PID	Pelvic inflammatory disease
PLD	Potentially lethal disease
PLP	Partial laryngopharyngectomy
PMH	Princess Margaret Hospital (Toronto, ON)
PMRT	Post mastectomy radiation therapy
PNET	Peripheral neuroectodermal tumor
PNI	Perineural invasion
PNS	Peripheral nervous system
po/po	Orally (per os) (by mouth)
POG	Pediatric Oncology Group
PORT	Post-operative radiotherapy
PORTEC	Post Operative Radiation Therapy in Endometrial Carcinoma
POS	Positive
pPR	Pathologic partial response
PR	Partial response
PR	Progesterone receptor
p.r.n.	L. pro re nata (according to circumstances)
PRV	Planning organ-at-risk volume
PS	Pyriform sinus
PSA	Prostate-specific antigen
PSF	Peak scatter factor
PTHRP	Parathyroid hormone-related protein
PTS/pts	Patients
PTV	Planning target volume
PUVA	Psoralen plus ultraviolet A
PVB	Platinum, vinblastine, bleomycin (regime)
PW	Pharyngeal wall
QA	Quality assurance
QD	Every day

QOD	Every other day
QOL	Quality of life
R	Roentgen
R&V	Record and verify
RAO	Right anterior oblique
Rb	Retinoblastoma
RBC	Red blood cells
RBE	Relative biological effectiveness
RCC	Renal cell cancer
R-CHOP	CHOP [cyclophosphamide, hydroxydaunomycin (doxorubicin), Oncovin (vincristine), and prednisone] plus rituximab
RCT	Randomized clinical trial
RFLP	Restriction fragment length polymorphism
RFS	Relapse-free survival
RFS	Recurrence-free survival
RM	Radical mastectomy
RMS	Rhabdomyosarcoma
RH	Radical hysterectomy
RILD	Radiation-induced lung disease
RMT	Retro molar trigone
RP	Radical prostatectomy
RPA	Recursive partitioning analysis
RPA	Replication protein A
RPLND	Retroperitoneal lymph node dissection
RPO	Right posterior oblique
RR	Recurrence rate
RR	Relative risk
RRP	Radical retropubic prostatectomy
RSC	Radiation Safety Committee
RSO	Radiation Safety Officer
RT	Radiation therapy
RTOG	Radiation Therapy Oncology Group
RUL	Right upper lobe
SAD	Source-to-axis distance
SAR	Scatter-air ratio
SBO	Small bowel obstruction
SBRT	Stereotactic body radiotherapy
SC	Subclavian
SCC	Squamous cell cancer
SC/IJ	Subclavian/internal jugular
SCCa	Squamous cell cancer
SCLC	Small-cell lung cancer
SCM	Sternocleidomastoid
SEER	Surveillance Epidemiology and End Results
SEM	Standard error of the mean

SEQ	Sequential
SGL	Supraglottic larynx
SI	Sacroiliac
SI	Système International d'Unités/International System of Units
SIADH	Syndrome of inappropriate antidiuretic hormone
SIB	Simultaneous integrated boost
SIOP	International Society of Paediatric Oncology
SLD	Sublethal damage
SLL	Small lymphocytic lymphoma
SLN	Sentinel lymph node
SMA	Superior mesenteric artery
SMF	Streptozocin, mitomycin, and 5-fluorouracil
sMLC	Static multileaf collimation
SOB	Shortness of breath
SPECT	Single photon emission computed tomography
SPEP	Serum protein electrophoresis
SPN	Single peripheral nodule
SQ	Subcutaneous
SRS	Stereotactic radiosurgery
ss	Statistically significant
SSB	Single-strand break
SSCP	Single-stranded conformation polymorphism
SSD	Source-to-surface distance
st	Statistical trend
STD	Sexually transmitted disease
STLI	Subtotal lymphoid irradiation
STNI	Subtotal nodal irradiation
STS	Soft-tissue sarcoma
SV	Seminal vesicle
Sv	Sievert
SVC	Superior vena cava
SWOG	Southwest Oncology Group
2-D	Two-dimensional
3-D	Three-dimensional
3D CRT	Three-dimensional conformal radiation therapy
T&O	Tandem and ovoid
TAC	Taxotere (docetaxel), adriamycin, cytoxan
TAH	Total abdominal hysterectomy
TAH-BSO	Total abdominal hysterectomy-bilateral salpingo-oophorectomy
TAH-USO	Total abdominal hysterectomy-unilateral salpingo-oophorectomy
TAR	Tissue-air ratio
TB	Tuberculosis
TBI	Total body irradiation
TCC	Transitional cell carcinoma
TCCa	Transitional cell cancer
TCR	Transcription-coupled repair

TF	Tray factor
TGF	Transforming growth factor
TLI	Total lymphoid irradiation
TI	Transport Index
TID (t.i.d.)	Three times a day
TIMP	Tissue inhibitors of metalloproteinases
TIPPB	Transperitoneal interstitial permanent prostate brachytherapy
TL	Total laryngectomy
TLD	Thermoluminescent dosimeter
TM	Temporomandibular
TM	Total mastectomy
TME	Total mesorectal excision
TMJ	Temporomandibular joint
TMR	Tissue-maximum ratio
TNF	Tumor necrosis factor
TNI	Total nodal irradiation
TNM	Tumor - regional lymph nodes - distant metastasis (staging)
T_{pot}	Potential doubling time
TPR	Tissue-phantom ratio
TR	Therapeutic ratio
TRT	Thoracic radiotherapy
TSH	Thyroid-stimulating hormone
TSS	Trans-sphenoidal surgery
TTP	Thrombotic thrombocytopenic purpura
TURBT	Transurethral resection of the bladder tumor
TURP	Transurethral resection of the prostate
TVC	True vocal cords
T_{vol}	Volume doubling time
UA	Urine analysis
UCSF	University of California at San Francisco
UF	Unfavorable
UF	University of Florida
UFH	Unfavorable histology
UIQ	Upper inner quadrant
UNSCEAR	United Nations Scientific Committee on the Effects of Atomic Radiation
UOO	Urinary outlet obstruction
UOQ	Upper outer quadrant
UPEP	Urine protein electrophoresis
UPSC	Uterine papillary serous carcinoma
USO	Unilateral salpingo-oophorectomy
UTI	Urinary tract infection
UV	Ultraviolet
VA	Veterans Association
VA	Vincristine and actinomycin D

VAA	Vincristine, actinomycin D, and adriamycin
VAC	Vincristine, dactinomycin, and cyclophosphamide (cytoxan)
VAClock	Vacuum lock device
VACS	Vacuum-assisted wound closure system
VAIN	Vaginal intraepithelial neoplasia
VALCSG	U.S. Department of Veterans Affairs Laryngeal Cancer Study Group
VB	Vertebral body
VC	Vincristine, cytoxan
VC	Vital capacity
VCR	Vincristine
VCP	Vincristine, CCNU, and prednisone
VEGF	Vascular endothelial growth factor
VF	Very favorable
VHL	von Hipple-Landau
VIP	vasoactive intestinal polypeptide
VMA	Vanillylmandelic acid
VNPI	Van Nuys Project Index
VP	Ventriculoperitoneal
VPL	Vertical partial laryngectomy
WART	Whole abdominal radiotherapy
WBRT	Whole brain radiation therapy
WDLL	Well-differentiated lymphocytic lymphoma
WF	Wedge factor
WHO	World Health Organization
WLE	Wide local incision
WPRT	Whole pelvis radiotherapy
XELOX	Xeloda plus oxaliplatin
XRT	External radiation therapy

Index

About the Editor

Hasan Murshed, M.D., M.S., earned his medical degree from the University of Dhaka, Bangladesh, and Master's degree in Medical Physics from Louisiana State University, Baton Rouge, Louisiana. He completed his residency in Radiation Oncology at the University of Alabama- Birmingham, Alabama, where he was the Chief Resident. Afterwards he served as Fellow at the University of Texas, M.D. Anderson Cancer Center, Houston, Texas.

Dr. Murshed is dual board certified by American Board of Radiology (ABR) in Radiation Oncology and in Medical Physics. He is a member of the American Society for Radiation Oncology (ASTRO).

Dr. Murshed has been in private practice for more than 15 years and is the Medical Director of Hope Regional Cancer Center, Panama City, Florida. He enjoys both educational and practicing aspects of radiation oncology. He is a passionate advocate for cancer patients and is involved in his community activities.

(Reach him at Hasan.Murshed@HopeRCC.com)

Printed and bound by CPI Group (UK) Ltd, Croydon, CR0 4YY

08/05/2025

01865003-0001